Lecture Notes in Computer Science　　1693

Edited by G. Goos, J. Hartmanis and J. van Leeuwen

T0223124

Springer

Berlin
Heidelberg
New York
Barcelona
Hong Kong
London
Milan
Paris
Singapore
Tokyo

Prasad Jayanti (Ed.)

Distributed Computing

13th International Symposium, DISC'99
Bratislava, Slovak Republic
September 27-29, 1999
Proceedings

Springer

Series Editors

Gerhard Goos, Karlsruhe University, Germany
Juris Hartmanis, Cornell University, NY, USA
Jan van Leeuwen, Utrecht University, The Netherlands

Volume Editor

Prasad Jayanti
Dartmouth College, Department of Computer Science
6211 Sudikoff Laboratory for Computer Science
Hanover, NH 03755, USA
E-mail: prasad@cs.dartmouth.edu

Cataloging-in-Publication data applied for

Die Deutsche Bibliothek - CIP-Einheitsaufnahme

Distributed computing : 13th international symposium ;
proceedings / DISC '99, Bratislava, Slovak Republic, September 27 -
29, 1999. Prasad Jayanti (ed.). - Berlin ; Heidelberg ; New York ;
Barcelona ; Hong Kong ; London ; Milan ; Paris ; Singapore ; Tokyo
: Springer, 1999
   (Lecture notes in computer science ; Vol. 1693)
   ISBN 3-540-66531-5

CR Subject Classification (1998): C.2.4, C.2.2, F.2.2, D.1.3, F.1, D.4.4-5

ISSN 0302-9743
ISBN 3-540-66531-5 Springer-Verlag Berlin Heidelberg New York

© Springer-Verlag Berlin Heidelberg 1999
Printed in Germany

Typesetting: Camera-ready by author
SPIN: 10705115   06/3142 – 5 4 3 2 1 0   Printed on acid-free paper

Preface

DISC, the International Symposium on DIStributed Computing, is an annual forum for research presentations on all facets of distributed computing. This volume includes 23 contributed papers and an invited lecture, all presented at DISC '99, held on September 27-29, 1999 in Bratislava, Slovak Republic.

In addition to regular submissions, the call for papers for DISC '99 also solicited Brief Announcements (BAs). We received 60 regular submissions and 15 brief announcement submissions. These were read and evaluated by the program committee, with the additional help of external reviewers when needed. At the program committee meeting on June 10-11 at Dartmouth College, Hanover, USA, 23 regular submissions and 4 BAs were selected for presentation at DISC '99. The extended abstracts of these 23 regular papers appear in this volume, while the four BAs appear as a special publication of Comenius University, Bratislava – the host of DISC '99. It is expected that the regular papers will be submitted later, in more polished form, to fully refereed scientific journals.

Of the 23 regular papers selected for the conference, 12 qualified for the *Best Student Paper* award. The program committee awarded this honor to the paper entitled "Revisiting the Weakest Failure Detector for Uniform Reliable Broadcast" by Marcos Aguilera, Sam Toueg, and Borislav Deianov. Marcos and Borislav, who are both students, share this award.

DISC '99 hosted three invited lectures, by Tushar Chandra (IBM), Faith Fich (University of Toronto), and Michael Fischer (Yale University). The extended abstract of Tushar Chandra's lecture appears in this volume. The extended abstracts of the other two invited lectures are expected to appear in next year's DISC proceedings.

The program committee for DISC '99 consisted of:

Angel Alvarez (Tech. U. of Madrid)   Srinivasan Keshav (Cornell)
Anindya Basu (Bell Labs)   Marios Mavronicolas (U. Connecticut)
Shlomi Dolev (Ben-Gurion)   Yoram Moses (Technion)
Cynthia Dwork (IBM)   Alessandro Panconesi (U. Bologna)
Rachid Guerraoui (E. Polytechnique)   Mike Reiter (Bell Labs)
Vassos Hadzilacos (U. Toronto)   Sam Toueg (Cornell)
Maurice Herlihy (Brown)   Moti Yung (CertCo)
Prasad Jayanti, Chair (Dartmouth)

Peter Ruzicka was the local arrangements chair for the conference. Miroslav Chladny and Rastislav Kralovic took charge of advertising and maintaining the web site for DISC '99. We thank all of them for a superb job.

We thank all the authors who submitted to DISC '99 and the keynote speakers for accepting our invitation. We thank ACM SIGACT for letting us use its automated submission server and the electronic program committee

(EPC) server. We are especially grateful to Steve Tate and Peter Shor for their help with the submission server and the EPC server, respectively. We thank Springer-Verlag for continuing the tradition and publishing these proceedings.

We gratefully acknowledge the generous support of the Slovak Society for Computer Science, Telenor, Comenius University, and Dartmouth College. The scope and the direction of DISC are supervised by the DISC steering committee which, for 1999, consisted of Bernadette Charron-Bost (Ecole Polytechnique), Vassos Hadzilacos (University of Toronto), Prasad Jayanti (Dartmouth College), Shay Kutten (Technion and IBM), Marios Mavronicolas (University of Connecticut), Andre Schiper – Vice Chair (Ecole Polytechnique, Lausanne), and Shmuel Zaks – Chair (Technion).

September 1999   Prasad Jayanti

External Reviewers

The program committee thanks the following persons who acted as referees for DISC '99:

Y. Afek
M. Aguilera
L. Alvisi
A. Amoroso
S. Arevalo
A. Arora
F. Ballesteros
M. Bearden
L. Bouge
H. Buhrman
B. Charron-Bost
V. Cholvi
P. De las Heras
R. De Prisco
A. Doudou
P. Fatourou
A. Fernandez-Anta
M. Franklin
J. Garay
L. Gargano
J. Gonzalez-Barahona
F. Guerra
N. Heintze
T. Herman
J. Hoepman

R. Jimenez-Peris
S. Kaxiras
E. Kushilevitz
K. Marzullo
J. Miranda
M. Moir
R. Ostrovsky
M. Pati
B. Patt-Shamir
A, Pietracaprina
R. Rajamohan
R. Rubinfeld
E. Santos
R. Segala
A. Shvartsman
R. Silvestri
A. Singh
K. Tan
G. Taubenfeld
J. Tromp
P. Vitanyi
E. Wimmers
A. Wool
B. Yener

Table of Contents

A Case for Message Oriented Middleware

Guruduth Banavar, Tushar Chandra, Robert Strom, and Daniel Sturman

IBM T. J. Watson Research Center, Hawthorne, New York
{banavar,tushar,strom,sturman}@watson.ibm.com

Abstract. With the emergence of the internet, independent applications are starting to be integrated with each other. This has created a need for technology for glueing together applications both within and across organizations, without having to re-engineer individual components. We propose an approach for developing this glue technology based on *message flows* and discuss the open research problems in realizing this approach.

1 Introduction

Recent advances in networking and the pervasive deployment of the internet have created new opportunities for computing research. Many applications are evolving from monolithic to distributed systems. Business processes are increasingly being automated and interconnected in spontaneous ways. Companies increasingly require the integration of once independent applications, either because they are vertically integrating components of the business, or because of mergers or outsourcing of function to separate organizations. In summary, there is a convergence to loosely integrated distributed systems, where each component can evolve independently.

In this paper, we make the case for research in "glue technology" for loosely integrating distributed systems. The basic observation underlying this technology is that widely disseminated, often real-time "events" (or messages) — e.g. stock quotations, advertisements, offers to buy and sell, weather reports, traffic conditions, etc. — are becoming ubiquitously available through the Internet. These public events, as well as internal events, such as orders, shipments, deliveries, manufacturing line changes, can form the "glue" to link applications within and across organizations. Since this technology is based on messages, we use the term Message Oriented Middleware, or MOM for short, to refer to it.

Consider the opportunities that arise within a single company. Today, most large companies consist of several smaller organizations that are supported by applications that were developed and have evolved largely independently of each other. In most cases, people provide the linkage between these smaller organizations. For example, when a sale occurs, the sales representative sends a request to manufacturing to produce the product. In such cases, what is needed is a technology that allows companies to automate such processes by tying together its organizations' independent applications. Once tied together, the integrated computing system is potentially cheaper to operate, faster and less prone to errors than the system in which humans glued together independent organizations. Further, this kind of integration opens up new opportunities for macroscopic analysis such as forecasting, and requirements analysis across the company that can further streamline operations.

The value of tying together applications can easily be extended to partnerships between companies. One obvious scenario is when two companies merge. Usually each company has its own set of independent applications — the challenge is to provide "computing glue" to tie these applications together. Another obvious scenario is when two companies do business with each other. In today's model, people are heavily involved in transacting business between companies. Business integration offers the opportunity to automate business interactions between companies by tying together their applications.

As more consumers shop, invest, pay bills and taxes, read, and perform cooperative work and play online, the same glue technology may be extended to support business-to-consumer interactions. Better integration between business software and end-user software such as web browsers offers the promise of more power and greater ease of use to the end-user.

We propose an approach for developing the glue technology required for message oriented middleware (MOM). Our proposed approach is derived from the publish and subscribe model [OPSS93] and event delivery systems [WIS]. In this model, the basic unit of data is a *message*, which corresponds to what are called "events" in publish/subscribe or event delivery systems. Clients register as publishers or subscribers of messages. Messages are sent to and delivered from *information spaces*, each of which has a predefined *message schema* [BKS+99]. Information spaces may be tied together via *message flow graphs* that specify how messages are propagated and transformed between producers and consumers. A message flow graph may route a filtered subset of messages from one information space to another, merge messages from multiple sources, or deliver a transformed version of a message from one information space to another. Some information spaces contain states summarizing the message history of other information spaces. This state can be re-mapped back into a message sequence, often in more than one way. Systems can exploit this non-determinism by relaxing the ordering of messages, by dropping obsolete messages, by compressing the past history being sent to a newly connecting subscriber or to a subscriber who has reconnected after being off-line.

In the near future, we envision a pervasive MOM environment that glues together a large number of stand-alone applications. Each application may evolve independently from the others in this environment. The MOM environment will support such evolution without requiring changes in other applications, and in fact, without requiring the other applications to be aware of the addition and removal of applications and clients. (The only exceptions would be those applications dealing with access control and security). The MOM environment will allow new applications to "tap into" information generated by existing applications without disturbing them. This will allow users to add higher order features such as auditing, monitoring, and data mining on top of existing information flows, after the fact, and without disrupting the underlying applications.

Several crucial research problems remain unsolved in the MOM approach, and even those that are solved have not been completely implemented yet. A complete and precise model for this approach has not yet emerged. Several key distributed computing problems remain open such as scalability, and how to provide end-to-end guarantees on message delivery. Some of the known algorithms tackle subsets of the overall problem. Questions related to fault-tolerance, security, message ordering, and topology changes that have been well studied in the context of other types of messaging systems are open areas for further research in the context of MOM.

There are several efforts from various other communities to provide glue technology to tie together applications, and it is not clear at this stage whether a single glue technology is best suited for all environments. The database community has extended the classical ideas underlying databases to distributed environments via distributed transactions [TGGL82] and federated databases [Hsi92]. The languages community has extended the concept of objects to a distributed environment via remote method invocation (CORBA [Gro98], RMI [BN83], etc.). Group communication systems such as Isis have also been used to glue together applications in a distributed environment [BCJ⁺90,Bir93,Pow96]. Finally, there exist higher-level approaches such as Workflow that are targeted towards specific subsets of the overall problem [WfM,PPHC98]. We will compare our proposed MOM approach with these other approaches.

The rest of this paper is organized as follows. In section 2 we examine several examples that motivate the need for message oriented middleware. In section 3 we elaborate on the message oriented middleware model. In section 4 we discuss open areas for further research in this area. In Section 5 we examine alternative approaches. Section 5 concludes with work related to content-based publish/subscribe systems.

2 Examples

In this section, we provide two examples that motivate the need for Message Oriented Middleware and illustrate the various requirements imposed by applications:

1. *Stock Trading.* This example illustrates the need for anonymity between message publishers and message subscribers. In addition it demonstrates the need for MOM-based systems to be highly scalable. It also demonstrates the need for MOM-based deployments that cross organizational boundaries. Finally, this example motivates the need for on-the-fly transformation of messages into formats suitable for different clients.
2. *Home Shopping.* In addition to anonymity between publishers and subscribers, this example illustrates the need for interpreting message streams to capture application-specific meaning. This example also shows the need for near real-time response from the MOM environment.

2.1 Stock Trading

To illustrate how MOM can support application integration, consider a publish-subscribe based stock trading application written for a particular stock exchange, say the New York Stock Exchange. In such an application, stock trades, bids, and sales are published as messages. Brokers affiliated with the NYSE access this information by subscribing to events of particular interest to them. Stock trade events are published in a format beginning with the following four attributes: (1) NYSE ticker symbol, (2) share price, (3) share volume, (4) broker id. A similar application running at another stock exchange, say the NASDAQ, may also publish events corresponding to trades, but with a different format for the first four attributes: (1) NASDAQ ticker symbol, (2) share price, (3) capital in this trade, (4) broker code. For both markets, message rates are very high, and there are large numbers of publishers and subscribers. Thus, an important requirement for MOM is performance and scalability.

Now let us suppose that brokers and analysts previously dealt separately with both the NYSE and NASDAQ exchanges, and that in future they wish to run the same analysis programs for trades on both exchanges. In order to run their internal analyses on information from both sources, they may wish to convert the data into a common internal format, and merge the two information streams into a single stream. For instance, Figure 1 shows both stock trade formats converted to a unified format consisting of the following first four attributes: (1) unique company name, (2) share price, (3) share volume, and (4) unique broker name. The MOM system should thus support transforming those messages it is delivering to clients requesting the common format while preserving the original format for legacy applications. Also, legacy NYSE client applications may wish to access NASDAQ trade events into the NYSE format and vice versa. That is, MOM-based transformation should enable clients accessing both stock exchanges to access this integrated data without disrupting the operation of legacy applications.

To extend the system to new applications, such as direct customer trading, it is simply necessary to "tap in" to the message streams. Provided that the infrastructure can scale from hundreds of brokers to hundreds of thousands of on-line investors, each investor can specify an appropriate selection of interest — such as the issues in his portfolio. Of course the applications used by customers and by professional stockbrokers will be very different, but the message stream "glue" will remain the same. This example illustrates both the importance of anonymity between producers and consumers, and the need to cross organizational barriers. Applications posting events need not be aware of their destinations; applications subscribing to events need not be aware of their sources. Extending the system to bring stock trade events directly to home computers may change the system load, but not the fundamental architecture.

2.2 Home Shopping

As a second example of the use of MOM, consider a home shopping application where consumers may request up-to-the-minute information and pricing on re-

5

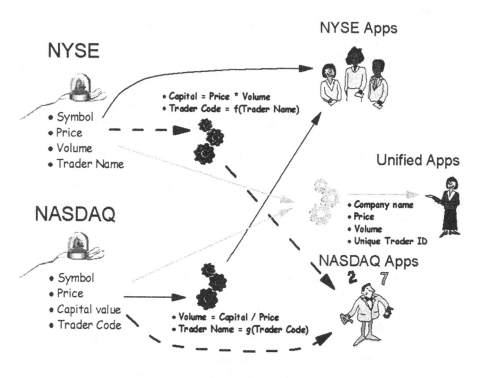

Fig. 1. Applications using both NASDAQ and NYSE to exchange data.

tail items from "virtual markets" for products such as automobiles, computers, or camera equipment. Each message represents a seller's ad: the seller's identity and location, the type of article, and attribute-value pairs representing the attributes of the article being sold. For example, automobile advertisements would include the make, model, year, mileage, and options. The price might either be fixed, or left open to competitive bidding in a real-time auction. Additional messages represent bids by buyers, and the open and closing of auctions. Consumers subscribe through a number of tests on these attributes. As in the previous example, messages must be routed to some subset of all subscribers based on their information content.

An important function that MOM must support for this scenario is the communication of dynamic changes in the availability and the price of items. The seller may lower the price or withdraw his ad in response to lack of interest by customers. Or buyers may raise the price as a result of competitive bidding. Typically a buyer would subscribe not just to a stream of events, but to a *state*, determined by the message history, such as the current price of items matching his criterion. As a result, new subscribers would not receive all messages from the beginning of time but instead only those messages representing the current valid prices for these selected items. Messages which have become superseded by updates or which correspond to items no longer available for sale need not be delivered. This example illustrates the importance of interpreting event histories as a state — specifying such a summarization requires the system to understand that a new price for the same item supersedes the previous price, and that the termination of an auction or the withdrawal of an ad cancels all previous prices for that item.

The ability to subscribe to a state summarizing a message history has additional effects on message delivery if the buyer wants to subscribe not merely to the current offer for each selected item, but instead wants to track for instance, the *lowest-priced* ad matching his criteria, plus any items for which the buyer is still the high bidder. In this case, messages which do not impact the lowest price because they are ads for articles with higher prices are not delivered. Note that if the low-priced ad is modified or withdrawn, or if its price is bid up in an auction so that it is no longer the low-priced ad, then it may be necessary to either deliver the ad for the second-low-priced item (if it had previously been suppressed) or to redeliver it. For example, consider the auto advertisements in Figure 2. The $20,000 price is the low price, so the $30,000 price is not delivered. However, once the $20,000 price is withdrawn or raised above $30,000, the ad for the $30,000 automobile is delivered to replace it.

Notice that, in this example, there is no real organizational boundary. Anyone might register as a publisher (potential seller) or as a subscriber (potential buyer) of an information space for a particular product.

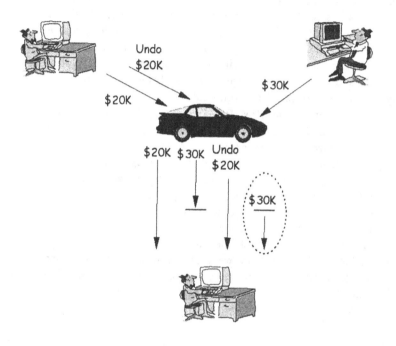

Fig. 2. Suppressing and delivering advertisements in a home shopping scenario.

3 A Flow-Graph Model for Message Oriented Middleware

For supporting the examples in the previous section, we desire a model which: (1) facilitates expression of clients' requirements; (2) is easy to reason about, both for validating specifications and implementations; (3) is rigorous, and (4) permits the widest possible latitude for the implementor.

Good models are founded upon a small number of basic concepts. For example, the key concepts underlying transactional database models are atomicity and serializability. The data, whether distributed and/or replicated, whether concurrently accessed or not, behave as if located at a single site and accessed one transaction at a time. Similarly, the key concepts underlying the Isis model [BCJ+90] are group membership [Bir93,Pow96] and virtual synchrony [BT87]. Once a model is chosen, we have a rigorous requirement for developing clever implementations for preserving the appearances of the model under a wide variety of design points and physical environments.

The Gryphon project at IBM Research is exploring a particular model for MOM based upon the concepts of *information spaces* and *message flows* (http://www.research.ibm.com/gryphon). A system is modeled as a *message flow graph:* an abstract representation of the propagation of the messages in a system, divorced from any realization on an actual network topology [BKS+99]. A message flow graph is a directed acyclic graph whose nodes are information spaces and whose arcs are message flows. Information spaces are either totally ordered *message histories* or *states* derived from message histories. Each information space has a schema that specifies the type of the messages or of the state. Publishers and subscribers are source and sink message histories respectively. Message flows specify the propagation of messages or the updating of state, in order to preserve specific relationships between information spaces as new messages are added to the system. These relationships include:

- *selection:* the destination message history receives a copy of the subset of the source message history that satisfies some boolean predicate P. For example, an analyst may request all trades of more than 1000 shares of XYZ company having a price greater than $40 per share.
- *transform:* the destination message history receives a copy of each message of the source message history after applying a transform T. For example, the conversion "Volume = Capital/Price" might be used to convert all messages from the NASDAQ format to the NYSE format.
- *merge:* when multiple message histories have arcs to a single destination, the destination receives a merge (in a non-deterministic order) of the all the messages of the sources. This operation is involved in any application involving multiple publishers.
- *collapse:* the destination state is computed by applying some summarization function S over all the messages in the source message history. In the home shopping example, a client may be interested in the lowest priced ad for Saab cars with less than 80,000 miles and a price under $6000.

– *expand: expand* is the inverse of *collapse*. The destination message history is (non-deterministically) computed to be any message history which summarizes to the source state under the summarization function S. All such message histories are said to be *equivalent* — the system is free to choose which one of the many message histories to deliver to a destination.

Message flow graphs can evolve dynamically, and in fact the changes to these graphs and requests to change the graph are themselves meta-events that can be subscribed to. As in similar systems, access control policies limit who may add and delete nodes and arcs, and where they may be added.

Notice that this model has some characteristics of database systems, some of group communication systems, and some unique characteristics of its own. Information spaces in MOM are analogous to tables in relational databases. Just as database tables have data schemas, information spaces have message schemas. The selection relation between information spaces is similar to the select operator between relational tables. Just as a relational database allows linkages between tables and views, MOM allows linkages between information spaces via message flow graphs.

Like group communication systems, messages flow from producers to consumers without explicit requests from consumers — i.e., both systems are push-based. In a push-based environment, it is natural that operations on the message flow, such as selections, transforms, and summarizations, are performed incrementally.

Defining and implementing the flow graph model gives rise to a number of open research issues. These issues are discussed in detail in the next section.

4 Research Issues

4.1 Model

The message flow graph is a useful abstraction for specifying many problems such as the ones discussed in the previous section. It is easy to explain to users familiar with dataflow graphs.

There are, however, a number of open issues. One is the type system for defining schemas for information spaces. Whereas it makes sense to organize relational databases as tables in normal form with each row consisting of a tuple of scalars, a similar "normal form" is probably not feasible for message histories. One reason is that while relational tables containing rows of different formats can be factored into separate tables, message histories cannot be so factored without losing the intrinsic total order characteristic of histories. It is probably necessary to allow messages to contain variant types, as well as embedded lists or bags.

Another open issue is the language for expressing the *selection* predicates, the *transforms*, and the summary functions used by *expand* and *collapse*. We want to be able to express problems like "cheapest current offer for a Saab" without elaborate programming. There is a tradeoff between convenience, expressive power, and analyzability.

Another issue is how to handle access control. In this model, access control can involve more than merely saying "this user may subscribe from this space". Some subscriptions require all messages to be archived forever, while others allow messages to be expired relatively quickly — these differences have consequences for physical resource requirements on broker servers, so there should be a way to allow access control to take these consequences into account.

4.2 Scalability

There are many dimensions of scalability. In this section, we deal with the potentially large fanout of select, transform, or summarization arcs from a single information space. In a large application, or in an anonymous environment such as home shopping where a single information space may be advertised very widely, the number of subscribers may be very large — perhaps in the tens of thousands or more. In this environment it becomes necessary to deploy algorithms that quickly match events against a large number of potential subscriptions — we refer to this problem as the *message matching* problem. Though the number of subscriptions to an information space may be large, say N (where N may be 10,000 or more), we expect only a few subscriptions to match any single event. Efficient algorithms exist for solving the message matching problem in messaging systems based on subject-based subscription, a simple table lookup based on the subject of the message yields a constant time algorithm, which is also optimal. In the more general content-based subscription systems, this approach does not work since different subscriptions may refer to different fields of the message schema. Naive solutions take $O(N)$ steps to solve the message matching problem. It is highly desirable to develop algorithms to solve the message matching problem that are sublinear in N. This is an active area of ongoing research [ASS+99].

Note that the message matching problem is complementary to the query problem in databases. In a database query, a single query (typically a select) is matched against a large amount of data — the challenge here is to develop algorithms that are sublinear in the amount of data in the database. In the message matching problem a single piece of data (a message) needs to be matched against a large number of standing queries (subscriptions). Note that the matching problem was first studied in the context of active databases. Efficient solutions to this problem are thus applicable in MOMs and in databases [HCKW90].

A problem similar to the message matching problem arises in the context of message flow graphs when there is a large fanout of arcs between a single information space and other information spaces representing states. By analyzing the multiple summarization functions we may be able to avoid the need to make multiple copies of the same state update and to exploit the fact that if one state doesn't change as a result of a message, a set of related states will also not change.

4.3   Distributed Implementation

The above solutions for matching have to be modified to reflect the fact that the message flow graph will typically be implemented over a geographically distributed network of server processes, which we call *message brokers*. Message brokers must combine the functions of routing and multicasting with the functions of implementing selections, transformations, and summarizations. Thus it becomes necessary to develop distributed solutions to these problems — this is an active area of ongoing research [BCM+99].

Consider two naive solutions to this problem:

- Perform message matching at the publisher and use the result of the matching to route to the destinations. With this solution, straightforward routing techniques will not work when there are a large number of clients, since (a) point-to-point routing will not take advantage of common paths, (b) routing based on destination lists could result in large message headers, and (c) routing based on multicast groups could require a very large number of groups (if there are N subscribers, the system may need as many as 2^N multicast groups).
- Broadcast the message to all message brokers and let each message broker match the message against its locally connected subscribers. This solution is likely to waste communication bandwidth in very large networks, since if subscriptions are sufficiently selective, messages will often be sent to a broker none of whose attached clients requires the message.

Approaches to the problem being studied include: (1) performing partial matching at each broker, forwarding messages (either by conventional point-to-point or by multicast) to the subset of neighboring brokers requiring the message; (2) matching messages to a combination of pre-allocated multicast groups; (3) exploiting the relationships between the subscriptions to reduce the combinatorial possibilities of multicast groups.

The existence of message transformations complicates the situation even further — some transformations can be moved and/or replicated on multiple brokers; others cannot, either because they involve data that cannot be moved (e.g. a large database mapping names to social security numbers), or because they involve "opaque" algorithms not visible to the middleware.

4.4   Message Reliability

The fault model that is typically implemented in traditional group communication systems — that a failed or slow process is automatically removed from the group [BT87] — is inappropriate for MOM-based applications. In MOM, the message flow graph is viewed as an abstract reliable entity: Subscriptions are persistent, and messages may not be lost, permuted, or duplicated, nor must spurious messages be generated (unless such distortions can be masked as a result of filtering or state equivalence). The implementation must preserve the appearances of persistence even though in the message distribution scenarios shown above, the distributed system may contain intermittently connected and intermittently faulty hardware components. This means that when a faulty subscriber reconnects, it must be possible to either deliver all the messages that it has missed, or else to compute (via analysis of the effects on the state of interest) a shorter set of messages which will re-create this state. Unlike with group communication systems, it is not sufficient to report to a faulty or disconnected subscriber that its subscription has been dropped. For example, the Replenishment Analysis teams must continue to receive inventory updates after a dropped connection is reestablished. We need algorithms to provide this appearance of persistence in a distributed network of message brokers. We also need algorithms to exploit the cases where state equivalence permits dropping of messages, and to exploit the properties of state equivalence to deliver compressed message sequences after a reconnection.

4.5 Message Ordering

Information spaces support the abstraction of a total order on messages. Since subscribers specify their interest in states derived from message histories, the middleware has the opportunity of relaxing total order deliveries for specific clients while preserving the meaning of the overall message history. This is in contrast with the approach taken by group communication systems in which ordering guarantees are driven by low level protocol options (e.g., publisher ordering, causal ordering, etc.) [BCJ+90].

For instance, if a subscriber is subscribing to the current price of a set of advertised items, the subscriber may be sensitive to the order of the last two updates to the same item, since the current price depends upon which update is first. The subscriber may not be sensitive to the order of earlier updates to that item or to the order of updates to different items. This gives the system the flexibility to weaken the ordering requirement where it is legitimate to do so while preserving it in the cases where it matters. However, it gives rise to open issues of how these situations are detected. It also creates the opportunity for optimistic delivery of out-of-order messages, as discussed below.

4.6 Optimistic Delivery

Efficient message delivery implementations that address fault-tolerance and ordering make a distinction between the receipt of a message and its actual delivery to a client — it is often necessary for the system to delay the delivery of a received message until certain control messages have arrived, such as for example, notifications that the data is stable and that no earlier messages are still en route. It is desirable wherever possible to deliver messages optimistically without waiting for this control information. In the simplest cases, the subscriber's state of interest doesn't depend upon order or isn't affected by extraneous unlogged messages. However, in more interesting cases, the state of interest does depend upon order, but the state interpretation makes it possible for "recovery" messages to retrieve the correct state after an out-of-order or unlogged message has arrived. For example, in the home shopping example, it may be that an offer to sell for $20000 is followed by an offer to sell for $30000. If the offer for $30000 arrives first, it can still be immediately delivered; when the offer for $20000 arrives later, the recovery action is to deliver it if it is for a different item than the $30000 offer, and to discard it as obsolete if it is for the same item.

It is an open problem to analyze a set of subscriptions to state derived from message histories, and determine (a) under which conditions messages can be optimistically delivered without waiting for control messages, and (b) what "recovery" messages must be inserted if it is later determined that the state needs to be corrected.

4.7 Topology Changes

End-users don't care about the topology of the underlying network. Ideally (a) it should be possible to reconfigure the topology of the underlying network non-disruptively, and (b) it should not require complex planning on the part of a network administrator to configure. Any approach to the topology reconfiguration problem must address scenarios in which multiple organizations may own parts of the communications links and logging disks, and these organizations must be able to reconfigure and/or control use of their facilities.

4.8 Security

MOM needs at least three varieties of security: (1) control of who may publish to, or subscribe from the information spaces of the virtual message flow graph, (2) control of the physical resources, (3) privacy protection of the data that flows between publishers and subscribers. Any security solution must accept the fact that there is no single "application" and no single owner of the whole network.

There are open issues about: (1) preventing a user from overloading system resources by either generating messages too quickly or by requesting states that make it impossible to discard any old messages; (2) how to deal with clients to the same information space from different organizations having different access rights; and (3) the tension between the requirement for brokers to do content-based matching and the requirement for some brokers not to be able to interpret the content.

5 Alternative Approaches

Other technologies, including object request brokers (ORBs) and database management systems (DBMSs) are being used to glue applications together in the kinds of scenarios presented in this paper [Gro98,Hsi92,WfM,BN83]. However, each of these approaches has its limitations for the purpose of MOM applications, as described below.

5.1 Remote Method Invocation (RMI) Systems

Object request brokers (e.g., [Gro98]) and in general RPC systems [BN83] can be used to glue applications by having one application call methods of objects in another remote application. The interfaces supported by an application are specified in an interface definition language (IDL) which are compiled into stubs for the caller and into language templates for the callee. RMI systems have several shortcomings that make them unsuitable for MOM applications:

- *Application evolution:* With this approach, applications tend to get tightly integrated, right from the design stage. Changes are difficult if not impossible to make after an application has been deployed. Also, since remote method invocation is a point-to-point concept, it is not possible to interpose new applications between existing information flows without disrupting the existing applications.
- *Disconnected operation:* RMI systems support a synchronous style of interaction — this makes them unsuitable in environments where clients may disconnect.

5.2 Database Systems

In general, database systems are optimized for a different set of applications than the ones that are presented in this paper. For example, databases are optimized for queries over a large amount of saved data as opposed to matching a message against a large number of standing queries or computing a summary state from a sequence of messages. Also, database systems usually support a small number of views whereas MOM systems must support a large number of views and must be optimized for frequent view updates. Furthermore, the overhead of distributed transactions in databases is prohibitively large for MOM applications.

The database community has developed a variety of techniques to use shared databases to glue together applications in a distributed environment. With this approach, one application adds data to a shared database and another application retrieves the data from it. Shared databases can be used in several configurations for this purpose, but all of them have their limitations:

- *Pull-based:* The receiving application may poll the shared database for new "incoming" data; this unnecessarily introduces extra network traffic.
- *Active Databases:* The receiving application may be alerted about new data in the database using a trigger mechanism. However, the trigger mechanism may not scale over a large number of receivers interested in different kinds of updates to the shared database.
- *Client-server architecture:* In this architecture, distributed clients access a centralized database. This approach offers limited scalability, and does not have the ability to cross organizational boundaries. Changes must first propagate to the centralized database before being sent to interested viewers.

- *Distributed database architecture:* In this architecture, the database is replicated at multiple sites. In many scenarios for glueing applications together, the replication guarantees provided by distributed databases may be too strong.
- *Federated databases:* In this architecture [KK90,Hsi92,GL94], a collection of independently designed databases is made to function as a single database. This involves name conflict resolution, schema conversion, and the execution of transactions on multiple databases as a single global transaction. Although this approach may be appropriate for organizing multiple databases within a single company, or for merging two companies together, it is unlikely to be feasible to run global serial transactions across multiple organizations and thousands of anonymous subscribers worldwide.

In general, a database used as a communication channel is too heavyweight as glue between applications. This approach has a significant administrative overhead and may not provide the same kind of communication throughput that a more specialized communication channel could provide. Thus, although databases cannot be a total solution, especially given heavyweight commit protocols that we often don't need in the message flow graph solutions, databases are still potential clients of MOM systems.

5.3 Group Communication Systems

Group communication systems (e.g., [Pow96]) can be used to glue applications by having applications join process groups meant for exchanging particular types of messages. This technique is commonly used to implement subject-based pub/sub, where a subject (or a channel) is implemented as a process group. In fact, we view MOM as a natural evolution of the group communication approach. However, this approach has several shortcomings if used to support the full spectrum of MOM applications:

- *Flexibility:* The group communication based approach imposes a fixed subject structure on all applications — this reduces the flexibility of the overall system. In large systems, it may be necessary for different applications to select messages based on different fields in a message — a subject structure cannot capture this requirement.
- *Scalability:* Group communication system implementations tend to be tightly coupled, thus it is natural to deploy group communication systems over small numbers of computers (100s) on a tightly coupled network (e.g., a LAN). Scaling group communication to larger numbers of computers and onto WAN environments is an open area of active research [BFH97].
- *Fault model:* The fault model that is typically implemented in group communication systems — that a failed process is automatically removed from the group — is inappropriate for MOM applications. In MOM, subscriptions are persistent, when a failed process recovers it needs to be updated with all the messages that it did not receive.

– *Opaque messages:* In general, group communication systems do not interpret the content of messages. This forces them to support qualities of service based on low level properties of the protocol, not on the semantics of messages. MOM systems can get more information from applications and use it to provide various qualities of service more effectively.

5.4 Workflow Systems

Workflow systems (e.g., [WfM,Lut94]) are used for coordinating potentially distributed tasks via a specification of the sequence and control of tasks. While these systems are typically used to solve problems at a "higher-level", they may also be used to glue applications by treating each application as an "activity" that communicates with other "activities" via a workflow manager (which is the software component that controls the flow of work between activities). However, the major shortcomings of this approach when used for integrating applications are:

– Workflow specifications are relatively static in nature — activities and their interactions do not change much once the flow has been defined. Applications requiring integration, on the other hand, may need to support changes to subscriptions at a frequent rate.
– Workflow managers are centralized in practice. This may limit the scalability and the throughput of the system. Building distributed workflow systems is an active area of ongoing research [PPHC98].

6 Related Work in Content-based Publish-Subscribe Systems

Several projects [WIS], such as SIENA [Car98], READY [GKP99], Elvin [SA97], and Gryphon (http://www.research.ibm.com/gryphon), are exploring the use of content-based publish-subscribe systems as the basis for various MOM applications. While the motivations for the work in these projects are similar, the approaches they are pursuing are different in important respects.

From a model point of view, all of the above systems support rich subscription languages which approach the expressiveness of SQL. Some of the systems, e.g., READY, also support the use of temporal relationships between messages for expressing "compound events". As described earlier, the content-based publish-subscribe model can be generalized to include transformations, merges, and stateful operations in the single framework of message flow graphs – this approach is being explored by the Gryphon project. None of the above projects has explored the notion of cross-domain message flows in any detail.

From an implementation point of view, none of the above projects has addressed all the research issues mentioned earlier in this paper. The first scalable solutions for matching and multicasting have appeared recently [ASS+99,BCM+99]. The SIENA project has explored issues relating to efficient propagation of subscriptions. Questions of efficient matching and multicast, message reliability, message ordering, and optimistic delivery are currently being explored in the Gryphon project.

References

[ASS+99] Marcos Aguilera, Rob Strom, Daniel Sturman, Mark Astley, and Tushar Chandra. Matching events in a content-based subscription system. In *Proceedings of the 18th ACM Symposium on the Principles of Distributed Computing, Atlanta, GA*, May 1999.

[BCJ+90] K. P. Birman, Robert Cooper, Thomas A. Joseph, Kenneth P. Kane, and Frank Bernhard Schmuck. *ISIS - A Distributed Programming Environment*, June 1990.

[BCM+99] Guruduth Banavar, Tushar Chandra, Bodhi Mukherjee, Jay Nagarajarao, Rob Strom, and Daniel Sturman. An efficient multicast protocol for content-based publish-subscribe systems. In *Proceedings of the International Conference on Distributed Computing Systems 1999, Austin, TX*, June 1999.

[BFH97] Ken Birman, Roy Friedman, and Mark Hayden. The maestro group manager: A structuring tool for applications with multiple quality of service requirements. Technical Report TR97-1619, Cornell University, Computer Science, feb 1997.

[Bir93] K. P. Birman. The process group approach to reliable distributed computing. *Communications of the ACM*, 36(12):36–53, Dec 1993.

[BKS+99] Guruduth Banavar, Marc Kaplan, Kelly Shaw, Rob Strom, Daniel Sturman, and Wei Tao. Information flow based event distribution middleware. In *Proceedings of the Middleware Workshop at the International Conference on Distributed Computing Systems 1999, Austin, TX*, June 1999.

[BN83] A. D. Birrell and B. J. Nelson. Implementing remote procedure calls. In *Proceedings of the ACM Symposium on Operating System Principles*, page 3, Bretton Woods, NH, October 1983. Association for Computing Machinery, Association for Computing Machinery.

[BT87] K. P. Birman and Joseph A. Thomas. Exploiting virtual synchrony in distributed systems. In *Proceedings of the Eleventh ACM Symposium on Operating Systems Principles*, pages 123–138, November 1987.

[Car98] Antonio Carzaniga. *Architectures for an Event Notification Service Scalable to Wide-area Networks*. PhD thesis, Politecnico di Milano, December 1998. Available from http://www.cs.colorado.edu/ carzanig/papers/.

[GKP99] R. Gruber, B Krishnamurthy, and E. Panagos. An architecture of the ready event notification system. In *Proceedings of the Middleware Workshop at the International Conference on Distributed Computing Systems 1999, Austin, TX*, June 1999.

[GL94] P. Gupta and E. Lin. Datajoiner: A practical approach to multi-database access. In *Parallel and Distributed Information Systems (PDIS '94)*, pages 264–264, Los Alamitos, Ca., USA, September 1994. IEEE Computer Society Press.

[Gro98] Object Management Group. Corba services: Common object service specification. Technical report, Object Management Group, July 1998.

[HCKW90] Eric N. Hanson, Moez Chaabouni, Chang-Ho Kim, and Yu-Wang Wang. A predicate matching algorithm for database rule systems. In *SIGMOD 1990, Atlantic City N. J.*, pages 271–280, May 1990.

[Hsi92]   D. Hsiao. Federated databases and systems: Part I – A tutorial on their data sharing. *VLDB Journal*, 1(1):127–179, July 1992.

[KK90]   Magdi N. Kamel and Nabil N. Kamel. The federated database management system: an architecture of distributed systems for the 90's. In *Proceedings, Second IEEE Workshop on Future Trends of Distributed Computing Systems*, pages 346–352, 1990.

[Lut94]   R. Lutz. IBM flowmark workflow manager - concept and overview. In G. Chroust and A. Benczur, editors, *Connectivity '94 - Workflow Management - Challenges, Paradigms and Products*, pages 65–68, Linz, Austria, October 1994. R. Oldenbourg, Vienna, Munich.

[OPSS93]   Brian Oki, Manfred Pfluegl, Alex Siegel, and Dale Skeen. The information bus - an architecture for extensible distributed systems. *Operating Systems Review*, 27(5):58–68, Dec 1993.

[Pow96]   David Powell. Group communication. *Communications of the ACM*, 39(4), April 1996. This is a collection of several papers in the area, Powell is guest editor.

[PPHC98]   S. Paul, E. Park, D. Hutches, and J. Chaar. RainMaker: Workflow execution using distributed, interoperable components. *Lecture Notes in Computer Science*, 1513:801–??, 1998.

[SA97]   Bill Segall and David Arnold. Elvin has left the building: A publish/subscribe notification service with quenching. In *Proceedings, AAUG97*, September 1997.

[SV97]   D. C. Schmidt and S. Vinoski. The OMG Events Service. *C++ Report*, 9(2):37–46, February 1997.

[TGGL82]   I. L. Traiger, J. N. Gray, C. A. Galtieri, and B. G. Lindsay. Transactions and consistency in distributed database management systems. *ACM Transactions on Database Systems*, pages 323–342, Sept 1982.

[WfM]   Workflow management coalition. http://www.aiai.ed.ac.uk/WfMC.

[WIS]   Workshop on internet scale event notification. See http://www.ics.uci.edu/IRUS/wisen/wisen98 for details.

Revisiting the Weakest Failure Detector for Uniform Reliable Broadcast*

Marcos Kawazoe Aguilera, Sam Toueg, and Borislav Deianov

Department of Computer Science, Upson Hall, Cornell University, Ithaca, NY
14853-7501, USA, {aguilera,sam,borislav}@cs.cornell.edu

Abstract. *Uniform Reliable Broadcast (URB)* is a communication primitive that requires that if a process delivers a message, then all correct processes also deliver this message. A recent paper [HR99] uses Knowledge Theory to determine what failure detectors are necessary to implement this primitive in asynchronous systems with process crashes and lossy links that are fair. In this paper, we revisit this problem using a different approach, and provide a result that is simpler, more intuitive, and, in a precise sense, more general.

1 Introduction

Uniform Reliable Broadcast (URB) is a communication primitive that requires that if a process delivers a message, then all correct processes also deliver this message [HT94]. A recent paper [HR99] uses Knowledge Theory to determine what failure detectors are necessary to implement this primitive in asynchronous systems with process crashes and fair links (roughly speaking, a fair link may lose an infinite number of messages, but if a message is sent infinitely often then it is eventually received).[1] In this paper, we revisit this problem using an algorithmic-reduction approach [CHT96], and provide a result that is simpler, more intuitive, and, in a precise sense, more general, as we now explain.

[HR99] considered systems where up to f processes may crash and links are fair, and used Knowledge Theory to show that solving URB in such a system requires a *generalized f-useful failure detector* (denoted G^f in here). Such a failure detector is parameterized by f and is described in Fig. 1. [HR99] shows that when $f = n$ or $f = n - 1$, G^f is equivalent to a *perfect failure detector*.

In this paper, we revisit this problem using the approach in [CHT96], and give a simpler characterization of the failure detectors that can solve URB in systems with process crashes and fair links. More precisely, we prove that the

---

* Research partially supported by NSF grant CCR-9711403 and by an Olin Fellowship.
[1] [HR99] actually studies a problem called *Uniform Distributed Coordination*. This problem, however, is isomorphic to URB: *init* and *do* in Uniform Distributed Coordination correspond to *broadcast* and *deliver* in URB, respectively.

A *generalized failure detector* [HR99] outputs a pair (S, k) where S is a subset of processes and k is a positive integer. Intuitively, the failure detector outputs (S, k) to report that k processes in S are faulty. In a run r, the failure detector event $suspect_p(S, k)$ is said to be *f-useful for* r if (a) S contains all processes that crash in r, and (b) $n - |S| > \min(f, n - 1) - k$. A generalized failure detector is *f-useful* if, for all runs r and processes p, the following two properties hold (where $r_p(t)$ denotes the prefix of run r at process p up to time t):

- If $suspect_p(S, k)$ is in $r_p(t)$ then there is a subset $S' \subseteq S$ such that $|S'| = k$ and for all $q \in S'$, we have that $crash_q$ is in $r_q(t)$.
- If p is correct, then there is a f-useful failure-detector event for r in $r_p(t)$, for some t.

Fig. 1. Definition of a generalized f-useful failure detectors.

weakest failure detector for this problem is a simple failure detector denoted Θ. Θ outputs a set of processes that are currently *trusted* to be up,[2] such that:

Completeness: There is a time after which processes do not trust any process that crashes.
Accuracy: If some process never crashes then, at every time, every process trusts at least one process that never crashes.

This simple characterization of the weakest failure detector for URB is more general than the one given in [HR99], in the sense that it holds for *any system with fair links, regardless of f or any other types of restrictions or dependencies on process crashes.*[3] To illustrate this point, consider the following three systems with n processors $\{p_1, p_2, \ldots, p_n\}$:

1. In system S_1, every processor may crash, except that we assume that p_1 and p_2 cannot both crash in the same run (this assumption makes sense if, for example, p_1 and p_2 are configured as symmetric primary/backup servers). Note that in S_1, up to $f = n - 1$ processors may crash in the same run.
2. In system S_2, every processor may crash, except that processor p_1 is a fault-tolerant highly-available computing server that crashes only when it is left alone in the system (this assumption is not unreasonable: in some existing systems, processes kill themselves if they are unable to communicate with a minimum number of processes). Note that in S_2, up to $f = n$ processors may crash in the same run.

---

[2] Some failure detectors in the literature output a set of processes suspected to be down; this is just the complement of the set of processes that are trusted to be up.
[3] If one assumes that a majority of processes does not crash, then URB can be solved without any failure detector [BCBT96]. As we explain in Sect. 11, this does not contradict our result.

3. In system S_3, the number of processes that crash is bounded, but this bound f is not given. Moreover, there are some additional restrictions and dependencies on process crashes (e.g., if more than half of the processes crash then a certain process p_1 commits suicide) but these are also not given.

What is the weakest failure detector for solving URB in each of S_1, S_2 and S_3? By our result, the answer is simply Θ.

In contrast, the result in [HR99] cannot be applied to S_1, S_2 and S_3, as we now explain. For S_3, this is obvious because f is not given. For S_1, the value of f, namely $n-1$, is given, but the result in [HR99] cannot be used, because it assumes that *every* set of (up to) $n-1$ processes may crash in a run — an assumption that does not hold for S_1. Similarly, for S_2, one cannot apply the result in [HR99].

Since, in some sense, both G^f and Θ are "minimal" for URB, an important question is now in order: What is the relation between G^f and Θ? To answer this question, we use the notions of *failure patterns* and *environments* [CHT96]. Roughly speaking, a *failure pattern* indicates, for each process p, whether p crashes and, if so, when. An *environment* $\mathcal{E}$ is a set of failure patterns; and a *system with environment* $\mathcal{E}$ is one where the process crashes must match one of the failure patterns in $\mathcal{E}$. Intuitively, environments allow us to express restrictions on process crashes, such as "either p_1 or p_2, but not both, may crash" (so environments can be used to formally define the systems S_1 and S_2 described earlier). A commonly-used environment in the literature is $\mathcal{E}^f$, the set of all failure patterns in which at most f processes crash: A system with environment $\mathcal{E}^f$ allows up to f process crashes, but there are no other constraints or dependencies, i.e., *any* subset of f process may crash, and these crashes can occur at *any* time.

We can now compare G^f and Θ. Roughly speaking, Θ is the weakest failure detector for URB regardless of the environment $\mathcal{E}$, while G^f is necessary and sufficient for URB in environment $\mathcal{E}^f$. When $\mathcal{E} = \mathcal{E}^f$, there is an algorithm that transforms G^f into Θ, and so Θ is at least as weak as G^f in environment $\mathcal{E}^f$.[4]

An important difference between [HR99] and this paper is that [HR99] uses Knowledge Theory [FHMV95] to establish and state its results, while we use algorithmic reductions [CT96]. An advantage of the algorithmic reduction method over the knowledge approach, is that the former allows the derivation of a stronger result: in a nutshell, the knowledge approach determines only what information about failures processes *know*, while the algorithmic reduction method determines what information about failures processes *know and can effectively compute*. Specifically, the result in [HR99] is that, in order to solve URB, processes must *know* the information provided by G^f. This does not automatically imply that processes can actually compute G^f.[5]

---

[4] This is modulo a technicality due to a difference in the two models: in [HR99] all the failure detector events are "seen" by processes, while here processes can "miss" some failure detector values.

[5] In Knowledge Theory, processes may know facts that they cannot actually compute. For example, if the system is sufficiently expressive, they know the answer to every

In contrast, the algorithmic reduction given in this paper shows that if processes can solve URB with some failure detector $\mathcal{D}$, then they can use $\mathcal{D}$ to *compute* failure detector Θ. This reduction implies that $\mathcal{D}$ is at least as strong as Θ in terms of problem solving: if processes can solve a problem with Θ, they can also solve it with $\mathcal{D}$ (by first using $\mathcal{D}$ to compute Θ). Note we would not be able to say that $\mathcal{D}$ is at least as strong as Θ (in terms of problem solving) if $\mathcal{D}$ only allowed processes to *know* (but not compute) the information provided by Θ.

Finally, there is another difference between our approach and the one in [HR99], namely, the universe of failure detectors that is being considered. To understand the meaning of a statement such as "$\mathcal{D}$ is the weakest failure detector...", or "$\mathcal{D}$ is necessary...", one needs to know the universe of failure detectors under consideration (because it is among these failure detectors that $\mathcal{D}$ is the "weakest" or "necessary"). In our paper, the universe of failure detectors is explicit and clear: a failure detector is a function of the failure pattern — a natural definition that is widely used [CT96, CHT96, ACT98, HMR97, OGS97, YNG98, LH94] etc. The universe of failure detectors in [HR99], however, is implicitly defined, and the exact nature and power of the failure detectors considered are not entirely clear. This issue is further discussed in Sect. 8.

In summary, in this paper we consider the problem of determining the weakest failure detector for solving URB in systems with process crashes and lossy links — a problem that was first investigated in [HR99]. In [HR99], this problem was studied using the framework of Knowledge Theory. In this paper, we tackle this problem using a different approach based on the standard failure detector models and techniques of [CHT96]. The results that we obtain are simple, intuitive and general. More precisely:

1. We provide a *single* failure detector Θ, and show that it is the weakest failure detector for URB, *in any environment*. In particular, our result holds even if f is not given.
   In environment $\mathcal{E}^f$, Θ is at least as weak as G^f.
2. Θ is simple and a natural candidate for solving URB. As a result, the algorithm that uses Θ to solve URB in any environment $\mathcal{E}$, is immediate.
3. Our results are derived and can be understood from first principles (they do not require Knowledge Theory).
4. Our "minimality" result is in terms of effective computation, not knowledge: roughly speaking, if processes can solve URB, we show how they can compute Θ (this implies knowledge of the information provided by Θ; but the converse does not necessarily hold).
5. The universe of failure detectors (with respect to which our minimality result holds) is given explicitly through a simple definition.

The paper is organized as follows. Our model is described in Sect. 2. In Sect. 3, we explain what it means for a failure detector to be weaker than another one.

---

unsolved problem in Number Theory, and they also know whether any given Turing Machine halts on blank tape.

Section 4 defines the uniform reliable broadcast problem. Failure detector Θ is defined in Sect. 5, and in Sect. 6, we show how to use it to implement uniform reliable broadcast in systems with process crashes and fair links. In Sect. 7 we show that Θ is actually the weakest failure detector for this problem. In Sect. 8, we briefly discuss the nature and power of failure detectors, and in Sect. 9 we consider the relation between G^f and Θ. Related work is discussed in Sect. 10 and we conclude the paper in Sect. 11.

2 Model

Throughout this paper, in all our results, we consider asynchronous message-passing distributed systems in which there are no timing assumptions. In particular, we make no assumptions on the time it takes to deliver a message, or on relative process speeds. The system consists of a set of n processes $\Pi = \{1, 2, \ldots, n\}$ that are completely connected by point-to-point (bidirectional) links. The system can experience both process failures and link failures. Processes can fail by crashing, and links can fail by dropping messages. The model, based on the one in [CHT96], is described next.

We assume the existence of a discrete global clock — this is merely a fictional device to simplify the presentation and processes do not have access to it. We take the range $\mathcal{T}$ of the clock's ticks to be the set of natural numbers.

2.1 Failure Patterns and Environments

Processes can fail by crashing, i.e., by halting prematurely. A *failure pattern F* is a function from $\mathcal{T}$ to 2^Π. Intuitively, $F(t)$ denotes the set of processes that have crashed through time t. Once a process crashes, it does not "recover", i.e., $\forall t : F(t) \subseteq F(t + 1)$. We define $\text{crashed}(F) = \bigcup_{t \in \mathcal{T}} F(t)$ and $\text{correct}(F) = \Pi \setminus \text{crashed}(F)$. If $p \in \text{crashed}(F)$ we say p *crashes (or is faulty) in F* and if $p \in \text{correct}(F)$ we say p is *correct in F*.

An environment $\mathcal{E}$ is a set of failure patterns. As we explained in the introduction, environments describe the crashes that can occur in a system.

Links can fail by dropping messages, but we assume that links are *fair*. Roughly speaking, a fair link from p to q may intermittently drop messages, and may do so infinitely often, but it must satisfy the following "fairness" property: if p repeatedly sends some message to q and q does not crash, then q eventually receives that message. This is made more precise in Sect. 2.3.

2.2 Failure Detectors

Each process has access to a local failure detector module that provides (possibly incorrect) information about the failure pattern that occurs in an execution. A *failure detector history H with range $\mathcal{R}$* is a function from $\Pi \times \mathcal{T}$ to $\mathcal{R}$. $H(p, t)$ is the output value of the failure detector module of process p at time t. *A failure detector $\mathcal{D}$* is a function that maps each failure pattern F to a non-empty *set* of failure detector histories with range $\mathcal{R}_{\mathcal{D}}$ (where $\mathcal{R}_{\mathcal{D}}$ denotes the range of the failure detector output of $\mathcal{D}$). $\mathcal{D}(F)$ denotes the set of possible failure detector histories permitted by $\mathcal{D}$ for the failure pattern F.

2.3   Runs of Algorithms

An algorithm $\mathcal{A}$ is a collection of n (possibly infinite-state) deterministic automata, one for each process in the system. Computation proceeds in atomic *steps* of $\mathcal{A}$. In each step, a process may: receive a message from a process, get an external input, query its failure detector module, undergo a state transition, send a message to a neighbor, and issue an external output.

A *run of algorithm $\mathcal{A}$ using failure detector $\mathcal{D}$* is a tuple $R = (F, H_{\mathcal{D}}, I, S, T)$ where F is a failure pattern, $H_{\mathcal{D}} \in \mathcal{D}(F)$ is a history of failure detector $\mathcal{D}$ for failure pattern F, I is an initial configuration of $\mathcal{A}$, S is an infinite sequence of steps of $\mathcal{A}$, and T is an infinite list of increasing time values indicating when each step in S occurs.

A run must satisfy some properties for every process p: If p has crashed by time t, i.e., $p \in F(t)$, then p does not take a step at any time $t' \geq t$; if p is correct, i.e., $p \in \text{correct}(F)$, then p takes an infinite number of steps; and if p takes a step at time t and queries its failure detector, then p gets $H_{\mathcal{D}}(p, t)$ as a response.

A run must also satisfy the following "fair link properties" for every pair of processes p and q:

- *Fairness*: If p sends a message m to q an infinite number of times and q is correct, then q eventually receives m from p.
- *Uniform Integrity*: If q receives a message m from p then p previously sent m to q; and if q receives m infinitely often from p, then p sends m infinitely often to q.

3   Failure Detector Transformations

As explained in [CT96, CHT96], failure detectors can be compared via algorithmic transformations. We now explain what it means for an algorithm $T_{\mathcal{D} \to \mathcal{D}'}$ to transform a failure detector $\mathcal{D}$ into another failure detector $\mathcal{D}'$ in an environment $\mathcal{E}$. Algorithm $T_{\mathcal{D} \to \mathcal{D}'}$ uses $\mathcal{D}$ to maintain a variable $\mathcal{D}'_p$ at every process p. This variable, reflected in the local state of p, emulates the output of $\mathcal{D}'$ at p. Let $H_{\mathcal{D}'}$ be the history of all the $\mathcal{D}'$ variables in a run R of $T_{\mathcal{D} \to \mathcal{D}'}$, i.e., $H_{\mathcal{D}'}(p, t)$ is the value of $\mathcal{D}'_p$ at time t in run R. Algorithm $T_{\mathcal{D} \to \mathcal{D}'}$ *transforms $\mathcal{D}$ into $\mathcal{D}'$ in $\mathcal{E}$* if and only if for every $F \in \mathcal{E}$ and every run $R = (F, H_{\mathcal{D}}, I, S, T)$ of $T_{\mathcal{D} \to \mathcal{D}'}$ using $\mathcal{D}$, we have $H_{\mathcal{D}'} \in \mathcal{D}'(F)$. Intuitively, since $T_{\mathcal{D} \to \mathcal{D}'}$ is able to use $\mathcal{D}$ to emulate $\mathcal{D}'$, $\mathcal{D}$ provides at least as much information about process failures as $\mathcal{D}'$ does, and we say that $\mathcal{D}'$ *is weaker than $\mathcal{D}$ in $\mathcal{E}$*.

Note that, in general, $T_{\mathcal{D} \to \mathcal{D}'}$ need not emulate *all* the failure detector histories of $\mathcal{D}'$ (in environment $\mathcal{E}$); what we do require is that all the failure detector histories it emulates be histories of $\mathcal{D}'$ (in that environment).

4 Uniform Reliable Broadcast

Uniform Reliable Broadcast (URB) is defined in terms of two primitives: broadcast(m) and deliver(m). We say that process p *broadcasts message* m if p invokes broadcast(m). We assume that every broadcast message m includes the following fields: the identity of its sender, denoted *sender*(m), and a sequence number, denoted *seq*(m). These fields make every broadcast message unique. We say that q *delivers message* m if q returns from the invocation of deliver(m). Primitives broadcast and deliver satisfy the following properties [HT94]:

- *Validity*: If a correct process broadcasts a message m, then it eventually delivers m.
- *Uniform Agreement*: If some process delivers a message m, then all correct processes eventually deliver m.
- *Uniform Integrity*: For every message m, every process delivers m at most once, and only if m was previously broadcast by *sender*(m).

Validity and Uniform Agreement imply that if a correct process broadcasts a message m, then all correct processes eventually deliver m.

5 Failure Detector Θ

We now define failure detector Θ. Each failure detector module of Θ outputs a *set of processes* that are trusted to be up, i.e., $\mathcal{R}_\Theta = 2^\Pi$. For each failure pattern F, $\Theta(F)$ is the set of all failure detector histories H with range $\mathcal{R}_\Theta$ that satisfy the following properties:

- *[Θ-completeness]*: There is a time after which correct processes do not trust any process that crashes. More precisely:

$$\exists t \in \mathcal{T}, \forall p \in \text{correct}(F), \forall q \in \text{crashed}(F), \forall t' \geq t : q \notin H(p, t')$$

- *[Θ-accuracy]*: If there is a correct process then, at every time, every process trusts at least one correct process. More precisely:

$$\text{crashed}(F) \neq \Pi \Rightarrow \forall t \in \mathcal{T}, \forall p \in \Pi \setminus F(t), \exists q \in \text{correct}(F) : q \in H(p, t)$$

Note that a process may be trusted even if it has actually crashed. Moreover, the correct processes trusted by a process p is allowed to change over time (in fact, it can change infinitely often), and it is not necessarily the same as the correct process trusted by another process q.

6 Using Θ to Implement Uniform Reliable Broadcast

The algorithm that implements URB using Θ is shown in Fig. 2. When ambiguities may arise, a variable local to process p is subscripted by p. To broadcast

```
1    For every process p:
2
3        To execute broadcast(m):
4            got[m] ← {p}
5            fork task diffuse(m)
6            return
7
8        task diffuse(m):
9            while true do
10               send m to all processes
11               d ← D_p                    { d is the list of processes trusted to be up }
12               if d ⊆ got[m] and p has not delivered m
13               then deliver(m)
14
15       upon receive m from q do
16           if task diffuse(m) has not been started yet then
17               got[m] ← {p, q}
18               fork task diffuse(m)
19           else got[m] ← got[m] ∪ {q}
```

Fig. 2. Implementing Uniform Reliable Broadcast using $\mathcal{D} = \Theta$

a message m, a process p first initializes $got_p[m]$ to $\{p\}$; this variable represents the processes that p knows to have received m so far. Process p then forks task $diffuse(m)$. In $diffuse(m)$, process p periodically sends m to all processes, and checks if $got[m]$ contains all processes that are currently trusted by p; when that happens, p delivers m if it has not done so already. When process p receives m from a process q, it starts task $diffuse(m)$ if it has not done so already.

Theorem 1. *Consider an asynchronous distributed system with process crashes and fair links, and with environment $\mathcal{E}$. The algorithm in Fig. 2 implements URB using Θ in $\mathcal{E}$.*

The proof is straightforward and can be found in [ATD99].

7 The Weakest Failure Detector for Uniform Reliable Broadcast

We now show that, in any environment, a failure detector $\mathcal{D}$ that can be used to solve URB can be transformed to Θ. More precisely, we have the following theorem:

Theorem 2. *Consider an asynchronous distributed system with process crashes and fair links, and with environment $\mathcal{E}$. Suppose failure detector $\mathcal{D}$ can be used to solve URB in $\mathcal{E}$. Then $\mathcal{D}$ can be transformed in $\mathcal{E}$ to the Θ failure detector.*

We now proceed to prove this theorem. Let $\mathcal{E}$ be an environment, $\mathcal{D}$ be a failure detector that can be used to solve URB in $\mathcal{E}$, and $\mathcal{A}_{URB}$ be the URB algorithm that uses $\mathcal{D}$. We describe an algorithm $T_{\mathcal{D}\to\Theta}$ that transforms $\mathcal{D}$ into Θ in $\mathcal{E}$. Intuitively, this algorithm works as follows.

Consider an arbitrary run of $T_{\mathcal{D}\to\Theta}$ using $\mathcal{D}$, with failure pattern $F \in \mathcal{E}$ and failure detector history $H \in \mathcal{D}(F)$. Processes periodically query their failure detector $\mathcal{D}$ and exchange information about the values of H that they see in this run. Using this information, processes construct a directed acyclic graph (DAG) that represents a "sampling" of failure detector values in H and some temporal relationships between the values sampled. To illustrate this, suppose that q_0 queries its failure detector $\mathcal{D}$ for the k_0-th time and sees value d_0; q_0 then reliably broadcasts the message $[q_0, d_0, k_0]$ (it can use $\mathcal{A}_{URB}$ to do so). When a process q_1 receives $[q_0, d_0, k_0]$, it can add vertex $[q_0, d_0, k_0]$ to its (current) version of the DAG. When q_1 later queries $\mathcal{D}$ and sees the value d_1 (say this is its k_1-th query), it adds vertex $[q_1, d_1, k_1]$ and edge $[q_0, d_0, k_0] \to [q_1, d_1, k_1]$ to its DAG: This edge indicates that q_0 saw d_0 (in its k_0-th query) *before* q_1 saw d_1 (in its k_1-th query). By periodically sending its current version of the DAG to all processes, and incorporating all the DAGs that it receives into its own DAG, a process can construct an ever increasing DAG that includes the failure detector values seen by processes and some of their temporal relationships.

It turns out that a process p can use its DAG to simulate runs of $\mathcal{A}_{URB}$ with failure pattern F and failure detector history H. These are runs that *could have occurred* if processes were running $\mathcal{A}_{URB}$ instead of $T_{\mathcal{D}\to\Theta}$.

To illustrate this, let p be a process, and consider a path in its DAG, say $[q_0, d_0, k_0], [q_1, d_1, k_1], \ldots, [q_\ell, d_\ell, k_\ell]$. In $T_{\mathcal{D}\to\Theta}$, process p uses this path to simulate a run R_{sim} of $\mathcal{A}_{URB}$. In R_{sim}, q_0 takes the 0-th step, q_1 takes the 1-st step, q_2 takes the 2-nd step, and so on. In the 0-th step, q_0 broadcasts m_0. Moreover, for every j, in the j-th step process q_j sees failure detector value d_j and receives the oldest message sent to it that it has not yet received (if there are no such messages, it receives nothing). It turns out that, if failure pattern F has some correct process, then process p can extract from R_{sim} a list of processes that contains at least one such a correct process. To see how, consider the step of R_{sim} when a process first delivers m_0, and suppose this is the k-th step. Then, among processes $\{q_0, \ldots, q_k\}$ (those that took steps before the delivery of m_0), there is at least one that never crashes in F. If that were not the case, we could construct another run R_{BAD} of $\mathcal{A}_{URB}$ with failure pattern F and failure detector history H, where (1) up to the k-th step, processes behave as in R_{sim}, (2) after the k-th step, processes $\{q_0, \ldots, q_k\}$ all crash, and all messages sent by these processes to other processes are lost and (3) from the $(k + 1)$-st step onwards, the correct processes (in F) take steps in a round-robin fashion. Note that in R_{BAD}, (1) process q_k delivers m_0 at the k-th step, (2) correct processes (in F) only take steps after the k-th step, (3) these processes never receive a message sent by the time of the k-th step, and so (4) correct processes (in F) never deliver m_0 — a contradiction. Thus, the list $\{q_0, \ldots, q_k\}$ contains at least one correct process (in F), and so p can achieve the Θ-accuracy property by outputting this list.

The list $\{q_0, \ldots, q_k\}$ that p generates, however, may contain processes that crash (in F). Thus, to achieve Θ-completeness, p must continuously repeat the simulation above to generate new $\{q_0, \ldots, q_k\}$ lists, such that eventually the lists contain only correct processes (in F). In order to guarantee that, p must ensure that the path $[q_0, d_0, k_0], [q_1, d_1, k_1], \ldots, [q_\ell, d_\ell, k_\ell]$ that it uses to extract $\{q_0, \ldots, q_k\}$ eventually includes only vertices of processes that do not crash. That will be true if all the processes that crash in F, do so before q_0 obtains d_0 at its k_0-th step. Therefore, process p can achieve Θ-completeness (as well as Θ-accuracy) by simply periodically reselecting a new path $[q_0, d_0, k_0], [q_1, d_1, k_1], \ldots, [q_\ell, d_\ell, k_\ell]$ so that $[q_0, d_0, k_0]$ is a "recent" vertex in its DAG.

Having given an overall account of how the transformation $T_{\mathcal{D} \to \Theta}$ works, we now explain it in more detail. In what follows, let S be a sequence of pairs consisting of a process name and a failure detector value, that is, $S :=$ $([q_0, d_0], [q_1, d_1], \ldots, [q_k, d_k])$. Let m_0 be an arbitrary fixed message. Given S, we can simulate an execution of $\mathcal{A}_{URB}$ in which (1) process q_0 initially invokes broadcast(m_0) and (2) for $j = 0, \ldots, k$, the j-th step of $\mathcal{A}_{URB}$ is taken by process q_j; in that step, q_j obtains d_j from its local failure detector module, and receives the oldest message addressed to it that it has not yet received (if there are no such messages, it receives nothing). We define $Delivered(S)$ to be true if process q_k delivers m_0 in the k-th step of this simulation.

The detailed algorithm that transforms $\mathcal{D}$ to Θ is given in Fig. 3. As we explained above, each process p maintains a directed acyclic graph DAG_p, whose nodes are triples $[q, d, seq]$. The transformation algorithm has three tasks; in the first task, a process p periodically queries its local failure detector, creates a new node $[p, d, curr]$ in DAG_p and adds an edge from all other nodes in DAG_p to this new node. Then, p uses $\mathcal{A}_{URB}$ to broadcasts its new DAG_p to all processes. In the second task, upon the delivery of $< DAG_q$ from a process q, process p merges its own DAG_p with DAG_q. In the third task, process p loops forever. In the loop, p first waits until its Task 1 adds a new node to DAG_p, and then waits until there is a path starting at this new node that satisfies $Delivered$. Once p finds such a path, it sets the output of $\mathcal{D}'$ to the set of all processes that appear in the path. Then, process p restarts the loop.

The detailed correctness proof of this algorithm is given in [ATD99].

8 On the Nature and Power of Failure Detectors

As we mentioned in the introduction, to understand the meaning of a statement such as "$\mathcal{D}$ is the weakest failure detector...", or "$\mathcal{D}$ is necessary...", we need to know the universe of failure detectors under consideration. For such minimality results to be significant, the universe of failure detectors should be reasonable. In particular, it should not include failure detectors that provide information that have nothing to do with failures, e.g., hints on which messages have been broadcast, information about the internal state of processes, etc. To see why, suppose that a "failure detector" is allowed to indicate whether a message m was broadcast; then processes could use it solve the URB problem without ever

```
 1    For every process p:
 2
 3        Initialization:
 4            DAG ← ∅
 5            curr ← −1
 6            𝒟'_p ← Π                                    { trust all processes }
 7
 8        cobegin
 9            ‖ Task 1:
10                while true do
11                    d ← 𝒟_p
12                    curr ← curr + 1
13                    add to DAG the node [p, d, curr] and edges from all other nodes to [p, d, curr]
14                    broadcast(DAG)        { use URB algorithm to broadcast }
15
16            ‖ Task 2:
17                upon deliver(DAG_q) from q do
18                    DAG ← DAG ∪ DAG_q
19
20            ‖ Task 3:
21                while true do
22                    next ← curr + 1
23                    wait until DAG contains a node of the form [p, *, next]
24                    wait until DAG contains a path P = ([q_0, d_0, seq_0], …, [q_k, d_k, seq_k]) such that
25                        (1) q_0 = p and seq_0 = next and
26                        (2) Delivered([q_0, d_0], …, [q_k, d_k]) is true
27                    𝒟'_p ← {q_0, …, q_k}              { all processes in this path }
28        coend
```

Fig. 3. Transformation of $\mathcal{D}$ to $\mathcal{D}' = \Theta$

sending any messages! Similarly, with the Consensus problem, if a "failure detector" could peek at the initial value of a process and provide this value to all processes, processes could use it to solve Consensus without messages and without $\diamond\mathcal{W}$ [CHT96]. Thus, a *failure* detector should be defined as an oracle that provides information about *failures* only.

In [HR99], it is not clear what information failure detectors are allowed to provide: On one hand, the formal model defines failure detectors as generic oracles;[6] on the other hand, their behavior is implicitly restricted by a closure axiom

---

[6] Even though the definition of a failure detector states that it must output a set S of processes, and that S should be "interpreted" as processes suspected of being faulty, there is nothing in the definition to enforce this interpretation: the model does not tie the output S to the crashes that occur in a run. Thus, the formal definition allows a failure detector to use its output S to encode information that has nothing to do with failures.

(on the set of runs of the system) that is introduced later in the paper.[7] The difficulty is that this axiom is technical and quite complex; furthermore, it does not mention failure detectors and it captures other assumptions that are not related to failure detection (e.g., the fact that processes are using a full-information protocol). Thus, the nature and power of the failure detectors that actually satisfy this axiom, and the universe of failure detectors under consideration, are not entirely clear.

9 Relation between G^f and Θ

In environment $\mathcal{E}^f$, Θ is at least as weak as G^f, that is, it is possible to transform G^f to Θ in $\mathcal{E}^f$. This transformation is given in Fig. 4. Initially, each process p sets its failure detector output to Π (trust all processes). There are three concurrent tasks. In the first task, p repeatedly sends "I-am-alive" to all processes in the system. In the second task, when p receives one such message from process q, it adds q to the set got. In the third task, process p loops forever. In each iteration, p checks whether at some time G^f has output a pair (S, k) such that $k > |S| - n + \min(f, n - 1)$ and got contains the complement of S. In that case, p sets its failure detector output to got, and then resets got to the empty set.

Theorem 3. *The algorithm in Fig. 4 transforms G^f into Θ in environment $\mathcal{E}^f$.*

The proof is simple, and can be found in [ATD99].

10 Related Work

The difference between the concepts of Agreement and Uniform Agreement was first pointed out in [Had86] in a comparison of Consensus versus Atomic Commitment. The term "Uniform" was introduced in [GT89, NT90], where it was studied in the context of Reliable Broadcast. In these papers, it is shown that with send and receive omission failures, URB can be solved if and only if a majority of processes are correct.

[BCBT96] consider systems with process crashes and fair (lossy) links, and addresses the following question: given any problem P that can be solved in a system where the only possible failures are process crashes, is P still solvable if links can also fail by losing messages? [BCBT96] shows that if P can be solved in systems with only process crashes, then P can also be solved in systems with process crashes *and* fair links, provided that (a) P is *correct-restricted*[8], or (b) a majority of processes are correct (i.e., $n > 2f$). As a corollary of this result (and the fact that URB is solvable in systems with only process crashes), we get that URB is solvable in systems with $f < n/2$ process crashes and fair links.

---

[7] This is axiom A4 in [HR99].

[8] Intuitively, a problem P is correct-restricted if its specification does not refer to the behavior of faulty processes [BN92, Gop92]. Note that URB is *not* correct-restricted.

```
1    For every process p:
2
3        Initialization:
4            𝒟′_p ← Π                                    { trust all processes }
5            got ← ∅
6
7        cobegin
8        ‖ Task 1:
9            while true do send (I-am-alive) to all processes
10
11       ‖ Task 2:
12           upon receive (I-am-alive) from q do
13               got ← got ∪ {q}
14
15       ‖ Task 3:
16           while true do
17               if there exists S, k such that
18                   (1) p got event suspect(S, k) (from G^f),
19                   (2) k > |S| − n + min(f, n − 1), and
20                   (3) got contains Π \ S
21                   then 𝒟′_p ← got; got ← ∅      { trust processes in got }
22       coend
```

Fig. 4. Transformation of G^f to $\mathcal{D}' = \Theta$ in $\mathcal{E}^f$.

[HR99] is the first paper to consider solving URB in systems with fair links and $f \geq n/2$. More precisely, [HR99] shows that if URB can be solved in a system S that satisfies some axioms A1–A5, then that system can "simulate" a system with failure detector G^f. This result holds even if system S has no failure detectors, but a different kind of oracle (axioms A1–A5 place restrictions on the allowable oracles). A discussion of other differences between [HR99] and this paper was given in Sect. 1.

11   Concluding Remarks

In some environments, URB can be solved without failure detectors at all, and this seems to contradict the fact that Θ is the weakest failure detector for URB in any environment. There is no contradiction, however, because in such environments Θ can be implemented.

For example, as we saw in the previous section, URB can be solved without failure detectors in an environment $\mathcal{E}_{maj}$ where a majority of processes are correct. This does not contradict Theorem 2 because Θ can be implemented in $\mathcal{E}_{maj}$, as we now explain.

To implement Θ in $\mathcal{E}_{maj}$, processes periodically send an "I-am-alive" message to all processes, and each process p keeps a list of processes $Order_p$. This list records the order in which the last "I-am-alive" message from each process is received. More precisely, $Order_p$ is initially an arbitrary permutation of the processes, and when p receives an "I-am-Alive" message from q, p moves q to the front of $Order$. To obtain Θ, a process p repeatedly outputs the first $\lceil (n+1)/2 \rceil$ processes in $Order_p$ as the set of trusted processes. It is easy to see why this implementation works: any process that crashes stops sending "I-am-alive" messages, and so it eventually moves towards the end of $Order_p$ and remains there forever afterwards. Since at most $\lfloor (n-1)/2 \rfloor$ processes crash, all processes that crash are eventually and permanently among the last $\lfloor (n-1)/2 \rfloor$ processes in $Order_p$ — so they do not appear among the first $\lceil (n+1)/2 \rceil$ processes. Thus our implementation satisfies Θ-completeness. To see that it also satisfies Θ-accuracy, note that among the first $\lceil (n+1)/2 \rceil$ processes in $Order_p$, there is *always* at least one correct process (since no majority of processes can crash in $\mathcal{E}_{maj}$).

In general, from the transformation algorithm in Fig. 3, the following obviously holds:

Remark 4. Consider an asynchronous distributed system with process crashes and fair links, and with environment $\mathcal{E}$. If URB can be solved in $\mathcal{E}$ without any failure detectors then Θ can be implemented in $\mathcal{E}$.

Acknowledgments

We would like to thank Joseph Halpern for discussing [HR99] with us and for providing useful suggestions for our paper.

References

[ACT98] Marcos Kawazoe Aguilera, Wei Chen, and Sam Toueg. Failure detection and consensus in the crash-recovery model. In *Proceedings of the 12th International Workshop on Distributed Algorithms*, Lecture Notes on Computer Science, pages 231–245. Springer-Verlag, September 1998. A full version is also available as Technical Report 98-1676, Computer Science Department, Cornell University, Ithaca, New York, April 1998.

[ATD99] Marcos Kawazoe Aguilera, Sam Toueg, and Borislav Deianov. Revisiting the weakest failure detector for uniform reliable broadcast. Technical Report 99-1741, Department of Computer Science, Cornell University, April 1999.

[BCBT96] Anindya Basu, Bernadette Charron-Bost, and Sam Toueg. Simulating reliable links with unreliable links in the presence of process crashes. In *Proceedings of the 10th International Workshop on Distributed Algorithms*, Lecture Notes on Computer Science, pages 105–122. Springer-Verlag, October 1996.

[BN92] R. Bazzi and G. Neiger. Simulating crash failures with many faulty processors. In A. Segal and S. Zaks, editors, *Proceedings of the 6th International Workshop on Distributed Algorithms*, volume 647 of *Lecture Notes on Computer Science*, pages 166–184. Springer-Verlag, 1992.

[CHT96]   Tushar Deepak Chandra, Vassos Hadzilacos, and Sam Toueg. The weakest
            failure detector for solving consensus. *Journal of the ACM*, 43(4):685–722,
            July 1996.

[CT96]   Tushar Deepak Chandra and Sam Toueg. Unreliable failure detectors for
            reliable distributed systems. *Journal of the ACM*, 43(2):225–267, March
            1996.

[FHMV95]   Ronald Fagin, Joseph Y. Halpern, Yoram Moses, and Moshe Y. Vardi.
            Reasoning About Knowledge. The MIT Press, 1995.

[Gop92]   Ajei Gopal. *Fault-Tolerant Broadcasts and Multicasts: The Problem of In-
            consistency and Contamination*. PhD thesis, Cornell University, January
            1992.

[GT89]   Ajei Gopal and Sam Toueg. Reliable broadcast in synchronous and asyn-
            chronous environments (preliminary version). In *Proceedings of the Third
            International Workshop on Distributed Algorithms*, volume 392 of *Lecture
            Notes on Computer Science*, pages 110–123. Springer-Verlag, September
            1989.

[Had86]   Vassos Hadzilacos. On the relationship between the atomic commitment
            and consensus problems. In *Proceedings of the Workshop on Fault-Tolerant
            Distributed Computing*, volume 448 of *Lecture Notes on Computer Science*,
            pages 201–208. Springer-Verlag, March 1986.

[HMR97]   Michel Hurfin, Achour Mostefaoui, and Michel Raynal. Consensus in asyn-
            chronous systems where processes can crash and recover. Technical Report
            1144, Institut de Recherche en Informatique et Systèmes Aléatoires, Uni-
            versité de Rennes, November 1997.

[HR99]   Joseph Y. Halpern and Aleta Ricciardi. A knowledge-theoretic analysis of
            uniform distributed coordination and failure detectors. In *Proceedings of
            the 18th ACM Symposium on Principles of Distributed Computing*, pages
            73–82, 1999.

[HT94]   Vassos Hadzilacos and Sam Toueg. A modular approach to fault-tolerant
            broadcasts and related problems. Technical Report 94-1425, Department
            of Computer Science, Cornell University, Ithaca, New York, May 1994.

[LH94]   Wai-Kau Lo and Vassos Hadzilacos. Using failure detectors to solve con-
            sensus in asynchronous shared-memory systems. In *Proceedings of the
            8th International Workshop on Distributed Algorithms*, Lecture Notes on
            Computer Science, pages 280–295. Springer-Verlag, 1994.

[NT90]   Gil Neiger and Sam Toueg. Automatically increasing the fault-tolerance
            of distributed algorithms. *Journal of Algorithms*, 11(3):374–419, 1990.

[OGS97]   Rui Oliveira, Rachid Guerraoui, and André Schiper.   Consensus
            in the crash-recover model.   Technical Report 97-239, Département
            d'Informatique, Ecole Polytechnique Fédérale, Lausanne, Switzerland,
            August 1997.

[YNG98]   Jiong Yang, Gil Neiger, and Eli Gafni. Structured derivations of con-
            sensus algorithms for failure detectors. In *Proceedings of the 17th ACM
            Symposium on Principles of Distributed Computing*, pages 297–306, June
            1998.

Efficient Algorithms to Implement Unreliable Failure Detectors in Partially Synchronous Systems *

Mikel Larrea[1]   Sergio Arevalo[2]   Antonio Fernández[2]

[1] Universidad Pública de Navarra, 31006 Pamplona, Spain.
[2] Universidad Rey Juan Carlos, 28933 Móstoles, Spain.
Email: mikel.larrea@unavarra.es, {s.arevalo, a.fernandez}@escet.urjc.es.

Abstract. Unreliable failure detectors, proposed by Chandra and Toueg [2], are mechanisms that provide information about process failures. In [2], eight classes of failure detectors were defined, depending on how accurate this information is, and an algorithm implementing a failure detector of one of these classes in a partially synchronous system was presented. This algorithm is based on all-to-all communication, and periodically exchanges a number of messages that is quadratic on the number of processes. To our knowledge, no other algorithm implementing these classes of unreliable failure detectors has been proposed.
In this paper, we present a family of distributed algorithms that implement four classes of unreliable failure detectors in partially synchronous systems. Our algorithms are based on a logical ring arrangement of the processes, which defines the monitoring and failure information propagation pattern. The resulting algorithms periodically exchange at most a linear number of messages.

1   Introduction

The concept of *unreliable failure detector* was introduced by Chandra and Toueg in [2]. These authors showed how unreliable failure detectors can be used to solve the *Consensus* problem [10] in asynchronous systems. (This was shown to be impossible in a pure asynchronous system by Fischer et al. [7].) Since then, a considerable amount of work has been devoted to study properties of the failure detection abstraction [1, 6, 9].

From the results of Fischer et al. and those of Chandra and Toueg, it can be derived the impossibility of, in asynchronous systems, implementing failure detectors precise enough to solve Consensus. Chandra and Toueg presented an algorithm that implements an unreliable failure detector in a partially synchronous system. To our knowledge, this is the only proposed algorithm implementing any of the classes of unreliable failure detectors defined in [2]. In this paper we present more efficient alternatives to that first algorithm.

* Partially supported by the Basque Government under grant number BFI96.043, and the Madrid Regional Research Council (CAM), contract number $CAM - 07T/00112/1998$.

1.1 Partial Synchrony

Distributed algorithms can be designed under different assumptions of system behaviors, i.e., system models. One of the main assumptions in which system models can differ is related to the timing aspects. Most models focus on two timing attributes: the time taken for message delivery across a communication channel, and the time taken by a processor to execute a piece of code. Depending on whether these attributes are bounded or not, and on the knowledge of these bounds, they can be classified as synchronous, asynchronous, or partially synchronous [5]. A timing attribute is *synchronous* if there is a known fixed upper bound on it. On the other hand, it is *asynchronous* if there is no bound on it. Finally, a timing attribute is *partially synchronous* if it is neither synchronous nor asynchronous. Dwork et al. [5] consider two kinds of partial synchrony. In the first one, the timing attribute is bounded, but the bound is unknown. In the second one, the timing attribute is bounded and the bound is known, but it holds only after an unknown stabilization interval. Chandra and Toueg [2] propose another kind of partial synchrony, in which the timing attribute is bounded, but the bound is unknown and holds only after an unknown stabilization interval. This will be the model of partial synchrony used in this paper.

Although the asynchronous model (in which at least one of the timing attributes is asynchronous) is attractive for designing distributed algorithms, it is well known that a number of synchronization distributed problems cannot be solved deterministically in asynchronous systems in which processes can fail. For instance, as we mentioned above, Consensus cannot be solved deterministically in an asynchronous system that is subject to even a single process failure [7], while it can be solved in both synchronous and partially synchronous systems [2, 4, 5]. In fact, the ability to solve these synchronization distributed problems closely depends on the ability to detect failures. In a synchronous system, reliable failure detection is possible. One can reliably detect failures using timeouts. (The timeouts can be derived from the known upper bounds on message delivery time and processing time.) In an asynchronous system, it is impossible to distinguish a failed process from a very slow one. Thus, reliable failure detection is impossible.

However, even if it is sufficient, reliable failure detection is not necessary to solve most of these problems. As we already mentioned, Chandra and Toueg [2] introduced unreliable failure detectors (failure detectors that can make mistakes), and showed how they can be used to solve Consensus and Atomic Broadcast. Guerraoui et al. [8] showed how unreliable failure detectors can be used to solve the Non-Blocking Atomic Commitment problem.

1.2 Unreliable Failure Detectors

An *unreliable failure detector* is a mechanism that provides (possibly incorrect) information about process failures. When it is queried, the failure detector returns a list of processes believed to have crashed (suspected processes). In [2], failure detectors were characterized in terms of two properties: *completeness* and

	Eventual strong accuracy	Eventual weak accuracy
Strong completeness	*Eventually Perfect* $\Diamond \mathcal{P}$	*Eventually Strong* $\Diamond \mathcal{S}$
Weak completeness	*Eventually Quasi-Perfect* $\Diamond \mathcal{Q}$	*Eventually Weak* $\Diamond \mathcal{W}$

Fig. 1. Four classes of failure detectors defined in terms of completeness and accuracy.

accuracy. Completeness characterizes the failure detector capability of suspecting every incorrect process (processes that actually crash) while accuracy characterizes the failure detector capability of not suspecting correct processes. Two kinds of completeness and four kinds of accuracy were defined, which combined yield eight classes of failure detectors.

In this paper we will focus on the two kinds of completeness and two of the four kinds of accuracy defined in [2], which are the following:

- *Strong completeness.* Eventually, every process that crashes is permanently suspected by *every* correct process.
- *Weak completeness.* Eventually, every process that crashes is permanently suspected by *some* correct process.

Note that completeness by itself is not very useful. We can trivially satisfy strong completeness by forcing every process to permanently suspect every other process in the system.

- *Eventual strong accuracy.* Eventually, no correct process is ever suspected by any correct process.
- *Eventual weak accuracy.* Eventually, some correct process is never suspected by any correct process.

Combining in pairs these completeness and accuracy properties, we obtain four different failure detector classes, which are shown in Fig. 1. Out of these, Chandra et al. [3] showed that $\Diamond \mathcal{W}$ is the weakest class of failure detectors required for solving Consensus.

Chandra and Toueg [2] proposed a timeout-based implementation of a $\Diamond \mathcal{P}$ failure detector in a system with partial synchrony (they recognize that, in practice, some synchrony is required to implement the failure detectors they propose). In their algorithm, all processes periodically send a message to every other process in order to inform them that it has not crashed. If there are n processes in the system and C of them do not crash, at least nC messages are periodically exchanged with this algorithm. We do not know of any other implementation of these classes of failure detectors.

1.3 Our Results

In this paper, we present a family of algorithms that implement unreliable failure detectors of the four classes defined in the previous section, in partially synchronous systems. Our algorithms have been designed, and are presented, in a gradual way. First, we present an algorithm that provides weak completeness. Next, we show how to extend this algorithm to provide eventual weak accuracy. This extended algorithm implements a $\Diamond \mathcal{W}$ failure detector. Next, we present two other extensions which strengthen the accuracy and the completeness, respectively, implementing the stronger failure detectors.

In all these algorithms, each correct process monitors only one other process in a cyclic fashion. The monitoring process performs this task by repeatedly polling the monitored process. Each polling involves only two messages exchanged between the monitoring and monitored processes. If the pollings were done periodically, a total of no more than $2n$ messages would be periodically exchanged. Eventually, this amount becomes at most $2\mathcal{C}$, which is a significant improvement over the at least $n\mathcal{C}$ messages of the previous algorithm (Chandra and Toueg's).

The rest of the paper is organized as follows. The next section describes our model of distributed system. In Section 3, we present a basic algorithm that provides weak completeness. In Section 4, we present an extension to the basic algorithm that provides eventual weak accuracy. In Section 5, we present another extension that provides eventual strong accuracy. In Section 6, we present an extension to the previous algorithms that provides strong completeness, while preserving accuracy. In Section 7, we study the performance of our algorithms in terms of the number and the size of the messages periodically exchanged. Finally, Section 8 summarizes the conclusions and presents future lines of work.

2 The Model

2.1 System Model

Our model of distributed system consists of a set Π of n processes, $\Pi = \{p_1, \ldots, p_n\}$, that communicate by exchanging messages. Every pair of processes is assumed to be connected by a reliable communication channel.

Processes can fail by *crashing*, that is, by prematurely halting. Crashed processes do not recover. In every execution of the system we identify two complementary subsets of Π: the subset of processes that do not fail, denoted *correct*, and the subset of processes that do fail, denoted *crashed*. We use $\mathcal{C}$ to denote the number of correct processes in the system, which we assume is at least one, i.e., $\mathcal{C} = |correct| > 0$. For every process p in *crashed* we use $Tcrash_p$ to denote the instant at which p crashes.

In the algorithms presented in this paper we consider the processes $p_1, \ldots, p_n$ arranged in a logical ring. This arrangement is known by all the processes. Without loss of generality, process p_i is followed in the ring by process $p_{(i \bmod n)+1}$. In general, we use $succ(p)$ to denote the process that follows process p in the ring, and $pred(p)$ to denote the process that precedes process p in the ring. Finally, we use $corr\_succ(p)$ and $corr\_pred(p)$ to denote the closest correct (i.e., belonging to the subset *correct*) successor and predecessor of p in the ring, respectively.

We consider the model of *partial synchrony* proposed by Chandra and Toueg [2]. In this model, there are bounds on both message delivery time and processing time, but these bounds are not known and only hold after an unknown, but finite, stabilization interval. We shall use T_s to denote the ending instant of this stabilization interval in the execution of interest. We also denote by Δ_{msg} the maximum time interval, after stabilization, since a process sends a message and that message is delivered and processed by its destination process (assuming that both the sender and the destination have not failed). Clearly, Δ_{msg} depends on the existing bounds on both message delivery time and processing time. Note that the exact value of Δ_{msg} exists, but it is unknown.

2.2 Implementation of Failure Detectors

A *distributed failure detector* can be viewed as a set of n failure detection modules, each one attached to a different process in the system. These modules cooperate to satisfy the required properties of the failure detector. Each module maintains a list of the processes it suspects to have crashed. These lists can differ from one module to another at a given time. We denote by L_p (G_p in Section 6) the list of suspected processes of the failure detection module attached to process p. Clearly, the contents of the list L_p (G_p) can be different at different times. We use $L_p(t)$ ($G_p(t)$ in Section 6) to denote the contents of L_p (G_p) at time t. A process p interacts only with its local failure detection module in order to get the current list of suspected processes.

In this paper, we only describe the behavior of the failure detection modules in order to implement a failure detector, but not the behavior of the processes they are attached to. For this reason, in the rest of the paper we will mostly use the term *process* instead of *failure detection module*. We consider that a process cannot crash independently of its attached failure detection module.

In any algorithm that implements any of the failure detector classes defined in Section 1.2, it is required that some processes monitor other processes. Monitoring allows a process to detect whether another process has crashed and to take proper action if so (usually suspect it). Clearly, there are several possible ways to implement the monitoring. Examples are the monitored process sending an I-AM-ALIVE message (a *heartbeat*) to the monitoring process or the later *polling* the former for such a message. In any case, the only way a process can show it has not crashed is by sending messages to those monitoring it. Hence, any monitoring protocol requires that the monitored process sends messages to the monitoring process.

Our algorithms use pollings instead of only sending heartbeats, because the former allow a finer control of the monitoring. To monitor process q, a process p sends an ARE-YOU-ALIVE? message to q and waits for an I-AM-ALIVE message from it. As soon as q receives the ARE-YOU-ALIVE? message, it sends the I-AM-ALIVE message to p. We will denote by $\Delta_{rtt} = 2\Delta_{msg}$ the maximum monitoring round-trip time after stabilization, i.e., the maximum time, after T_s, elapsed between the sending of an ARE-YOU-ALIVE? message to a correct process, and the reception and processing of the corresponding I-AM-ALIVE reply message.

Since a monitoring process p does not know Δ_{rtt}, it has to use an estimated value (timeout) that tells how much time it has to wait for the reply from the monitored process q. This time value is denoted by $\Delta_{p,q}$. Then, if after $\Delta_{p,q}$ time p did not receive the reply from q, it suspects that q has crashed. We need to allow these time values to vary over time in our algorithms. We use $\Delta_{p,q}(t)$ to denote the value of $\Delta_{p,q}$ at time t.

3   A Basic Algorithm that Provides Weak Completeness

In this section, we present an algorithm that will be used as a framework for all the failure detector implementations presented in this paper. This first algorithm satisfies the weak completeness property. In the following sections we will extend the algorithm to satisfy also eventual weak accuracy, eventual strong accuracy, and strong completeness. This algorithm is presented here for the sake of clarity but is not very useful by itself, since it does not satisfy any of the accuracy properties previously defined.

The algorithm executes as follows: initially, every process starts monitoring its successor in the ring. If a process p does not receive the reply from the process q it is monitoring, then p suspects that q has crashed, and starts monitoring the successor of q in the ring. This monitoring scheme is repeated, so that p always suspects all processes in the ring between itself and the process it is monitoring (not included). If, later on, p receives a message from a suspected process q while it is monitoring another process r, then p stops suspecting q and all the processes between q and r in the ring, and starts monitoring q again.

Fig. 2 presents the algorithm in detail. Each process p has a variable $target_p$ which holds the process being monitored by p at a given time. As we said above, all processes between p and $target_p$ in the ring (and only them) are suspected by p, and these are the only processes included in the list L_p of suspected processes of p. (Initially, no process is suspected, i.e., $\forall p : L_p(0) = \emptyset$.) The $mutex_p$ variable is used to avoid race conditions in process p.

We now show that weak completeness holds with this algorithm. Given an incorrect process p, the following theorem states that it will be permanently suspected by $corr\_pred(p)$ (the first correct process preceding p in the ring).

Theorem 1. $\exists t_0 : \forall p \in crashed$, p has failed at time t_0 and $\forall t \geq t_0, p \in L_{corr\_pred(p)}(t)$.

Proof. Let p be a process that crashes. We claim that p will be permanently included in $L_{corr\_pred(p)}$. The proof uses strong induction on the distance from $corr\_pred(p)$ to p. Let first consider that such distance is 1, i.e., $corr\_pred(p) = pred(p)$. Before p fails, $corr\_pred(p)$ and p exchange ARE-YOU-ALIVE? and I-AM-ALIVE messages (see Fig. 2). Eventually p crashes, and there is an ARE-YOU-ALIVE? message sent by $corr\_pred(p)$ that reaches p after $Tcrash_p$. Since p has already crashed by then, it will never reply to that message. If such a message was sent at time t', then $\Delta_{corr\_pred(p),p}(t')$ time later, $corr\_pred(p)$ will include

Every process p executes:

$target_p \leftarrow succ(p)$
$L_p \leftarrow \emptyset$
$\forall q \in \Pi : \Delta_{p,q} \leftarrow$ default timeout

cobegin
|| Task 1:
  loop
    $wait(mutex_p)$
    send ARE-YOU-ALIVE? to $target_p$
    $t_{out} \leftarrow \Delta_{p,target_p}$
    $received \leftarrow false$
    $signal(mutex_p)$
    delay t_{out}
    $wait(mutex_p)$
    if not $received$
      $L_p \leftarrow L_p \cup \{target_p\}$
      $target_p \leftarrow succ(target_p)$
    end if
    $signal(mutex_p)$
  end loop

|| Task 2:
  loop
    receive message m from a process q
    $wait(mutex_p)$
    case
      $m =$ ARE-YOU-ALIVE?:
        send I-AM-ALIVE to q
        if $q \in L_p$
        $L_p \leftarrow L_p - \{q,\ldots,pred(target_p)\}$
        $target_p \leftarrow q$
        $received \leftarrow true$
      end if
      $m =$ I-AM-ALIVE:
        case
          $q = target_p$:
            $received \leftarrow true$
          $q \in L_p$:
            $L_p \leftarrow L_p - \{q,\ldots,pred(target_p)\}$
            $target_p \leftarrow q$
            $received \leftarrow true$
          else discard m
        end case
    end case
    $signal(mutex_p)$
  end loop
coend

Fig. 2. Algorithm that provides weak completeness.

p in $L_{corr\_pred(p)}$. Since no message will ever be received by $corr\_pred(p)$ from p after that, it will never be removed from $L_{corr\_pred(p)}$.

We will now prove that if the claim holds for any distance $1 \leq d \leq i - 1$, it also holds for distance i. Let us assume the distance from $corr\_pred(p)$ to p be $i > 1$. Then, for any process $q \in \{succ(corr\_pred(p)),\ldots,pred(p)\}$, it can be easily seen that $corr\_pred(q) = corr\_pred(p)$ and the distance d from $corr\_pred(p)$ to q verifies $1 \leq d \leq i - 1$. Hence, from the induction hypothesis, all processes in $\{succ(corr\_pred(p)),\ldots,pred(p)\}$ will eventually be permanently in $L_{corr\_pred(p)}$. After that, they will never be monitored again by $corr\_pred(p)$. The situation then is similar to the distance-1 case considered above and, by a similar argument, p will eventually be permanently included in $L_{corr\_pred(p)}$.

Corollary 1. *The algorithm of Fig. 2 provides weak completeness.*

4 Extending the Basic Algorithm to Provide Eventual Weak Accuracy

The algorithm presented in the previous section does not satisfy any of the accuracy properties defined in Section 1.2. It does not prevent the erroneous suspicion of any correct process, and these incorrect suspicions, although not permanent (if the suspected process is correct, the reply message will eventually be received), can happen infinitely often. This is due to the fact that the message delivery time could be greater than the fixed *default timeout* (see Fig. 2). In order to provide some useful accuracy, the timeout values must be augmented when processes are aware of having erroneously suspected a correct process. In this section, we present an extension to the basic algorithm of Fig. 2, based on augmenting the timeout values, which satisfies the eventual weak accuracy property.

Eventual weak accuracy requires that, eventually, some correct process is never suspected by any correct process. In order to provide it, it is enough that this is satisfied for only one correct process. Our extension to the basic algorithm guarantees the existence of such a process, which we denote *leader*. Clearly, if we knew beforehand a correct process, eventual weak accuracy could be obtained by making all processes augment their timeout value with respect to this process each time they suspect it. This correct process would be *leader*. But since we cannot know in advance the correctness of any process, we need to devise another way to eventually have a correct and not-suspected process.

In our extension of the algorithm of Fig. 2, processes behave as follows. Initially, every process will consider a pre-agreed process (e.g. p_1) as an *initial candidate* to be *leader*. When a process that monitors this candidate suspects it, it considers its successor in the ring as new candidate and monitors it. This scheme is repeated every time the current candidate is suspected. (Note that a process not monitoring a candidate cannot suspect it.) If a process p stops suspecting a process q, previously considered as candidate, then p will augment its timeout value $\Delta_{p,q}$ [1]. If the previously suspected process q was not considered as candidate, then p will not change $\Delta_{p,q}$. This way, *leader* will be the first correct process in the ring starting from the *initial candidate* (inclusive). All processes monitoring it will eventually stop suspecting it, and processes that do not monitor it will never suspect it. This gives us the eventually weak accuracy property. Fig. 3 presents the extended algorithm in detail.

We now show that eventual weak accuracy holds with this algorithm, i.e., eventually some correct process is never suspected by any correct process.

Lemma 1. *After T_s, any correct process p will suspect leader for no more than Δ_{rtt} time, each time it does.*

Proof. Remember that, after T_s, Δ_{rtt} is a bound on the monitoring round-trip time. A correct process p suspects *leader* after sending an ARE-YOU-ALIVE? message to it at time t and not receiving an I-AM-ALIVE reply message in $\Delta_{p,leader}(t)$

---
[1] For simplicity of the algorithm, instead of increasing timeouts when we stop suspecting, we increase timeouts as soon as we suspect a candidate.

Every process p executes:

$initial\_cand_p \leftarrow$ pre-agreed process
$target_p \leftarrow succ(p)$
$L_p \leftarrow \emptyset$
$\forall q \in \Pi : \Delta_{p,q} \leftarrow$ default timeout

cobegin
‖ Task 1:
  loop
    wait($mutex_p$)
    send ARE-YOU-ALIVE? to $target_p$
    $t_{out} \leftarrow \Delta_{p,target_p}$
    $received \leftarrow false$
    signal($mutex_p$)
    delay t_{out}

wait($mutex_p$)
if not $received$
  if $initial\_cand_p \in \{succ(p), \ldots, target_p\}$
    $\Delta_{p,target_p} \leftarrow \Delta_{p,target_p} + 1$
    $L_p \leftarrow L_p \cup \{target_p\}$
    $target_p \leftarrow succ(target_p)$
  end if
  signal($mutex_p$)
end loop

‖ Task 2:
  $\ldots$ {Same as algorithm in Fig. 2}
coend

Fig. 3. Extension to the algorithm of Fig. 2 to provide eventual weak accuracy.

time. Since, by definition, *leader* is a correct process, the I-AM-ALIVE message will arrive at most at time $t + \Delta_{rtt}$ ($T_s + \Delta_{rtt}$ if $t < T_s$). At this moment *leader* is removed from L_p, the list of suspected processes of p.

Lemma 2. *Any correct process p will suspect leader a finite number of times.*

Proof. Let p be some correct process. Since the value of T_s is finite, p suspects *leader* a finite number of times before T_s. After that, from the algorithm, each time p suspects *leader*, the value of $\Delta_{p,leader}$ is incremented by one. After suspecting *leader* a finite number of times, $\Delta_{p,leader}$ will be greater than Δ_{rtt}. After this moment, p never suspects *leader* anymore.

Theorem 2. $\exists t_1 : \forall p \in correct, \forall t > t_1, leader \notin L_p(t)$

Proof. Let t_1^p be the instant at which a correct process p stops suspecting *leader* for the last time. (If p never suspects *leader*, $t_1^p = 0$.) Such an instant exists from Lemma 1 and Lemma 2. Then, after instant $t_1 = \max\limits_{p \in correct} \{t_1^p\}$ no correct process p has *leader* in its list L_p.

Corollary 2. *The algorithm of Fig. 3 provides eventual weak accuracy.*

Observation 1 *The only difference between this algorithm and the algorithm of Fig. 2 is that in the former the values of $\Delta_{p,q}$ can change. Clearly, this does not affect the proof of Theorem 1. Hence, Corollary 1 also applies to this algorithm.*

Corollary 3. *The algorithm of Fig. 3 implements a failure detector of class $\Diamond W$.*

Proof. Follows from Corollary 2, Observation 1, and Corollary 1.

Every process p executes:

```
target_p ← succ(p)                      wait(mutex_p)
L_p ← ∅                                 if not received
∀q ∈ Π : Δ_{p,q} ← default timeout          Δ_{p,target_p} ← Δ_{p,target_p} + 1
                                            L_p ← L_p ∪ {target_p}
cobegin                                     target_p ← succ(target_p)
|| Task 1:                              end if
  loop                                 signal(mutex_p)
    wait(mutex_p)                    end loop
    send ARE-YOU-ALIVE? to target_p
    t_out ← Δ_{p,target_p}           || Task 2:
    received ← false                    ...          {Same as algorithm in Fig. 2}
    signal(mutex_p)                  coend
    delay t_out
```

Fig. 4. Extension to the algorithm of Fig. 2 to provide eventual strong accuracy.

5 Extending the Basic Algorithm to Provide Eventual Strong Accuracy

Eventual strong accuracy requires that, eventually, no correct process is ever suspected by any correct process. In this section, we propose another extension to the basic algorithm of Section 3 which satisfies this property. Broadly, the extension consists in each process augmenting its timeout values with respect to all processes it incorrectly suspects. This way every process will augment the timeout value with respect to its closest correct successor in the ring, and will thus eventually stop suspecting it (and hence, any other correct process). This gives us the eventually strong accuracy property. Fig. 4 presents the extended algorithm in detail.

We now show that eventual strong accuracy holds with the algorithm in Fig. 4. We start with two lemmas, whose proofs are similar to those of Lemma 1 and Lemma 2, respectively, and are omitted.

Lemma 3. *After T_s, any correct process p will suspect $corr\_succ(p)$ for no more than Δ_{rtt} time, each time it does.*

Lemma 4. *Any correct process p will suspect $corr\_succ(p)$ a finite number of times.*

Theorem 3. $\exists t_2 : \forall p \in correct, \forall q \in correct, \forall t > t_2, q \notin L_p(t)$

Proof. Let t_2^p be the instant at which a correct process p stops suspecting $corr\_succ(p)$ for the last time. (If p never suspects $corr\_succ(p)$, $t_2^p = 0$.) Such an instant exists from Lemma 3 and Lemma 4. Then, after instant $t_2 = \max_{p \in correct} \{t_2^p\}$ no correct process p has $corr\_succ(p)$ in its list L_p. Then, after t_2, each correct process p only suspects processes in $succ(p), \ldots, pred(corr\_succ(p))$, which are not correct by the definition of $corr\_succ(p)$. Therefore, no correct process q is in L_p after t_2.

Corollary 4. *The algorithm of Fig. 4 provides eventual strong accuracy.*

Note that Observation 1 still applies to this algorithm. Hence, the following corollary, that follows from Corollary 4, Observation 1, and Corollary 1.

Corollary 5. *The algorithm of Fig. 4 implements a failure detector of class $\Diamond Q$.*

6 Extending the Previous Algorithms to Provide Strong Completeness

In this section we present an extension to the previous algorithms to provide strong completeness, while preserving accuracy. By combining this extension with the algorithms that implement failure detectors of classes $\Diamond W$ and $\Diamond Q$, presented in previous sections, we obtain implementations of failure detectors of classes $\Diamond S$ and $\Diamond P$, respectively.

Strong completeness requires that, eventually, every process that crashes is permanently suspected by every correct process. In [2], Chandra and Toueg presented a distributed algorithm that transforms weak completeness into strong completeness. Broadly, in their algorithm, every process periodically *broadcasts* (sends to every other process) its *local* list of suspected processes. Upon reception of these lists, each process builds a *global* list of suspected processes, which provides strong completeness. Clearly, in this algorithm each correct process periodically sends n messages, with the total number of messages exchanged being at least $n\mathcal{C}$.

In our extension, we follow a similar approach. Besides its local list L_p of suspected processes, each process p has a global list G_p of suspected processes. While L_p only holds the suspected processes between p and the process p is monitoring ($target_p$), G_p holds all the processes that are being suspected in the system. Now, the global lists are the ones providing strong completeness.

In order to correctly build the global lists, processes need to propagate their local lists. However, instead of periodically broadcasting its local list, every process will only send its global list (which contains the local list) to the process it is monitoring. This process, upon reception of that list, updates its global list and further propagates it. Note that, since we use the ring arrangement of processes, each process at most sends and receives one message periodically, and the total number of messages exchanged is $O(n)$ in the worst case, which eventually becomes $O(\mathcal{C})$. Furthermore, instead of using specific messages to send the global lists, we can piggyback the global lists in the ARE-YOU-ALIVE? messages inherent to the monitoring action. This way, there is no increment in message exchanges from the previous algorithms. Fig. 5 presents the extended algorithm in detail. We now show that strong completeness holds, while accuracy is preserved, with this algorithm.

Every process p executes:

{if the algorithm needs it:
$initial\_cand_p \leftarrow$ pre-agreed process}
$target_p \leftarrow succ(p)$
$L_p \leftarrow \emptyset$
$G_p \leftarrow \emptyset$
$\forall q \in \Pi : \Delta_{p,q} \leftarrow$ default timeout

cobegin
|| Task 1:
  loop
    wait($mutex_p$)
    send ARE-YOU-ALIVE?
       —with G_p— to $target_p$
    $t_{out} \leftarrow \Delta_{p,target_p}$
    $received \leftarrow false$
    signal($mutex_p$)
    delay t_{out}
    wait($mutex_p$)
    if not $received$
      {Update $\Delta_{p,target_p}$ if required}
      $G_p \leftarrow G_p \cup \{target_p\}$
      $L_p \leftarrow L_p \cup \{target_p\}$
      $target_p \leftarrow succ(target_p)$
    end if
    signal($mutex_p$)
  end loop

|| Task 2:
  loop
    receive message m from a process q
    wait($mutex_p$)
    case
      $m =$ ARE-YOU-ALIVE? —with G_q—:
        send I-AM-ALIVE to q
        if $q \in L_p$
          $L_p \leftarrow L_p - \{q, \ldots, pred(target_p)\}$
          $target_p \leftarrow q$
          $received \leftarrow true$
        end if
        $G_p \leftarrow G_q \cup L_p - \{p,q\}$
      $m =$ I-AM-ALIVE:
        case
          $q = target_p$:
            $received \leftarrow true$
          $q \in L_p$:
            $L_p \leftarrow L_p - \{q, \ldots, pred(target_p)\}$
            $G_p \leftarrow G_p - \{q\}$
            $target_p \leftarrow q$
            $received \leftarrow true$
          else discard m
        end case
    end case
    signal($mutex_p$)
  end loop
coend

Fig. 5. Extension to the previous algorithms to provide strong completeness.

Observation 2 *The only difference between this algorithm and the previous ones is the handling of the global lists of suspected processes G_p, while the local lists L_p are handled as before. Hence, Theorem 1 and whichever corresponds of Theorem 2 and Theorem 3 are still applicable to this algorithm.*

Observation 3 $\forall p \in \Pi, \forall t, L_p(t) \subseteq G_p(t)$.

Observation 4 $\forall p \in correct, \forall t,$ *p will eventually receive* ARE-YOU-ALIVE? *messages after t.*

Lemma 5. $\exists t_3 : \forall q \in crashed, \forall p \in correct, \forall t \geq t_3, q \in G_p(t)$.

Proof. Let us assume we are at least at instant t_0 as defined in Theorem 1. We know that at this instant any process $q \in crashed$ has already failed and has been permanently included in $L_{corr\_pred(q)}$.

Let us assume now that we have a process $q \in crashed$ and a process $p \in correct$. We claim that q will eventually be permanently included in G_p. We use strong induction on the number of correct processes in the set $\{corr\_pred(q),\ldots,p\}$. For the base case we assume there is only one correct process in the set, i.e., $p = corr\_pred(q)$. Hence, from Theorem 1, q is permanently in L_p and, from Observation 3, q will be permanently in G_p in this case.

We will now prove that, if the claim holds for any number $1 \le c \le i - 1$ of correct processes in the set $\{corr\_pred(q),\ldots,p\}$, it also holds when the number of correct processes in the set is i. To do so, we show first that there is a time t' after which p receives ARE-YOU-ALIVE? messages and all of them carry global lists containing q. From that, it is immediate to see in the algorithm that, after receiving the first such ARE-YOU-ALIVE? message, q will be permanently included in G_p. Let us assume the number of correct processes in the set $\{corr\_pred(q),\ldots,p\}$ be $i > 1$. By induction hypothesis, there is a time t'' at which any correct process $r \in \{corr\_pred(q),\ldots,corr\_pred(p)\}$ permanently contains q in its global list G_r. Also, there is a time $t' = \max(t'', T_s) + \Delta_{msg}$ at which all the ARE-YOU-ALIVE? messages sent to p before t'' have been received. From Observation 4, process p will receive new ARE-YOU-ALIVE? messages after t'. Let be an ARE-YOU-ALIVE? message received by p from a process s at a time $t > t'$. There are two cases to consider:

- $s \in \{corr\_pred(q),\ldots,corr\_pred(p)\}$. In this case, from the induction hypothesis and the definition of t', we know that the global list G_s carried by the ARE-YOU-ALIVE? message contains q.
- $s \in \{p,\ldots,corr\_pred(corr\_pred(q))\}$. In this case, it can be seen from the algorithm that if p receives an ARE-YOU-ALIVE? message from s, then necessarily, at the time of sending the message, $p = target_s$ and L_s contained q. Therefore, from Observation 3, the G_s carried by the ARE-YOU-ALIVE? message contains q.

The following lemma states that the algorithm of Fig. 5 preserves eventual accuracy.

Lemma 6. *Let p be any correct process. If there is a time after which no correct process q contains p in L_q, then there is a time after which no correct process q contains p in G_q.*

Proof. Let us assume we are at least at instant t_0 as defined in Theorem 1. We know that at this instant any process in *crashed* has already failed. Let p be a correct process and $t''' \ge t_0$ be an instant such that $\forall t \ge t''', \forall q \in correct, p \notin L_q$.

Let us assume now that we have a process $q \in correct$. We claim that there is a time after which p is never in G_q. We use strong induction on the number of correct processes in the set $\{p,\ldots,q\}$. For the base case, we assume there is only one correct process in the set, i.e., $p = q$. It is easy to observe from the algorithm that p will never include itself in G_p.

We will now prove that, if the claim holds for any number $1 \le c \le i - 1$ of correct processes in the set $\{p,\ldots,q\}$, it also holds when the number of correct processes in the set is i. To do so, we show first that there is a time t' after which q receives ARE-YOU-ALIVE? messages and all of them carry global lists not containing p. From that, it is immediate to see in the algorithm that, after receiving the first such ARE-YOU-ALIVE? message, p will be removed (if needed) and never included again in G_q. Let us assume the number of correct processes in the set $\{p, \ldots, q\}$ be $i > 1$. By induction hypothesis, there is a time t'' after which any correct process $r \in \{p, \ldots, corr\_pred(q)\}$ does not contain p in its global list G_r. Also, there is a time $t' = \max(t'', T_s) + \Delta_{msg}$ at which all the ARE-YOU-ALIVE? messages sent to q before t'' have been received. From Observation 4, process q will receive new ARE-YOU-ALIVE? messages after t'. Let be an ARE-YOU-ALIVE? message received by q from a process s at a time $t > t'$. There are two cases to consider:

- $s \in \{p, \ldots, corr\_pred(q)\}$. In this case, from the induction hypothesis and the definition of t', we know that the global list G_s carried by the ARE-YOU-ALIVE? message does not contain p.
- $s \in \{q, \ldots, corr\_pred(p)\}$. This case cannot happen, because it would imply that p is in the local list L_s.

Combining both lemmas it is immediate to derive the following theorem.

Theorem 4. *The algorithm of Fig. 5 provides strong completeness while preserving accuracy.*

Corollary 6. *The algorithm of Fig. 5, combined with the algorithm of Fig. 3 or Fig. 4, implements failure detectors of classes $\Diamond S$ and $\Diamond P$, respectively.*

7 Performance Analysis

In this section, we will evaluate the performance of the presented algorithms in terms of the number and size of the exchanged messages. Observe that failure detection is an on-going activity that inherently requires an infinite number of messages. Furthermore, the pattern of message exchange between processes can vary over time (and need not be periodic), and different algorithms can have completely different patterns. For these reasons, we have to make some assumptions in order to use the number of messages as a meaningful performance measure. We will first assume that the algorithms execute in a periodic fashion, so that we can count the number of messages exchanged in a period. Secondly, to be able to compare the number of messages exchanged by different algorithms, we must assume that their respective periods have the same length.

Under the above assumptions, in our algorithms each correct process periodically polls only one other process. Each polling involves two messages. Thus, a total of no more than $2n$ messages would be periodically exchanged. Eventually, this amount becomes $2C$, since there will be only C correct processes remaining in the system. This compares favorably with Chandra and Toueg's algorithm, which requires a periodic exchange of at least nC messages.

Concerning the size of the messages, our algorithms implementing failure detectors with weak completeness ($\Diamond W$ and $\Diamond Q$) require messages of $\Theta(\log n)$ bits (to identify the sender). On the other hand, the algorithms implementing failure detectors with strong completeness ($\diamond\mathcal{S}$ and $\diamond\mathcal{P}$) require messages of $\Theta(n)$ bits, since we can code the global list G_p of suspected processes in n bits (one bit per process).

Chandra and Toueg's algorithm, which only implements $\diamond\mathcal{P}$, requires messages of $\Theta(\log n)$ bits. This size is smaller than the size needed by our $\diamond\mathcal{P}$ algorithm. However, the total amount of information periodically exchanged in our algorithm is $\Theta(n^2)$ bits, while in theirs it is $\Theta(n^2 \log n)$ bits. Furthermore, each message that is sent involves a fixed overhead. In this sense, our algorithm presents an edge, since it involves less messages.

8 Conclusions and Future Work

In this paper we have proposed several algorithms to implement failure detectors of classes $\diamond\mathcal{W}$, $\diamond\mathcal{Q}$, $\diamond\mathcal{S}$ and $\diamond\mathcal{P}$. These algorithms are efficient alternatives to the algorithm implementing $\diamond\mathcal{P}$ proposed by Chandra and Toueg [2].

Apparently, the time to propagate the failure information in our algorithms is larger than the time in Chandra and Toueg's algorithm. We need to further study this performance parameter both theoretically and empirically.

As pointed out in the previous section, the number of messages periodically exchanged is not a general enough performance measure, since algorithms need not be periodic. We are studying new ways of evaluating the performance of this kind of algorithms.

References

1. M. Aguilera and S. Toueg. Heartbeat: A Timeout-Free Failure Detector for Quiescent Reliable Communication. *Proceedings of the 11th International Workshop on Distributed Algorithms (WDAG)*, LNCS, Springer-Verlag, Germany, Sep. 1997.
2. T. D. Chandra and S. Toueg. Unreliable Failure Detectors for Reliable Distributed Systems. *Journal of the ACM*, 43 (2), pages 225-267, Mar. 1996.
3. T. D. Chandra, V. Hadzilacos, and S. Toueg. The Weakest Failure Detector for Solving Consensus. *Journal of the ACM*, 43 (4), pages 685-722, Jul. 1996.
4. D. Dolev, C. Dwork, and L. Stockmeyer. On the Minimal Synchronism Needed for Distributed Consensus. *Journal of the ACM*, 34 (1), pages 77-97, Jan. 1987.
5. C. Dwork, N. Lynch, and L. Stockmeyer. Consensus in the Presence of Partial Synchrony. *Journal of the ACM*, 35 (2), pages 288-323, Apr. 1988.
6. C. Fetzer and F. Cristian. Fail-Aware Failure Detectors. *Proceedings of the 15th Symposium on Reliable Distributed Systems (SRDS)*, Canada, Oct. 1996.
7. M. Fischer, N. Lynch, and M. Paterson. Impossibility of Distributed Consensus with One Faulty Process. *Journal of the ACM*, 32 (2), pages 374-382, Apr. 1985.
8. R. Guerraoui, M. Larrea, and A. Schiper. Non-Blocking Atomic Commitment with an Unreliable Failure Detector. *Proceedings of the 14th Symposium on Reliable Distributed Systems (SRDS)*, Germany, Sep. 1996.
9. R. Guerraoui and A. Schiper. Gamma-Accurate Failure Detectors. *Proceedings of the 10th International Workshop on Distributed Algorithms (WDAG)*, LNCS, Springer-Verlag, Italy, Oct. 1996.
10. M. Pease, R. Shostak, and L. Lamport. Reaching Agreement in the Presence of Faults. *Journal of the ACM*, 27 (2), pages 228-234, Apr. 1980.

Solving Consensus Using Chandra-Toueg's Unreliable Failure Detectors: A General Quorum-Based Approach

Achour Mostéfaoui and Michel Raynal

IRISA - Campus de Beaulieu, 35042 Rennes Cedex, France,
{mostefaoui,raynal}@irisa.fr

Abstract. This paper addresses the Consensus problem in asynchronous distributed systems (made of n processes, at most f of them may crash) equipped with unreliable failure detectors. A *generic* Consensus protocol is presented: it is quorum-based and works with any failure detector belonging to the class S (provided that $f \le n-1$) or to the class $\diamond S$ (provided that $f < n/2$). This quorum-based generic approach for solving the Consensus problem is new (to our knowledge). Moreover, the proposed protocol is conceptually simple, allows early decision and uses messages shorter than previous solutions.

The generic dimension and the surprising design simplicity of the proposed protocol provide a better understanding of the basic algorithmic structures and principles that allow to solve the Consensus problem with the help of unreliable failure detectors.

Keywords: Asynchronous Distributed System, Consensus, Crash Failure, Perpetual/Eventual Accuracy, Quorum, Unreliable Failure Detector.

1 Introduction

The *Consensus* problem is now recognized as being one of the most important problems to solve when one has to design or to implement reliable applications on top of an unreliable asynchronous distributed system. Informally, the Consensus problem is defined in the following way. Each process proposes a value, and all non-crashed processes have to agree on a common value which has to be one of the proposed values. The Consensus problem is actually a fundamental problem. This is because the most important practical agreement problems (*e.g.*, Atomic Broadcast, Atomic Multicast, Weak Atomic Commitment) can be reduced to it (see, for example, [2], [5] and [6] for each of the previous problems, respectively). The Consensus problem can be seen as their "*greatest common denominator*".

Solving the Consensus problem in an asynchronous distributed system where processes can crash is far from being a trivial task. More precisely, it has been shown by Fischer, Lynch and Paterson [4] that there is no deterministic solution to the Consensus problem in those systems as soon as processes (even only one) may crash. The intuition that underlies this impossibility result lies in the inherent difficulty of safely distinguishing a crashed process from a "slow" process, or from a process with which communications are "very slow". This result has challenged and motivated researchers to find a set of minimal properties that, when satisfied by the runs of a distributed system, allows to solve Consensus despite process crashes.

The major advance to circumvent the previous impossibility result is due to Chandra and Toueg who have introduced [2] (and studied with Hadzilacos [3]) the *Unreliable Failure Detector* concept. A failure detector can be seen as a set of modules, each associated with a process. The failure detector module attached to a process provides it with a list of processes it suspects to have crashed. A failure detector module can make mistakes by not suspecting a crashed process or by erroneously suspecting a correct process. In their seminal paper [2] Chandra and Toueg have introduced several classes of failure detectors. A class is defined by a *Completeness* property and an *Accuracy* property. A completeness property is on the actual detection of crashes. The aim of an accuracy property is to restrict erroneous suspicions. Moreover an accuracy property is *Perpetual* if it has to be permanently satisfied. It is *Eventual* if it is allowed to be permanently satisfied only after some time.

In this paper, we are interested in solving the Consensus problem in asynchronous distributed systems equipped with a failure detector of the class S or with a failure detector of the class $\Diamond S$. Both classes are characterized by the same completeness property, namely, "Eventually, every crashed process is suspected by every correct process". They are also characterized by the same basic accuracy property, namely, "There is a correct process that is never suspected". But these two classes differ in the way (modality) their failure detectors satisfy this basic accuracy property. More precisely, the failure detectors of S perpetually satisfy the basic accuracy property, while the failure detectors of $\Diamond S$ are allowed to satisfy it only eventually.

Several Consensus protocols based on such failure detectors have been designed. Chandra and Toueg have proposed a Consensus protocol that works with any failure detector of the class S [2]. This protocol tolerates any number of process crashes. Several authors have proposed Consensus protocols based on failure detectors of the class $\Diamond S$: Chandra and Toueg [2], Schiper [9] and Hurfin and Raynal [8]. All these $\Diamond S$-based Consensus protocols require a majority of correct processes. It has been shown that this requirement is necessary [2]. So, these protocols are optimal with respect to the number of crashes they tolerate. Moreover, when we consider the classes of failure detectors that allow to solve the Consensus problem, it has ben shown that $\Diamond S$ is the weakest one [3].

S-based Consensus protocols and $\Diamond S$-based Consensus protocols are usually considered as defining two distinct families of failure detector-based Consensus protocols. This is motivated by (1) the fact that one family assumes perpetual accuracy while the other assumes only eventual accuracy, and (2) the fact that the protocols of each family (and even protocols of a same family) are based on different algorithmic principles. In this paper, we present a generic failure detector-based Consensus protocol which has several interesting characteristics. The most important one is of course its "generic" dimension: it works with any failure detector of the class S (provided $f < n$) or with any failure detector of the class $\Diamond S$ (provided $f < n/2$) (where n and f denote the total number of processes and the maximum number of processes that may crash, respectively). This protocol is based on a single algorithmic principle, whatever is the class of the underlying failure detector. Such a generic approach for solving the Consensus problem is new (to our knowledge). It has several advantages. It favors a better understanding of the basic algorithmic structures and principles that are needed to solve the Consensus problem with the help of a failure detector. It also provides a better insight into the "perpetual/eventual" attribute of the accuracy property, when using unreliable failure detectors to solve the Consensus problem. (So, it allows to provide a single proof, where the use of this attribute is perfectly identified.) Moreover, the algorithmic unity of the protocol is not obtained to the detriment of its efficiency. Last but not least, the design simplicity of the protocol is also one of its noteworthy properties.

The paper is composed of seven sections. Section 2 presents the distributed system model and the failure detector concept. Section 3 defines the Consensus problem. The next two sections are devoted to the generic protocol: it is presented in Section 4 and proved in Section 5. Section 6 discusses the protocol and compares it with previous failure detector-based Consensus protocols. Finally Section 7 concludes the paper.

2 Asynchronous Distributed System Model

The system model is patterned after the one described in [2, 4]. A formal introduction to failure detectors is provided in [2, 3].

2.1 Asynchronous Distributed System with Process Crash Failures

We consider a system consisting of a finite set Π of $n > 1$ processes, namely, $\Pi = \{p_1, p_2, \ldots, p_n\}$. A process can fail by *crashing*, *i.e.*, by prematurely halting. It behaves correctly (*i.e.*, according to its specification) until it (possibly) crashes. By definition, a *correct* process is a process that does not crash. Let f denote the maximum number of processes that can crash ($f \leq n - 1$). Processes communicate and synchronize by sending and receiving messages through channels. Every pair of processes is connected by a channel. Channels are not required to be FIFO, they may also duplicate messages. They are only assumed to be reliable in the following sense: they do not create, alter or lose messages. This means that a message sent by a process p_i to a process p_j is assumed to be eventually received by p_j, if p_j is correct[1]. The multiplicity of processes and

---

[1] The "no message loss" assumption is required to ensure the Termination property of the protocol. The "no creation and no alteration" assumptions are required to ensure its Validity and Agreement properties (see Sections 3 and 4).

the message-passing communication make the system *distributed*. There is no assumption about the relative speed of processes or the message transfer delays. This absence of timing assumptions makes the distributed system *asynchronous*.

2.2 Unreliable Failure Detectors

Informally, a failure detector consists of a set of modules, each one attached to a process: the module attached to p_i maintains a set (named *suspected$_i$*) of processes it currently suspects to have crashed. Any failure detector module is inherently unreliable: it can make mistakes by not suspecting a crashed process or by erroneously suspecting a correct one. Moreover, suspicions are not necessarily stable: a process p_j can be added to or removed from a set *suspected$_i$* according to whether p_i's failure detector module currently suspects p_j or not. As in papers devoted to failure detectors, we say "process p_i suspects process p_j" at some time, if at that time we have $p_j \in suspected_i$.

As indicated in the introduction, a failure detector class is formally defined by two abstract properties, namely a *Completeness* property and an *Accuracy* property. In this paper, we consider the following completeness property [2]:

- **Strong Completeness**: Eventually, every process that crashes is permanently suspected by every correct process.

Among the accuracy properties defined by Chandra and Toueg [2] we consider here the two following ones:

- **Perpetual Weak Accuracy**: Some correct process is never suspected.
- **Eventual Weak Accuracy**: There is a time after which some correct process is never suspected by correct processes.

Combined with the completeness property, these accuracy properties define the following two classes of failure detectors [2]:

- $\mathcal{S}$: The class of *Strong* failure detectors. This class contains all the failure detectors that satisfy the strong completeness property and the perpetual weak accuracy property.
- $\Diamond\mathcal{S}$: The class of *Eventually Strong* failure detectors. This class contains all the failure detectors that satisfy the strong completeness property and the eventual weak accuracy property.

Clearly, $\mathcal{S} \subset \Diamond\mathcal{S}$. Moreover, it is important to note that any failure detector that belongs to $\mathcal{S}$ or to $\Diamond\mathcal{S}$ can make an arbitrary number of mistakes.

3 The Consensus Problem

3.1 Definition

In the Consensus problem, every correct process p_i *proposes* a value v_i and all correct processes have to *decide* on some value v, in relation to the set of proposed values. More precisely, the *Consensus problem* is defined by the following three properties [2, 4]:

– Termination: Every correct process eventually decides on some value.
– Validity: If a process decides v, then v was proposed by some process.
– Agreement: No two correct processes decide differently.

The agreement property applies only to correct processes. So, it is possible that a process decides on a distinct value just before crashing. *Uniform Consensus* prevents such a possibility. It has the same Termination and Validity properties plus the following agreement property:

– Uniform Agreement: No two processes (correct or not) decide differently.

In the following we are interested in the Uniform Consensus problem.

3.2 Solving Consensus with Unreliable Failure Detectors

The following important results are associated with the Consensus problem when one has to solve it in an asynchronous distributed system, prone to process crash failures, equipped with an unreliable failure detector.

– In any distributed system equipped with a failure detector of the class S, the Consensus problem can be solved whatever the number of crashes is [2].
– In any distributed system equipped with a failure detector of the class $\Diamond S$, at least a majority of processes has to be correct (*i.e.*, $f < n/2$) for the Consensus problem to be solvable [2].
– When we consider the classes of failure detectors that allow to solve the Consensus problem, $\Diamond S$ is the weakest one [3]. This means that, as far as failure detection is concerned, the properties defined by $\Diamond S$ constitute the borderline beyond which the Consensus problem can not be solved[2].
– Any protocol solving the Consensus problem using an unreliable failure detector of the class S or $\Diamond S$, solves also the Uniform Consensus problem [6].

4 The General Consensus Protocol

4.1 Underlying Principles

The algorithmic principles that underly the protocol are relatively simple. The protocol shares some of them with other Consensus protocols [2, 8, 9]. Each process p_i manages a local variable est_i which contains its current estimate of the decision value. Initially, est_i is set to v_i, the value proposed by p_i. Processes proceed in consecutive asynchronous rounds. Each round r (initially, for each

---

[2] The "weakest class" proof is actually on the class $\Diamond W$ of failure detectors [3]. But, it has been shown that $\Diamond W$ and $\Diamond S$, that differ in the statement of their completeness property, are actually equivalent: the protocol that transforms any failure detector of the class $\Diamond W$ in a failure detector of the class $\Diamond S$ is based on a simple gossiping mechanism [2].

process p_i, $r_i = 0$) is managed by a predetermined process p_c (*e.g.*, c can be defined according to the round robin order). So, the protocol uses the well-known *rotating coordinator* paradigm[3].

Description of a round A round (r) is basically made of two phases (communication steps).

First phase of a round. The current round coordinator p_c sends its current estimate (est_c) to all processes. This phase terminates, for each process p_i, when p_i has received an estimate from p_c or when it suspects p_c. In addition to est_i, p_i manages a local variable $est\_from\_c_i$ that contains either the value it has received from p_c, or the default value $\bot$. So, $est\_from\_c_i = \bot$ means that p_i has suspected p_c, and $est\_from\_c_i \neq \bot$ means that $est\_from\_c_i = est_c$. If we assumed that all non-crashed processes or none of them have received p_c's estimate and they all have the same perception of crashes, then they would get the same value in their $est\_from\_c_i$ local variables. Consequently, they could all "synchronously" either decide (when $est\_from\_c_i \neq \bot$) or proceed to the next round (when $est\_from\_c_i = \bot$).

Second phase of a round. Unfortunately, due to asynchrony and erroneous failure suspicions, some processes p_j can have $est\_from\_c_j = est_c$, while other processes p_k can have $est\_from\_c_k = \bot$ at the end of the first phase. Actually, the aim of the first phase was to ensure that $\forall\ p_i$: $est\_from\_c_i = est_c$ or $\bot$. The aim of the second phase is to ensure that the Agreement property will never be violated. This prevention is done in the following way: if a process p_i decides $v = est_c$ during r and if a process p_j progresses to $r+1$, then p_j does it with $est_j = v$. This is implemented by the second phase that requires each process p_i to broadcast the value of its $est\_from\_c_i$ local variable. A process p_i finishes the second phase when it has received est_from_c values from "enough" processes. The meaning of "enough" is captured by a set Q_i, dynamically defined during each round. Let rec_i be the set of est_from_c values received by p_i from the processes of Q_i. We have: $rec_i = \{\bot\}$ or $\{v\}$ or $\{v, \bot\}$ (where v is the estimate of the current coordinator). Let p_j be another process (with its Q_j and rec_j). If $Q_i \cap Q_j \neq \emptyset$, then there is a process $p_x \in Q_i \cap Q_j$ that has broadcast $est\_from\_c_x$ and both p_i and p_j have received it. It follows that rec_i and rec_j are related in the following way:

$$rec_i = \{v\} \Rightarrow (\forall\ p_j : (rec_j = \{v\}) \ \lor \ (rec_j = \{v, \bot\}))$$
$$rec_i = \{\bot\} \Rightarrow (\forall\ p_j : (rec_j = \{\bot\}) \ \lor \ (rec_j = \{v, \bot\}))$$
$$rec_i = \{v, \bot\} \Rightarrow (\forall\ p_j : (rec_j = \{v\}) \ \lor \ (rec_j = \{\bot\}) \ \lor \ (rec_j = \{v, \bot\}))$$

The behavior of p_i is then determined by the content of rec_i:

– When $rec_i = \{v\}$, p_i knows that all non-crashed processes also know v. So, p_i is allowed to decide on v provided that all processes that do not decide consider v as their current estimate.

---

[3] Due to the completeness property of the underlying failure detector, this paradigm can be used without compromising the protocol termination. More precisely, the completeness property can be exploited by a process to not indefinitely wait for a message from a crashed coordinator.

- When $rec_i = \{\bot\}$, p_i knows that any set rec_j includes $\bot$. In that case, no process p_j is allowed to decide and p_i proceeds to the next round.
- When $rec_i = \{v, \bot\}$, according to the previous items, p_i updates its current estimate (est_i) to v to achieve the Agreement property. Note that if a process p_j decides during this round, any process p_i that proceeds to the next round, does it with $est_i = v$.

Definition of the Q_i set As indicated previously, the definition of the Q_i sets has to ensure that the predicate $Q_i \cap Q_j \neq \emptyset$ holds for every pair (p_i, p_j). The way this condition is realized depends on the class to which the underlying failure detector belongs.

Let us first consider the case where the failure detector belongs to the class S. In that case, there is a correct process that is never suspected. Let p_x be this process. If Q_i contains p_x, then p_i will obtain the value of $est\_from\_c_x$. If follows that if $(\forall\, p_i)$ Q_i is such that $\Pi = Q_i \cup suspected_i$, then, $\forall\, (p_i, p_j)$, we have $p_x \in Q_i \cap Q_j$.

Let us now consider the case where the failure detector belongs to the class $\Diamond S$. In that case, $f < n/2$ and there is a time after which some correct process is no longer suspected. As we do not know the time from which a correct process is no longer suspected, we can only rely on the majority of correct processes assumption. So, by taking $(\forall\, p_i)$ Q_i equal to a majority set, it follows that, $\forall\, (p_i, p_j)$, $\exists p_x$ such that, $p_x \in Q_i \cap Q_j$.

Note that in both cases, Q_i is not statically defined. In each round, its actual value depends on message receptions and additionally, in the case of S, on process suspicions.

On the quorum-based approach The previous principles actually define a quorum-based approach. As usual, (1) each quorum must be *live*: it must include only non-crashed processes (this ensures processes will not block forever during a round). Furthermore, (2) each quorum must be *safe*: it must have a non-empty intersection with any other quorum (this ensures the agreement property cannot be violated). As indicated in the previous paragraph, the quorum safety requirement is guaranteed by the "perpetual" modality of the accuracy property (for S), and by the majority of correct processes assumption (for $\Diamond S$).

Other combinations of eventual weak accuracy (to guarantee eventual termination) and live and safe (possibly non-majority) quorums would work[4]. Bringing a quorum-based formulation to the fore is conceptually interesting. Indeed, the protocol presented in the next section works for any failure detector satisfying strong completeness, eventual weak accuracy and the "quorum" conditions.

---

[4] As an example, let us consider quorums defined from a $\sqrt{n} * \sqrt{n}$ grid (with $n = q^2$). This would allow the protocol to progress despite $n - (2 * \sqrt{n} - 1)$ crashes or erroneous suspicions in the most favorable case. Of course, in the worst case, the use of such quorums could block the protocol in presence of only $\sqrt{n}$ crashes or erroneous suspicions. Details on quorum definition can be found in [1].

4.2 The Protocol

The protocol is described in Figure 1. A process p_i starts a Consensus execution by invoking Consensus(v_i). It terminates it when it executes the statement **return** which provides it with the decided value (lines 12 and 16).

It is possible that distinct processes do not decide during the same round. To prevent a process from blocking forever (*i.e.*, waiting for a value from a process that has already decided), a process that decides, uses a reliable broadcast [7] to disseminate its decision value (similarly as protocols described in [2, 8, 9]). To this end the Consensus function is made of two tasks, namely, $T1$ and $T2$. $T1$ implements the previous discussion. Line 12 and $T2$ implement the reliable broadcast.

Function Consensus(v_i)
cobegin
(1) **task** $T1$: $r_i \leftarrow 0$; $est_i \leftarrow v_i$; % $v_i \neq \perp$ %
(2)   **while** *true* **do**
(3) $c \leftarrow (r_i \bmod n) + 1$; $est\_from\_c_i \leftarrow \perp$; $r_i \leftarrow r_i + 1$; % round $r = r_i$ %
(4)   **case** $(i = c)$ **then** $est\_from\_c_i \leftarrow est_i$
(5) $(i \neq c)$ **then wait** $(($EST(r_i, v) is received from $p_c) \vee (c \in suspected_i))$;
(6)   **if** (EST(r_i, v) has been received) **then** $est\_from\_c_i \leftarrow v$
(7)   **endcase**;   % $est\_from\_c_i = est_c$ or $\perp$ %
(8) $\forall j$ **do send** EST$(r_i, est\_from\_c_i)$ **to** p_j **enddo**;
(9)   **wait until** $(\forall p_j \in Q_i$: EST(r_i, est_from_c) has been received from $p_j)$;
                     % Q_i has to be a *live* and *safe* quorum %
                     % For $\mathcal{S}$: Q_i is such that $Q_i \cup suspected_i = \Pi$ %
                     % For $\Diamond\mathcal{S}$: Q_i is such that $|Q_i| = \lceil (n+1)/2 \rceil$ %
(10)   **let** $rec_i = \{est\_from\_c \mid$ EST(r_i, est_from_c) is received at line 5 or 9\};
                     % $est\_from\_c = \perp$ or v with $v = est_c$ %
                     % $rec_i = \{\perp\}$ or $\{v\}$ or $\{v, \perp\}$ %
(11)   **case** $(rec_i = \{\perp\})$ **then skip**
(12) $(rec_i = \{v\})$ **then** $\forall j \neq i$ **do send** DECIDE(v) **to** p_j **enddo**; **return**(v)
(13) $(rec_i = \{v, \perp\})$ **then** $est_i \leftarrow v$
(14)   **endcase**
(15) **enddo**

(16) **task** $T2$: **upon reception of** DECIDE(v):
                     $\forall j \neq i$ **do send** DECIDE(v) **to** p_j **enddo**; **return**(v)
coend

Fig. 1. The Consensus Protocol

5   Correctness Proof

5.1   Validity

Lemma 1. *Let us consider a round r and a process p_i. The round r is coordinated by p_c. We have:*
(1) If p_c participates in round r, then est_c is equal to an initial value proposed by a process.
(2) If p_i computes rec_i during round r, then: $rec_i = \{\bot\}$ or $rec_i = \{v\}$ or $rec_i = \{v, \bot\}$, where v is equal to est_c. Moreover, if $v \in rec_i$, p_c has participated in round r.
(3) If p_i starts round $r+1$, it does it with an estimate (est_i) whose value is equal to an initial value.

Proof The proof is by induction on the round number.

- Base case. Let us consider the round $r = 1$. It is coordinated by $p_c = p_1$, and est_c is equal to v_c (p_c's proposal, line 1). The local variable $est\_from\_c_j$ of any process p_j that (during this round) executes line 8, is equal either to est_c (if p_j has received an estimate from p_c -line 4- or if $p_j = p_c$ -line 6-) or to $\bot$ (if p_j has suspected p_c, line 5). So, if p_j executes line 8, it broadcasts either the value of est_c ($= v_c$) or $\bot$. It follows that any p_i that computes rec_i during the first round, can only receive v_c or $\bot$ at line 9. Consequently, we have: $rec_i = \{\bot\}$ or $rec_i = \{v_c\}$ or $rec_i = \{v_c, \bot\}$.
  Now, let us first note that, initially, $est_i = v_i$ (line 1). Due to lines 11-13, if p_i starts $r + 1$, it does it either with the value of est_i left unchanged (line 11) or with $est_i = v_c$ (line 13). So, the lemma is true for $r = 1$.
- Assume the lemma is true until r, $r \geq 1$. This means that if p_c (the round $r + 1$ coordinator) participates in $r + 1$, then we had (at the end of r) $rec_c = \{\bot\}$ or $rec_c = \{v\}$ or $rec_c = \{v, \bot\}$, where v is an initial value. Due to the induction assumption and to the **case** statement (lines 11-14) executed by p_c at the end of r, it follows that p_c starts $r + 1$ with est_c equal to an initial value proposed by a process. Now, the situation is similar to the one of the base case, and consequently, the same argument applies to the round $r + 1$ case, which proves the lemma.

$$\square_{Lemma\ 1}$$

Theorem 1. *If a process p_i decides v, then v was proposed by some process.*

Proof If a process decides at line 16, it decides the value decided by another process at line 12. So we only consider the case where a value that has been decided at line 12. When a process p_i decides v at line 12, it decides on the value ($\neq \bot$) of the rec_i singleton. Due to the items (1) and (2) of Lemma 1, v is an initial value of a process.

$$\square_{Theorem\ 1}$$

5.2   Termination

Lemma 2. *If no process decides during $r' \leq r$, then all correct processes start $r + 1$.*

Proof   The proof is by contradiction. Suppose that no process has decided during a round $r' \leq r$, where r is the smallest round number in which a correct process p_i blocks forever. So, p_i is blocked at line 4 or at line 9.

Let us first examine the case where p_i blocks at line 4. Let p_c be the round r coordinator. If $p_i = p_c$, it cannot block at line 4, as it does not execute this line. Moreover, in that case, it executes the broadcast at line 8 or crashes. If $p_i \neq p_c$, then:
- Either p_i suspects p_c. This is due to an erroneous suspicion or to the strong completeness property of the failure detector.
- Or p_i never suspects p_c. Due to the strong completeness property, this means that p_c is correct. From the previous observation, p_c has broadcast its current estimate at line 8, and p_i eventually receives it.
It follows that p_i cannot remain blocked at line 4.

Let us now consider the case where p_i blocks at line 9. For this line there are two cases to consider, according to the class of the underlying failure detector.

- The failure detector belongs to S and $f \leq n - 1$. In that case, the set Q_i of processes from which p_i is waiting for messages is such that $Q_i \cup suspected_i = \Pi$. As, no correct process blocks forever at line 4, each of them executes a broadcast at line 8. It follows from these broadcasts and from the strong completeness property that, $\forall p_j$, p_i will receive a round r estimate from p_j or will suspect it. Consequently, p_i cannot block at line 9.
- The failure detector belongs to the class $\Diamond S$ and $f < n/2$. In that case Q_i is defined as the first majority set of processes p_j from which p_i has received a EST(r, est_from_c) message. As there is a majority of correct processes, and as (due to the previous observation) they do not block forever at line 4, they broadcast a round r estimate message (line 8). It follows that any correct process receives a message from a majority set of processes. Consequently, p_i cannot block at line 9.

Finally, let us note that, due to the item (2) of Lemma 1, a correct process p_i terminates correctly the execution of the **case** statement (lines 11-14). It follows that if p_i does not decide, it proceeds to the next round. A contradiction.

$\square_{Lemma\ 2}$

Theorem 2. *If a process p_i is correct, then it decides.*

Proof   If a (correct or not) process decides, then, due to the sending of DECIDE messages at line 12 or at line 14, any correct process will receive such a message and decide accordingly (line 14).

So, suppose that no process decides. The proof is by contradiction. Due to the accuracy property of the underlying failure detector, there is a time t after which there is a correct process that is never suspected. Note that $t = 0$ if the failure detector belongs to S, and $t \geq 0$ if it belongs to $\Diamond S$ (assuming the protocol starts executing at time $t = 0$).

Let p_x be the correct process that is never suspected after t. Moreover, let r be the first round that starts after t and that is coordinated by p_x. As by assumption no process decides, due to Lemma 2, all the correct processes eventually start round r.

The process p_x starts round r by broadcasting its current estimate value (est_x), which, due to Lemma 1, is equal to an initial value. Moreover, during r, p_x is not suspected. Consequently, all processes p_i that participate in round r (this set includes the correct processes) receive est_x at line 4, and adopt it as their $est\_from\_c_i$ value. If follows that no value different from est_x can be broadcast at line 8; consequently, est_x is the only value that can be received at line 9. Hence, for any correct process p_i, we have $rec_i = \{est_x\}$ at line 10. It follows that any correct process executes line 12 and decides accordingly. $\Box_{Theorem\ 2}$

The following corollary follows from the proof of the previous theorem.

Corollary 1. *If the underlying failure detector belongs to the class S, the maximum number of rounds is n. Moreover, there is no bound on the round number when the underlying failure detector belongs to the class $\Diamond S$.*

5.3 Uniform Agreement

Lemma 3. *If two processes p_i and p_j decide at line 12 during the same round, they decide the same value.*

Proof If both p_i and p_j decide during the same round r, at line 12, we had $rec_i = \{v\}$ and $rec_j = \{v'\}$ at line 10. Moreover, from item (2) of Lemma 1, we have $v = v' = est_c$ (where est_c is the value broadcast during r by its coordinator). $\Box_{Lemma\ 3}$

Theorem 3. *No two processes decide differently.*

Proof Let r be the first round during which a process p_i decides. It decides at line 12. Let v be the value decided by p_i. Let us assume another process decides v' during a round $r' \geq r$. If $r' = r$, then due to Lemma 3, we have $v = v'$. So, let us consider the situation where $r' > r$. We show that the estimate values (est_j) of all the processes p_j that progress to $r + 1$ are equal to v. This means that no other value can be decided in a future round[5].

---

[5] When we consider the terminology used in $\Diamond S$-based protocols, this means the value v is *locked*. This proof shows that the "*value locking*" principle is not bound to the particular use of $\Diamond S$. With S, a value is locked as soon as it has been forwarded by the (first) correct process that is never suspected. With $\Diamond S$, a value is locked as soon as it has been forwarded by a majority of processes.

Let us consider any process p_k that terminates the round r. Let us first note that there is a process p_x such that $p_x \in Q_i \cap Q_k$. This follows from the following observation:

- If the failure detector belongs to S, then by considering p_x, the correct process that is never suspected, we have $p_x \in Q_i \cap Q_k$.
- If the failure detector belongs to the class $\Diamond S$, as Q_i and Q_k are majority sets, we have $Q_i \cap Q_k \neq \emptyset$, and there is a p_x such that $p_x \in Q_i \cap Q_k$.

As p_i has decided v at line 12 during r, we had during this round $rec_i = \{v\}$. This means that p_i has received v from all the processes of Q_i, and so from p_x. Thus, p_k has also received v from p_x, and consequently, $rec_k = \{v\}$ or $rec_k = \{v, \bot\}$. It follows that if p_k proceeds to the next round, it executes line 13. Consequently, for all processes p_j that progress to $r + 1$, we have $est_j = v$. This means that, from round $r + 1$, all estimate values are equal to v. As no value different from v is present in the system, the only value that can be decided in a round $> r$ is v. $\square_{Theorem\ 3}$

6 Discussion

6.1 Cost of the Protocol

Time complexity of a round As indicated in Corollary 1, the number of rounds of the protocol is bounded by n, when used with a failure detector of the class S. There is no upper bound when it is used with a failure detector of the class $\Diamond S$. So, to analyze the time complexity of the protocol, we consider the length of the sequence of messages (number of communication steps) exchanged during a round. Moreover, as on one side we do not master the quality of service offered by failure detectors, but as on the other side, in practice failure detectors can be tuned to very seldom make mistakes, we do this analysis considering the underlying failure detector behaves reliably. In such a context, the time complexity of a round is characterized by a pair of integers. Considering the most favorable scenario that allows to decide during the current round, the first integer measures its number of communication steps. The second integer considers the case where a decision can not be obtained during the current round and measures the minimal number of communication steps required to progress to the next round. Let us consider these scenarios.

- The first scenario is when the current round coordinator is correct and is not suspected. In that case, 2 communication steps are required to decide. During the first step, the current coordinator broadcasts its value (line 8). During the second step, each process forwards that value (line 8), waits for "enough" messages (line 9), and then decides (line 12). So, in the most favorable scenario that allows to decide during the current round, the round is made of two communication steps.
- The second scenario is when the current round coordinator has crashed and is suspected by all processes. In that case, as processes correctly suspect the

coordinator (line 5), they actually skip the first communication step. They directly exchange the $\perp$ value (line 8) and proceed to the next round (line 11). So, in the most favorable scenario to proceed to the next round, the round is made of a single communication step.

So, when the underlying failure detector behaves reliably, according to the previous discussion, the time complexity of a round is characterized by the pair $(2, 1)$ of communication steps.

Message complexity of a round During each round, each process sends a message to each process (including itself). Hence, the message complexity of a round is upper bounded by n^2.

Message type and size There are two types of message: EST and DECIDE. A DE-CIDE message carries only a proposed value. An EST message carries a proposed value (or the default value $\perp$) plus a round number. The size of the round number is bounded by $log_2(n)$ when the underlying failure detector belongs to S (Corollary 1). It is not bounded in the other case.

6.2 Related Work

Several failure detector-based Consensus protocols have been proposed in the literature. We compare here the proposed protocol (in short MR) with the following protocols:
- The S-based Consensus protocol proposed in [2] (in short, CT_S).
- The $\Diamond S$-based Consensus protocol proposed in [2] (in short, $CT_{\Diamond S}$).
- The $\Diamond S$-based Consensus protocol proposed in [9] (in short, $SC_{\Diamond S}$).
- The $\Diamond S$-based Consensus protocol proposed in [8] (in short, $HR_{\Diamond S}$).

As MR, all these protocols proceed in consecutive asynchronous rounds. Moreover, all, but CT_S, are based on the rotating coordinator paradigm. It is important to note that each of these protocols has been specifically designed for a special class of failure detectors (either S or $\Diamond S$). Differently from MR, none of them has a generic dimension. Let us also note that only MR and both CT protocols cope naturally with message duplications (*i.e.*, they do not require additional statements to discard duplicate messages).

Let $V = \{$ initial values proposed by processes $\} \cup \{\perp\}$. Table 1 compares CT_S and MR (when used with S). Both protocols use n^2 messages during each round. A round is made of one or two communication steps in MR, and of a single communication step in CT_S. The first column indicates the total number (k) of communication steps needed to reach a decision. For MR, this number depends on the parameter f. As indicated, CT_S does not allow early decision, while MR does. The second column indicates the size of messages used by each protocol. As the current round number is carried by messages of both protocols, it is not indicated.

	# communication steps	Message size
CT_S	$k = n$	An array of n values $\in V$
MR with S	$2 \leq k \leq 2(f + 1)$	A single value $\in V$

Table 1. Comparing MR with CT_S

Table 2 compares MR (when used with $\Diamond S$) with $CT_{\Diamond S}$, $SC_{\Diamond S}$ and $HR_{\Diamond S}$. In all cases, there is no bound on the round number and all protocols allow early decision. So, the first column compares the time complexity of a round, according to the previous discussion (Section 6.1). The second column is devoted to the message size. As each protocol uses messages of different size, we only consider their biggest messages. Moreover, as in all protocols, each of those messages carries its identity (sender id, round number) and an estimate value, the second column indicates only their additional fields. Let us additionally note that, differently from $SC_{\Diamond S}$ and $HR_{\Diamond S}$, MR does not require special statements to prevent deadlock situations.

	Time complexity of a round	Message size
$CT_{\Diamond S}$	$(3, 0)$	An integer timestamp
$SC_{\Diamond S}$	$(2, 2)$	A boolean and a process id
$HR_{\Diamond S}$	$(2, 1)$	A boolean
MR with $\Diamond S$	$(2, 1)$	No additional value

Table 2. Comparing MR with $CT_{\Diamond S}$, $SC_{\Diamond S}$ and $HR_{\Diamond S}$

Finally, let us note that MR provides a (factorized) proof, that is shorter and simpler to understand than the proofs designed for the other protocols.

7   Conclusion

This paper has presented a *generic* Consensus protocol that works with any failure detector belonging to the class S (provided that $f \leq n - 1$) or to the class $\Diamond S$ (provided that $f < n/2$).

The proposed protocol is conceptually simple, allows early decision and uses messages shorter than previous solutions. It has been compared to other Consensus protocols designed for specific classes of unreliable failure detectors. Among its advantages, the design simplicity of the proposed protocol has allowed the design of a simple (and generic) proof. The most noteworthy of its properties lie in its quorum-based approach and in its generic dimension.

It is important to note that a Consensus protocol initially designed to work with a failure detector of the class S will not work when S is replaced by $\Diamond S$. Moreover, a Consensus protocol initially designed to work with a failure detector of $\Diamond S$ requires $f < n/2$; if $\Diamond S$ is replaced by S, the protocol will continue to work, but will still require $f < n/2$ which is not a necessary requirement in that context. Actually, modifying a $\Diamond S$-based Consensus protocol to work with S and $f < n - 1$ amounts to design a new protocol. The generic dimension of the proposed protocol prevents this drawback. In that sense, the proposed protocol is the first failure detector-based Consensus protocol that is not bound to a particular class of failure detectors.

Last but not least, the design of this generic protocol is a result of our effort to understand the relation linking S on one side, and $\Diamond S$ plus the majority requirement on the other side, when solving the Consensus problem with unreliable failure detectors.

Acknowledgments

The authors are grateful to Jean-Michel Hélary who made insightful comments on a first draft of this paper.

References

1. Agrawal D. and El Abbadi A., Exploiting Logical Structures in Replicated Databases. *Information Processing Letters*, 33:255-260, 1990.
2. Chandra T. and Toueg S., Unreliable Failure Detectors for Reliable Distributed Systems. *Journal of the ACM*, 43(2):225-267, March 1996.
3. Chandra T., Hadzilacos V. and Toueg S., The Weakest Failure Detector for Solving Consensus. *Journal of the ACM*, 43(4):685-722, July 1996.
4. Fischer M.J., Lynch N. and Paterson M.S., Impossibility of Distributed Consensus with One Faulty Process. *Journal of the ACM*, 32(2):374-382, April 1985.
5. Fritzke U., Ingels P., Mostefaoui A. and Raynal M., Fault-Tolerant Total Order Multicast to Asynchronous Groups. *Proc. 17th IEEE Symposium on Reliable Distributed Systems*, Purdue University, pp. 228-235, October 1998.
6. Guerraoui R., Revisiting the Relationship between Non-Blocking Atomic Commitment and Consensus. *Proc. 9th Int. Workshop on Distributed Algorithms (WDAG95)*, Springer-Verlag LNCS 972 (J.M. Hélary and M. Raynal Eds), pp. 87-100, September 1995.
7. Hadzilacos V. and Toueg S., Reliable Broadcast and Related Problems. In *Distributed Systems*, ACM Press (S. Mullender Ed.), New-York, pp. 97-145, 1993.
8. Hurfin M. and Raynal M., A Simple and Fast Asynchronous Consensus Protocol Based on a Weak Failure Detector. *Distributed Computing*, 12(4), 1999.
9. Schiper A., Early Consensus in an Asynchronous System with a Weak Failure Detector. *Distributed Computing*, 10:149-157, 1997.

A Dynamic Primary Configuration Group Communication Service

Roberto De Prisco[1], Alan Fekete[2], Nancy Lynch[3], and Alex Shvartsman[4]

[1] MIT Laboratory for Computer Science, Cambridge, MA 02139, USA and
Dip. di Informatica ed Applicazioni, University of Salerno, Italy.
`robdep@theory.lcs.mit.edu`
[2] Basser Dept. of Computer Science, University of Sydney, NSW 2006, Australia
`fekete@theory.lcs.mit.edu`
[3] MIT Laboratory for Computer Science, Cambridge, MA 02139, USA.
`lynch@theory.lcs.mit.edu`
[4] Dept. of Computer Science and Eng., University of Connecticut, Storrs, CT, USA,
and MIT Laboratory for Computer Science, Cambridge, MA 02139, USA.
`alex@theory.lcs.mit.edu`

Abstract. Quorum-based methods for managing replicated data are
popular because they provide availability of both reads and writes in
the presence of faulty behavior by some sites or communication links.
Over a very long time, it may become necessary to alter the quorum
system, perhaps because some sites have failed permanently and others have joined the system, or perhaps because users want a different
trade-off between read-availability and write-availability. There are subtle issues that arise in managing the change of quorums, including how
to make sure that any operation using the new quorum system is aware
of all information from operations that used an old quorum system, and
how to allow concurrent attempts to alter the quorum system.

In this paper we use ideas from group management services, especially
those providing a dynamic notion of primary view; with this we define
an abstract specification of a system that presents each user with a consistent succession of identified *configurations*, each of which has a membership set, and a quorum system for that set. The key contribution here
is the intersection property, that determines how the new configurations
must relate to previous ones. We demonstrate that our proposed specification is neither too strong, by showing how it can be implemented, nor
too weak, by showing the correctness of a replicated data management
algorithm running above it.

1 Introduction

In distributed applications involving replicated data, a well known way to en-
hance the availability and efficiency of the system is to use *quorums*. A quorum
is a subset of the members of the system, such that any two quorums have non-
empty intersection. An update can be performed with only a quorum available,
unlike other replication techniques where all of the members must be available.

The intersection property of quorums guarantees consistency. Quorum systems have been extensively studied and used in applications, e.g., [1, 7, 8, 18, 23, 24, 34, 38]. The use of quorums has been proven effective also against Byzantine failures [32, 33].

Pre-defined quorum sets can yield efficient implementations in settings which are relatively static, i.e., failures are transient. However they work less well in settings where processes routinely join and leave the system, or where the system can suffer multiple partitions. These settings require the on-going modification of the choice of quorums. For example, if more sites join the system, quorums must be reconfigured to make use of the new sites. If many sites fail permanently, quorums must be reconfigured to maintain availability. The most common proposal has been to use a two-phase commit protocol which stops all application operations while all sites are notified of the new configuration. Since two-phase commit is a blocking protocol, this solution is vulnerable to a single failure during the configuration change. In a setting of database transactions, [23] showed how to integrate fault-tolerant updates of replicated information about quorum sizes (using the same quorums for both data item replicas, and for quorum information replicas).

Here we offer a different approach, based on ideas of dynamic primary views from group management systems. *View-oriented group communication services* have become important as building blocks for fault-tolerant distributed systems. Such a service enables application processes located at different nodes of a fault-prone distributed network to operate collectively as a group, using the service to multicast messages to all members of the group. Each such service is based on a *group membership service*, which provides each group member with a *view* of the group; a view includes a list of the processes that are members of the group. Messages sent by a process in one view are delivered only to processes in the membership of that view, and only when they have the same view. Within each view, the service offers guarantees about the order and reliability of message delivery. Examples of view-oriented group communication services are found in Isis [9], Transis [15], Totem [37], Newtop [20], Relacs [3], Horus [46] and Ensemble [45].

For many applications, some views must be distinguished as *primary views*. Primary views have stronger properties, which allow updates to occur consistently. Traditionally, a primary view was defined as one containing a majority of all possible sites, but other, dynamic, definitions are possible, based on intersection properties between successive primary views. One possibility is to define a primary view as a view containing a majority of the previous primary view. Several papers define primary views adaptively, e.g., [6, 13, 14, 17, 27, 35, 41, 43, 47]. Producing good specifications for view-oriented group communication services is difficult, because these services can be complicated, and because different such services provide different guarantees about safety, performance, and fault-tolerance. Examples of specifications for group membership services and view-oriented group communication services appear in [4, 5, 10, 12, 16, 21, 22, 25,

$26, 36, 39, 42, 44$]. Extending these definitions to specify dynamic primary views was the focus of [14, 47].

In this paper we combine the notion of dynamic primary view with that of a quorum system, and call the result a *configuration*. We integrate this with a group communication service, resulting in a *dynamic primary configuration group communication service*. The main difficulty in combining quorum systems with the notion of dynamic primary view is the intersection property between quorums from different views, which is required to maintain consistency. With configurations the simple intersection property (i.e., a primary view contains a majority of the previous primary) that works for primary views, is no longer enough. Indeed updated information might be only at a quorum and the processors in the intersection might be not in that quorum. A stronger intersection property is required. We propose one possible intersection property that allows applications to keep consistency across different primary configurations. Namely, we require that there be a quorum of the old primary configuration which is included in the membership set of the new primary configuration. This guarantees that there is at least one process in the new primary configuration that has the most up to date information. This, similarly to the intersection property of dynamic primary views, allows flow of information from the old configuration to the new one and thus permits one to preserve consistency.

The specific configurations we consider use two sets of quorums, a set of *read* quorums and a set of *write* quorums, with the property that any read quorum intersects any write quorum. (This choice is justified by the application we develop, an atomic read/write register.) With this kind of configuration the intersection property that we require for a new primary configuration is that there be one read quorum and one write quorum both of which are included in the membership set of the new primary configuration. The use of read and write quorums (as opposed to just quorums) can be more efficient in order to balance the load of the system (see for example [18]).

We provide a formal automaton specification, called DC for "dynamic configurations", for the safety guarantees made by a dynamic primary configuration group communication service. We remark that we do not address liveness properties here, but that they can be expressed as conditional performance properties, similar to those in [21], or with other techniques such as failure-detectors [11].

Clearly the DC specification provides support for primary configurations. However it also has another important feature, namely, it provides support for state-exchange. When a new configuration starts, applications generally require some pre-processing, such as an exchange of information, to prepare for ordinary computation. Typically this is needed in order to bring every member of the configuration up to date. For example, processes in a coherent database application may need to exchange information about previous updates in order to bring everyone in the new configuration up to date. We will refer to the up-to-date state of a new configuration as the *starting state* of that configuration. The starting state is the state of the computation that all members should have in order to perform regular computation. When the notification of a new configuration is given to its members, the DC specification allows these members to submit their current state. Then the service takes care of collecting all the states and computing the starting state for the new configuration and delivering it to the members. When all members have been notified of the starting state for a configuration c, all information about the membership set and the quorums of previous configurations is not needed anymore, and the service no longer needs to ensure intersection in membership between configurations before c and any subsequent ones that are formed. This is the basis of a garbage-collection mechanism which was introduced in [47].

The DC specification offers a broadcast/convergecast communication service which works as follows: a process p submits a message to the service; the service forwards this message to the members of the current configuration and upon receiving acknowledgment values from a quorum of members it computes a response for the message sent by process p and gives the response to p. This communication mechanism has been introduced in [30], though in the setting of that paper there is no group-oriented computation.

We demonstrate the value of our DC specification by showing both how it can be implemented and how it can be used in an application. Both pieces are shown formally, with assertional proofs.

We implement DC by using a variant of the group membership algorithm of [47]. Our variant integrates communication with the membership service, provides state-exchange support at the beginning of a new configuration, and uses a static configuration-oriented service internally. We prove that this algorithm implements DC, in the sense of trace inclusion. The proof uses a simulation relation and invariant assertions.

We develop an atomic read/write shared register on top of DC. The algorithm is based on the work of Attiya, Bar-Noy and Dolev [2] and follows the approach used in [19, 30]. The application exploits the communication and state-exchange services provided by DC. The proof of correctness uses a simulation relation and invariant assertions.

2 Mathematical foundations and notation

We describe the services and algorithms using the the I/O automaton model of Lynch and Tuttle [31] (without fairness). The model and associated methodology is described in Chapter 8 of [29].

Next we provide some definitions used in the rest of the paper.

We write λ for the empty sequence. If a is a sequence, then $|a|$ denotes the length of a. If a is a sequence and $1 \leq i \leq |a|$ then $a(i)$ denotes the ith element of a. Given a set S, $seqof(S)$ denotes the set consisting of all finite sequences of elements of S. If s and t are sequences, the concatenation of s and t, with s coming first, is denoted by $s+t$. We say that sequence s is a *prefix* of sequence t, written as $s \leq t$, provided that there exists u such that $s+u = t$. The "head" of a sequence a is $a(1)$. A sequence can be used as a queue: the *append* operation modifies the sequence by concatenating the sequence with a new element and the *remove* operation modifies the sequence by deleting the head of the sequence.

If R is a binary relation, then we define $dom(R)$, the *domain* of R to be the set (without repetitions) of first elements of the ordered pairs comprising relation R.

We denote by $\mathcal{P}$ the universe of all processors[1] and we assume that $\mathcal{P}$ is totally ordered. We denote by $\mathcal{M}$ the universe of all possible messages. We denote by $\mathcal{G}$ a totally ordered set of identifiers used to distinguish configurations. Given a set S, the notation $S_\perp$ refers to the set $S \cup \{\perp\}$. If a set S is totally ordered, we extend the ordering of S to the set $S_\perp$ by letting $\perp < s$ for any $s \in S$.

A *configuration* is a quadruple, $c = \langle g, P, \mathcal{R}, \mathcal{W} \rangle$, where $g \in \mathcal{G}$ is a unique identifier, $P \subseteq \mathcal{P}$ is a nonempty set of processors, and $\mathcal{R}$ and $\mathcal{W}$ are nonempty sets of nonempty subsets[2] of P, such that $R \cap W \neq \{\}$ for all $R \in \mathcal{R}$, $W \in \mathcal{W}$. Each element of $\mathcal{R}$ is called a *read quorum* of c, and each element of $\mathcal{W}$ a *write quorum*. We let $\mathcal{C}$ denote the set of all configurations.

Given a configuration $c = \langle g, P, \mathcal{R}, \mathcal{W} \rangle$, the notation $c.id$ refers to the configuration identifier g, the notation $c.set$ refers to the membership set P, while $c.rqrms$ and $c.wqrms$ refer to $\mathcal{R}$ and $\mathcal{W}$, respectively. We distinguish an initial configuration $c_0 = \langle g_0, P_0, \mathcal{R}_0, \mathcal{W}_0 \rangle$, where g_0 is a distinguished configuration identifier.

3 The DC specification

In many applications significant computation is performed only in special configurations called *primary configurations*, which satisfy certain intersection properties with previous primary configurations. In particular, we require that the membership set of a new primary configuration must include the members of at least one read quorum and one write quorum of the previous primary configuration. The DC specification provides to the client only configurations satisfying this property. This is similar to what the DVS service of [14] does for ordinary views.

An important feature of the DC specification is that it allows for state-exchange at the beginning of a new primary configuration. State-exchange at the beginning of a new configuration is required by most applications. When a new configuration is issued each member of the configuration is supposed to submit its current state to the service which, once obtained the state from all the members of the configuration computes the most up to date state over all the members, called the *starting state*, and delivers this state to each member. This way, each member begins regular computation in the new configuration knowing the starting state. We remark that this is different from the approach used by the DVS service of [14] which lets the members of the configuration compute

---

[1] In the rest of the paper we will use *processor* as synonymous of *process*. The differences between the two terms are immaterial in our setting.

[2] Expressing each quorum as a set of subsets is a generalization of the common technique where the quorums are based on integers n_r and n_w such that $n_r + n_w \geq |P|$; the two approaches are related by defining the set of read quorums as consisting of those subsets of P with cardinality at least n_r, and the set of write quorums as consisting of those subsets of P of cardinality at least n_w.

the starting state. Some existing group communication services also integrate state-exchange within the service [43].

Finally, the DC specification offers a broadcast/convergecast communication mechanism. This mechanism involves all the members of a quorum, and uses a condenser function to process the information gathered from the quorum. More specifically, a client that wants to send a message (request) to the members of its current configuration submits the message together with a *condenser* function to the service; then the DC service broadcasts the message to all the members of the configuration and waits for a response from a quorum (the type of the quorum, read or write, is also specified by the client); once answers are received from a quorum, the DC service applies the condenser function to these answers in order to compute a response to give back to the client that sent the message.

We remark that this kind of communication is different from those of the VS service [21] and the DVS service [14]. Instead, it is as the one used in [30]. We integrate it into DC because we want to develop a particular application that benefits from this particular communication service (a read/write register as is done in [30]).

Prior to providing the code for the DC specification, we need some notation and definitions, which we introduce in the following while giving an informal description of the code.

Each operation requested by the client of the service is tagged with a unique identifier. Let OID be the set of operation identifiers, partitioned into sets OID_p, $p \in \mathcal{P}$. Let $\mathcal{A}$ be a set of "acknowledgment" values and let $\mathcal{R}$ be a set of "response" values. A *value condenser function* is a function from $(\mathcal{A}_\perp)^n$ to $\mathcal{R}$. Let Φ be the set of all value condenser functions. Let $\mathcal{S}$ be the set of states of the client (this does not need to be the entire client's state, but it may contain only the relevant information in order for the application to work). A *state condenser function* is a function from $(\mathcal{S}_\perp)^n$ to $\mathcal{S}$. Let Ψ be the set of all state condenser functions. Given a function $f : \mathcal{P} \to D$ from the set of processors $\mathcal{P}$ to some domain value D and given a subset $P \subseteq \mathcal{P}$ of processors we write $f|P$ to denote the function f' defined as follows: $f'(p) = f(p)$ if $p \in P$ and $f'(p) = \perp$ otherwise.

We use the following data type to describe an operation: $\mathcal{D} = \mathcal{M} \times \Phi \times \{\text{"read"}, \text{"write"}\} \times 2^{\mathcal{P}} \times (\mathcal{A}_\perp)^n \times Bool$ and we let $\mathcal{O} = OID \to \mathcal{D}_\perp$. Given an operation descriptor, selectors for the components are msg, cnd, sel, dlv, ack, and rsp. Given an operation descriptor $d \in \mathcal{D}$ for an operation i, $d.msg$ is the message of operation i which is delivered to all the processes (it represents the request of the operation, like read a register or write a register), $d.cnd$ is the condenser of operation i which is used to compute a response when acknowledgment values are available from a quorum of processes, $d.sel$ is a selector that specifies whether to use a read or a write quorum, $d.dlv$ is the set of processes to which the message has been delivered, $d.ack$ contains the acknowledgment values, and, finally, $d.rsp$ is a flag indicating whether or not the client has received a response for the operation. Operation descriptors maintain information about the operations. When an operation i is submitted its descriptor $d = pending[g](i)$ is initialized to $d = (m, \phi, b, \{\}, \{\}, \texttt{false})$ where m, ϕ and b come with the operation submission (i.e., are provided by the client). Then $d.dlv, d.ack$ and $d.rsp$ are updated while the operation is being serviced. Once a response has been given back to the client and thus $d.rsp$ is set to true, the operation is completed.

For each process p we define the current configuration of p as the last configuration c given to p with a NEWCONF$(c)_p$ event (or a predefined configuration if no such event has happened yet). The identifier of the current configuration of process p is stored into variable $cur\text{-}cid_p$. When a configuration c has been notified to a processor p we say that processor p has "attempted" configuration c. We use the history variable $attempted$ to record the set of processors that have attempted a particular configuration c. More formally $p \in attempted[c.id]$ iff processor p has attempted c.

Next we define an important notion, the one of "dead" configuration. Informally a dead configuration c is a configuration for which a member process p went on to newer configurations, that is, it executed action NEWCONF$(c')_p$ with $c'.id > c.id$, before receiving the notification, that is the NEWCONF$(c)_p$ event, for configuration c (which can no longer be notified to that processor, and thus is dead because processor p cannot participate and it is impossible to compute the starting state). More formally we define $dead \in 2^C$ as $dead = \{c \in C | \exists p \in c.set : cur\text{-}cid_p > c.id$ and $p \notin attempted[c.id]\}$.

DC (Signature and state)

Signature:

Input:
SUBMIT$(m, \phi, b, i)_p$, $m \in \mathcal{M}$, $\phi \in \Phi$,
  $b \in \{$"read", "write"$\}$, $p \in \mathcal{P}, i \in OID_p$
ACKDLVR$(a, i)_p$, $a \in A$, $i \in OID$, $p \in \mathcal{P}$
SUBMIT-STATE$(s, \psi)_p$, $s \in \mathcal{S}$, $\psi \in \psi$

Internal: CREATECONF(c), $c \in \mathcal{C}$
Output:
NEWCONF$(c)_p$, $c \in \mathcal{C}$, $p \in c.set$
NEWSTATE$(s)_p$, $s \in \mathcal{S}$
RESPOND$(a, i)_p$, $a \in A$, $i \in OID_p$, $p \in \mathcal{P}$
DELIVER$(m, i)_p$, $m \in \mathcal{M}$, $i \in OID$, $p \in \mathcal{P}$

State:
$created \in 2^C$, init $\{c_0\}$
for each $p \in \mathcal{P}$: $cur\text{-}cid[p] \in \mathcal{G}_\perp$,
  init g_0 if $p \in P_0$, $\perp$ else
for each $g \in \mathcal{G}$: $attempted[g] \in 2^{\mathcal{P}}$,
  init P_0 if $g = g_0$, $\{\}$ else

for each $g \in \mathcal{G}$:
$got\text{-}state[g] = \mathcal{P} \to \mathcal{S}_\perp$, init everywhere $\perp$
$condenser[g] = \mathcal{P} \to \psi_\perp$, init everywhere $\perp$
$state\text{-}dlv[g] \in 2^{\mathcal{P}}$, init P_0 if $g = g_0$, $\{\}$ else
$pending[g] \in \mathcal{O}$, init everywhere $\perp$

Fig. 1. The DC signature and state

We say that a configuration c is *totally attempted* in a state s of DC if $c.set \subseteq attempted[c.id]$. We denote by TotAtt the set of totally attempted configurations. Informally a totally attempted configuration is a configuration for which all members have received notification of the new configuration. Similarly, we say that a configuration c is *attempted* in a state s of DC if $attempted[c.id] \neq \{\}$. We denote by $\mathcal{A}tt$ the set of attempted configurations. Clearly $\mathcal{A}tt \subseteq \mathit{TotAtt}$.

DC (Transitions)

Actions:

internal CREATECONF(c)
  Pre: For all $w \in created$: $c.id \neq w.id$
    if $c \notin dead$ then
      For all $w \in created, w.id < c.id$:
        $w \in dead$ or
        $(\exists x \in Tot\mathcal{E}st: w.id{<}x.id{<}c.id)\vee$
        $(\exists R \in w.rqrms, \exists W \in w.wqrms$:
          $R \cup W \subseteq c.set)$
      For all $w \in created, w.id > c.id$
        $w \in dead$ or
        $(\exists x \in Tot\mathcal{E}st: c.id{<}x.id{<}w.id)\vee$
        $(\exists R \in c.rqrms, \exists W \in c.wqrms$:
          $R \cup W \subseteq w.set)$
  Eff: $created := created \cup \{c\}$

output NEWCONF$(c)_p$, $p \in c.set$
  Pre: $c \in created$
    $c.id > cur\text{-}cid[p]$
  Eff: $cur\text{-}cid[p] := c.id$
    $attempted[c.id]$
      $:= attempted[c.id] \cup \{p\}$

input SUBMIT-STATE$(s, \psi)_p$
  Eff: if $cur\text{-}cid[p] \neq \bot$ and
    $got\text{-}state[cur\text{-}cid[p]](p) = \bot$ then
    $got\text{-}state[cur\text{-}cid[p]](p) := s$
    $condenser[cur\text{-}cid[p]](p) := \psi$

output NEWSTATE$(s)_p$ choose c
  Pre: $c.id = cur\text{-}cid[p]$
    $c \in created$
    $\forall q \in c.set: got\text{-}state[c.id](q) \neq \bot$
    $s = condenser[c.id](p)(got\text{-}state[c.id])$
    $p \notin state\text{-}dlv[c.id]$
  Eff: $state\text{-}dlv[c.id]$
      $:= state\text{-}dlv[c.id] \cup \{p\}$

input SUBMIT$(m, \phi, b, i)_p$
  Eff: if $cur\text{-}cid[p] \neq \bot$ then
    $pending[cur\text{-}cid[p]](i)$
      $:= (m, \phi, b, \{\}, \{\}, \textbf{false})$

output DELIVER$(m, i)_p$ choose g
  Pre: $g = cur\text{-}cid[p]$
    $p \notin pending[g](i).dlv$
    $pending[g](i).msg = m$
  Eff: $pending[g](i).dlv$
      $:= pending[g](i).dlv \cup \{p\}$

input ACKDLVR$(a, i)_p$
  Eff: if $cur\text{-}cid[p] \neq \bot$ and
    $pending[cur\text{-}cid[p]](i).ack(p) \neq \bot$
    then
    $pending[cur\text{-}cid[p]](i).ack(p)$
      $:= a$

output RESPOND$(r, i)_p$ choose c, Q
  Pre: $c.id = cur\text{-}cid[p]$
    $c \in created$
    $i \in OID_p$
    $pending[c.id](i).rsp = \textbf{false}$
    if $pending[c.id].sel =$ "read"
      then $Q \in c.rqrms$
    if $pending[c.id].sel =$ "write"
      then $Q \in c.wqrms$
    let $f = pending[c.id](i).ack$
    $\forall q \in Q : f(q) \neq \bot$
    $r = pending[c.id](i).cnd(f|Q)$
  Eff: $pending[c.id](i).rsp := \textbf{true}$

Fig. 2. The DC transitions

After a processor p has attempted a new configuration, it submits its state by means of action SUBMIT-STATE$(s, \psi)_p$. Variable $got\text{-}state[g](p)$ records the state s submitted by processor p for the current configuration of p whose identifier is g. Similarly, the state condenser function submitted by p is recorded into variable $condenser[g](p)$. After all processors members of a configuration c have submitted their state, the starting state for c can be computed, by using the appropriate condenser function, and can be given to the members of c. Note that the state condensor is used when all members have submitted a state, in contrast to message convergecast which applies the value condensor once a quorum of values are known. Variable $state\text{-}dlv[g]$ records the set of processors to which the starting state for the configuration with identifier g has been delivered.

When the starting state for a configuration c has been delivered to processor p we say that c is *established* (at p). A configuration is totally established when it is established at all processors members of the configuration. More formally a configuration c is *totally established* in a state s of DC if, in state s, we have $c.set \subseteq state\text{-}dlv[c.id]$. We denote by $Tot\mathcal{E}st$ the set of totally established configurations. When a configuration c becomes totally established, information about the membership set and quorums of configurations previous to c can be discarded, because the intersection property will be guaranteed between c and later configurations.

The code of the DC specification is given in Figures 1 and 2.

The second precondition of CREATECONF(c) is the key to our specification. It states that when a configuration c is created it must either be already dead or for any other configuration w such that there are no intervening totally established configurations, the earlier configuration (i.e., the one with smaller identifier) has one read quorum and one write quorum whose members are included in the membership set of the later configuration (i.e., the one with bigger identifier). The above precondition is formalized in the following key invariant:

Invariant 1 *Let* $c_1, c_2 \in created \setminus dead$, *with* $c_1.id < c_2.id$. *Then either exists* $w \in Tot\mathcal{E}st, c_1.id < w.id < c_2.id$, *or else exist* R, W *quorums of* c_1 *such that* $R \cup W \subseteq c_2.set$

The property stated by this invariant is used to prove correct the application that we build on top of DC. We remark that dead configurations are excluded, that is, the intersection property may not hold for dead configurations. However, in a dead configuration it is not possible to make progress because for such a configuration there is at least one process that will not participate and thus the configuration will never become established.

The need for considering dead configurations comes from the implementation of the specification that we provide. It is possible to give a stronger version of DC by requiring that the intersection property in the precondition of action CREATECONF holds also for dead configurations, however this stronger version might not be implementable. Moreover, as we have said above, there is no loss of generality since no progress is made anyway in dead configurations.

4 An implementation of DC

The DC specification can be implemented, in the sense of trace inclusion, with an algorithm similar to that used in [14] to implement the DVS service. Hence it uses ideas from [47]. This implementation consists of an automaton DC-CODE$_p$ for each $p \in \mathcal{P}$. Due to space constraints we omit the code and the proof of correctness and provide only an overall description.

4.1 The implementation

The automaton DC-CODE$_p$ uses special messages, tagged either with "*info*", used to send information about the active and ambiguous configurations, or with "*got-state*", used to send the state submitted by a process to all the members of the configuration. The former information is needed to check the intersection property that new primary configurations have to satisfy according to the DC specification. The latter information is needed in order to compute the starting state for a new configuration.

The major problem is that the DC specification requires a global intersection property (i.e., a property that can be checked only by someone that knows the entire system state), while each single process has a local knowledge of the system. So, in order to guarantee that a new configuration satisfies the requirement of DC, each single process needs information from other processes members of the configuration.

Informally, the filtering of configurations works as follows. Each process keeps track of the latest totally established configuration, called the "active" configuration, recorded into variable *act*, and a set of "ambiguous" configurations, recorded into variable *amb*, which are those configurations that were notified after the active configuration but did not become established yet. We define *use* = *act* ∪ *amb*. When a new configuration is detected, process p sends out an "*info*" message containing its current act_p and amb_p values to all other processors in the new configuration, using an underlying broadcast communication mechanism, and waits to receive the corresponding "*info*" messages for configuration c from all the other members of c. After receiving this information (and updating its own act_p and amb_p accordingly), process p checks whether c has the required intersection property with each view in the use_p set. If so, configuration c is given in output to the client at p by means of action NEWCONF$(c)_p$.

When a new primary configuration c has been given in output to processor p by means of action NEWCONF$(c)_p$, the client at p submits its current state together with a condenser function to be used to compute the starting state when all other members have submitted their state (such a condenser function depends on the application). Clearly the state of p is needed by other processors in the configuration while p needs the state of the other processors. Hence when a SUBMIT-STATE$(s, \psi)_p$ is executed at p, the state s submitted by processor p is sent out with a "*got-state*" message to all other members of the configuration. Upon receiving the state of all other processors, DC-CODE$_p$ uses the state condenser function ψ provided by the client at p in order to compute the starting state to be output, by means of action NEWSTATE$(s)_p$, to the client at p.

Finally, the broadcast/convergecast communication mechanism of DC is simulated by using the underlying broadcast communication mechanism (this simulation is quite straightforward).

4.2 Proof

The proof that DC-IMPL implements DC in the sense of trace inclusion is done by using invariants and a simulation relation. The proof is similar to the one in [14] used to prove that DVS-IMPL implements DVS. There is a key difference in the implementation which provides new insights for the DVS specification and implementation, as we explain below.

The DVS specification requires a global intersection property which is the following: given two primary views w and v with no intervening totally established view, we must have that $w.set \cup v.set \neq \{\}$. The DVS implementation, when delivering a new view v, checks *a stronger property* locally to the processors, which requires that $|v.set \cup w.set| \geq |w.set|/2$ for all the views w, $w.id < v.id$, known by the processor performing the check.

The DC specification requires a global intersection property which is the following: given two primary configurations, both of which are not dead, with no intervening totally established configuration, then it must be that there exists a read and write quorum of the configuration with a smaller identifier which are included in the membership set of the configuration with bigger identifier. The DC implementation checks *the same property* locally to each processor. The intuitive reason why by checking locally the same property we can prove it also globally is that we exclude dead configurations. This suggest that also for DVS we can prove the stronger intersection property (the one checked locally) or we can use a weaker local check (the intersection required globally) if we do exclude dead views.

5 Atomic Read/Write Shared Memory Algorithm

In this section we show how to use DC to implement an atomic multi-writer multi-reader shared register. The algorithm is an extension of the single-writer multi-reader atomic register of Attiya, Bar-Noy and Dolev [2]. A similar extension was provided in [30]. The overall algorithm is called ABD-SYS and consists of an automaton ABD-CODE$_p$ for each $p \in \mathcal{P}$, and DC. Due to space constraint the code of automaton ABD-CODE$_P$ is omitted from this extended abstract.

5.1 The algorithm

Each processor keeps a copy of the shared register, in variable *val* paired with a tag, in variable *tag*. Tags are used to establish the time when values are written: a value paired with a bigger tag has been written after a value paired with a smaller tag. Tags consists of pairs $\langle j, p \rangle$ where j is a sequence number (an integer) and p is a processor identifier. Tags are ordered according to their sequence numbers with processors identifiers breaking ties. Given a tag $\langle j, p \rangle$ the notation *t.seq* denotes the sequence number j.

The algorithm has two modes of operation: a *normal mode* and a *reconfiguration mode*. The latter is used to establish a new configuration. It is entered when a new configuration is announced (action NEWCONF) and is left when the configuration becomes established (action NEWSTATE). The former is the mode where read and write operations are performed and it is entered when a configuration is established and is left when a new configuration is announced. During the reconfiguration mode pending operations are delayed until the normal mode is restored.

Clients of the service can request read and write operations by means of actions READ$_p$ and WRITE$(x)_p$. We assume that each client does not invoke a new operation request before receiving the response for the previous request. Both type of requests (read and write) are handled in a similar way: there is a *query* phase and a subsequent *propagate* phase. During the query phase the server receiving the request "queries" a read-quorum in order to get the value of the shared register and the corresponding tag for each of the members of the read-quorum. From these it selects the value x corresponding to the max tag t. This concludes the query phase. In the propagation phase the server sends a new value and a new tag (which are (t, x) for the case of a READ$_p$ operation and $(\langle t.seq + 1, p \rangle, y)$ for a WRITE$(y)_p$ operation) to the members of a write quorum. These processors update their own copy of the register if the tag received is greater than their current tag; then they send back an acknowledgment to the server p. When p gets the acknowledgment message from the members of a write quorum, the propagate phase is completed. At this point the server can respond to the client that issued the operation with either the value read, in the case of a read operation, or with just a confirmation, in the case of a write operation.

We remark that when a configuration change happens during the execution of a requested operation, the completion of the operation is delayed until the normal mode is restored. However if the query phase has already been completed it is not necessary to repeat it in the new configuration.

5.2 Proof

The proof that ABD-SYS implements an atomic read/write shared register is omitted from this extended abstract. The proof uses an approach similar to that used in [14] and in [21] to prove the correctness of applications built on top of DVS and VS, respectively.

We remark that the intersection property of DC, namely that there exist a read quorum R and a write quorum W of a previous primary configuration both belonging to the next primary configuration comes from this particular application. For other applications one might have different (maybe weaker) intersection properties. For example, one might require that the new primary configuration contains a read quorum of the previous one (and not a write one). In our case, we must require both a read quorum and a write quorum in the new primary because we want to implement an atomic register and if, for example we only require a read quorum to be in the new configuration, it is possible that other read quorums of the old configuration will be able to read old values making the register not atomic anymore.

6 Conclusions

In this paper we have combined the notion of dynamic primary views with that of quorum systems, to identify a service that provides *configurations*. Our key contribution in solving the problem of making quorums dynamic, that is, adaptable to the set of processors currently connected, is to identify a suitable intersection property which can be used to maintain consistency across different configurations. An interesting direction of research is to identify which properties have to be satisfied in order to transform a "static" service or application into a "dynamic" one. For example, some data replication algorithms are based on views with a distinguished leader (e.g., [28, 40]) and these applications tolerate transient failures, i.e., they work well in a static setting. We think that it is possible to follow an approach similar to the one used in this paper to transform these applications into ones that adapt better to dynamic settings, where processes can leave the system forever and new members can join the system.

References

1. D. Agrawal and A. El Abbadi. An efficient and fault-tolerant solution for distributed mutual exclusion. *ACM Transactions on Computer Systems*, 9(1):1–20, 1991.
2. H. Attiya, A. Bar-Noy, and D. Dolev. Sharing memory robustly in message passing systems. *Communications of the ACM*, 42(1):124–142, 1996.
3. Ö. Babaoğlu, R. Davoli, L. Giachini, and M. Baker. Relacs: A communication infrastructure for constructing reliable applications in large-scale distributed systems. In *Proceedings of Hawaii International Conference on Computer and System Science*, 1995, vol II, pp 612–621.
4. Ö. Babaoğlu, R. Davoli, L. Giachini, and P. Sabattini. The inherent cost of strong-partial view synchronous communication. In *Proceedings of Workshop on Distributed Algorithms on Graphs*, pages 72–86, 1995.
5. Ö. Babaoğlu, R. Davoli, and A. Montresor. Group Communication in Partitionable Systems: Specifications and Algorithms. TR UBLCS99-01, Department of Computer Science, University of Bologna, 1998.
6. A. Bartoli and Ö. Babaoğlu, Selecting a "Primary Partition" in Partitionable Asynchronous Distributed Systems, In *Proceedings of the 16th Symposium on Reliable Distributed Systems* pages 138–145, 1997.
7. M. Bearden and R. Bianchini Jr. The synchronization cost of on-line quorum adaptation. In *10th (ISCA) International Conference on Parallel and Distributed Computing Systems (PDCS'97)*, pages 598–605, 1997.
8. M. Bearden and R. Bianchini Jr. A fault-tolerant algorithm for decentralized on-line quorum adaptation. In *Proceedings of the 28th Annual International Symposium on Fault-Tolerant Computing (FTCS)*, 1998.
9. K.P. Birman and R. van Renesse. *Reliable Distributed Computing with the Isis Toolkit*. IEEE Computer Society Press, Los Alamitos, CA, 1994.
10. T. Chandra, V. Hadzilacos, S. Toueg, and B. Charron-Bost. On the impossibility of group membership. In *Proceedings of the Fifteenth Annual ACM Symposium on Principles of Distributed Computing*, pages 322–330, 1996.
11. T. Chandra, and S. Toueg, Unreliable failure detectors for reliable distributed systems. *Journal of the ACM*, 43(2):225–267, March 1996.

12. F. Cristian. Group, majority and strict agreement in timed asynchronous distributed systems. In *Proceedings of the 26th Conference on Fault-Tolerant Computer Systems*, pages 178–187, 1996.

13. D. Davcev and W. Buckhard. Consistency and recovery control for replicated files. In ACM Symp. on Operating Systems Principles, volume 10, pages 87–96, 1985.

14. R. De Prisco, A. Fekete, N. Lynch, and A.A. Shvartsman. A dynamic view-oriented group communication service. In *Proceedings of the 17th ACM Symposium on Principle of Distributed Computing (PODC)*, pages 227–236, 1998.

15. D. Dolev and D. Malkhi. The Transis approach to high availability cluster communications. *Communications of the ACM*, 39(4):64–70, 1996.

16. D. Dolev, D. Malkhi, and R. Strong. A framework for partitionable membership service. Technical Report TR95-4, Institute of Computer Science, Hebrew University, Jerusalem, Israel, March 1995.

17. A. El Abbadi and S. Dani. A dynamic accessibility protocol for replicated databases. *Data and knowledge engineering*, 6:319–332, 1991.

18. A. El Abbadi and S. Toueg. Maintaining availability in partitioned replicated databases. *ACM Transactions on Database Systems*, 14(2):264–290, 1989.

19. B. Englert and A.A. Shvartsman. Non-obstructive quorum reconfiguration in a robust emulation of shared memory. Manuscript.

20. P. D. Ezhilchelvan, A. Macedo, and S. K. Shrivastava. Newtop: a fault tolerant group communication protocol. In *15th International Conference on Distributed Computing Systems (ICDCS)*, 1995.

21. A. Fekete, N. Lynch, and A.A. Shvartsman. Specifying and using a partitionable group communication service. In *Proceedings of the 16th ACM Symposium on Principle of Distributed Computing (PODC)*, pages 53–62, 1997.

22. R. Friedman and R. van Renesse. Strong and weak virtual synchrony in Horus. Technical Report TR95-1537, Department of Computer Science, Cornell University, Ithaca, NY, 1995.

23. D. Gifford. Weighted voting for replicated data. In *Proceedings of the ACM Symposium on Operating Systems Principles*, pages 150–162, 1979.

24. M. Herlihy. A quorum-consensus replication method for abstract data types. *ACM Transactions on Computer Systems*, 4(1):32–53, 1986.

25. M. Hiltunen and R. Schlichting. Properties of membership services. In *Proceedings of the 2nd International Symposium on Autonomous Decentralized Systems*, pages 200–207, 1995.

26. F. Jahanian, S. Fakhouri, and R. Rajkumar. Processor group membership protocols: Specification, design and implementation. In *Proceedings of the 12th IEEE Symposium on Reliable Distributed Systems*, pages 2–11, 1993.

27. S. Jajodia and D. Mutchler. Dynamic voting algorithms for maintaining the consistency of a replicated database. *ACM Trans. Database Systems*, 15(2):230–280, 1990.

28. L. Lamport. The part-time parliament. *ACM Transactions on Computer Systems*, 16(2):133–169, May 1998. Also Research Report 49, DEC SRC, Palo Alto, CA, 1989.

29. N. Lynch. *Distributed Algorithms*. Morgan Kaufmann Publishers, Inc., San Mateo, CA, March 1996.

30. N. Lynch and A.A. Shvartsman. Robust emulation of shared memory using dynamic quorum-acknowledged broadcasts. In *Proceedings of the 27th IEEE International Symposium on Fault-Tolerant Computing (FTCS)*, pages 272–281, 1997.

31. N. Lynch and M. R. Tuttle. An introduction to input/output automata. *CWI-Quarterly*, 2(3):219–246, September 1989. Centrum voor Wiskunde en Informatica, Amsterdam, The Netherlands. Technical Memo MIT/LCS/TM-373, Laboratory for Computer Science, Massachusetts Institute of Technology, Cambridge, MA 02139, November 1988.

32. D. Malkhi and M.K. Reiter. Byzantine quorum systems. *Distributed Computing*, 11:203–13, 1998.

33. D. Malkhi, M.K. Reiter, and A. Wool. The load and availability of byzantine quorum systems. In *Proceedings of the 16th ACM Symposium on Principle of Distributed Computing (PODC)*, pages 249–257, 1997.

34. D. Malkhi, M.K. Reiter, and R. Wright. Probabilistic quorum systems. In *Proceedings of the 16th ACM Symposium on Principle of Distributed Computing (PODC)*, pages 267–273, 1997.

35. C. Malloth and A. Schiper. View synchronous communication in large scale networks. In *2nd Open Workshop of the ESPRIT project BROADCAST (Number 6360)*, July 1995 (also available as a Technical Report Nr. 94/84 at Ecole Polytechnique Fédérale de Lausanne (Switzerland), October 1994).

36. L. Moser, Y. Amir, P. Melliar-Smith, and D. Agrawal. Extended virtual synchrony. In *Proceedings of the 14th IEEE International Conference on Distributed Computing Systems*, pages 56–65, 1994. Full version appears in TR ECE93-22, Dept. of Electrical and Computer Engineering, University of California, Santa Barbara, CA.

37. L. E. Moser, P. M. Melliar-Smith, D. A. Agarwal, R. K. Budhia, and C. A. Lingley-Papadopoulos. Totem: A fault-tolerant multicast group communication system. *Communications of the ACM*, 39(4), April 1996.

38. M. Naor and A. Wool. The load, capacity and availability of quorum systems. *SIAM Journal on Computing*, 27(2):423–447, 1998.

39. G. Neiger. A new look at membership services. In *Proceedings of the 15th Annual ACM Symposium on Principles of Distributed Computing*, pages 331–340, 1996.

40. B. Oki and B. Liskov. Viewstamped replication: A general primary copy method to support highly available distributed systems. In *Proceedings of the Seventh ACM Symposium on Principles of Distributed Computing*, pages 8–17, 1988.

41. J. Paris and D. Long. Efficient dynamic voting algorithms. In *Proceedings of the 13th International Conference on Very Large Data Base*, pages 268–275, 1988.

42. A. Ricciardi. The group membership problem in asynchronous systems. Technical Report TR92-1313, Department of Computer Science, Cornell University, Ithaca, NY, 1992.

43. A. Ricciardi and K.P. Birman. Using process groups to implement failure detection in asynchronous environments. In *Proceedings of the 10th ACM Symposium on Principle of Distributed Computing (PODC)*, pages 341–352, 1991.

44. A. Ricciardi, A. Schiper, and K.P. Birman. Understanding partitions and the "no partitions" assumption. Technical Report TR93-1355, Department of Computer Science, Cornell University, Ithaca, NY, 1993.

45. R. van Renesse, K.P. Birman, M. Hayden, A. Vaysburd, and D. Karr, Building adaptive systems using Ensemble. *Software- Practice and Experience*, 29(9):963–979, 1998.

46. R. van Renesse, K.P. Birman, and S. Maffeis. Horus: A flexible group communication system. *Communications of the ACM*, 39(4):76–83, 1996.

47. E. Yeger Lotem, I. Keidar, and D. Dolev. Dynamic voting for consistent primary components. In *Proceedings of the Sixteenth Annual ACM Symposium on Principles of Distributed Computing*, pages 63–71, 1997.

Asynchronous Group Membership with Oracles

Kal Lin and Vassos Hadzilacos

University of Toronto
kal@cs.utoronto.ca
vassos@cs.utoronto.ca

Abstract. We present a model of distributed systems intended for the description of group membership services. The model incorporates a generalization of failure detectors [9], which we call *oracles*. Oracles provide information about processes that may be included into or excluded from the group. Based on this model, we provide a specification of a group membership service in asynchronous systems augmented with oracles. We also present an algorithm that implements such a service provided that the information supplied by the oracles is of sufficient quality.

1 Introduction

Several researchers have argued that the design and implementation of complex distributed systems, especially those for which fault-tolerance and high availability are primary goals, is facilitated by the use of "process groups" (for an overview see [16]). Speaking very informally, a process group consists of a collection of processes that cooperate in carrying out a common task — such as maintaining a database, supporting users who are collaborating in a complex design, or carrying out a massively parallel computation. In such applications, processes benefit from multicast capabilities, so that they can efficiently disseminate information about their own state to the entire group.

For multicasts to be meaningful, processes must have a fairly well coordinated view of the group's membership. One complicating factor is that the membership of the group changes over time. This is certainly due to failures and recoveries; it may also be due to other, application-specific, reasons: Subscribers to a database change over time, the participants in the complex design change as the design progresses through different phases, and nodes whose spare cycles are used for a massively parallel computation may drop in or out of the task as their load (and consequently the availability of spare cycles) changes. These requirements call for some system-level facilities that allow the (ever-changing) members of the group to have consistent views of the (ever-changing) membership. A second complicating factor is that often the maintenance of a consistent view of the group's membership must be accomplished in *asynchronous* distributed systems; that is, systems where the speeds of (non-faulty) processes and the delays of messages are finite but unbounded.

Many systems have been developed that provide a group membership service. The first of these systems is the Isis toolkit [6]. Others include the Highly

Available System [10], Amoeba [15], Transis [2], Horus [19], Relacs [5], Newtop [12], and Totem [3]. Group membership services can be classified in one of two categories: *primary partition* and *partitionable*. A primary-partition group membership service ensures that at each (logical) time there is only one view of the group, by restricting changes in the membership to only one partition.[1] A partitionable group membership service allows multiple independent views to coexist at the same (logical) time in different partitions. In this paper, we focus exclusively on primary-partition services.

Despite the existence of many systems that offer a group membership service, there is no satisfactory rigorous and abstract specification for that service in the context of *asynchronous* systems that encompasses both *safety* and *liveness* requirements. Cristian [11] gave such a specification for *synchronous* systems. Ricciardi and Birman [18] gave a specification for asynchronous systems but this specification contains serious flaws, as pointed out by Enceaume et al. [4]. In particular, the liveness property of the specification is too strong, and it is not at all obvious how to weaken it so as to ensure that the resulting property is both useful to applications using the service and implementable. De Prisco et al. [17] gave a rigorous I/O automata-based specification for group membership in asynchronous systems but, as the authors expressly acknowledge, their specification encompasses only safety properties.

Guerraoui and Schiper [14] propose a solution to Group Membership that has similarities to our approach. They advocate using Consensus to solve a variety of agreement problems such as Group Membership — but also Nonblocking Atomic Commitment, View Synchronous Communication and Atomic Multicast — in the context of asynchronous systems with failure detectors. The scope of their paper, therefore, is wider than ours, which addresses only Group Membership. Their specification of Group Membership, however, is incomplete.

The difficulty of formulating a useful, yet implementable, specification for (primary-partition) group membership services in asynchronous systems is, perhaps, not surprising if the matter is considered in the light of the well-known impossibility result by Fischer, Lynch and Paterson [13]. This result states that in asynchronous systems where (even) one process can crash, any algorithm that satisfies the safety property that correct processes should never reach inconsistent decisions, must violate the liveness property that each correct process should eventually reach a decision. It is true that there are differences between the sort of agreement that must be reached in the Consensus problem (to which this impossibility result applies), and the sort of agreement that must be achieved by (primary partition) group membership services. Chandra et al., however, showed that these differences do not render the Fischer, Lynch and Paterson result inapplicable: (even) a very weak type of group membership service is susceptible to a similar impossibility result [8].

In view of this, it is reasonable to try resolving the problem of formulating a useful and implementable specification of group membership by bringing

---

[1] Roughly speaking, a partition is a maximal set of processes that can communicate with one another.

to bear the approaches which allowed researchers to get around the Fischer-Lynch-Paterson impossibility result for Consensus. The use of unreliable failure detectors, pioneered by Chandra and Toueg [9], seems especially well-suited to the task: One of the reasons why the membership of a group changes is that processes fail. We can use information provided by (unreliable) failure detectors both to determine the membership of the group (this helps in formulating a useful specification) and to achieve agreement among the surviving members of the group (this helps in designing an implementation for the specification).

Considerable modifications to the original model of failure detectors are required, however. In part, these are due to the fact that the set of processes in the system is no longer fixed but changes over time. Furthermore, as we stated earlier, failures (and recoveries) are only *one* cause of changes in the membership of a group. We would like our model to be general enough that we can also describe other causes. A difficulty we must overcome here is that these causes are application-specific while we want our model to be application-independent.

In this paper, we introduce a model based on an abstraction we call *oracles*. Each process has access to an *include oracle* and to an *exclude oracle*, from which the process can obtain information about processes it should include into or exclude from the group. The information provided by oracles regarding which processes to include or exclude incorporates whatever (possibly imperfect) information the oracles have about failures in the system, but may also incorporate application-specific information. For example, in a database application a process might be included because its owner subscribed to the database; in a massively-parallel computation a process might be excluded because it runs on a node that suddenly became heavily loaded and has no spare cycles. We do not model the *reasons* for inclusion or exclusion — merely the fact. This makes the model application-independent. Oracles, and the model of computation, are described in Section 2.

Using this model, we present a rigorous and abstract specification for a group membership service in asynchronous systems. Our specification addresses both safety and liveness requirements. It is described in Section 3.2.

Finally, we present an algorithm to implement this specification. The algorithm is based on Chandra and Toueg's rotating coordinator algorithm [9], and is given in Section 4. Due to space limitations, the proof of correctness of the algorithm is omitted.

2   The Model

The system consists of an unbounded set of processes, $\Pi = \{p_1, p_2, p_3, \ldots\}$, connected by reliable links. The unbounded set of processes Π represents the set of processes that *may* participate in the computation. In the course of any particular computation only *some* of these processes will actually participate. Informally speaking, we say that a process p is *participating* if p is executing steps of the protocol and some process (possibly p) wishes p to join the computation[2].

To simplify the model, we assume the existence of a fictional global clock, whose output is the set of positive integers denoted by $\mathcal{T}$. The processes do not have access to this clock.

To model the set of processes that actually participate in a computation, and the duration of their participation, we define a participation pattern. Formally, a *participation pattern* is a function $PP : \mathcal{T} \to 2^{\Pi}$ where intuitively $PP(t)$ denotes the set of processes that are participating in the computation at time t. We restrict the participation pattern so that there is at most one (possibly infinite) interval of time during which a process is participating. More precisely, $\forall p \in \Pi,\ \forall t, t', t'' \in \mathcal{T},\ t < t' < t'',\ (p \in PP(t) \wedge p \notin PP(t')) \Rightarrow p \notin PP(t'')$.

We define the set of *persistently participating* processes in a participation pattern as $Persist(PP) = \{p : \exists t \in \mathcal{T},\ \forall t' \geq t,\ p \in PP(t')\}$.

2.1 Oracles

Every process has access to an *exclude oracle* and an *include oracle*. Each process may query its oracles at any time to obtain a set of processes that the oracle wishes to exclude from or include into the group. An exclude oracle may wish to exclude a process because it believes (as a failure detector might) that the process is no longer participating in the protocol. It may also wish to exclude a process for application-specific reasons. Similarly, an include oracle may wish to include a process because it believes that the process has recovered, or because of application-specific reasons. We do not assume that oracles are "perfect"; they reflect possibly imperfect (and possibly contradictory) information available to the processes. Thus, the mere fact that a process p is in some process q's exclude (or include) oracle, does not necessarily mean that p will be excluded from (or included into) the group. However, as it will become clearer when we present the liveness properties of our Group Membership specification in Section 3, if the information of oracles is persistent and non-contradictory, then the group's membership must conform to the information of the oracles.

Oracles — in particular exclude oracles — are intended as a generalization of failure detectors [9, 7]. It is tempting to define oracles in a similar manner. There are, however, some differences that complicate somewhat the definition. In particular, the set of processes in the system is no longer fixed; it varies as processes join or leave the group. In fact, the set of *potential* processes in the system may be infinite. Consider one of the most interesting failure detectors, the so-called *eventually strong* failure detector. This is defined in terms of the following two properties: (1) all faulty processes must eventually be suspected permanently by all correct processes in the system (eventual strong completeness); and (2) some correct process must eventually cease being suspected by all correct processes in the system (eventual weak accuracy).

---

[2] Consider two processes, p and q. Process p is participating in the computation but experiences a failure and stops participating without executing another step. Process q is participating in the computation and executes all its steps and terminates. We model both p and q as no longer participating.

In our new setting, "all correct processes in the system" is a huge (possibly infinite) set. Furthermore, most processes in this set are irrelevant to the group: they will never become members of it. It makes no sense to require the exclude oracle to exclude the many processes that may fail but which are not part of the group. More importantly, the existence of *some* process in the system that is eventually not excluded by any correct one is small comfort: we want to be assured that such a process will exist in the group, not in the entire system at large. In other words, we would like to state the completeness and accuracy properties relative to the set of processes in "the group". The trouble is that there is no such thing as "the group" yet: we are trying to define a formal model in which to describe "the group"!

We resolve this apparent circularity by defining the behavior of the exclude oracle in terms of a parameter which specifies a set of processes, and is intended to be "the current membership of the group". The exclude oracle, formally speaking, must be prepared to respond to a query where the set of processes specified in this parameter could be any set of processes whatsoever. In fact, processes are restricted to querying the exclude oracle using the current membership of the group as the actual parameter in the course of an execution. (This will become clearer when we define "well-formed runs" in the discussion of computations.) With these remarks in mind to help guide our intuition, we are now ready to formally define exclude and include oracles.

An *exclude oracle history* is a function $XOH : \Pi \times \mathcal{T} \times 2^{\Pi} \to 2^{\Pi}$. $XOH(p, t, \varrho)$ is the set of processes that the exclude oracle of process p, at time t, believes should be excluded. The parameter ϱ is intended to represent the current set of processes in the group. Thus, informally, an exclude oracle history represents a possible behavior of the exclude oracle. An *exclude oracle XO* is a function that maps a participation pattern PP to a set of exclude oracle histories $XO(PP)$. This definition reflects the intuition that the behavior of the exclude oracle depends, in part, on the participation pattern. The participation pattern, however, does not completely determine the behavior of the exclude oracle[3] — hence the exclude oracle maps the participation pattern to a *set* of possible behaviors.

An *include oracle history* is a function $IOH : \Pi \times \mathcal{T} \to 2^{\Pi}$. $IOH(p, t)$ represents the set of processes that the include oracle of process p believe should be included into the group at time t, and is precisely the set it will return if it is queried by p at that time. An *include oracle IO* is a function that maps a participation pattern PP to a set of include oracle histories $IO(PP)$. Note that the parameter ϱ used in the definition of an exclude oracle history does not apply here. ϱ is intended to represent the set of processes currently in the group; it does not contain processes that are trying to join the group but have not yet succeeded in doing so.

In order to circumvent the impossibility result of [8], we must place some restrictions on the behavior of the oracles. These restrictions are the analogues of the eventual completeness and accuracy properties of the eventual strong

---

[3] Application semantics and inaccuracies are also reflected in the behavior of the exclude oracle.

failure detector mentioned earlier, adapted to the setting of exclude oracles. We say that an exclude oracle XO is an *Eventually Strong XO* if the following two properties are satisfied:

Property 1 (XO Eventual Completeness). Eventually every persistently participating process in the current group excludes forever every process in the current group that isn't persistently participating.

$\forall PP, \forall XOH \in XO(PP), \forall \varrho \in 2^{\Pi}, \exists t \in \mathcal{T}, \forall t' \geq t,$

$\forall q \in \varrho \cap (\Pi - Persist(PP)), \forall p \in \varrho \cap Persist(PP), q \in XOH(p, t', \varrho)$

Property 2 (XO Eventual Accuracy). If the current group contains a persistently participating process then there is a time after which some persistently participating process in the current group is never excluded by any persistently participating process in the current group.

$\forall PP, \forall XOH \in XO(PP), \forall \varrho \in 2^{\Pi} (\varrho \cap Persist(PP) \neq \emptyset \Rightarrow \exists t \in \mathcal{T},$

$\exists q \in \varrho \cap Persist(PP), \forall t' \geq t, \forall p \in \varrho \cap Persist(PP), q \notin XOH(p, t', \varrho))$

We define an include oracle IO as an *Eventually Strong IO* if the following properties are satisfied:

Property 3 (IO Eventual Completeness). Eventually every persistently participating process permanently includes every persistently participating process.

$\forall PP, \forall IOH \in IO(PP), \exists t \in \mathcal{T}, \forall t' \geq t,$

$\forall q \in Persist(PP), \forall p \in Persist(PP), q \in IOH(p, t')$

Property 4 (IO Eventual Accuracy). Eventually no process includes a process that is not persistently participating.

$\forall PP, \forall IOH \in IO(PP), \exists t \in \mathcal{T}, \forall t' \geq t,$

$\forall q \in \Pi - Persist(PP), \forall p \in \Pi, q \notin IOH(p, t')$

2.2 Views

The term "view" is traditionally used to refer to the current membership of the group (at some process). It is appealing to define a view simply as a set of processes, but upon reflection this turns out to be inadequate. To see why, consider the following situation: Suppose that the membership of the group is originally $\{p, q\}$. A process r is then added, so that the membership becomes $\{p, q, r\}$. Process r is then removed, and the membership becomes $\{p, q\}$, again. We would like to distinguish the initial view from the final view. Yet, considered as sets, the two views are identical.

This example leads us to define views as identifiers in some set (for the sake of concreteness, $\mathbf{Z}^{+}$). We assume that a function can "decode" each identifier v by mapping it into the set of processes that makes up the group's membership when the view is represented by v. Formally, a *view* is an identifier from the set $\Psi = \mathbf{Z}^+ \cup \{nil, fin\}$. The special view nil (the null view) represents that no view has been installed, and the special view fin (the final view) represents the end of a process's participation in the group. We define $\hat{\Psi} = \Psi - \{nil, fin\}$. The "decoding" function is $Members : \Psi \to 2^{\Pi}$, where $Members(v)$ is the set of processes in the view $v \in \Psi$. We assume that $Members(nil) = Members(fin) = \emptyset$. Note that, in general, it is possible to have two views $v, v' \in \hat{\Psi}$ such that $v \neq v'$, but $Members(v) = Members(v')$. If $p \in Members(v)$, we say that view v *contains* process p.

We assume that the state of a process includes information about the most recently installed view. We define $ViewState(\sigma)$ to be the view corresponding to state σ. $ViewState(\sigma)$ is nil if no view from $\hat{\Psi}$ has been installed and fin if the process is no longer participating after having installed a view from $\hat{\Psi}$.

2.3 Computations

A *configuration* is a pair $\langle s, M \rangle$ where s is a function that maps a process p to its local state and M is a set of messages (intuitively, the set of messages sent and not yet received). An *algorithm* is a collection of deterministic automata, one per process. In a single *step* of a given algorithm, a process p may perform one of the following actions:

- $\langle send, p, m \rangle$ send the message m;
- $\langle recv, p, m \rangle$ receive the message m;
- $\langle excl, p, \varrho, \gamma \rangle$ query the exclude oracle of process p about set ϱ with result γ;
- $\langle incl, p, \delta \rangle$ query the include oracle of process p with result δ;
- $\langle change, p, \sigma \rangle$ change the state of process p to σ.

If a process p has state σ then a step e by p is *applicable* in configuration $C = \langle s, M \rangle$ if p's automaton stipulates that the step e can be taken in state σ and, in addition, $m \in M$ for a receive step $e = \langle recv, p, m \rangle$. $e(C)$ denotes the configuration resulting from the application of step e to C.

A *schedule* S of an algorithm A is a sequence of steps of A. $S[i]$ is the ith step of the sequence. A schedule S of an algorithm A is applicable to a configuration C if and only if (a) S is the empty schedule, or (b) $S[1]$ is applicable to C and $S[2]$ is applicable to $S[1](C)$ and $S[3]$ is applicable to $S[2](S[1](C))$, etc.

An initial configuration $I = \langle s, M \rangle$ is *valid* if $M = \emptyset$ and there exists a unique $v^* \in \hat{\Psi}$ such that for each process p the state function s provides: $ViewState(s(p)) = v^*$ if $p \in Members(v^*)$ and $ViewState(s(p)) = nil$ otherwise. We define $Input(I)$ to be v^*.

Let A be an algorithm, XO be an exclude oracle, and IO be an include oracle. A *run* of A with XO and IO is a tuple $R = \langle PP, XOH, IOH, I, S, T \rangle$ where PP is a participation pattern, $XOH \in XO(PP)$ is an exclude oracle history, $IOH \in IO(PP)$ is an include oracle history, I is an initial configuration of A, S is an infinite schedule of A that is applicable to I, and T is an infinite sequence of increasing time values (indicating when each step in S occurred according to the fictional global clock). We define $ViewRun(p, i, R)$ to be $ViewState(s(p))$, where s is the process state function of the configuration after the first i steps of schedule S starting from initial configuration I in the run R; we define $ViewSet(p, i, R) = Members(ViewRun(p, i, R))$.

A run, R, is *well-formed* if $\forall i \in \mathbf{Z}^{+}$ and $\forall p \in \Pi$ it satisfies the following properties:

- I is a valid initial configuration;
- if $S[i] = \langle excl, p, \varrho, \gamma \rangle$ then $\varrho = ViewSet(p, i, R)^{4}$ and $\gamma = XOH(p, T[i], \varrho)$;
- if $S[i] = \langle incl, p, \delta \rangle$ then $\delta = IOH(p, T[i])$;
- if $p \in Persist(PP)$ then p takes an infinite number of steps in S;
- every message sent to a process $p \in Persist(PP)$ is eventually received;
- if $p \notin PP(T[i])$ then $XOH(p, T[i], \varrho) = \emptyset$ for any ϱ;
- if $p \notin PP(T[i])$ then $IOH(p, T[i]) = \emptyset$;
- if $p \notin PP(T[i])$ and $\exists i' < i$ such that $ViewRun(p, i', R) \in \hat{\Psi}$ then $\forall i'' \geq i, ViewRun(p, i'', R) = fin$.

From now on, we consider only well-formed runs.

3 The Specification

In this section, we give a specification that captures the basic notions of Group Membership. We say that algorithm A solves Group Membership (GM) with oracles XO and IO if every run $R = \langle PP, XOH, IOH, I, S, T \rangle$ of A satisfies the safety properties and liveness properties described in this section.

3.1 Safety Properties

The first three safety properties, which we call "validity properties" require that the group's membership does not change unless there is a good reason. First we explain the motivation for such properties. Some previously proposed specifications for group membership allow two kinds of undesirable behavior [4]: Capricious removal causes processes to expel others from the group for no reason; collective suicide causes processes to leave the group for no reason. Such behavior is undesirable because it allows for trivial (and useless) implementations of the group membership service, which force the group to be the empty set for no reason! Our specification avoids this pitfall by insisting that processes be removed from or added to the group *only* if the include or exclude oracles justify the change. Notice that unlike other specifications, in which changes to the membership are caused by processes executing "join" and "leave" events which are under their own control, the output of the include and exclude oracles is *not* under the process' control. More precisely, we require the following properties:

Property 5 (Exclude Validity). If p installs view $v \in \hat{\Psi}$ and, later, view $v' \in \hat{\Psi}$ where v contains q and v' does not contain q then q was previously in the output of some exclude oracle.

Property 6 (Final View Validity). If p installs fin then p was previously in the output of some exclude oracle or p is not persistently participating.

---

[4] As mentioned in the discussion leading up to the definition of an exclude oracle, the exclude oracle may only be queried about the current group.

Property 7 (Include Validity). If p installs view $v \in \hat{\Psi}$ where $v \neq Input(I)$ and v contains q then q was in the output of some include oracle.

The validity properties require that the group's membership should conform to the information given by the oracles. Ideally, one would like the members of the group at any time to reflect the *participation pattern*. However, the include and exclude oracles are the only means that processes have at their disposal to "sense" the participation pattern. Thus, if these oracles provide very inaccurate information about the participation pattern, the membership of the group may be far from the ideal. This is not a weakness of our specification. On the contrary, we believe that it is an advantage of our approach that it can meaningfully capture situations where the information about the state of the group is highly inaccurate due to unanticipated delays, inappropriately short settings of timeout timers or a variety of other reasons that can arise in practice.

The next two safety properties, which we call "integrity properties" formalize the semantics of the special views *nil* and *fin*.

Property 8 (Null View Integrity). If p installs a view $v \neq nil$ then p cannot subsequently install *nil*.

Property 9 (Final View Integrity). If p installs *fin* then p does not subsequently install another view.

Final View Integrity prohibits a process from leaving a group and then joining it again. In practice, the same "computational entity" can repeatedly leave and rejoin the group under a different name from Π.

The last safety property, which we call "agreement", stipulates that the sequence of views installed by the different processes fit together in a global sense: there is a single sequence of views such that each process installs a sequence of views that is a "window" to this one sequence.

Property 10 (Agreement). There exists a sequence $G = \langle v_0, v_1, v_2, \ldots \rangle$ of distinct views $v_i \in \hat{\Psi}$ such that $v_0 = Input(I)$ and the sequence of views from $\hat{\Psi}$ installed by any process p is a contiguous subsequence of G.

3.2 Liveness Properties

The validity properties state that the membership does not change without good reason. Conversely, the liveness properties state that if a compelling reason does exist then the membership of the group will change. We say that a property P holds *almost always* in a run if there is a time after which the property P always holds.

Property 11 (Exclude Progress). Let p be a persistently participating process that installs some view. If almost always p excludes process q and almost always all processes do not include q then almost always p's view does not contain q.

Property 12 (Include Progress). Let p be a persistently participating process that installs some view. If almost always p includes q and q never installs *fin* then almost always p's view contains q.

Property 11 states that if there is good reason to exclude a process p from the group and no good reasons to include p in the group then p must eventually be dropped from the group. Property 12 states a similar progress requirement for inclusion into the group.

Property 13 (Quiescent Progress). If almost always all processes do not exclude q and almost always all processes do not include q then almost always all views contain q or almost always no view contains q.

Property 13 states that the views eventually become stable with respect to processes that the oracles are silent about. Suppose the current view at process p contains $\{p, q, r\}$. r stops participating. p's oracle requests the removal of r successfully and the next view at p contains $\{p, q\}$. All the oracles then give imperfect information and request the inclusion of r. Our specification allows the next view at p to contain $\{p, q, r\}$. As long as the oracles are colluding to exclude and then include r, our specification allows this to happen repeatedly. When the oracles become silent with respect to r, Property 13 requires that the views become stable with respect to r.

Property 14 (Include Notification). If p installs $v \in \hat{\Psi}$ and v contains a persistently participating process q, then q eventually installs v.

Property 14 requires that processes that have been included into the group, actually participate in the group.

Several of the properties in our specification refer to the behavior of the oracles. This is a departure from the way in which Consensus is specified in the analogous situation where we have failure detectors rather than oracles. There, the specification makes reference to the failure pattern (the analogue to our participation pattern) but not to the behavior of the failure detectors (the analogue to our oracles). Why not specify Group Membership with reference only to the participation pattern? The reason is the difference in the nature of the two problems. In Group Membership processes must compute something (the new view) that is related to the participation pattern. Their ability to do so depends on the oracles, which are the only means processes have for observing the participation pattern. It is therefore natural that the problem specification refers to the oracles. In contrast, what processes compute in Consensus is not in any way related to the failure pattern. It therefore stands to reason that the problem should be specifiable without reference to the failure detectors, which are the only means the processes have for observing the failure pattern. By requiring stronger properties of the oracles it is possible to limit and even to completely eliminate the reference to the oracles in the specification of Group Membership. The resulting specification, however, is meaningful only for restricted classes of oracles. We felt that the loss of generality is too high a price to pay for the gain in specification simplicity.

4 The Algorithm

In our model with an infinite number of processes and a computation that is "long-lived", it is possible that an infinite number of processes may stop participating in the computation. However, if too many processes stop participating simultaneously our algorithm will not be able to make progress. Thus we require a minimal level of participation to satisfy the liveness part of the specification. The safety properties are never violated. In the case of our group membership algorithm, we require a majority of processes in any view to be currently in the participation pattern. Formally, $\forall i \in \mathbf{Z}^+$, $\forall p \in \Pi$, $(PP(T[i]) \neq \emptyset \wedge ViewSet(p, i, R) \neq \emptyset \Rightarrow |ViewSet(p, i, R) \cap PP(T[i])| > |ViewSet(p, i, R)|/2)$.

The algorithm assumes that the exclude oracle is an eventually strong XO (Properties 1 and 2) and that the include oracle is an eventually strong IO (Properties 3 and 4).

In our pseudo-code, we use the notation $xvar \leftarrow XO$ to indicate that variable $xvar$ gets the value of the local exclude oracle when queried about the set of processes corresponding to the current view. The notation $ivar \leftarrow IO$ indicates the variable $ivar$ gets the value of the local include oracle.

We assume all messages that arrive at a process are kept in a local message pool. The pool can be searched by any task of a process for messages satisfying certain criteria. We assume that all messages have a tuple form. We define an *retrieve* primitive to extract messages from the pool.

The *retrieve* primitive takes as an argument a tuple consisting of two types of parameters: "extract" parameters and "pattern" parameters. Parameters that are preceded with a ? are extract parameters and parameters that are not preceded by a ? are pattern parameters. $retrieve\langle a_1, a_2, \ldots, a_n \rangle$ returns *false* if there is no message in the pool that consists of n parameters where each of the pattern parameters in the argument to *retrieve* matches in position and value with the parameters of the message in the pool. $retrieve\langle a_1, a_2, \ldots, a_n \rangle$ returns *true* if there is such a message. Further, each of the extract parameters in the argument to *retrieve* is assigned the value of the corresponding parameter in the message. If more than one such message exists in the pool, one is selected arbitrarily.

4.1 View Consensus

At the heart of our GM algorithm lies a variant of the well-known Consensus problem, that we call View Consensus (VC). In this section, we define the problem and give an algorithm that solves it. VC is defined in terms of two primitives, VC-propose(v, v') and VC-decide(v, v'') where v, v' and v'' are views. Intuitively, a process invokes VC-propose(v, v') to propose v' as a possible view to succeed v. If a process executes VC-decide(v, v'') it has decided on v'' as the view to succeed v. We use the notation VC-propose$(v, -)$ and VC-decide$(v, -)$ to indicate that the second parameter can be any view. VC is specified by the following properties:

Property 15 (VC-Uniform Agreement). If p executes VC-decide(v, v') and q executes VC-decide(v, v'') then $v' = v''$.

Property 16 (VC-Termination). If a process p executes VC-propose$(v, -)$ where $p \in Members(v)$ and p does not stop participating while in the view v then p executes VC-decide$(v, -)$.

Property 17 (VC-Uniform Integrity). Every process that executes VC-decide$(v, -)$ does it at most once.

Property 18 (VC-Uniform Validity). If p executes VC-decide(v, v') some process previously executed VC-propose(v, v').

In Figure 1 we use the rotating coordinator algorithm of Chandra and Toueg to implement VC.

4.2 Group Membership Service

In Figure 2, we give a protocol to satisfy the specification for GM. The protocol runs through three phases. Phase A is only applicable to processes that are not part of the initial group. These processes wait until a message of type J arrives with the first view to be installed. Once this message is retrieved, processes proceed to phase B. Processes in the initial group proceed directly to phase B.

In phase B of the protocol, each process tries to build, in the variable *tryset*, a set of processes to propose as the next view. Each process does this by querying its local include and exclude oracles. Any process that is successful in building a new *tryset* sends its *tryset* to all members of the current view. By the end of phase B, each member of the current view has some *tryset* (whether it was sent by some other member of the current view or successfully built by querying the oracles) to propose for View Consensus.

Phase C begins with View Consensus for the current view with the proposal created in phase B. The process then waits for the resulting new view from View Consensus. If the current process is a member of the new view then the process installs the new view. Otherwise, the process installs *fin*. We keep track of all processes that have been removed from the group in the variable *dropped*. These processes are prevented from being included again during phase B. At the end of phase C, messages of type J are sent to any new processes joining the group (which are still in phase A). Finally, the processes that have not installed *fin* at the end of phase C, begin again at phase B.

The protocol satisfies some common notions of Group Membership that are not part of the GM specification. For example, the protocol satisfies Self Inclusion[5] which is not required by the specification. Our model assumes that each of the views installed contain a majority of participating processes. A natural modification to the algorithm is to ensure the protocol only proposes *tryset*'s of sufficient size to accurately reflect the assumptions of the model.

5 Concluding Remarks

By using oracles, we have abstracted, into well defined modules, the reasons a process might be included into or excluded from a group by a group membership

---

[5] If p installs a view $v \in \hat{\Psi}$ then $p \in Members(v)$.

Every process p executes the following:

cobegin
procedure VC-propose (v, v')
    $n \leftarrow |Members(v)|$ ▷ *no. of processes in the view*
    $est \leftarrow v'$ ▷ *the current estimate*
    $tsp \leftarrow 0$ ▷ *timestamp est was adopted*
    $rnd \leftarrow 0$ ▷ *the current round*
    while p has not executed VC-decide$(v, -)$ **do**
        $rnd \leftarrow rnd + 1$
        $coord \leftarrow$ the $(rnd \bmod n) + 1$ member of $Members(v)$
        send $\langle P1, v, p, rnd, est, tsp \rangle$ to $coord$ ▷ *PHASE 1: send estimates*
        if $p = coord$ **then**   ▷ *PHASE 2: gather estimates*
            wait   **until**   [any $\lceil(n + 1)/2\rceil$ processes q: retrieve
           $\langle P1, v, q, rnd, ?rep, ?reptsp \rangle]$
           $msgs[rnd] \leftarrow$ the set of messages retrieved above
           $t \leftarrow \max reptsp : \langle -, -, -, -, -, reptsp \rangle \in msgs[rnd]$
           $est \leftarrow$ select one $rep : \langle -, -, -, -, rep, t \rangle \in msgs[rnd]$
           send $\langle P2, v, coord, rnd, est \rangle$ to $Members(v)$
        $exc \leftarrow \emptyset$ ▷ *PHASE 3: adopt an estimate*
        wait until [retrieve $\langle P2, v, coord, rnd, ?newest \rangle$ or $coord \in (exc \leftarrow XO)]$
        if $coord \notin exc$ **then**
           $est \leftarrow newest$
           $tsp \leftarrow rnd$
           send $\langle P3, v, p, rnd, ACK \rangle$ to $coord$
        else
           send $\langle P3, v, p, rnd, NAK \rangle$ to $coord$
        if $p = coord$ **then**   ▷ *PHASE 4: count acks*
           wait until [any $\lceil(n+1)/2\rceil$ processes q: retrieve $\langle P3, v, q, rnd, ACK \rangle$ or
           $\langle P3, v, q, rnd, NAK \rangle]$
           if $\lceil(n+1)/2\rceil$ ACK messages retrieved above **then**
              send $\langle D, v, p, est \rangle$ to p

task VC-decide
    while *true* **do**
        if retrieve $\langle D, ?v, ?q, ?newview \rangle$ **then**
           if p has not executed VC-decide$(v, -)$ **then**
              send $\langle D, v, q, newview \rangle$ to $Members(v)$
              VC-decide$(v, newview)$
coend

Fig. 1. View Consensus

service. Further research is needed into more refined specifications of oracles for specific applications, as well as implementations of such application-specific oracles.

In this paper, we did not discuss group communication primitives (multicasts). This can be an extensive topic with a wide variety of interesting ordering

Every process p executes the following:

```
v = nil                                        ▷ the current view
if p is in the initial view then
    v = initial view
dropped ← ∅                                     ▷ all processes removed
while v = nil do                                ▷ PHASE A: first view
    if retrieve ⟨J, ?v, ?dropped⟩ then
        install(v)
while v ≠ fin do                                ▷ PHASE B: build tryset
    tryset ← Members(v)                         ▷ set possible in next view
    while tryset = Members(v) do
        joins ← IO − dropped − Members(v)       ▷ the set of processes to add
        quits ← (XO − IO) ∩ Members(v)          ▷ the set of processes to drop
        tryset ← (Members(v) ∪ joins) − quits
        if retrieve ⟨T, v, ?sometryset⟩ then
            tryset ← sometryset
    send ⟨T, v, tryset⟩ to Members(v)
    v' ← view encoding such that Members(v') = tryset and v' > v
    VC-propose(v, v')                           ▷ PHASE C: view consensus
    wait until [some newv: p has executed VC-decided(v, newv)]
    oldv ← v
    if p ∈ Members(newv) then
        v ← newv
    else
        v ← fin
    install(v)
    dropped ← dropped ∪ (Members(oldv) − Members(newv))
    send ⟨J, newv, dropped⟩ to Members(newv) − Members(oldv)
```

Fig. 2. Group Membership Service

and delivery requirements. We believe this group membership specification will provide a good basis upon which to study multicasts and are currently working on the issue.

In our model, we assume reliable links. We plan to investigate the work of Aguilera, Chen and Toueg [1] on intermittent connectivity with respect to our model and algorithms.

Acknowledgments

We would like to thank Rachid Guerraoui, Wai-Kau Lo, André Schiper and the anonymous reviewers for their useful comments.

References

1. M. K. Aguilera, W. Chen, and S. Toueg. Heartbeat: A timeout-free failure detector for quiescent reliable communication. Technical Report TR97-1631, Department of Computer Science, Cornell University, May 1997.

2. Y. Amir, D. Dolev, S. Kramer, and D. Malki. Transis: a communication sub-system for high availability. In *Proceedings of the 22nd Annual International Symposium on Fault-Tolerant Computing*, pages 76–84, July 1992.
3. Y. Amir, L. Moser, P. Melliar-Smith, D. Agarwal, and P. Ciarfella. The totem single-ring ordering and membership protocol. In *ACM Transactions on Computer Systems 13 4*, pages 311–342, Nov. 1995.
4. E. Anceaume, B. Charron-Bost, P. Minet, and S. Toueg. On the formal specification of group membership services. Technical Report 95-1534, Department of Computer Science, Cornell University, Aug. 1995.
5. O. Babaoglu, R. Davoli, L.-A. Giachini, and M. G. Baker. Relacs: a communications infrastructure for constructing reliable applications in large-scale distributed systems. In *BROADCAST Project*. Department of Computer Science, University of Newcastle upon Tyne, UK, 1994.
6. K. P. Birman. The process group approach to reliable distributed computing. In *Communications of the ACM*, pages 36–53, Dec. 1993.
7. T. D. Chandra, V. Hadzilacos, and S. Toueg. The weakest failure detector for solving Consensus. *Journal of the ACM*, 43(4):685–722, July 1996.
8. T. D. Chandra, V. Hadzilacos, S. Toueg, and B. Charon-Bost. On the impossibility of group membership. In *Proceedings of the 15th ACM Symposium on Principles of Distributed Computing*, May 1996.
9. T. D. Chandra and S. Toueg. Unreliable failure detectors for reliable distributed systems. *Journal of the ACM*, 43(2):225–267, Mar. 1996.
10. F. Cristian. Reaching agreement on processor group membership in synchronous distributed systems. In *Distributed Computing 4(4)*, pages 9–16, July 1987.
11. F. Cristian. Reaching agreement on processor group membership in synchronous distributed systems. *Distributed Computing*, 4:175–187, Apr. 1991.
12. P. Ezhilchelvan, R. Macêdo, and S. Shrivastava. Newtop: a fault-tolerant group communication protocol. In *Proceedings of the 15thInternational Conference on Distributed Computing Systems*, June 1995.
13. M. Fischer, N. Lynch, and M. Paterson. Impossibility of distributed consensus with one faulty process. *Journal of the ACM*, 32(2):374–382, April 1985.
14. R. Guerraoui and A. Schiper. The generic consensus service. Technical Report TR 98/282, Ecole Polytechnique Fédérale de Lausanne, July 1998. Revised version appeared in *Proceedings of the 26th IEEE International Symposium on Fault-Tolerant Computing (FTCS-26)*, Sendai, Japan, June 1996.
15. M. F. Kaashoek and A. S. Tanenbaum. Group communication in the amoeba distributed operating system. In *Proceedings of the 11th International Conference on Distributed Computer Systems*, pages 222–230, May 1991.
16. D. Powell. Special issue on group communication. *Communications of the ACM*, pages 50–97, Apr. 1996.
17. R. D. Prisco, A. Fekete, N. Lynch, and A. Shvartsman. A dynamic view-oriented group communication service. In *Proceedings of the 17th ACM Symposium on Principles of Distributed Computing*, pages 227–236, 1998.
18. A. Ricciardi and K. Birman. Process membership in asynchronous environments. Technical report, Department of Computer Science, Cornell University, Apr. 1994. available by anonymous ftp from ftp.cs.cornell.edu in pub/aleta/AsyncMembService.ps.
19. R. van Renesse, K. P. Birman, R. Cooper, B. Glade, and P. Stephenson. The horus system. In *Reliable Distributed Computing with the Isis Toolkit*, pages 133–147, 1993.

Generic Broadcast*

Fernando Pedone and André Schiper

Département d'Informatique
Ecole Polytechnique Fédérale de Lausanne
CH-1015 Lausanne EPFL, Switzerland
{Fernando.Pedone, Andre.Schiper}@epfl.ch

Abstract. Message ordering is a fundamental abstraction in distributed systems. However, usual ordering guarantees are purely "syntactic", that is, message "semantics" is not taken into consideration, despite the fact that in several cases, semantic information about messages leads to more efficient message ordering protocols. In this paper we define the *Generic Broadcast* problem, which orders the delivery of messages only if needed, based on the semantics of the messages. Semantic information about the messages is introduced in the system by a conflict relation defined over messages. We show that Reliable and Atomic Broadcast are special cases of Generic Broadcast, and propose an algorithm that solves Generic Broadcast efficiently. In order to assess efficiency, we introduce the concept of *delivery latency*.

1 Introduction

Message ordering is a fundamental abstraction in distributed systems. Total order, causal order, view synchrony, etc., are examples of widely used ordering guarantees. However, these ordering guarantees are purely "syntactic" in the sense that they do not take into account the "semantics" of the messages. Active replication for example (also called state machine approach [12]), relies on total order delivery of messages on the active replicated servers. By considering the semantics of the messages sent to active replicated servers, total order delivery may not always be needed. This is the case for example if we distinguish *read* messages from *write* messages sent to active replicated servers, since read messages do not need to be ordered with respect to other read messages. As message ordering has a cost, it makes sense to avoid ordering messages when not required.

In this paper we define the *Generic Broadcast* problem (defined by the primitives *g-Broadcast* and *g-Deliver*), which establishes a partial order on

* Research supported by the EPFL-ETHZ DRAGON project and OFES under contract number 95.0830, as part of the ESPRIT BROADCAST-WG (number 22455).

message delivery. Semantic information about messages is introduced in the system by a *conflict* relation defined over the set of messages. Roughly speaking, two messages m and m' have to be g-Delivered in the same order only if m and m' are conflicting messages. The definition of message ordering based on a conflict relation allows for a very powerful message ordering abstraction. For example, the Reliable Broadcast problem is an instance of the Generic Broadcast problem in which the conflict relation is empty. The Atomic Broadcast problem is another instance of the Generic Broadcast problem, in which all pair of messages conflict.

Any algorithm that solves Atomic Broadcast trivially solves any instance of Generic Broadcast (i.e., specified by a given conflict relation), by ordering more messages than necessary. Thus, we define a Generic Broadcast algorithm to be *strict* if it only orders messages when necessary. The notion of strictness captures the intuitive idea that total order delivery of messages has a cost, and this cost should only be paid when necessary.

In order to assess the cost of Generic Broadcast algorithms, we introduce the concept of *delivery latency* of a message. Roughly speaking, the delivery latency of a message m is the number of communication steps between *g-Broadcast(m)* and *g-Deliver(m)*. We then give a strict Generic Broadcast algorithm that is less expensive than known Atomic Broadcast algorithms, that is, in runs where messages do not conflict, our algorithm ensures that the delivery latency of every message is always equal to 2 (known Atomic Broadcast algorithms have at least delivery latency equal to 3).

The rest of the paper is structured as follows. Section 2 defines the Generic Broadcast problem. Section 3 defines the system model and introduces the concept of delivery latency. Section 4 presents a solution to the Generic Broadcast problem. Section 5 discusses related work, and Section 6 concludes the paper.

2 Generic Broadcast

2.1 Problem Definition

Generic Broadcast is defined by the primitives g-Broadcast and g-Deliver.[1] When a process p invokes g-Broadcast with a message m, we say that p g-Broadcasts m, and when p returns from the execution of g-Deliver with

---

[1] g-Broadcast has no relation with the GBCAST primitive defined in the Isis system [1].

message m, we say that p g-Delivers m. Message m is taken from a set $\mathcal{M}$ to which all messages belong. Central to Generic Broadcast is the definition of a (symmetric) conflict relation on $\mathcal{M} \times \mathcal{M}$ denoted by $\mathcal{C}$ (i.e., $\mathcal{C} \subseteq \mathcal{M} \times \mathcal{M}$). If $(m, m') \in \mathcal{C}$ then we say that m and m' conflict. Generic Broadcast is specified by (1) a conflict relation $\mathcal{C}$ and (2) the following conditions:

gB-1 (VALIDITY) If a correct process g-Broadcasts a message m, then it eventually g-Delivers m.

gB-2 (AGREEMENT) If a correct process g-Delivers a message m, then all correct processes eventually g-Deliver m.

gB-3 (INTEGRITY) For any message m, every correct process g-Delivers m at most once, and only if m was previously g-Broadcast by some process.

gB-4 (PARTIAL ORDER) If correct processes p and q both g-Deliver messages m and m', and m and m' conflict, then p g-Delivers m before m' if and only if q g-Delivers m before m'.

The conflict relation $\mathcal{C}$ determines the pair of messages that are sensitive to order, that is, the pair of messages for which the g-Deliver order should be the same at all processes that g-Deliver the messages. The conflict relation $\mathcal{C}$ renders the above specification *generic*, as shown in the next section.

2.2 Reliable and Atomic Broadcast as Instances of Generic Broadcast

We consider in the following two special cases of conflict relations: (1) the empty conflict relation, denoted by $\mathcal{C}_\emptyset$, where $\mathcal{C}_\emptyset = \emptyset$, and (2) the $\mathcal{M} \times \mathcal{M}$ conflict relation, denoted by $\mathcal{C}_{\mathcal{M} \times \mathcal{M}}$, where $\mathcal{C}_{\mathcal{M} \times \mathcal{M}} = \mathcal{M} \times \mathcal{M}$. In case (1) no pair of messages conflict, that is, the partial order property gB-4 imposes no constraint. This is equivalent to having only the conditions gB-1, gB-2 and gB-3, which is called *Reliable Broadcast* [4]. In case (2) any pair (m, m') of messages conflict, that is, the partial order property gB-4 imposes that all pairs of messages be ordered, which is called *Atomic Broadcast* [4]. In other words, Reliable Broadcast and Atomic Broadcast lie at the two ends of the spectrum defined by Generic Broadcast. In between, any other conflict relation defines an instance of Generic Broadcast.

Conflict relations lying in between the two extremes of the conflict spectrum can be better illustrated by an example. Consider a replicated

Account object, defined by the operations *deposit(x)* and *withdraw(x)*. Clearly, *deposit* operations commute with each other, while *withdraw* operations do not, neither with each other nor with *deposit* operations.[2] Let $\mathcal{M}_{deposit}$ denote the set of messages that carry a *deposit* operation, and $\mathcal{M}_{withdraw}$ the set of messages that carry a *withdraw* operation. This leads to the following conflict relation $\mathcal{C}_{Account}$:

$$\mathcal{C}_{Account} = \{ (m, m') \; : \; m \in \mathcal{M}_{withdraw} \text{ or } m' \in \mathcal{M}_{withdraw}\}.$$

Generic Broadcast with the $\mathcal{C}_{Account}$ conflict relation for broadcasting the invocation of deposit and withdraw operations to the replicated *Account* object defines a weaker ordering primitive than Atomic Broadcast (e.g., messages in $\mathcal{M}_{deposit}$ are not required to be ordered with each other), and a stronger ordering primitive than Reliable Broadcast (which imposes no order at all).

2.3 Strict Generic Broadcast Algorithm

From the specification it is obvious that any algorithm solving Atomic Broadcast also solves any instance of the Generic Broadcast problem defined by $\mathcal{C} \subseteq \mathcal{M} \times \mathcal{M}$. However, such a solution also orders messages that do not conflict. We are interested in a *strict* algorithm, that is, an algorithm that does not order two messages if not required, according to the conflict relation $\mathcal{C}$. The idea is that ordering messages has a cost (in terms of number of messages, number of communication steps, etc.) and this cost should be kept as low as possible. More formally, we define an algorithm that solves Generic Broadcast for a conflict relation $\mathcal{C} \subset \mathcal{M} \times \mathcal{M}$, denoted by $A_{\mathcal{C}}$, *strict* if it satisfies the condition below.

> (STRICTNESS) Consider an algorithm $A_{\mathcal{C}}$, and let $\mathcal{R}_{\mathcal{C}}^{NC}$ be the set of runs of $A_{\mathcal{C}}$. There exists a run R in $\mathcal{R}_{\mathcal{C}}^{NC}$, in which at least two correct processes g-Deliver two non-conflicting messages m and m' in a different order.

Informally, the strictness condition requires that algorithm $A_{\mathcal{C}}$ allow runs in which the g-Deliver of non conflicting messages is not totally ordered. However, even if $A_{\mathcal{C}}$ does not order messages, it can happen that total order is spontaneously ensured. So we cannot require violation of total order to be observed in every run: we require it in at least one run of $A_{\mathcal{C}}$.

---

[2] This is the case for instance if we consider that a *withdraw(x)* operation can only be performed if the current balance is larger than or equal to x.

3 System Model and Definitions

3.1 Processes, Failures and Failure Detectors

We consider an asynchronous system composed of n processes $\Pi = \{p_1, \ldots, p_n\}$. Processes communicate by message passing. A process can only fail by crashing (i.e., we do not consider Byzantine failures). Processes are connected through reliable channels, defined by the two primitives $send(m)$ and $receive(m)$. We assume that the asynchronous system is augmented with failure detectors allowing to solve Consensus (e.g., the class of failure detector $\Diamond S$ allows Consensus to be solved if the maximum number of failures is smaller than $n/2$) [2].

3.2 Delivery Latency

In the following, we introduce the delivery latency as a parameter to measure the efficiency of algorithms solving a Broadcast problem (defined by the primitives α-Broadcast and α-Deliver). The deliver latency is a variation of the Latency Degree introduced in [11], which is based on modified Lamport's clocks [7].

- a *send* event and a *local* event on a process p do not modify p's local clock,
- let $ts(send(m))$ be the timestamp of the $send(m)$ event, and $ts(m)$ the timestamp carried by message m: $ts(m) \stackrel{def}{=} ts(send(m)) + 1$,
- the timestamp of $receive(m)$ on a process p is the maximum between $ts(m)$ and p's current clock value.

The delivery latency of a message m α-Broadcast in a run R of an algorithm A solving a Broadcast problem, denoted by $dl^R(m)$, is defined as the difference between the largest timestamp of all α-Deliver(m) events (at most one per process) in run R, and the timestamp of the α-Broadcast(m) event in run R.

Let $\pi^R(m)$ be the set of processes that α-Deliver message m in run R, and α-Deliver$_p(m)$ the α-Deliver(m) event at process p. The deliver latency of m in run R is formally defined as

$$dl^R(m) \stackrel{def}{=} \underset{p \in \pi^R(m)}{MAX} (ts(\alpha\text{-Deliver}_p(m)) - ts(\alpha\text{-Broadcast}(m))).$$

For example, consider a broadcast algorithm where a process p, wishing to broadcast a message m, (1) sends m to all processes, (2) each process q on receiving m sends an acknowledge message $ACK(m)$ to all processes, and (3) as soon as q receives n_{ack} messages of the type $ACK(m)$, q delivers m. Let R be a run of this algorithm where only m is broadcast. We have $dl^R(m) = 2$.

4 Solving Generic Broadcast

4.1 Overview of the Algorithm

Processes executing our Generic Broadcast algorithm progress in a sequence of stages numbered $1, 2, ..., k, ...$. Stage k terminates only if two conflicting messages are g-Broadcast, but not g-Delivered in some stage $k' < k$.

g-Delivery of non-conflicting messages. Let m be a message that is g-Broadcast. When some process p receives m in stage k, and m does not conflict with some other message m' already received by p in stage k, then p inserts m in its $pending_p^k$ set, and sends an $ACK(m)$ message to all processes. As soon as p receives $ACK(m)$ messages from n_{ack} processes, where

$$n_{ack} \geq (n+1)/2, \tag{1}$$

p g-Delivers m.

g-Delivery of conflicting messages. If a conflict is detected, Consensus is launched to terminate stage k. The Consensus decides on two sets of messages, denoted by $NCmsgSet^k$ (NC stands for Non-Conflicting) and $CmsgSet^k$ (C stands for Conflicting). The set $NCmsgSet^k \cup CmsgSet^k$ is the set of all messages that are g-Delivered in stage k. Messages in $NCmsgSet^k$ are g-Delivered before messages in $CmsgSet^k$, and messages in $NCmsgSet^k$ may be g-Delivered by some process p in stage k before p executes the k-th Consensus. The set $NCmsgSet^k$ does not contain conflicting messages, while messages in $CmsgSet^k$ may conflict. Messages in $CmsgSet^k$ are g-Delivered in some deterministic order. Process p starts stage $k + 1$ once it has g-Delivered all messages in $CmsgSet^k$.

Properties. To be correct, our algorithm must satisfy the following properties:

(a) If two messages m and m' conflict, then at most one of them is g-Delivered in stage k before Consensus.

(b) If message m is g-Delivered in stage k by some process p before Consensus, then m is in the set $NCmsgSet^k$.

(c) The set $NCmsgSet^k$ does not contain any conflicting messages.[3]

Property (a) is ensured by condition (1). Property (b) is ensured as follows. Before starting Consensus, every process p sends its $pending_p^k$ set to all processes (in a message of type *checking*, denoted by CHK), and waits for messages of type CHK from exactly n_{chk} processes. Only if some message m is at least in $\lceil (n_{chk} + 1)/2 \rceil$ messages of type CHK, then m is inserted in $majMSet_p^k$, the initial value of Consensus that decides on $NCmsgSet^k$. So, if m is in less than $\lceil (n_{chk}+1)/2 \rceil$ messages of type CHK, m is not inserted in $majMSet_p^k$. Indeed, if condition

$$2n_{ack} + n_{chk} \geq 2n + 1 \tag{2}$$

holds, then m could not have been g-Delivered in stage k before Consensus. To understand why, notice that from (2), we have

$$(n - n_{chk}) + \lceil (n_{chk} + 1)/2 \rceil \leq n_{ack}, \tag{3}$$

where $(n - n_{chk})$ is the number of processes from which p knows nothing. From (3), if m is in less than $\lceil (n_{chk} + 1)/2 \rceil$ messages of type CHK, then even if all processes from which p knows nothing had sent $ACK(m)$, there would not be enough $ACK(m)$ messages to have m g-Delivered by some process in stage k before Consensus.

Property (c) is ensured by the fact that m is inserted in $majMSet_p^k$ only if m is in at least $\lceil (n_{chk} + 1)/2 \rceil$ messages of type CHK received by p (majority condition). Let m and m' be two messages in $majMSet_p^k$. By the majority condition, the two messages are in the $pending_q^k$ set of at least one process q. This is however only possible if m and m' do not conflict.

Minimal number of correct processes. Our Generic Broadcast algorithm waits for n_{ack} messages before g-Delivering non-conflicting messages, and n_{chk} messages if a conflict is detected before starting Consensus. So our algorithm requires $max(n_{ack}, n_{chk})$ correct processes. The minimum of this expression happens to be $(2n + 1)/3$, when $n_{ack} = n_{chk}$.

---

[3] Property (c) does not follow from (a) and (b). Take for example two messages m and m' that conflict, but are not g-Delivered in stage k without the cost of Consensus: neither property (a), nor property (b) applies.

4.2 The Generic Broadcast Algorithm

Provided that the number of correct processes is at least $max(n_{ack}, n_{chk})$, $n_{ack} \geq (n+1)/2$, and $2n_{ack} + n_{chk} \geq 2n + 1$, Algorithm 1 solves Generic Broadcast for any conflict relation $\mathcal{C}$. All tasks in Algorithm 1 execute concurrently, and Task 3 has two entry points (lines 12 and 31). Process p in stage k manages the following sets.

- $R\_delivered_p$: contains all messages R-delivered by p up to the current time,
- $G\_delivered_p$: contains all messages g-Delivered by p in all stages $k' < k$,
- $pending_p^k$: contains every message m such that p has sent an ACK message for m in stage k up to current time, and
- $localNCg\_Deliver_p^k$: is the set of non conflicting messages that are g-Delivered by p in stage k, up to the current time (and before p executes the k-th Consensus).

When p wants to g-Broadcast message m, p executes R-$broadcast(m)$ (line 8). After R-delivering a message m, the actions taken by p depend on whether m conflicts or not with some other message m' in $R\_delivered_p \setminus G\_delivered_p$.

No conflict. If no conflict exists, then p includes m in $pending_p^k$ (line 14), and sends an ACK message to all processes, acknowledging the R-deliver of m (line 15). Once p receives n_{ack} ACK messages for a message m (line 31), p includes m in $localNCg\_Deliver_p^k$ (line 35) and g-Delivers m (line 36).

Conflict. In case of conflict, p starts the terminating procedure for stage k. Process p first sends a message of the type $(k, pending_p^k, CHK)$ to all processes (line 17), and waits the same information from exactly n_{chk} processes (line 18). Then p builds the set $majMSet_p^k$ (line 20).[4] It can be proved that $majMSet_p^k$ contains every message m such that for any process q, $m \in localNCg\_Deliver_q^k$. Then p starts consensus (line 21) to decide on a pair $(NCmsgSet^k, CmsgSet^k)$ (line 22). Once the decision is made, process p first g-Delivers (in any order) the messages in $NCmsgSet^k$ that is has not g-Delivered yet (lines 23 and 25), and then p g-Delivers (in some deterministic order) the messages in $CmsgSet^k$ that it has not g-Delivered yet (lines 24 and 26). After g-Delivering all messages decided in Consensus execution k, p starts stage $k + 1$ (lines 28-30).

---

[4] $majMSet_p^k = \{m : |Chk_p^k(m)| \geq (n_{chk} + 1)/2\}$

Algorithm 1 Generic Broadcast

1: Initialisation:
2:   $R\_delivered \leftarrow \emptyset$
3:   $G\_delivered \leftarrow \emptyset$
4:   $k \leftarrow 1$
5:   $pending^1 \leftarrow \emptyset$
6:   $localNCg\_Deliver^1 \leftarrow \emptyset$

7: To execute g-$Broadcast(m)$:   {*Task 1*}

8:   R-$broadcast(m)$

9: g-$Deliver(-)$ occurs as follows:

10:   **when** R-$deliver(m)$ {*Task 2*}
11:     $R\_delivered \leftarrow R\_delivered \cup \{m\}$

12:   **when** $(R\_delivered \setminus G\_delivered) \setminus pending^k \neq \emptyset$ {*Task 3*}
13:     **if** [for all $m, m' \in R\_delivered \setminus G\_delivered,\ m \neq m' : (m, m') \notin Conflict$]
        then
14:       $pending^k \leftarrow R\_delivered \setminus G\_delivered$
15:       send($k, pending^k, ACK$) to all
16:     **else**
17:       send($k, pending^k, CHK$) to all
18:       **wait until** [for n_{chk} processes $q : p$ received $(\underline{k}, pending_q^k, \underline{CHK})$ from q]
19:       #Define $Chk^k(m) = \{q : p$ received $(\underline{k}, pending_q^k, \underline{CHK})$ from q **and**
                                                                    $m \in pending_q^k\}$
20:       $majMSet^k \leftarrow \{m : |Chk^k(m)| \geq \lceil (n_{chk} + 1)/2 \rceil\}$
21:       propose($k, (majMSet^k, (R\_delivered \setminus G\_delivered) \setminus majMSet^k)$)
22:       **wait until** decide($\underline{k}, (NCmsgSet^k, CmsgSet^k)$)
23:       $NCg\_Deliver^k \leftarrow (NCmsgSet^k \setminus localNCg\_Deliver^k) \setminus G\_delivered$
24:       $Cg\_Deliver^k \leftarrow CmsgSet^k \setminus G\_delivered$
25:       g-Deliver messages in $NCg\_Deliver^k$ in any order
26:       g-Deliver messages in $Cg\_Deliver^k$ using some deterministic order
27:       $G\_delivered \leftarrow (localNCg\_Deliver^k \cup NCg\_Deliver^k \cup Cg\_Deliver^k) \cup$
                                                                    $G\_delivered$
28:       $k \leftarrow k + 1$
29:       $pending^k \leftarrow \emptyset$
30:       $localNCg\_Deliver^k \leftarrow \emptyset$

31:   **when** receive($\underline{k}, pending_q^k, \underline{ACK}$) from q
32:     #Define $Ack^k(m) = \{q : p$ received $(\underline{k}, pending_q^k, \underline{ACK})$ from q **and**
                                                                    $m \in pending_q^k\}$
33:     $ackMSet^k \leftarrow \{m : |Ack^k(m)| \geq n_{ack}\}$
34:     $localNCmsgSet^k \leftarrow ackMSet^k \setminus (G\_delivered \cup NCmsgSet^k)$
35:     $localNCg\_Deliver^k \leftarrow localNCg\_Deliver^k \cup localNCmsgSet^k$
36:     g-Deliver all messages in $localNCmsgSet^k$ in any order

4.3 Proof of Correctness

Due to space limitations, we have only included some of the proofs in this section. All proofs (Agreement, Partial Order, Validity, and Integrity) can be found in [9]. In the following, we prove that the three properties ((a)-(c)) presented in Section 4.1 hold.

Lemma 1 states that the set $pending^k$ does not contain conflicting messages. It is used to prove Lemmata 2 and 5 below.

Lemma 1. *For any process p, and all $k \geq 1$, if messages m and m' are in $pending_p^k$, then m and m' do not conflict.*

PROOF: Suppose, by way of contradiction, that there is a process p, and some $k \geq 1$ such that m and m' conflict and are in $pending_p^k$. Since m and m' are in $pending_p^k$, p must have R-delivered m and m'. Assume that p first R-delivers m and then m'. Thus, there is a time t after p R-delivers m' such that p evaluates the *if* statement at line 13, and $m' \in R\_delivered_p$, $m' \notin G\_delivered_p$, and $m' \notin pending_p^k$. At time t, $m \in R\_delivered_p$ (by the hypothesis m is R-delivered before m'), and $m \notin G\_delivered_p$ (if $m \in G\_delivered$, from lines 27-29 m and m' cannot be both in $pending_p^k$). Therefore, when the *if* statement at line 13 is evaluated, m and m' are in $R\_delivered \setminus G\_delivered$, and since m and m' conflict, the condition evaluates false, and m' is not included in $pending_p^k$, a contradiction that concludes the proof. $\square$

Lemma 2 proves property (a).

Lemma 2. *If two messages m and m' conflict, then at most one of them is g-Delivered in stage k before Consensus.*

PROOF: The proof is by contradiction. Assume that there are two messages m and m' that conflict and are g-Delivered in stage k before Consensus. Without lack of generality, consider that m is g-Delivered by process p, and m' is g-Delivered by process q. From the Generic Broadcast algorithm (lines 31-36), p (q) has received n_{ack} messages of the type $(k, pending^k, ACK)$ such that $m \in pending^k$ ($m' \in pending^k$). Since $n_{ack} > (n + 1)/2$, there must be a process r that sends the message $(k, pending_r^k, ACK)$ to processes p and q, such that m and m' are in $pending_r^k$, contradicting Lemma 1. $\square$

Lemma 3 relates (1) the set $Ack^k(m)$ of processes that send an acknowledgement for some message m in stage k and (2) the set Chk_p^k of processes from which some process p receives CHK messages in stage k, with (3) the set $Chk_p^k(m)$ of processes from which p receives a CHK message containing m in stage k.

Lemma 3. *Let $Ack^k(m)$ be a set of processes that execute the statement $send(k, pending^k, ACK)$ (line 15) in stage k with $m \in pending^k$, and let Chk_p^k be the set of processes from which some process p receives messages of the type $(k, pending^k, CHK)$ in stage k (line 18). If $Ack^k(m) \geq n_{ack}, Chk_p^k \geq n_{chk}$, and $2n_{ack} + n_{chk} \geq 2n + 1$, then there are at least $\lceil (n_{chk} + 1)/2 \rceil$ processes in $Chk_p^k(m) \stackrel{def}{=} Chk_p^k \cap Ack^k(m)$.*

PROOF: We prove the contrapositive, that is, if $|Chk_p^k(m)| < \lceil (n_{chk} + 1)/2 \rceil$ then $|Ack^k(m)| < n_{ack}$. From the definitions of $Ack^k(m)$ and $Chk_p^k(m)$, it follows that $|Ack^k(m)| \leq (n - n_{chk}) + |Chk_p^k(m)|$ (1). To see why, notice that set $Chk_p^k(m)$ contains all processes from set Chk_p^k that sent an acknowledgement message for m. Process p does not know anything about the remaining processes in $\Pi \setminus Chk_p^k$, but even if all of them acknowledged message m, the number of acknowledges is at most equal to $(n - n_{chk})$.

From (1) and the fact that $|Chk_p^k(m)| < \lceil (n_{chk} + 1)/2 \rceil$, we have $|Ack^k(m)| - (n - n_{chk}) \leq |Chk_p^k(m)| < \lceil (n_{chk} + 1)/2 \rceil$. Thus, $(n - n_{chk}) > |Ack^k(m)| - \lceil (n_{chk} + 1)/2 \rceil$ (2). From $2n_{ack} + n_{chk} \geq 2n + 1$, and the fact that n_{ack}, n_{chk}, and n are integers, we have that $(n - n_{chk}) \leq n_{ack} - \lceil (n_{chk} + 1)/2 \rceil$ (3). Therefore, from (2) and (3), we conclude that $|Ack^k(m)| < n_{ack}$. □

Lemma 4 proves property (b) presented in Section 4.1. It states that any message g-Delivered by some process q during stage k, before q executes Consensus in stage k will be included in the set $NCmsgSet^k$ decided by Consensus k.

Lemma 4. *For any two processes p and q, and all $k \geq 1$, if p executes $decide(k, (NCmsgSet^k, -))$, then $localNCg\_Deliver_q^k \subseteq NCmsgSet^k$.*

PROOF: Let m be a message in $localNCg\_Deliver_q^k$. We first show that if p executes the statement $propose(k, majMSet_p^k, -))$, then $m \in majMSet_p^k$. Since $m \in localNCg\_Deliver_q^k$, q must have received n_{ack} messages of the type $(k, pending^k, ACK)$ (line 31) such that $m \in pending^k$. Thus, there are n_{ack} processes that sent m to all processes in the $send$ statement at line 15. From Lemma 3, $Chk^k(m) \geq (n_{chk} + 1)/2$, and so, from the algorithm line 20, $m \in majMSet_p^k$. Therefore, for every process q that executes $propose(k, (majMSet_q^k, -))$, $m \in majMSet_q^k$. Let $(NCmsgSet^k, -)$ be the value decided on Consensus execution k. By the uniform validity of Consensus, there is a process r that executed $propose(k, (majMSet_r^k, -))$ such that $NCmsgSet^k = majMSet_r^k$, and so, $m \in NCmsgSet^k$. □

Lemma 5 proves property (c).

Lemma 5. *If two messages m and m' conflict, then at most one of them is in $NCmsgSet^k$.*

PROOF: The proof is by contradiction. Assume that there are two messages m and m' that conflict, and are both in $NCmsgSet^k$. From the validity property of Consensus, there must be a process p that executes $propose(k, (majMSet_p^k, -))$, such that $NCmsgSet^k = majMSet_p^k$. Therefore, m and m' are in $majMSet_p^k$, and from the algorithm, p receives $\lceil (n_{chk} + 1)/2 \rceil$ messages of the type $(k, pending^k, CHK)$ such that m is in $pending^k$, and p also receives $\lceil (n_{chk} + 1)/2 \rceil$ messages of the type $(k, pending^k, CHK)$ such that m' is in $pending^k$. Since p waits for n_{chk} messages of the type $(k, pending^k, CHK)$, there must exist at least one process q in Chk_p^k such that m and m' are in $pending_q^k$, contradicting Lemma 1. □

4.4 Strictness and Cost of the Generic Broadcast Algorithm

Proposition 5 states that the Generic Broadcast algorithm of Section 4.2 is a strict implementation of Generic Broadcast.

Proposition 5. *Algorithm 1 is a strict Generic Broadcast algorithm.*

We now discuss the cost of our Generic Broadcast algorithm. Our main result is that for messages that do not conflict, the Generic Broadcast algorithm can deliver messages with a delivery latency equal to 2, while for messages that conflict, the delivery latency is at least equal to 4. Since known Atomic Broadcast algorithms deliver messages with a delivery latency of at least 3,[5] this results shows the tradeoff of the Generic Broadcast algorithm: if messages conflict frequently, our Generic Broadcast algorithm may become less efficient than an Atomic Broadcast algorithm, while if conflicts are rare, then our Generic Broadcast algorithm leads to smaller costs compared to Atomic Broadcast algorithms.

---

[5] An exception is the Optimistic Atomic Broadcast algorithm [8], which can deliver messages with delivery latency equal to 2 if the *spontaneous total order property* holds.

Propositions 6 and 7 assess the cost of the Generic Broadcast algorithm when messages do not conflict. In order to simplify the analysis of the delivery latency, we concentrate our results on runs with one message (although the results can be extended to more general runs). Proposition 6 defines a lower bound on the delivery latency of the algorithm, and Proposition 7 shows that this bound can be reached in runs where there are no process failures. We consider a particular implementation of Reliable Broadcast that appears in [2].[6]

Proposition 6. *Assume that Algorithm 1 uses the Reliable Broadcast implementation presented in [2]. If $\mathcal{R}_C$ is a set of runs generated by Algorithm 1 such that m is the only message g-Broadcast and g-Delivered in runs in $\mathcal{R}_C$, then there is no run R in $\mathcal{R}_C$ where $dl^R(m) < 2$.*

Proposition 7. *Assume that Algorithm 1 uses the Reliable Broadcast implementation presented in [2]. If $\mathcal{R}_C$ is a set of runs generated by Algorithm 1, such that in runs in $\mathcal{R}_C$, m is the only message g-Broadcast and g-Delivered, and there are no process failures, then there is a run R in $\mathcal{R}_C$ where $dl^R(m) = 2$.*

The results that follow define the behaviour of the Generic Broadcast algorithm in runs where conflicting messages are g-Broadcast. Proposition 8 establishes a lower bound for cases where messages conflict, and Proposition 9 shows that the *best* case with conflicts can be reached when there are no process failures nor failure suspicions.

Proposition 8. *Assume that Algorithm 1 uses the Reliable Broadcast implementation presented in [2], and the Consensus implementation presented in [11]. Let $\mathcal{R}_C$ be a set of runs generated by Algorithm 1, such that m and m' are the only messages g-Broadcast and g-Delivered in $\mathcal{R}_C$. If m and m' conflict, then there is no run R in $\mathcal{R}_C$ where $dl^R(m) < 4$ and $dl^R(m') < 4$.*

Proposition 9. *Assume that Algorithm 1 uses the Reliable Broadcast implementation presented in [2], and the Consensus implementation presented in [11]). Let $\mathcal{R}_C$ be a set of runs generated by Algorithm 1, such that m and m' are the only messages g-Broadcast and g-Delivered in $\mathcal{R}_C$, and there are no process failures nor failure suspicions. If m and m' conflict, then there is a run R in $\mathcal{R}_C$ where m is g-Delivered before m' and $dl^R(m) = 2$ and $dl^R(m') = 4$.*

---

[6] Whenever a process p wants to R-broadcast a message m, p sends m to all processes. Once a process q receives m, if $q \neq p$ then q sends m to all processes, and q R-delivers m.

5 Related Work

Group communication aim at extending traditional one-to-one communication, which is insufficient in many settings. One-to-many communication is typically needed to handle replication (replicated data, replicated objects, etc.). Classical techniques to manage replicated data are based on voting and quorum systems (e.g., [3, 5, 6] to cite a few). Early quorum systems distinguish read operations from write operations in order to allow for concurrent read operations. These ideas have been extended to abstract data types in [5]. Increasing concurrency, without compromising the strong consistency guarantees on replicated data, is a standard way to increase the performance of the system. Lazy replication [10] is another approach that aims at increasing the performance by reducing the cost of replication. Lazy replication also distinguishes between read and write operations, and relaxes the requirement of total order delivery of read operations. Consistency is ensured at the cost of managing timestamps outside of the set of replicated servers; these timestamps are used to ensure Causal Order delivery on the replicated servers.

Our approach also aims at increasing the performance of replication by increasing concurrency in the context of group communication. Similarly to quorum systems, our Generic Broadcast algorithm allows for concurrency that is not possible with traditional replication techniques based on Atomic Broadcast. From this perspective, our work can be seen as a way to integrate group communications and quorum systems. There is even a stronger similarity between quorum systems and our Generic Broadcast algorithm. Our algorithm is based on two sets: an acknowledgement set and a checking set.[7] These sets play a role similar to quorum systems. However, quorum systems require weaker conditions to keep consistency than the condition required by the acknowledgement and checking sets.[8] Although the reason for this discrepancy is very probably related to the guarantees offered by quorum systems, the question requires further investigation.

6 Conclusions

The paper has introduced the Generic Broadcast problem, which is defined based on a conflict relation on the set of messages. The notion of

---

[7] Used respectively for g-Delivering non-conflicting messages during a stage, and determining non-conflicting messages g-Delivered at the termination of a stage.

[8] Let n_r be the size of a read quorum, and n_w the size of a write quorum. Quorum systems usually requires that $n_r + n_w \geq n + 1$.

conflict can be derived from the semantic of the messages. Only conflicting messages have to be delivered by all processes in the same order. As such, Generic Broadcast is a powerful message ordering abstraction, which includes Reliable and Atomic Broadcast as special cases. The advantage of Generic Broadcast over Atomic Broadcast is a cost issue, where cost is defined by the notion of delivery latency of messages.

On a different issue, our Generic Broadcast algorithm uses mechanisms that have similarities with quorum systems. As future work it would be interesting to investigate this point to better understand the differences between replication protocols based on group communication (e.g., Atomic Broadcast, Generic Broadcast) and replication protocols based on quorum systems.

Finally, as noted in Section 4.1, our Generic Broadcast algorithm requires at least $(2n + 1)/3$ correct processes. Such a condition is usual in the context of Byzantine failures, but rather surprising in the context of crash failures.

References

1. K. Birman and T. Joseph. Reliable Communication in the Presence of Failures. *ACM Transactions on Computer Systems*, 5(1):47–76, February 1987.
2. T. D. Chandra and S. Toueg. Unreliable failure detectors for reliable distributed systems. *Journal of the ACM*, 43(2):225–267, March 1996.
3. D.K. Gifford. Weighted Voting for Replicated Data. In *Proceedings of the 7th Symposium on Operating Systems Principles*, pages 150–159, December 1979.
4. V. Hadzilacos and S. Toueg. Fault-Tolerant Broadcasts and Related Problems. In *Distributed Systems*, chapter 5. Addison Wesley, second edition, 1993.
5. M. Herlihy. A Quorum-Consensus Replication Method for Abstract Data Types. *ACM Transactions on Computer Systems*, 4(1):32–53, February 1986.
6. S. Jajodia and D. Mutchler. Dynamic Voting. In *Proc. of the ACM SIGMOD Int. Conference on Management of Data*, pages 227–238, May 1987.
7. L. Lamport. Time, clocks, and the ordering of events in a distributed system. *Communications of the ACM*, 21(7):558–565, July 1978.
8. F. Pedone and A. Schiper. Optimistic Atomic Broadcast. In *Proc. of 12th International Symposium on Distributed Computing*, pages 318–332, September 1998.
9. F. Pedone and A. Schiper. Generic broadcast. Technical Report SSC/1999/012, EPFL, Communication Systems Department, April 1999.
10. S. Ghemawat R. Ladin, B. Liskov. Providing High Availability Using Lazy Replication. *ACM Transactions on Computer Systems*, 10(4):360–391, November 1992.
11. A. Schiper. Early consensus in an asynchronous system with a weak failure detector. *Distributed Computing*, 10(3):149–157, 1997.
12. F. B. Schneider. Implementing fault-tolerant services using the state machine approach: A tutorial. *ACM Computing Surveys*, 22(4):299–319, December 1990.

Non-blocking Asynchronous Byzantine Quorum Systems

Rida A. Bazzi

Department of Computer Science and Engineering
Arizona State University
Tempe, AZ 85287-5406 U.S.A.
bazzi@asu.edu

Abstract. Quorum systems have been used to implement many coordination problems in distributed systems. In this paper, we propose a reformulation of the definition of Byzantine quorum systems. Our reformulation captures the requirement for non-blocking access to quorums in asynchronous systems. We formally define the asynchronous access cost of quorum systems and we show that the asynchronous access cost and not the size of a quorum is the right measure of message complexity of protocols using quorums in asynchronous systems. We also show that previous quorum systems proposed in the literature have a very high asynchronous access cost. We present new quorum systems with low asynchronous access cost and whose other performance parameters match those of the best Byzantine quorum systems proposed in the literature. In particular, we present a construction for the disjoint failure pattern that outperforms previously proposed systems for that pattern.

Keywords: quorum, tolerance, Byzantine, failures, distributed, asynchronous, access cost.

1 Introduction

A quorum system is a collection of sets (quorums) that mutually intersect. Quorum systems have been used to implement mutual exclusion [1, 8], replicated data systems [7], commit protocols [15], and distributed consensus [11]. For example, in a typical implementation of mutual exclusion using a quorum system, processors request access to the critical section from all members of a quorum. A processor can enter its critical section only if it receives permission from all processors in a quorum.[1] Work on quorum systems traditionally considered crash failures [1, 2, 4, 5, 6, 7, 8, 14, 13]. Malkhi and Reiter [9] proposed the interesting notion of Byzantine quorums - quorum systems that can tolerate Byzantine failures. They showed that the traditional definition of quorums is not adequate to handle Byzantine failures: in the presence of Byzantine failures, the intersection of two quorums should contain enough correct processors so that correct

---

[1] Additional measures are needed to insure that the implementation is fair and deadlock free.

processors can unambiguously access the quorums. They presented protocols to implement a distributed shared register variable using Byzantine quorums. Their implementation requires a client accessing a quorum to wait for responses from every processor in a quorum set, but they did not study the problem of finding a quorum set whose elements are available - an available quorum.

In this paper, we study the cost of finding an available quorum in the presence of Byzantine failures. We introduce non-blocking Byzantine quorum systems and show that they can be achieved at a low cost and we present non-blocking Byzantine quorum constructions for two failure models. The constructions we present are the first that do not require blocking and that have a low cost. Also, the construction we present for the Disjoint failure model yields a Byzantine quorum system that has better performance parameters than previously proposed systems. Our construction rely on a new access model we call *partial access*. With partial access, a processor need not wait for a reply from each process in a quorum set. The quorum system should be designed to ensure that any two partial accesses have a large enough intersection to ensure consistency. It turns out that the set of partial accesses of a non-blocking Byzantine quorum system is a Byzantine quorum system as defined in [9].

It should be emphasized that partial access is relevant for general quorum access in asynchronous systems and is not only relevant to asynchronous Byzantine quorum systems. In this paper, we only consider partial access for the case of Byzantine failures. The same methods we propose are applicable to cases in which the failures are not Byzantine, but that are restricted to a predefined failure pattern. A probabilistic model of failure does not have a predefined failure pattern and therefore our results are not directly applicable to it.

The rest of the paper is organized as follows. Section 2 discusses related work and Section 3 summarizes our contributions. Section 4 presents basic definitions and introduces the notion of asynchronous access cost. Section 5 gives examples of the asynchronous access cost of two Byzantine quorum systems. Section 6 reformulates the definition of Byzantine quorums to capture the asynchronous access cost as a design objective. Section 7 presents non-blocking quorum systems with low asynchronous access cost and whose other performance parameters match those of the best Byzantine quorum systems proposed in the literature. Section 8 concludes the paper.

2 Related Work

The problem of finding an available quorum has been addressed by researchers for the case of detectable crash failures [2, 13]. In [13], the *probe complexity* of a quorum system is defined. The probe complexity is the minimum number of processors that need to be contacted to establish the existence or non-existence of an available quorum. In the definition of probe complexity, processors can be probed incrementally and the identity of the processor to be probed next can depend on the responses received from previous probes. In [2], the author formally defined the concept of *cost of failures*, which can be thought of as the probe complexity per failures. Both [2] and [13] assume that failures can be detected. Their incremental access methods are not directly applicable to asynchronous systems subject to Byzantine failures.

The problem of finding an available quorum in the presence of Byzantine failures has not been studied by other researchers. Due to the nature of Byzantine failures and system asynchrony, the definition of Byzantine quorums proposed in [9] requires that an available quorum exists in the system. Unfortunately, that requirement does not say anything about the cost of finding an available quorum. The availability requirement of Byzantine quorum systems was relaxed in [3] for systems in which timeouts can be used to detect failures. In such systems, any quorum set Q can be accessed without a need to access servers that do not belong to Q.

3 Contributions

To our knowledge, this is the first work that studies the cost of accessing Byzantine quorum systems in asynchronous systems. We define the asynchronous access cost of a Byzantine quorum and introduce non-blocking Byzantine quorum systems. Unlike Byzantine quorum systems, non-blocking Byzantine quorum systems capture the asynchronous access cost as well the probe complexity. In that respect, they are similar to synchronous Byzantine quorum [3].

We propose optimal non-blocking quorum systems and show that they are not equivalent to previously proposed Byzantine quorum systems. For the disjoint failure pattern, we propose a non-blocking quorum system that yields the best known Byzantine quorum system for that failure model.

4 Definitions and System Model

4.1 System Model

We assume that the system consists of a set $\mathcal{P}$ of n server processors and a number of client processors that are distinct from the servers. All processors can communicate using reliable message passing. We assume that there are no bounds on message delivery time or on processors speeds and that there are no failure detectors in the system.

4.2 Failure Model

Server processors can fail.[2] The assumptions about failures affect the way a quorum can be used. In the Byzantine failure model, it is usually assumed that there is a *known bound* on the number of failures that can occur in the system and that failed processors do not recover. In this paper we adopt a model of failures introduced in [9]. The set *faulty* denotes the set of faulty processors in

---

[2] We do not consider client failures in this paper.

the system. A *failure pattern* $\mathcal{F}$ identifies the possible sets of faulty processors in the system. We write $\mathcal{F} = \{F_1, F_2, \ldots, F_m\}$. There exists an element F of $\mathcal{F}$ such that at any given instant, the faulty processors belong to F. The processors do not necessarily know F. A common example of a failure pattern is the *f-threshold* pattern in which $\mathcal{F} = \{F \in \mathcal{P} : |F| = f\}$. Another interesting failure pattern is the *disjoint* pattern in which all elements of $\mathcal{F}$ are disjoint [9].

4.3 Quorum Systems

The standard definition of a quorum system is the following.

Definition 1. A *quorum system* Q over $\mathcal{P}$ is a set of subsets (called *quorums*) of $\mathcal{P}$ such that any two quorums have a non-empty intersection.

The intersection property of quorums is essential for their use in coordination problems.

Processors access a quorum to coordinate their actions. The following is the typical way to access a quorum. A processor, the *client*, sends a request to every processor, *server*, in a quorum set. Upon receiving a request, a correct processor updates its state and sends a reply. The client waits until it receives a reply from every processor in the quorum. If the client receives replies from all processors in a quorum then the access is considered successful. If one of the servers failed, then the client attempts to access another quorum that does not have any faulty processor (the question of finding a quorum with no faulty processors has been addressed in [2, 13]). Since processors access a quorum only if all its members are correct, two clients are always guaranteed to receive a response from a common correct server which belongs to a non-empty intersection of two quorums. The correctness of quorum-based protocols rely on this intersection property. A quorum is said to be *available* if all its elements are correct processors [12].

4.4 Byzantine Quorums in Asynchronous Systems

If failures are arbitrary, a processor might receive conflicting replies from faulty and correct processors. It follows that a processor must base its coordination decisions on replies that it *knows* to be from correct processors. Motivated by this requirement, Malkhi and Reiter gave the following definition [9]:

Definition 2. A quorum system tolerates failure pattern $\mathcal{F}$ if

1. $\forall Q_1, Q_2 \in Q \ \forall F_1, F_2 \in \mathcal{F} : (Q_1 \cap Q_2) - F_1 \not\subseteq F_2$.
2. $\forall F \in \mathcal{F} \ \exists Q \in Q : F \cap Q = \emptyset$

The first condition requires that the intersection of two quorums is not contained in the intersection of two sets in $\mathcal{F}$. This guarantees that the replies of correct processors can be identified . To see why this is the case, consider, as an example, the *f*-threshold failure pattern. For that pattern, the condition reduces to a familiar-looking condition: $Q_1 \cap Q_2 \geq 2f + 1$. So, it is always possible to have

$f + 1$ identical replies in the intersection of two quorums. One of these replies must be the reply of a correct processor.

The second condition requires that some quorum consists of correct processors. The second condition is needed in asynchronous systems because there is no way to differentiate a slow processor from a faulty one. To access a quorum in an asynchronous system, a processor cannot simply send requests to all processors in a quorum set and waits for replies. In the worst case, even in a failure-free execution, a processor might have to send requests to every processor in the system and then waits for replies from a quorum that consists of correct processor (we give an example below). The availability condition (also called resiliency requirement in [10]) is needed to ensure that some quorum is available in the system. The work of Malkhi and Reiter [9] and their subsequent work [10] does not address the problem of ensuring that a response is received. Addressing this problem is an important contribution of this paper.

4.5   Cost of Access

In this section we introduce the *asynchronous access cost* of a quorum system. In asynchronous systems, a processor cannot use timeouts to detect failures. As pointed above, to access a quorum set, a processor cannot simply send requests to every element of the quorum set and then wait for replies. This is due to system asynchrony and the fact that failed processes might never reply. Byzantine quorum systems as defined in [9] get around this difficulty by requiring that for every faulty set F there exists a quorum set Q such that $F \cap Q = \emptyset$. It follows that one way to guarantee replies from some quorum is to send requests to every processor in the system and then wait for replies from some quorum. Obviously, sending requests to every processor is too costly and eliminates the benefits of using quorum systems.

In practice, a system might not be fully asynchronous and quorums can be accessed without the need to contact every processor in the system. For example, a client can send request to a set of servers in a quorum and then send requests to more server if no response is received within some time limit, until a response is received from a quorum set. In this paper, we are considering the question of accessing quorums in systems that are fully asynchronous in which there are no bounds on message delivery delays or processors speed. For such systems, our aim is to improve on the worst-case scenario in which every server needs to be contacted to guarantee a response from some quorum set.

In this paper, we consider the *direct access model* in which processes access a quorum by sending all requests at once and then wait for replies. The direct access model is not the most general model of accessing quorums. For instance, a process might incrementally access a quorum system by sending requests to some processes, then send further requests based on the replies it receives. We call such an incremental strategy a fault-tolerant access strategy (see [2] for a formal definition, also see [13] for a related notion). We believe that an incremental fault-tolerant access strategy is more appropriate for systems with detectable failures than for asynchronous systems with undetectable failures. In fact, an incremental strategy would require more than one round of message exchange which can be prohibitively high in a fully asynchronous system. Studying the cost of access of incremental strategy is a subject for future research.

Definition 3. Let Q be a Byzantine quorum system. A set A is an *access set* of a quorum set $Q \in Q$ if $Q \subseteq A$ and

$$\forall F \in \mathcal{F} \exists Q' \in \mathcal{Q} : Q' \subseteq A - F$$

Note that a quorum Q might have more than one access set.

Definition 4. Let $\mathcal{Q}$ be a Byzantine quorum system. The *asynchronous access cost* of a quorum set $Q \in \mathcal{Q}$ is the size of the smallest access set of Q.

Note that by the definition of a Byzantine quorum system, the set $\mathcal{P}$ of all servers is an access set of each quorum set, and therefore the asynchronous access cost is well defined.

Definition 5. The *asynchronous access cost* of a Byzantine quorum system $\mathcal{Q}$ is

$$cost(\mathcal{Q}) = \min\{|A| : \forall F \in \mathcal{F} \exists Q \in \mathcal{Q} : Q \subseteq A - F\}$$

In the direct access model, the asynchronous access cost gives the minimum number of servers that need to be contacted to ensure that a response is received from some quorum set.

As the following theorem shows, in a fully asynchronous system, a client needs to send requests to $cost(\mathcal{Q})$ servers each time it needs to access a quorum set.

Theorem 6. *Let $\mathcal{Q}$ be a Byzantine quorum system. In the direct access model, a client needs to send requests to $cost(\mathcal{Q})$ servers to guarantee a response from each server in some quorum set.*

Proof. In the direct access model, a client c sends all request at the beginning to some set of servers A. If $|A| < cost(\mathcal{Q})$, then, by definition of the asynchronous access cost, there is a faulty set such that $A - F$ contains no quorum set. If processes in F fail, c will not receive a response from every server in any quorum set.

4.6 Strategies and Load

This section presents the formal definitions of strategy and load as in [12]. It discusses the implications of the asynchronous access cost on the load of a quorum system.

A protocol using a quorum system chooses a quorum to access according to some rules. A strategy is a probabilistic rule to choose a quorum. Formally, a strategy is defined as follows.

Definition 7. Let $Q = \{Q_1, \ldots, Q_m\}$ be a quorum system. A *strategy* $w \in [0,1]^m$ for Q is a probability distribution over Q.

For every processor $q \in \mathcal{P}$, a strategy w induces a probability that q is chosen to be accessed. This probability is called the load on q. The *system load* is the load of the *busiest* element induced by the best possible strategy.

Definition 8. Let w be a strategy for a quorum system $Q = \{Q_1, \ldots, Q_m\}$. For any $q \in \mathcal{P}$, the *load* induced by w on q is $l_w(q) = \Sigma_{Q_j \ni q} w_j$. The *load* induced by w on Q is

$$\mathcal{L}_w(Q) = \max_{q \in \mathcal{P}} l_w(q)$$

The *system load* on Q is

$$\mathcal{L}(Q) = \min_w \{\mathcal{L}_w(Q)\},$$

where the minimum is taken over all strategies.

The definition of load implicitly assumes that no extra servers need to be contacted when a particular quorum is accessed. This is not the case for Byzantine failures because extra servers need to be accessed even in failure-free runs to guarantee a response (assuming clients do not know that the run is failure-free). From the discussion about the cost of access, it follows that the load definition should take the cost of access into consideration. The definition of load can simply be changed by replacing a quorum with the access set of the quorum, while allowing for different access sets for the same quorum at different times. If the only access set of any quorum is the set $\mathcal{P}$ of all servers, it follows that the load is 1, regardless of the quorum size.

5 Asynchronous Access Cost Examples

In this section we give examples of the asynchronous access cost for two Byzantine quorum systems. The first system, the *Paths* system, has optimal quorum size and load (as traditionally defined) combination and high availability in the presence of crash failures. We show that it has a large asynchronous access cost. The second system, the threshold system, has a small asynchronous access cost relative to the size of its quorums.

5.1 Paths System

The *Paths* system [10] is defined for the f-threshold failure pattern. It is defined as follows. Let $n = d^2$, be the number of servers arranged in a square grid of the triangular lattice. A quorum consists of $\sqrt{2f+1}$ non-intersecting top-bottom paths and $\sqrt{2f+1}$ non-intersecting left-right paths. In [10], it is shown that any two quorums intersect in $2f + 1$ distinct vertices and that the path system can tolerate no more than $\sqrt{n}$ failures.

The *Paths* systems has small quorum size, small load (not taking access cost into consideration) and high availability in the presence of crash failures. Unfortunately, the asynchronous access cost of the *Paths* system is high as we show below.

Lemma 9. $cost(Path) = \Omega((f + \sqrt{f+1})d)$.

Proof. If a set A is of size $|A| < (f + \sqrt{f+1})d$, then A cannot contain more than $(f + \sqrt{f+1}) - 1$ disjoint left-right paths because each left-right path is of size at least d. It follows that a maximum cut set of A is of size at most $(f + \sqrt{f+1}) - 1$. Removing f vertices from the maximum cut set yields a set with cut set of size at most $\sqrt{f+1} - 1$. Such a set cannot have $\sqrt{f+1}$ disjoint paths.

In particular, the access cost of the *Paths* system is very high if $f = \Omega(d)$.

Corollary 10. *If* $f = \Omega(d)$, *then* $cost(Path) = \Omega(n)$.

5.2 Threshold System

The threshold system is defined for the f-threshold failure pattern. A quorum of the threshold system consists of any set of $f + \lceil \frac{n+1}{2} \rceil$. Any two quorums are guaranteed to intersect in at least $2f + 1$ elements. For the threshold system, the cost of the system is not much different from the quorum size, but the quorum size is large.

Lemma 11. *The asynchronous access cost of the Threshold system is* $O(2f + \lceil \frac{n+1}{2} \rceil)$.

Proof. In fact, a set A of size $2f + \lceil \frac{n+1}{2} \rceil$ vertices is guaranteed to contain a quorum if any f elements are removed from A. Also, a set A of size less than $2f + \lceil \frac{n+1}{2} \rceil$ vertices is not guaranteed to contain a quorum if f elements are removed from A.

6 Non-Blocking Quorum Systems

The goal of defining non-blocking quorum systems is to emphasize the importance of the asynchronous access cost as a design parameter, as well as to provide a more uniform definition of Byzantine quorum systems. In the examples above, there is no clear relationship between the cost of access and the size of the quorum. Our aim is to reformulate the definition of the quorum system so that the cost of access is found as part of the design of the quorum system and not after the quorum is already designed. So, instead of designing the quorum sets, we directly design the access sets. We should note here that access sets have not been considered previously by other researchers.

We define a *non-blocking Byzantine quorum system* as follows.

Definition 12. A set system Q is a *non-blocking masking quorum system* that tolerates failure pattern $\mathcal{F}$ if and only if:

$$\forall Q_1, Q_2 \in Q \;\; \forall F_1, F_2, F_3, F_4 \in \mathcal{F} : ((Q_1 - F_1) \cap (Q_2 - F_2) - F_3 \not\subseteq F_4$$

Note that this definition is similar to the first condition of Definition 2. In fact, given a non-blocking quorum system Q, the set $\{Q - F : Q \in Q \wedge F \in \mathcal{F}\}$ is a Byzantine Quorum system as defined by Malkhi and Reiter in [9] on the one hand. On the other hand, finding a non-blocking quorum system corresponding to a particular Byzantine quorum system is not straightforward always.

We define partial access sets of a non-blocking Byzantine quorum system as follows.

Definition 13. The *partial access sets* of a non-blocking Byzantine quorum system Q that tolerates failure pattern $\mathcal{F}$ are the sets of the form $Q - F$, where $Q \in Q$ and $F \in \mathcal{F}$.

Our definition requires that the client be able to determine a correct response from any partial access set; to have successful partial accesses, it is enough to guarantee that the quorum system can handle the worst-case failure scenario. To access a quorum Q, a client sends requests to all servers in Q, and then waits for a response from all servers in a partial access set of Q. Such a response is guaranteed by the definition of non-blocking Byzantine quorum systems. Once a response from a partial access set is received, the client can proceed as in [9].

The following theorem gives a sufficient condition for a collection of sets to be a non-blocking Byzantine quorum system.

Theorem 14. *A set Q is a* non-blocking quorum system *that tolerates failure pattern $\mathcal{F}$ if:*

1. $\forall Q_1, Q_2 \in Q \ \forall F_1, F_2 \in \mathcal{F} : (Q_1 \cap Q_2) - F_2 \not\subseteq F_2$, *and*
2. $\forall Q_1 \in Q \ \forall F_1, F_2 \in \mathcal{F} \exists Q_2 \in Q : Q_2 \subseteq (Q_1 - F_1) \cup F_2$.

Proof. The proof is by contradiction. Let Q_1 and Q_2 be two quorum sets such that $\exists F_1, F_2, F_3, F_4 \in \mathcal{F} : ((Q_1 - F_1) \cap (Q_2 - F_2) - F_3 \subseteq F_4$ It follows that $(Q_1 - F_1) \cap (Q_2 - F_2) \subseteq F_3 \cup F_4$ and $((Q_1 - F_1) \cup F_3) \cap ((Q_2 - F_2) \cup F_4) \subseteq F_3 \cup F_4$. By Condition 2 of the theorem, it follows that there exists two quorum sets Q and Q' such that $Q \cap Q' \subseteq F_3 \cup F_4$. This contradicts Condition 1 of the theorem. $\blacksquare$

As we saw, to each non-blocking Byzantine quorum system corresponds a Byzantine quorums system as defined in [9]. The importance of the reformulation lies in the fact that it ties the quorum size to the asynchronous access cost. When designing a non-blocking quorum system, one would have to design a quorum system with small quorums sets (all other parameters being equal), which means that the resulting asynchronous access cost is small. This is due to the fact that the quorums of a non-blocking quorum system are access sets of the underlying Byzantine quorum system. On the other hand, when designing Byzantine quorum systems as defined in the formulation of [9], the asynchronous cost of access is not directly related to the quorum size even if the quorum systems have good performance parameters. One might argue that it is always possible to construct Byzantine quorum systems with low access cost and without the need for a reformulation of the definition. Intuitively, we believe that this is not true unless the access cost is an explicit design parameter, in which case one has to use a definition similar to ours. Also, we believe that our definition provides a natural expression of the access cost as a design parameter. Finally, previous Byzantine quorum constructions in the literature did not take the access cost into account as we saw in Section 5.

6.1 Existence of Non-Blocking Quorum Systems

Given a failure pattern, we are interested in deciding whether there exists a quorum system that tolerates the failure pattern. The following two propositions give necessary and sufficient conditions.

Proposition 15. *There exists a non-blocking quorum system that tolerates failure pattern $\mathcal{F}$ if and only if $\mathcal{Q} = \{\mathcal{P}\}$ tolerates $\mathcal{F}$.*

Proof. If $\mathcal{Q} = \{\mathcal{P}\}$ tolerates $\mathcal{F}$, then there exists a quorum system that tolerates $\mathcal{F}$. If there exists a quorum system $\mathcal{Q}$ that tolerates $\mathcal{F}$, then there exists a quorum in $\mathcal{Q}$ that cannot be contained in the union of less than five elements of $\mathcal{F}$. It follows that $\mathcal{P}$ is not equal to the union of less than five elements in $\mathcal{F}$ and that $\{\mathcal{P}\}$ tolerates $\mathcal{F}$.

Proposition 16. *There exists a non-blocking quorum system that tolerate failure pattern $\mathcal{F}$ if and only if*

$$\forall A, B, C, D \in \mathcal{F}: \quad \mathcal{P} \neq A \cup B \cup C \cup D.$$

Proof. Direct application of Proposition 15.

It is interesting to note that the necessary and sufficient condition for the existence of a non-blocking Byzantine quorum system is also a necessary and sufficient condition for the existence of a quorum system [9]. This is expected, given the extremal nature of the system used in the proofs.

Corollary 17. *There exists a quorum system that tolerates the f-threshold failure pattern if and only if $n \geq 4f + 1$.*

7 Non-Blocking Quorum Systems Constructions

Depending on the failure patterns, constructing a non-trivial non-blocking Byzantine quorum systems can be harder than constructing a Byzantine quorum system (the set $\mathcal{Q} = \{\mathcal{P}\}$ is a trivial system if a non-blocking quorum system exist). In this section we present two constructions of non-blocking Byzantine quorum systems, one for the threshold failure pattern and one for the disjoint failure pattern.

7.1 Threshold Failure Pattern

Consider a system of $n = d^2$ processors arranged in a $d \times d$ square grid, $d > 4$ in the presence of the f-threshold failure pattern, $f < (n-1)/4$. Two vertices (x_1, y_1) and (x_2, y_2) of the grid are connected if: $x_1 = x_2 \wedge y_1 = y_2 + 1$, $x_1 = x_2 \wedge y_2 = y_1 + 1$, $x_1 = x_2 + 1 \wedge y_1 = y_2$, $x_2 = x_1 + 1 \wedge y_1 = y_2$, $x_1 = x_2 + 1 \wedge y_1 = y_2 + 1$, or $x_2 = x_1 + 1 \wedge y_2 = y_1 + 1$.

Similar to the *Paths* system [10], we define a non-blocking quorum system Q_{fn} that consists of $2\lceil \sqrt{f+1} \rceil$ disjoint left-right paths and $2\lceil \sqrt{f+1} \rceil$ top-bottom paths. Using the same arguments as in [10], it is easy to show that any two quorums are guaranteed to intersect in $4f + 1$ elements. It follows that the quorum system is a non-blocking quorum system. The quorum system Q_{fn} has better fault tolerance than the *Paths* system which can tolerate no more than $\sqrt{n}$ in the worst case. The reason is that the *Paths* system requires that each row have a number of available vertices for the system to be available. In contrast, Q_{fn} can function as long as the intersection property is satisfied and regardless of the availability in each row.

More importantly, the cost of accessing Q_{fn} is $4\lceil \sqrt{f+1} \rceil d$, compared to $\Omega((f + \sqrt{f+1})d)$ for the *Paths* system.

Finally, the Byzantine quorum system $Q_f = \{Q - F : Q \in Q_{fn} \text{ and } F \in \mathcal{F}\}$ is not directly related to the *Paths* system. In fact, many quorums of Q_f do not contain a quorum of the *Paths* system and vice versa. This can be easily shown by considering the discussion on the fault tolerance of the two systems and the fact that the quorums of the *Paths* system are smaller than those of Q_f. This example shows the advantage of using the definition of non-blocking quorum systems.

7.2 Disjoint Failure Pattern

In this section we provide an efficient construction of a non-blocking quorum system Q_{dn} for a failure pattern $\mathcal{F}$ whose elements are disjoint. The construction is similar to the construction given in [3]. We present the construction in some detail to show that our definition of non-blocking Byzantine quorum systems yields quorum systems that are not easily designed for the original definition. In fact, the Byzantine quorum system Q_d defined by the partial access sets of Q_{dn} outperforms the ones proposed in [9] for the disjoint failure pattern. Also, we do not know how to express Q_d other than as the set of partial access sets of Q_{dn}. We do not provide proofs for most of our claims because they are almost identical to those of [3].

Let $\mathcal{F} = \{F_1, F_2, \ldots, F_m\}$ be the set of failure sets ordered in decreasing size. We assume without loss of generality that $m > 4$. Let $\alpha = n - (\Sigma_{i=1}^{4} |F_i|)$.

Our construction will proceed as follows. First we show that there are five disjoint sets of size greater than $\frac{\alpha}{10}$ such that no two of them will have an non-empty intersection with the same faulty set. Then, on each of the five sets S_i, $i = 0, \ldots, 4$, we construct a traditional quorum system whose load is $O(\frac{1}{\sqrt{|S_i|}})$.

On $\mathcal{P}$, we construct a quorum system whose elements consist of the union of five quorums, one from each of the five sets.

Let $m_0 = 4$ and define m_i, $i = 1, \ldots, 4$ as follows:

$$m_i = \min\{j : |F_i \cup \bigcup_{m_{i-1} < k \leq j+1} F_k| \geq \frac{\alpha}{10}\}$$

Note that j and k are bound variables in the definition of m_i. Also, m_i, $1 \leq i \leq 4$, are always guaranteed to exist.

Now, define the five sets S_i, $0 \leq i \leq 4$, as follows:

- $S_i = F_i \cup \bigcup_{m_i < k \leq m_i} F_k$, if $i < 4$, and
- $S_4 = \bigcup_{m_4 < k} F_k$

Proposition 18. $S_i \cap S_j = \emptyset$, $0 \leq i \neq j \leq 4$.

Proposition 19. $S_i \geq \frac{\alpha}{10}$ for $0 \leq i \leq 4$.

Now, we describe the non-blocking quorum system $\mathcal{Q}_{dn}$. On S_i, $0 \leq i \leq 4$, define a quorum system with load $O(\frac{1}{\sqrt{|S_i|}})$. Many such systems exist. One such system is the triangle lattice system [2]. In the triangle lattice system over S_i, we can choose $\sqrt{2|S_i|}$ quorums such that each processor belongs to exactly two quorums. If we choose each quorum with a probability $\frac{1}{\sqrt{2|S_i|}}$, it follows that the load of the triangle lattice system on S_i is at most $\frac{2}{\sqrt{2|S_i|}} = \sqrt{\frac{2}{|S_i|}}$. Define a quorum on $\mathcal{P}$ to be the union of five quorum sets one from each of the triangle lattices defined on S_i, $0 \leq i \leq 4$.

Proposition 20. *The resulting system $\mathcal{Q}_{dn}$ is a non-blocking quorum system that tolerates $\mathcal{F}$.*

Proof. In fact, any two quorums intersect in five servers, no two of which belong to the same faulty set. Therefore the intersection of two quorums does not belong to the union of four faulty sets.

Let $\mathcal{Q}_d$ be the Byzantine quorum system defined by the access sets of $\mathcal{Q}_{dn}$. $\mathcal{Q}_d = \{Q - F : Q \in \mathcal{Q}_{dn} \text{ and } F \in \mathcal{F}\}$. It follows that $\mathcal{Q}_d$ tolerates the disjoint failure pattern $\mathcal{F}$.

Proposition 21. *The load of the quorum system $\mathcal{Q}_d$ is $O(\frac{1}{\sqrt{\alpha}})$.*

Lemma 22. *The load of $\mathcal{Q}_d$ is optimal.*

Proof. The proof uses the same techniques as those used in [3] and is omitted.

The load of $\mathcal{Q}_d$ stated above is the traditional load. Nevertheless, the load of $\mathcal{Q}_{dn}$ is of the same order as the load of $\mathcal{Q}_d$ and is therefore optimal. Finally, we know of no simpler way to express $\mathcal{Q}_d$ or to obtain a Byzantine quorum system that tolerate $\mathcal{F}$ and has a better load.

8 Conclusion

An important contribution of this paper is the recognition that in asynchronous systems, it is not enough to design a quorum systems with small quorum sets, but it is more important to design a quorum set that is amenable to efficient access. We proposed a new definition of Byzantine quorum systems that lend themselves to non-blocking access. We have shown that designing non-blocking Byzantine quorums with small access cost is possible in asynchronous systems.

One might think that the only difference between Byzantine quorum systems and non-blocking Byzantine quorum systems is that of how access is achieved, and that it is possible to come up with a new definition of access for Byzantine quorum systems to achieve non-blocking access. While this is possible, the resulting non-blocking quorum system is not guaranteed to have a small access cost. To design Byzantine quorum system with a small access cost, we believe that a formulation similar to ours is needed.

Finally, it is interesting to study incremental access strategies and the corresponding cost of access. We leave that as a subject for future research.

References

1. D. Agrawal and A. El-Abbadi. An efficient and fault-tolerant solution for distributed mutual exclusion. *ACM Transactions on Computer Systems*, 9(1):1–20,1991.
2. R. A. Bazzi. Planar Quorums In *Proceedings of the 10th International Workshop on Distributed Algorithms*, pages 251-268, October 1996.
3. R. A. Bazzi. Synchronous Byzantine Quorum Systems In *Proceedings of the Sixteenth ACM Symposium on Principles of Distributed Computing*, Santa Barbara, California, 1997. Full version submitted for publication.
4. H. Garcia–Molina and D. Barbara. How to assign votes in a distributed system. *Journal of the ACM*, 32(4):481–860, 1985.
5. D. K. Gifford. Weighted Voting for Replicated Data *Proceeding of 7th ACM Symposium on Operating Systems Principles*, pages 150–162, December 1979.
6. A. Kumar. Hierarchical quorum consensus: A new algorithm for managing replicated data. *IEEE Transactions of Computers*, 40(9):996–1004,1991.
7. A. Kumar., M. Rabinovich, and R. Sinha. A performance study of general grid structures for replicated data. In *Proceedings of International Conference on Distributed Computing Systems*, pages 178–185, May, 1993.
8. M. Maekawa. A $\sqrt{n}$ algorithm for mutual exclusion in decentralized systems. *ACM Transactions on Computer Systems*, 3(2):145–159,1985.
9. D. Malkhi and M. Reiter. Byzantine Quorum Systems. In *Proceedings of ACM 29th Symposium on Theory of Computing*, May, 1997.
10. D. Malkhi, M. Reiter, and A. Wool. The load and availability of Byzantine quorum systems. In *Proceedings of the Sixteenth ACM Symposium on Principles of Distributed Computing*, August, 1997.
11. M. L. Neilsen *Quorum Structures in Distributed Systems*. Ph.D. Thesis, Department of Computer and Information Sciences, Kansas State University, 1992.

12. M. Naor and A. Wool The Load, capacity and availability of quorum systems. In *Proceedings of the 35th IEEE Symposium on Foundations of Computer Science*, pages 214–225. 1994.
13. D. Peleg and A. Wool. How to be an Efficient Snoop, or the Probe Complexity of Quorum Systems. In *Proceedings of the 15th ACM Symposium on Principles of Distributed Computing*, pages 290-299, 1996.
14. D. Peleg and A. Wool. The availability of quorum systems. *Information and Computation*, 123(2):210-223, 1995.
15. D. Skeen. A quorum–based commit protocol. In *Proceedings of 6th Berkeley Workshop on Distributed Data Management and Computer Networks*, pages 69–80, 1982.

Byzantine Agreement Secure against General Adversaries in the Dual Failure Model*

Bernd Altmann and Matthias Fitzi and Ueli Maurer

{altmann,fitzi,maurer}@inf.ethz.ch

Department of Computer Science
Swiss Federal Institute of Technology (ETH), Zurich
CH-8092 Zurich, Switzerland

Abstract. This paper introduces a new adversary model for Byzantine agreement and broadcast among a set P of players in which the adversary may perform two different types of player corruption: active (Byzantine) corruption and fail-corruption (crash). As a strict generalization of the results of Garay and Perry, who proved tight bounds on the maximal number of actively and fail-corrupted players, the adversary's capability is characterized by a set $\mathcal{Z}$ of pairs (A, F) of subsets of P where the adversary may select an arbitrary such pair (A_i, F_i) from $\mathcal{Z}$ and corrupt the players in A_i actively and fail-corrupt the players in F_i.
For this model we prove that the exact condition on $\mathcal{Z}$ for which perfectly secure agreement and broadcast are achievable is that for no three pairs (A_i, F_i), (A_j, F_j), and (A_k, F_k) in $\mathcal{Z}$ we have $A_i \cup A_j \cup A_k \cup (F_i \cap F_j \cap F_k) = P$. Achievability is demonstrated by efficient protocols. Moreover, for a slightly stronger condition on $\mathcal{Z}$, which covers the previous mixed (active and fail-corruption) threshold condition and the previous purely-active non-threshold condition, we demonstrate agreement and broadcast protocols that are substantially more efficient than all previous protocols for these two settings.

Key words. Broadcast, Byzantine agreement, unconditional security, active adversary, fail-corruption.

1 Introduction

Byzantine agreement and broadcast are two closely related fundamental problems in distributed systems and cryptography, in particular in secure multi-party computation. In this paper we consider Byzantine agreement (and broadcast) protocols among a set of players in a standard model with a complete synchronous network of pairwise authenticated channels among the players.

1.1 Player Corruption

We demand the protocols to be perfectly secure (i.e. unconditionally secure with no probability of error) against an adversary that may corrupt players in two different ways:

---
* Research supported by the Swiss National Science Foundation (SNF), SPP project no. 5003-045293

Active corruption: The adversary takes full control over the corrupted players and makes them deviate from the protocol in an arbitrary way.

Fail-corruption: At an arbitrary time during the protocol, chosen by the adversary, the communication from and to the corrupted player is stopped.

The players that are fail-corrupted or uncorrupted are called *non-malicious* since they do not deviate from the protocol as long as they participate. A player is called *correct* if he is non-malicious and has not failed yet at the described point of time. Thus correctness describes a temporal property of the players and only a player that is correct at the end of the protocol is actually uncorrupted.

For a fail-corrupted player to *fail during some communication round* means that he is correct up to this point and, during this round, stops communicating with at least one correct player.[1] The player sends no messages during any subsequent round of the protocol.

1.2 Byzantine Agreement and Broadcast

A *Byzantine agreement* protocol is defined for a set of n players with every player initially holding an input value and finally deciding on an output value such that the following conditions are satisfied:

Agreement: All uncorrupted players decide on the same output value.

Validity: If all initially correct players hold the same input value v then all uncorrupted players decide on v.

Termination: For all non-malicious players the protocol terminates after a finite number of rounds.

In contrast to agreement, *broadcast* is defined with respect to one particular player called the dealer who initially inputs a value. Again, every player decides on some output value. For broadcast the former agreement and termination conditions are still required. The validity condition transforms into

Validity ': If the dealer is uncorrupted then all uncorrupted players decide on the dealer's input value.

Note that it suffices to focus on bit-agreement (or bit-broadcast) protocols where the domain of values is restricted to $\{0, 1\}$ since protocols for any finite domain with cardinality m can be easily obtained by applying $\lceil \log m \rceil$ bit-protocols in parallel. This does not change the round complexity and increases the communication complexity only by a factor $\lceil \log m \rceil$.

1.3 Previous Work

In the threshold model with an active adversary, Lamport, Shostak and Pease [PSL80,LSP82] proved that Byzantine agreement is achievable if and only

---

[1] Our model includes that in the round during which a player fails, some correct players may still receive a valid message by this player whereas others may not. Hence the correct players' views about which players have failed can be inconsistent, and this must be taken into account in the design and analysis of the protocols.

if less than one third of the players are actively corrupted ($t < n/3$). For this model numerous protocols with optimal resilience have been proposed in the literature [DFF+82,BDDS87,TPS87,FM88,BGP89,CW92,GM93], which all have communication and computation complexities polynomial in the number n of players. In the threshold model with an adversary that may only perform fail-corruptions, Lamport and Fischer [LF82] proved that agreement is achievable for any $t < n$.

These results have been unified in [GP92] for the threshold model where an adversary is considered who may corrupt arbitrary t players, but at most $b \leq t$ of them actively (the rest is only fail-corrupted). They proved that $t + 2b < n$ is a tight bound on agreement to be achievable and proposed protocols with optimal resilience and polynomial complexities.

In the more general context of secure multi-party computation, Hirt and Maurer [HM97] introduced the concept of a general adversary that is characterized by an adversary structure which is a set of subsets of the player set. The adversary may corrupt the players of exactly one of these subsets. For the same model, with respect to an active adversary, Fitzi and Maurer [FM98] proposed optimally resilient broadcast protocols with computation complexity polynomial in the size of the adversary structure and communication complexity polynomial in the number n of players.

1.4 Contributions

This paper unifies the models of [GP92] and [FM98] to the new model with a general adversary that may simultaneously corrupt some players actively and some other players to fail. For this model a tight condition on the adversary structure is proven for Byzantine agreement to be achievable. Efficient protocols are proposed for every structure that meets this condition. This condition for example guarantees that, quite surprisingly, agreement is possible among four players p_1, p_2, p_3, and p_4 if any player p_i is actively corrupted and all the remaining players except $p_{((i+1) \bmod 4)}$ are fail-corrupted.

Furthermore we present a protocol that, when restricting this model to the special cases of [GP92] and [FM98], is even more efficient than any protocol previously known for these special cases.

Although all these results (tight condition and protocols) are only presented for agreement they immediately hold for broadcast as well since, with only minor modifications, a broadcast protocol can be easily obtained from any agreement protocol and vice versa. Our proposed agreement protocols can even be turned into a broadcast protocol with no loss of efficiency.

1.5 Definitions and Notation

The *player set* is denoted by $P = \{p_1, \ldots, p_n\}$ and its *cardinality* by $n = |P|$. The adversary is defined by a *general adversary structure* $\mathcal{Z}$ which is a set of *classes* (A, F) with $A \subseteq P$ and $F \subseteq P$ where the players of exactly one class (A, F) may be corrupted — actively corrupted for the players in A and corrupted to fail for the players in F. Without loss of generality we demand $A \cap F = \emptyset$ since active corruption is strictly more general than fail-corruption.

A class (A', F') is *contained* in a class (A, F) (written $(A', F') \subseteq (A, F)$) if $A' \subseteq A$ and $F' \subseteq A \cup F$, and a class (A', F') is *strictly contained* in a class (A, F) if it is contained, and $A' \subset A$ or $F' \subset F$ (written $(A', F') \subset (A, F)$).

The adversary structure $\mathcal{Z}$ is defined to be *monotone* with respect to inclusion, i.e.,

$$(A, F) \in \mathcal{Z} \wedge (A', F') \subseteq (A, F) \Longrightarrow (A', F') \in \mathcal{Z}.$$

The *basis* $\overline{\mathcal{Z}}$ of an adversary structure $\mathcal{Z}$ is the set of all maximal elements of $\mathcal{Z}$

$$\overline{\mathcal{Z}} = \left\{ (A, F) \in \mathcal{Z} \mid \nexists (A', F') \in \mathcal{Z} : (A, F) \subset (A', F') \right\}.$$

A set A is called an *active set* of an adversary structure $\mathcal{Z}$ if $(A, \emptyset) \in \mathcal{Z}$. A set F is called a *fail set* of $\mathcal{Z}$ if $(\emptyset, F) \in \mathcal{Z}$. The set of all active sets of an adversary structure $\mathcal{Z}$ is denoted by $\mathcal{Z}_A$.

The following predicates $Q(P, \mathcal{Z})$ and $R(P, \mathcal{Z})$ on adversary structures $\mathcal{Z}$ with respect to a player set P will be needed later in this paper:

$$Q(P, \mathcal{Z}) := \forall (A_1, F_1), (A_2, F_2), (A_3, F_3) \in \mathcal{Z} : A_1 \cup A_2 \cup A_3 \cup F_1 \neq P.$$

$$R(P, \mathcal{Z}) := \forall (A_1, F_1), (A_2, F_2), (A_3, F_3) \in \mathcal{Z} : A_1 \cup A_2 \cup A_3 \cup (F_1 \cap F_2 \cap F_3) \neq P.$$

Note that $Q(P, \mathcal{Z})$ implies $R(P, \mathcal{Z})$ and that, because of symmetry, $Q(P, \mathcal{Z})$ is equivalent to $R(P, \mathcal{Z})$ in the threshold case.

2 Necessary Condition

Given the tight bound of $t + 2b < n$ for the threshold model[2] in [GP92] it might be obvious to conclude that $Q(P, \mathcal{Z})$ is a necessary condition for the general model, i.e., for any three classes in $\mathcal{Z}$ the union of all active sets with one of the fail sets must not cover the full player set P. However, as a consequence of the (generally) asymmetric properties of general adversary structures, agreement can still be achievable when this bound is violated since the failure of one particular player may rule out certain classes of the structure to be selected by the adversary. Thus only a weaker condition can be proven to be necessary which we prove to be tight in the next section: $R(P, \mathcal{Z})$, i.e., for any three classes in $\mathcal{Z}$ the union of all active sets with the intersection of all fail sets must not cover the full player set P.

Theorem 1. *For a set P of n players and any adversary structure $\mathcal{Z}$, $R(P, \mathcal{Z})$ is necessary for Byzantine agreement to be achievable.*

Proof. For the sake of contradiction suppose that there is an agreement protocol for some adversary structure $\mathcal{Z}$ violating $R(P, \mathcal{Z})$. Hence there are three classes $(A_1, F_1), (A_2, F_2), (A_3, F_3) \in \mathcal{Z}$ such that $A_1 \cup A_2 \cup A_3 \cup (F_1 \cap F_2 \cap F_3) = P$. Due to the monotonicity of the adversary structure we can assume without loss of generality that $F_1 = F_2 = F_3 =: F$ and that the sets A_1, A_2, A_3 and F are pairwise disjoint. One possible strategy for the adversary is to make all players

---

[2] i.e. three times the number of actively corrupted plus once the number of fail-corrupted players must be less than n

in F fail at the beginning of the protocol. Hence this protocol can be easily modified into a secure agreement protocol for the player set $P' = P \setminus F$ with respect to $\mathcal{Z}$ restricted to the players in P' since by assumption this protocol is correct even if no player in F ever sends any message. Since $A_1 \cup A_2 \cup A_3 = P'$ this contradicts the result of [PSL80,HM97] that agreement is impossible in this case.

3 Optimally Resilient Protocols

This section describes protocols for any player set P and adversary structure $\mathcal{Z}$ satisfying $R(P, \mathcal{Z})$.

3.1 Protocol Elements and Code Notation

The protocols are constructed basically along the lines of the protocols of [GP92] which are based on several subprotocols. The main idea of these subprotocols is that every player enters them with his *preferred* value he inclines to decide on and exits them with an updated (potentially different) preferred value such that the following two conditions are satisfied

Persistence: If all correct players enter the subprotocol with the same preferred value then, after the execution of the subprotocol, all correct players[3] still prefer this value. In other words, the subprotocol has no effect when agreement had previously been achieved.

Consistence: In any case (also if the correct players enter the subprotocol with distinct preferred values) the values preferred by the correct players at the end of the subprotocol are consistent (in a way to be defined separately for each particular subprotocol).

The effect of such subprotocols can be interpreted as getting the correct players closer to a state of agreement whereas, once achieved, agreement cannot be reversed anymore by the corrupted players. In this paper, often a weaker form of consistence is used that depends on whether some fail-corrupted (i.e. non-actively corrupted) player fails during the execution of the according subprotocol.

Conditional consistence: Consistence provided that no fail-corrupted player fails during the execution of the subprotocol in consideration.

All pseudo code descriptions of protocols are stated with respect to the local view of one particular player. The complete protocols consist of all players executing their local codes in parallel. Variables that have no subscript (e.g. v) are stated with respect to an arbitrary player and variables with a subscript p (e.g. v_p) denote the corresponding variable of the particular player p. For every player p, two global[4] variables are used throughout all subprotocols, v_p and L_p. v_p denotes the preferred value by player p. L_p is a set in which player p collects all players that he has detected to be corrupted (active or fail). L is initialized to the empty set and (for a correct player) will never contain any correct player.

---

[3] i.e. all players who are *still* correct — remember the temporal definition of correctness.

[4] with respect to p's scope

3.2 Value Unification

This section describes the crucial subprotocol of the agreement protocol: MakeUnique. It satisfies the persistence property according to Section 3.1 and conditional consistency in a way that at the end no two correct players prefer distinct values in $\{0, 1\}$ if no fail-corrupted player fails during the execution of the subprotocol. In order to achieve this the original bit domain is extended by an invalidity value 2. However, the preferred value v is still required to be in $\{0, 1\}$ *before* the execution of MakeUnique.

MakeUnique:

1. SendToAll(v);   // i.e. send v to every other player
2. $L := L \cup \{ r \in P \mid$ no value received from r or value outside $\{0, 1\} \}$;
3. $C^0 := \{ r \in P \mid r$ sent $0 \} \setminus L$;
4. $C^1 := \{ r \in P \mid r$ sent $1 \} \setminus L$;
5. if $(C^1, L) \in \mathcal{Z}$ then $v := 0$
6.   elseif $(C^0, L) \in \mathcal{Z}$ then $v := 1$
7.   else $v := 2$
8. fi;

If, at the end of MakeUnique, a player p holds some value $v_p \in \{0, 1\}$ we say that player p accepts value v_p. On the other hand $v_p = 2$ means that player p rejects any value from $\{0, 1\}$. More precisely, a correct player accepts a value $v \in \{0, 1\}$ exactly if, according to his view, agreement on v could have been achieved before the execution of MakeUnique. For $v \in \{0, 1\}$ we define $\bar{v}$ as $\bar{v} := 1 - v$.

Lemma 1 (Persistence of MakeUnique). *If all correct players initially hold the same value $v \in \{0, 1\}$, then after the execution of MakeUnique every correct player p holds the value $v_p = v$.*

Proof. Let p be a player who is correct at the end of MakeUnique. Since all correct players initially hold the same value v every such player either sends this value to p or fails during this communication round. Hence $\bar{v}$ will only be received from an actively corrupted player, and $(C_p^{\bar{v}}, L_p) \in \mathcal{Z}$ holds. Hence also $(C_p^v, L_p) \notin \mathcal{Z}$ must hold since otherwise $R(P, \mathcal{Z})$ would be violated (because $P = C_p^v \cup C_p^{\bar{v}} \cup (L_p \cap L_p)$). Thus $v_p = v$ after the execution of MakeUnique.

Lemma 2 (Conditional Consistency of MakeUnique). *If after the execution of MakeUnique, two correct players p and q hold values $v_p \neq 2$ and $v_q \neq 2$, respectively, then either $v_p = v_q$ or at least one fail-corrupted player failed during the execution of MakeUnique.*

Proof. Suppose for the sake of contradiction that no fail-corrupted player fails between sending his value to the players p and q and that $v_p = v$ and $v_q = \bar{v}$ for some $v \in \{0, 1\}$ and hence $(C_p^{\bar{v}}, L_p) \in \mathcal{Z}$ and $(C_q^v, L_q) \in \mathcal{Z}$. We have $P = C_p^{\bar{v}} \cup C_p^v \cup L_p$ and hence P can be decomposed as

$$C_p^{\bar{v}} \cup \underbrace{(C_p^v \cap C_q^v)}_{\subseteq C_q^v} \cup \underbrace{(C_p^v \setminus C_q^v) \cup (L_p \setminus L_q)}_{=:A} \cup (L_p \cap L_q) = P. \tag{1}$$

Since no fail-corrupted player failed during the execution of this protocol all players in $A = (C_p^v \setminus C_q^v) \cup (L_p \setminus L_q)$ must be actively corrupted and hence $(A, L_p \cap L_q) \in \mathcal{Z}$ must hold. Thus we have $(C_p^{\bar{v}}, L_p) \in \mathcal{Z}$, $(C_q^v, L_q) \in \mathcal{Z}$ and $(A, L_p \cap L_q) \in \mathcal{Z}$, and by Equation (1) $C_p^{\bar{v}} \cup C_q^v \cup A \cup (L_p \cap L_q) = P$, which contradicts $R(P, \mathcal{Z})$.

3.3 Agreement Protocol

The agreement protocol consists of a loop over a sequence of statements where one single iteration of the loop can be interpreted in the following way:

The players run the MakeUnique protocol in order to guarantee that no two correct players continue with distinct values in $\{0, 1\}$. In the next round all players report their (unified) values to every other player. Then every player accepts a value $v \in \{0, 1\}$ if, according to his view, at least one correct player reported on v — otherwise he rejects by setting $v := 2$. Finally some distinguished player, called the *king*, reports on his particular value v which is adopted exactly by those players who know that at least one correct player rejected after MakeUnique (which implies that agreement did not hold before this particular iteration of the loop).

Agreement(VAR v) (**Agreement Protocol 1**):
1. $L := \emptyset$;
2. for $i := 1$ to $\lceil \log n \rceil n$ do
3. $k := ((i - 1) \bmod n) + 1$;   // Assign king
4.   MakeUnique;   // Communication Phase 1
5.   SendToAll(v);   // Communication Phase 2
6. $L := L \cup \{ r \in P \mid$ no value received from r or value outside $\{0, 1, 2\} \}$;
7. $D^i := \{ r \in P \mid r$ sent $i \} \setminus L$ for $i \in \{0, 1, 2\}$;
8.   if $(D^0, L) \notin \mathcal{Z}$ then $v := 0$
9.   elseif $(D^1, L) \notin \mathcal{Z}$ then $v := 1$
10.   else $v := 2$
11.   fi;
12. p_k (only): SendToAll(v);   // Communication Phase 3
13. $w :=$ value received by p_k;   // if no value is received then set $w := 0$
14.   if $(D^2, L) \notin \mathcal{Z}$ then $v := \min(1, w)$ fi;
15. od;

Every single iteration of the for-loop can be seen as a subprotocol with persistence and conditional consistence properties according to Section 3.1. These properties are stated in the next lemmas.

Lemma 3 (Conditional Consistence). *At the end of any iteration of the for-loop with a correct king p_k during which no fail-corrupted player fails, every correct player p holds the same value $v_p = v$.*

Proof. Consider some k^{th} iteration of the for-loop with p_k being correct and during which no fail-corrupted player fails. If all correct players replace their values v by $\min(1, w)$, we are done since all correct players receive the same value w from player p_k.

Suppose now that at least one correct player p ignores the value sent by the king since $(D_p^2, L_p) \in \mathcal{Z}$ holds. Hence $v_p \neq 2$ since otherwise, according to the Lines 8 to 10 of the protocol, also $(D_p^0, L_p) \in \mathcal{Z}$ and $(D_p^1, L_p) \in \mathcal{Z}$ would hold in contradiction to $R(P, \mathcal{Z})$. Let $v := v_p$. $(D_p^v, L_p) \notin \mathcal{Z}$ ($v \neq 2$ and Lines 8 to 10) implies that at least one correct player sent v during Communication Phase 2 and, due to the (conditional) consistence of $\mathtt{MakeUnique}$, no correct player sent $\bar{v}$ during the same phase. Hence, for every correct player q, $D_q^{\bar{v}}$ can only contain actively corrupted players and hence $(D_q^{\bar{v}}, L_q) \in \mathcal{Z}$ holds.

Suppose, for the sake of contradiction, that there is a correct player q who enters Communication Phase 3 with a value $v_q \neq v$, i.e., $(D_q^v, L_q) \in \mathcal{Z}$. $P = D_p^{\bar{v}} \cup D_p^v \cup D_p^2 \cup L_p$ can be decomposed as

$$\underbrace{D_p^{\bar{v}} \cup (D_p^v \setminus D_q^v)}_{=:A_1} \cup \underbrace{(D_p^v \cap D_q^v)}_{\subseteq D_q^v} \cup D_p^2 \cup \underbrace{(L_p \setminus L_q)}_{=:A_2} \cup (L_p \cap L_q) = P.$$

All players in $A = A_1 \cup A_2$ are actively corrupted since they sent either $\bar{v}$ or distinct values to the players p and q or failed[5] in p's view but not in q's view. Hence $(A, L_p \cap L_q) \in \mathcal{Z}$ which leads to a contradiction with condition $R(P, \mathcal{Z})$ since together with $(D_p^2, L_p) \in \mathcal{Z}$ and $(D_q^v, L_q) \in \mathcal{Z}$ we have $D_p^2 \cup D_q^v \cup A \cup (L_p \cap L_q) = P$.

Thus every correct player q enters Communication Phase 3 with $(D_q^v, L_q) \notin \mathcal{Z}$ and hence $v_q = v = v_p$. Since especially the king p_k is correct every player who accepts p_k's value accepts $v_{p_k} = v = v_p$.

Lemma 4 (Persistence). *If at the beginning of any iteration of the for-loop every correct player p holds the same value $v_p = v \neq 2$, then every correct player holds v at the end of the iteration even if some fail-corrupted players fail.*

Proof. Due to the persistence property of $\mathtt{MakeUnique}$ (Lemma 1) every correct player p holds $v_p = v$ after $\mathtt{MakeUnique}$ and hence, after $\mathtt{SendToAll}$, $(D_q^{\bar{v}}, L_q) \in \mathcal{Z}$ and $(D_q^2, L_q) \in \mathcal{Z}$. Because of the condition $R(P, \mathcal{Z})$ also $(D_q^v, L_q) \notin \mathcal{Z}$ must hold. Thus every correct player p ignores the king in Communication Phase 3 and holds value $v_p = v$ at the end of the loop.

The following theorem together with Theorem 1 shows that the condition $R(P, \mathcal{Z})$ is tight:

Theorem 2. *For a set P of n players and an adversary structure $\mathcal{Z}$ perfectly secure Byzantine agreement is achievable if $R(P, \mathcal{Z})$ is satisfied. For every structure $\mathcal{Z}$ satisfying $R(P, \mathcal{Z})$ there is such a protocol with communication complexity polynomial in n and computation complexity polynomial in $|\overline{\mathcal{Z}}|$.*[6]

Proof. We first show by contradiction that, in Agreement Protocol 1, all uncorrupted players finally decide on the same value. Thus assume that two uncorrupted players decide on distinct values. Then, according to Lemma 3, there was

---

[5] note that we suppose no fail-corrupted player to fail during this loop

[6] Under the natural assumption that there exists an algorithm polynomial in n to decide whether a given class (A, F) is an element of the adversary structure $\mathcal{Z}$, the computation complexity is also polynomial in n.

no iteration of the for-loop with a correct king during which no fail-corrupted player failed. Let $C(0) = P$ and $C(i)$ denote the set of players that are still correct at the end of iteration i of the for-loop, and let $c(0) = n$ and $c(i) = |C(i)|$. We argue that during any n sequential iterations $i = j, \ldots, j + n - 1$ at least $c(j - 1)/2$ fail-corrupted players failed. The failure of one single fail-corrupted player can prevent agreement for at most two iterations with a king from the set $C(j - 1)$ — one correct king's iteration and his own one[7]. Hence at least half of the players in $C(j - 1)$ must have failed. Hence, for any l with $0 < l \leq \lceil \log n \rceil$, $c(ln) \leq c((l - 1)n)/2$ and $c(ln) \leq c(0)/2^l$, i.e. for $l = \lceil \log n \rceil$ (after the last iteration of the for-loop) we have

$$c(\lceil \log n \rceil n) \leq c(0)/2^{\lceil \log n \rceil} \leq c(0)/n = 1,$$

in contradiction to the fact that at least two players are uncorrupted and hence $c(\lceil \log n \rceil n) > 1$. Hence there is a first iteration of the for-loop with a correct king during which no fail-corrupted player fails. After this iteration agreement holds (Lemma 3) and due to Lemma 4 agreement holds also at the end of the protocol.

The validity and termination properties are obviously satisfied. The efficiency can be easily verified by code inspection.

4 Efficiency Improvements by Early Stopping

A major disadvantage of Agreement Protocol 1 of Section 3 is that the players must continue to iterate the for-loop even if agreement on some value has already been reached. The goal of this section is to derive a protocol that can be terminated as soon as agreement is achieved, i.e., a protocol that terminates early if only few players are corrupted. This is achieved by some modifications of Agreement Protocol 1.

However, a full description and correctness proof of our early stopping protocols for condition $R(P, \mathcal{Z})$ would exceed the limits of this extended abstract. Instead, we give an early stopping protocol with respect to the stronger condition $Q(P, \mathcal{Z})$ which can be handled more easily.[8] Moreover these protocols, when applied to the case of a mixed (active and fail-corruption) threshold adversary [GP92] or a purely-active non-threshold adversary [FM98], are even more efficient than any previously known protocols for these special cases.[9]

4.1 Protocol Modifications

As a consequence of the somewhat stronger condition $Q(P, \mathcal{Z})$ on P and $\mathcal{Z}$, explicit failure detection becomes unnecessary (i.e. L drops out of the algorithms). The main idea is to achieve the following property which is important for the correctness of the protocol:

---

[7] after he has already failed during the correct player's iteration

[8] Note that $Q(P, \mathcal{Z})$ still implies the achievability bounds for [GP92,FM98].

[9] in contrast to our early stopping protocols for $R(P, \mathcal{Z})$ (not described in this extended abstract), which are less efficient than those of [GP92] for their special model.

Stop-Implication: A correct player (only) stops early if it is guaranteed that every correct player already prefers the same value v and if it is guaranteed that even after his early stopping v is preferred by every correct player.

Since the Stop-Implication is a property of the final agreement protocol its correctness is proven only later, in the proof of Lemma 10. In order for the subprotocols to still satisfy the persistence property, even if correct players stop early, the following rule is introduced.

Substitution-Rule: Whenever, during any communication round, a player p expects a value x to be sent by a player q but does not receive any value, then x is set to the value x_p that has been sent by himself during the same communication round.[10]

This rule together with the Stop-Implication guarantees that, after a correct player p has stopped early, every correct player q replaces any future message by p correctly as if p would still participate in the protocol.[11]

4.2 Value Unification

Subprotocol `MakeUnique` of Section 3.2 can be simplified when condition $Q(P, \mathcal{Z})$ is satisfied. Since `MakeUnique` will be applied in two different contexts, we use the variable parameter x in the following pseudo-code description.

`MakeUnique(VAR x):`

1. `SendToAll(x)`;
2. $C^0 := \{ r \in P \mid r \text{ sent } 0 \}$;
3. $C^1 := \{ r \in P \mid r \text{ sent } 1 \}$;
4. if $C^1 \in \mathcal{Z}_A$ then $x := 0$
5. elseif $C^0 \in \mathcal{Z}_A$ then $x := 1$
6. else $x := 2$
7. fi;

It is easy to see that together with the Substitution Rule, persistence (according to Lemma 1) is still satisfied. In contrast to the conditional consistence in Lemma 2 even *unconditional* consistence can be proven.

Lemma 5 (Consistence of `MakeUnique`). *If, after the execution of* `MakeUnique`, *two correct players p and q hold values $v_p \neq 2$ and $v_q \neq 2$, then $v_p = v_q$.*

Proof. Let p and q be two correct players and, for the sake of contradiction, suppose that $v_p = v \neq 2$ and $v_q = 1 - v = \bar{v}$.

---

[10] This substitution value is well-defined since communication is symmetric in the sense that during any specific round all players report on their particular view of the same variable or fact. The only exception is the king's round wherein only the king sends his preferred value. In this case simply the own preferred value is taken.

[11] Whenever it is argued that every correct player behaves in a certain way, only players that have not stopped yet are considered.

Suppose that no correct player has stopped so far during the protocol and let A (and F) be the sets of players that are actively corrupted (and fail corrupted), and hence $C_p^{\bar{v}} \in \mathcal{Z}_A$, $C_q^v \in \mathcal{Z}_A$ and $(A, F) \in \mathcal{Z}$. Since a correct player sends the same value (in $\{0, 1\}$) to both players p and q we have $C_p^{\bar{v}} \cup C_q^v \cup A \cup F = P$ in contradiction to $Q(P, \mathcal{Z})$.

On the other hand, if any correct player has stopped the protocol before then, due to the Stop-Implication, the players p and q hold the same value $v_p = v_q$ after MakeUnique because of the persistence property.

4.3 Unicast

In order to enable a player to detect that all correct players prefer the same value (and even will after he stops), Communication Phase 2 of Agreement Protocol 1 is replaced by the more powerful primitive Unicast. Note that the for-loop can be parallelized into one communication round.

Unicast(VAR D^0, D^1, D^2):

1. SendToAll(v);
2. for $l := 1$ to n do
3. $\quad R^l :=$ value received from p_l;
4. $\quad S^l := \begin{cases} 0, \text{ if } R^l \in \{0, 1\} \\ 1, \text{ if } R^l = 2 \end{cases}$
5. $\quad$ MakeUnique(S^l);
6. od;
7. $D^0 := \{ p_l \in P \mid R^l = 0 \wedge S^l = 0 \}$;
8. $D^1 := \{ p_l \in P \mid R^l = 1 \wedge S^l = 0 \}$;
9. $D^2 := \{ p_l \in P \mid R^l = 2 \wedge S^l = 1 \}$;
10. if $D^0 \notin \mathcal{Z}_A$ then $v := 0$
11. $\quad$ elseif $D^1 \notin \mathcal{Z}_A$ then $v := 1$
12. $\quad$ else $v := 2$
13. fi;

We say that player p accepts value $v \in \{0, 1, 2\}$ from player q or, as a short hand, that p accepts $\langle v, q \rangle$ if $q \in D_p^v$. The following lemma follows directly from the consistence and persistence properties of MakeUnique.

Lemma 6 (Consistence of Unicast). *The value v sent by a correct player p is accepted by every correct player q, i.e., $p \in D_q^v$. Moreover, if a correct player p accepts $\langle v, r \rangle$ for $v \in \{0, 1\}$ and $r \in P$, then no correct player q accepts $\langle 2, r \rangle$, i.e., $D_q^2 \subseteq (P \setminus D_p^v)$ for any two correct players p and q.*

Lemma 7 (Persistence of Unicast). *If all correct players prefer the same value $v \in \{0, 1\}$ before the execution of Unicast then all players from which a correct player p does **not** accept v are actively corrupted. In particular $(P \setminus D_p^v) \in \mathcal{Z}_A$ (and hence $D_p^2 \in \mathcal{Z}_A$), and $v_p = v$ at the end of Unicast.*

Proof. According to Lemma 6 the value of every correct player is accepted. It remains to show that even a value is accepted from every fail-corrupted player p_i: A correct player either does not receive a value from p_i during SendToAll and hence replaces this value by v or he still receives a value from p_i but then this value must be v since p_i was correct until the execution of Unicast and therefore preferred v by assumption. Hence $S^i \equiv 0$ for all correct players which persists after MakeUnique according to the persistence property.

4.4 Agreement Protocol

Agreement(VAR v) (Agreement Protocol 2):

```
1. for k := 1 to n do
2.     MakeUnique(v);                 // Communication Phase 1
3.     Unicast(D⁰,D¹,D²);             // Communication Phase 2
4.     pₖ (only): SendToAll(v);       // Communication Phase 3
5.     w := value received from pₖ;
6.     if (v = 2 ∨ D² ∉ Z_A) then v := min(1, w)
7.        elseif (v ≠ 2 ∧ P \ Dᵛ ∈ Z_A) then stop
8.     fi;
9. od;
```

Persistence and consistence can be proven in a similar way as for Agreement Protocol 1 of Section 3. Moreover even *unconditional consistence* can be proven.

Lemma 8 (Persistence). *If, at the beginning of some for-loop, all correct players prefer the same value $v \neq 2$ then they still do so at the end of the loop.*

Proof. According to the persistence of MakeUnique and Unicast $D_p^v \notin \mathcal{Z}_A$, $D_p^{\bar{v}} \in \mathcal{Z}_A$ and $D_p^2 \in \mathcal{Z}_A$ are satisfied for every correct player p and hence $v_p = v$ and the king's value is ignored by p.

The following two lemmas (Lemma 9 and 10) are needed for the proof of the consistence property of Agreement Protocol 2. Lemma 10 assures that the Stop-Implication indeed holds — a fact which also the previous proofs for MakeUnique and Unicast rely on.

Lemma 9. *If a correct player p ignores the king's value according to Line 6 of the protocol, then every correct player prefers the same value v_p before Communication Phase 3.*

Proof. Suppose that p ignores the king since $v_p = v \neq 2$ (and hence $D_p^v \notin \mathcal{Z}_A$) and $D_p^2 \in \mathcal{Z}_A$ hold. $D_p^v \notin \mathcal{Z}_A$ implies that at least one correct player entered Unicast with value v and hence every correct player entered Unicast with value v or 2.

For the sake of contradiction suppose that some correct player q enters this phase with some value $v_q \neq v$. Due to Lemma 6 all values by correct players are accepted. Hence, for some set A of actively corrupted players and some set F of fail-corrupted players, we can write the player set as $P = D_p^{\bar{v}} \cup D_p^v \cup D_p^2 \cup A \cup F$ which can be decomposed as

$$\underbrace{D_p^{\bar{v}}}_{=A_1} \cup \underbrace{(D_p^v \setminus D_q^v)}_{=A_2 \cup F_2} \cup \underbrace{(D_p^v \cap D_q^v)}_{\subseteq D_q^v} \cup D_p^2 \cup A \cup F = P$$

where $A_1 \cup A_2 \subseteq A$ and $F_2 \subseteq F$. Hence we get $D_p^2 \in \mathcal{Z}_A$ (since p ignores the king), $D_q^v \in \mathcal{Z}_A$ (since $v_q \neq v$) and $(A, F) \in \mathcal{Z}$ in contradiction to $Q(P, \mathcal{Z})$.

Lemma 10 (Stop-Implication). *If a correct player stops early then every correct player already prefers the same value v and will do so during every subsequent communication round.*

Proof. Consider the first iteration of the for-loop in which some correct players stop. Let p be such a player and $v = v_p \neq 2$ be his preferred value. Player p's stopping implies that the king's value is ignored by p and hence every correct player q prefers the same value $v_q = v$ by Lemma 9. Due to Lemma 6, $D_q^2 \subseteq P \setminus D_p^v$ holds and since $P \setminus D_p^v \in \mathcal{Z}_A$ by the stop condition for player p we immediately get $D_q^2 \in \mathcal{Z}_A$. Hence every correct player q ignores the king's value and $v_p = v_q = v$ at the end of the loop. By Lemma 8 agreement on this value persists for every further communication round.

Lemma 11 (Consistence). *At the end of any for-loop with a correct king all correct players prefer the same value.*

Proof. If any correct player has stopped so far then consistence follows by the Lemmas 8 and 10. Hence suppose that no correct player has stopped so far, and suppose some k^{th} iteration of the for-loop with p_k being correct. If all correct players replace their values $v := \min(1, w)$ we are done. Suppose now that at least one correct player p ignores the value sent by the king. Hence, by Lemma 9, every correct player prefers the same value v_p before Communication Phase 3. Hence especially the king prefers v_p and every correct player who replaces his value replaces it with v_p.

Lemma 12. *Let C be the set of players that are actively or fail-corrupted. Agreement Protocol 2 achieves agreement and all correct players terminate the protocol after at most $|C| + 2$ iterations of the for-loop.*

Proof. That Agreement Protocol 2 achieves agreement follows immediately by the Lemmas 8 and 11, and the fact that there is at least one iteration of the for-loop with a correct king. It remains to show that, at the end of the first loop which is entered by all correct players with the same value $v \neq 2$, all correct players have stopped with value v. Suppose that all correct players enter some loop with the same value v. Due to the persistence property of `MakeUnique` they also enter `Unicast` with this value and hence, due to Lemma 7, they still hold this value after `Unicast` and $P \setminus D^v \in \mathcal{Z}_A$. Hence every correct player stops according to Line 7 of the protocol.

4.5 Optimizations

Agreement Protocol 2 can be optimized in the following ways.

I. Depending on the concrete adversary structure $\mathcal{Z}$ the for-loop does not necessarily have to run over all n possible kings since it is only required that at least one of the kings be correct.

II. Every correct player may stop the protocol immediately after the loop in which he plays the king because all correct players will start the next loop with his value.

III. In order to save one communication round in each loop, Communication Phase 3 (i.e. king's value distribution) can be integrated into Unicast by the king already computing his distribution value in advance after the SendToAll round of Unicast:

1. $\widetilde{D}^i := \{ p_l \in P \mid R^l = i \}$ for $i \in \{0, 1, 2\}$;

2. $\widetilde{v} := \begin{cases} 0, \text{ if } \widetilde{D}^0 \notin \mathcal{Z}_A \\ 1, \text{ if } \widetilde{D}^1 \notin \mathcal{Z}_A \\ 2, \text{ else.} \end{cases}$

This value $\widetilde{v}$ can be sent by the king p_k already during the MakeUnique round of Unicast without harming the protocol's correctness. In order to see this suppose the king to be correct.

- If all correct players consider the king then they all prefer the same value at the end of this loop. The king is only considered if agreement did not hold at the beginning of the loop and hence it does not matter which value is sent by the king.
- If at least one correct player ignores the king then for some $v \in \{0, 1\}$ $D_p^v \notin \mathcal{Z}_A$ holds for every correct player p by Lemma 9. But since $D_{p_k}^v \subseteq \widetilde{D}_{p_k}^v$ this is the value $\widetilde{v} = v$ that is sent by p_k.

Theorem 3. *For any player set P and adversary structure $\mathcal{Z}$ satisfying $Q(P, \mathcal{Z})$, Agreement Protocol 2 (by including the optimizations of this section) reaches agreement. Let C be the set of players that actually misbehave in the protocol (by failing or sending false values), then all correct players terminate the protocol after at most $3(|C| + 2)$ communication rounds.*

Proof. The theorem follows by Lemma 12 and Optimization III of this section.

4.6 Comparison with Previous Results

Agreement Protocol 2 (with optimizations) can be applied to the threshold model in [GP92] as well as to the general active adversary model in [FM98].

The protocols of [GP92] for the threshold model with actively and fail-corrupted players involve $5(t + 1)$ communication rounds in the worst case. Provided that only some $c \leq b$ players are actually corrupted, then only $5(c + 2)$ communication rounds are needed (whereas early stopping is not proven for $b < c < t$). Our improvement of these protocols is two-fold. First, the worst case round complexity is only $3(t + 1)$. Second, we achieve early stopping independently of any additional constraint on the number c of actually corrupted players, i.e., provided that some $c < t$ players are actually corrupted, the round complexity is at most $3(c + 2)$.

In the general adversary model of [FM98] with only active player corruption the tight bound for broadcast and agreement to be achievable is that no three adversary sets $A_i \in \mathcal{Z}_A$ ($i \in \{1, 2, 3\}$) cover the player set P. This implies that there is at least one player set $S \notin \mathcal{Z}_A$ of cardinality $|S| \leq \lceil \frac{n}{3} \rceil$ since otherwise this condition would be violated. According to Optimization I, it therefore suffices to define the for-loop over the set S since this set contains at least one correct player. Hence Agreement Protocol 2 involves at most $3 \lceil \frac{n}{3} \rceil \leq n + 2$ communication rounds. Provided that c players are actually corrupted then only

$\min(3(c+2), 3\lceil\frac{n}{3}\rceil)$ communication rounds are needed. In contrast to these results the protocols of [FM98] need $2n$ communication rounds in order to achieve polynomial communication complexity.

5 Acknowledgments

The authors would like to thank Ronald Cramer, Juan Garay and Martin Hirt for helpful comments and interesting discussions.

References

[BDDS87] A. Bar-Noy, D. Dolev, C. Dwork, and H. R. Strong. Shifting gears: Changing algorithms on the fly to expedite Byzantine agreement. In *Proceedings of the Sixth Annual ACM Symposium on Principles of Distributed Computing*, pp. 42–51, Vancouver, British Columbia, Canada, 10–12 Aug. 1987.

[BGP89] P. Berman, J. A. Garay, and K. J. Perry. Towards optimal distributed consensus (extended abstract). In *30th Annual Symposium on Foundations of Computer Science*, pp. 410–415, Research Triangle Park, North Carolina, 30 Oct.–1 Nov. 1989. IEEE.

[CW92] B. A. Coan and J. L. Welch. Modular construction of a Byzantine agreement protocol with optimal message bit complexity. *Information and Computation*, 97(1):61–85, Mar. 1992.

[DFF+82] D. Dolev, M. J. Fischer, R. Fowler, N. A. Lynch, and H. R. Strong. An efficient algorithm for Byzantine agreement without authentication. *Information and Control*, 52(3):257–274, Mar. 1982.

[FM88] P. Feldman and S. Micali. Optimal algorithms for Byzantine agreement. In *Proc. 20th ACM Symposium on the Theory of Computing (STOC)*, pp. 148–161, 1988.

[FM98] M. Fitzi and U. Maurer. Efficient Byzantine agreement secure against general adversaries. In *Distributed Computing — DISC*, volume 1499, pp. 134–148, 1998.

[GM93] J. A. Garay and Y. Moses. Fully polynomial Byzantine agreement in $t+1$ rounds (extended abstract). In *Proceedings of the Twenty-Fifth Annual ACM Symposium on Theory of Computing*, pp. 31–41, San Diego, California, 16–18 May 1993.

[GP92] J. A. Garay and K. J. Perry. A continuum of failure models for distributed computing. In A. Segall and S. Zaks, editors, *Distributed Algorithms, 6th International Workshop, WDAG '92*, volume 647 of *Lecture Notes in Computer Science*, pp. 153–165, Haifa, Israel, 2–4 Nov. 1992. Springer.

[HM97] M. Hirt and U. Maurer. Complete characterization of adversaries tolerable in secure multi-party computation. In *Proc. 16th ACM Symposium on Principles of Distributed Computing (PODC)*, pp. 25–34, Aug. 1997.

[LF82] L. Lamport and M. J. Fischer. Byzantine generals and transaction commit protocols. Technical report, SRI International (Menlo Park CA), TR, 1982.

[LSP82] L. Lamport, R. Shostak, and M. Pease. The Byzantine generals problem. *ACM Transactions on Programming Languages and Systems*, 4(3):382–401, July 1982.

[PSL80] M. Pease, R. Shostak, and L. Lamport. Reaching agreement in the presence of faults. *Journal of the ACM*, 27(2):228–234, Apr. 1980.

[TPS87] S. Toueg, K. J. Perry, and T. K. Srikanth. Fast distributed agreement. *SIAM Journal on Computing*, 16(3):445–457, June 1987.

Randomness Recycling in Constant-Round Private Computations

(EXTENDED ABSTRACT)

Carlo Blundo, Clemente Galdi, and Pino Persiano

Dipartimento di Informatica ed Applicazioni
Università di Salerno, 84081 Baronissi (SA), Italy
E-mail:{carblu, clegal, giuper}@dia.unisa.it

Abstract. In this paper we study the randomness complexity needed to distributively perform k XOR computation in a t-private way using constant-round protocols.

We show that cover-free families allow the recycling of random bits for constant-round private protocols. More precisely, we show that after an 1-round initialization phase during which random bits are distributed among the players, it is possible to perform each of k XOR computations using 2-rounds of communication. In each phase the random bits are used according to a cover-free family and this allows to use each random bit for more than one computation.

For $t = 2$, we design a protocol that uses $O(n \log k)$ random bits instead of $O(nk)$ bits if no recycling is performed. More generally, if $t > 1$ then $O(kt^2 \log n)$ random bits are sufficient to accomplish this task, for $t = O(n^{1/2-\epsilon})$ for constant $\epsilon > 0$.

1 Introduction

Consider a set of n players $\mathcal{P} = \{P_1, \ldots, P_n\}$, each possessing a private input x_i, who wish to compute a certain function f of these variables. A *private* protocol allows the players to distributively compute the value of the function $f(x_1, \ldots, x_n)$, in such a way that at the end of the protocol each player knows the value of the function but no player has information about the other players' input more than what can be inferred from its own input and from the value of the function. Obviously some players can collude together in order to infer information about other players' inputs. A protocol is said to be t-private if any coalition consisting of at most t-players cannot learn additional information from the protocol execution.

This problem has been widely studied in the last years and several information theoretic and computationally secure protocols have been proposed ([1, 4, 6, 7, 12, 14]) and relations among the basic ingredients of private multiparty computation have been established ([5, 8, 11]). It is well known that randomness is an essential resource for private protocols and this has motivated the quantitative study of randomness in the context of private protocols. In [5], lower bounds on the amount of randomness for t-private protocols have been given. Moreover, the efficiency of a distributed protocol critically depends on the number of rounds of communication needed for its execution. Surprisingly, most of the work done in this field actually focused on minimizing the randomness and the message complexity of the protocols, designing algorithms that run in a number of rounds that depends on the number of players n or on the security threshold t. For example [11] show how to use small sample spaces to reduce the number of random bits in private computations. However, the algorithm proposed requires a non-constant number of rounds of communication. Some of the papers exploring the case of constant round private protocols are [3, 2]. In [3] constant round protocols are shown for the case of computational privacy. In [2] the authors show that for any boolean function f, there exists an information-theoretic t-private protocol that runs in constant number of rounds using $\Omega(tn \log n)$ random bits. Notice that to run k different computations of the function f, $\Omega(ktn \log n)$ random bits are needed as opposed to $O(kt^2 \log n)$ random bits used by our protocol (see below). In [13], it is shown that it is possible to recycle the random bits used for a 1-private XOR computation to perform $O(n)$ 1-private XOR computations.

In this paper, we show that recycling random bits in constant round private computation is possible not only for the case of minimal privacy but even when the more stringent requirement of t-privacy is imposed. Our proposed protocols consist of $k + 1$ phases: An initialization phase in which some of the players pick random bits and distribute them to all the other players and k computation phases. During the i-th computation phase, each player sends a single *one bit message* to a designated player for phase i that will then compute and announce the result of the computation. The choice of the random bits to use is based on the construction of families of subsets with the "cover-freeness" properties.

For sake of ease of presentation, we start by describing a simple 2-private k-phase 2-round protocol that uses $O(n\sqrt{n})$ random bits and 2 rounds of communication per phase. We will then show how to improve the randomness complexity of this protocol achieving a $O(n \log k)$. We show further how to use the random bits generated during the initialization phase according to a cover free family and present a t-private protocol that uses $O(kt^2 \log n)$ random bits and still runs in 2-round per phase.

2 Preliminaries

Let $\mathcal{P} = \{P_1, \ldots, P_n\}$ denote the set of players. Each P_i holds a vector of k private inputs $\boldsymbol{x}_i = (x_i^1, \ldots, x_i^k) \in \{0, 1\}^k$. The players are connected by means of a complete network of private channels; these are channels in which only the sender can write and only the receiver can read the transmitted message. The player have unbounded computational resources and, they are honest, i.e., they follow the protocol, but curious in sense that at the end of the protocol some of them can collude together to infer information about the private input of other players.

The players wish to compute the k sums[1] of their inputs, i.e.,

$$\operatorname{xor}(x_1^1, \ldots, x_n^1); \operatorname{xor}(x_1^2, \ldots, x_n^2); \ldots; \operatorname{xor}(x_1^k, \ldots, x_n^k).$$

Notations. We denote random variables by capital letters, any value that a random variable can take by the corresponding lower letter and use the writing $\boldsymbol{x}$ to denote a vector.

We denote by $\boldsymbol{x}^j = (x_1^j, \ldots, x_n^j) \in \{0, 1\}^n$, the vector of inputs for phase j, $\boldsymbol{x} = (\boldsymbol{x}^1, \ldots, \boldsymbol{x}^k) \in \{0, 1\}^{kn}$, the vector of all the inputs. Moreover, let us denote by $\boldsymbol{f}^{(k)}(\boldsymbol{x}) = (f(\boldsymbol{x}^1), \ldots, f(\boldsymbol{x}^k))$, the vector of the value of the function in all the phases, $\boldsymbol{C}_i^j$ the random variable describing the communication string seen by P_i during the phase j (including incoming and outgoing messages), and by $\boldsymbol{C}_i$ the communication seen during the execution of all the phases of the protocol. Similarly denote by $\boldsymbol{C}_S^j$ (resp., $\boldsymbol{C}_S$) the communication string seen by a subset S of players during the phase j (resp., the entire execution) of the protocol. Moreover we denote by $\boldsymbol{R}_i$ (resp., $\boldsymbol{R}_S$) be the random bits received (or distributed) by P_i (resp., players in S) during the entire execution of the protocol.

Definition 1 (Privacy). *A k-phase n-player protocol for computing a function f is t-private if for any subset $S \subseteq \mathcal{P}$ of at most t players, for any input vectors $\boldsymbol{x}, \boldsymbol{y}$ such that $\boldsymbol{f}^{(k)}(\boldsymbol{x}) = \boldsymbol{f}^{(k)}(\boldsymbol{y})$ and such that $\boldsymbol{x}_i = \boldsymbol{y}_i$ for each $i \in S$, for any communication string c and for any random string r_S,*

$$Pr\left[C_S = c | R = r_S, X = x\right] = Pr\left[C_S = c | R = r_S, X = y\right]$$

where the distribution probability is taken on the random string of the other players.

---

[1] All the summation in this work are intended to be bitwise xor.

Definition 2. *A d-random protocol is a protocol such that, for every input assignment x, the total number of random coins tossed by all the players in every execution is at most d.*

In a distributed protocol, a *round* could be defined as the sequence: The players receive messages, execute some local computation, send some messages.

Definition 3. *A k-phase r-round protocol is a protocol such that, for every input assignment x and for any sequence of random coins tossed by the players, the number of rounds to compute the value of some function f in each phase is at most r.*

Let a and b be two l-dimensional vector on some finite field, we will denote by $a \cdot b = \sum_{i=1}^{l} a_i b_i$ the inner product of the two vectors.

A 0-1 vector v of length l can be thought of as the characteristic vector of an ordered set $\langle P_1, \ldots, P_l \rangle$. With a slight abuse of notation, we say that $P_i \in v$ iff the i-th component in v is equal to 1.

3   The Protocols

In this section we start by describing the protocol for $t = 2$ and then we present the general protocol for $t > 1$.

3.1   A 2-Private $O(n)$-Phase 2-Round Protocol

In this section, we present a simple protocol consisting of a 1-round initialization phase and k 2-round computation phases to perform $k = O(n)$ XOR evaluations. The protocol uses $O(n\sqrt{n})$ random bits improving on the protocol that uses $O(n^2)$ random bits, $O(1)$-rounds of communication, and consists of k independent executions of the protocol for computing the XOR.

Although, we will later show a more efficient 2-private protocol that uses $O(n \log n)$ random bits and then a protocol for the case $t > 2$. The protocol we present in this section contains all the main ideas of the more complex protocols in a crisp and compact way.

The n players $P_1, \ldots, P_n$ are partitioned into $k = O(n)$ *collecting* players $P_1, \ldots, P_k$, $d = \Theta(\sqrt{n})$ *distributing* players $P_{k+1}, \ldots, P_{k+d}$, and $n - d - k$ *regular* players. The distributing players are the only players that have random bits. Each of them, during the initialization phase, gives one bit to each other player (regular, collecting or distributing) and thus each player receives exactly d random bits. Each computation is associated with one collecting player with each collecting player serving for exactly one phase.

Each player computes $k = d(d - 1)/2$ bits, $b_i^{(1)}, b_i^{(2)}, \ldots, b_i^{(k)}$, by performing the xor of each possible pair of the random bits received during the initialization phase. We also assume that the players have agreed upon a standard enumeration of the pairs of random bits so that the j-th bits constructed by the players are the xor of the random bits generated by the same two distributing players. Phase j is thus associated to two distributing players and one collecting player which we call the phase-managers.

Phase j can be described as follows: Each player P_i, excluding the managers, computes $x_i^{(j)} + b_i^{(j)}$, i.e., the xor of his input for the j-th phase, $x_i^{(j)}$, and the random bit for this phase and sends the result to the collecting player. Each of the two distributing players P_i of the phase compute the xor of his input, the bit $b_i^{(j)}$, and all the random bits they have sent to the players during the initialization phase. The collecting player compute the xor of all the messages received with his input and the bit $b_j^{(j)}$ computed and announces the result to the other players.

A more formal description of the protocol is found in Figure 1. It is easy to see that the result is correct since all the random bits cancel out when the messages received by the collecting player are summed up.

The 2-privacy of the protocol derives from the following easy observations.

- Each coalition that does not include any collecting player has no information on the inputs of the other players;
- Each coalition consisting of two collecting players has no information on the inputs of the other players. Indeed, the messages of each player at two different phases have been masked with different pairs of random bits;
- Each coalition of one collecting and one distributing player does not get information on the inputs of the other players since at each phase the inputs of the player have been masked using random bits generated by two different distributing players.

We stress that each collecting player collects messages at most once during the entire execution. This is because if a player works as collector during two different phases then he could cancel out by himself the random bits used in both phases by simply xoring the messages received by

---

Protocol XOR(n,k)

Initialization Phase

0. Choose d such that $\binom{d}{2} \geq k$.
1. Each distributing player $P_{k+i}, i = 1, 2, \ldots, d$, generates uniformly and independently n random bits, $r_1^{(i)} \ldots r_n^{(i)}$, and sends $r_j^{(i)}$ to player P_j.
2. Denote by $r_i = (r_i^{(1)}, \ldots, r_i^{(d)})$ the vector of random bits received by P_i.
3. Each player computes the sequence $\mathcal{F} = \{v_1, \ldots, v_k\}$ of characteristic vectors of all the subsets of two elements on $\{1, 2, \ldots, d\}$ according to a standard enumeration of pairs.

Phase j=1,2,...,k

1. Each distributing player $P_i \in v_j$ computes $m_i^{(j)} = x_i^{(j)} + r_i \cdot v_j^T + \sum_{s=1}^n r_s^{(i)}$
2. Each distributing player $P_i \notin v_j$ computes: $m_i^{(j)} = x_i^{(j)} + r_i \cdot v_j^T$
3. Each collecting or regular player P_i sends $m_i^{(j)}$ to P_j.
4. P_j computes the sum of the messages received and announces the result.

Fig. 1. A simple 2-private k-phase 2-round protocol.

each single player. Since it holds that the sets of distributing players and collecting players are disjoint, the number, n, of players involved in the execution must be at least $k + d$.

Theorem 1. *Protocol $XOR(n, k)$ is a 2-private k-phase 2-round $O(n\sqrt{n})$-random n-player protocol to compute the XOR function, for any $k < n - O(\sqrt{n})$.*

Proof. The correctness can be derived as follows. During phase j, collecting player P_j computes:

$$\sum_{i=1}^n m_i^{(j)} = \sum_{i \in v_j} (x_i^{(j)} + r_i \cdot v_j^T + \sum_{s=1}^n r_s^{(i)}) + \sum_{i \in \mathcal{P} \setminus v_j} (x_i^{(j)} + r_i \cdot v_j^T)$$

$$= \sum_{i=1}^n x_i^{(j)} + \sum_{i=1}^n r_i \cdot v_j^T + \sum_{i \in v_j} \sum_{i=1}^n r_i^{(s)}$$

$$= \sum_{i=1}^n x_i^{(j)} + \sum_{i=1}^n r_i \cdot v_j^T + \sum_{i=1}^n \sum_{i \in v_j} r_i^{(s)}$$

$$= \sum_{i=1}^n x_i^{(j)} + \sum_{i=1}^n r_i \cdot v_j^T + \sum_{i=1}^n r_i \cdot v_j^T$$

$$= \sum_{i=1}^{n} x_i^{(j)}$$

Let us consider the privacy condition. We will first consider the coalition S composed of two collecting players $\{i_1, i_2\}$ and then we will extend the proof to a coalition composed by a collecting player and another player (regular or distributing) and, by what has been claimed above, this will conclude the proof.

W.l.o.g., let $S = \{1, 2\}$. Let x, y be two vectors such that $f^{(k)}(x) = f^{(k)}(y)$ and $x_i = y_i$ for each $i \in \{1, 2\}$, let $r_S = (r_1^{(1)}, \ldots, r_1^{(d)}, r_2^{(1)}, \ldots, r_2^{(d)})$ be the random string assigned to players in S, let $B_1 = (M_1^3, \ldots, M_1^k)$, $B_2 = (M_2^3, \ldots, M_2^k)$ and let $F^{(k)}$ be the random variable describing the values of the function. The communication string seen by the coalition is a sequence $C_S = (M_1^1, \ldots, M_n^1, M_1^2, \ldots, M_n^2, B_1, B_2, F^{(k)})$ of $2n + 2(n-2) + k$ messages, i.e., the messages received by the players in the coalition during phases 1 and 2, the massages sent by these players during the remaining phases and the values of the function during the entire protocol. Fix an arbitrary communication string $c = (c_1^1, \ldots, c_n^1, c_1^2, \ldots, c_n^2, b_1, b_2, f)$. Let $C_S^m = (M_1^1, \ldots, M_n^1, M_1^2, \ldots, M_n^2, B_1, B_2)$ (resp. $c_S^m = (c_1^1, \ldots, c_n^1, c_1^2, \ldots, c_n^2, b_1, b_2)$), i.e., the communication seen be the coalition excluding the values of the function, then

$$
\begin{aligned}
Pr[C_S = c | X = x, R_S = r_S] &= Pr[C_S^m = c_S^m, F^{(k)} = f | X = x, R_S = r_S] \\
&= Pr[F^{(k)} = f | X = x, R_S = r_S, C_S^m = c_S^m] \quad (1) \\
&\quad Pr[C_S^m = c_S^m | X = x, R_S = r_S]. \quad (2)
\end{aligned}
$$

Let us consider separately the two factors: Since $f^{(k)}(x) = f^{(k)}(y)$, the factor (1) is equal to

$$Pr[F^{(k)} = f | X = y, R_S = r_S, C_S^m = c_S^m]. \quad (3)$$

On the other hand, (2) can be rewritten as:

$$
\begin{aligned}
Pr[C_S^m = c_S^m | X = x, R_S = r_S] &= \\
&= Pr[M_1^1 = c_1^1, \ldots, M_n^1 = c_n^1, M_1^2 = c_1^2, \ldots, M_n^2 = c_n^2, \\
&\quad B_1 = b_1, B_2 = b_2, | X = x, R_S = r_S] \\
&= \Pi_{i=1}^2 Pr[M_i^1 = c_i^1, M_i^2 = c_i^2, B_i = b_i | X = x, R_S = r_S] \cdot \quad (4) \\
&\quad \Pi_{i=3}^n Pr[M_i^1 = c_i^1, M_i^2 = c_i^2 | X = x]. \quad (5)
\end{aligned}
$$

This is because the messages sent by different players are independent since their inputs and the random bits they receive are independent and the messages sent by the players in $\mathcal{P} \setminus S$ are independent from the random bits received by the players in S.

By hypothesis, $x_i = y_i$ for each $i \in S$, hence we compute (4) as

$$\Pi_{i=1}^2 Pr[M_i^1 = c_i^1, M_i^2 = c_i^2, B_i = b_i | X = y, R = r_S]. \qquad (6)$$

For (5) recall that each message is the xor of the input and two random bits. Fix one player $P_i \in \mathcal{P} \setminus S$. The messages that P_i sends to P_1 and P_2 are $m_i^{(1)} = x_i^{(1)} + r_1 + r_2$ and $m_i^{(2)} = x_i^{(2)} + r_3 + r_4$, with r_1, r_2, r_3, r_4 taken among the random bits P_i has received during the initialization phase.

As v_1, v_2 are two (distinct) 2-subsets of $\{1, \ldots, d\}$, the set with characteristic vector v_1 is not a proper subset of v_2 and vice versa. This implies that in $\{r_1, r_2\}$ there is at least one element that does not belong to $\{r_3, r_4\}$ and vice versa. As a worst case example, suppose that r_2 and r_4 are the *same* element. This means that $M_i^{(1)} = X_i^{(1)} + R_1 + R_2$ and $M_i^{(2)} = X_i^{(2)} + R_2 + R_3$.

If we fix the value of these messages to be m_1, m_2, for each possible input sequence $X_i^{(1)} = x_i^{(1)}, X_i^{(2)} = x_i^{(2)}$, P_i can, starting from his inputs along with the value of $R_2 = r_2$, construct the messages m_1, m_2 by properly choosing the random bits r_1, r_3. In other words the messages sent by the players in $\mathcal{P} \setminus S$ to the ones in S are independent on the particular value of the inputs so we can write the following:

$$\Pi_{i=3}^n Pr[M_i^1 = c_i^1, M_i^2 = c_i^2 | X = x] = \Pi_{i=3}^n Pr[M_i^1 = c_i^1, M_i^2 = c_i^2 | X = y]. \qquad (7)$$

By grouping together (3),(6) and (7) we have:

$$Pr[C_S = c | x, r_S] = Pr[C_S = c | y, r_S].$$

To conclude, we have to prove the that theorem holds for a coalition composed by a collecting player, w.l.o.g. P_1 and another non-collecting player P_j. Here we have two possible cases: Either P_j is a regular player or P_j is a distributing one. It suffices to notice that in both these cases P_j does not receive any message, thus the only messages the coalition can use are the ones received by P_i, i.e., $X_i^{(1)} + R_1 + R_2$.

Thus, if P_j is a regular player, then the coalition cannot cancel out any random bit, while if P_j is a distributing player, the coalition can cancel at most one random bit. Since each player uses at least two random bits during each phase, the privacy condition is still satisfied.

Let us now consider the randomness complexity of the protocol. Recall that d is the number of distributing players and n is the number of players involved in the protocol. We have chosen $\mathcal{F}$ as the family of the characteristic vectors of all the 2-subsets of $\{1, \ldots, d\}$ thus $|\mathcal{F}| = k = \binom{d}{2} = d(d-1)/2$. Since $n \geq k+d = d(d-1)/2+d = O(d^2)$, we have that $d = O(\sqrt{n})$. Recall that each distributing player selects n random bits, thus the total number of random bits used is $n \cdot d = O(n\sqrt{n})$.

□

3.2 Improving Randomness Complexity for 2-Private Protocols

In the previous section we have given a simple k-phase 2-round protocol that allows to reuse the same random bits for several computations. A better randomness complexity can be obtained if we use more sophisticated combinatorial structures. Indeed, notice that our proof of security of the previous section relies on the property that the symmetric difference between any two vectors v_i and v_j has weight at least 2.

A Sperner family $\mathcal{F} = \{S_1, \ldots, S_{|\mathcal{F}|}\}$ on a ground set $G = \{g_1, \ldots, g_{|G|}\}$ is a subset of 2^G, with the property that $S_i \not\subseteq S_j$, for each $i \neq j$. In this case we say that S_j does not *cover* S_i. The size of the family $\mathcal{F}$ is the number of elements in $\mathcal{F}$. A Sperner family is t-uniform if it contains only t-subsets of the ground set G.

Notice that the set of vectors used by the protocol XOR presented in Figure 1 is a 2-uniform Sperner family on ground set $\{P_{k+1}, \ldots, P_{k+d}\}$. In the following, let $\mathcal{F}$ be a family of vectors of ground set $\{P_{k+1}, \ldots, P_{k+d}\}$ and $k \leq |\mathcal{F}|$. Each $v_i \in \mathcal{F}$ is the characteristic vector of a subset of the ground set. A generalization of the protocol presented in Figure 1 is given in Figure 2.

The proof of the following lemma uses similar argument of Theorem 1 and is thus omitted.

Lemma 1. *Let $\mathcal{F}$ be a Sperner family on the ordered set $\langle P_{k+1}, \ldots, P_{k+d} \rangle$ of size d such that for each $v_i \in \mathcal{F}$ it results that $|v_i| \geq 2$. Let $k \leq |\mathcal{F}|$ such that $n \geq k+d$. Protocol XOR($n,\mathcal{F},k$) is a 2-private k-phase 2-round n-player protocol to compute the XOR function using $n \cdot d$ random bits.*

By well known properties of the Sperner families, in order to maximize the size of $\mathcal{F}$, we will use the $d/2$-uniform ones. Thus it is possible to write the following:

Protocol XOR(n,$\mathcal{F}$,k)

Let $\mathcal{F} = \{v_1, v_2, \ldots, v_k\}$.

Initialization Phase

1. Each distributing player $P_{k+j}, 1 \leq j \leq d$ generates uniformly and independently n random bits, $r_1^{(j)} \ldots r_n^{(j)}$, and sends $r_i^{(j)}$ to player P_i.
2. Denote by $r_i = (r_i^{(1)}, \ldots, r_i^{(d)})$ the vector of random bits received by P_i.

Phase ℓ =1,2,...,k

1. Each distributing player $P_i \in v_\ell$ computes $m_i^{(\ell)} = x_i^{(\ell)} + r_i \cdot v_\ell^T + \sum_{s=1}^n r_s^{(i)}$
2. Each distributing player $P_i \notin v_\ell$ computes: $m_i^{(\ell)} = x_i^{(\ell)} + r_i \cdot v_\ell^T$
3. Each collecting or regular player P_i sends $m_i^{(\ell)}$ to P_ℓ.
4. P_ℓ computes the sum of the messages received and announces the result.

Fig. 2. A Generic Constant-Round Protocol Using a family $\mathcal{F}$

Theorem 2. *For each $\epsilon > 0$, all sufficiently large n, and $k = (1 - \epsilon)n$ there exists a 2-private k-phase 2-round n-player protocol to compute the xor function that uses $O(n \log k)$ random bits.*

Sketch of Proof. It is well known that there exists a Sperner family, over d elements of size $\binom{d}{\lceil d/2 \rceil}$. Thus, we choose d as the minimum integer such that $k \leq \binom{d}{\lceil d/2 \rceil}$, i.e., $d = O(\log k)$ and construct such a Sperner family $\mathcal{F}$ to be used in the protocol $XOR(n, \mathcal{F}, k)$. $\qquad \square$

4 A t-Private 2-Round Protocol

In this section we focus our attention on the concept of a t-cover free family as introduced in [10]. A t-cover free family $\mathcal{F} = \{S_1, \ldots, S_{|\mathcal{F}|}\}$ on the ground set G is a subset of 2^G, with the property that each set in the family is not covered by the union of t others. We will denote by $\mathcal{F}_w$ a w-uniform t-cover free family. It is easy to verify that the following holds:

Property 1. Let $\mathcal{F}_w$ be a w-uniform t-cover free family of size k over a ground set of size $d < \lambda$. Then, there exists a w-uniform t-cover free family $\mathcal{F}_w^*$ of size at least $k - d$ such that each element of the ground set belongs to at least 2 sets of $\mathcal{F}_w^*$.

The following property of t-cover free families will be used in proving the t-privacy of our protocol.

Lemma 2. *Let $\mathcal{F}_w$ be a w-uniform t-cover free family over a ground set G, with $w \geq t$. Then, for any $1 \leq \ell \leq t$ and for any ℓ sets $v_1, \ldots, v_\ell \in \mathcal{F}_w$ and $t - \ell$ sets $u_1, \ldots, u_{t-\ell} \subseteq G$ of size 1, for any $v \in \mathcal{F}_w$ we have that $v \not\subseteq \bigcup_{i=1}^{\ell} v_i \cup \bigcup_{i=1}^{t-\ell} u_i$.*

Proof. Suppose that $v \subseteq \bigcup_{i=1}^{\ell} v_i \cup \bigcup_{i=1}^{t-\ell} u_i$ and choose $w_1, \ldots, w_{t-\ell} \in \mathcal{F}_w$ such that $u_i \subseteq w_i$ and $w_i \neq v$. Such w_i's certainly exist since, by Property 1 each element of the ground set belongs to at least 2 sets of the family $\mathcal{F}_w$. Now we have that $v \subseteq \bigcup_{i=1}^{\ell} v_i \cup \bigcup_{i=1}^{t-\ell} w_i$ which contradicts the t-cover freeness of the family.

A sketch of the proof of the following lemma is given in the appendix.

Lemma 3. *Let $\mathcal{F}_w$ be a w-uniform $(t-1)$-cover free family on a ground set of size d such that $w \geq t$. For any $k \leq |\mathcal{F}_w|$, such that $n \geq k + d$, Protocol $XOR(n, \mathcal{F}_w, k)$ is a t-private k-phase 2-round n-player protocol to compute the XOR function using $n \cdot d$ random bits.*

In order to evaluate the randomness complexity of the protocol presented we recall the following:

Lemma 4 ([9]). *There is a deterministic algorithm that, for any fixed t, k, constructs a w-uniform t-cover-free family $\mathcal{F}_w$ of size k with $w = \lceil d/4t \rceil$ on a ground set of size d with*

$$d \leq 16t^2 \left(\frac{\log(k/2)}{\log 3} + 1 \right).$$

Note that it is possible to construct a t-cover free family $\mathcal{F}_w$ with $w \geq t$. By Lemma 3 and 4, it is possible to write the following:

Lemma 5. *For any n, t and for any k such that $n \geq k + t^2 \log k$, there exists an explicitly constructible t-private k-phase 2-round n-player protocol to compute the XOR function that uses $O(nt^2 \log k)$ random bits.*

Thus we have the following:

Theorem 3. *For $t = O(n^{1/2-\epsilon})$ and sufficiently large n, there exists a t-private k-phase 2-round n-player protocol that uses $O(nt^2 \log k)$ if $k \leq n/2$ and $O(kt^2 \log n)$ random bits if $k \geq n/2$.*

Sketch of Proof. Lemma 5 actually proves the theorem for $k \leq n/2$. Let $s = n/2$. If $k \geq n/2$, we can run $O(k/s)$ independent executions of the t-private s-phase protocol using $O(kt^2 \log n)$ random bits. $\qquad \square$

5 Conclusion

We have shown how to run k disjoint 2-private XOR computations using only $O(n \log k)$ random bits and 2 rounds per phase. One important feature of our algorithm is that each phase is run independently from each other, i.e., we do not require all k inputs to be available at the same time. We have also shown how to achieve, in constant round per phase, t-privacy for the k-phase setting. We have presented a t-private k-phase 2-round protocol that uses $O(nt^2 \log k)$ random bits improving on the $O(tkn)$ of the constant-round "naive" solution.

References

1. J. Bar-Ilan and D. Beaver. Non-cryptographic fault-tolerant computing in a constant number of round of interaction. In *Proceedings of 8th ACM Symposium on Principles of Distributed Computing*, pages 36–44, 1989.
2. D. Beaver, J. Feigenbaum, J. Kilian, and P. Rogaway. Security with low communication overhead. In *Advances in Cryptology – CRYPTO 90*, pages 62–76, 1990.
3. D. Beaver, S. Micali, and P. Rogaway. The round complexity of secure protocols. In *Proceedings of 22th Symposium on Theory of Computation*, pages 503–513, 1990.
4. M. Ben-Or, S. Goldwasser, and A. Wigderson. Completeness theorems for non-cryptographic fault-tolerant distributed computation. In *Proceedings of 20th Symposium on Theory of Computation*, pages 1–10, 1988.
5. C. Blundo, A. De Santis, G. Persiano, and U. Vaccaro. Randomness complexity of private multiparty protocols. *To appear in Computational Complexity (preliminary version ICALP 95)*, 1998.
6. D. Chaum, C. Crepeau, and I. Damgård. Multiparty unconditionally secure protocols. In *Proceedings of 20th Symposium on Theory of Computation*, pages 11–19, 1988.
7. B. Chor and E. Kushilevitz. A communication-privacy tradeoff for modular addition. *Information Processing Letters*, 45:205–210, 1991.
8. B. Chor and E. Kushilevitz. A zero-one law for boolean privacy. *SIAM Journal of Disc. Mat.*, 4(1):36–46, 1991.
9. D.Z. Du and F.K. Hwang. *Combinatorial Groups Testing and its Applications.* World Scientific, Singapore, 1993.
10. P. Erdös, P. Frankl, and Z. Füredi. Families of finite sets in which no set is covered by the union of r others. *Israel Journal of Mathematics*, 51:79–89, 1985.
11. E. Kushilevitz and Y. Mansour. Small sample spaces and privacy. In *Proceedings of 15th ACM Symposium on Principles of Distributed Computing*, 1996.
12. E. Kushilevitz, R. Ostrovsky, and A. Rosèn. Characterizing linear size circuit in terms of privacy. In *Proceedings of 28th ACM Symposium on Theory of Computing*, 1996.
13. E. Kushilevitz, R. Ostrovsky, and A. Rosèn. Amortizing randomness in private multiparty computations. In *Proc. Seventeenth ACM Symposium on Principles of Distributed Computing*, 1998.
14. E. Kushilevitz and A. Rosèn. A randomness-round tradeoff in private computation. *SIAM Journal of Disc. Mat.*, 11(1):61–80, 1998.

Appendix

Proof's Sketch of Lemma 3. The proof of correctness uses similar argument of Theorem 1 and is thus omitted.

Consider an arbitrary coalition S of at most t players composed by ℓ collecting players, $1 \leq \ell \leq t$, and $t - \ell$ distributing players. W.l.o.g., suppose that $S = \{P_1, \ldots, P_\ell, P_{k+1}, \ldots, P_{k+t-\ell}\}$. The view of the coalition can be written as a sequence of $n - |S|$ systems of linear equations in the unknowns $r_i^{(j)}$:

$$
\begin{bmatrix}
m_i^{(1)} = x_i^{(1)} + r_i \cdot v_1 \\
\vdots \\
m_i^{(\ell)} = x_i^{(\ell)} + r_i \cdot v_\ell \\
a_i^{(1)} = r_i^{(1)} \\
\vdots \\
a_i^{(t-\ell)} = r_i^{(t-\ell)}
\end{bmatrix}
. \tag{8}
$$

Since the random bits distributed to different players are independent, we can consider the systems one at a time. (Actually, this is not completely accurate as we need to impose the condition that the sum of the inputs of each phase equals the sum of the inputs for that phase. However this detail can be easily accommodated.) By Lemma 2, for each $1 \leq j \leq l$, there exists $r_i^{(i_j)}$ such that $r_i^{(i_j)}$ appears only in the j-th equality. Therefore we can write (8) as:

$$
\begin{bmatrix}
m_i^{(1)} = x_i^{(1)} + r_i^{(i_1)} + R_{i_1} \\
\vdots \\
m_i^{(l)} = x_i^{(l)} + r_i^{(i_l)} + R_{i_l} \\
a_i^{(1)} = r_i^{(1)} \\
\vdots \\
a_i^{(t-l)} = r_i^{(t-l)}
\end{bmatrix}
.
$$

This shows that the view of the coalition consisting of

$$
(m_i^{(1)}, \ldots, m_i^{(l)}, a_i^{(1)}, \ldots, a_i^{(t-l)})
$$

is independent from the vector of the inputs. □

Abuse-Free Multi-party Contract Signing

JUAN A. GARAY[*]   PHILIP MACKENZIE[*]

Information Sciences Research Center
Bell Laboratories
600 Mountain Ave
Murray Hill, NJ 07974

Abstract. In the contract-signing problem, participants wish to sign a contract m in such a way that either all participants obtain each others' signatures, or nobody does. A contract-signing protocol is *optimistic* if it relies on a trusted third party, but only uses it when participants misbehave (e.g., try to cheat, or simply crash).

We construct an efficient general multi-party optimistic contract-singing protocol. The protocol is also *abuse-free*, meaning that at no point can a participant prove to others that he is capable of choosing whether to validate or invalidate the contract. This is the first abuse-free optimistic contract-signing protocol that has been developed for $n > 3$ parties. We also show a linear lower bound on the number of rounds of any n-party optimistic contract-signing protocol.

1 Introduction

A contract is a non-repudiable agreement on a given text [7]. Contract signing is an important part of any business transaction, in particular in settings where participants do not trust each other to some extent already. Thus, the World Wide Web is probably the best example of a setting where contract signing schemes are needed. Still, even though a great amount of research has gone into developing methods for contract signing over a network such as the WWW, the case of contract signing by an arbitrary number of signatories was only recently considered, with most of the work concentrating on the case of two parties. In this paper we present a general n-party optimistic contract-signing protocol.

Electronic contract signing. Contract signing is part of the broader problem of fair exchange [8, 11, 17, 21, 2]. More specifically, it can be considered fair exchange of digital signatures [4]. The term "contract signing" was first introduced in [7].

Early work on electronic contract signing, or more generally, fair exchange of secrets/signatures, focused on the gradual release of secrets to obtain simultaneity, [6, 15, 19] (see [12] for more recent results). The idea is that if each party alternately releases a small portion of the secret, then neither party has a considerable advantage over the other. Unfortunately, such a solution has several

---

[*] E-mail: {garay,philmac}@research.bell-labs.com.

drawbacks. Apart from being expensive in terms of computation and communication, it has the problem in real situations of uncertain termination: if the protocol stops prematurely and one of the participants does not receive a message, he will never be sure whether the other party is continuing with the protocol, or stopped—and perhaps even engaged in another contract-signing protocol!

More recently, considerable efforts have been devoted to develop efficient protocols that mimic the features of "paper contract signing," especially *fairness*. A contract-signing protocol is *fair* if at the end of the protocol, either both parties have valid signatures for a contract, or neither does. In some sense, this corresponds to the "simultaneity" property of traditional paper contract signing. That is, a paper contract is generally signed by both parties at the same place and at the same time, and thus is fair.

An alternative approach to achieving fairness instead of relying on the gradual release of secrets has been to use a *trusted third party* (TTP). A TTP is essentially a judge that can be called in to handle disputes between contract signers. This was the case in the early work of [14], where the contract is only valid if a "center of cancellation" does not object. The TTP can be *on-line* in the sense of mediating after every exchange as in [11, 13, 17], at the expense of the TTP becoming a potential bottleneck, or *off-line*, meaning that it only gets involved when something goes wrong (e.g., a participant attempts to cheat, or simply crashes, or the communication delays between the participants are intolerably high, etc.). The latter approach has been called *optimistic* [2], and fair contract-signing protocols have been developed in this model [2, 4, 3]. Although the TTP is (by definition) trusted, it is, in some protocols, possible for the TTP to be accountable for his actions. That is, it can be determined if the TTP misbehaved.

However, until recently, "fair" contract-signing protocols had the conceptual drawback of allowing a party (say, Alice) at some point to show to outside parties that she has a *potentially signed contract* (say, with Bob), as well as control over whether the contract will be validated. (In some cases protocols are even asymmetric, in the sense of not giving the other party (Bob) the same ability.) Alice may take advantage of this feature by coercing another party, say Carol, into another contract on the threat of signing the contract with Bob. and then cancelling the contract with Bob. (Bob would probably not appreciate this.) Another example of abuse would be in "We will beat your best deal" scenarios, in which Alice can take a validated price on some merchandise from vendor Val and present it to merchant Mary to achieve a better price, and later renege on the deal with Val.

In [18] this type of attack was pointed out, and an efficient *abuse-free* optimistic contract-signing protocol was presented. Although not mentioned, a protocol for fair exchange of digital signatures presented in [4] is also abuse-free; however, that protocol is inefficient in that it requires cut-and-choose techniques.

In [23] the optimal efficiency of optimistic contract-signing protocols is considered, and they give tight lower bounds on the message and round complexity of 2-party protocols.

Most of the protocols previously developed are for two-party contract sign-ings. In [18] an intricate protocol for three parties is presented. Independently and concurrently to our work, the case of multi-party contract signing was considered in [1,5]. In [1], an optimistic multi-party contract-signing protocol is given for the case of synchronous networks, while in [5], an optimistic multi-party contract-signing protocol is given for asynchronous networks; these protocols, however, are not abuse-free. To our knowledge, there has been no proposal on how to produce general n-party abuse-free contract signings.

Our results. We give a construction of an optimistic abuse-free contract-signing protocol for an arbitrary number of participants n. The construction is modular, requires $O(n^3)$ messages and $O(n^2)$ rounds of interaction (in an asynchronous environment), and tolerates an arbitrary number of faulty (Byzantine) parties. The protocol uses *private contract signatures*, introduced in [18]. We also show a lower bound of n rounds for any optimistic contract-signing protocol (i.e., even if it is not abuse-free).

Other related work. As pointed out in [23], contract signing bears some resemblance to atomic commitment [25] and Byzantine agreement [22]. Contract signing is to be robust against malicious participants while providing a non-repudiable agreement; on the other hand, atomic commitment tolerates only benign failures (is unattainable otherwise) and does not require that participants reach a decision (also, when they do, *all* decisions—including those of the faulty participants—must be consistent). The failure model of contract signing is similar to that of Byzantine agreement—although in the TTP version the trusted third party is assumed to remain uncorrupted. However, contract signing achieves more than reaching agreement: all the participants should be able to prove it afterwards.

Organization of the paper. The remainder of the paper is organized as follows. Section 2 describes the model and states the relevant definitions. Section 3 describes the cryptographic tools that we need for the design. The multi-party abuse-free contract-signing protocol is presented in Section 4, and the proof of correctness and security is given in Section 5. Section 6 presents the efficiency analysis and the lower bound on the number of rounds. Section 7 offers some final remarks.

2   Model and Definitions

Our basic model is similar to that of [4]. We have a set of participants $S = \{P_1, P_2, \cdots, P_n\}$, and a trusted third party T. Participants may be correct or faulty (Byzantine). Formally, the participants and the trusted third party are modelled by probabilistic interactive Turing machines. We assume all participants have public/private keys which will be specified later. T acts like a server, responding (atomically) to requests from the participants, with responses defined later. We assume that communication between any participants and T is over a private channel.

The network model we consider is the same as in [4]. Namely, it is an asynchronous communication model with no global clocks, where messages can be delayed arbitrarily, but with messages sent between correct participants and the trusted third party guaranteed to be delivered eventually. In general, we assume an adversary may schedule messages, and possibly insert its own messages into the network.

The participants, $\{P_1, \ldots, P_n\}$, wish to "sign" a contract m.[1] By signing a contract, we mean providing public, non-repudiable evidence that they have agreed to the contract. The type of evidence is either universally agreed upon, or is part of the contract m itself. For instance, valid evidence may include either valid signatures by all participants on m, or valid signatures by all participants on the concatenation of m and the public key of T, signed together by T.

Obviously, in the asynchronous model of [16], an adversary may prevent a contract from being signed simply by delaying all messages between players. Thus in order to force contract-signing protocols to be non-trivial, we specify a completeness condition using a slightly restricted adversary. An optimistic contract-signing protocol is *complete* if the (slightly restricted) adversary cannot prevent a set of correct participants from obtaining a valid signature on a contract. This adversary has signing oracles that can be queried on any message except m, can interact with T, and can arbitrariliy schedule messages from the participants to T. However, it cannot delay messages between the correct participants enough to cause any timeouts.

An optimistic contract-signing protocol is *fair* if

1. it is impossible for a set of corrupted participants, A, to obtain a valid contract without allowing the remaining set of participants, B, to also obtain a valid contract;

2. once a correct participant obtains a cancellation message from the TTP T, it is impossible for any other participant to obtain a valid contract; and

3. every correct participant is guaranteed to complete the protocol.

Effectively, condition 2 provides a *persistency* condition, stating that correct participants cannot have their outcomes overturned by other participants. In previous two-party protocols, this condition was never explicitly discussed, although the condition was trivially satisfied by those protocols. With multi-party protocols, the condition is much more difficult to satisfy.

We assume the corrupted participants have a signing oracle to obtain signatures from the remaining participants B on any message except m. The corrupted participants may also interact with T and the messages from B to T may be arbitrarily scheduled.

---

[1] In general, each participant might need to sign different pieces of text. Extension to this case is trivial.

An optimistic contract-signing protocol is *abuse-free* if it is impossible for any set of participants, A, at any point in the protocol to be able to prove to an outside party that they have the power to terminate (abort) or successfully complete the contract.

We say an optimistic contract-signing protocol is *secure* if it is fair, complete, and abuse-free.

3 Cryptographic Tools

3.1 Discrete logs

For a prime q, we will be working in a group G_q of order q with generator g. For a specific example, we could use a group form by integer modular arithmetic as follows. Let p be a prime of the form $lq + 1$ for some value l co-prime to q, and let Z_p^* be the group, with g a generator of order q in Z_p^*. Then G_q would be the subgroup generated by g.

We assume the hardness of the *Decision Diffie-Hellman problem* (DDH). In this problem, it is the goal of the polynomial-time adversary to distinguish the following two distributions with a non-negligible advantage over a random guess:

1. (g_1, g_2, y_1, y_2) with $g_1, g_2, y_1, y_2 \in_R G_q$, and
2. (g_1, g_2, g_1^r, g_2^r) with $g_1, g_2 \in_R G_q$ and $r \in_R Z_q$.

The security of the digital signatures described in the next section relies on the DDH assumption.

3.2 Private contract signatures

Our protocols use *private contract signatures* (PCS), a type of digital signatures that were introduced in [18]. Roughly, the properties of these signatures can be summarized as follows: These signatures are:

- **Undeniable** [9]: they are not self-authenticating or universally verifiable—they cannot be transferred;
- **designated-verifier** [20]: only a selected receiver chosen by the signatory can verify them and convince himself of their validity;
- **designated-converter** [10]: a third party (designated by the signatory) can convert them into self-authenticating signatures; and
- **non-interactive**: the receiver of the signature knows beforehand that the third party can convert the signature, without the need for a verification session.

That is, upon receiving a PCS, a party convinces himself of its validity, but cannot convince anybody else, and he also knows that the third party appointed by the signatory can convert it into a regular (self-authenticating) signature.

For completeness, we include the full formal definition here.

Definition 1. *A* private contract signature (PCS) *scheme* Σ *is a tuple of probabilistic polynomial-time algorithms* {PCS-Sign, S-Convert, TP-Convert, PCS-Ver, S-Ver, TP-Ver} *defined as follows, and having the security properties defined below.*

(1) PCS-Sign *executed by party A on m for B with respect to third party T, denoted* PCS-Sign$_A(m, B, T)$, *outputs a private contract signature, denoted* PCS$_A(m, B, T)$. *A private contract signature can be verified using* PCS-Ver, *i.e.,*

$$\text{PCS-Ver}(m, A, B, T, S) = \begin{cases} \text{true } \textit{if } S = \text{PCS}_A(m, B, T); \\ \text{false } \textit{otherwise.} \end{cases}$$

(2) S-Convert *executed by A on a private contract signature $S = \text{PCS}_A(m, B, T)$ generated by A, denoted* S-Convert$_A(S)$, *produces a universally-verifiable signature by A on m,* S-Sig$_A(m)$.

(3) **TP-Convert** *executed by T on a private contract signature $S = \text{PCS}_A(m, B, T)$, denoted* TP-Convert$_T(S)$, *produces a universally-verifiable signature by A on m,* TP-Sig$_A(m)$.

(4) S-Sig$_A(m)$ *can be verified using* S-Ver, *and* TP-Sig$_A(m)$ *can be verified using* TP-Ver, *i.e.,*

$$\text{S-Ver}(m, A, T, S) = \begin{cases} \text{true } \textit{if } S = \text{S-Sig}_A(m); \\ \text{false } \textit{otherwise;} \end{cases}$$

and

$$\text{TP-Ver}(m, A, T, S) = \begin{cases} \text{true } \textit{if } S = \text{TP-Sig}_A(m); \\ \text{false } \textit{otherwise.} \end{cases}$$

The security properties of a PCS *scheme are:*

(1) **Unforgeability of** $\text{PCS}_A(m, B, T)$**:** *For any m, it is infeasible for anyone but A or B to produce T and S such that* PCS-Ver(m, A, B, T, S) = true.

(2) **Designated verifier property of** $\text{PCS}_A(m, B, T)$**:** *For any B, there is a polynomial-time algorithm* FakeSign *such that for any m, A, and T,* FakeSign$_B(m, A, T)$ *outputs S, where* PCS-Ver(m, A, B, T, S) = true.

(3) **Unforgeability of** S-Sig$_A(m)$ **and** TP-Sig$_A(m)$**:** *For any m, A, B, T, assuming $P = \text{PCS}_A(m, B, T)$ is known and was produced by* PCS-Sign$_A(m, B, T)$, *it is infeasible*

    (3.1) *for anyone but A or T to produce S such that* S-Ver(m, A, T, S) = true *and* TP-Ver(m, A, T, S) = true;

    (3.2) *for anyone but A to produce S such that* S-Ver(m, A, T, S) = true *and* TP-Ver(m, A, T, S) = false; *and*

    (3.3) *for anyone but T to produce S such that* TP-Ver(m, A, T, S) = true *and* S-Ver(m, A, T, S) = false.

Definition 2. *A* PCS *scheme Σ is* third party-accountable *if for any* $\text{PCS}_A(m, B, T)$, *the distributions of* S-Sig$_A(m)$ *and* TP-Sig$_A(m)$, *produced by* S-Convert *and* TP-Convert, *respectively, are disjoint and efficiently distinguishable.*

That is, it is impossible to have S-Ver(m, A, T, S) = TP-Ver(m, A, T, S) = true for any S, and thus it is possible for a verifier to distinguish whether the conversion was performed by the signatory or by the third pary. This property might be useful if the signatories are concerned about the third party's trustworthiness. A somewhat complementary property is the following.

Definition 3. *A* PCS *scheme* Σ *is* third party-invisible *if for any* PCS$_A(m, B, T)$, *the distributions of* S-Sig$_A(m)$ *and* TP-Sig$_A(m)$, *produced by* S-Convert *and* TP-Convert, *respectively, are identical.*

In other words, for any S, S-Ver(m, A, T, S) = TP-Ver(m, A, T, S), meaning no one can determine if a conversion was performed by the original signer or the trustee. This property might be useful in some scenarios where signatories may not want possible "bad publicity" associated with a contract needing to be converted by the third party.

In [18] it is shown:

Theorem 1 ([18]). *Assuming the security of* DDH, *there exists a* PCS *scheme (in the random oracle model).*

4 The Multi-party Contract-Signing Protocol

4.1 Alternating contract-signing protocols

The basic structure of an optimistic 2-party protocol (e.g., [18]) is shown in Figure 1. (The protocol of [4] has the same structure, except that the underlying primitives are different, and provide different functionality.) The protocol has an alternating structure, with a previously agreed-upon initiator, say, party A. If no problems occur, A sends a "promise" (i.e., a private contract signature of Section 3) that she will sign the message to B. B verifies A's PCS and gets convinced of A's intentions—but cannot convince anybody else, and responds with his PCS. Then A converts her PCS into a universally-verifiable signature, and then B does the same.

If problems occur, A or B may run protocols to *abort* or *resolve* the contract signing, depending on what step has been attained in the protocol. These protocols are run between A or B and T, the trusted party. Since A sends her message first and might not hear from B, or the PCS she receives could be wrong, the purpose of abort is to give A the power to terminate the protocol. If resolve is invoked, the participant converts his own PCS into a regular signature, and sends it to T together with what he received from the other participant. Depending on the state of the protocol that it keeps, T grants an abort or converts the PCS into a regular signature and sends it back to the participant who invoked the resolve protocol. (T is able to perform the signature conversions given its designated-converter status.) It is shown in [18] that, assuming the security of DDH, the protocol of Fig. 1 is a secure contract-signing protocol for two parties.

Notice that in the protocol only A can abort the protocol. The reason for this is that if also B could abort, then the abuse freeness condition would be violated.

Specifically, after receiving A's converted signature, $\text{S-Sig}_A(m)$, B could prove to an outside party that he has a valid contract signed by A, as well as the power to terminate it. There is also a reason for the protocol being alternating (first A sends a message, then B does, and so forth), for if it were not (i.e., both parties could start "simultaneosuly"), then the same type of scenario as the one above could occur, with one party being able to prove that he has a valid contract.

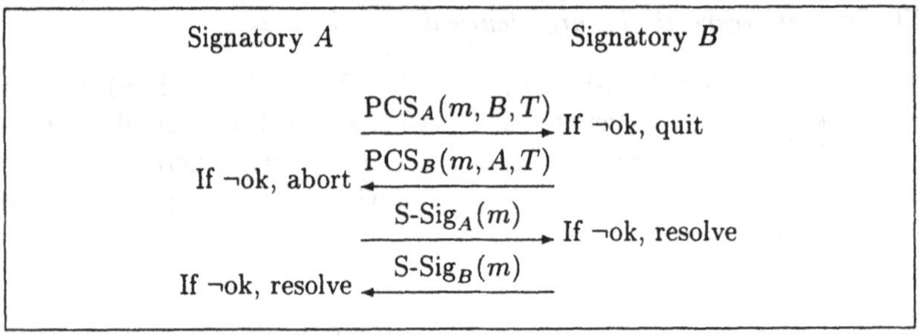

Fig. 1. *A secure contract-signing protocol for two parties*

It was pointed out in [18] that this type of protocol does not extend easily to the multi-party case; specifically, it is unclear whether to let the "middle" parties abort or not. In the next section we present a contract-signing protocol for $n \geq 3$ parties that is secure. The approach we take is to let aborts be overturned, but in a way that avoids the violations of fairness and abuse freeness pointed out in [18]. Naturally, we use the private contract signatures of Section 3 as "promises."

4.2 Protocol description

Our protocol can be described recursively. For i participants P_1 through P_i to sign a contract, P_i indicates its willingness to sign the contract to P_1 through P_{i-1}, then participants P_1 through P_{i-1} come to an agreement about the contract (with promises, not signatures), letting P_i know about this (again with promises). Then all participants exchange promises to sign the contract. Only when all recursive levels are finished do the participants exchange signatures on a contract.

To apply this recursive approach, we use different "strengths" of promises for the different levels of recursion. We denote the strength of a promise by an integer "level." Specifically, an "i-level promise from A to B on a message m" is denoted $\text{PCS}_A((m,i),B,T)$. Our approach is shown in Figure 2. Note that the order of participants is reversed (P_i down to P_1) to match the recursion levels.

If there is no misbehavior by any participants, there is never a need to contact the trusted third party T. If T is contacted, it needs to store some information to handle the abort and/or resolve messages it may receive. Specifically, if there is a positive resolution (meaning the contract must be honored) it needs to store a completely signed contract (with the promises possibly converted to universal signatures by T itself). If there has not been a positive resolution, T needs to store an "abort list" containing indices of all the parties that have aborted, or tried to resolve unsuccessfully. T will also store the first abort message it received, along with another "forced abort list" that will be explain in the protocol below.

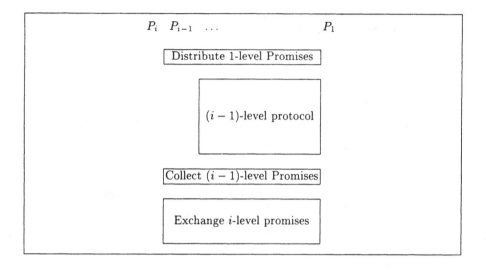

Fig. 2. *Secure contract-signing protocol: ith recursive level*

Protocol for participant P_i:

(1) **(Wait for all higher recursive levels to start)** P_i waits for 1-level promises from $P_{i+1}, \ldots, P_n$ on m. If it does not receive them in a timely manner, P_i simply quits.

(2) **(Start recursive level i)** P_i runs PCS-Sign$_{P_i}((m,1), P_j, T)$ for $1 \leq j \leq i-1$ and sends each PCS$_{P_i}((m,1), P_j, T)$ to P_j.

(3) **(Wait for recursive level $i-1$ to finish)** P_i waits for $(i-1)$-level promises from $P_1, \ldots, P_{i-1}$ on m. If it does not receive them in a timely manner, P_i runs the **Abort** procedure.

(4) **(Send i-level promises to all parties)** P_i runs PCS-Sign$_{P_i}((m,i), P_j, T)$ for $1 \leq j \leq i-1$ and sends each PCS$_{P_i}((m,i), P_j, T)$ to P_j.

(5) **(Finish recursive level i when i-level promises are received)** P_i waits for i-level promises from $P_1, \ldots, P_{i-1}$ on m. If it does not receive them in a timely manner, P_i runs the **Resolve** procedure.

(6) **(Complete all higher recursive levels)** For $a = i+1$ to n, P_i does the following:

(6.1) P_i runs PCS-Sign$_{P_i}((m, a-1), P_j, T)$ and sends PCS$_{P_i}((m, a-1), P_a, T)$ to P_a.

(6.2) P_i waits for a-level promises from $P_{i+1}, \ldots, P_a$ on m. If it does not receive them in a timely manner, P_i runs the **Resolve** procedure.

(6.3) P_i runs PCS-Sign$_{P_i}((m,a), P_j, T)$ for $1 \leq j \leq i - 1$ and sends each PCS$_{P_i}((m,a), P_j, T)$ to P_j.

(6.4) P_i waits for a-level promises from $P_1, \ldots, P_{i-1}$ on m. If it does not receive them in a timely manner, P_i runs the **Resolve** procedure.

(6.5) P_i runs PCS-Sign$_{P_i}((m,a), P_j, T)$ for $i + 1 \leq j \leq a$ and sends each PCS$_{P_i}((m,a), P_j, T)$ to P_j.

(7) P_i waits for signatures and $n + 1$-level promises[2] from $P_{i+1}, \ldots, P_n$ on m. If it does not receive them in a timely manner, P_i runs the **Resolve** procedure.

(8) P_i runs PCS-Sign$_{P_i}((m, n+1), P_j, T)$ and S-Convert$_{P_i}($PCS$_{P_i}((m,1), P_j, T))$ for $1 \leq j \leq n$, and sends each result (PCS$_{P_i}((m, n+1), P_j, T),$ S-Sig$_{P_i}((m,1)))$ to P_j.

Protocol P_i-Abort: To abort, P_i sends $[m, P_i, (P_1, \ldots, P_n),$ abort$]_{P_i}$ to T.

Protocol P_i-Resolve: For P_i to resolve, it runs S-Convert$_{P_i}($PCS$_{P_i}((m,1), P_j, T))$ (for any $j \in \{1, \ldots, n\}$) to produce S-Sig$_{P_i}((m,1))$, and then sends the message

$$[\{PCS_{P_j}((m, k_j), P_i, T)\}_{j \in \{1, \ldots, n\} \setminus \{i\}}, \text{S-Sig}_{P_i}((m,1))]_{P_i}$$

to T, where for $j > i$, k_j is the maximum level of a promise received from P_j on m, and for $j < i$, k_j is the maximum level of promises received from *all* participants $P_{j'}$, with $j' < i$. (For example, if the maximum level of the promises received by P_4 from P_3 and P_2 was 6, and the maximum level received by P_4 from P_1 was 5, then it would send the 5-level promises for P_1, P_2 and P_3.)

Protocol for T: For each contract[3] m with participants P_1 through P_n, when T learns about this contract (through an abort or receive message) it sets up a record that stores a boolean variable `validated`(m) which is true if the contract has been validated, and T has a full set of signatures (many would be converted by T from promises, most likely). If `validated`(m) is false, then T maintains the set S_m of indices of parties that have aborted, or resolved and failed to overturn a previous abort. T also maintains a set F_m of indices of parties that have not themselves aborted, but whom T will force to abort in certain situations. This set F_m is needed because at a particular point in our protocol, standard tests for whether to overturn an abort would allow unfairness. Specifically, they would allow groups of participants to conspire and receive a valid contract after a correct participant already received a cancellation from the T.

    The protocol when T receives an abort message from P_i, $[m, P_i, (P_1, \ldots, P_n),$ abort$]_{P_i}$, is as follows:

(1)   If the signature is correct, and there has not been a positive resolution, T does the following. If i is larger than the maximum index in S_m, T clears

---

[2] We include these to simplify the TTP's protocol.

[3] Without loss of generality, we may assume all contracts are distinct.

F_m. In any case, T stores i in the set S_m. T sends $[[m, P_j, (P_1, \ldots, P_n),$ abort$]_{P_j}]_T$ and $[m, S_m, \text{abort}]_T$ to P_i. If this is the first player in the list, T sets validated(m) to false, and stores $[[m, P_i, (P_1, \ldots, P_n), \text{abort}]_{P_i}]_T$.

(2) If there has been a positive resolution, T sends the valid (signed) contract to P_i, i.e., $\{\text{S-Sig}_{P_j}((m, k_j))\}_{j \in \{1, \ldots, n\}}$, where k_j is the level of the promise from P_j that was converted to a universally-verifiable signature.

The protocol when T receives a resolve message from P_i,

$$[\{\text{PCS}_{P_j}((m, k_j), P_i, T)\}_{j \in \{1, \ldots, n\} \setminus \{i\}}, \text{S-Sig}_{P_i}((m, 1))]_{P_i},$$

is as follows:

(1) If $i \in S_m$, T ignores the message.

(2) T checks to make sure all promises and signatures are consistent (i.e., m is the same, etc.) and valid. If not, then it ignores the message.

(3) If there has been no previous query to T on m, it sends

$$[\{\text{TP-Convert}_T(\text{PCS}_{P_j}((m, k_j), P_i, T))\}_{j \in \{1, \ldots, n\} \setminus \{i\}}]$$

to P_i, stores all the signatures, and sets validated(m) to true

(4) If there has been a positive resolution, T sends the stored valid contract to P_i, i.e., $\{\text{S-Sig}_{P_j}((m, k'_j))\}_{j \in \{1, \ldots, n\}}$, where k'_j is the level of the promise from P_j that was converted to a universally-verifiable signature.

(5) If there has not been a positive resolution, T runs as follows:

    (5.1) If $i \notin F_m$, then

        (5.1.1) if for any $\ell \in S_m$ there is a $j \in S_m$ such that $j > k_\ell$, then T adds i to S_m, and sends the stored abort message $[[m, P_j, (P_1, \ldots, P_n), \text{abort}]_{P_j}]_T$ and $[m, S_m, \text{abort}]_T$ to P_i. Let a be the maximum value in S_m. If $a > i$, then for all j with $k_j = a - 1$, T adds j to F_m. If $a = i$, T clears F_m.

        (5.1.2) Otherwise, T sends

$$[\text{TP-Convert}_T(\text{PCS}_{P_j}((m, k_j), P_i, T))\}_{j \in \{1, \ldots, n\} \setminus \{i\}}]$$

to P_i, stores all the signatures, and sets validated(m) to true

    (5.2) Else $(i \in F_m)$

        (5.2.1) Let a be the maximum value in S_m. If for all $i < j \leq a$, $k_j > a$ and for all $j < i$, $k_j \geq a$, then T sends

$$[\text{TP-Convert}_T(\text{PCS}_{P_j}((m, k_j), P_i, T))\}_{j \in \{1, \ldots, n\} \setminus \{i\}}]$$

to P_i, stores all the signatures, and sets validated(m) to true

(5.2.2)   Otherwise, T adds i to S_m, and sends the stored abort message $[[m, P_j, (P_1, \ldots, P_n), \text{abort}]_{P_j}]_T$ and $[m, S_m, \text{abort}]_T$ to P_i. Let a be the maximum value in S_m. If $a > i$, then for all j with $k_j = a - 1$, T adds j to F_m. If $a = i$, T clears F_m.

5 Protocol Correctness

Theorem 2. *Assuming the security of DDH, the protocol above is a secure optimistic contract-signing protocol (in the random oracle model), with TTP-invisibility if the PCS scheme is third-party invisible, and TTP-accountability if the PCS scheme is third-party accountable.*

Proof. Recall that we say that an optimistic contract-signing protocol is secure if it is complete, fair and abuse-free.

Complete: Completeness follows directly from the definition of private contract signatures.

Fair: To show fairness for P_i we must prove two results:

(1) If any other party or parties can obtain a valid contract on m, so can P_i, and

(2) If P_i gets a cancellation from T, then no other party or parties can obtain a valid contract.

Result (1) can be seen from the following two cases:

(1) Say P_i has sent out a universally-verifiable signature on m. Then P_i has $(n + 1)$-level promises from P_{i+1} through P_n, and n-level promises from P_1 through P_{i-1}, so P_i can contact T and T will overturn any set of aborts S_m, even if $i \in F_m$.

(2) Say P_i has not sent out a universally-verifiable signature on m. Then by the security of the PCS, for some party to obtain a valid contract, some P_j would have to obtain the contract from T. Then P_i can send an abort or resolve message to T and obtain the contract also.

Result (2) can be seen from the following cases:

(1) Say P_i sends an abort to T in Step 3 of the protocol and receives a signed abort message back from T. Since P_i is correct, $i > 1$, parties P_1 through P_{i-1} have a 1-level promise from P_i, and parties P_{i+1} through P_n have no promise from P_i. Since T is honest, T stores i in S_m and will never allow any resolve request to overturn the abort, since any resolve request will have k_i (the level of i's promise) at most 1, and thus $i > k_i$.

(2) Say P_i sends a resolve request to T in Step 5 of the protocol and receives a signed abort message back from T. Since P_i is correct, P_i must have sent $(i - 1)$-level promises to T from P_1 through P_{i-1}, and P_1 through P_{i-1} have at most i-level promises from P_i. Since T is honest, there

must be a $j \in S_m$ with $j > i$, so T stores i in S_m and will never allow any resolve request to overturn the abort, since any resolve request will have k_i (the level of i's promise) at most i, and thus $j > k_i$.

(3) Say P_i sends a resolve request to T in Step (6.2) of the protocol and receives a signed abort message back from T. Since P_i is correct, P_i must have sent $(a-1)$-level or a-level promises to T from P_1 through P_{i-1} and P_{i+1} thorugh P_{a-1}, and P_1 through P_{i-1} and P_{i+1} through P_a have at most $(a-1)$-level promises from P_i. Since T is honest, there must be a $j \in S_m$ with $j \geq a$, so T stores i in S_m and will never allow any resolve request to overturn the abort, since any resolve request will have k_i (the level of i's promise) at most $a-1$, and thus $j > k_i$.

(4) Say P_i sends a resolve request to T in Step (6.4) of the protocol and receives a signed abort message back from T. Since P_i is correct, P_i must have sent to T (1) a-level promises from P_1 through P_{i-1} and (2) $(a-1)$-level promises from P_{i+1} thorugh P_{a-1}. Also, P_1 through P_{i-1} have at most a-level promises from P_i, and P_{i+1} through P_a have at most $(a-1)$-level promises from P_i. Since T is honest, there are two cases:

(4.1) There is a $j \in S_m$ with $j > a$, so T stores i in S_m and will never allow any resolve request to overturn the abort, since any resolve request will have k_i (the level of i's promise) at most a, and thus $j > k_i$.

(4.2) There is no $j \in S_m$ with $j > a$, but $a \in S_m$, and there is also a $j' \in S_m$ with $j < i$. In this case, T stores i in S_m and all $j < i$ in F_m, and will never allow any resolve request to overturn the abort, since any resolve request will either have k_i at most $a-1$ (and thus $a > k_i$), or will have $k_i = a$ and be from a party with index in F_m.

Abuse-free: To show abuse-freeness for P_i we must show that no party obtains publicly verifiable information about (honest) P_i signing the contract until P_i has the power to validate the contract over any other parties' aborts. This follows by the designated verifier property of PCS, and the fact that once P_i sends S-Sig$_{P_i}((m,1))$, P_i will have received $(n+1)$-level promises from P_{i+1} through P_n and n-level promises from P_1 through P_{i-1}, so P_i either has all the signatures from all other parties, or could contact T and obtain a valid contract over any other parties' aborts.

TTP-Invisibility or TTP-Accountability: Straightforward from the definitions.

□

6 Efficiency

By inspection of the recursive construction, it is easy to see that the number of messages required by our protocol is $O(n^3)$, and the number of rounds is $O(n^2)$.

We now show a lower bound in the number of rounds which holds even if the contract-signing protocol is not abuse-free.

Theorem 3. *Any complete and fair optimistic contract-signing protocol with n participants requires at least n rounds in an optimistic run.*

Proof. (Sketch) Since the optimistic protocol is complete, there must be a way for the n participants to obtain a universally-verifiable contract without contacting the TTP. Thus there must be some party, say P_1[4] that sends a message during some round containing information that can be used along with information provided by other participants to validate the contract. At this point, since the protocol is fair, P_1 must have received messages in previous rounds from other participants, say P_2 through P_n, such that regardless of the actions of those participants, P_1 could send a message to the TTP and obtain a validated contract.

Specifically, there must be a previous round in which a participant, say P_2, sends a message to P_1 that allows this. At this point, since the protocol is fair, P_2 must have received messages in previous rounds from participants P_3 through P_n so that regardless of the actions of those participants P_2 could send a message to the TTP and obtain a validated contract. (Otherwise, P_2 could not obtain a validated contract, but P_1 would be able to (possibly much later), and thus the protocol would not be fair for P_2.)

In a similar manner, given that a set of participants, say P_1 through P_i have received messages so that for each $j \in \{1, \ldots, i\}$, participant P_j could send a message to the TTP and obtain a validated contract regardless of the actions of participants P_{j+1} through P_n, there must be a previous round in which a participant, say P_{i+1}, sends the message that allows this to P_i.

Therefore, by an inductive argument, we show the number of rounds is at least n. $\square$

7 Conclusions

In this paper we presented an optimistic abuse-free contract-signing protocol for an arbitrary number of participants n. The protocol tolerates an arbitrary number of faulty (Byzantine) parties. and requires $O(n^3)$ messages and $O(n^2)$ rounds of interaction (in an asynchronous environment). Waidner [26] recently suggested a way to add abuse freeness to any optimistic contract signig protocol using verifiable encryption. Applying this transformation to the protocol of [5] yields an abuse-free optimistic contract signing protocol requiring $O(n)$ rounds.

---

[4] The indices here are unrelated to the indices used in the protocol of Section 4

References

1. N. Asokan, B. Baum-Waidner, M. Schunter, and M. Waidner. Optimistic synchronous multi-party contract signing. IBM Research Report RZ3089, 1998.
2. N. Asokan, M. Schunter, and M. Waidner. Optimistic protocols for fair exchange. In *ACM Conf. on Computer and Comm. Security '97*, pp. 6–17.
3. N. Asokan, V. Shoup, and M. Waidner. Asynchronous protocols for optimistic fair exchange. In *IEEE Symp. on Research in Security and Privacy*, pp. 86–99, 1998.
4. N. Asokan, V. Shoup, and M. Waidner. Fair exchange of digital signatures. In *EUROCRYPT '98*, pp. 591–606.
5. B. Baum-Waidner and M. Waidner. Optimistic asynchronous multi-party contract signing. IBM Research Report RZ3078, 1998.
6. M. Blum. How to exchange (secret) keys. *ACM Transactions on Computer Systems*, 1(2):175–193, May 1983.
7. M. Blum. Coin flipping by telephone: A protocol for solving impossible problems. In *CRYPTO 81*, pp. 11–15.
8. H. Bürk and A. Pfitzmann. Value exchange systems enabling security and unobservability. *Computers and Security*, 9:715–721, 1990.
9. D. Chaum. Blind signatures for untraceable payments. In *CRYPTO 82*, pp. 199–203.
10. D. Chaum. Designated confirmer signatures. In *EUROCRYPT 94*, pp. 86–91.
11. B. Cox, J. D. Tygar, and M. Sirbu. Netbill security and transaction protocol. In *First USENIX Workshop on Electronic Commerce*, pp. 77–88, 1995.
12. I. Damgård. Practical and provably secure release of a secret and exchange of signatures. *J. of Cryptology*, 8(4):201–222, Autumn 1995.
13. R. Deng, L. Gong, A. Lazar, and W. Wang. Practical protocols for certified electronic mail. *J. of Network and Systems Management*, 4(3), 1996.
14. S. Even. A protocol for signing contracts. *ACM SIGACT News*, 15(1):34–39, 1983.
15. S. Even, O. Goldreich, and A. Lempel. A randomized protocol for signing contracts. *Communications of the ACM*, 28(6):637–647, June 1985.
16. M. Fischer, N. Lynch, and M. Paterson. Impossibility of distributed commit with one faulty process. *Journal of the ACM*, 32(2), 1985.
17. M. Franklin and M. Reiter. Fair exchange with a semi-trusted third party. In *ACM Conf. on Computer and Comm. Security '97*, pp.1–5.
18. J. Garay, M. Jakobsson, and P. MacKenzie. Abuse-free optimistic contract signing. To appear in *CRYPTO 99*, August 1999.
19. O. Goldreich. A simple protocol for signing contracts. In *CRYPTO 83*, pp. 133–136.
20. M. Jakobsson, K.Sako, and R. Impagliazzo. Designated verifier proofs and their applications. In *EUROCRYPT 96*, pp. 143–154.
21. S. Micali. Certified e-mail with invisible post offices. Presented at the 1997 RSA Security Conference, 1997.
22. M. Pease, R. Shostak, and L. Lamport. Reaching agreement in the presence of faults. *Journal of the ACM*, 27(2):228–234, 1980.
23. B. Pfitzmann, M.Schunter, and M. Waidner. Optimal efficiency of optimistic contract signing. In *PODC '98*, pp. 113–122.
24. C. P. Schnorr. Efficient identification and signatures for smart cards. In *CRYPTO'89*, pp. 239–252.
25. A. Silberschatz, H. Korth, and S. Sudarshan. *Database System Concepts*. McGraw-Hill, 1997.
26. M. Waidner. Personal communication.

Fair and Efficient Mutual Exclusion Algorithms (Extended Abstract)*

K. Alagarsamy and K. Vidyasankar

Department of Computer Science,
Memorial University of Newfoundland,
St. John's, Newfoundland, Canada, A1B 3X5.
(alagar, vidya)@cs.mun.ca

Abstract. Peterson's n-process mutual exclusion algorithm [P81] has been widely touted for elegance and simplicity. It has been analyzed extensively, and yet certain properties have eluded the researchers. This paper illustrates, and expands on, several properties of Peterson's algorithm: (1) We reiterate that the number of processes that can overtake a process, called *unfairness index*, is unbounded in Peterson's algorithm; (2) With a slight modification of the algorithm, we obtain the unfairness index of $n(n-1)/2$; (3) We identify an inherent characteristic of that algorithm that sets the lower bound of $n(n-1)/2$ for the unfairness index; (4) By modifying the characteristic, we obtain algorithms with unfairness index $(n-1)$; (5) We show that the new algorithms are amenable to reducing shared space requirement, and to improving time efficiency (where the number of steps executed is proportional to the current contention); and (6) We also extend the algorithms to solve l-exclusion problem in a simple and straightforward way.

1 Introduction

We assume a system of n independent cyclic processes competing for a shared resource R. In a process p, the part of the code segment that accesses R is called *a critical section (CS) of p for the resource R* [D65]. The *mutual exclusion problem* is to design an algorithm that assures the following properties :

- *Safety* : At any time, at most one process is allowed to be in the CS.
- *Liveness* : When one or more processes have expressed their intentions to enter the CS, one of them eventually enters.

In addition, it is desirable to have the following property.

- *Freedom from Starvation* : Any process that expresses its intention to enter the CS will be able to do so in finite time.

The following assumptions are made in any mutual exclusion algorithm.

---

* This research is supported in part by the Natural Sciences and Engineering Research Council of Canada Individual Research Grant OGP0003182.

Assumption 1. *The execution speed of any process is finite but unpredictable.*

Assumption 2. *Critical section execution time of any process is finite but unpredictable.*

The mutual exclusion problem is one of the important problems in concurrent programming. Dekker was the first to give a correct software solution to mutual exclusion problem for two processes case. Dijkstra proposed a solution for n processes [D65]. Following Dijkstra's solution, many solutions appeared in the literature for n processes. Peterson presented an elegant solution for n processes in 1981 [P81]. Ever since the publication of Peterson's algorithm, it has become de facto example of mutual exclusion algorithm for many researchers and most text books on operating systems and concurrent programming, due to its simplicity [P81, R86, BD93, S97, VFG97] and elegance [D81, H90, S97, VFG97, T98]. Many correctness proofs for this algorithm have been presented in the literature [D81, R86, H90, VFG97].

That Peterson's algorithm satisfies safety, liveness, and freedom from starvation properties can be proved easily. However there is some confusion about the "fairness" of Peterson's algorithm.

When several processes are competing for the CS, a process may overtake another process, which started competing for the CS earlier, in entering the CS. As an example, assume n seats (shared resource) are available for a concert when a request r is submitted to reserve a seat. If the algorithm allows high overtakings, then all the n seats may be taken by the requests which arrive after r, and r is left unserved. This may occur due to different execution speeds of the processes. Such overtakes are normally considered unfair from the user point of view since the speed of a process may be constrained by the system's internal state and may not be an inherent property of any particular process.

We formalize the unfairness notion as follows.

Definition 1. *If a process i completes its first write operation on a shared variable of a mutual exclusion algorithm A before a process j does and subsequently j completes its CS execution before i does, then* **the process j overtakes the process i in CS access.**

Definition 2. *In an algorithm A, the maximum number of possible CS access overtakes over a process by other processes is called the* **unfairness index of the algorithm A.**

Definition 3. *In an algorithm A, the maximum number of CS access overtakes a process i can make over another process j is called the* **overtake index of the process i over j.** *The maximum of the overtake indices of i over other processes is called the* **overtake index of i in A.** *The maximum of the overtake indices of all the processes is called* **overtake index of the algorithm A.**

The unfairness index of an algorithm A indicates the worst possible amount of denial of service that the algorithm may cause to any process, and the overtake index indicates the best possible amount of favor of service that the algorithm may give to any process.

Raynal [R86] calculates the unfairness index of Peterson's algorithm as $n(n-1)/2$. Kowaltowski and Palma [KP84] believe it to be $n-1$ and Hofri [H90] shows it to be $n-1$ under certain liveness assumptions. However, it is widely known that the unfairness index of Peterson's algorithm is unbounded. (Problem 10.12 in Lynch's book [L96], page 329, asks for checking whether the unfairness index is bounded, stated as whether *bounded bypass* is guaranteed. Unbounded bypass of the n-process tournament algorithm, whose components are Peterson's algorithm for the case $n = 2$, is shown on page 293 in that book.) We reiterate in this paper that the unfairness index is not bounded, by showing that the overtake index is not bounded. We then show that by slightly modifying Peterson's algorithm a bounded unfairness index of $n(n-1)/2$, and overtake index of $(n-1)$ can be obtained.

We identify an inherent characteristic of Peterson's algorithm that sets the lower bound for the unfairness index as $n(n-1)/2$. By changing this characteristic, we obtain new mutual exclusion algorithms and achieve overtake index of 1 (that is, no process can overtake any other process more than once) and unfairness index of $(n-1)$.

The new algorithms suggest a way of reducing the shared space requirements. We give two space-efficient algorithms, one with the characteristic of Peterson's algorithm and unfairness index $n(n-1)/2$ and the other with a new characteristic and unfairness index $(n-1)$. These two algorithms bring out the difference between the two characteristics in a clear-cut manner.

We also find ways of reducing the number of instructions a process has to execute before entering the CS. For our improved algorithms, this number is proportional to the contention for the CS.

We also show that many of our algorithms can be extended in a very simple manner to solve l-exclusion problem [FLBB79, ADGMS94, AM94]. Here upto l $(l \geq 1)$ processes can be in the critical section simultaneously. This may be regarded as a resource allocation problem, with l identical copies of a non-sharable resource, where each process can request one copy of that resource. The algorithms proposed in the literature either assume higher level synchronization primitives, *test-and-set* in [FLBB79], and atomic queue procedures, *acquire* and *release* [AM94], or use a concurrent timestamp system [ADGMS94]. Designing a concurrent timestamp system itself is a nontrivial problem [DS97]. In contrast, our algorithms are simple and straightforward extensions of mutual exclusion algorithms. It is noteworthy that all our new algorithms preserve the elegance of Peterson's algorithm.

In section 2, Peterson's algorithm is given and its unfairness aspect discussed. In section 3, new algorithms with unfairness index $n-1$ are given. Space efficient algorithms are presented in section 4. Time efficient algorithms are given in section 5. Section 6 deals with l-exclusion algorithms, and section 7 presents the concluding remarks.

2 Peterson's Algorithm and Bounding its Unfairness Index

The basic idea behind Peterson's n-process mutual exclusion algorithm [P81] is that each process passes through $n-1$ stages before entering the critical section. These stages are designed to block one process per stage so that after $n-1$ stages only one process will be eligible to enter the critical section (which we consider as stage n). The algorithm uses two integer arrays *step* and *pos* of sizes $n-1$ and n respectively: *pos* is an array of 1-writer multi-reader variables and *step* is an array of multi-writer multi-reader variables. The value at *step*[j] indicates the *latest* process at step j, and *pos*[i] indicates the latest stage that the process i is passing through. (Peterson uses Q for *pos*, and $TURN$ for *step*.) The array *pos* is initialized to 0. The process id's, *pids*, are assumed to be integers between 1 and n. The code segment for process i is given in Figure 1[1].

Process i:

1. *for* $j = 1$ *to* $n - 1$ *do*
2. *begin*
3.   *pos*[i] := j;
4.   *step*[j] := i;
5.   *wait until* $(\forall k \neq i, pos[k] < j)$
          $\lor (step[j] \neq i)$
6. *end*;
7. *cs.i*;
8. *pos*[i] := 0;

Figure 1 : Algorithm $PH1$ [P81]

Process i:

1. *for* $j = 1$ *to* $n - 1$ *do*
2. *begin*
3.   *pos*[i] := j;
4.   *step*[j] := i;
5.   *wait until* $(\forall k \neq i, pos[k] < j)$
          $\lor (step[j] \neq i)$
6. *end*;
7. *wait until* $(\forall k \neq i, (pos[k] = 0)$
          $\lor (step[pos[k]] = k))$
8. *cs.i*;
9. *pos*[i] := 0;

Figure 2 : Algorithm $PH2$

We use the following terminology.

- A process p is said to be at *stage* j if $pos[p] = j$. A process is said to be *blocked at stage* j $(1 \leq j \leq n - 1)$ if it is waiting for a condition to become true at stage j. A process is *blocked* if it is blocked at some stage j; it is *unblocked* otherwise.
- If the condition $step[j] \neq p$ is true (after the process p sets $step[j] = p$), then we say that the process p has been *pushed* (out of stage j, to enter stage $j + 1$).
- A process p that has set $step[j] = p$ and is not blocked at stage j is said to have *crossed* stage j.

---

[1] The labels of all the algorithms in this paper start with P, to indicate 'Peterson-style'. The meaning of the second letter will be indicated later on.

Lemma 1. *The algorithm PH1 assures that at any time the number of processes that have crossed stage j is at most $n - j$, for $1 \leq j \leq n - 1$, $n > 1$.*

Proof. The proof is by induction on j. Let $C = (\forall k \neq p, pos[k] < j) \vee (step[j] \neq p)$.

For $j = 1$, we need to consider only the case where all n processes are competing for the CS and, every process has set $step[1]$. The process, say p, which sets its *pid* to $step[1]$ last is blocked at stage 1, because the condition C, for $j = 1$, is false for p. The assertion follows.

Assume as induction hypothesis that for some m, between 1 and $n - 2$, the number of processes that have crossed stage m is at most $n - m$. Only these processes will enter stage $m+1$ and set $step[m+1]$. The last process among them, say p, that sets $step[m + 1]$ is blocked, because the condition C, for $j = m + 1$, is false for p. Therefore the number of processes that could cross stage $m + 1$ is at most $n - (m + 1)$. The assertion follows. □

Theorem 1. *The algorithms PH1 assures mutual exclusion.*

Proof. By Lemma 1, at any time, the number of processes that can cross stage $n - 1$, and enter the CS, is $n - (n - 1)$, that is, 1. □

Lemma 2. *At any time, (a) the number of processes blocked at any stage is at most 1, and (b) at least one process with the highest pos value is unblocked.*

Proof. Part (a) follows from the fact that the only process that can be blocked at a stage k is the process whose *pid* is equal to $step[k]$. This fact also implies part (b) when there are two or more processes with the highest *pos* value. When there is only one process with the highest *pos* value, say j, we have $(\forall k \neq j, pos[k] < j)$ and therefore this process is not blocked. □

Theorem 2. *The algorithm PH1 assures freedom from starvation, that is, a competing process will enter the critical section in a finite time.*

Proof. We need to show only that no process will remain blocked at any particular stage for ever. Since a process may get blocked at most $n - 1$ times, the assertion would then follow.

Consider a process p blocked at some stage k. Suppose the condition $step[j] \neq i$ never becomes true for p. Then, there must be a set Q of one or more processes at stages higher than k. By Lemma 2(b), at any time, at least one process with the highest *pos* value is unblocked (different processes in Q may have the highest *pos* value at different times, and different processes may be unblocked at different times). By Assumption 1 every unblocked process will complete the execution of its current instruction in finite time and, by Assumption 2, every process which enters the CS will complete the CS execution in a finite time. This guarantees that all processes in Q will eventually complete their CS executions in finite time, and then the condition $(\forall k \neq i, pos[k] < j)$ will be satisfied for p. Then, p will become unblocked and can move up to the next stage. □

The unfairness index of the algorithm $PH1$ is not bounded, if $n > 2$. The following scenario illustrates this. The processes p_1, p_2, and p_3 are currently competing for the CS.

- Process p_1 starts first, sets $pos[p_1] = 1$,
- p_3 starts and assigns its pid to $step[1]$,
- p_2 sets its pid to $step[1]$ and so p_3 is pushed,
- since the condition $(\forall k \neq p_2, pos[k] < 1) \vee (step[1] \neq p_2)$ is not true, p_2 is blocked at stage 1,
- p_3 crosses stage 1 to stage 2,
- since the condition $(\forall k \neq p_3, pos[k] < j)$ is true, for $j \geq 2$, it keeps proceeding further, enters the CS, and completes its CS execution,
- p_3 starts competing again for the CS, and sets its pid to $step[1]$,
- the condition $(step[1] \neq p_2)$ becomes true, that is, p_2 is unblocked and p_3 is blocked at stage 1,
- p_2 moves up all the way, enters and leaves the CS, starts competing again, and sets its pid to $step[1]$,
- this time p_2 gets blocked and p_3 is unblocked, at stage 1, and
- p_2 and p_3 can overtake p_1, alternately, several times until p_1 sets $step[1] = p1$.

This implies that the unfairness index of $PH1$ is not bounded.

Note : The above result holds even if we replace the "first write operation" by "a bounded number of write operations" in Definition 1.1, as long as the bound is less than $2(n-2)$. Any number of overtakes on a process p is possible at stage j, for every j up to $n-2$. When p is in stage $n-1$, that is, after $2(n-2)$ write operations, it can be overtaken by at most one process.

The unfairness index can be bounded by modifying the algorithm slightly. One such modification is shown in $PH2$, in Figure 2. As seen from the above scenario, the unboundedness is due to the fact that unblocked processes may "sleep" for a long time or may execute very slowly compared to other processes. Algorithm $PH2$ "speeds up" such slow processes; really, it "slows down" fast processes until slower ones progress considerably: each process ready to enter the CS waits until all other competing processes progress at least until the end of their current stages. The proof of the safety property of $PH2$ is similar to that of $PH1$.

Theorem 3. *The algorithm PH2 has (a) unfairness index $n(n-1)/2$ and (b) overtake index $(n-1)$.*

Proof. In $PH2$, every process executes line 7 before entering the CS. There, it waits until every other competing process is blocked (when it observes that process; later on, that process might have become unblocked and moved up). This assures that every unblocked process reaches at least the end of its current stage, and if it has already crossed the current stage and not yet entered the next stage, then it reaches at least the end of the next stage.

Consider a process p at or about to enter stage j. By Lemma 1, at most $n - (j - 1)$ processes can (cross stage $j - 1$ and) enter stage j. In the worst case, all the other $n - j$ processes can overtake p in stage j. When the first among these executes line 7, p would be blocked at stage j. It will remain blocked at most until all these $n - j$ processes finish their CS executions. At that time, p will notice that the condition $(\forall k \neq p, pos[k] < j)$ is satisfied and will cross stage j.

Thus, at most $n - j$ processes can overtake p in stage j. Therefore the maximum number of overtakes, that is, the unfairness index, is $\sum_{j=1}^{n}(n - j) = n(n - 1)/2$.

Part (b) follows from the fact that a process q can overtake a process p at every stage. $\qquad\square$

3   Reducing Unfairness Index and Overtake Index

The unfairness index of $n(n - 1)/2$ can be attributed to the following characteristics of Peterson's algorithm.

(1) A process crosses a stage by being pushed by another process.
(2) Only the (single) process at the highest stage can also cross, by itself, without being pushed.

Therefore, unless being pushed, a process p blocked at a stage is not allowed to cross that stage until all processes at higher stages finish the CS executions. Then, when p finally crosses, several new processes may overtake p. In the following, we derive new algorithms by keeping (1) but modifying (2). We show that the new strategies help to reduce the unfairness index. We consider two alternatives to (2):

(2a) Processes at all stages can also cross without being pushed, *under certain safe conditions*.
(2b) Only the process at the lowest stage can also cross without being pushed, *under certain safe conditions*.

The safe conditions of (2a) and (2b) are different.

Algorithm $PA1$, described in Figure 3, implements (2a)[2]. Here $l(j)$ is the number of processes whose *pos* value is less than j. A process is allowed to cross stage j if there are at least j processes in stages 0 to $j - 1$. We note that when there is no process in the CS, (2) is automatically satisfied for the single process in the highest stage; it will observe $l(j) = n - 1$. Using $l(j)$ notation the algorithm $PH1$ can be stated as $PH1'$, in Figure 4. (We note that $l(j)$ is simply the value computed by the current process by reading the *pos* values. It is not a "global" value.)

---

[2] Our convention in labeling the algorithms is that the second letter indicates whether the highest stage process (H), all processes (A), or the lowest stage process (L) can cross by themselves without being pushed.

Process i: Process i:

1. *for $j = 1$ to $n - 1$ do*   1. *for $j = 1$ to $n - 1$ do*
2. *begin*   2. *begin*
3.   *$pos[i] := j$;*   3.   *$pos[i] := j$;*
4.   *$step[j] := i$;*   4.   *$step[j] := i$;*
5.   *wait until $(l(j) \geq j) \vee (step[j] \neq i)$*   5.   *wait until $(l(j) = n - 1) \vee (step[j] \neq i)$*
6. *end;*   6. *end;*
7. *$pos[i] := 0$;*   7. *$pos[i] := 0$;*

Figure 3 : Algorithm $PA1$ **Figure 4 : Algorithm $PH1'$**

Lemma 3. *The algorithm $PA1$ assures that at any time the number of processes that have crossed the stage j is at most $n - j$, for $(1 \leq j \leq n - 1)$, $n > 1$.*

The proof is same as for Lemma 1 with $C = (l(j) \geq j) \vee (step[j] \neq p)$.

Theorem 4. *The algorithm $PA1$ assures mutual exclusion.*

The proof follows from Lemma 3.

The unfairness index of the algorithm $PA1$ is also not bounded, if $n > 2$. The following scenario illustrates this. Suppose that processes p_1 and p_2 are currently competing for the CS.

- Process p_1 starts first, sets $pos[p_1] = 1$,
- p_2 starts, sets $pos[p_2] = 1$, and $step[1] = p_2$,
- since $l(1) = n - 2 \geq 1$ for p_2, p_2 crosses stage 1,
- $l(j) = n - 1 \geq j$, for all j from 2 to $n - 1$, for p_2 and so it moves up all the stages, enters the CS, and leaves the CS,
- p_2 starts competing again, sets $pos[p_2] = 1$, $step[1] = p_2$, and
- this cycle may repeat many times until p_1 sets $step[1] = p_1$.

Thus the number of overtakes of p_2 over p_1 is unbounded. Hence the unfairness index of the algorithm $PA1$ is not bounded.

Here also the unboundedness is due to (unblocked) processes being too slow relative to other competing processes. Again, slowing down faster processes until the slower ones progress considerably, we can bound the unfairness index. One way of accomplishing this is given in $PA2$, in Figure 5. Here $l_p(j)$ is the number of processes whose *pos* value is less than j but not zero. This algorithm has unfairness index $(n - 1)$ and overtake index 1. The proofs are similar to those for algorithm $PL1$ given in Figure 6.

Algorithm $PL1$ implements the characteristic (2b). Here N_{p0} is the number of processes whose *pos* values is 0 (again as observed by the current process).

Lemma 4. *The algorithm $PL1$ assures that at any time the number of processes that have crossed the stage j is at most $n - j$, for $(1 \leq j \leq n - 1)$, $n > 1$.*

Process i:

1. *for $j = 1$ to $n - 1$ do*
2. *begin*
3.   *pos[i] := j;*
4.   *step[j] := i;*
5.   *wait until $(l(j) \geq j) \vee (step[j] \neq i)$*
6.   *wait until $(l_p(j) = 0) \vee (l(j) \leq j - 1)$*
7. *end;*
8. *cs.i;*
9. *pos[i] := 0;*

Figure 5 : Algorithm $PA2$

Process i:

1. *for $j = 1$ to $n - 1$ do*
2. *begin*
3.   *pos[i] := j;*
4.   *step[j] := i;*
5.   *wait until $((l_p(j) = 0) \wedge (N_{p0} \geq j)$*
           $\vee (step[j] \neq i)$
6. *end;*
7. *cs.i;*
8. *pos[i] := 0;*

Figure 6 : Algorithm $PL1$

The proof is same as for Lemma 1 with $C = ((l_p(j) = 0) \wedge (N_{p0} \geq j)) \vee (step[j] \neq p)$.

Theorem 5. *The algorithm $PL1$ assures mutual exclusion.*

The proof follows from Lemma 4.

We show that $PL1$ has unfairness index $n - 1$.

Theorem 6. *The algorithm $PL1$ has overtake index 1.*

Proof. Suppose a process p overtakes another process q in $PL1$. That is, q sets $pos[q] = 1$ before p sets $pos[p] = 1$, but p enters the CS before q does. Then the wait condition in line 5 for $j = n - 1$ can be satisfied for p only by p being pushed, since it would observe at least two processes, namely p and q, to be competing and so will compute $N_{p0} \not\geq n - 1$.

When p is pushed off stage $n - 1$, let q be in stage m. If $m = n - 1$, then since at most two competing processes could cross the stage $n - 2$, by Lemma 4, q would have been the only process other than p in stage $n - 1$, and so q would have pushed p to the CS, and would be blocked at stage $n - 1$. Now, suppose $m < n - 1$. Then p would have crossed stages $m + 1$ and above only by being pushed, since it will observe $l_p(j) \neq 0$ due to q in stage less than $m + 1$. Then, (i) there must be a blocked process at every stage above m, (ii) the number of processes at stages m or above, can only be $n - (m - 1)$ including q, by Lemma 4, (iii) the number of stages above m is $n - m$, and these imply that q is the only process at stage m. Also, due to this number of processes being $n - (m - 1)$, the last process that crossed stage m would have observed $N_{p0} \leq m - 1$, and so, would have crossed only by being pushed, by the only remaining process at stage m, namely q. That is, q is blocked at stage m.

So, after p completes CS execution, q will move up to the next stage, either by itself or by being pushed. In any case, no other process can enter the stage $m + 1$, until q pushes the process blocked in that stage, and gets itself blocked. This pattern continues until q enters the critical section. That is, q cannot be overtaken by any process, including p if it starts competing again. Hence the overtake index of $PL1$ is 1. $\qquad\square$

Theorem 7. *The algorithm $PL1$ has unfairness index $n - 1$.*

Proof. By Theorem 6, each process can overtake another process at most once. Since the total number of processes in the system is n, at most $n - 1$ overtakes are possible before a process enters the CS. Hence the unfairness index of $PL1$ is $n - 1$. $\qquad\square$

4 Improving Space Efficiency

It turns out that the wait condition of $PL1$ can be simplified to $(N_{p0} \geq j) \lor (step[j] \neq i)$, still yielding unfairness index $n - 1$. The resulting algorithm would have the characteristic (2a) instead of (2b).

To compute N_{p0}, we need to know only whether pos value is zero or nonzero, that is, whether a process p is competing or not. Therefore the algorithm can be simplified with boolean $door$ value instead of integer pos. The array $door$ is initialized to 0. The algorithm is $PA3$, in Figure 7.

Process i:

1. $door[i] := 1;$
2. $for\ j = 1\ to\ n - 1\ do$
3. $begin$
4. $step[j] := i;$
5. $wait\ until\ (n - \sum_{k=1}^{n} door[k] \geq j)$
              $\lor (step[j] \neq i)$
6. $end;$
7. $cs.i;$
8. $door[i] := 0;$

Figure 7 : Algorithm $PA3$

Process i:

1. $door[i] := 1;$
2. $for\ j = 1\ to\ n - 1\ do$
3. $begin$
4. $step[j] := i;$
5. $wait\ until\ (\sum_{k=1}^{n} door[k] \leq j)$
              $\lor (step[j] \neq i)$
6. $end;$
7. $cs.i;$
8. $door[i] := 0;$

Figure 8 : Algorithm $PH3$

It is interesting to note that an algorithm with characteristic (2) and unfairness index $n(n - 1)/2$ can be obtained by a simple modification of the wait condition. This is algorithm $PH3$, given in Figure 8.

Suppose m processes are competing. In both $PH2$ and $PH3$, a process p can cross without being pushed only if all other processes are in the lower stages. An additional requirement in $PH3$ is that p must be in stage m or above, whereas in $PH2$, p could be anywhere, even in a stage below m. This additional requirement in $PH3$ ensures that, when p moves up without being pushed, each stage j, for j between 1 and $m - 1$, has exactly one process, and this process will cross stage j after at most $n - j$ processes overtake it.

The proofs of the properties for $PA3$ and $PH3$ are similar, respectively, to those of $PA2$ and $PH2$.

5 Improving Time Efficiency

The algorithms shown in the Figures 7 and 8 are also amenable to improving time efficiency. We observe that when the number of competing processes is less than n, it is unnecessary for a process to start from stage 1. For example, if there is only one process competing for the CS, then the process can 'jump' directly to the CS (to the stage n). In general, if there are k processes competing for the CS, a process can jump directly to the stage $n - k + 1$, and continue with the rest of the algorithm from thereon. This is done with algorithm $PA3$. The resulting algorithm would have characteristic (2b) instead of (2a). This is algorithm $PL2$, given in Figure 9. (The same modification is applicable to $PH3$ also.) Here, the number of iterations in the loop, and hence the number of shared variable accesses, depends on the contention observed by the process.

This modification in $PL2$ also assures additional fairness in the following sense: if a process p sets its *door* value after another process q made its initial jump, then p cannot overtake q. That is, the maximum number of overtakes depends only on the current contention.

Process i:

1. $door[i] := 1$;
2. *for* $j = n - \sum_{k=1}^{n} door[k] + 1$ *to* $n - 1$ *do*
3. *begin*
4. $\quad step[j] := i$;
5. $\quad$ *wait until* $(n - \sum_{k=1}^{n} door[k] \geq j) \vee (step[j] \neq i)$
6. *end*;
7. $cs.i$;
8. $door[i] := 0$;

Figure 9 : Algorithm $PL2$

6 Algorithms for l-exclusion Problem

This section deals with a generalization of mutual exclusion problem, called l-exclusion problem, introduced by Fischer et al. in [FLBB79], and subsequently studied in [ADGMS94, AM94]. The required properties of an l-exclusion algorithm are:

- *Safety (l-exclusion):* At any time, at most l processes are allowed to be in the critical section simultaneously.
- *Liveness (l-lockout avoidance):* When there are strictly less than l processes in the critical section, at least one process from the group of processes waiting for the CS should reach the CS in a finite time.

Fischer et al. [FLBB79] discussed a way of reducing l-exclusion problem to one-exclusion problem and then applying known solutions to the later problem. This solution is commonly used in banks for scheduling people waiting for a teller. The main drawback of this approach is that, if $l \geq 2$ copies of the resource are free, instead of allowing the first l processes to move "simultaneously" to "tellers", the algorithm requires them to file past to the front of the line one at a time. If the process at the front of the line is slow, then $l - 1$ processes behind it are forced to wait. In fact, if the process at the front of the line "fails", then the processes behind it wait forever and the system stops functioning. In this case, one failure can tie up all of the system's resources [FLBB79].

As noted in [AM94], all prior l-exclusion algorithms for shared memory systems either require unrealistic atomic operations or perform badly. We show that many of the mutual exclusion algorithms in this paper can be modified very slightly to obtain l-exclusion algorithms.

Except $PH1$ and $PH2$, all the algorithms presented in the previous sections can be easily modified to solve l-exclusion problem, simply by changing $n - 1$ to $n - l$ in the 'for statement' of each algorithm. We present the l-exclusion version of $PL2$ only, in Figure 10.

Process i:

1. $door[i] := 1;$
2. $for\ j = n - \sum_{k=1}^{n} door[k] + 1$
   $to\ n - l\ do$
3. $begin$
4. $\quad step[j] := i;$
5. $\quad wait\ until\ (n - \sum_{k=1}^{n} door[k] \geq j)$
   $\quad\quad \vee (step[j] \neq i)$
6. $end;$
7. $cs.i;$
8. $door[i] := 0;$

Figure 10 : Algorithm l-PL2

Process i:

1. $for\ j = 1\ to\ n - l\ do$
2. $begin$
3. $\quad pos[i] := j$
4. $\quad step[j] := i;$
5. $\quad wait\ until\ (l(j) \geq n - l) \vee (step[j] \neq i)$
6. $end;$
7. $cs.i;$
8. $pos[i] := 0;$

Figure 11 : Algorithm l-PH1'

To extend Peterson's algorithm, $PH1$, to solve the l-exclusion problem (problem 10.13 in Lynch book [L96]), the simple modification adopted for our algorithms, that is just changing the number of stages to be crossed, is not appropriate. Instead the condition for a process to cross a stage without being pushed has to be modified. In $PH1'$, the modification would be $l(j) \geq n - l$ instead of $l(j) = n - 1$, in the wait statement. In addition, the above modification, that is, changing $n - 1$ to $n - l$, can also be done to improve efficiency. The resulting algorithm is shown in Figure 11.

The correctness of these algorithms follows from the correctness proofs of their one-exclusion versions. In contrast to the algorithm of [FLBB79], our l-

exclusion algorithms can tolerate up to $l-1$ failures and therefore can be used to build fault-tolerant distributed systems.

7 Concluding Remarks

Peterson's n-process mutual exclusion algorithm has intrigued researchers since its publication. It has been extensively analyzed, and yet certain properties have eluded the researchers. This paper attempts to fill the gap in the analysis. We have (i) shown the unboundedness of the unfairness index of the algorithm and that the algorithm can easily be modified to bound the unfairness index to $n(n-1)/2$, and (ii) captured the underlying characteristic of the algorithm that sets the bound to the above value. Then, employing complementary characteristics, we have devised new mutual exclusion algorithms with unfairness index $n-1$. We have also given, through simple extensions, several elegant algorithms that improve space and time efficiency, and for solving l-exclusion problem.

Though the first software solutions for the mutual exclusion problem were presented as early as 1965, new solutions keep emerging for this problem either to meet the needs of different technologies (such as multiprogramming, multitasking, multiprocessing, parallel processing, distributed processing, and multithreading), or to achieve newly conceived criteria (such as self stabilization, scalability, and adaptiveness), or to effectively exploit some of the system characteristics (such as sparse situation where the total number of potentially contending processes is very large but the number of processes expected to be competing at any time is very small, distributed shared memory machines where the access of each shared variable involves traversing of interconnection network, and thread synchronization (threads are created within a single process, normally they are not large in number, and mostly all are executed in the same processor)), or to improve over existing ones with respect to certain quantitative or qualitative measures. This diversity in the classes of mutual exclusion algorithms makes a meaningful global comparison difficult.

Fairness is a crucial attribute of distributed algorithms. This criterion determines for how long a process, after performing the first write operation on a shared variable, indicating its interest in the CS, has to wait. All the solutions to the mutual exclusion problem are expected to be starvation free. However, ensuring starvation-freedom alone may not be sufficient in many applications; stronger fairness criteria are desirable. This paper focuses on two such criteria, unfairness and overtake index.

References

[ADGMS94] Y. Afek, D. Dolev, E. Gafni, M. Merrit and N. Shavit, A bounded First-In, First-Enabled Solution to the l-exclusion Problem, ACM TOPLAS, 16(3): 939-953, 1994.
[AM94] J. H. Anderson and M. Moir, Using k-exclusion to implement Resilient, Scalable Shared Objects, PODC '94, 141-150, 1994.

[BD93]   A. Burns and G. Davies, Concurrent Programming, Addison Wesley, 1993.

[CS94]   M. Choy and A. K. Singh, Adaptive Solutions to the Mutual Exclusion Problem, Distributed Computing, 8:1-17, 1994.

[DS97]   D. Delov and N. Shavit, Bounded Concurrent Time-stamping, SIAM Journal of Computing, 26(2):418-455, 1997.

[D65]   E.W. Dijkstra, Solution of a Problem in Concurrent Programming Control, CACM, 8(9):569, 1965.

[D81]   E.W. Dijkstra, An assertional proof of a program by G.L. Peterson, EWD 779, 1981.

[FLBB79] M. Fischer, N. Lynch, J. Burns, and A. Borodin, Resource Allocation with immunity to Process Failure, Proc. of the 20th Annual IEEE symposium on FOCS, 78-92, 1979.

[H90]   M. Hofri, Proof of a mutual exclusion algorithm - A 'class'ic example, ACM SIGOSR 24(1):18-22, 1990.

[KP84]   T. Kowaltowski and A. Palma, Another Solution of the Mutual Exclusion Problem, IPL 19(3):145-146, 1984.

[L87]   L. Lamport, A Fast Mutual Exclusion Algorithm, ACM TOCS, 5(1), 1-11, 1987.

[L96]   N. Lynch, Distributed Algorithms, Morgan Kaufmann Publishers, Inc., 1996.

[P81]   G.L. Peterson, Myths about the mutual exclusion problem, IPL 12(3):115-116, 1981.

[R86]   M. Raynal, Algorithms for Mutual Exclusion, MIT Press, 1986.

[S97]   F.B. Schneider, On Concurrent Programming, Graduate texts in computer science series, Springer 1997.

[T98]   Y. Tsay, Deriving Scalable Algorithms for Mutual Exclusion, DISC '98, 1998.

[VFG97]   F.W. van der Sommen, W.H.J. Feijen and A.J.M. van Gasterm, Peterson's Mutual Exclusion Algorithm Revisited, SCP 29:327-334, 1997.

Fast *and* Scalable Mutual Exclusion*

James H.Anderson and Yong-Jik Kim

Department of Computer Science
University of North Carolina at Chapel Hill

Abstract. We present an N-process algorithm for mutual exclusion under read/write atomicity that has $O(1)$ time complexity in the absence of contention and $\Theta(\log N)$ time complexity under contention, where "time" is measured by counting remote memory references. This is the first such algorithm to achieve these time complexity bounds. Our algorithm is obtained by combining a new "fast-path" mechanism with an arbitration-tree algorithm presented previously by Yang and Anderson.

1   Introduction

Recent work on mutual exclusion [3] has focused on the design of "scalable" algorithms that minimize the impact of the processor-to-memory bottleneck through the use of *local spinning*. A mutual exclusion algorithm is *scalable* if its performance degrades only slightly as the number of contending processes increases. In local-spin mutual exclusion algorithms, good scalability is achieved by requiring all busy-waiting loops to be read-only loops in which only locally-accessible shared variables are accessed that do not require a traversal of the processor-to-memory interconnect. A shared variable is locally accessible on a distributed shared-memory multiprocessor if it is stored in a local memory module, and on a cache-coherent multiprocessor if it is stored in a local cache line.

A number of queue-based local-spin mutual exclusion algorithms have been proposed in which only $O(1)$ remote memory references are required for a process to enter and exit its critical section [1, 4, 6]. In each of these algorithms, waiting processes form a "spin queue". Read-modify-write instructions are used to enqueue a blocked process on this queue. Performance studies presented in [1, 4, 6] have shown that these algorithms scale well as contention increases.

In subsequent work, Yang and Anderson showed that performance comparable to that of the queue-lock algorithms cited above could be achieved using only read and write operations [8]. In particular, they presented a read/write mutual exclusion algorithm with $\Theta(\log N)$ time complexity and experimentally showed that this algorithm is only slightly slower than the fastest queue locks. In Yang and Anderson's algorithm, instances of a local-spin mutual exclusion algorithm for two processes are embedded within a binary arbitration tree, as depicted in Fig. 1(a). The entry and exit sections associated with the two links connecting

---

* Work supported by NSF grant CCR 9732916. The first author was also supported by an Alfred P. Sloan Research Fellowship.

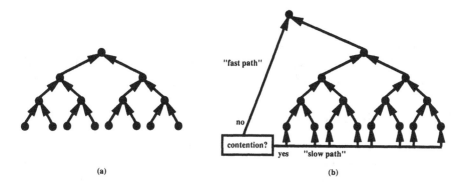

Fig. 1. Yang and Anderson's arbitration-tree algorithm (inset (a)) and its fast-path variant (inset (b)).

a given node to its sons constitute a two-process mutual exclusion algorithm. Initially, all processes start at the leaves of the tree. To enter its critical section, a process traverses the path from its leaf to the root, executing the entry section of each link on this path. Upon exiting its critical section, a process traverses this path in reverse, executing the exit section of each link.

Although Yang and Anderson's algorithm exhibits scalable performance, in complexity-theoretic terms, there is still a gap between the $\Theta(\log N)$ time complexity of their algorithm and the constant time complexity of algorithms based on stronger synchronization primitives. This gap is particularly troubling when considering performance in the absence of contention. Even without contention, the arbitration-tree algorithm forces each process to perform $\Theta(\log N)$ remote memory references in order to enter and exit its critical section. To alleviate this problem, Yang and Anderson presented a variant of their algorithm that includes a "fast-path" mechanism that allows the arbitration tree to be bypassed in the absence of contention. This variant is illustrated in Fig. 1(b). This algorithm has the desirable property that contention-free time complexity is $O(1)$. Unfortunately, it has the undesirable property that time complexity under contention is $\Theta(N)$ in the worst case, rather than $\Theta(\log N)$. In Yang and Anderson's fast-path algorithm, a process checks whether the fast path can be reopened after a period of contention ends by "polling" each process individually to see if it is still contending. This polling loop is the reason why the time complexity of their algorithm is $\Theta(N)$ in the worst case.

To this day, the problem of designing a read/write mutual exclusion algorithm with $O(1)$ time complexity in the absence of contention and $\Theta(\log N)$ time complexity under contention has remained open. In this paper, we close this problem by presenting a fast-path mechanism that achieves these time complexity bounds when used in conjunction with Yang and Anderson's arbitration-tree algorithm. Our fast-path mechanism has the novel feature that it can be reopened after a period of contention without having to poll each process individually to see if it is still contending.

The rest of this paper is organized as follows. In Sec. 2, we present our fast-path algorithm. In Sec. 3, we prove that the algorithm is correct. We end the paper with concluding remarks in Sec. 4.

2 Fast-Path Algorithm

Our fast-path algorithm is shown in Fig. 2. In this section, we explain informally how the algorithm works. We begin with a brief overview of the code. We assume that each labeled sequence of statements in Fig. 2 is atomic; each such sequence reads or writes at most one shared variable. A process determines if it can access the fast path by executing statements 1-9. If a process p detects any other competing process while executing these statements, then p is "deflected" out of the fast path and invokes either $SLOW1$ or $SLOW2$. $SLOW1$ is invoked if p has not updated any variables that must be reset in order to reopen the fast path. Otherwise, $SLOW2$ is invoked. A detailed explanation of the deflection mechanism is given below. If a process is not deflected, then it successfully acquires the fast path, which consists of statements 10-20. A process that either acquires the fast path or is deflected to $SLOW2$ attempts to reopen the fast path by executing statements 13-20 or 29-37, respectively. A detailed explanation of how the fast path is reopened is given below.

Before entering its critical section, a fast-path process must perform the entry code of the two-process mutual exclusion algorithm on top of the arbitration tree, as shown in Fig. 1(b). It executes this code using 0 as a virtual process identifier. This is denoted as "ENTRY_2(0)" in Fig. 2 (see statement 11). The corresponding two-process exit code is denoted "EXIT_2(0)" (statement 19). Each process p that is deflected to $SLOW1$ or $SLOW2$ must first compete within the N-process arbitration tree (using its own process identifier). The entry and exit code for the arbitration tree are denoted "ENTRY_N(p)" and "EXIT_N(p)", respectively (statements 21, 25, 26, and 39). After competing within the arbitration tree, a deflected process accesses the two-process algorithm on top of the tree using 1 as a virtual process identifier. The entry and exit code for this are denoted "ENTRY_2(1)" and "EXIT_2(1)", respectively (statements 22, 24, 27, and 38).

We now explain our fast-path acquisition mechanism in detail. At the heart of this mechanism is the following code fragment from Lamport's fast mutual exclusion algorithm [5].

```
shared variable  X: 0..N − 1; Y: boolean initially true
process p::
    Noncritical Section;
    X := p;
    if ¬Y then "compete with other processes (slow path)"
    else Y := false;
        if X ≠ p then "compete with other processes (slow path)"
        else "take the fast path"
```

type *Ytype* = **record** *free*: boolean; *indx*: $0..N-1$ **end**   /* stored in one word */

shared variable
    $X: 0..N-1$;
    Y, *Reset*: *Ytype* **initially** $(true, 0)$;
    Slot, *Proc*: **array**$[0..N-1]$ **of** boolean **initially** *false*;
    Infast: **boolean initially** *false*

private variable *y*: *Ytype*

process *p*::   /* $0 \le p < N$ */
while *true* **do**
0: Noncritical Section;
1: $X := p$;
2: $y := Y$;
    if $\neg y.free$ **then** $SLOW1()$
    else
3:    $Y := (false, 0)$;
4:    $Proc[p] := true$;
5:    **if** $(X \ne p \vee$
6:        *Infast*) **then** $SLOW2()$
    else
7:    $Slot[y.indx] := true$;
8:    **if** $Reset \ne y$ **then**
9:        $Slot[y.indx] := false$;
        $SLOW2()$
    else
10:        *Infast* := *true*;
        /* fast path */
11:        ENTRY_2(0);
12:        Critical Section;
13:        $Proc[p] := false$;
14:        $Reset := (false, y.indx)$;
15:        **if** $\neg Proc[y.indx]$ **then**
16:            $Reset :=$
                $(true, y.indx + 1 \bmod N)$;
17:            $Y :=$
                $(true, y.indx + 1 \bmod N)$
            fi;
18:        $Slot[y.indx] := false$;
19:        EXIT_2(0);
20:        *Infast* := *false*
    fi fi fi
od

procedure $SLOW1()$
21:ENTRY_N(p);
22:    ENTRY_2(1);
23:        Critical Section;
24:    EXIT_2(1);
25:EXIT_N(p)

procedure $SLOW2()$
26:ENTRY_N(p);
27:    ENTRY_2(1);
28:        Critical Section;
29:        $Y := (false, 0)$;
30:        $X := p$;
31:        $y := Reset$;
32:        $Proc[p] := false$;
33:        $Reset := (false, y.indx)$;
34:        **if** $(\neg Slot[y.indx] \wedge$
35:            $\neg Proc[y.indx])$ **then**
36:            $Reset :=$
                $(true, y.indx + 1 \bmod N)$;
37:            $Y :=$
                $(true, y.indx + 1 \bmod N)$
            fi;
38:    EXIT_2(1);
39:EXIT_N(p)

Fig. 2. Fast-path algorithm.

This code ensures that at most one process will "take the fast path". Moreover, with the stated initial conditions, if one process executes this code fragment in isolation, then that process will take the fast path. The problem with using this code is that, after a period of contention ends, it is difficult to "reopen" the fast path so that it can be acquired by other processes. If a process does succeed in taking the fast path, then that process can reopen the fast path itself by simply resetting Y to *true*. On the other hand, if no process succeeds in taking the fast path, then the fast path ultimately must be reopened by one of the slow-path processes. Unfortunately, because processes are asynchronous and communicate only by means of atomic read and write operations, it can be difficult for a slow-path process to know whether the fast path has been acquired by some process.

As a stepping stone towards our algorithm, consider the algorithm shown in Fig. 3, which uses unbounded memory to solve the problem. In this algorithm, Y has an additional field, which is an identifier that is used to "rename" any process that acquires the fast path. This identifier will increase without bound over time, so we will never have to worry about the possibility that two processes are renamed with the same identifier. With this added field, a slow-path process has a way of identifying a process that has taken the fast path. To see how this works, consider what happens when, starting from the initial state, some set of processes execute their entry sections. At least one of these processes will read $Y = (true, 0)$ at statement 2 and assign $Y := (false, 0)$ at statement 3. By properties of Lamport's fast-path code, of the processes that assign Y, at most one will reach statement 6. A process that reaches statement 6 will either acquire the fast path by reaching statement 9, or will be deflected to $SLOW2$ at statement 8.

This gives us two cases to analyze: Of the processes that read $Y = (true, 0)$ and assign Y, either all are deflected to $SLOW2$, or one, say p, acquires the fast path. In the former case, at least one of the processes that executes $SLOW2$ will increment the *indx* field of Y and set the *free* field of Y to *true* (statement 28). This has the effect of reopening the fast path. In the latter case, we must argue that (i) the fast-path process p reopens the fast path after leaving it, and (ii) no $SLOW2$ process "prematurely" reopens the fast path before p has left the fast path. Establishing (i) is straightforward. Process p will reopen the fast path by incrementing the *indx* field of Y and setting the *free* field of Y to *true* (statement 13). Note that the *Infast* variable prevents the reopening of the fast path from actually taking effect until after p has finished executing EXIT_2(0). To establish (ii), suppose, to the contrary, that some $SLOW2$ process q reopens the fast path by executing statement 28 while p is executing within statements 9-15. For this to happen, q must have read $Slot[0]$ at statement 26 before p assigned $Slot[0] := true$ at statement 6. This in turn implies that q executed statement 25 before p executed statement 7. Thus, p must have found $Reset \neq y$ at statement 7, i.e., it was deflected to $SLOW2$, which is a contradiction. It follows from the explanation given here that after an initial period of contention ends, we must have $Y.free = true$ and $Y.indx > 0$. This argument can be applied inductively

type *Ytype* = **record** *free*: **boolean**; *indx*: $0..\infty$ **end**   /* stored in one word */

shared variable   /* other variable declarations are as in Fig. 2 */
    Slot: **array**$[0..\infty]$ **of boolean initially** *false*

process *p*::   /* $0 \le p < N$ */
while *true* **do**   **procedure** *SLOW*1()
0: Noncritical Section;   16: ENTRY_N(p);
1: $X := p$;   17:   ENTRY_2(1);
2: $y := Y$;   18:   Critical Section;
   if $\neg y.free$ **then** *SLOW*1()   19:   EXIT_2(1);
   else   20: EXIT_N(p)
3:   $Y := (false, 0)$;
4:   **if** $(X \neq p \vee$
5:       *Infast*) **then** *SLOW*2()   **procedure** *SLOW*2()
     else   21: ENTRY_N(p);
6:     $Slot[y.indx] := true$;   22:   ENTRY_2(1);
7:     **if** $Reset \neq y$ **then**   23:   Critical Section;
8:       $Slot[y.indx] := false$;   24: $y := Reset$;
         *SLOW*2()   25: $Reset := (false, y.indx)$;
       else   26:   **if** $\neg Slot[y.indx]$ **then**
9:       *Infast* := *true*;   27: $Reset := (true, y.indx + 1)$;
         /* fast path */   28: $Y := (true, y.indx + 1)$
10:      ENTRY_2(0);   **fi**;
11:        Critical Section;   29:   EXIT_2(1);
12:        $Reset := (true, y.indx + 1)$; 30: EXIT_N(p)
13:        $Y := (true, y.indx + 1)$;
14:      EXIT_2(0);
15:      *Infast* := *false*
     fi fi fi
od

Fig. 3. Fast-path algorithm with unbounded memory.

to show that the fast path is properly reopened after each period of contention ends.

Of course, the problem with this algorithm is that the *indx* field of Y that is used for renaming will continue to grow without bound. The algorithm of Fig. 2 solves this problem by requiring $Y.indx$ to be incremented modulo-N. With $Y.indx$ being updated in this way, the following potential problem arises. A process p may reach statement 7 in Fig. 2 with $y.indx = k$ and then get delayed. While delayed, other processes may repeatedly increment $Y.indx$ (in *SLOW*2) until it "cycles back" to k. At this point, another process q may reach statement 7 with $y.indx = k$. This is a problem because p and q may interfere with each other in updating $Slot[k]$. The algorithm in Fig. 2 prevents such a scenario from happening by preventing $Y.indx$ from cycling while some process executes within statements 7-18. To see how this is prevented, note that before reaching statement 7, a process p must first assign $Proc[p] := true$ at statement 4. Note further that before a process can increment $Y.indx$ from n to $n+1$ **mod**

N (statement 17 or 37), it must first check $Proc[n]$ (statement 15 or 35) and find it to be false. This check prevents $Y.indx$ from cycling while p executes within statements 7-18. As shown in the next section, the correctness of the code that reopens the fast path (statements 13-18 and 29-37) rests heavily on the fact that this code is executed within a critical section.

3 Correctness Proof

In this section, we prove that the algorithm in Fig. 2 is correct. Specifically, we prove that the mutual exclusion property (at most one process executes critical section at any time) holds and that the fast path is always open in the absence of contention. (The algorithm is easily seen to be starvation-free, given the correctness of ENTRY and EXIT calls.) The following notational conventions will be used in the proof.

Notational Conventions: Unless stated otherwise, we assume i, j, and k range over $\{0..N-1\}$. We use $n.i$ to denote the statement with label n of process i, and $i.y$ to represent i's private variable y. Let S be a subset of the statement labels in process i. Then, $i@\{S\}$ holds iff the program counter for process i equals some value in S. □

Definition: We define a process i to be *FAST-possible* if the condition $F(i)$, defined below, is true.

$$F(i) \equiv i@\{3..8, 10..20\} \land$$
$$(i@\{3..5\} \Rightarrow X = i) \land (i@\{3..8\} \Rightarrow Reset = i.y) \qquad \square$$

Informally, this condition indicates that process i may *potentially* acquire the fast path. It does not necessarily mean that i is *guaranteed* to acquire the fast path: if $F(i)$ holds, then process i still can be deflected to $SLOW1$ or $SLOW2$. If a process i is at $\{3..9\}$ and is not FAST-possible, then we define it to be *FAST-disabled*. We will later show that a FAST-disabled process cannot acquire the fast path. We now turn our attention to the mutual exclusion property.

3.1 Mutual Exclusion

We will establish the mutual exclusion property by proving that the conjunction of a number of assertions is an invariant. This proves that each of these assertions individually is an invariant. These invariants are numbered (I1) through (I22) and are stated on the following pages. Informally, invariants (I1) through (I4) give conditions that must hold if a process is FAST-possible. Invariants (I5) through (I9) prevent "cycling". These invariants are used to show that if $i@\{6..9\}$ holds and process i is FAST-disabled, then $Reset.indx$ must be "trapped" between $i.y.indx$ and i. Therefore, there is no way $Reset$ can cycle back, erroneously making process i FAST-enabled again. Invariants (I10) through (I15) show that certain regions of code are mutually exclusive. Invariants (I16) through (I21) are all simple invariants that follow almost directly from the code. Invariant (I22) is the mutual exclusion property, our goal.

In establishing these invariants, statements that might potentially establish $F(i)$ must be repeatedly considered. The following lemma shows that only one such statement must be considered.

Lemma 1: *If t and u are consecutive states such that $F(i)$ is false at t but true at u, and if each of (I1) through (I22) holds at t, then u is reached from t via the execution of statement 2.i.*

Proof: The only statements that could potentially establish $F(i)$ are 2.i (which establishes $i@\{3..8, 10..20\}$ and may establish $Reset = i.y$), 5.i (which falsifies $i@\{3..5\}$), 8.i (which falsifies $i@\{3..8\}$), 1.i (which establishes $X = i$), and 31.i, 14.j, 16.j, 33.j, and 36.j, where j is any arbitrary process (which may establish $Reset = i.y$). We now show that none of these statements other than 2.i can establish $F(i)$.

Statement 5.i can establish $i@\{6\}$, and hence $F(i)$, only if $X = i$ holds at t. But, by (I5), this implies that $Reset = i.y$ holds at t as well. By the definition of $F(i)$, this implies that $F(i)$ holds at t, a contradiction.

Statement 8.i can establish $i@\{10\}$, and hence $F(i)$, only if $Reset = i.y$ holds at t. But this implies that $F(i)$ holds at t, a contradiction.

Statements 1.i and 31.i establish $i@\{2, 32\}$. Thus, they cannot establish $F(i)$.

Statements 14.j and 33.j could establish $F(i)$ only if $i@\{3..8\} \wedge Reset \neq i.y$ holds at t, and upon executing 14.j or 33.j, $Reset = i.y$ is established. However, by (I3) and (I16), 14.j and 33.j can change the value of $Reset$ only by changing the value of $Reset.free$ from $true$ to $false$. By (I20), if $i@\{3..8\}$ holds at t, then $i.y.free = true$ holds as well. Thus, statements 14.j and 33.j cannot possibly establish $Reset = i.y$, and hence cannot establish $F(i)$.

Statements 16.j and 36.j likewise can establish $F(i)$ only if $i@\{3..8\} \wedge Reset \neq i.y$ holds at t. We consider two cases, depending on whether $i@\{3..5\}$ or $i@\{6..8\}$ holds at t. If $i@\{3..5\} \wedge Reset \neq i.y$ holds at t, then by (I5), $X \neq i$ holds at t. This implies that $X \neq i$ holds at u as well, i.e., $F(i)$ is false at u.

Now, suppose that $i@\{6..8\} \wedge Reset \neq i.y$ holds at t. By (I17), statements 16.j and 36.j increment $Reset.indx$ by 1 modulo-N. Therefore, they may establish $F(i)$ only if $Reset.indx = (i.y.indx - 1) \bmod N$ holds at t. By (I6), this implies that $i = Reset.indx$ or $i = i.y.indx$ holds at t. By (I8), the latter implies that $i = Reset.indx$ holds at t. Hence, in either case, $i = Reset.indx$ holds at t. Because we have assumed that $i@\{6..8\} \wedge j@\{16, 36\}$ holds at t, by (I7), we have a contradiction. Therefore, statements 16.j and 36.j cannot establish $F(i)$. □

We now prove each invariant listed above. It is easy to see that each invariant hold initially, so we will not bother to prove this. For each invariant I, we show that for any pair of consecutive states t and u, if all invariants hold at t, then I holds at u. In proving this, we do not consider statements that trivially don't affect I.

invariant $F(i) \wedge i@\{4..8, 10..17\} \Rightarrow Y = (false, 0)$ (I1)

Proof: To prove that (I1) is not falsified, it suffices to consider only those statements that may establish the antecedent or falsify the consequent. By Lemma 1, the only statement that can establish $F(i)$ is $2.i$. However, $2.i$ establishes $i@\{3\}$ and thus cannot establish the antecedent. The condition $i@\{4..8, 10..17\}$ may be established only by statement $3.i$, which also establishes the consequent.

The consequent may be falsified only by statements $17.j$ or $37.j$, where j is any arbitrary process. If $j = i$, then both $17.j$ and $37.j$ establish $i@\{18, 38\}$, which implies that the antecedent is false.

Suppose that $j \neq i$. By (I10) and (I11), the antecedent and $j@\{17\}$ cannot hold simultaneously (recall that $j@\{17\}$ implies $F(j)$, by definition). Hence, statement $17.j$ cannot be executed while the antecedent holds. Similarly, by (I12), (I13), and (I14), the antecedent and $j@\{37\}$ cannot both hold. Hence, statement $37.j$ also cannot be executed while the antecedent holds. $\quad\square$

invariant $F(i) \wedge i@\{8, 10..17\} \Rightarrow Slot[i.y.indx] = true$ $\qquad$ (I2)

Proof: By Lemma 1, the only statement that can establish $F(i)$ is $2.i$. However, $2.i$ establishes $i@\{3\}$ and hence cannot establish the antecedent. The condition $i@\{8, 10..17\}$ may be established only by statement $7.i$, which also establishes the consequent.

The consequent may be falsified only by statements $2.i$, $31.i$, $9.j$, and $18.j$, where j is any arbitrary process. Statements $2.i$ and $31.i$ establish $i@\{3, 21, 32\}$, which implies that the antecedent is false. If $j = i$, then $9.j$ and $18.j$ establish $i@\{19, 26\}$, which implies that the antecedent is false.

Suppose that $j \neq i$. In this case, statement $9.j$ may falsify the consequent only if $i.y.indx = j.y.indx$ holds. By (I15) (with i and j exchanged), $j@\{9\} \wedge i.y.indx = j.y.indx$ implies that the antecedent of (I2) is false. Thus, $9.j$ cannot falsify (I2). Similarly, by (I11), if $j@\{18\}$ holds (which implies that $F(j)$ holds), then the antecedent of (I2) is false. Thus, $18.j$ also cannot falsify (I2). $\quad\square$

invariant $i@\{10..16\} \Rightarrow Reset.indx = i.y.indx$ $\qquad$ (I3)

Proof: The antecedent may be established only by statement $8.i$, which does so only if $Reset = i.y$ holds. Therefore, statement $8.i$ preserves (I3).

The consequent may be falsified only by statements $2.i$, $31.i$, $14.j$, $16.j$, $33.j$, and $36.j$, where j is any arbitrary process. The antecedent is false after the execution of $2.i$ and $31.i$ and also after the execution of $16.j$, $33.j$, and $36.j$ if $j = i$. If $j = i$, then statement $14.j$ preserves the consequent.

Consider $14.j$, $16.j$, $33.j$, and $36.j$, where $j \neq i$. By (I11), the antecedent of (I3) and $j@\{14, 16\}$ cannot hold simultaneously (recall that $i@\{10..16\} \Rightarrow F(i)$ and $j@\{14, 16\} \Rightarrow F(j)$). Similarly, by (I14), the antecedent and $j@\{36\}$ cannot hold simultaneously. Hence, statements $14.j$, $16.j$, and $36.j$ can be executed only when the antecedent is false, and thus do not falsify (I3). By (I16), statement $33.j$ cannot change $Reset.indx$. Hence, it does not falsify (I3). $\quad\square$

invariant $i@\{11..20\} \Rightarrow Infast = true$ $\qquad$ (I4)

Proof: The antecedent may be established only by statement $10.i$, which also establishes the consequent. The consequent may be falsified only by statement $20.j$, where j is any arbitrary process. If $j = i$, then statement $20.j$ also falsifies the antecedent. If $j \neq i$, then by (I11), the antecedent and $j@\{20\}$ cannot both hold. Hence, the antecedent is false after the execution of statement $20.j$. □

invariant $i@\{3..5\} \wedge X = i \Rightarrow Reset = i.y$ (I5)

Proof: The antecedent may be established only by statements $1.i$ (which establishes $X = i$) and $2.i$ (which may establish $i@\{3..5\}$). However, $1.i$ establishes $i@\{2\}$ and hence cannot establish the antecedent. Also, by (I19), statement $2.i$ establishes the consequent.

The consequent may be falsified only by statements $2.i$, $31.i$, $14.j$, $16.j$, $33.j$, and $36.j$, where j is any arbitrary process. However, statement $2.i$ preserves (I5) as shown above. Furthermore, the antecedent is false after the execution of $31.i$ and also after the execution of each of $14.j$, $16.j$, $33.j$, and $36.j$ if $j = i$.

Consider $14.j$, $16.j$, $33.j$, and $36.j$, where $j \neq i$. If the antecedent and consequent of (I5) both hold, then $F(i)$ holds by definition. If $j \neq i$, then by (I10) and (I12), $j@\{14, 16, 33, 36\}$ cannot hold as well. Hence, these statements cannot falsify (I5). □

invariant $i@\{6..9\} \Rightarrow (i.y.indx \leq Reset.indx \leq i) \vee$
$(Reset.indx \leq i \leq i.y.indx) \vee$
$(i \leq i.y.indx \leq Reset.indx)$ (I6)

Proof: The antecedent may be established only if $5.i$ is executed when $X = i$ holds. In this case, by (I5), $Reset = i.y$ holds, so the consequent is preserved.

The consequent may be falsified only by statements $2.i$, $31.i$, $14.j$, $16.j$, $33.j$, and $36.j$, where j is any arbitrary process. The antecedent is false after the execution of $2.i$ and $31.i$ and also after the execution of each of $14.j$, $16.j$, $33.j$, and $36.j$ if $j = i$.

Consider statements $16.j$ and $36.j$, where $j \neq i$. By (I17), these statements increment $Reset.indx$ by 1 modulo-N. Therefore, these statements may falsify the consequent only if $Reset.indx = i$ holds before execution. However, in this case, by (I7), the antecedent of (I6) is false. Thus, statements $16.j$ and $36.j$ cannot falsify (I7).

Finally, consider $14.j$ and $33.j$, where $j \neq i$. By (I3) and (I16), $14.j$ and $33.j$ don't change $Reset.indx$. Hence, they can't falsify the consequent. □

invariant $i@\{6..9\} \wedge Reset.indx = i \Rightarrow \neg(\exists j :: j@\{16, 36\})$ (I7)

Proof: The antecedent may be established only by statements $5.i$, $14.k$, $16.k$, $33.k$, and $36.k$, where k is any arbitrary process. Statement $5.i$ establishes the antecedent only if executed when $X = i$ holds. In this case, by (I5), $Reset = i.y$, and hence $F(i)$, holds as well. By (I10) and (I12), this implies that $\neg(\exists j :: j@\{16, 36\})$ also holds. This implies that statement $5.i$ cannot falsify (I7).

If $k = i$, then the antecedent is false after the execution of each of $14.k$, $16.k$, $33.k$, and $36.k$. If $k \neq i$, then by (I22), $(\forall j :: k@\{16, 36\} \wedge j@\{16, 36\} \Rightarrow k = j)$ holds. Therefore, $16.k$ and $36.k$ both establish $(\forall j :: \neg j@\{16, 36\})$, which is equivalent to the consequent. Now, consider statements $14.k$ and $33.k$, where $k \neq i$. By (I3) and (I16), these statements do not change $Reset.indx$. It follows that, although statements $14.k$ and $33.k$ may preserve the antecedent, they do not establish it.

The consequent may be falsified only by statements $15.j$ and $35.j$, which may do so only if $Proc[j.y.indx] = false$. However, if the antecedent of (I7) and $j@\{15, 35\}$ both hold, then the following hold: $Reset.indx = j.y.indx$, by (I17), $Reset.indx = i$, by the antecedent, and $Proc[i] = true$, by (I21). Taken together, these assertions imply that $Proc[j.y.indx] = true$. Therefore, statements $15.j$ or $35.j$ cannot falsify the consequent while the antecedent holds. □

invariant $i@\{6..9\} \wedge i.y.indx = i \Rightarrow Reset.indx = i.y.indx$ (I8)

Proof: The antecedent may be established only by statements $2.i$, $5.i$, and $31.i$. However, statements $2.i$ and $31.i$ establish $i@\{3, 32\}$, which implies that the antecedent is false. Furthermore, by (I5), statement $5.i$ preserves the consequent.

The consequent may be falsified only by statements $2.i$, $31.i$, $14.j$, $16.j$, $33.j$, and $36.j$, where j is any arbitrary process. However, the antecedent is false after the execution of $2.i$ and $31.i$ and also after the execution of each of $16.j$, $33.j$, and $36.j$ if $j = i$.

Consider statements $14.j$, $16.j$, $33.j$, and $36.j$, where $j \neq i$. By (I3) and (I16), statements $14.j$ and $33.j$ do not change $Reset.indx$, and hence cannot falsify the consequent. Note also that, by (I7), the antecedent, the consequent, and $j@\{16, 36\}$ cannot all hold simultaneously. Hence, statements $16.j$ and $36.j$ cannot falsify the consequent when the antecedent holds. □

invariant $i@\{9\} \wedge Reset.indx = i.y.indx \Rightarrow Reset.free = false$ (I9)

Proof: (I9) may be falsified only by statements $2.i$, $8.i$, $31.i$, $14.j$, $16.j$, $33.j$, and $36.j$, where j is any arbitrary process. Statements $2.i$ and $31.i$ establish $i@\{3, 32\}$, which implies that the antecedent is false. Statement $8.i$ establishes the antecedent only if executed when $Reset \neq i.y \wedge Reset.indx = i.y.indx$ holds, which implies that $Reset.free \neq i.y.free$. However, by (I20), $i.y.free = true$. Thus, $Reset.free = false$.

If $j = i$, then each of $14.j$, $16.j$, $33.j$, and $36.j$ establishes $i@\{15, 17, 34, 37\}$, which implies that the antecedent is false.

Consider statements $14.j$, $16.j$, $33.j$, and $36.j$, where $j \neq i$. Statements $14.j$ and $33.j$ trivially establish or preserve the consequent. By (I17), statements $16.j$ and $36.j$ increment $Reset.indx$ by 1 modulo-N. Therefore, these statements may establish the antecedent of (I9) only if executed when $i@\{9\} \wedge Reset.indx = (i.y.indx - 1) \bmod N$ holds. In this case, by (I6), $i = Reset.indx$ or $i = i.y.indx$ holds. By (I8), the latter implies that $i = Reset.indx$ holds. In either case, $i = Reset.indx$ holds. By (I7), this implies that $i@\{9\}$ is false. It follows that statements $16.j$ and $36.j$ cannot falsify (I9). □

invariant $F(i) \wedge F(j) \wedge i \neq j \Rightarrow \neg(i@\{3..6\} \wedge j@\{3..8, 10..17\})$ (I10)

Proof: By Lemma 1, the only statement that can establish $F(i)$ is $2.i$. Therefore, the only statements that may falsify (I10) are $2.i$ and $2.j$. Without loss of generality, it suffices to consider only statement $2.i$.

Statement $2.i$ may establish $F(i) \wedge i@\{3..6\}$ only if $Y.free = true$. We consider two cases. First, suppose that $(\exists j : j \neq i :: F(j) \wedge j@\{3..5\})$ holds before $2.i$ is executed. In this case, $X = j$ holds by the definition of $F(j)$. Hence, $X \neq i$, which implies that $2.i$ does not establish $F(i)$. Second, suppose that $(\exists j : j \neq i :: F(j) \wedge j@\{6..8, 10..17\})$ holds before $2.i$ is executed. In this case, by (I1), $Y.free = false$. In either case, statement $2.i$ cannot establish $F(i) \wedge i@\{3..6\}$. □

invariant $F(i) \wedge F(j) \wedge i \neq j \Rightarrow \neg(i@\{7, 8, 10..20\} \wedge j@\{7, 8, 10..20\})$ (I11)

Proof: By Lemma 1, the only statement that can establish $F(i)$ is $2.i$. However, $2.i$ establishes $i@\{3\}$ and hence cannot falsify (I11). The only other statements that could potentially falsify (I11) are $6.i$ and $6.j$. Without loss of generality, it suffices to consider only statement $6.i$.

By Lemma 1, statement $6.i$ may establish $F(i) \wedge i@\{7, 8, 10..20\}$ only if $F(i) \wedge Infast = false$ holds before execution. We consider two cases. First, suppose that $(\exists j : j \neq i :: F(j) \wedge j@\{7, 8, 10..17\})$ holds before the execution of $6.i$. In this case, by (I10), $F(i) \wedge i@\{6\}$ is false. This implies that $6.i$ cannot establish $F(i) \wedge i@\{7, 8, 10..20\}$. Second, suppose that $(\exists j : j \neq i :: F(j) \wedge j@\{18..20\})$ holds before $6.i$ is executed. In this case, by (I4), $Infast = true$. Hence, statement $6.i$ cannot establish $i@\{7..20\}$. □

invariant $F(i) \Rightarrow \neg(i@\{3..5\} \wedge j@\{31..37\})$ (I12)

Proof: By Lemma 1, the only statement that can establish $F(i)$ is $2.i$. Therefore, the only statements that may falsify (I12) are $2.i$ and $30.j$.

Statement $2.i$ may falsify (I12) only if executed when $Y.free = true \wedge j@\{31..37\}$ holds, but this is precluded by (I18). Statement $30.j$ may falsify (I12) only if executed when $F(i) \wedge i@\{3..5\} \wedge i \neq j$ holds. Because statement $30.j$ falsifies $X = i$, it also falsifies $F(i) \wedge i@\{3..5\}$. Thus, it preserves (I12). □

invariant $F(i) \Rightarrow \neg(i@\{6, 7\} \wedge j@\{34..37\})$ (I13)

Proof: By Lemma 1, the only statement that can establish $F(i)$ is $2.i$. However, $2.i$ establishes $i@\{3\}$ and hence cannot falsify (I13). The only other statements that may potentially falsify (I13) are $5.i$ and $33.j$.

Statement $5.i$ may falsify (I13) only if executed when $F(i) \wedge j@\{34..37\}$ holds, but this is precluded by (I12). Statement $33.j$ may falsify (I13) only if executed when $F(i) \wedge i@\{6, 7\}$ holds, which, by (I20), implies that $i.y.free = true$ holds. Because statement $33.j$ establishes $Reset.free = false$, $Reset \neq i.y$ holds after its execution, which implies that $F(i) \wedge i@\{6, 7\}$ is false. Therefore, statement $33.j$ preserves (I13). □

invariant $F(i) \Rightarrow \neg(i@\{8, 10..19\} \wedge j@\{35..37\})$ (I14)

Proof: By Lemma 1, the only statement that can establish $F(i)$ is $2.i$. However, $2.i$ establishes $i@\{3\}$ and hence cannot falsify (I14). The only other statements that could potentially falsify (I14) are $7.i$ and $34.j$. Statement $7.i$ may falsify (I14) only if executed when $F(i) \wedge j@\{35..37\}$ holds, but this is precluded by (I13).

Statement $34.j$ may falsify (I14) only if executed when $F(i) \wedge i@\{8, 10..19\} \wedge Slot[j.y.indx] = false$ holds. By (I22), $i@\{17..19\}$ and $j@\{34\}$ cannot hold simultaneously. Thus, $34.j$ could potentially falsify (I14) only if executed when $F(i) \wedge i@\{8, 10..16\} \wedge Slot[j.y.indx] = false$ holds. In this case, $Slot[i.y.indx] = true$ holds as well, by (I2), as does $Reset.indx = i.y.indx$, by the definition of $F(i)$ and (I3). In addition, by (I17), $j@\{34\}$ implies that $Reset.indx = j.y.indx$ holds. Combining these assertions, we have $Slot[j.y.indx] = false \wedge Slot[j.y.indx] = true$, which is a contradiction. Hence, statement $34.j$ cannot falsify (I14). $\square$

invariant $i@\{6..9\} \wedge j@\{6..17\} \wedge i \neq j \Rightarrow i.y.indx \neq j.y.indx$ (I15)

Proof: The only statements that may falsify the consequent are $2.i$, $31.i$, $2.j$, and $31.j$. However, the antecedent is false after the execution of each of these statements. The only statements that can establish the antecedent are $5.i$ and $5.j$. We show that $5.i$ does not falsify (I15); the reasoning for $5.j$ is similar. Statement $5.i$ can establish the antecedent only if executed when $X = i$ holds. By (I5), this implies that $Reset = i.y$ holds, which in turn implies that $F(i)$ is true. So, assume that $X = i \wedge Reset = i.y \wedge F(i)$ holds before $5.i$ is executed. We analyze three cases, which are defined by considering the value of process j's program counter.

- **Case 1:** $j@\{6..8\}$ holds before $5.i$ is executed. In this case, because $F(i)$ is true, by (I10), $F(j)$ does not hold. Thus, we have $j@\{6..8\} \wedge \neg F(j)$, which implies that $Reset \neq j.y$. Because $Reset = i.y$, this implies that $i.y \neq j.y$. In addition, by (I20), we have $i.y.free = true \wedge j.y.free = true$. Thus, the consequent of (I15) holds before, and hence after, $5.i$ is executed.
- **Case 2:** $j@\{9\}$ holds before $5.i$ is executed. In this case, we show that the consequent of (I15) holds before, and hence after, $5.i$ is executed. Assume to the contrary that $i.y.indx = j.y.indx$ holds before $5.i$ is executed. Then, because $Reset = i.y$ holds, we have $j.y.indx = Reset.indx$. By (I9), this implies that $Reset.free = false$. Because $Reset = i.y$ holds, this implies that $i.y.free = false$ holds. However, by (I20), we have $i.y.free = true$, which is a contradiction.
- **Case 3:** $j@\{10..17\}$ holds before $5.i$ is executed. In this case, by (I10), $F(i) \wedge i@\{5\}$ is false, which is a contradiction. $\square$

The following invariants are straightforward and are stated without proof.

invariant $i@\{32, 33\} \Rightarrow Reset = i.y$ (I16)
invariant $i@\{15, 16, 34..36\} \Rightarrow Reset = (false, i.y.indx)$ (I17)
invariant $i@\{30..37\} \Rightarrow Y = (false, 0)$ (I18)

invariant $Y.free = true \Rightarrow Y = Reset$ (I19)

invariant $i@\{3..20\} \Rightarrow i.y.free = true$ (I20)

invariant $(i@\{5..13, 26..32\}) = (Proc[i] = true)$ (I21)

invariant (Mutual exclusion) $|\{i :: i@\{12..19, 23, 24, 28..38\}\}| \leq 1$ (I22)

Proof: From the specification of ENTRY_2/EXIT_2 and ENTRY_N/EXIT_N, (I22) may fail to hold only if two processes simultaneously execute within statements 10-20. However, this is precluded by (I11). □

3.2 Fast Path is Always Open in the Absence of Contention

Having shown that the mutual exclusion property holds, we now prove that when all processes are within their noncritical sections, the fast path is open. This property is formally captured by (I26) given below. Before proving (I26), we first present three other invariants; two of these are quite straightforward and are stated without proof.

invariant $Slot[k] = true \Rightarrow (\exists i :: i@\{8..18\} \wedge k = i.y.indx)$ (I23)

invariant $(\forall i :: i@\{0..2, 18..25, 38, 39\}) \Rightarrow Y.free = true$ (I24)

Proof: The only statements that can establish the antecedent are $15.i$, $17.i$, $34.i$, $35.i$, and $37.i$. Both $17.i$ and $37.i$ establish the consequent.

Statements $15.i$ and $35.i$ can establish the antecedent only if $Proc[k] = true$, where $k = i.y.indx$. By (I21), $Proc[k] = true$ implies that $k@\{5..13, 26..32\}$ holds, which implies that the antecedent is false.

Similarly, statement $34.i$ can establish the antecedent only if $Slot[i.y.indx] = true$. By (I23), this implies that $(\exists j :: j@\{8..18\} \wedge i.y.indx = j.y.indx)$ holds. By (I22), $j@\{12..18\} \wedge i@\{34\}$ is false. It follows that $(\exists j :: j@\{8..11\} \wedge i.y.indx = j.y.indx)$ holds, which implies that the antecedent is false.

The only statements that can falsify the consequent are $3.i$ and $29.i$. Both establish $i@\{4, 30\}$, which implies that the antecedent is false. □

invariant $Infast = true \Rightarrow (\exists i :: i@\{11..20\})$ (I25)

invariant (Fast path is open in the absence of contention)
$(\forall i :: i@\{0\}) \Rightarrow Y.free = true \wedge Infast = false \wedge Y = Reset$ (I26)

Proof: If $(\forall i :: i@\{0\})$ holds, then $Y.free = true$ holds by (I24), and $Infast = false$ holds by (I25). By (I19), $Y = Reset$ holds as well. □

4 Concluding Remarks

In presenting our fast-path algorithm, we have abstracted away from the details of the underlying algorithms used to implement the ENTRY and EXIT calls.

With the ENTRY_2/EXIT_2 calls in Fig. 2 implemented using Yang and Anderson's two-process algorithm, our fast-path algorithm can be simplified slightly. In particular, the writes to the variable *Infast* can be removed, and the test of *Infast* in statement 6 can be replaced by a test of a similar variable (specifically the variable $C[0]$ — see [8]) used in Yang and Anderson's algorithm.

Results by Cypher have shown that read/write atomicity is too weak for implementing mutual exclusion with a constant number of remote memory references per critical section access [2]. The actual lower bound established by him is a slow growing function of N. We suspect that $\Omega(\log N)$ is probably a tight lower bound for this problem. At the very least, we know from Cypher's work that time complexity under contention must be a function of N. Thus, mechanisms for achieving constant time complexity in the absence of contention should remain of interest even if algorithms with better time complexity under contention are developed.

The problem of implementing a fast-path mechanism bears some resemblance to the wait-free long-lived renaming problem [7]. Indeed, thinking about connections to renaming led us to discover our fast-path algorithm. In principle, a fast-path mechanism could be implemented by associating a name with the fast path and by having each process attempt to acquire that name in its entry section; a process that successfully acquires the fast-path name would release it in its exit section. Despite this rather obvious connection, the problem of implementing a fast-path mechanism is actually a much easier problem than the long-lived renaming problem. In particular, while a renaming algorithm must be wait-free, most of the steps involved in releasing a "fast-path name" can be done within a process's critical section. Our algorithm heavily exploits this fact.

References

1. T. Anderson. The performance of spin lock alternatives for shared-memory multiprocessors. *IEEE Trans. on Parallel and Distributed Sys.*, 1(1):6–16, 1990.
2. R. Cypher. The communication requirements of mutual exclusion. In *Proceedings of the Seventh Annual ACM Symposium on Parallel Algorithms and Architectures*, pages 147–156, 1995.
3. E. Dijkstra. Solution of a problem in concurrent programming control. *Communications of the ACM*, 8(9):569, 1965.
4. G. Graunke and S. Thakkar. Synchronization algorithms for shared-memory multiprocessors. *IEEE Computer*, 23:60–69, 1990.
5. L. Lamport. A fast mutual exclusion algorithm. *ACM Trans. on Computer Sys.*, 5(1):1–11, 1987.
6. J. Mellor-Crummey and M. Scott. Algorithms for scalable synchronization on shared-memory multiprocessors. *ACM Trans. on Computer Sys.*, 9(1):21–65, 1991.
7. M. Moir and J. Anderson. Wait-free algorithms for fast, long-lived renaming. *Science of Computer Programming*, 25(1):1–39, 1995.
8. J.-H. Yang and J. Anderson. Fast, scalable synchronization with minimal hardware support. In *Proceedings of the 12th Annual ACM Symposium on Principles of Distributed Computing*, pages 171–182. 1993.

The Congenial Talking Philosophers Problem in Computer Networks*
(Extended Abstract)

Yuh-Jzer Joung

joung@ccms.ntu.edu.tw
Department of Information Management
National Taiwan University
Taipei, Taiwan

Abstract. The design issues for asynchronous group mutual exclusion have been modeled as the *Congenial Talking Philosophers*, and solutions for shared-memory models have been proposed [4]. This paper presents an efficient and highly concurrent distributed algorithm for computer networks where processes communicate by message passing.

1 Introduction

The design issues for mutual exclusion between groups of processes have been modeled by Joung [4] as the *Congenial Talking Philosophers*. The problem concerns a set of N philosophers $p_1, p_2, \ldots, P_N$ which spend their time thinking alone and talking in a forum. Initially, all philosophers are thinking. From time to time, when a philosopher is tired of thinking, it wishes to attend a forum of its choice. Given that there is only one meeting room—the shared resource, a philosopher attempting to enter the meeting room to attend a forum can succeed only if the meeting room is empty (and in this case the philosopher starts the forum), or some philosopher interested in the forum is already in the meeting room (and in this case the philosopher joins this ongoing forum). We assume that when a philosopher has attended a forum, it spends an unpredictable but finite amount of time in the forum. After a philosopher leaves a forum (that is, exits the meeting room), it returns to thinking.[1] The problem is to design an algorithm for the philosophers satisfying the following requirements:

Mutual Exclusion: if some philosopher is in a forum, then no other philosopher can be in a different forum simultaneously.

Bounded Delay: a philosopher attempting to attend a forum will eventually succeed.

Concurrent Entering: if some philosophers are interested in a forum and no philosopher is interested in a different forum, then the philosophers can attend the forum concurrently.

---

* This research was supported in part by the National Science Council, Taipei, Taiwan, under Grants NSC 86-2213-E-002-053 and NSC 87-2218-E-002-050, and by the 1998 Research Award of College of Management, National Taiwan University.

[1] Throughout the paper, "in a forum" is used synonymously with "in the meeting room." So, "to attend/leave a forum" is synonymously with "to enter/exit the meeting room."

The requirement of "concurrent entering" is to prevent an unnecessary synchronization on philosophers in attending the same forum when no other philosophers is interested in a different forum. For example, solutions that simply adopt a conventional n-process mutual exclusion algorithm for the problem are obviously an overkill. (For a survey of such algorithms see the books [8, 1, 12, 7].) Moreover, solutions that may allow philosophers to be in a forum simultaneously, but still require them to compete with one another in some mutually exclusive style in order to *enter* the meeting room are also not proper to this problem.

As usual, we are interested in completely decentralized solutions for the problem. A "semi-centralized" solution can be easily derived, for example, by employing a "concierge" for each forum. A philosopher interested in a particular forum first issues a request to the concierge of the forum. The concierges then compete with one another in a mutually exclusive style to obtain a privilege for their philosophers to use the meeting room. The algorithm is "semi-centralized" because although the contention to the meeting room is resolved decentralizedly by the concierges, the decision as when a set of philosophers interested in the same forum can enter the meeting room is determined centralizedly by the concierge of the forum. So, like other centralized solutions, the algorithm is vulnerable to any fault and performance bottleneck of the concierges. Furthermore, the "semi-centralized" solution must process each request for a forum in two stages: one between the requesting philosopher and the corresponding concierge, and the other among the concierges for mutual exclusion.

In this paper we focus the Congenial Talking Philosophers problem on computer networks where philosophers communicate by reliable and FIFO message passing. Solutions for shared-memory models are treated in [4]. While it is true that shared-memory algorithms can be systematically converted to message passing (or the other way around, see, e.g., Ch. 17 of [7]), such transformation is generally costly. For example, the transformation of the shared-memory algorithm presented in [4] may result in an asymmetric solution where some processes are designated to maintain the shared variables, usually in a centralized fashion, and so the processes are often the bottleneck of the performance; the solution also requires many messages (more than $6(N-1)$) per entry to the critical section. Thus, it is worth investigating solutions that directly take advantage of the underlying features of the execution model. For example, a communication imposes a causal ordering between the initiator (the information provider) and its target (the information recipient), and the **send** and **receive** commands in the message-passing paradigm implicitly assumes this causal ordering in the execution. In contrast, a more sophisticated technique is required in a completely decentralized shared-memory model to ensure that two asynchronous processes engaged in a communication are appropriately synchronized so that the information provider will not overwrite the information before the other process has observed the content.

Indeed, as we shall see shortly in Section 3, a symmetric and completely decentralized solution satisfying the three basic requirements—mutual exclusion, bounded delay, and concurrent entering—can be easily devised by modifying Ricart and Agrawala's algorithm [10] for n-process mutual exclusion. This is not the case we have experienced in the shared-memory model; the algorithm presented in [4] is somewhat complex and is not a straightforward adaption from existing algorithms for mutual exclusion. Nevertheless, one is easy to be deceived by this simple algorithm: its behavior appears to be fine from static analysis until we put it on simulation and learned that it is only slightly better than one imposing mutual exclusion on every entry to the critical section! Therefore, it is also interesting to see why such a simple modification does not work and how a more efficient algorithm can be devised for the problem.

The rest of the paper is organized as follows: Section 2 presents some criteria for evaluating solutions for the Congenial Talking Philosophers problem. In Section 3 we present the straightforward solution descried above and show why the solution has a surprisingly poor performance. Section 4 then presents a more concurrent solution. Conclusions and future work are offered in Section 5.

2   Complexity Measures

Solutions for the Congenial Talking Philosophers problem can be evaluated by the following four perspectives: *messages, time, context switches*, and *degree of concurrency*. Like the conventional mutual exclusion problem, message complexity is concerned with the number of messages the system generates per entry to the critical section—the meeting room. The other three complexity measures are defined below.

Definition 1. A *passage* by p_i through the meeting room is an interval $[t_1, t_2]$, where t_1 is the time p_i enters the meeting room, and t_2 the time it exits the meeting room. The passage is *initiated* at t_1, and is *completed* at t_2. The passage is *ongoing* at any time in between t_1 and t_2. The *attribute* of the passage is $\langle p_i, X \rangle$, where X is the forum p_i is attending.

When no confusion is possible, we use intervals and attributes interchangeably to represent passages. The phrase "a passage through X by p_i" refers to a passage with attribute $\langle p_i, X \rangle$.

Definition 2. Let S be a set of intervals. A subset R of S is a *minimal cover* of S if for every $\alpha \in S$, every time instance in α is in some $\beta \in R$ (that is, $\forall [t_1, t_2] \in S, t_1 \leq t \leq t_2 \Rightarrow \exists [t_3, t_4] \in R, t_3 \leq t \leq t_4$) and the size of R is minimal. The *dimension* of S, denoted by $\Omega(S)$, is the size of a minimal cover of S.

For example, suppose that a philosopher p_i has to wait for the following passages before it can enter the meeting room: $\langle p_1, X \rangle$, $\langle p_2, X \rangle$, $\langle p_3, X \rangle$, $\langle p_4, Y \rangle$, $\langle p_5, Y \rangle$, $\langle p_6, Y \rangle$, $\langle p_7, Z \rangle$, and $\langle p_8, Z \rangle$ (see Fig. 1). Then the five passages $\langle p_1, X \rangle$, $\langle p_3, X \rangle$, $\langle p_4, Y \rangle$, $\langle p_7, Z \rangle$, and $\langle p_8, Z \rangle$ constitute a minimal cover of the set of all eight passages drawn in the figure. So, the dimension of the set of the eight passages is 5. Because passages may overlap, when measuring the "time" a philosopher may wait in terms of passages, we cannot directly count all the passages it has to wait, but rather the dimension of them. So in this case the five passages $\langle p_1, X \rangle$, $\langle p_3, X \rangle$, $\langle p_4, Y \rangle$, $\langle p_7, Z \rangle$, and $\langle p_8, Z \rangle$ suffice to account for p_i's wait.

Likewise, the *time* complexity of a solution for the Congenial Talking Philosophers problem is measured by $\Omega(T)$, where T is the maximal set of passages that may be initiated after a philosopher p_i has made a request for a forum, and that must be completed before p_i can enter the meeting room. Note that the definition of T does not include those passages that are initiated after p_i has made its request, but p_i needs not wait for them to be completed in order to enter the meeting room; that is, we do not count those passages that may be concurrently ongoing with p_i's.

In practice, a "context switch" occurs when a shared resource is "cleaned" for a new group of processes. Depending on the applications, some context switches may be very time-consuming. So in the Congenial Talking Philosophers problem a philosopher waiting for more passages through the same forum may in practice

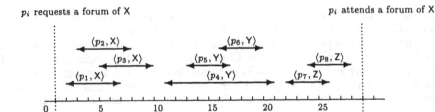

p_i requests a forum of X p_i attends a forum of X

Fig. 1. A layout of passages.

need less time than one waiting for fewer passages through different fora. So, in addition to time complexity, we also need a measurement of "context switches", which requires the following definition.

Definition 3. Let U_X be a set of passages through forum X. Let $t_s = \min\{t \mid [t, t'] \in U_X\}$, and $t_f = \max\{t' \mid [t, t'] \in U_X\}$. Then, U_X is a *round of passages through* X (or simply *a round of* X) if:

1. No passage other than that of U_X is initiated in between t_s and t_f; and
2. The last passage initiated before t_s and the first passage initiated after t_f, if any, must be for a different forum.

In other words, a round of X is a maximal set of consecutive passages through forum X. If U_X is a round of X, then we say that the round is *initiated* at t_s, and *completed* at t_f.

The *context-switch complexity* is measured by the maximum number of rounds of passages that may be initiated after a philosopher has made a request for X, but before a round of X is initiated in which p_i can make a passage through X. For example, in Fig. 1, suppose that no passage is initiated before $\langle p_1, X \rangle$. Then, p_i waits for 3 rounds of passages for its request: a round of X, a round of Y, and a round of Z.

We measure the *degree of concurrency* by the maximum number of entries to the meeting room that can still be made while some philosopher is in the meeting room and another philosopher is waiting for a different forum. (Obviously, if no philosopher is waiting for a different forum while a philosopher is in the meeting room, then, in the presence of concurrent entering, every philosopher interested in the same forum can enter/re-enter the meeting room without any restriction.) We choose this measurement because when a philosopher p is in the meeting room, no other philosopher interested in a different forum can use the meeting room. Given that p decides on its own when it will leave the meeting room, a better resource utilization can be achieved if we will allow more philosophers interested in the same forum to share the meeting room with p.

Note that the above complexity measures all concern worst-case scenarios. It is undoubtedly that an average-case analysis would be more appealing for the evaluation. However, due to the dynamic nature of the problem, an average-case analysis is extremely complicated. Simulation studies [6] are therefore encouraged to provide some insight into the average-case behavior of a proposed solution.

3   A Straightforward Decentralized Solution

Recall that in Ricart and Agrawala's algorithm [10] for n-process mutual exclusion, a process requiring entry to the critical section multicasts a request message to every other process, and enters the critical section only when all the other processes have replied to this request. To ensure mutual exclusion and bounded delay, each process maintains a sequence number SN that is to be updated according to Lamport's causality rules [5]. Each process's SN is initialized to 0. On issuing a request, a process p_i increases its SN by 1, and attaches the pair $\langle i, sn_i \rangle$ to the request, where i is the unique identity of the process and sn_i is the new value of SN. Formally, $\langle i, sn_i \rangle$ is the *priority* of the request. Upon receiving a request with a priority $\langle i, sn_i \rangle$, a process p_j adjusts the value of its SN to $\max(SN, sn_i)$, and uses the following rules to decide when to reply to the request:

1. p_j replies immediately if it does not require entry to the critical section, or it requires entry to the critical section and the priority of its request is lower than $\langle i, sn_i \rangle$.
2. the reply is delayed if p_j also requires entry to the critical section and the priority of its request is higher than $\langle i, sn_i \rangle$. The reply is delayed until p_j has exited the critical section.

The priority is ordered as follows: a priority $\langle i, sn_i \rangle$ is *higher* than $\langle j, sn_j \rangle$, denoted by $\langle i, sn_i \rangle > \langle j, sn_j \rangle$, if and only if $sn_i < sn_j$, or $sn_i = sn_j$ and $i < j$.

Ricart and Agrawala's algorithm can be straightforwardly modified for the Congenial Talking Philosophers problem as follows: A philosopher wishing to attend forum X multicasts a request to every other philosopher, and enters the meeting room when all philosophers have replied to its request. A request message is of the form $Req(\langle i, sn_i \rangle, X)$, which additionally bears the name of the forum the philosopher wishes to attend. Upon receipt of the request, a philosopher p_j uses the following rules to decide when to reply to the request:

1. p_j replies immediately if it is not interested in a different forum, or it is interested in a different forum and the priority of its request is lower than that of p_i's request. (A philosopher is *interested* in a forum if it has issued a request for the forum, and either it is still waiting for attending the forum, or it is already in the forum.)
2. the reply is delayed if p_j is interested in a different forum and the priority of its request is higher than that of p_i's request.

We refer to the modified algorithm as RA1. It is easy to see that RA1 satisfies the three requirements—mutual exclusion, bounded delay, and concurrent entering. For mutual exclusion, observe that by the way sequence numbers are maintained, if a philosopher p_j requests a forum after it has received a request $Req(\langle i, sn \rangle, X)$ issued by p_i, then p_j must obtain a priority for its request lower than $\langle i, sn \rangle$. So, when p_j's request arrives at p_i, if the request is for a different forum, then the reply to the request must be deferred by p_i until p_i has left X (for which the request $Req(\langle i, sn \rangle, X)$ is issued). Therefore, p_j cannot attend a different forum while p_i is in X. Moreover, given that priorities are unique, when two philosophers request different fora concurrently, the request issued by the low-priority philosopher will be delayed by the high-priority one until the high-priority philosopher has passed through a forum. So, the two philosophers cannot be in different fora simultaneously. Because neither logically dependent requests nor concurrent requests can violate mutual exclusion, mutual exclusion is therefore guaranteed.

For bounded delay, observe that after p_i has issued a request $Req(\langle i, sn \rangle, X)$, for each p_j, p_i can receive at most one request from p_j with a priority higher than that of p_i's request. This is because messages over a communication link are delivered in the order sent. So, if p_i receives a request from p_j after p_i has issued $Req(\langle i, sn \rangle, X)$, then before p_j makes a new request, it must have received p_i's reply to its previous request, and so it must have received p_i's request $Req(\langle i, sn \rangle, X)$ sent before the reply. So, p_j's new request must have a priority lower than that of p_i's request. So, in between the time (call this t_1) p_i issues a request and the time (call this t_2) it receives replies from all other philosophers, p_j can have at most two requests with a priority higher than that of p_i's request: one that p_i receives before t_1, and the other that p_i receives after t_1. (We assume that a request *ceases to exist* once the requesting philosopher has completed a passage through a forum for the request.) Overall, in between t_1 and t_2, there are at most $2(N-1)$ requests having a priority higher than that of p_i's request. Because the reply to a request can be deferred only if the receiving philosopher is interested in a different forum and its request for the forum has a priority higher than that of the former request, and because a philosopher spends only finite time in a forum, p_i's request will eventually be replied by all other philosophers. Hence, bounded delay is guaranteed.

For concurrent entering, observe that if a set of philosophers attempt to attend a given forum X, then they will not delay one another's request. So if no philosopher is interested in a different forum, then each of the philosophers interested in X will be able to obtain a reply from every other philosopher. Since no extra synchronization is imposed on how a philosopher replies to the requests for X, the requesting philosophers attend X in a purely concurrent style.

To evaluate the algorithm, consider first message complexity. It is easy to see that, like Ricart and Agrawala's algorithm, RA1's message complexity is $2(N-1)$: each entry to the meeting room requires $N-1$ requests and $N-1$ replies.

For time complexity, let T be the set of passages that are initiated after p_i has sent out a request, and that must be completed before p_i can enter the meeting room. Recall from the previous discussion that in between the time p_i issues a request and the time it receives replies from all other philosophers, there are at most $2(N-1)$ requests having a priority higher than that of p_i's request. Clearly, only these requests can result in passages in T. So, $|T| \leq 2(N-1)$. It is easy to see that the dimension of T is also $2(N-1)$. This is because, in the worst case, the passages in T may be mutually disjoint. So the time complexity of RA1 is $2(N-1)$. Moreover, from the above discussion it is easy to see that RA1's context-switch complexity is also $2(N-1)$.

Finally, from the above discussion it is also easy to see that if p_i has issued a request for X, then while a philosopher is occupying the meeting room for forum Y, at most $2(N-2)$ entries to the meeting room can be made before p_i enters the meeting room. Therefore, the maximum degree of concurrency offered by the algorithm is $2(N-2)$.

The simulation results are summarized in Fig. 4 in the appendix. The results indicate that the behavior of the system is only slightly better than the case where the philosophers use the meeting room in a mutually exclusive style!

We now analyze the simulation results from a more static point of view. Assume there are m fora $X_1, \ldots, X_m$. Let $N = m \cdot k$, and assume that all N philosophers wish to attend a forum, where for each of the m fora k philosophers have requested the forum. Suppose that the philosophers' priorities are ordered decreasingly as follows:

$$p_{1,1}, p_{2,1}, \cdots, p_{m,1}, p_{1,2}, p_{2,2}, \cdots, p_{m,2}, \cdots, p_{1,k}, p_{2,k}, \cdots, p_{m,k}$$

where $p_{i,j}$ denotes the jth philosopher that is interested in X_i. By the algorithm, the $m \cdot k$ requests will yield $m \cdot k$ rounds of passages (because the philosophers will enter the meeting room in the order of their priorities), where each round consists of only one passage.

Consider the expected concurrency behavior of the above example. Observe that the total number of rounds of passages these $m \cdot k$ requests may generate depends on how their priorities are ordered. Suppose that of the $(m \cdot k)!$ possible orderings, the $m \cdot k$ requests have an equal probability to assume each ordering. Let $E(m, k)$ be the expected number of rounds of passages the requests may generate. In combinatorics, $E(m, k)$ is equivalent to the expected number of runs $m \cdot k$ balls, k balls per color, may generate when they are randomly placed on a line, where a *run* is defined to be a maximal sequence of balls of the same color. By a combinatorial analysis [2], we have

$$E(m, k) = mk - k + 1$$

Given that there are $m \cdot k$ requests, the expected number of passages per round is

$$\frac{mk}{mk - k + 1} < \frac{mk}{mk - k} = \frac{m}{m - 1}$$

(One may compare this value with the measured average round size in our simulation for RA1.) Therefore, when m is large, the expected number of passages per round is nearly 1, meaning that the concurrency of RA1 is almost the same as one applying a conventional mutual exclusion algorithm such as Ricart and Agrawala's to strictly impose mutual exclusion on every entry to the meeting room!

4 A Highly Concurrent Solution

The poor average-case concurrency behavior of RA1 is due to the fact that if two philosophers p_i and p_j are interested in the same forum, but a third philosopher p_k interested in a different forum has obtained a priority in between p_i's and p_j's, then p_i and p_j cannot attend a forum concurrently because the low-priority philosopher (say p_j) must wait for p_k to finish a forum before it can attend a forum. Intuitively, p_j should be allowed to join p_i's forum, for otherwise concurrency would not be increased. To do so, while p_i is in a forum, if it receives p_j's request for the same forum, then we let p_i reply to p_j with a start message to inform p_j that it can directly enter the meeting room to join the ongoing forum. That is, we allow a high-priority philosopher to *capture* a low-priority one to join a forum. (A captured philosopher cannot in turn capture other philosophers to avoid a possibility of livelock, e.g., two philosophers repeatedly capturing each other to attend a forum while blocking a third philosopher waiting for a different forum.) Obviously, p_j's entry to the meeting room must be known by p_k because p_k may have already received p_j's reply and is waiting for only p_i's reply. So, when p_i leaves the forum, in the reply to p_k's request, p_i must inform p_k that it has captured p_j to attend a forum. p_k then uses this information to decide if it has an "up-to-date" reply from p_j. If so, then p_k is sure that p_j has also exited the forum and so can enter the meeting room without violating mutual exclusion. On the other hand, if the most recent reply from p_j is "out-of-date", then p_k must wait until p_j sends it a new reply. Clearly, p_j must send such a reply on exiting the meeting room.

Note that because p_j may have already replied to p_k's request before it is captured by p_i, it may reply to p_k's request twice (where the other is sent upon exiting the meeting room). The extra reply is offset by the dispensation of p_k's reply to p_j's request because p_j's request has already been granted by p_i. So the overall messages required per entry to the meeting room are not increased by the extra reply. However, p_j's request may arrive at p_i before p_i enters the meeting room. Because philosophers interested in the same forum will not block each other's request (so as to ensure concurrent entering), upon receipt of p_j's request p_i must reply to the request immediately. When later p_i is allowed to use the meeting room, it has to send a start message to capture p_j. So, p_i may respond to p_j's request twice, yielding the number of messages required per entry to the meeting room to be increased by $N-1$ in the worst case (where all philosophers have requested the same forum).

Moreover, from the above discussion we see that sequence numbers along do not convey enough information for philosophers to decide whether a reply to a request is out-of-date. So, in the new algorithm, which we shall refer to as RA2, we let each philosopher p_i maintain a *vector sequence number* VSN_i [9, 11]. VSN_i is a vector of natural numbers of length N and is initialized to contain all zeros. The value $VSN_i[j]$ represents a count of requests that have occurred at p_j and that are known at p_i, either because they originate there (when $j = i$) or because their existence is known about through message passing. Let $\mathcal{VSN}$ denote the set of vectors of natural numbers of length N, and $\mathcal{N}$ denote the set of natural numbers. The binary relation '$<$' on $\mathcal{N} \times \mathcal{VSN}$ is defined as follows:

$$\langle k, v \rangle < \langle j, u \rangle \text{ iff } \sum_l v[l] > \sum_l u[l] \text{ or } \left(\sum_l v[l] = \sum_l u[l] \wedge k > j \right)$$

It can be seen that the binary relation '$<$' on $\mathcal{N} \times \mathcal{VSN}$ is antisymmetric and transitive; and for any two distinct pairs $\langle j, u \rangle$ and $\langle k, v \rangle$, either $\langle j, u \rangle < \langle k, v \rangle$ or $\langle k, v \rangle < \langle j, u \rangle$.

Furthermore, p_i also maintains a vector VF_i of natural numbers of length N, where $VF_i[j]$, initialized to 0, represents a count of entries to the meeting room that are made by p_j and that are known at p_i.

When a philosopher p_i wishes to attend a forum X, it increments $VSN_i[i]$ by 1 and, like RA1, p_i multicasts a request message $Req(\langle i, vsn_i \rangle, X)$ to every other philosopher, where vsn_i is the new value of VSN_i. The value $\langle i, vsn_i \rangle$ is the *priority* of the request. A priority $\langle j, u \rangle$ is *higher than* $\langle k, v \rangle$ if and only if $\langle j, u \rangle > \langle k, v \rangle$. Unlike RA1, however, p_i may enter the meeting room either because every philosopher has replied to its request with an "up-to-date" acknowledgment Ack, or because some philosopher has replied to its request with a message $Start$. In the former case, we say that p_i enters the meeting room as a *captor* (and acts as a captor in the meeting room), while in the latter case p_i enters the meeting room as a *captive*.

Upon receiving a message $Req(\langle i, vsn_i \rangle, X)$, p_j updates VSN_j to $merge(VSN_j, vsn_i)$, where function $merge(u, v)$ is defined as follows:

$$merge(u, v)[k] = \max(u[k], v[k]), \quad 1 \le k \le N$$

It can be seen that if a request with priority $\langle j, u \rangle$ (logically) happens before a request with priority $\langle k, v \rangle$, then $\sum_l u[l] < \sum_l v[l]$ and, so, $\langle j, u \rangle > \langle k, v \rangle$.

The rules to decide when and how to reply to the request are as follows:

1. p_j replies with an acknowledgment $Ack(j, vsn_i[i], vf_j)$ (where vf_j is the current value of VF_j) immediately if either (1) it is also interested in X but is not currently acting as a captor in the meeting room, or (2) it is not interested in X, is not in the meeting room, and has a priority lower than

$\langle i, vsn_i \rangle$. (We assume that a philosopher p_j possesses a priority all the time, where the priority is set to a minimal value $\langle j, \infty \rangle$ if p_j is not interested in a forum, and is set to $\langle j, vsn_j \rangle$ if p_j has requested a forum and the priority of its request is $\langle j, vsn_j \rangle$.)

2. p_j replies with a message $Start(\langle j, vsn_j \rangle, vsn_i[i])$ if it is in forum X and is acting as a captor in the meeting room. Note that the reply bears p_j's current priority $\langle j, vsn_j \rangle$.

3. Otherwise, p_j must be interested in a different forum, and either p_j is in the meeting room, or it has a priority higher than $\langle i, vsn_i \rangle$. In this case, p_j delays the reply until it has exited the meeting room, and then replies with an acknowledgment.

Observe that an acknowledgment $Ack(j, vsn_i[i], vf_j)$ in the algorithm additionally carries two values: $vsn_i[i]$—p_i's sequence number in its request, and vf_j—p_j's knowledge (at the time the acknowledgment is sent) of the counts of entries to the meeting room made by each philosopher. The value $vsn_i[i]$ is used by p_i to determine whether the acknowledgment is for its current request, or for a previous request (and in this case the acknowledgment is "out-of-date" and must be discarded). A philosopher may receive an out-of-date acknowledgment because it can enter the meeting room (as a captive) before it receives all acknowledgments for its request. So, p_i's request $Req(\langle i, vsn_i \rangle, X)$ may have already ceased to exist when p_i receives $Ack(j, vsn_i[i], vf_j)$. By comparing $vsn_i[i]$ with p_i's sequence number in its current request, p_i can decide whether the acknowledgment is out-of-date.

The value of vf_j is for p_i to update its VF_i: On receipt of $Ack(j, vsn_i[i], vf_j)$, p_i updates VF_i to $merge(VF_i, vf_j)$. The new value of VF_i then is used by p_i to check if every acknowledgment $Ack(k, vsn_i[i], vf_k)$ it possesses remains up-to-date. In the algorithm, $VF_i[k]$ must be no greater than $vf_k[k]$ in order for $Ack(k, vsn_i[i], vf_k)$ to remain up-to-date. The intuition for this is as follows: $VF_k[k]$ must always have a correct count of the number of entries to the meeting room p_k has made. So, after p_i receives $Ack(k, vsn_i[i], vf_k)$, p_i's $VF_i[k]$ must be updated to $vf_k[k]$. Suppose p_k is interested in a different forum. Let $Req(\langle k, vsn_k \rangle, Y)$ be p_k's request. If p_k does not enter the meeting room before p_i does, then p_k's acknowledgment remains up-to-date because $VF_i[k]$ continues to have a value equal to $vf_k[k]$. The fact that p_k acknowledges p_i's request guarantees that p_k's request has a priority lower than that of p_i's request. So, p_k cannot receive p_i's acknowledgment until p_i's request $Req(\langle i, vsn_i \rangle, X)$ ceases to exist. So, until p_i has left forum X, p_k cannot enter the meeting room as a captor.

However, if some philosopher p_l is currently in forum Y acting as a captor, then p_l may reply to p_k's request with a message $Start(\langle l, vsn_l \rangle, vsn_k[k])$. So, p_k may enter the meeting room before p_i. Note again that the fact that p_l is in the meeting room acting as a captor guarantees that p_l's request must have a priority higher than that of p_i's request. So p_i cannot enter the meeting room as a captor until p_l has replied to its request with an acknowledgment, which cannot be sent until p_l has exited the meeting room. When p_l replies to p_i's request with an acknowledgment $Ack(l, vsn_i[i], vf_l)$, for p_i to learn from p_l that p_k has been captured to enter the meeting room (and so p_k's acknowledgment $Ack(k, vsn_i[i], vf_k)$ is out-of-date), the count $vf_l[k]$ is set to $vsn_k[k]$ (which must be equal to $vf_k[k] + 1$). When p_i receives p_l's acknowledgment and updates its VF_i, it knows that the current value of $VF_i[k]$ is one greater than $vf_k[k]$ carried by $Ack(k, vsn_i[i], vf_k)$. So, it knows that the acknowledgment is out-of-date and it must wait for a new acknowledgment from p_k in order for it to enter the meeting room as a captor.

The complete code of the algorithm is given in Fig. 2 as a CSP-like repetitive command consisting of five guarded commands A, B, C, D, and E [3].

The variables used in the algorithm are listed below:

- *state*: the state of p_i (see Fig. 3). The initial state is *thinking*.
- VSN_i: a vector of natural numbers of length N, where $VSN_i[j]$, initialized to 0, represents a count of requests that are made by p_j and that are known at p_i.
- VF_i: a vector of natural numbers of length N, where $VF_i[j]$, initialized to 0, represents a count of entries to the meeting room that are made by p_j and that are known at p_i.
- *priority*: the priority of p_i. It is initialized to a minimal value $\langle i, \infty \rangle$.
- *target*: the forum p_i wishes to attend, or $\bot$ otherwise. It is initialized to $\bot$.
- *is_captor*: a boolean variable indicating if p_i is acting as a captor in the meeting room. It is initialized to false.
- *request_queue*: a queue of requests of size at most $N - 1$. It is initialized to $\emptyset$, and is used to store the most recent requests by every other philosopher.
- *friend_requests*: a queue of requests that are for the same forum as p_i's request and that are received while p_i is in the meeting room.
- *ack_queue*: the set of acknowledgments to p_i's request. It is initialized to $\emptyset$

In the algorithm, request messages are processed by guarded command B. Note that after p_i has replied to $Req(\langle j, vsn_j \rangle, \mathsf{Y})$ with an acknowledgment $Ack(i, vsn_j[j], VF_i)$, p_i may need to send a new reply to the request. This happens when (1) p_i subsequently enters the meeting room as a captor and wishes to capture p_j to join the forum, or (2) p_i is captured to attend the meeting room and needs to send a new acknowledgment to p_j after it has exited the meeting room. Therefore, a request message may need to be saved for another reply. In the algorithm, request messages are kept in *request_queue*. Obviously, only the most recent request per philosopher needs to be saved. Lines B.7-13 implement the three rules described earlier regarding how request messages are processed. Each new request is kept in *request_queue* (line B.6) no matter how p_i responds to the request (unless the request is out-of-date; see the comment at the end of this section).

Acknowledgments are processed by guarded command C. p_i enters the meeting room as a captor when its request has been acknowledged by all the other philosophers (line C.10). Then, for each request for X in *request_queue*, p_i must send a start message to capture the requesting philosopher to enter the meeting room (lines C.17-20). Moreover, the requests in *request_queue* bearing a priority higher than that of p_i's request can also be deleted (lines C.21-22) because the requesting philosophers must have already entered the meeting room for their requests (for otherwise they will not acknowledge p_i's request). If p_i instead enters the meeting room as a captive (line D.3), then it removes the captor's request and the requests in *request_queue* that bear a priority higher than that of the captor's request (lines D.7-9). Again, this is because the requests must have already ceased to exist; for, otherwise, p_i's captor would not be able to enter the meeting room to capture p_i. The captor's priority carried by each start message is used for this purpose.

On exiting the meeting room, p_i must reply to the requests that are held in *request_queue*, including those that p_i may have already replied (p_i's replies to them become out-of-date because p_i has been captured to enter the meeting room). Clearly, not every request needs to be replied. For example, if the value of $vsn_j[j]$ in a request $Req(\langle j, vsn_j \rangle, \mathsf{Y})$ is less than or equal to $VF_i[j]$, then, obviously, the request has been granted and so no reply is needed. Moreover,

A.1   *[wish to attend a forum of X $\longrightarrow$
A.2 $VSN_i[i] := VSN_i[i] + 1;$
A.3 $target := X;$
A.4 $priority := \langle i, VSN_i \rangle;$ /* obtain a priority for its request */
A.5 $state := waiting;$
A.6   **multicast** $Req(\langle i, VSN_i \rangle, X)$ to every other philosopher; /* issue a request */

B.1 $\square$ **receive** $Req(\langle j, vsn_j \rangle, Y) \longrightarrow$
B.2 $VSN_i := merge(VSN_i, vsn_j);$ /* adjust VSN_i */
B.3   **if** $\exists\, Req(\langle j, vsn'_j \rangle, Z) \in request\_queue$ **then** /* remove p_j's previous request */
B.4   remove $Req(\langle j, vsn'_j \rangle, Z)$ from $request\_queue;$
B.5   **if** $VF_i[j] < vsn_j[j]$ **then** {
B.6   add $Req(\langle j, vsn_j \rangle, Y)$ to $request\_queue;$
B.7   **if** $(target = Y \bigwedge \neg is\_captor) \bigvee (target \neq Y \bigwedge state \neq talking \bigwedge$
              $priority < \langle j, vsn_j \rangle)$ **then**
B.8   **send** $Ack(i, vsn_j[j], VF_i)$ to $p_j;$
B.9   **else if** $target = Y \bigwedge is\_captor$ **then** {
B.10   **send** $Start(priority, vsn_j[j])$ to $p_j;$ /* p_i captures p_j */
B.11   /* p_i is sure that p_j will make its $vsn_j[j]$th entry to the meeting room */
B.12 $VF_i[j] := max(VF_i[j], vsn_j[j]);$ }
B.13   /* otherwise, $target \neq Y \bigwedge (state = talking \bigvee priority > \langle j, vsn_j \rangle)$ */
B.14   **if** $target = Y \bigwedge state = talking$ **then**
B.15   /* p_i needs not re-send a reply to the request on exiting the
             meeting room */
B.16   add $Req(\langle j, vsn_j \rangle, Y)$ to $friend\_requests;$
B.17   } /* else the request is out-of-date */

C.1 $\square$ **receive** $Ack(j, sn, vf_j) \longrightarrow$
C.2 $VF_i := merge(VF_i, vf_j);$ /* adjust VF_i */
C.3   **let** priority be $\langle i, vsn_i \rangle;$
C.4   **if** $vsn_i[i] = sn \bigwedge state \neq talking$ **then** {
       /* otherwise the acknowledgment is out-of-date */
C.5   **if** $\exists\, Ack(j, sn', vf'_j) \in ack\_queue$ **then** /* remove p_j's previous reply */
C.6   remove $Ack(j, sn', vf'_j)$ from $ack\_queue;$
C.7   add $Ack(j, sn, vf_j)$ to $ack\_queue;$
C.8   **for each** $Ack(k, sn'', vf_k) \in ack\_queue$ **do**
         /* remove out-of-date acknowledgments */
C.9   **if** $vf_k[k] < VF_i[k]$ **then** remove $Ack(k, sn'', vf_k)$ from $ack\_queue;$
C.10   **if** $|ack\_queue| = N - 1$ **then** {
C.11   /* receive acknowledgments from every other philosopher */
C.12 $state := talking;$ /* enter the meeting room as a captor */
C.13 $VF_i[i] := VF_i[i] + 1;$
C.14 $is\_captor := true;$
C.15 $ack\_queue := \emptyset;$
C.16   **for each** $Req(\langle l, vsn_l \rangle, Y) \in request\_queue$ **do**
C.17   **if** $target = Y \wedge VF_i[l] < vsn_l[l]$ **then** {
C.18   /* capture the congenial philosopher */
C.19   **send** $Start(priority, vsn_l[l])$ to $p_l;$
C.20 $VF_i[l] := max(VF_i[l], vsn_l[l]);$ }
C.21   **else if** $\langle l, vsn_l \rangle > priority$ **then** /* the request is out-of-date */
C.22   remove $Req(\langle l, vsn_l \rangle, Y)$ from $request\_queue;$
C.23   } /* end of if-then statement in line C.10 */
C.24   } /* end of if-then statement in line C.4 */

Fig. 2. Algorithm RA2 executed by philosopher p_i.

D.1   □ **receive** $Start(\langle j, vsn_j \rangle, sn) \longrightarrow$
D.2   **let** *priority* be $\langle i, vsn_i \rangle$;
D.3   **if** $vsn_i[i] = sn \wedge state \neq talking$ **then** { /* captured by p_i */
D.4 $state := talking$; /* enter the meeting room as a captive */
D.5 $VF_i[i] := VF_i[i] + 1$;
D.6 $ack\_queue := \emptyset$;
D.7   **for each** $Req(\langle l, vsn_l \rangle, \mathsf{Y}) \in request\_queue$ **do**
D.8   /* remove the captor's request and the requests that bear a priority */
       /* higher than that of the captor */
D.9   **if** $\langle l, vsn_l \rangle \geq \langle j, vsn_j \rangle$ **then** remove $Req(\langle l, vsn_l \rangle, \mathsf{Y})$ from *request_queue*;
D.10   /* else, out-of-date message */ }

E.1   □ **exit a forum of** *target* $\longrightarrow$
E.2   **for each** $Req(\langle j, vsn_j \rangle, \mathsf{Y}) \in request\_queue$ **do**
E.3   **if** $VF_i[j] < vsn_j[j] \wedge Req(\langle j, vsn_j \rangle, \mathsf{Y}) \notin friend\_requests$ **then**
E.4   send $Ack(i, vsn_j[j], VF_i)$ **to** p_j;
E.5   **else if** $VF_i[j] \geq vsn_j[j]$ **then** /* the request is out-of-date */
E.6   remove $Req(\langle j, vsn_j \rangle, \mathsf{Y})$ from *request_queue*;
E.7 $target := \bot$;
E.8 $friend\_requests := \emptyset$;
E.9 $priority := \langle i, \infty \rangle$;
E.10 $is\_captor := false$;
E.11 $state := thinking$;
E.12]

Fig. 2. Algorithm RA2 executed by philosopher p_i (continued).

if a request $Req(\langle j, vsn_j \rangle, \mathsf{Y})$ arrives while p_i is in forum Y, then even though p_i does not act as a captor in the meeting room, p_i must still acknowledge the request immediately so as to guarantee concurrent entering. Clearly, the acknowledgment must carry the most up-to-date count of entries p_i has made to the meeting room (including the one p_i has just made to enter the forum Y). A new acknowledgment sent by p_i upon leaving the forum therefore does not carry more information than is needed and, so, can be saved. The queue *friend_requests* is used to store such requests (lines B.14-16 and E.3). The rule for determining which request needs to be replied and which needs to be removed is given in lines E.2-6.

Note that after p_i has replied to a request (say, by p_j) of the same interest (say, forum Y), p_i may still need to keep the request in *request_queue* because there is no guarantee that p_j's request will be granted before or concurrently with p_i's regardless of whose priority is higher. For example, suppose p_i is captured by p_k to attend Y. Suppose further that p_j's request arrives at p_k after p_k has left Y (so that p_k is unable to capture p_j in time), and p_j's request arrives at p_i before p_k has captured p_i. Then, when p_i acknowledges p_j's request, p_j's knowledge of $VF_i[i]$ is one less than the count p_k will inform p_j via p_k's acknowledgment. So, p_j will consider p_i's acknowledgment out-of-date and will be waiting for a new acknowledgment from p_i. So, p_i must send the acknowledgment for. otherwise, the system would be deadlocked. Moreover, after p_i has sent the new acknowledgment, p_i may request another forum and then be captured again to enter the meeting room before p_j is allowed to enter the meeting room. So, p_i's second acknowledgment may again become out-of-date. So, in the worst case, p_i has to maintain p_j's request until it has learned that p_j's request has ceased to exist (or is about to cease to exist).

The fact that a philosopher may be captured over and over again also reveals that the algorithm provides a virtually unbounded degree of concurrency. Note, however, that this does not mean that a captor can capture a philosopher an infinite number of times; for otherwise, it would contradict our assumption that every philosopher spends only finite time in the meeting room.

Finally, because a philosopher p_k sets its $VF_k[j]$ to $vsn_j[j]$ upon capturing p_j with a request $Req(\langle j, vsn_j \rangle, \mathsf{X})$, at some point $VF_k[j]$ may be greater than $VF_j[j]$ (whose value must be equal to $vsn_j[j] - 1$ when p_j makes the request $Req(\langle j, vsn_j \rangle, \mathsf{X})$). Moreover, another philosopher p_i may learn of the new $VF_k[j]$ before p_j has received p_k's start message (and so before p_j has made its $vsn_j[j]$th entry to the meeting room). As a result, care must be taken to prevent p_j from miscounting the number of entries it has made to the meeting room; otherwise, the algorithm could err. In the algorithm, a $Req(\langle j, vsn_j \rangle, \mathsf{X})$ arrives at p_i is considered out-of-date and is removed right away if $VF_i[j] \geq vsn_j[j]$ (line B.5). Therefore, p_j will never receive an acknowledgment $Ack(i, vsn_j[j], vf_i)$ from p_i whose $vf_i[j]$ is greater than $VF_j[j]$.

Due to the space limitation, the correctness of RA2 and its performance will be analyzed in the full paper.

5 Conclusions and Future Work

We have presented an efficient and highly concurrent distributed algorithm RA2 for the Congenial Talking Philosophers problem. The algorithm requires, on an average, N to $3(N-1)$ messages per entry to the meeting room. In terms of context-switch complexity, when a philosopher requests a forum X, at most $2(N-1)$ rounds of passages can be initiated before a round of X is initiated in which the philosopher can make a passage through X. Within each round, at most $O(N)$ passages suffice to account for the blocking of another philosopher's request. So the time complexity is $O(N^2)$. In terms of concurrency, RA2 can offer a virtually unbounded degree of concurrency.

For comparison, we have also presented RA1, which is a straightforward modification from Ricart and Agrawala's algorithm for n-process mutual exclusion. RA1 requires $2(N-1)$ messages per entry to the meeting room. Its context-switch complexity and time complexity are both $2(N-1)$, and offers a maximum degree of concurrency of $2(N-2)$. Although, statically, the two algorithms do not differ very much from various perspectives, the difference between their dynamic performance is quite significant. As illustrated by the simulation, RA1 performs poorly as compared to RA2; it out-performs RA2 only in message complexity, but only by a slight margin.

The comparison between RA1 and RA2 also highlights several directions for future work. For example, RA2 requires, in the worst case, $3(N-1)$ messages per entry to the meeting room (although in simulation the number of messages required is approximately $2.3(N-1)$), but RA1 needs only $2(N-1)$ messages. Moreover, in RA2 each request bears a vector timestamp, while only a timestamp is needed in RA1. The use of vector timestamps compromises the scalability of RA2. Thus, it is interesting to see if RA2 can be further improved to reduce its message size and the number of messages needed per entry to the meeting room.

References

1. M. Ben-Ari. *Principles of Concurrent and Distributed Programming*. Prentice-Hall, 1990.
2. F. N. David and D. E. Barton. *Combinatorial chance*. Charles Griffin & Co., 1962.
3. C. A. R. Hoare. Communicating sequential processes. *CACM*, 21(8):666–677, August 1978.
4. Y.-J. Joung. Asynchronous group mutual exclusion (extended abstract). In *Proc. 17th ACM PODC*, pp. 51–60, 1998.
5. L. Lamport. Time, clocks and the ordering of events in a distributed system. *CACM*, 21(7):558–565, July 1978.
6. A. M. Law and W. D. Kelton. *Simulation modeling & analysis*. McGraw-Hill, 1991.
7. N. A. Lynch. *Distributed Algorithms*. Morgan-Kaufmann, 1996.
8. M. Raynal. *Algorithms for Mutual Exclusion*. MIT Press, 1986.
9. M. Raynal. About logical clocks for distributed systems. *ACM Operating Systems Review*, 26(1):41–48, January 1992.
10. G. Ricart and A. K. Agrawala. An optimal algorithm for mutual exclusion in computer networks. *CACM*, 24(1):9–17, January 1981.
11. R. Schwarz and F. Mattern. Detecting causal relationships in distributed computations: In search of the holy grail. *Distributed Computing*, 7(3):149–174, March 1994.
12. A. Silberschatz and P. Galvin. *Operating System Concepts*. Addison-Wesley, fourth edition, 1994.

Appendix A: Some simulation results

The Appendix presents some simulation results for both RA1 and RA2. In the simulation, we have set up a system of N philosophers and m fora. Each time a philosopher wishes to attend a forum, it randomly chooses one of the m fora to attend, and the choice follows a uniform distribution. The time a philosopher stays in states *thinking* and *talking* follows an exponential distribution with means $\mu_{thinking}$ and $\mu_{talking}$ respectively. The message transmission time also follows an exponential distribution with a mean μ_{link_delay}. We measure the following values:

- The average time a philosopher spends in state *waiting*; i.e., the average waiting time.
- The average number of rounds of passages a philosopher has bypassed in state *waiting*; i.e., the average number of context switches a philosopher has to wait per request.
- The average number of passages per round; i.e., the average round size.
- The average capacity; i.e., on an average, the maximum number of philosophers that can be in the meeting room simultaneously per round.
- The average number of messages required per entry to the meeting room.
- Throughput; i.e., the average number of entries to the meeting room per second.

The simulation program is written in Java using Java Development Kit V1.02. Fig. 4 summarizes some of our simulation results.[2] For comparison, we have also measured the behavior of the algorithm when philosophers use the meeting room in a mutually exclusive style. This is done by designating one unique forum to each philosopher. In the figure, we use $m = N^*$ to denote this scenario. We have

---

[2] Some java applets animating the algorithms for the Congenial Talking Philosophers problem can be found in http://joung.im.ntu.edu.tw/congenial/.

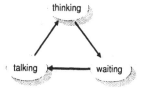

Fig. 3. State transition diagram of a philosopher.

$N = 30$, $\mu_{thinking} = 50ms$, $\mu_{talking} = 250ms$, $\mu_{link\_delay} = 2ms$

	$m = 1$	$m = 3$	$m = 5$	$m = 10$	$m = 20$	$m = 30^*$
average waiting time (ms)	112.58	6007.79	6655.4	7092.94	7397.53	7537.88
average context switches	0	19.10	23.17	25.91	27.36	28.82
average round size	NA	1.51	1.24	1.11	1.05	1
average capacity	30	1.51	1.24	1.11	1.05	1
average messages per entry	58	58	58	58	58	58
average throughput (entry/sec)	71.74	4.75	4.31	4.05	3.89	3.82

Simulation results for Algorithm RA1.

$N = 30$, $\mu_{thinking} = 50ms$, $\mu_{talking} = 250ms$, $\mu_{link\_delay} = 2ms$

	$m = 1$	$m = 3$	$m = 5$	$m = 10$	$m = 20$	$m = 30^*$
average waiting time (ms)	583.85	1151.15	1749.65	2908.77	4270.66	7791.74
average context switches	0	1.20	2.28	4.80	8.99	28.86
average round size	NA	23.95	12.58	5.98	3.20	1
average capacity	29	16.27	10.57	5.62	3.11	1
average messages per entry	66.60	66.83	63.40	60.79	59.41	58
average throughput (entry/sec)	32.41	20.21	14.49	9.30	6.54	3.70

Simulation results for Algorithm RA2.

Fig. 4. Some simulation results

also set up the case $m = 1$ where maximum concurrency should be allowed as no two requests will conflict. It is not difficult to see that the setting of Fig. 4 represents a very high contention situation to the meeting room.

From Fig. 4 we can see that RA1 provides virtually no concurrency. For example, when $m = 3$, it is likely that one third of the waiting requests are targeting at the same forum very often. However, the simulation results indicate that the behavior of the system is only slightly better than the case $m = 30^*$ where the philosophers use the meeting room in a mutually exclusive style. On the other hand, the performance is improved significantly by RA2. For example, when $m = 3$, the average context switches per request is 1.2, as opposed to 19.1 for Algorithm RA1. Moreover, on an average, up to 16.27 philosophers can be in the meeting room simultaneously per round for RA2, as opposed to 1.51 for RA1. Note that the number of messages required per entry to the meeting room is $2(N - 1) = 58$ for RA1, but this number is not fixed for different values of m. As we can see, the message complexity is $2(N - 1)$ when no two philosophers may request the same forum simultaneously; otherwise, the message complexity ranges in between N and $3(N - 1)$. The message complexity increases as m decreases. This is also witnessed by the simulation results. For example, when $m = 20$, the average number of messages required per entry to the meeting room is $59.41 = 2.05(N - 1)$. The number increases to $66.83 = 2.30(N - 1)$ for $m = 3$, and remains about the same value for the worst case where $m = 1$.

Software Fault Tolerance of Concurrent Programs Using Controlled Re-execution *

Ashis Tarafdar[1] and Vijay K. Garg[2]

[1] Dept. of Computer Sciences, The Univ. of Texas at Austin, Austin, TX 78712
ashis@cs.utexas.edu
[2] Dept. of Electr. and Comp. Engg., The Univ. of Texas at Austin, Austin, TX 78712
garg@ece.utexas.edu

Abstract. Concurrent programs often encounter failures, such as races, owing to the presence of synchronization faults (bugs). One existing technique to tolerate synchronization faults is to roll back the program to a previous state and re-execute, in the hope that the failure does not recur. Instead of relying on chance, our approach is to control the re-execution in order to avoid a recurrence of the synchronization failure. The control is achieved by tracing information during an execution and using this information to add synchronizations during the re-execution.

The approach gives rise to a general problem, called the *off-line predicate control problem*, which takes a computation and a property specified on the computation, and outputs a "controlled" computation that maintains the property. We solve the predicate control problem for the mutual exclusion property, which is especially important in synchronization fault tolerance.

1 Introduction

Concurrent programs are difficult to write. The programmer is presented with the task of balancing two competing forces: safety and liveness [8]. Frequently, the programmer leans too much in one of the two directions, causing either safety failures (e.g. races) or liveness failures (e.g. deadlocks). Such failures arise from a particular kind of software fault (bug), known as a *synchronization fault*. Studies have shown that synchronization faults account for a sizeable fraction of observed software faults in concurrent programs [6]. Locating synchronization faults and eliminating them by reprogramming is always the best strategy. However, many systems must maintain availability in spite of software failures. It is, therefore, desirable to be able to bypass a synchronization fault and recover from the resulting failure. This problem of software fault tolerance for synchronization faults in concurrent programs [1] is the primary motivation for this paper.

---

* supported in part by the NSF ECS-9414780, CCR-9520540, a General Motors Fellowship, Texas Education Board ARP-320 and an IBM grant

[1] By concurrent programs, we include all parallel programming paradigms such as: multi-threaded programs, shared-memory parallel programs, message-passing distributed programs, distributed shared-memory programs, etc. We will refer to a parallel entity as a process, although in practice it may also be a thread.

Traditionally, it was believed that software failures are permanent in nature and, therefore, they would recur in every execution of the program with the same inputs. This belief led to the use of design diversity to recover from software failures. In approaches based on design diversity [1, 13], redundant modules with different designs are used, ensuring that there is no single point-of-failure. Contrary to this belief, it was observed that many software failures are, in fact, *transient* - they may not recur when the program is re-executed with the same inputs [3]. In particular, the failures caused by synchronization faults are usually transient in nature.

The existence of transient software failures motivated a new approach to software fault tolerance based on rolling back the processes to a previous state and then restarting them (possibly with message reordering), in the hope that the transient failure will not recur in the new execution [5, 17]. Methods based on this approach have relied on chance in order to recover from a transient software failure. In the special case of synchronization faults, however, it is possible to do better. Instead of leaving recovery to chance, our approach ensures that the transient synchronization failure does not recur. It does so by controlling the re-execution, based on information traced during the failed execution.

Our mechanism involves (i) tracing an execution, (ii) detecting a synchronization failure, (iii) determining a control strategy, and (iv) re-executing under control. Each of these problems is also of independent interest. Our requirements for tracing an execution and re-execution under control are very similar to trace-and-replay techniques in concurrent debugging. Trace-and-replay techniques have been studied in various concurrent paradigms such as message-passing parallel programs [12], shared-memory parallel programs [11], distributed shared memory programs [15], and multi-threaded programs [2]. Among sychronization failures, this paper will focus on races. Race detection has been previously studied [4, 10]. We will discuss tracing, failure detection, and re-execution under control in greater depth in Section 4. This paper addresses the remaining problem of determining a control strategy.

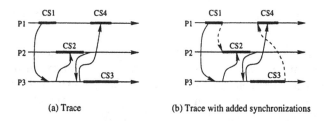

(a) Trace   (b) Trace with added synchronizations

Fig. 1. Example: Tracing and Controlling During Rollback Recovery

To illustrate what determining a control strategy involves, consider the execution shown in Figure 1(a). CS1 - CS4 are the critical sections of the execution. The synchronizations between processes are shown as arrows from one process execution to another. A synchronization ensures that the execution after the head of the arrow can proceed only after the execution before the tail has completed. A race occurs when two critical sections execute simultaneously. For example, CS1 and CS2 may have a race, since the synchronizations do not prevent them from executing simultaneously. A control strategy is a set of *added synchronizations* that would ensure that a race does not occur. The race can be avoided by adding synchronizations, shown as broken arrows in Figure 1(b).

The focus of this paper is the problem of determining which synchronizations to add to an execution trace in order to tolerate a synchronization fault in the re-execution. This proves to be an important problem in its own right and can be applied in areas other than software fault tolerance, such as concurrent debugging. We generalize the problem using a framework known as the *off-line predicate control* problem. This problem was introduced in [16], where it was applied to concurrent debugging. Informally, off-line predicate control specifies that, given a computation and a property on the computation, one must determine a controlled computation (one with more synchronizations) that maintains the property. (We will use the term *computation* for a formal model of an *execution*.) The previous work [16] solved the predicate control problem for a class of properties called *disjunctive predicates*. Applying the results of that study to software fault tolerance would mean avoiding synchronization failures of the form: $l_1 \wedge l_2 \wedge l_3$, where l_i is a local property specified on process P_i. For example, if l_i specifies that a server is unavailable, the synchronization failure is that all servers are unavailable at the same time.

In this paper, we address a class of off-line predicate control problems, characterized by the mutual exclusion property, that is especially useful in tolerating races. We consider four classes of mutual exclusion properties: *off-line mutual exclusion*, *off-line readers writers*, *off-line independent mutual exclusion*, and *off-line independent read-write mutual exclusion*. For each of these classes of properties, we determine necessary and sufficient conditions under which the problem may be solved. Furthermore, we design an efficient algorithm that solves the most general of the problems, off-line independent read-write mutual exclusion, and thus also solves each of the other three problems. The algorithm takes $O(np)$ time, where n is the number of concurrent processes and p is the number of critical sections.

The problems have been termed *off-line* problems to distinguish them from their more popular *on-line* variants (i.e. the usual mutual exclusion problems [14]). The difference between the on-line and off-line problems is that in the on-line case, the computation is provided on-line, whereas in the off-line case, the computation is known *a priori*. Ignorance of the future makes on-line mutual exclusion a harder problem to solve. In general, in on-line mutual exclusion, one cannot avoid deadlocks without making some assumptions (e.g. critical sections do not block). Thus, on-line mutual exclusion is impossible to solve. To understand why this is true, consider the scenario in Figure 1. Any on-line algorithm, being unaware of the future computation, would have a symmetric choice of entering CS1 or CS2 first. If CS2 is entered first, it would result in a deadlock. An off-line algorithm, being aware of the future computation, could make the correct decision to enter CS1 first and add a synchronization from CS1 to CS2. A proof of the impossibility of on-line mutual exclusion follows along similar lines as the proof of Theorem 3 in [16]. Thus, there will always be scenarios where on-line mutual exclusion algorithms will fail, resulting in either race conditions or deadlocks. In such scenarios, controlled re-execution based on off-line mutual exclusion becomes vitally important.

2 Model and Problem Statement

The model that we present is of a single execution of the concurrent program. The model is not at the programming language level, but at a lower level, at which the execution consists of a sequence of states for each process and the communications that occurred among them (similar to the happened before model[7]).

Let S be a finite set of elementary entities known as *states*. S is partitioned into subsets $S_1, S_2, \cdots, S_n$, where $n > 1$. These partitions correspond to n processes in the system. A subset G of S is called a *global state* iff $\forall i : |G \cap S_i| = 1$. Let G_i denote the unique element in $G \cap S_i$. A *global predicate* is a function that maps a global state onto a boolean value.

A *computation* is a partial order $\rightarrow$ on S such that $\forall i : \rightarrow_i$ is a total order on S_i, where $\rightarrow_i$ represents $\rightarrow$ restricted to the set S_i. Note that the states in a single process are totally ordered while the states across processes are partially ordered. We will use $\rightarrow, \rightarrow^k, \rightarrow^c$ to denote computations, and $\|, \|^k, \|^c$ to denote the respective incomparability relations (e.g. $s \| t \equiv (s \not\rightarrow t) \wedge (t \not\rightarrow s)$). Given a computation $\rightarrow$ and a subset K of S, $\rightarrow$-*consistent*$(K) \equiv \forall s, t \in K : s \| t$. In particular, a global state may be $\rightarrow$-consistent. The notion of consistency tells us when a set of states could have occurred concurrently in a computation.

A computation $\rightarrow$ is *extensible* in S iff:

$\forall K \subseteq S : \rightarrow$-consistent$(K) \Rightarrow \exists$ global state $G \supseteq K : \rightarrow$-consistent$(G)$

Intuitively, extensibility allows us to extend a consistent set of states to a consistent global state. Any computation in S can be made extensible by adding "dummy" states to S. Therefore, we implicitly assume that any computation is extensible.

Given a computation $\rightarrow$, let $\leq$ be a relation on global states defined as: $G \leq H \equiv \forall i : (G_i \rightarrow_i H_i) \vee (G_i = H_i)$. It is a well-known fact that the set of $\rightarrow$-consistent global states is a lattice with respect to the $\leq$ relation [9]. In particular, we will use $\rightarrow$-glb(G, H) for the greatest lower bound of G and H with respect to $\rightarrow$ (so, $\rightarrow$-glb$(G, H)_i = \rightarrow_i$-min(G_i, H_i)). If G and H are $\rightarrow$-consistent, then $\rightarrow$-glb(G, H) is also $\rightarrow$-consistent.

Given a computation $\rightarrow$ and a global predicate B, a computation $\rightarrow^c$ is called a *controlling computation* of B in $\rightarrow$ iff (1) $\rightarrow \subseteq \rightarrow^c$, and (2) $\forall G : \rightarrow^c$-consistent$(G) \Rightarrow B(G)$. This tells us that a controlling computation is a stricter partial order (containing more synchronizations). Further, any global state that may occur in the controlling computation must satisfy the specified global predicate. Thus, the problem of finding a controlling computation is to add synchronizations until all global states that violate the global predicate are made inconsistent. More formally,

The Off-line Predicate Control Problem: Given a computation $\rightarrow$ and a global predicate B, find a controlling computation of B in $\rightarrow$

3 Solving the Off-line Predicate Control Problem

In [16], it was proved that the Off-line Predicate Control is NP-Hard. Therefore, it is important to solve useful restricted forms of the Off-line Predicate Control Problem. Since we are interested in avoiding race conditions, we restrict the general problem by letting B specify the mutual exclusion property.

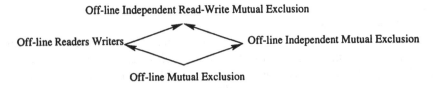

Fig. 2. Variants of Off-line Mutual Exclusion

The simplest specification for mutual exclusion is: no two critical sections execute at the same time. This corresponds to the semantics of a single exclusive lock for all the critical sections. We call the corresponding problem the *Off-line Mutual Exclusion Problem*. We can generalize this to the *Off-line Readers Writers Problem* by specifying that only critical sections that "write" must be exclusive, while critical sections that "read" need not be exclusive. This corresponds to the semantics of read-exclusive-write locks. Another way to generalize the Off-line Mutual Exclusion Problem is to allow the semantics of independent locks. In this *Off-line Independent Mutual Exclusion Problem*, no two critical sections of the same lock can execute simultaneously. Finally, we can have critical sections with the semantics of independent read-exclusive-write locks. This is the *Off-line Independent Read-Write Mutual Exclusion Problem*. Figure 2 illustrates the relative generality of the four problems.

In traditional *on-line* mutual exclusion, there has been no "independent" variant, since it trivially involves applying the same algorithm for each lock. However, in off-line mutual exclusion, such an approach will not work, since the synchronizations added by each independent algorithm may cause deadlocks when applied together.

For the practitioner, an algorithm which solves Off-line Independent Read-Write Mutual Exclusion would suffice, since it can be used to solve all other variants. However, for the purpose of presentation we will start with the simplest Off-line Mutual Exclusion Problem and then generalize it in steps. For each problem, we will determine the necessary and sufficient conditions for finding a solution. Finally, we will make use of the results in the design of an algorithm which solves the most general of the four problems.

3.1 Off-line Mutual Exclusion

Off-line Mutual Exclusion is a specialization of Off-line Predicate Control to the following class of global predicates:

$$B_{mutex}(G) \equiv \forall \; distinct \; s, t \in G : \neg(critical(s) \land critical(t))$$

where $critical$ is a function that maps a state onto a boolean value. Thus, B_{mutex} specifies that at most one process may be critical in a global state.

Based on the $critical$ boolean function on states, we define $critical$ $sections$ as maximal intervals of critical states. More precisely: given a $critical$ function on S and a computation $\rightarrow$ on S, a $critical$ $section$, CS, is a non-empty, maximal subset of an S_i such that: (1) $\forall s \in CS : critical(s)$, and (2) $\forall s, t \in CS : \forall u \in S_i : s \rightarrow u \rightarrow t \Rightarrow u \in CS$.

Let $CS.first$ and $CS.last$ be the minimum and maximum states respectively in CS (w.r.t. $\rightarrow_i$). Let $\mapsto$ be a relation on critical sections defined as: $CS \mapsto CS' \equiv CS.first \rightarrow CS'.last \land CS \neq CS'$ Thus, $\mapsto$ orders a critical section before another if some state in the first happened before some state in the second. Note that $\mapsto$ may have cycles.

We will be dealing with different computations. All computations will have the same total order $\rightarrow_i$ for each S_i. Therefore, the set of critical sections will not change for each computation. However, the $\mapsto$ relation will change, in general. For computations $\rightarrow$, $\rightarrow^k$, and $\rightarrow^c$, the relation on critical sections will be denoted as $\mapsto$, $\mapsto^k$ and $\mapsto^c$ respectively.

Theorem 1 (Necessary Condition) *For a computation* $\rightarrow$ *of* S, *and a global predicate* B_{mutex},
  a controlling computation of B_{mutex} *in* $\rightarrow$ *exists* $\Rightarrow$ $\mapsto$ *has no cycles*

Proof: We prove the contrapositive. Let $\mapsto$ have a cycle, say $CS_1 \mapsto CS_2 \mapsto \cdots CS_m \mapsto CS_1$, $(m \geq 2)$ and let $\rightarrow^c$ be a computation such that $\rightarrow \subseteq \rightarrow^c$. Since $\rightarrow^c$ cannot have a cycle, at least one of:
$CS_1.last \not\rightarrow^c CS_2.first$, $CS_2.last \not\rightarrow^c CS_3.first$, $\cdots$, and $CS_m.last \not\rightarrow^c CS_1.first$ must hold. Without loss of generality, let $CS_1.last \not\rightarrow^c CS_2.first$. We also have $CS_2.last \not\rightarrow^c CS_1.first$ (since $CS_1 \mapsto CS_2$). Since $\rightarrow^c$ is extensible, we can define s_2 as the maximum state in S_2 such that $CS_1.last \parallel^c s_2$, and s_1 as the maximum state in S_1 such that $CS_2.last \parallel^c s_1$. By extensibility of $\rightarrow^c$, we can find $\rightarrow^c$-consistent global states G_1 and G_2 containing $\{CS_1.last, s_2\}$ and $\{CS_2.last, s_1\}$ respectively. We now have two cases:

  Case 1: $[s_1 \in CS_1 \lor s_2 \in CS_2]$ In this case $\neg B_{mutex}(G_2) \lor \neg B_{mutex}(G_1)$.

  Case 2: $[s_1 \notin CS_1 \land s_2 \notin CS_2]$ Since $s_1 \notin CS_1$, there are two ways to position s_1: (a) $s_1 \rightarrow^c CS_1.first$ or (b) $CS_1.last \rightarrow^c s_1$. In sub-case (a), since $CS_2.last \not\rightarrow^c CS_1.first$, either $CS_2.last \parallel^c CS_1.first$ or $CS_1.first \rightarrow^c CS_2.last$, which gives us $s_1 \rightarrow^c CS_2.last$. Both possibilities contradict the definition of

s_1. This leaves sub-case (b) as the only possibility. Therefore, $CS_1.last \rightarrow^c s_1$. Similarly, we can prove $CS_2.last \rightarrow^c s_2$. Let $H = \rightarrow^c$-glb(G_1, G_2). H contains $CS_1.last$ and $CS_2.last$ and, so, $\neg B_{mutex}(H)$. Further, H is $\rightarrow^c$-consistent (by the lattice property).

So in either case, $\rightarrow^c$ is not a controlling computation of B_{mutex} in $\rightarrow$. □

Theorem 2 (Sufficient Condition) *For a computation $\rightarrow$ of S, and a global predicate B_{mutex},*

$$\mapsto \text{ has no cycles} \quad \Rightarrow \quad \text{a controlling computation of } B_{mutex} \text{ in } \rightarrow \text{ exists}$$

Proof: Since $\mapsto$ has no cycles, we can arrange all of the critical sections in a sequence: $CS_1, CS_2, \cdots CS_m$ such that $CS_i \mapsto CS_j \Rightarrow i < j$. Let $\rightarrow^c$ be defined as $(\rightarrow \cup \{(CS_i.last, CS_{i+1}.first) \mid 1 \leq i \leq m-1\})^+$, where $()^+$ is the transitive closure. Clearly $\rightarrow \subseteq \rightarrow^c$. In the next paragraph, we will prove that $\rightarrow^c$ is a partial order. Assume that there is a global state G such that $\neg B_{mutex}(G)$. Therefore, we can find states s and t such that $critical(s)$ and $critical(t)$. Let CS_i and CS_j be the two critical sections to which s and t belong respectively. w.l.o.g, let $i < j$. Therefore, $s \rightarrow^c t$, and $\neg \rightarrow^c$-consistent(G). Therefore, $\rightarrow^c$-consistent$(G) \Rightarrow B_{mutex}(G)$. So $\rightarrow^c$ is a controlling computation of B_{mutex} in $\rightarrow$.

Our remaining proof obligation is to prove that $\rightarrow^c$ is a partial order. To this end, let $\rightarrow^k$ be defined as: $(\rightarrow \cup \{(CS_i.last, CS_{i+1}.first) \mid 1 \leq i \leq k-1\})^+$. We make the following claim:

Claim: $\forall 1 \leq k \leq m$: (1) $\rightarrow^k$ is a partial order, and (2) $CS_i \mapsto^k CS_j \Rightarrow i < j$

Clearly $\rightarrow^c = \rightarrow^m$ and so this claim implies that $\rightarrow^c$ is a partial order.

Proof of Claim: (by Induction on k)

Base Case: Immediate from $\rightarrow = \rightarrow^1$.

Inductive Case: We make the inductive hypothesis that $\rightarrow^{k-1}$ is a partial order, and that $CS_i \mapsto^{k-1} CS_j \Rightarrow i < j$. We may rewrite the definition of $\rightarrow^k$ as: $(\rightarrow^{k-1} \cup \{(CS_{k-1}.last, CS_k.first)\})^+$. First we demonstrate that $\rightarrow^k$ is irreflexive and transitive (which together imply asymmetry).

(i) *Irreflexivity:* Let $s \rightarrow^k t$. There are two possibilities: either $s \rightarrow^{k-1} t$ or $s \rightarrow^{k-1} CS_{k-1}.last \wedge CS_k.first \rightarrow^{k-1} t$. In the first case, the inductive hypothesis tells us that $\rightarrow^{k-1}$ is irreflexive and so $s \neq t$. In the second case, part (1) of the inductive hypothesis tells us that $\rightarrow^{k-1}$ is transitive, and part (2) of the inductive hypothesis tells us that $CS_k.first \not\rightarrow^{k-1} CS_{k-1}.last$ and so $s \neq t$.

(ii) *Transitivity:* This is immediate from the definition of $\rightarrow^k$.

Therefore, $\rightarrow^k$ is a partial order. We now show the second part of the claim. Suppose $CS_i \mapsto^k CS_j$. This implies that $CS_i.first \rightarrow^k CS_j.last \wedge i \neq j$. There are two cases: either $CS_i.first \rightarrow^{k-1} CS_j.last \wedge i \neq j$ or $CS_i.first \rightarrow^{k-1} CS_{k-1}.last \wedge CS_k.first \rightarrow^{k-1} CS_j.last \wedge i \neq j$. In the first case, we have $CS_i \mapsto^{k-1} CS_j$ and so by the inductive hypothesis, $i < j$. In a similar manner, the second case would give us $i \leq k-1 \wedge k \leq j$ and so $i < j$. □

In conclusion, the necessary and sufficient condition for finding a controlling computation for B_{mutex} is that there is no cycle of critical sections with respect to $\mapsto$. Further note that, since the proof of Theorem 2 is constructive, we can use it to design a naive algorithm to find a controlling computation. (We will see why this algorithm is naive in Section 3.5).

3.2 Off-line Readers Writers Problem

Let *read_critical* and *write_critical* be functions that map a state onto a boolean value. Further, no state can be both *read_critical* and *write_critical* (any read and write locked state is considered to be only write locked). Let $critical(s) \equiv read\_critical(s) \lor write\_critical(s)$. The Off-line Readers Writers Problem is a specialization of the Off-line Predicate Control Problem to the following class of global predicates:

$$B_{rw}(G) \equiv \forall \ distinct \ s, t \in G : \neg(write\_critical(s) \land critical(t))$$

Given a *read_critical* function and a *write_critical* function on S and a computation $\rightarrow$ on S, we define a *read critical section* and a *write critical section* in an analogous fashion to the critical sections that we defined before. Note that, since no state is both *read_critical* and *write_critical*, critical sections in a process do not overlap.

Let $\mapsto$ be a relation on both read and write critical sections defined as: $CS \mapsto CS' \equiv CS.first \rightarrow CS'.last \land CS \neq CS'$

Theorem 3 (Necessary Condition) *For a computation $\rightarrow$ of S, and a global predicate B_{rw},*

a controlling computation of	$\Rightarrow$	*all cycles in $\mapsto$ contain*
B_{rw} in $\rightarrow$ exists		*only read critical sections*

Proof: The proof is similar to the proof of Theorem 1. We will prove the contrapositive. Let $\mapsto$ have a cycle, say $CS_1 \mapsto CS_2 \mapsto \cdots CS_m \mapsto CS_1$. Without loss of generality, let CS_1 be a write critical section. Let $\rightarrow^c$ be a computation such that $\rightarrow \subseteq \rightarrow^c$.

First, we claim that there is at least one critical section in the cycle say CS_k (where $k \neq 1$), such that $CS_1.last \not\rightarrow^c CS_k.first$ and $CS_k.last \not\rightarrow^c CS_1.first$. To prove this, we assume the opposite:
$$\forall CS_k \ (k \neq 1) : \ CS_1.last \rightarrow^c CS_k.first \lor CS_k.last \rightarrow^c CS_1.first - (i)$$
and prove a contradiction as follows. $CS_m \mapsto CS_1$ implies $CS_1.last \not\rightarrow^c CS_m.first$. Therefore, by (i), $CS_m.last \rightarrow^c CS_1.first$. This allows us to define j as the smallest integer such that $CS_j.last \rightarrow^c CS_1.first$. $CS_1 \mapsto CS_2$ implies that $CS_2.last \not\rightarrow^c CS_1.first$. Therefore, $j \neq 2$. In particular, CS_{j-1} and CS_1 are distinct. By our choice of j, $CS_{j-1}.last \not\rightarrow^c CS_1.first$. So, using (i), $CS_1.last \rightarrow^c CS_{j-1}.first$. We now have a cycle: $CS_1.last \rightarrow^c CS_{j-1}.first$ (as above), $CS_{j-1}.first \rightarrow^c CS_j.last$ (since $CS_{j-1} \mapsto CS_j$), $CS_j.last \rightarrow^c CS_1.first$ (by our choice of j), and $CS_1.first \rightarrow^c CS_1.last$ (by the definition of *first* and *last*). This cycle contradicts the fact that $\rightarrow^c$ is a partial order.

Since we have demonstrated the existence of a CS_k such that $CS_1.last \not\rightarrow^c CS_k.first$ and $CS_k.last \not\rightarrow^c CS_1.first$, we can use a proof similar to the one in Theorem 1 to show that $\rightarrow^c$ is not a controlling computation of B_{rw} in $\rightarrow$. □

Theorem 4 (Sufficient Condition) *For a computation $\mapsto$ of S, and a global predicate B_{rw},*

> all cycles in $\mapsto$ contain $\quad \Rightarrow \quad$ a controlling computation of
> only read critical sections $\qquad\qquad B_{rw}$ in $\rightarrow$ exists

Proof: Consider the set of strongly connected components of the set of critical sections with respect to the $\mapsto$ relation. Define the $\hookrightarrow$ relation on strongly connected components as $SCC \hookrightarrow SCC' \equiv \exists CS \in SCC, CS' \in SCC' : CS \mapsto CS' \wedge SCC \neq SCC'$. It is verifiable that $\hookrightarrow$ is a partial order. Therefore, we can linearize it to get a sequence of all strongly connected components, say $SCC_1, SCC_2, \cdots SCC_l$ such that $SCC_i \hookrightarrow SCC_j \Rightarrow i < j$. Let $\rightarrow^c$ be defined as $(\rightarrow \cup \{(CS_i.last, CS_j.first) \mid CS_i \in SCC_k, CS_j \in SCC_{k+1}$ for some $1 \leq k \leq l-1\})^+$. Clearly $\rightarrow \subseteq \rightarrow^c$. We can show that $\rightarrow^c$ is a partial order along similar lines as the proof of Theorem 2.

We now show that $\rightarrow^c$ is a controlling computation of B_{rw} in $\rightarrow$. Suppose G is a global state such that $\neg B_{rw}(G)$. Therefore, we can find states s and t such that $write\_critical(s)$ and $critical(t)$. Let CS be a write critical section that contains s and let CS' be a critical section that contains t. Let SCC_i and SCC_j be the strongly connected components that contain CS and CS' respectively. SCC_i is distinct from SCC_j since, otherwise, there would be a cycle in $\mapsto$ that contains a write critical section. Without loss of generality, let $i < j$. By the definition of $\rightarrow^c$, we have $s \rightarrow^c t$ and, therefore, $\neg \rightarrow^c$-consistent(G). Therefore, $\rightarrow^c$ is a controlling computation of B_{rw} in $\rightarrow$. $\square$

Note, as before, that the proof of Theorem 4 can be used to design an algorithm to find a controlling computation.

3.3 Off-line Independent Mutual Exclusion

Let $critical_1, critical_2, \cdots critical_m$ be functions that map an event onto a boolean value. The Off-line Independent Mutual Exclusion Problem is a specialization of the Off-line Predicate Control Problem to the following class of global predicates:

$$B_{ind}(G) \equiv \forall \text{ distinct } s, t \in G : \forall i : \neg(critical_i(s) \wedge critical_i(t))$$

Given a function $critical_i$ on S and a computation $\rightarrow$ on S, we define an *i-critical section* in an analogous fashion to the critical sections that we defined before. Note that the definition allows independent critical sections on the same process to overlap. In particular the same set of states may correspond to two different critical sections (corresponding to a critical section with multiple locks). Let $\mapsto$ be a relation on all critical sections defined as before.

Theorem 5 (Necessary Condition)
For a computation $\rightarrow$ of S, and a global predicate B_{ind},

> a controlling computation of $\quad \Rightarrow \quad \mapsto$ has no cycles of i-critical
> B_{ind} in $\rightarrow$ exists $\qquad\qquad$ sections, for some i

Proof: The proof is almost identical to the proof of Theorem 1. □

Theorem 6 (Sufficient Condition) *For a computation → of S, and a global predicate B_{ind},*

$\mapsto$ *has no cycles of i-critical* $\Rightarrow$ *a controlling computation of*
sections, for some i   *B_{ind} in → exists*

Proof: The proof is along similar lines to the proof of Theorem 4. In this case we take strongly connected components as before, but make use of the fact that no two *i*-critical sections may be in the same strongly connected component (otherwise, there would be a cycle of *i*-critical sections). □

3.4 Off-line Independent Read-Write Mutual Exclusion

Using similar definitions, the Off-line Independent Read-Write Mutual Exclusion Problem is a specialization of the Off-line Predicate Control Problem to the following class of global predicates:

$$B_{ind-rw}(G) \equiv \forall \text{ distinct } s,t \in G : \forall i : \neg(write\_critical_i(s) \wedge critical_i(t))$$

As before, we define *i-read critical sections* and *i-write critical section* ($1 \leq i \leq m$). Similarly, let $\mapsto$ be a relation on all critical sections. The necessary and sufficient condition is a combination of that of the previous two sections. Since the proofs are similar to the previous ones, we simply state:

Theorem 7 (Necessary and Sufficient Condition)
For a computation → of S, and a global predicate B_{ind-rw},

a controlling computation of $\equiv$ *all cycles of i-critical sections in $\mapsto$*
B_{ind-rw} in → exists   *contain only read critical sections*

3.5 Algorithm

Figure 3 shows the algorithm to find a controlling computation of B_{ind-rw} in →. Since the other forms of mutual exclusion are special cases of B_{ind-rw}, this algorithm can be applied to any of them.

The input to the algorithm is the computation, represented by n lists of critical sections $C_1, \cdots, C_n$. For now, to simplify presentation, we assume that critical sections are totally ordered on each process. Each critical section is represented as its process id, its first and last states, a type identifier cs_id that specifies the $critical_{cs\_id}$ function, and a flag indicating if it is a write or read critical section. The partial order is implicitly maintained by vector clocks [9] associated with the first and last states of each critical section. The algorithm outputs the $\rightarrow^c$ relation specified as a list of ordered pairs of states.

The first while loop of the algorithm builds *ordered*, a totally ordered set of strongly connected components of critical sections (called scc's from here on). The second while loop simply uses *ordered* to construct the $\rightarrow^c$ relation.

```
Types:    state:              (pid: int; v: vector_clock);
          critical_section:   (pid: int; first: state; last: state;
                                 cs_id: integer; write_critical: boolean);
          strongly_conn_component:  set of critical_section;
Input:    C₁,C₂,···,Cₙ:      list of critical_section
Output:   O:                 list of (state, state), initially null
Vars:     scc_set, crossable: set of strongly_conn_component
          crossed, prev, curr:  strongly_conn_component
          cs, cs':              critical_section
          ordered:             list of strongly_conn_component


while (∀i :  Cᵢ ≠ null) do
    scc_set := get_scc(C₁.head, C₂.head, ···, Cₙ.head)
    crossable := { s ∈ scc_set | ∀s' ∈ scc_set, s' ≠ s :  s' ↛ s }
    crossed := select(crossable);
    if (not_valid(crossed)) then
        exit("No Controlled Computation Exists");
    for each cs in crossed do
        C_{cs.pid}.delete_head();
    ordered.add_head(crossed);
prev := ordered.delete_head();
while (ordered ≠ null) do
    curr := ordered.delete_head();
    for each cs in prev and cs' in curr do
        if (cs.last ↛ cs'.first) then
            O.add_head(cs.last, cs'.first);
```

Fig. 3. Algorithm for Off-line Independent Read-Write Mutual Exclusion

The goal of each iteration of the first while loop is to add an scc, which is min-imal w.r.t. $\hookrightarrow$, to *ordered* (where $\hookrightarrow$ is the relation on scc's defined in the proof of Theorem 4). To determine this scc, it first computes the set of scc's among the leading critical sections in $C_1, \cdots C_n$. Since no scc can contain two critical sections from the same process, it is sufficient to consider only the leading critical sections. From the set of scc's, it determines the set of minimal scc's, *crossable*. It then randomly selects one of the minimal scc's. Finally, before adding the scc to *ordered*, it must check if the scc is *not_valid*, where $not\_valid(crossed) \equiv \exists cs, cs' \in crossed : cs.cs\_id = cs'.cs\_id \wedge cs.write\_critical$. If an invalid scc is found, no controlling computation exists (by Theorem 7).

The main while loop of the algorithm executes p times in the worst case, where p is the number of critical sections in the computation. Each iteration takes $O(n^2)$, since it must compute the scc's. Thus, a simple implementation of the algorithm will have a time complexity of $O(n^2 p)$. However, a better im-plementation of the algorithm would amortize the cost of computing scc's over multiple iterations of the loop. Each iteration would compare each of the critical sections that have newly reached the heads of the lists with the existing scc's, thus forming new scc's. Therefore, each of the p critical section reaches the head of the list just once, when it is compared with $n-1$ critical sections to determine the new scc's. The time complexity of the algorithm with this improved implementation is, therefore, $O(np)$. Note that a naive algorithm based directly on the constructive proof of the sufficient condition in Theorem 7 would take $O(p^2)$. We have reduced the complexity significantly by using the fact that the critical sections in a process are totally ordered.

The algorithm has implicitly assumed a total ordering of critical sections in each process. However, as noted before, independent critical sections on the same process may overlap, and may even coincide exactly (a critical section with multiple locks is treated as multiple critical sections that completely overlap). The algorithm can be extended to handle such cases by first determining the scc's within a process. These scc's correspond to maximal sets of overlapping critical sections. The input to the algorithm would consist of n lists of such process-local scc's. The remainder of the algorithm remains unchanged.

4   Application to Software Fault Tolerance

Our proposed scheme for software fault tolerance consists of four parts: (i) tracing an execution, (ii) detecting a synchronization failure, (iii) determining a control strategy, and (iv) re-executing under control. This paper has focused mainly on the problem of determining a control strategy. We have designed an efficient algorithm that determines which synchronizations to add in order to avoid very general forms of mutual exclusion violation. As mentioned before, the other three parts of our scheme have been addressed as independent problems. We now put all the pieces together for a comprehensive look at how race failures (mutual exclusion violations) can be tolerated.

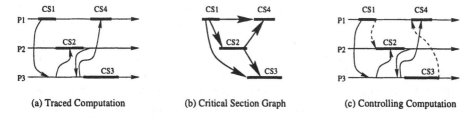

| (a) Traced Computation | (b) Critical Section Graph | (c) Controlling Computation |

Fig. 4. Example: Tolerating Races in a Concurrent Execution

The problem of determining a control strategy was placed in a very general model of concurrent execution. However, tracing, detection, and controlled re-execution depend greatly on the particular concurrent paradigm. We choose a simple example that demonstrates the key issues that will arise in most concurrent paradigms. Consider a distributed system of processes that write to a single shared file. The file system itself does not synchronize accesses and so the processes are responsible for synchronizing their accesses to the file. If they do not do so, the writes may interleave and the data may get corrupted. Since the file data is very crucial, we must ensure that races can be tolerated. Synchronization occurs through the use of explicit message passing between the processes.

The first part of our mechanism involves tracing the execution. The concern during tracing is to reduce the space and time overhead, so that tolerating a possible fault does not come at too great a cost. Much work has been done in implementing tracing in various paradigms, while keeping the overhead low [2, 11, 12, 15]. In our example, we use a vector clock mechanism [9], updating the vector clock at each send and receive point. This vector clock needs to be logged for each of the writes to the file (for our algorithm). The vector clock values must also be logged for each receive point (for replay). When a write is initiated, and when it returns, the vector clock must be logged. In our example, the writes are typically very long and therefore are performed asynchronously. Thus, execution continues while the write is in progress. In particular, the process may receive a message from another process during its write to the file. Inserting some computation at the send, receive, write initiation, and write completion points can be achieved either by code instrumentation, or by modifying the run-time environment (message-passing interface and the file system interface).

The second part of our mechanism is detecting when a race occurs. Many existing tools have been built to solve exactly this problem [4, 10]. Since we use message passing as our synchronization mechanism, the methods described in [10] are particularly applicable.

Once a race has been detected, we roll-back all processes to a consistent global state prior to the race. We also roll-back the file to a version consistent with the rolled-back state of the processes. (We assume a versioned file system with the ability to roll back.) We then take the section of the traced vector clock values that occur after the rolled-back state. These indicate the critical section entry and exit points required by our algorithm. The algorithm would take $O(np)$ time, where n is the number of processes and p is the number of critical sections that have been rolled back. The output of the algorithm is the set of added synchronizations specified as pairs of critical section boundary points. Figure 4 demonstrates a possible scenario. Here the semantics of mutual exclusion correspond to a single exclusive lock. Therefore, the necessary and sufficient condition is that there are no cycles in the critical section graph shown in Figure 4(b). Applying the algorithm would add synchronizations to give the controlling computation shown in Figure 4(c).

The next step is to replay the processes using the logged vector clock values of the receive points. Each receive point must be blocked until the same message arrives as in the previous execution. This is a standard replay mechanism (e.g. [12]). In addition to this replay, we must impose additional synchronizations. For example, suppose (s, t) is one of the synchronizations output by our algorithm. The state s is a critical section exit point while t is a critical section entry point. Each of these additional synchronizations is implemented by a control message sent from s and received before t. Thus, at each critical section exit point, we must check the added synchronizations to decide if a control message must be sent. At each critical section entry point, we must check the added synchronizations to decide if the process must block waiting for a control message. As in tracing, the points at which computation must be added are the write initiation and completion points, and the send and receive points. Again, we can accomplish this by code instrumentation or run-time environment modification.

We have chosen an example in which the processes only write to the file. If the processes were to read from the file as well, then that would cause causal dependencies between processes. Then we would have to track these causal dependencies as we did for messages. Another option would be to assume that these causal dependencies do not affect the message communications, in which case, we do not have to track them. However, if we take this approach, we would have to check to see that our traced computation is the same as the one being replayed. In case of a divergence, we would leave the execution to proceed uncontrolled from the point of divergence.

5 Concluding Remarks

We have presented an approach for tolerating synchronization faults in concurrent programs based on rollback and controlled re-execution. Our focus in this paper has been on races, which form a particular type of synchronization fault. In order to determine a control strategy that avoids races while re-executing, we have solved the off-line predicate control problem for various forms of mutual exclusion properties. We have determined the necessary and sufficient conditions for solving off-line predicate control for simple mutual exlusion, read-write mutual exclusion, independent mutual exclusion, and independent read-write mutual exclusion. We have presented an efficient algorithm that solves for the most general property, independent read-write mutual exclusion. The algorithm takes $O(np)$ time, where n is the number of processes and p is the number of critical sections. Finally, we have demonstrated how races can be tolerated using our algorithm. An implementation of software fault tolerance using controlled re-execution is currently being developed in order to evaluate the performance and effectiveness of the technique in practice.

It may be argued that mutual exclusion could be simply handled at the programming language level using locks (in other words, on-line mutual exclusion, as opposed to off-line mutual exclusion). However, there are good reasons for our approach. Firstly, as noted in Section 1, it is impossible to ensure that there will be no deadlocks with on-line locking unless some assumptions are made, such as non-blocking critical sections. In off-line mutual exclusion, no such assumptions are required. Secondly, programmers make mistakes, being prone to reduce locking for greater efficiency. Thirdly, source code is often unavailable for modification, while requirements change dynamically. In modern component-based systems, different components may come from different vendors and it may be difficult to ensure a consistent locking discipline throughout the code. The best approach is to use both good programming discipline and a sofware fault tolerance technique to make programs more resistant to failures.

References

1. A. Avizienis and L. Chen. On the implementation of n-version programming for software fault tolerance during execution. In *Proc. of the First IEEE-CS International Conference on Computer Software and Applications*, pages 149 – 155, November 1977.
2. J. D. Choi and H. Srinivasan. Deterministic replay of java multithreaded applications. In *2nd SIGMETRICS Symp. on Parallel and Distr. Tools*, pages 48 – 59, Aug. 1998.
3. F. Cristian. Understanding fault-tolerant distributed systems. *CACM*, 34(2):56 – 78, Feb 1991.
4. M. Feng and C. E. Leiserson. Efficient detection of determinacy races in cilk programs. In *Proc. of 9th Annual ACM Symposium on Parallel Algorithms and Architectures*, pages 22–25, Newport, USA, June 1997.
5. Y. Huang and C. Kintala. Software implemented fault tolerance: technologies and experience. In *Proc. IEEE Fault-Tolerant Comp. Symp.*, pages 138 – 144, June 1993.
6. R. K. Iyer and I. Lee. Software fault tolerance in computer operating systems. In M. R. Lyu, editor, *Software Fault Tolerance*, Trends in Software Series, chapter 11, pages 249 – 278. John Wiley & Sons, Inc., 1995.
7. L. Lamport. Time, clocks, and the ordering of events in a distributed system. *Communications of the ACM*, 21(7):558 – 565, July 1978.
8. D. Lea. *Concurrent Programming in Java: Design Principles and Patterns*, chapter 3.1.2. The Java Series. Addison Wesley Longman, Inc., 1997.
9. F. Mattern. Virtual time and global states of distributed systems. In *Parallel and Distributed Algorithms: Proc. of the International Workshop on Parallel and Distributed Algorithms*, pages 215 – 226. Elsevier Science Publishers B. V. (North Holland), 1989.
10. R. H. B. Netzer. *Race condition detection for debugging shared-memory parallel programs*. PhD thesis, University of Wisconsin-Madison, 1991.
11. R. H. B. Netzer. Optimal tracing and replay for debugging shared-memory parallel programs. In *Proc. of ACM/ONR Workshop on Parallel and Distributed Debugging*, pages 1 – 11, May 1993. Also available as ACM SIGPLAN Notices Vol. 28, No. 12.
12. R. H. B. Netzer and B. P. Miller. Optimal tracing and replay for debugging message-passing parallel programs. In *Supercomputing '92*, pages 502 – 511, November 1992.
13. B. Randell. System structure for software fault-tolerance. *IEEE Transactions on Software Engineering*, 1(2):220 – 232, June 1975.
14. M. Raynal. *Algorithms for mutual exclusion*. MIT Press, 1986.
15. M. Ronnse and W. Zwaenepoel. Execution replay for treadmarks. In *Proc. of the 5th EUROMICRO Workshop on Parallel and Distributed Processing (PDP'97)*, pages 343–350, January 1997.
16. A. Tarafdar and V. K. Garg. Predicate control for active debugging of distributed programs. In *Proc. of the 9th Symposium on Parallel and Distributed Processing*, Orlando, USA, April 1998. IEEE.
17. Y. M. Wang, Y. Huang, W. K. Fuchs, C. Kintala, , and G. Suri. Progressive retry for software failure recovery in message-passing applications. *IEEE Trans. on Computers*, 46(10):1137–1141, October 1997.

DUALITY: An Architecture Independent Design Model for Parallel Systems Based on Partial Order Semantics

Camelia Zlatea and Tzilla Elrad

Illinois Institute of Technology, Computer Science Department,
Chicago, Illinois, 60616, USA
{camelia, elrad}@charlie.iit.edu
http://www.iit.edu/~concur

Abstract. This paper introduces DUALITY, a design model that provides a more structured style of parallel programming and refines causality from concurrency. We investigate semantic and syntactic transformations that support identifying the structure of a parallel program, as the basis for reducing the design complexity. The initial focus is on specification and correctness, then gradually adding architectural details and finally addressing efficiency. A parallel program is viewed as a *Meta-Program* - the result of causally composing an architecture-independent algorithm - the specification, with an architecture-dependent program - the mapping. This approach supports the derivation of efficient parallel implementations from program specifications. Consequently, transparent and architecture-independent specifications can be transformed into forms that match particular target architectures. Correctness of the implementation is inferred from correctness of the specification, by gradually imposing temporal and causal order and by transforming any property of the specification into a property of the parallel program. DUALITY relates data and process parallelism and aims to reuse design knowledge from sequential patterns. DUALITY is developed in the context of the UNITY formalism and the principle and algebraic laws of Communication Closed Layers (CCL), and illustrated through the algorithm of all-points shortest path.

1 Introduction

It has been stressed in the recent years the effectiveness of a more abstract model for the design of parallel programs. This results in a separation between the structure of the parallel program from the organization of the parallel architecture.

Chandy and Misra's UNITY formalism [1] provides a simple implementation-independent notation and a proof system based on temporal logic. A UNITY program is decoupled from its implementation. It derives much of its simplicity by abstracting away from the notion of control flow. The programs are bags of multiple assignments executed nondeterministically, under the weak fairness assumption that each assignment is selected infinitely often. The formalism is suitable for specifying and verifying various safety and progress properties of concurrent programs whose semantics is modeled by weakly fair transition systems. A strong aspect determined by the simplicity of the notation is the capacity to develop parallel or distributed applications jointly with correctness proofs. UNITY enforces the idea of representing parallel or distributed systems as collections of guarded actions, without any apparent algebraic structure. The motivation is that the algebraic syntactic structure of the programming notation is too close to the actual architecture of the target machines and that this aspect should not influence the (initial) design of the systems. The work in [1] stresses the design of parallel or distributed systems starting with an initial phase, which is architecture and implementation independent. From here the difficulty and the challenge of balancing UNITY's absence of control structures with the goal to devise efficient UNITY implementations on existing parallel or distributed architectures. This aspect can become a drawback for complex systems like mobile distributed systems or real-time embedded systems.

Bouge [2] and Snyder [11] argue as well for a more abstract model for the design of parallel and distributed programs based on the separation between the structure of the program, from the organization of the architecture. Their work shows that the data-parallel programming model can make a clear separation between the programming model and the execution model.

Another school of thoughts evolved from the algebraic approach often referred as modularity or compositionality principle [7], [9]. Although there is an agreement with the idea that initial design should ignore architectural details, the compositionality principle states that a (parallel or distributed) system can be derived from specifications of its components, by ignoring their internal algebraic structure. However, in contrast with [1], this trend does not consider that algebraic syntactic structure of the programming notation is too close to the target architecture. Much more, it is claimed that what leads to dependency, on one or other architecture, is due to certain language operations such as sequential operation. A model for concurrency is proposed. It allows distinction between parallel program composition F [] G [9], classical sequential composition F ; G and a weak sequential composition, called layer composition, $F \bullet G$ (inspired by Elrad and Francez [3] Communication Closed Layers principle). For the *layer composition* $F \bullet G$, any event f from F precedes any event g from G, with which is in conflict, in causal dependence. By comparison, *sequential composition*, denoted with ";", is a representation of the temporal dependence. Work in [7, 9] formulates the algebraic laws of the layer composition, providing that there is no conflict between the programs F and K and between H and G respectively:

$$(F[]H) \bullet (G[]K) = (F \bullet G)[](H \bullet K).$$

This law is not valid if causal order, expressed by the layer composition, is replaced with temporal order, represented by the sequential composition. The Communication Closed Layers (CCL) principle enables a direct representation of properties involving temporal and causal order. Identifying causality of the events helps in bounding the nondeterminism. Serializability is a property that encompasses causal order and concurrency. It is very useful for program refinement, preserving mapping in the syntactic domain, for the purpose of efficient implementations on parallel architectures.

Our paper presents DUALITY [14], an extension of the UNITY concurrency model with compositional programming abstractions and partial order based structures. One reason to build on UNITY is given by the availability of an architecture-independent programming notation and logic, within the same formalism. We believe that our design model can be also supported by partial-order temporal logic specifications like ISTL [8], or at some extent, by branching time logic or CTL^* [5]. DUALITY strongly adheres to the idea of ignoring implementation or architectural details during the initial design phases. Yet, our goals are to balance transparency and adaptation for applications running on various classes of parallel or distributed machines, including mobile or hybrid architectures.

DUALITY framework integrates both UNITY and the compositional, algebraic principle and intends to add more expressiveness and modularity to parallel programs. UNITY programs can be represented under the interleaved model of concurrency i.e. one distinguishes between execution sequences, which are not significantly different. The execution sequences are equivalent because they either, differ by the ordering of independent events or by the number of times a state is adjacently repeated. If an ordering is given in the specification, then it is assumed that the mapping also preserves the ordering. This could unnecessarily lead to an increased complexity of the design and verification. Partial-order semantics has been developed for modeling concurrency in a more abstract and faithful manner. The ordering is enforced in specification and mapping, only for the cases of *dependent* events, since independent events can be executed in any order. Under partial-order semantics, UNITY specifications no longer make distinction between equivalent execution sequences, thus reducing the size of the explored state-space. Instead of representing all possible interleavings, all possible execution sequences, it is sufficient to represent at least one sequence per equivalence class. UNITY properties by definition apply globally on programs. The idea helps in introducing new properties based on partial-order semantics in UNITY formalism.

The outline of this paper is as follows. Section 2 gives a brief review of the background concepts and the formal semantics for the partial-order structures, defined in in terms of UNITY. Section 3 presents an informal description of the DUALITY design model. Section 4 illustrates a case of program transformation and design reuse. Finally, Section 5 concludes and discusses on future research directions.

2 Extending UNITY with Partial Order Based Structures

UNITY formalism [1] provides a language to construct well-founded formulas and a logic to construct proofs. This section gives a brief overview of UNITY. It also introduces the constructs that support a structured style of parallel programming, and the method to integrate Communication Closed Layers as a compositional abstraction in UNITY.

UNITY notation allows an abstract representation of the parallel computation. A program has a section for variable declarations, a section specifying the initial values for the variables (the *INITIALLY* predicate) and a finite set of assignments. A program is similar to a "bag" of assignments. Each assignment can be selected non-deterministically and eventually executed, and returned to the "bag". The execution model for UNITY programs is based on sequences of tuples (a tuple being a state). Each element of a sequence models an execution step of the program. A sequence denotes a possible run. A program can terminate if it reaches a *fixed point*, where no state transition is possible. In a UNITY program there is no notion of control structures or control flow (considered implementation aspects). A program can be mapped then implemented on different types of architectures. The correctness of the UNITY program is independent of the target architecture and the manner in which the program is executed. However, efficiency must be evaluated with reference to the target architecture.

Notations: s, t - UNITY assignments; $s.r$ - the set of variables read by s; $s.w$ - the set of variables written by s; L, F - UNITY programs; $L.a$ - the set of all assignments, belonging to L; $L.r$ - the set of all variables read by L; $L.w$ - the set of all variables written by L; p - a precondition that must be true before the execution of s and q - a postcondition, resulting after the execution of s. Proofs in UNITY are based on assertions of type $\{p\}$ s $\{q\}$. A property P(p,q) applies globally to a program F, i.e. $\{p\}$ F $\{q\}$, if and only if $< \forall s : s \in F :: \{p\} s \{q\} >$. For brevity, this paper focuses on three of the UNITY logic properties: *invariant* and *co* - safety properties and *leads-to* - progress property.

"*invariant* $p \equiv (INITIALLY \Rightarrow p) \wedge (\{p\} F \{p\})$". To illustrate the property, "invariant x>0" states that the variable x is positive in any state of the program execution.

"$p\ co\ q \equiv\ < \forall s:$ s in F :: $\{p\}$ s $\{q\} >$"; it signifies that if a state satisfying p occurs anywhere in the execution, the next state must satisfy q.

"$p\ leads$-$to\ q$" - signifies that once p becomes true q will be true eventually. However, it cannot be asserted that p will remain true as long as q is not. To illustrate, "x=0 *leads-to* x>0", states that whenever x is equal to 0 during a program execution, then it will eventually become positive at some later state in the execution.

UNITY defines *union* as a nondeterministic parallel composition. The union of the programs S_1 and S_2 is denoted $S_1 \ [] \ S_2$ and has the following properties:

  (i) $INITIALLY(S_1 \ [] \ S_2) = INITIALLY(S_1) \wedge INITIALLY(S_2)$
  (ii) $(S_1 \ [] \ S_2).a = S_1.a \cup S_2.a$.

The main idea is that the safety of the composite program follows from the safety of its components. A shared-memory or a distributed program can be represented as a union: $F = S_1 \ [] \ S_2 \ [] \ .. \ [] \ S_n$. Nevertheless, the absence of control structures in UNITY limits the expressiveness of the *union* when composing specifications and mappings for various parallel or distributed architectures. This leads us to the conclusion that UNITY notation for the mappings should provide certain forms of control structures. A more structured style of parallel programming can be provided, by isolating weak sequential phases and their interrelationship. Communication Closed Layers principle [3] and algebraic laws [7] formalize the concept of weak sequential composition. The idea is that actions which are not dependent (unilateral or bilateral data dependent) do not have to wait for one another to proceed, even if they are composed sequentially. In the DUALITY framework, we relate UNITY model with the interleaving and the partial-order semantics. The interleaved execution of a UNITY program can be interpreted as a succession of partial order executions. We extend UNITY with programming abstractions that involve temporal and causal order and help in identifying the interface between program structures.

Property 1 Strong Enable s. If s labels an assignment, we define *s.event* a predicate that is true whenever s is selected and the guard is true (eventually this leads to a program state transition): *strong enable s* $\equiv$ *s.event.*

Property 2 Weak Enable s. If a selected statement s has false guard, *s.event* is false: *weak enable s* $\equiv \neg(s.event)$. (This is equivalent to the execution of a skip statement).

Definition 1 Progress Condition. *L.event* denotes a predicate, which is true if exists an assignment s $\in$ L.a, such that *s.event* is true (i.e., *strong enable s* holds). All the states where *L.event* holds make a consistent set of local states associated with the program L: *L.event* $\equiv <\exists s : s{\in}L.a \land s.event >$.

Definition 2 Activation Condition. *L.init* denotes a predicate associated with the initial set of states, which precedes the selection and execution of any assignment belonging to L.a.

Definition 3 Fixed Point. A *Fixed Point, FP_L*, for the program L is a state predicate such that the execution of any statement s $\in$ L.a in that state leaves the state unchanged: $FP_L \equiv <\forall s : s \in L.a \land p :: \{p\} s \{p\} >$.

Definition 4 Group-of-Actions. A *Group-of-Actions* is a program structure L identified by the activation condition, progress condition and respectively the Fixed-Point such that following properties hold:
  (i) *L.init* co (*L.event* $\lor$ *L.init*)
  (ii) *L.event* leads-to FP_L
  Property (i) states that the execution of the *Group-of-Actions* L is always enabled from its activation condition. Property (ii) states that the progress condition for the program L causally precedes the eventual Fixed Point.

Example: Program F uses Sieve Algorithm to compute the first count = K prime numbers from a sequence of natural numbers seq.i ($1 \leq i \leq N$, N>K). F (Fig. 1)is a union composition $F = <[] \ j : 1 \leq j \leq N :: L_j >$. The interfaces of L_j are specified by the activation condition,

L_j.init $\equiv$ count = j - 1 $\wedge$ j $\leq$ K $\wedge$ seq.i = j < N; $FP_{L_j} \equiv$ j < seq.i < N; and respectively by the progress condition

L_j.event $\equiv$ seq.i $\geq$ j $\wedge$ count $\leq$ K.

Program L_j initially count = j - 1 $\wedge$ j $\leq$ K $\wedge$ seq.i = j < N
assign
count, i := count +1, i+1 if seq.i = j []
i := i +1 if (seq.i > j) $\wedge$ (seq.i mod j = 0) []
seq.j+1, i := seq.i, i+1 if (seq.i > j) $\wedge$ (seq.i mod j $\neq$ 0)
end

Fig. 1. Program F - Sieve Algorithm

We introduce new compositional abstractions that restrict nondeterminism and enable a direct representation of properties that involve temporal and causal order. (Notations used L_i and L_j groups of actions and s, t UNITY assignments).

Definition 5 Mutual-Dependence. "s mutual-dependent t" iff
(s data-bilateral-dependent t) $\wedge$ (s temporal-bilateral-dependent t).
Example: s: x:=1 if y=0 [] t: y:=0 if x=1; s.w =t.r={x} s.r=t.w={ y }; data bilateral dependence is expressed (s.w $\cap$ t.r $\neq \emptyset$) $\wedge$ (s.r $\cap$ t.w $\neq \emptyset$)) and temporal bilateral dependence, (s.event before t.event) $\vee$ (t.event before s.event).
"Li mutual-dependent Lj" iff $\exists s \in L_i$.a $\wedge$ $\exists t \in L_j$.a, such that the property "s mutual-dependent t" holds.

Definition 6 Safe-Dependence. "s safe-dependent t" iff
(s temporal-unilateral-dependent t) $\vee$ (s data-unilateral-dependent t).
Example: s: y:= x -1 [] t: x:=x+1 where s.r={ x } s.w={ y } t.r=t.w={ x } or always s.event precedes t.event.
"L_i safe-dependent L_j" iff $\forall$ s $\in L_i$.a $\wedge$ $\forall$ t $\in L_j$.a, the property "s safe-dependent t" holds.

Definition 7 Communication Closed Layer (CCL Structure). A group of actions L_j (j = 1..k) is called a *CCL structure* in the context of a program F, if there exists a partitioning of the program F, F.a = $\bigcup L_j$.a (j = 1..k), such that for any two groups of actions L_j, L_{j+1} (j = 1..k-1), "L_j safe-dependent L_{j+1}".

Definition 8 Partial-Order Layer (POL Structure). A *CCL structure* L_j (j = 1..k) is called a *POL structure* in the context of a program F, iff for L_j the relation "mutual-dependence " is a transitive closure.

Lemma 1 CCL Progress/Safety Properties. If L_j (j = 1..k) is a *POL structure* in the context of a program F, there exists LI_j a predicate, such that:

a) *"invariant LI_j"* holds in all consistent local states (also called global snapshot [12]) determined by the executions of the program L_j.

b) *"LI_j leads-to LI_{j+1}"* and *"$\neg(LI_{j+1}$ co $LI_j)$"* holds for the program resulted by reunion of L_j and L_{j+1}.

Proof:

a) From definition 7, for any *POL structure* L_j (j = 1..k), $\exists$ predicate LI_j such that: $<\forall$ s, t $\in L_j$.a , "s mutual-dependent t"$> \equiv$
$(L_j$.init $\Rightarrow LI_j) \wedge$ ({ LI_j } F { LI_j }) $\equiv$ invariant LI_j.

b) For any POL structures L_j and L_{j+1} (j = 1..k-1) $\exists$ predicate LI_j such that: "L_j temporal-unilateral dependent L_{j+1}"$\Rightarrow$
"L_j safe-dependent L_{j+1}"$\Rightarrow$ "LI_j leads-to LI_{j+1}"
or "L_j data-unilateral dependent L_{j+1}"$\Rightarrow$
"L_j safe-dependent L_{j+1}"$\Rightarrow$ "LI_j leads-to LI_{j+1}".
The *co* property is proved by contradiction; we demonstrate that
"L_j safe-dependent L_{j+1}" $\Rightarrow$ "$\neg(LI_{j+1}$ co $LI_j)$"

Lemma 2 CCL-POL Transformation. Any *CCL structure* L can be represented as a safe dependent layer composition (denoted "•") of *POL structures* L_i 1≤i≤m, with the following properties :

a) L $\equiv L_1$ • L_2 • .. • L_m.

b) $\exists$ *"invariant LI"* that holds in all consistent local states determined by the executions of L.

Proof:

a) Apply definition 7 and 8.

b) For example: *"invariant LI"* = *"invariant LI_1"*$\vee$ ..$\vee$ *"invariant LI_m"*

Lemma 3 Union-CCL Transformation. Given a program F as a union composition: F = S_1 [] S_2 [] .. [] S_n. If there exists a partitioning of F,
F.a = $\bigcup$Lj.a (j=1..k), such that any L_j (j=1..k) is a *CCL structure*, then the union and the Communication Closed Layer compositions (denoted "•") are equivalent:

F = S_1 [] S_2 [] .. [] S_n $\equiv L_1$ • L_2 • .. • L_k

Discussion: The union composition can be transformed into an equivalent Communication Closed Layer composition, providing that no mutual interlayer, "conflict" communications occur during the execution of any program L_j (j=1,k). Therefore, the union composition F can be equivalently rewritten as a composition of Communication Closed Layers, based on the causal order of the events.

3 DUALITY Design Model

DUALITY, our design model for parallel programs, divides the solution space into two synergistically coordinated representations of the specifications and mappings.

(i) *The problem-oriented specification,* "What?," is an architecture-independent representation of the computations. This is the premise to achieve transparency, for applications running in a parallel or distributed environment. Correctness, safety and progress properties apply globally to the transparent specification.

(ii) *The mapping,* "How? When? Where?," is an abstract description of how to execute a specification on a target parallel or distributed architecture. Mapping represents architectural details, e.g. parallelism constraints, location awareness, adaptation to interprocessor communication constraints. Complexity and efficiency are major concerns of the mapping.

We introduce *Meta-Program* as a consistent coordination of architecture-independent specifications and efficient implementations. A *Meta-Program* is a causal and concurrent, dual, composition of the adaptive mapping and the transparent specification. This notion extends Chandy and Misra's program-schema [1].

Controlling the effect of nondeterminism is one problem that affects the design of parallel applications In a *Meta-Program* there is a duality of causal and concurrent relations between specification and mapping events. This fact is due to the asynchronous character of the system components. However, one can identify the duality of causal and concurrent relations between *Meta-Program* events. Let consider two agents, a_1 and a_2, sending the messages b_1 and respectively b_2 to the same host, h, in mailbox B. To represent the two actions one uses labeled assignments, $x: B_h := b_1$ and respectively $y: B_h: = b_2$. The mapping expresses how the assignments are executed. To illustrate, for a mobile concurrent system, mapping can represent channel availability abstractions, $m_x: connect(a_1,h)$ and $m_y: connect(a_2,h)$, respectively. Notation for nondeterministic interleaving of specification and mapping events:

$Concurrent(m_x: connect(a_1,h), m_y: connect(a_2,h), x: B_h := b_1, y: B_h := b_2)$;

using a simplified notation:

$Concurrent(m_x, m_y, x, y)$.

Under the interleaving semantics [6], a single execution of the *Meta-Program* is considered a totally ordered sequence of events. The semantics of the *Meta-Program* is given by the set of all possible total order executions: $(x\ m_y)$, $(m_y\ x)$, $(x\ m_x)$, $(m_x\ x)$, $(y\ m_y)$, $(m_y\ y)$, $(y\ m_x)$, $(m_x\ y)$. The two total-orders of independent events, $(x\ m_y)$ and $(m_y\ x)$ are equivalent, and so are the total-orders $(y\ m_y)$ and $(m_y\ y)$. One calls the unordered sequence of the events x or m_y a partial-order. Under this semantics, a single execution is considered to be a partially-ordered sequence of events. The *Meta-Program* semantics is given by six partial-order executions: $(x\ m_y, m_y\ x)$, $(x\ m_x)$, $(m_x\ x)$, $(y\ m_y)$, $(m_y\ y)$, $(y\ m_x, m_x\ y)$. Partial-order semantics makes distinction between causality and concurrency, and allows for a more expressive specification. Therefore, one can determine equivalent sequences of events. In this way, instead of analyzing all possible interleavings, we can only consider at least one representative from each equivalence class. This approach has two folds:

1. It allows for a simplified, less expensive and more efficient verification of the system's properties.

2. It supports better decisions among the number of possible alternatives, consequently a reduced design complexity.

The semantics of *POL structures* and *CCL structures* allow verification of the properties of the parallel systems, without exploring all possible interleavings of nondeterministic executions. One benefit is the capacity to manipulate the *layer composition* as a partial-order, mapping operator. Initially, the *Meta-Program* is represented:

$$MP_S = Concurrent(m_x, m_y, x, y) \equiv m_x[]m_y[]x[]y \tag{1}$$

For all executions of the Meta-Program, there is a causal order between the events, m_x and x and respectively m_y and y. Providing that there is no conflict between x and m_y and respectively y and m_x, the ordering between non-conflicting events can be ignored. By applying definitions 5, 6, 7, 8 and Lemma 2, one identifies two POL structures: the specification (2) and the mapping (3).

$$S = Concurrent(x, y) \equiv x[]y \tag{2}$$

$$M_S = Concurrent(m_x, m_y) \equiv m_x[]m_y \tag{3}$$

The Meta-Program expresses that the two POL structures are in safe-dependent, causal relation:

$$MP_S = Causal(M_S, S) \tag{4}$$

The relation Concurrent(s,t) means that the actions s and t can happen in any order, consequently: "s mutual-dependent t" $\equiv$ Concurrent(s,t). The relation Causal(s,t) expresses the data or temporal causality between actions s and t, therefore we can write: "s safe-dependent t" $\equiv$ Causal(s,t). From (2), (3) and (4), the Meta-Program expression

$MP_S = Causal(Concurrent(m_x, m_y), Concurrent(x, y))$ can be denoted in terms of layer and union composition:

$$M_S \bullet S = (m_x[]m_y) \bullet (x[]y) \tag{5}$$

This design strategy leads us to the algebraic law of Communication Closed Layers, that allow for gradually adding details of temporal ordering to a Meta-Program that is already proven correct.
$Causal(Concurrent(m_x, m_y), Concurrent(x, y)) =$
$Concurrent(Causal(m_x, x), Causal(m_y, y))$
Consequently we write an equivalent expression of the Meta-Program:

$$MP_S = (m_x[]m_y) \bullet (x[]y) = (m_x \bullet x)[](m_y \bullet y) \tag{6}$$

The algebraic law is reformulated (MP_x, MP_y are Meta-Program components) in (7):

$$MP_S = MP_x[]MP_y = M_S \bullet S \tag{7}$$

To make a generalization, let assume an architecture independent, transparent specification,

$$S = Concurrent(S_1, .., S_n) \equiv S_1[]..[]S_n. \tag{8}$$

A possible mapping to a shared memory parallel architecture is a union of n communication channels, denoted

$$M_S = Concurrent(M_{S1}, .., M_{Sn}) \equiv (M_{S1}[]..[]M_{Sn}). \tag{9}$$

In a Meta-Program, which describes a parallel application, the mapping component is an adaptive layer that causally coordinates the events of the specification layer. The mapping program acts as a regulator that controls the specification. It can delay or inhibit basic interactions (assignments) or it can reallow them, in accordance with implementation constraints. The Meta-Program expression to reflect this idea is given by (10).

$$MP_S = Causal(Concurrent(M_{S1}, .., M_{Sn}), Concurrent(S_1, .., S_n)) \tag{10}$$

We formulate, in terms of UNITY, the generalized Communication Closed Layers algebraic law [7, 9], to allow transformations of the Meta-Program in forms that match shared memory or distributed parallel architectures. Each transformation step is carried out in conjunction with a formal verification phase, to increase confidence in the design correctness and to allow earlier error detection. This method is highly applicable in the initial stages of the design. Given L_{ij} and L_{kl} CCL structures, if there is a causal dependence between L_{ij} and L_{kl} then either i=k or j=l is satisfied, for $1 \leq i, j, k, l \leq n$. The generalized algebraic law of Communication Closed Layers is formulated,

$Concurrent(Causal(L_{11}, .., L_{1m}), .., Causal(L_{n1}, .., L_{nm})) =$
$Causal(Concurrent(L_{11}, .., L_{n1}), .., Concurrent(L_{1m}, .., L_{nm}))$

or an equivalent notation in terms of layer and union compositions:

$$(L_{11} \bullet .. \bullet L_{1m})[]..[](L_{n1} \bullet .. \bullet L_{nm}) = (L_{11}[]..[]L_{n1}) \bullet .. \bullet (L_{1m}[]..[]L_{nm}) \tag{11}$$

Applying (11) on the Meta-Program MP_S (10), we obtain the DUALITY principle in practice:

$MP_S = Causal(M_S, S) =$
$Causal(Concurrent(M_{S1}, .., M_{Sn}), Concurrent(S_1, .., S_n)) =$
$Concurrent(Causal(M_{S1}, S_1), .., Causal(M_{Sn}, S_n)) =$
$Concurrent(MP_{S1}, .., MP_{Sn}))$

DUALITY principle formulated in terms of layer and union composition:

$MP_S = M_S \bullet S$ and

$$(M_{S1}[]..[]M_{Sn}) \bullet (S_1[]..[]S_n) = (M_{S1} \bullet S_1)[]..[](M_{Sn} \bullet S_n) = MP_{S1}[]..[]MP_{Sn} \tag{12}$$

By transforming the initial representation of the *Meta-Program* (4), we coordinate parallel architectural constraints with specific clusters of actions (assignments). Consistent coordination implies that if the architecture independent specification of an application is S_i, the correspondent parallel application,

MP_{Si}, can reuse S_i's design knowledge. DUALITY supports the derivation of consistent parallel implementations from program specifications. Consequently, transparent and architecture-independent specifications can be transformed efficiently into forms that match particular target architectures. Our approach relates data and process parallelism and aims to reuse design knowledge from classes of sequential design patterns, therefore, it is the basis to reduce the overall complexity. The correctness of the Meta-Program is deduced from the correctness of the architecture-independent specifications, preserved at each refinement step. More specifically, the correctness of the *Meta-Program* is inferred from the individually identified program modules: *Groups-of-Actions*, *POL structures* or *CCL structures*.

Lemma 4 Safety of Duality. If invariant I holds for union $(MP_1 \; [] \; MP_2)$ and the same invariant I holds for the layer composition $(M_S \bullet S)$, then the two forms are input/output equivalent: $MP_1 \; [] \; MP_2 \equiv M_S \bullet S$.

Lemma 5 Progress-Safety of Duality. Given $MP_S = M_S \bullet S$, invariant I_{MS} holds for M_S, invariant I_S holds for S, then the formula (invariant I_{MS}) leads-to (invariant I_S) holds for the Meta-Program MP_S.

Discussion: I_{MS} is an assertion, on the global snapshot, associated with the layer M_S. Also, I_S is an assertion, on the global snapshot, associated with the layer S. No matter how the Meta-Program evolves, if I_{MS} is possible at some time, then I_S is also possible at a later time. This property applies on the safe-dependent composition of the mapping and the specification, i.e. on the Meta-Program MP_S. It supports a specification consistent implementation model for a parallel program, based on the duality of causality and concurrency.

Related work has investigated manual proofs for Communication Closed Layers [3, 12] and mechanized verification based on partial-order model checkers. Partial global snapshots in UNITY have been suggested in [10] as recording predicates that hold at some point in the computation.

4 Example of Formal Transformation and Design Reuse

To illustrate, we use the Floyd-Warshall algorithm [13], the shortest distance between all pairs of nodes.

Notations: Quantified compositions,
$<[] \; i : 1 \leq i \leq n : S_i> = S_1 \; [] \; .. \; [] \; S_n$ - union composition
$<\| \; i : 1 \leq i \leq n : S_i> = S_1 \; \| \; .. \; \| \; S_n$ - synchronous parallel composition
$<\bullet \; i : 1 \leq i \leq n : L_i> = L_1 \; \bullet .. \bullet \; L_n$ - layer composition

(I) Initial solution - an architectural independent, transparent specification. A model of the program is a weighted, directed graph, G, with n nodes The weight of the edge connecting nodes t and u is denoted by w[t,u]. If nodes are not connected, w[t,u]=∞. In Fig. 2 is the initial specification (t, u, v - nodes and d[t,u] - distance between nodes t and u). We address the issue of correctness by expressing the safety and the progress properties and by verifying them against the initial specification.

invariant(d[t,u] is shortest path from nodes t to u) holds for F1.

Program F1
initially $<\|$ t,u :: d[t,u] = w[t,u]$>$
assign $<[]$ t,u,v : $1 \leq$ t,u,v $\leq$n:: d[t,u]:=min(d[t,u], d[t,v]+d[v,u])$>$
end

Fig. 2. Program F1 (Floyd-Warshall) - architecture independent specification

(II) Transformations of the initial solution based on causal and temporal order. We transform (see Lemma 3) a union composition into a functionally equivalent composition of *CCL structures*. The quantified layered representation is given by program F2 (Fig. 3).

Program F2
assign
$<[]$t,u : $1 \leq$ t,u $\leq$n :: d[t,u] = w[t,u]$>$ •
$<$ • v :: $1 \leq$ v$\leq$n :: $<[]$ t,u : $1 \leq$ t,u $\leq$n:: d[t,u]: =min(d[t,u], d[t,v]+d[v,u])$> >$
end

Fig. 3. Program F2 - the transformation in CCL structures

Next we explain why this solution can be more efficiently mapped to an asynchronous shared memory architecture or to a static distributed architecture. We need to introduce some notations.

$L_0 = <[]$ t,u : $1\leq$t,u$\leq$n :: d[t,u] = w[t,u]$>$ is the initial *CCL structure*. L_0 initializes the shortest distance between any nodes, t and u. Q_{tu} is the notation for d[t,u]=w[t,u], therefore $L_0 = <[]$ t,u : $1\leq$t,u$\leq$n :: $Q_{tu} >$.

For any $1\leq$ i $\leq$n, $L_i = <[]$ t,u : $1 \leq$t,u $\leq$n:: d[t,u]: =min(d[t,u], d[t,i]+d[i,u])$>$ is a *CCL structure*, which calculates the shortest distance between any nodes t and u, through an intermediate node i.

For the assignment d[t,u]: =min(d[t,u], d[t,i]+d[i,u]) we use the notation $P_{tu}{}^i$ and obtain $L_i = <[]$ t,u : $1 \leq$t,u $\leq$n :: $P_{tu}{}^i >$, where $1\leq$ i $\leq$n . Applying Lemma 3, the specification is rewritten as a layer composition of *CCL structures*:

$$F2 = L_0 • L_1 •..• L_n \tag{13}$$

$I_i = $ *invariant*(d[t,u] is shortest path from t to u, through i)

I_i is an assertion about the global virtual state associated with the *CCL structure* L_i. By applying Lemma 5 and transitivity, we prove that formula: "I_{k-1} *leads-to* I_k" holds for any $1 \leq k \leq n$.

(III) Transformations of the layered solution to match a distributed architecture, preserving safety and progress properties. From (13) and using the notations defined previously, the program F2 is rewritten:

F2 = <[] t,u : $1 \leq t,u \leq n$:: Q_{tu} > •
<[] t,u : $1 \leq t,u \leq n$:: P_{tu}^1 > • .. •
<[] t,u : $1 \leq t,u \leq n$ :: P_{tu}^n>

By explicitly representing the quantified expressions we obtain:

$$F2 = (Q_{11}[]..[]Q_{nn}) \bullet (P_{11}^1[]..[]P_{nn}^1) \bullet .. \bullet (P_{11}^n[]..[]P_{nn}^n) \tag{14}$$

Form (14) applies to asynchronous shared memory architectures. We can take advantage of the minimal communication conflict closed ordering. Thus, if we apply the general algebraic laws of CCL to a program F2 we obtain:

$$F2 = (Q_{11} \bullet P_{11}^1 \bullet .. \bullet P_{11}^n)[](Q_{12} \bullet P_{12}^1 \bullet .. \bullet P_{12}^n)[]..[](Q_{nn} \bullet P_{nn}^1 \bullet .. \bullet P_{nn}^n) \tag{15}$$

Form (15) is more appropriate for implementation on distributed architectures.

(IV) The Meta-Program MP_{F2} - a coordinated composition of the specification (F2) with a mapping program (M_{F2}) to a distributed architecture. $MP_{F2} = \text{Causal}(M_{F2}, F2) = M_{F2} \bullet F2$

To illustrate, the mapping program (M_{F2}) stipulates an initial number of implementation details, which are related to communication channels.

$M_{F2} = M_{11} [] M_{12} [] .. [] M_{nn}$

The notation M_{tu} stands for a mapping program component that represents the actions on the communication channel c_{tu}, connecting the nodes t and u. The Meta-Program representation is given by the CCL composition of the mapping program with the specification F2 (13), provided in a form that matches a distributed architecture (15).

$MP_{F2} = (M_{11} [] M_{12} [] .. [] M_{nn}) \bullet (L_0 \bullet L_1 \bullet .. \bullet L_n)$

$MP_{F2} =$
$(M_{11} [] M_{12} [] .. [] M_{nn}) \bullet$
$((Q_{11} \bullet P_{11}^1 \bullet .. P_{11}^n) [] (Q_{12} \bullet P_{12}^1 \bullet .. P_{12}^n) [] (Q_{nn} \bullet P_{nn}^1 \bullet .. \bullet P_{nn}^n)$

By applying the generalized laws of CCL on the Meta-Program MP_{F2} we obtain:

$MP_{F2} =$
$(M_{11} \bullet (Q_{11} \bullet P_{11}^1 \bullet .. \bullet P_{11}^n)) []$
$(M_{12} \bullet (Q_{12} \bullet P_{12}^1 \bullet .. \bullet P_{12}^n)) [] .. []$
$(M_{nn} \bullet (Q_{nn} \bullet P_{nn}^1 \bullet P_{nn}^2 \bullet .. \bullet P_{nn}^n))$

We distribute the mapping component on all program specification components and obtain the quantified representation of the Meta-Program MP_{F2}:

$$MP_{F2} = < []t, u : 1 \leq t, u \leq n :: (M_{tu} \bullet Q_{tu}) \bullet < \bullet k : 1 \leq k \leq n :: M_{tu} \bullet P_{tu}^k >> \tag{16}$$

DUALITY principle applied on (16) indicates a consistent decomposition of the parallel program, coordinating the specification and mapping components.

$$MP_{F2} = MP_{11}[]MP_{12}[]..[]MP_{nn} \tag{17}$$

The Meta-Program MP_{F2} is a causal coordinated composition of mapping and specification events. Specification is transparent and architecture-independent. Mapping deals with the implementation details of the parallelism. This separation of concerns gives more modularity. It helps in systematically identifying architectural and behavioral patterns, an aspect that can become the basis for a reduced design cost and less complexity.

(V) The verification of the coordinated *Meta-Program.* We can infer the safety and progress properties in the Meta-Program MP_{F2} by causally composing mapping and specification data and temporal properties and by applying Lemma 4, Lemma 5 and the generalized algebraic laws of CCL.

5 Summary and Future Work

This paper describes DUALITY, a design model for parallel and distributed applications, based on the systemic duality of causality and concurrency. Compared to data-parallel model [2], DUALITY, acts as a specification-consistent coordination model for parallel program executions. It specifies temporal and causal ordering of events, both process and data parallelism. We integrate the simplicity of UNITY's notation and logic with the modular structure of the Communication Closed Layers. In this way, we provide a more structured style of parallel programming, while stressing the separation of concerns of correctness and efficiency. The correctness of parallel programs should not rely on implementation details related to a certain target machine or concerning issues of some particular programming language or operating system. By introducing DUALITY, the correctness of parallel and distributed systems is addressed in a systematic manner with each transformation of the specification. Applicable for initial phases of the design, DUALITY principle supports a simple formalism that, in the end, can be mapped onto real programming languages. This approach leads to fewer, but more relevant design alternatives, therefore less design complexity. Our definition of *Meta-Program* extends the UNITY's notion of program-schema. The *Meta-Program* reflects the duality of concurrency and causality relations between events in a parallel system. DUALITY allows the reuse of architectural patterns and proofs of sequential algorithms in the design of parallel programs.

We are currently working on to extend formalism of Communication Closed Layers composition, defined in terms of UNITY and branching temporal logic.

Ongoing work integrates a partial-order model checker [6] to provide a mechanized verification for specifications and mappings of parallel and distributed programs.

References

1. Chandy, K., Misra, J.: Parallel Programs Design: A Foundation. Addison-Wesley, New York, N.Y.,(1988).
2. Bouge, Luc: The Data Parallel Programming Model: A Semantic Perspective. Research Report-96-27, LIP, Lyon, (1996).
3. Elrad, T., Francez, N.: Decomposition of Distributed Programs into Communication Closed Layers. Science of Programming, 2, N.H., (1982) 155-173
4. Elrad, T., K, Nambi, K.: Scheduling Cooperative Work: Viewing Distributed Systems as Both CSP and SCL. In Proceedings of the 13th International Conference on Distributed Computing Systems, Pittsburgh, May (1993)
5. Emerson, A.: Temporal and Modal Logic. Handbook of Theoretical Computer Science, Elsevier Science Publisher B.V., (1990)
6. Godefroid, P., Peled, D., Staskauskas, M.: Using Partial-Order Methods in the Formal Validation of Industrial Concurrent Programs. IEEE Transactions on Software Engineering, 2:7, (1996) 496-507
7. Janssen, W., Poel, M, Zwiers, J.: Actions System and Action Refinement in the Development of Parallel Systems. In Proc. of CONCUR'91, Springer-Verlag, LNCS 527, (1991) 298-316
8. Katz, S., Peled, D.: Interleaving Set Temporal Logic. Theoretical Computer Science, 75(2), (1990)
9. Poel, M, Zwiers, J.: Layering Techniques for Development of Parallel Systems. Proc. of ACM PODC, (1992)
10. Sanders, B., Meyer, D.: Composing Lead-to Properties. Technical Report, UF-CISE, ftp://ftp.cise.ufl.edu/cis/tech-reports/tr96/tr96-013.ps, (1996)
11. Snyder, L.: Applications of the phase abstraction for portable and scalable parallel programming. Languages, Compilers and Run-Time Environments, (1992)
12. Stomp, F.A., de Roever, W.P.: Designing distributed algorithms by means of formally phased reasoning. Proc. of the 3rd International Workshop on Distributed Algorithms, LNCS 392, Springer-Verlag, (1989) 242-253
13. Warshall, S.: A Theorem on Boolean Matrices. Journal of the ACM, 9, (1962) 11-12
14. Zlatea, C., Elrad, T.: Brief Announcement: A Design Methodology for Mobile Distributed Applications based on UNITY Formalism and Communication Closed Layering, Proc. of 18th Symposium ACM PODC, Atlanta, May (1999)

A New Rewrite Method for Proving Convergence of Self-Stabilizing Systems

Joffroy Beauquier[1], Béatrice Bérard[2] and Laurent Fribourg[2]

[1] LRI, CNRS URA 410, Université Paris-Sud 91405 Orsay cedex, France
jb@lri.fr
[2] LSV, CNRS UMR 8643, ENS de Cachan, 61 av. du Prés. Wilson,
94235 Cachan cedex, France
{berard,fribourg}@lsv.ens-cachan.fr

Abstract. In the framework of self-stabilizing systems, the convergence proof is generally done by exhibiting a measure that strictly decreases until a legitimate configuration is reached. The discovery of such a measure is very specific and requires a deep understanding of the studied transition system. In contrast we propose here a simple method for proving convergence, which regards self-stabilizing systems as string rewrite systems, and adapts a procedure initially designed by Dershowitz for proving termination of string rewrite systems.

1   Introduction

Introduced by Dijkstra, with three mutual exclusion algorithms on a ring of processes [10], the notion of self-stabilization has been largely studied for the last ten years (see [28,30] for surveys). In this paper, we consider a system which consists of a ring of machines controlled by a "central demon". Its configuration is the concatenation of the components local states and it is characterized by a set R of transitions defined over configurations. The system is *self-stabilizing* with respect to a subset L of *legitimate* configurations when, regardless of the initial configuration and regardless of the transition selected each time by the central demon, it is guaranteed to arrive in a configuration of L within a finite number of steps. The set L is assumed to have a *closure* property: from a legitimate configuration in L, the system persistently remains in L. It is also frequent to assume that there is *no-deadlock*. With these two hypotheses, it is easy to show that a system is self-stabilizing iff it has the *no-cycle* property: there is no cyclic sequence of transitions which contains some configuration $w \notin L$. This property is often shown by exhibiting a *norm function* defined over the set of configurations, whose value strictly decreases after each transition (or each bounded sequence of transitions) as long as the configuration is not legitimate [30]. Since such a measure is usually very specific to the considered system, finding one is very difficult and requires a deep understanding of this system (see e.g.[22,13,4]).

We propose here a new approach for proving the absence of cycle. Configurations are viewed as words of a formal language, transitions of R as rewrite rules, and the no-cycle property as a variant of the nontermination property for rewrite rules. More precisely, we will attack the no-cycle property under the following equivalent form: there is no infinite sequence of transitions of R^{-1} (the reverse system obtained from R by switching origin and target configurations) starting from a configuration $w \notin L$. The absence of such infinite sequences will then be shown by refining the generation procedure of *reduction chains*[1], first proposed by Dershowitz for proving string rewriting termination [7]. The method proposed here is new in that: 1) it uses a general technique of string-rewriting to deal with self-stabilization; 2) instead of working with the direct rewriting relation from arbitrary configurations towards the legitimate ones, it uses the inverse relation; 3) it does not consider all the possible rewrite derivations, but only "representative" ones, using a restricted rewriting strategy.

Related work on self-stabilization proofs. [10] is without proof. In [11], a correctness proof is given for the third (3-state) algorithm of [10], by showing properties of executions using behavioral reasoning. As already pointed out, almost all further proof methods (cf. [30]) are based on norm functions (see an example in [18]) but, as expressed by Gouda [14]: "It has been my experience that the ratio of time to design a stabilizing system to the time to verify its stabilization is about one to ten". For simplifying proof process, general paradigms have been proposed: various protocol compositions making proofs modular ([3,15]), attractor or staircase methods ([14,28]), automatic transformations into stabilizing systems [2]. Some ideas in [17] are also used in our approach, as discussed in Section 7. Note that, recently, some works were done for proving convergence without appealing to a norm function: [31] uses techniques borrowed from control theory and [1] induction techniques over the set of configurations.

Related work on rewrite techniques applied to distributed systems. Although viewing transitions as rewrite rules is rather natural, the application of general rewrite techniques for proving properties of distributed systems has not been explored to our knowledge, except in [24–26] where graph rewriting techniques (with priorities) are used to prove the correctness of various distributed algorithms (election, spanning-tree construction,...). However this work does not address the issue of self-stabilization.

Plan of the paper. Section 2 gives an intuitive presentation of the method with the example of Ghosh's 4-state algorithm. Section 3 shows how self-stabilization can be viewed as a property of string rewriting systems. Our basic method and the underlying correctness result are explained in Section 4, then refined in Section 5. Section 6 relates compositionality results in the field of self-stabilization and in the field of rewriting. Section 7 concludes with final remarks and perspectives.

2 An illustrating example: Ghosh's 4-state algorithm

Ghosh's algorithm is a variant of Dijkstra's 4-state self-stabilizing algorithm [13]. The system consists of a parametric number N of machines $(0, 1, \cdots, N-1)$, which have four states: $\{0, 1, 2, 3\}$, except the *top* machine $N-1$ (resp. *bottom* machine 0) which has only two states: $\{0, 2\}$ (resp. $\{1, 3\}$). The configuration of the system is the string of all machine states, delimited by special end symbols '#'. Writing X, Y for nonempty string variables, the transitions correspond to the following system $R = Middle \cup Top \cup Bottom$ of rewrite rules.

- *Middle* is made of rules of the form:

$$M_1: \quad \#X(q+1)qY\# \rightarrow \#X(q+1)(q+1)Y\#$$

---

[1] also called *forward closures* in [8].

M_2 : $\#Xq(q+1)Y\# \rightarrow \#X(q+1)(q+1)Y\#$

where $q \in \{0, 1, 2, 3\}$ and '+' is addition modulo 4.

- *Top* is made of rules of the form:

T_1 : $\#X32\# \rightarrow \#X30\#$ and T_2 : $\#X10\# \rightarrow \#X12\#$

- *Bottom* is made of rules of the form:

B_1 : $\#12X\# \rightarrow \#32X\#$ and B_2 : $\#30X\# \rightarrow \#10X\#$

Ghosh proves the convergence by considering a norm function (Br, Ds) such that either Br or Ds *strictly* decreases each time a transition is done. Individually Br and Ds are non-increasing functions. Br is the number of *breaks*, i.e. the number of neighbouring states q, q' of the string which differ by at least one unit. Ds is a very subtle function measuring the sum of distances between pairs of neighbouring breaks of the string. All the difficulty of Ghosh's proof comes from the discovery of such a measure Ds. In contrast, we now informally explain how our method proves the convergence, with the help of measure Br only. Our first idea is to consider not the original system R but the inverse R^{-1} obtained by switching lefthand and righthand sides. Since Br is non-increasing via R, it is non-decreasing via R^{-1}. Our second idea is to prove convergence by showing that there is no infinite derivation via R^{-1} (except those among legitimate configurations, which are not displayed here for lack of space). We will focus on Br-preserving infinite derivations, i.e. infinite derivations which preserve the number of breaks: since Br is non-decreasing and bounded by the total number N of system components, any infinite derivation has an infinite Br-preserving suffix, so there is no loss of generality. For instance, the two following reductions (with underlines indicating positions of a substring to be reduced) are discarded because they increase Br by one:

$\#\underline{11}23(0123)\cdots(0123)2\cdots2\# \rightarrow \#1023(0123)\cdots(0123)2\cdots2\#$

$\#1123(0123)\cdots(0123)2\cdots\underline{222}\cdots2\# \rightarrow \#1123(0123)\cdots(0123)2\cdots212\cdots2\#$

Our third and main idea is to generate not all the possible Br-preserving derivations via R^{-1} but only "representative" ones, in the sense that an infinite derivation exists iff an infinite representative one exists. As explained later, representative derivations are obtained by reasoning with 1st-order variables that represent arbitrary sets of strings, and instantiating these variables in a "minimal" way through successive steps. For pedagogical reasons, we first assume that appropriate instantiations are known from the beginning, and present the treatment of Ghosh's algorithm, starting from a string s_0 with all its variables already instantiated.

Generation of representative strings.

We start from:

s_0 : $\#\pi(0123)\cdots(0123)3\cdots\underline{30}\#$, where π is either 3 or 123. Now s_0 reduces via T_1^{-1} to

s_1 : $\#\pi(0123)\cdots(0123)3\cdots\underline{332}\#$, which reduces via a (possibly empty) sequence of M_1^{-1}

to

s_2 : $\#\pi(0123)\cdots(0123)3\cdots\underline{332}\cdots2\#$.

At some point, one generates

s_3 : $\#\pi(0123)\cdots(0123)(0123)32\cdots2\#$, which reduces via M_2^{-1} successively to

s_4 : $\#\pi(0123)\cdots(0123)(01\underline{22}3)2\cdots2\#$,

s_5 : $\#\pi(0123)\cdots(0123)(01\underline{1}23)2\cdots2\#$,

s_6 : $\#\pi(0123)\cdots(0123)(\underline{00}123)2\cdots2\#$,

s_7 : $\#\pi(0123)\cdots(0123)(30123)2\cdots2\#$

A generalized form for s_3 and s_7 is

s_8 : $\#\pi(0123)\cdots(0123)(012\underline{33})(0123)\cdots(0123)2\cdots2\#$,

which contains a substring (01233) between a left and right sequences of (0123)'s.

s_8 rewrites via M_2^{-1} successively to

s_9 : $\#\pi(0123)\cdots(0123)(01\underline{22}3)(0123)\cdots(0123)2\cdots2\#$,

s_{10} : $\#\pi(0123)\cdots(0123)(01\underline{1}23)(0123)\cdots(0123)2\cdots2\#$,

s_{11} : $\#\pi(0123)\cdots(0123)(\underline{00}123)(0123)\cdots(0123)2\cdots2\#$,

s_{12} : $\#\pi(0123)\cdots(012\underline{3})(\underline{3}0123)(0123)\cdots(0123)2\cdots2\#$.

which can be seen as a copy of s_8 where an element (0123) of the left sequence has moved to the right sequence. Such an iterated application of M_2^{-1} always ends when the left sequence is empty, thus yielding:

s_{end} : $\#\pi(30123)(0123)\cdots(0123)2\cdots2\#$.

In case π is 3 there is no possible Br-preserving rule application.

In case π is 123, there are two ultimate applications of M_2^{-1} yielding successively:

s'_{end} : $\#1\underline{22}3(0123)(0123)\cdots(0123)2\cdots2\#$,

s''_{end} : $\#1123(0123)(0123)\cdots(0123)2\cdots2\#$,

with no Br-preserving rule applicable to s''_{end}.

This result shows that there is no infinite Br-preserving derivation starting from s_0. It remains to explain how the initial string s_0 was inferred. The basic idea is to reason on strings with variables at the first-order level. Variables are instantiated in a "minimal" manner so that reduction rules become applicable. We start with the left-hand side $\#X30\#$ of top rule T_1^{-1}, which is reduced to $\#X32\#$. Then X is bound to X_13, and instance $\#X_1332\#$ reduces via M_1^{-1} to $\#X_1322\#$. This operation is iterated, yielding $\#X_n32^n2\#$. Then X_n is instantiated with $Y3$, but now M_2^{-1} is applied, which yields $\#Y232^n2\#$. Then Y is instantiated with $Z2$, and application of M_2^{-1} yields $Z1232^n2\#$. Iterating this operation generates strings of the form $\#W_1(0123)2^n2\#$, $\cdots$, $\#W_m(0123)^m2^n2\#$, $\cdots$. Similarly, another representative string derivation can be obtained, starting from the other top rule righthand side $\#X12\#$.

As a recapitulation, our strategy consists in generating "representative" chains of derivations by starting from righthand sides of top rules and applying Br-preserving rules (from right to left). One then shows that only finite derivations are obtained (except over legitimate configurations). The finiteness of derivations will be proved formally by finding a generic set Π of "growing patterns", i.e. a set of strings such that any Br-preserving rule applied to any element $t \in \Pi$ yields an element $u \in \Pi$ greater than t, for some ordering $>$ over Π. In the case of Ghosh's algorithm, Π is of the form: $\{\#X\pi'(0123)^m2^n2\# \mid m \geq 0, n \geq 0\}$ where π' is 3, 23, 123 or 0123. The associated relation $>$ merely orders elements of Π according to the number m of substrings (0123) they contain. (m is increased by one, each time four rules are applied consecutively.) Our underlying claim is that such a strictly monotonic ordering $>$ is much simpler to find than Ghosh's strictly monotonic norm (Br, Ds) because we focus on "representative" derivations using a restricted strategy of rule application, instead of considering all the possible configurations. The rest of the paper is devoted to the formal description of our strategy and a proof of its correctness.

3 Self-stabilizing systems as string rewrite systems

We first recall some basic definitions from (string) rewrite systems ([9],[5]). The words considered here are generally delimited by a leftmost and rightmost special symbol '#'. The symbols appearing between them belong to a finite alphabet Σ or a set $V = \{W, X, Y \ldots\}$ of variable symbols. A *string* is an element of Σ^*, with ε for the empty string. A *ground word* is an element of $\#\Sigma^*\#$ and an *(open) word* is an element of $\#(\Sigma \cup V)^*\#$. A substitution is a mapping θ from V to $(\Sigma \cup V)^*$ with $\theta(W) = W$ almost everywhere except on a finite set of variables denoted $Dom(\theta)$. A substitution θ is represented by a finite set of pairs of the form $\{W/\theta(W)\}_{W \in Dom(\theta)}$. A substitution θ is *ground* when $\theta(W)$ is in Σ^*, for all $W \in Dom(\theta)$.

String rewrite systems. The string rewrite systems considered here contain length-preserving rules, divided into three subsets: *top rules* in $Tops$ are applied to the rightmost part of words; *bottom rules* in $Bottoms$ are applied to the leftmost part of words (or simultaneously at both ends); the rest of rules in $Middles$ are called *middle rules*. More precisely, let ℓ, r (resp. ℓ_i, r_i for $i = 1, 2$) be nonempty strings of Σ^* of the same length, and X, Y variables,
- $Middles$ is made of rules of the form: $\#X\ell Y\# \to \#XrY\#$
- $Tops$ is made of rules of the form: $\#X\ell\# \to \#Xr\#$
- $Bottoms$ is made of rules of the form:
$$\#\ell X\# \to \#rX\# \quad \text{or} \quad \#\ell_1 X\ell_2\# \to \#r_1 X r_2\#.$$
We are going to apply these rules either to ground words or to words of the form $\#uWv\#$ where u, v denote strings over Σ^*, and W a variable.

Example.[2]
B_1^{-1} : $\#1X2\# \to \#2X1\#$ is a bottom-rule. T_4^{-1} : $\#X21\# \to \#X12\#$ is a top-rule. M_1^{-1} : $\#X01Y\# \to \#X10Y\#$ and M_4^{-1} : $\#X20Y\# \to \#X02Y\#$ are middle rules.

Ground reduction. A ground word w is *reducible* via a rule of the form $\#X\ell_1 Y\# \to \#Xr_1 Y\#$ iff $w = \#u\ell_1 v\#$ for some strings $u, v \in \Sigma^*$. One also says that w is an instance of the rule lefthand side via the ground substitution $\{X/u, Y/v\}$. The *reduced form* of w is $w' = \#ur_1 v\#$. Reduction via a rule of the form $\#\ell_1 X\ell_2\# \to \#r_1 X r_2\#$ is defined in a similar way.

A word w reduces to w' via S, written $w \to_S w'$ (or sometimes simply $w \to w'$), if w' is the reduced form of w via some rule of S. We say that S is *non terminating* iff there exists an infinite sequence of reductions via S starting from some ground word w. Otherwise, S is said to be *terminating*.

Example. The word w : $\#1012\#$ reduces via rule B_1^{-1} : $\#1X2\# \to \#2X1\#$ to w' : $\#2011\#$, using the substitution $\{X/01\}$.

Self-stabilization. We are now able to give a formal definition of self-stabilization for a system modeled as a string rewrite system R. From now on, configurations are regarded as ground words. Writing L_N for the set of legitimate configurations in a system with N machines, we define the *global set of legitimitate configurations*, as $\mathcal{L} = \cup_{N \geq 2} L_N$.

Definition 1. A rewrite system R is *self-stabilizing* with respect to set $\mathcal{L}$ iff:
  (0) Each ground word is reducible via R.
  (1) $\mathcal{L}$ is *closed via* R, i.e: $w \in \mathcal{L} \wedge w \to_R w' \Rightarrow w' \in \mathcal{L}$, for all ground words w, w'.
  (2) There is no ground cyclic derivation of the form $w_1 \to_R \cdots \to_R w_n = w_1$ with $w_1 \notin \mathcal{L}$.

---
[2] these rules are the inverse of B_1, T_4, M_1, M_4 from Beauquier-Debas algorithm (see section 5).

Statement (0) expresses a *no-deadlock* property, (1) a *closure* property for $\mathcal{L}$, and (2) a *no-cycle* property. It easily follows from this definition that any "maximal" derivation is infinite and reaches the set $\mathcal{L}$: this corresponds to a *convergence* property (also called *no-livelock* property in [6]).

Assuming (1), we have two equivalent versions for (2):
(2′) There is no ground cyclic derivation via $S \equiv R^{-1}$, of the form $w_1 \to_S \cdots \to_S w_n = w_1$ with $w_1 \notin \mathcal{L}$.
(2″) There is no infinite ground derivation via $S \equiv R^{-1}$ starting from a word $w \notin \mathcal{L}$.

Proof. (2) $\Leftrightarrow$ (2′) $\Leftrightarrow$ (2″). One has clearly (2) $\Leftrightarrow$ (2′) and (2″) $\Rightarrow$ (2′). Let us show (2′) $\Rightarrow$ (2″) by showing $\neg$(2″) $\Rightarrow \neg$(2′). Suppose $\neg$(2″): there is an infinite ground derivation Δ via S: $u_1 \to_S \cdots \to_S u_i \to_S \cdots$ with $u_1 \notin \mathcal{L}$. Since S is length-preserving there should be a cycle in this derivation, so there is an initial part of Δ which is of the form: $u_1 \to_S \cdots \to_S u_j \to_S \cdots \to_S u_n = u_j$, for some j and n. Since $u_1 \to_S^* u_j$, we have $u_j \to_R^* u_1$. It follows $u_j \notin \mathcal{L}$ because, otherwise, u_1 would be itself in $\mathcal{L}$ by assumption (1) of closure. Therefore the subpart $u_j \to_S \cdots \to_S u_n = u_j$ is a cycle with $u_j \notin \mathcal{L}$. One has thus exhibited a cycle via S containing an element not in $\mathcal{L}$, which proves $\neg$(2′).

Remark 2. Note that equivalence between (2) and (2″) does not hold any longer if R is used instead of R^{-1} within (2″).

4 A first-order characterization of cycles

Assuming now that R satisfies (0) and (1), we will focus on the problem of proving the *no-cycle* property, stated under form (2″). Our method relies on a first-order characterization of cycles: we will show that an infinite ground derivation via R^{-1} (as mentioned in (2″)) is actually an instance of an infinite derivation at the "first-order" level. In order to state our main result, we need the notion of top chains, which is transposed from [7] in our particular context.

Minimal reductions and top chains. We now deal with one-variable words t of the form $\#uWv\#$, with $u, v \in \Sigma^*$ and $W \in V$, and we consider the minimal complete set of substitutions $\mu_1, ..., \mu_k$ which make t reducible via a given rule of the form $\ell \to r$, i.e, the set of most general unifiers of t with a rule lefthand side ℓ. The general unification problem for words is complex, and was solved by Makanin [27]. However our particular unification problem here is simple, because t and ℓ do not share variables, and are "linear" (i.e. contain at most one occurrence of the same variable). In such a case the number of most general unifiers is finite: roughly speaking, it suffices to consider all the manners in which t and ℓ overlap depending on the possible instantiations of their variables (see, e.g., [20]). Suppose now that t and ℓ are unifiable via a set of most general unifiers $\mu_1, ..., \mu_k$ ($t\mu_i = \ell\mu_i$ for $i = 1, ..., k$), so that each instance $t\mu_i$ of t reduces to $r\mu_i$. We will disregard unifiers μ_j which instantiate t at a "variable position". We then say that t is *minimally reducible at a nonvariable position* via the set of unifiers $\{\mu_1, ..., \mu_k\}$. (This corresponds to the operation called "narrowing" in first-order rewrite systems [29,12,19].) The corresponding set of minimal reduction steps is $\{t\mu_i \to r\mu_i\}_{i=1,...,k}$.

Example.
Suppose we have a rule of the form $\#X11Y\# \rightarrow \#X22Y\#$. The word $t : \#1W1\#$ unifies
with lefthand side $\#X11Y\#$ via most general unifiers:
$\mu_1 : \{W/1W'\} \cup \{X/\varepsilon, Y/W'1\}$, $\mu_2 : \{W/W'1\} \cup \{X/1W', Y/\varepsilon\}$,
$\mu_3 : \{W/\varepsilon\} \cup \{X/\varepsilon, Y/\varepsilon\}$ and $\mu_4 : \{W/W_111W_2\} \cup \{X/1W_1, Y/W_21\}$.
The last unifier μ_4 (with the associated reduction) is discarded because it corresponds
to a unification taking place at a variable position of t. The minimal reductions of t
corresponding to μ_1, μ_2, μ_3 are: $\#11W'1\# \rightarrow \#22W'1\#$, $\#1W'11\# \rightarrow \#1W'22\#$ and
$\#11\# \rightarrow \#22\#$.

Definition 3. The *top minimal reduction chains* (or simply *top chains*) of rewrite system
S form a set of derivations inductively defined as follows:
- Every top rule $\#X\ell_1\# \rightarrow \#Xr_1\#$ of S is a top minimal reduction chain.
- If $C : v \rightarrow \cdots \rightarrow w$ is a top minimal reduction chain and $\ell \rightarrow r$ is a rule of S
such that w unifies with ℓ at a nonvariable position via the set of most general unifiers
$\{\mu_1, ..., \mu_k\}$, then $v\mu_i \rightarrow \cdots \rightarrow w\mu_i \rightarrow r\mu_i$ (for $i = 1, ..., k$) is a top minimal reduction
chain, called *successor* of C via $\ell \rightarrow r$.

The transitive closure of the successor relation is called "iterated successor". It is easy
to see that, due to the form of the rules of the string rewrite system S, a top chain
$t_1 \rightarrow t_2 \rightarrow ... \rightarrow t_n$ is such that either all the words $t_1, ..., t_n$ are ground, or each t_i
$(1 \leq i \leq n)$ is of the form $\#u_iWv_i\#$ where the u_is (resp. v_is) are strings of Σ^* of the
same length.

Example. Consider the top rule $T_4^{-1} : \#W21\# \rightarrow \#W12\#$ viewed as a top chain.
Its righthandside $\#W12\#$ unifies with the lefthand side of $B_1^{-1} : \#1X2\# \rightarrow \#2X1\#$
via the set of most general unifiers $\mu_1 : \{W/\varepsilon\} \cup \{X/\varepsilon\}$ and $\mu_2 : \{W/1W'\} \cup \{X/X'1\}$.
Therefore the successors of T_4^{-1} via B_1^{-1} are:
$\#21\# \rightarrow \#12\# \rightarrow \#21\#$ and $\#1W'21\# \rightarrow \#1W'12\# \rightarrow \#2W'11\#$.

Note that the requirement that the starting chain is a top rule instead of a general
rule of S is new with respect to Dershowitz's definition [7]. Such a requirement is made
possible because we will assume additionally that system $S - Tops$ is terminating (see
Theorem 5).

Definition 4. A top chain (resp. ground derivation) $t_1 \rightarrow \cdots \rightarrow \cdots \rightarrow t_n$ is *quasi-cyclic*
if $t_i = t_n$ for some $i < n$, and $t_p \neq t_q$ for all distinct p, q less than n.

A characterization of self-stabilization. We can now state our main result:

Theorem 5. *Let $R = Middle_R \cup Top_R \cup Bottom_R$ be a rewrite system and let $\mathcal{L}$ be a
set of configurations such that:*
(0) each ground word is reducible via R,
(1) $\mathcal{L}$ is closed via R, and
(3) $R - Top_R$ (or, equivalently, $(R - Top_R)^{-1}$) is terminating.
*Then R is self-stabilizing w.r.t. $\mathcal{L}$ iff there is no quasi-cyclic top chain $t_1 \rightarrow \cdots \rightarrow t_n$ via
R^{-1}, such that $t_1' \notin \mathcal{L}$ for some ground instance t_1' of t_1.*

The proof of theorem 5 involves additional notions of "active" or "inactive" steps
within infinite ground derivations, as introduced by Dershowitz [7]. The corresponding

definitions and properties, as well as the proof, are given in the Appendix.

In order to mechanically check point (3) of theorem 5, i.e. termination of $R - Top_R$, one can use classical well-founded orderings used in rewriting theory [9]. One can also use Dershowitz's chain test: generate all the general chains until either one "cycles" in the sense of [7] (non-termination detection) or all terminate (termination proof). Dershowitz's procedure can also be refined if one knows that $R - Top_R - Bottom_R$ is itself terminating. Then, in order to prove termination of $R - Top_R$, it suffices to generate only the "bottom" chains via $R - Top_R$, i.e. chains that start from a bottom rule, and check that none of them has a cycle. (Of course, in this case, one has to check additionally the termination of $R - Top_R - Bottom_R$, but this is generally easier.)

5 A practical proof method

We now present our basic procedure, as well as a fully treated example of application.

5.1 Basic procedure and ϕ-refinement

Theorem 5 suggests to prove self-stabilization by generating all top chains via R^{-1} and checking the condition over the initial word t_1 for quasi-cyclic chains. Unfortunately, top chains, when generated in a brute manner, are frequently in infinite number. However it is often possible to discover some recurrent forms, called "patterns", for words t_n appearing at the end of chains. For example, starting from word $\#2W11\#$, and applying Beauquier-Debas system $S \equiv R'^{-1}$ (see below) with rules $\#X20Y\# \rightarrow \#X02Y\#$ and $\#X01Y\# \rightarrow \#X10Y\#$ (with $Y \neq \varepsilon$), one generates chains that all end with words of the form $\#0^j2W10^k1\#$ with $j, k \geq 0$. Formally:

Definition 6. A *set of patterns* Π is a set of the form
$$\{ \#a_1^{i_1}...a_p^{i_p}Wb_1^{j_1}...b_q^{j_q}\# \mid \psi(i_1, ..., i_p, j_1, ..., j_q) \}$$
where $a_1, ..., a_p, b_1, ..., b_q$ are letters of Σ, $i_1, ..., i_p, j_1, ..., j_q$ are natural numbers, and ψ an arithmetical relation.

The discovery of such patterns allows us to characterize finitely an infinite number of top chains. These patterns will be required to be *closed* via S, i.e.: for all $\pi \in \Pi$ and all minimal reduction of π to π' via S using unifier μ ($\pi\mu \rightarrow \pi'$), π' is in Π. Additionally, π' will be required to be greater than $\pi\mu$ for some ordering $>$ over words, *compatible* with substitution i.e. such that: $t_1 > t_2 \Longrightarrow t_1\theta > t_2\theta$, for any ground substitution θ. Such requirements prevent cycles within derivations of the form $t_1 \rightarrow \cdots \rightarrow t_n \rightarrow t_{n+1} \rightarrow ... \rightarrow t_{n+m}$, as far as $t_n \in \Pi$ and no word of Π unifies with t_i ($1 \leq i < n$). More precisely:

Definition and Property 7. An *S-closed set of growing patterns* Π is a set of patterns such that, for all $\pi \in \Pi$ and all minimal reduction of π to π' via S using μ ($\pi\mu \rightarrow \pi'$): $\pi' \in \Pi$ and $\pi' > \pi\mu$ for some ordering $>$ compatible with substitution.
If a non quasi-cyclic chain $C : t_1 \rightarrow \cdots \rightarrow t_n$ is such that t_n belongs to an S-closed set Π of growing patterns nonunifiable with any $t_1, ..., t_{n-1}$, then any iterated successor of C of the form: $t_1(\mu_1 \cdots \mu_m) \rightarrow \cdots \rightarrow t_n(\mu_1 \cdots \mu_m) \rightarrow t_{n+1}(\mu_1 \cdots \mu_m) \rightarrow \cdots \rightarrow t_{n+m}(\mu_1 \cdots \mu_m)$ is itself non quasi-cyclic.

Example. Consider the set $\Pi : \{\#0^j2W10^k1\# \mid j \geq 0, k \geq 0\}$. The only rules of

Beauquier-Debas system $S \equiv R'^{-1}$ (see section 5.2) that are applicable to Π are:
$\#X20Y\# \to \#X02Y\#$ and $\#X01Y\# \to \#X10Y\#$, with $Y \neq \varepsilon$.
Given $\pi : \#0^j2W10^k1\#$, the first rule (resp. second rule) minimally reduces it to
$\pi'_1 : \#0^{j+1}2W10^k1\#$ (resp. $\pi'_2 : \#0^j2W10^{k+1}1\#$), which belongs to Π and is greater than π with respect to the number of '0's to the left of '2' (resp. number of '0's to the right of leftmost occurrence of '1'). Therefore Π is an S-closed set of growing patterns.

Using theorem 5 and property 7, and assuming $(0), (1), (3)$ for R, we obtain:

Basic Procedure
Start with set of top rules $Tops$ (with $S \equiv R^{-1}$) as an initial set of chains.
For each chain $t_1 \to \cdots \to t_n$, compute iteratively its successors via rules of S unless:
  - $t_1 \in \mathcal{L}$, or
  - $t_n \in \Pi$, for some S-closed set Π of growing patterns nonunifiable with any $t_1, ..., t_{n-1}$.
If, among all the generated chains, there is one quasi-cyclic chain $t_1 \to \cdots \to t_i \to \cdots \to t_n = t_i$ such that t_1 has a ground instance $t'_1 \notin \mathcal{L}$, then R is not self-stabilizing. Otherwise R is self-stabilizing.

Remark 7. In order to detect if, given t_1, there exists a ground instance not belonging to $\mathcal{L}$, one may assume that $\mathcal{L}$ is characterized by a *regular language* (see [17]). If t_1 is ground, then the problem reduces to $t_1 \notin \mathcal{L}$, which is decidable. If t_1 is not ground, then t_1 is of the form $\#uWv\#$, and the problem reduces to test $\#u\Sigma^*v\# \cap \overline{\mathcal{L}} \neq \emptyset$, which is also decidable. Note besides that the assumption of regularity for $\mathcal{L}$ allows us to mechanically check property (1) of closure via R. This is equivalent to check that the image of $\mathcal{L}$ via $\to_R$ is included into $\mathcal{L}$. Since $\mathcal{L}$ is regular and $\to_R$ can be seen as a rational transduction, this inclusion problem is decidable (see [23],[17]).

Our basic procedure can be refined by using a measure, say ϕ, over ground words which "never increases" when applying a rule, such as Br in section 2. Finding such a measure is generally much easier than finding a norm, which must "always decrease" when applying a rule (or a bounded number of rules) of R. Formally, we assume given a measure ϕ from words over $(\Sigma \cup \mathcal{V})^*$ to $\mathbb{N}$, with the following properties:
  - ϕ is *non-increasing with R*, i.e., is such that $t \to_R t'$ implies $\phi(t) \geq \phi(t')$.
  - ϕ is *compatible with substitution:* $\phi(t) > \phi(t')$ implies $\phi(t\theta) > \phi(t'\theta)$ for any ground substitution θ.

Given ϕ, it is easy to show that the basic procedure can be refined by generating only ϕ-*preserving* successors via $S \equiv R^{-1}$ instead of all the possible successors. (A successor $t_1\mu \to \cdots \to t_n\mu \to t_{n+1}\mu$ of $t_1 \to \cdots \to t_n$ is ϕ-preserving iff $\phi(t_n\mu) = \phi(t_{n+1}\mu)$.)

5.2   Beauquier-Debas algorithm

This system originates from [4], and is an adaptation of Dijkstra's third (3-state) algorithm [10]. In our formalism, it corresponds to the following system R:

Bottom	B_1 :	$\#2X1\# \to \#1X2\#$
Top	T_1 :	$\#X00\# \to \#X21\#$
	T_2 :	$\#X10\# \to \#X01\#$
	T_3 :	$\#X20\# \to \#X11\#$

	T_4 :	$\#X12\# \rightarrow \#X21\#$	
	T_5 :	$\#X22\# \rightarrow \#X01\#$	
Middle	M_1 :	$\#X10Y\# \rightarrow \#X01Y\#$	(with $Y \neq \epsilon$)[3]
	M_2 :	$\#X11Y\# \rightarrow \#X02Y\#$	(with $Y \neq \epsilon$)
	M_3 :	$\#X12Y\# \rightarrow \#X00Y\#$	(with $Y \neq \epsilon$)
	M_4 :	$\#X02Y\# \rightarrow \#X20Y\#$	(with $Y \neq \epsilon$)
	M_5 :	$\#X22Y\# \rightarrow \#X10Y\#$	(with $Y \neq \epsilon$)

$\mathcal{L}$ is defined as: $\#0^*20^*1\# \ \cup \ \#0^*10^*2\#$.

In this example, it is assumed that the sum of the elements of the initial configuration is null, modulo 3. This property is preserved when applying the rules of R. One checks easily that any ground word (with a null sum of elements) is reducible via R, and $\mathcal{L}$ is closed via R (see [4]). Therefore, R is self-stabilizing iff there is no ground cyclic derivation via R containing an element $w \notin \mathcal{L}$. As remarked in [4], one can see that T_1, T_2, T_3 are applied at most once. As a consequence R is self-stabilizing iff there is no ground cyclic derivation via $R_0 \equiv R - \{T_1, T_2, T_3\}$ containing an element $w \notin \mathcal{L}$. The measure ϕ over a word $t \in (\Sigma \cup \mathcal{V})^*$, is defined as the number of nonnull elements contained by t. Obviously, ϕ is non-increasing with R_0 and compatible with substitution. Besides, among rules of R_0 only rules $B_1^{-1}, M_1^{-1}, M_4^{-1}, T_4^{-1}$ preserve the number of nonnull elements. The ϕ-refinement of the basic procedure thus consists in generating top chains via $R'^{-1} \equiv \{B_1^{-1}, M_1^{-1}, M_4^{-1}, T_4^{-1}\}$ instead of R_0^{-1}. The chains generated this way are all derived from the single initial top chain (corresponding to T_4^{-1}):

(c_0) $\#X21\# \rightarrow \#X12\#$.

Immediate successors of (c_0) are obtained by minimally reducing word $\#X12\#$ either via M_1^{-1} or via B_1^{-1}. In the first case, we generate:

(c_0^1) $\#X021\# \rightarrow \#X012\# \rightarrow \#X102\#$.

In the second case, we generate:

(c_{11}) $\#21\# \rightarrow \#12\# \rightarrow \#21\#$.

(c_{12}) $\#1X21\# \rightarrow \#1X12\# \rightarrow \#2X11\#$.

More generally, the first successors of (c_0) are obtained by applying i times ($i \geq 0$) rule M_1^{-1}, then possibly rule B_1^{-1}. The application of rule M_1^{-1} i times to (c_0) yields:

(c_0^i) $\#X0^i21\# \rightarrow \#X0^i12\# \rightarrow \#X0^{i-1}102\# \rightarrow \cdots \rightarrow \#X10^i2\#$.

The application of B_1^{-1} then yields:

(c_{11}^i) $\#0^i21\# \rightarrow \#0^i12\# \rightarrow \#0^{i-1}102\# \rightarrow \cdots \rightarrow \#10^i2\# \rightarrow \#20^i1\#$.

(c_{12}^i) $\#1X0^i21\# \rightarrow \#1X0^i12\# \rightarrow \#1X0^{i-1}102\# \rightarrow \cdots \rightarrow \#1X10^i2\# \rightarrow \#2X10^i1\#$.

The first element $\#0^i21\#$ of (c_{11}^i) belongs to $\mathcal{L}$, so there is no need to compute the successors of (c_{11}^i). The last element $\#2X10^i1\#$ of (c_{12}^i) belongs to $\Pi : \{\#0^j2X10^k1\# \mid j \geq 0, k \geq 0\}$, which is an R'^{-1}-closed set of growing patterns (see example above). Furthermore, the other elements of (c_{12}^i): $\#1X0^i21\#$, $\#1X0^i12\#$, $\cdots$, $\#1X10^i2\#$ cannot unify with any element of Π (as they start with 1 instead of 0 or 2). Therefore we do not need to compute the successors of (c_{12}^i) either. So the procedure of top chain generation ends. The only quasi-cyclic chain generated is $(c_{11}^0) \equiv (c_{11}) \equiv \#21\# \rightarrow \#12\# \rightarrow \#21\#$, which starts with an element of $\mathcal{L}$. Self-stabilization is thus proved for Beauquier-Debas's variant of Dijkstra's 3-state algorithm. Self-stabilization of Ghosh's algorithm [13] can be proved formally along the same lines, as sketched out in section 2.

---

[3] Such a rule M_1 with condition $Y \neq \epsilon$ should be regarded as an abbreviation for 3 rules M_{1a} : $\#X10aY\# \rightarrow \#X01aY\#$, with $a \in \{0, 1, 2\}$.

6 Compositionality

It is interesting to relate compositionality results obtained in the context of self-stabilizing systems with those obtained in the context of rewrite systems. Similarly to what Dershowitz proved w.r.t. composition of terminating systems (see theorem in [7], p.456), one can derive from theorem 5 sufficient conditions for self-stabilization of the combination of two self-stabilizing systems.

Theorem 8. *Assume that:*
- *R_1 is self-stabilizing w.r.t. $\mathcal{L}_1$.*
- *R_2 is self-stabilizing w.r.t. $\mathcal{L}_2$ when starting from $\mathcal{L}_1$.* [4]
- *there is no overlap between lefthand sides of R_1 and righthand sides of R_2.*
- *all executions are fair w.r.t. both R_1 and R_2.* [5]
Then $R_1 \cup R_2$ is self-stabilizing w.r.t. $\mathcal{L}_2$.

This can be seen as a version Herman's compositionality result [16] in our context.

7 Conclusion and perspectives

In contrast with methods relying on the existence of a strictly decreasing norm function [4,13,18,22], our method requires only little specific knowledge and proposes a uniform framework for the full proof of several non trivial examples, as shown here on Ghosh's 4-state algorithm [13] and Beauquier-Debas's 3-state algorithm [4]. These examples are simple ones, which allow us to give a clear view of the procedure. Besides, the corresponding problem is interesting in itself because it is related to mutual exclusion and has a non trivial specification. Our procedure is inspired by Dershowitz's chain generation procedure [7], and proves convergence of self-stabilizing algorithms much in the same way as Dershowitz proves the termination of rewrite systems. The method is not fully automatic: we need in particular to infer by hand generic "patterns" of configurations from words produced recurrently throughout derivations. Note that patterns have been also used in previous works on self-stabilization, e.g. in [17] where they are expressed under the form of regular languages. The main differences with [17] (and other traditional proof methods of self-stabilization) come from:

1. considering the *reverse* transition relation R^{-1} instead of R;

2. focusing on derivations (via R^{-1}) originating from *top-* configurations instead of derivations (via R) starting from any configuration.

3. deriving new configurations (via R^{-1}) through a restricted strategy of rule application (top chain generation) instead of deriving all the possible successor configurations (via R).

We have also given a natural counterpart of Herman's compositionality result in our framework. We are currently investigating an extension of our proof method in two directions. We first want to consider more realistic token ring algorithms, like different versions of the IBM token ring or FDDI protocols, involving a change from the state reading model to the message passing model. In this case, channel states must be modeled

---

[4] "when starting from $\mathcal{L}_1$" means that condition (0) is replaced with "(0') Each ground word of $\mathcal{L}_1$ is reducible via R_2" in definition 1 of self-stabilization for R_2 w.r.t. $\mathcal{L}_2$.

[5] See, e.g., [30], p. 476, for a formal definition of "fairness".

and the hypotheses must be slightly modified to consider self-stabilization. The second natural way is an extension to algorithms running on arbitrary (non-ring) networks. In this framework, strings must be replaced by graphs. We would then have to use graph rewriting techniques, as proposed in [24–26] for other properties of distributed systems. As a promising first step, we consider the case of tree networks, in which leaves can receive markers, in the same way that top and bottom nodes receive '#'.

Acknowledgement

We would like to thank Nachum Dershowitz for his encouragement and pointing out reference [31].

References

1. G. Antonoiu and P.K. Srimani. "A Self-Stabilizing Leader Election Algorithm for Tree Graphs", *Journal of Parallel and Distributed Computing, 34:2*, May 1996, pp. 227–232.
2. Y. Afek, S. Kutten and M. Yung M.. "Memory efficient self stabilizing protocols for general networks", *Proc. 7th WDAG*, LNCS 725, Springer-Verlag, 1990, pp. 15-28.
3. A. Arora, M.G. Gouda and T. Herman. "Composite routing protocols". *Proc. 2nd IEEE Symp. on Parallel and Distributed Processing*, 1990.
4. J. Beauquier and O. Debas. "An optimal self-stabilizing algorithm for mutual exclusion on uniform bidirectional rings". *Proc. 2nd Workshop on Self-Stabilizing Systems*, Las Vegas, 1995, pp. 226-239.
5. R.V. Book and F. Otto. *String-Rewriting Systems*. Springer-Verlag, 1993.
6. J.E. Burns and J. Pachl. "Uniform Self-Stabilizing Rings". *TOPLAS* 11:2, 1989.
7. N. Dershowitz. "Termination of Linear Rewriting Systems". *Proc. ICALP*, LNCS 115, Springer-Verlag, 1981, pp. 448-458.
8. N. Dershowitz and C. Hoot. "Topics in termination". *Proc. Rewriting Techniques and Applications*, LNCS 690, Springer-Verlag, 1993, pp. 198-212.
9. N. Dershowitz and J.-P. Jouannaud. "Rewrite Systems". *Handbook of Theoretical Computer Science*, vol. B, Elsevier - MIT Press, 1990, pp. 243-320.
10. E.W. Dijkstra. "Self-stabilizing systems in spite of distributed control". *Comm. ACM* 17:11, 1974, pp. 643-644.
11. E.W. Dijkstra. "A Belated Proof of Self-stabilization". *Distributed Computing* 1:1, 1986, pp. 5-6.
12. M. Fay. "First-order unification in an equational theory". *Proc. 4th Workshop on Automated Deduction*, Austin, Texas, 1979, pp. 161-167.
13. S. Ghosh. "An Alternative Solution to a Problem on Self-Stabilization". *ACM TOPLAS* 15:4, 1993, pp. 735-742.
14. M.G. Gouda. "The triumph and tribulation of system stabilization". *Proc. 9th WDAG*, LNCS 972, Springer-Verlag, 1995, pp. 1-18.
15. M.G. Gouda and T. Herman. "Adaptative programming". *IEEE Transactions on Software Engineering* 17, 1991, pp.911-921.
16. T. Herman. *Adaptativity through distributed convergence*. Ph.D. Thesis, University of Texas at Austin. 1991.
17. J.-H. Hoepman. "Uniform Deterministic Self-Stabilizing Ring-Orientation on Odd-Length Rings". *Proc. 8th Workshop on Distributed Algorithms*, LNCS 857, Springer-Verlag. 1994, pp.265-279.
18. S.C. Hsu and S.T. Huang. "A self-stabilizing algorithm for maximal matching". *Information Processing Letters* 43:2, 1992, pp. 77-81.

19. J.-M. Hullot. "Canonical Forms and Unification". *Proc. 5th Conf. on Automated Deduction*, LNCS, Springer-Verlag, 1980, pp. 318-334.

20. J. Jaffar. "Minimal and Complete Word Unification". *J. ACM* 37:1, 1990, pp. 47-85.

21. S. Katz and K.J. Perry. "Self-stabilizing extensions for message-passing systems". *Distributed Computing* 7, 1993, pp. 17-26.

22. J.L.W. Kessels. "An Exercise in proving self-stabilization with a variant function". *Information and Processing Letters* 29, 1988, pp. 39-42.

23. Y. Kesten, O. Maler, M. Marcuse, A. Pnueli and E. Shahar. "Symbolic Model-Checking with Rich Assertional Languages". *Proc. CAV'97*, LNCS 1254, Springer-Verlag, 1997, pp. 424-435.

24. I. Litovski and Y. Métivier. "Computing with Graph Rewriting Systems with Priorities". *Theoretical Computer Science* 115:2, 1993, pp. 191-224.

25. I. Litovski, Y. Métivier and E. Sopena. "Different Local Controls for Graph Relabeling Systems". *Mathematical Systems Theory* 28:1, 1995, pp. 41-65.

26. I. Litovski, Y. Métivier and W. Zielonka. "On the Recognition of Families of Graphs with Local Computations". *Information and Computation* 118:1, 1995, pp. 110-119.

27. G.S. Makanin. "The problem of solvability of equations in a free semigroup". *Matematiceskij Sbornik* 103, 1977, pp. 147-236.

28. M. Schneider. "Self-Stabilization". *ACM Computing Surveys* 25:1, 1993.

29. J.R. Slagle. "Automated Theorem-Proving for Theories with Simplifiers, Commutativity, and Associativity." *J. ACM* 21:4, 1974, pp. 622-642.

30. G. Tel. *Introduction to Distributed Algorithms*. Cambridge University Press, 1994.

31. O. Theel and F.C. Gärtner. "An Exercise in Proving Convergence through Transfer Functions". *Proc. 4th Workshop on Self-stabilizing Systems*, Austin, Texas, 1999, pp. 41-47.

Appendix: proof of theorem 5

The proof of theorem 5 relies on properties involving the notions of active or inactive steps for derivations, as defined by Dershowitz [7].

Definition 9. The *active area* of a ground word w_i in a ground derivation $w_1 \to w_2 \to \cdots \to w_n$ is that part of w_i that has been created by the nonvariable portions of the righthand sides of the rules that have been applied. Only the top letter (i.e., the rightmost letter) of the initial word w_1 is considered active.

More precisely, suppose that a rule of the form $\#X\ell_1 Y\# \to \#Xr_1 Y\#$ (resp. $\#\ell_1 X\ell_2\# \to \#r_1 Xr_2\#$) is applied to a ground word w of the form $\#u_1\ell_1 u_2\#$ (resp. $\#\ell_1 u_1 \ell_2\#$) to obtain a ground word w' of the form $\#u_1 r_1 u_2\#$ (resp. $\#r_1 u_1 r_2\#$). Then, in w', all the letters of r_1 (resp. r_1 and r_2) are active if at least one letter of ℓ_1 (resp. ℓ_1 or ℓ_2) was active; besides, all the letters of u_1, u_2 that were already active in w remain active in w'. We say that a ground word is *active* if its top letter is (active letters will be overlined).

Definition 10. An *active ground derivation* via S (resp. *inactive ground derivation* via S) is a ground derivation $w_1 \to w_2 \to \cdots \to w_n$ in which rules of S are applied only in the active area (resp. inactive area) of words.

We will denote by $\xrightarrow{act}$ (resp. $\xrightarrow{inact}$) an application of a rule at an active area (resp. inactive area) of a ground word.

We now give a property A.1, which is the counterpart of the relation between reduction sequences and narrowing sequences in first-order terms theory [19], and a property A.2, which was proved by Dershowitz [7].

Property A.1 (lifting lemma).

For all active ground derivation $\Delta : w_1 \xrightarrow{act} w_2 \xrightarrow{act} \cdots \xrightarrow{act} w_n$ via S, there exists a top chain $C : t_1 \to t_2 \to \cdots \to t_n$ via S which has Δ as an instance (i.e. such that $w_1 = t_1\theta, w_2 = t_2\theta, ..., w_n = t_n\theta$, for some ground substitution θ).

Property A.2 (semi-commutation).

Let w_1, w_2, w_3 be ground words such that $w_1 \xrightarrow{act} w_2 \xrightarrow{inact} w_3$. Then there exists a ground word w_2' such that $w_1 \xrightarrow{inact} w_2' \xrightarrow{act} w_3$.

We finally give two properties A.3 and A.4, which are adapted from [7] in our context.

Property A.3. Let S be a rewrite sytem such that $S - Top_S$ is terminating. Then any infinite ground derivation via S has only a finite number of inactive steps.

Proof. Consider an infinite ground derivation $\Delta : w_1 \to \cdots \to w_n \to \cdots$ via S. Applying a rule at an active area of a ground word cannot create any new inactive letters, while applying a rule at an inactive area only replaces a certain portion of inactive area by another inactive portion of the same length. Therefore either (a) all the inactive subareas of Δ disappear after a finite number of steps, or (b) at least one of them remains, but between two fixed positions. In case (b), there is a subpart Δ' of Δ of the form $w_i \to \cdots \to w_n \to \cdots$, such that every w_n is of the form $x_n v_n y_n$, all the x_n's (resp. v_n's, w_n's) have the same length, and the v_n's always remain inactive. Since the active application of rules over subparts of x_n or y_n have no influence over the inactive portion v_n, one can extract from Δ' an infinite inactive ground derivation Δ'' affecting only the v_n's. This infinite derivation Δ'' never makes use of a top rule since the top letter is active. This is in contradiction with assumption that $S - Top_S$ is terminating. The only possible case is therefore (a): all the inactive subareas disappear after a finite number of steps.

Property A.4. Suppose that $S - Top_S$ is terminating, and $\mathcal{L}$ is closed via S^{-1}. Then there is an infinite ground derivation via S starting from a word $w \notin \mathcal{L}$ if and only if there is a quasi-cyclic top chain via S, starting from a word t such that $t\theta \notin \mathcal{L}$ for some ground substitution θ.

Proof. The if part is obvious. To prove the only-if part, consider an infinite ground derivation Δ starting from a word $w \notin \mathcal{L}$. By property A.3 (since $S - Top_S$ is terminating) this infinite derivation contains only a finite number of inactive steps. Applying iteratively property A.2, one can push back these inactive steps to the beginning of the derivation, thus obtaining a reordered infinite ground derivation Δ'. Frome some point on, there are only active steps in derivation Δ'. Let $\Delta'' : w_i \to w_{i+1} \to \cdots$ denote this active infinite ground part of derivation. Since $\mathcal{L}$ is closed via S^{-1}, we must have $w_i \notin \mathcal{L}$. Besides, since the rules are length-preserving, there is an initial part of Δ'' of the form $w_i \to \cdots \to w_j \to \cdots \to w_n$ such that $w_j = w_n$ and $w_p \neq w_q$ for all $p < q < n$. By the lifting lemma, there is a top chain $C : t_i \to \cdots \to t_j \to \cdots \to t_n$ with $C\theta = \Delta$, for some ground substitution θ. In particular $t_j\theta = w_j = w_n = t_n\theta$. But t_j and t_n are either both ground or of the form $\#u_j W v_j\#$ and $\#u_n W v_n\#$ with $|u_j| = |u_n|$ and $|v_j| = |v_n|$. So $t_j = t_n$ follows from $t_j\theta = t_n\theta$. Besides, for all $p < q < n$, t_p and t_q are distinct since their instances w_p, w_q via θ are distinct. Therefore $t_i \to \cdots \to t_j \to \cdots \to t_n$ is a quasi-cyclic top chain, starting from t_i with $t_i\theta = w_i \notin \mathcal{L}$.

Now theorem 5 directly results from property A.4 above and the definition of self-stabilization.

Stabilization-Preserving Atomicity Refinement

Mikhail Nesterenko[1] * and Anish Arora[2] **

[1] Mathematics and Computer Science,
Kent State University, Kent, OH 44242 USA,
mikhail@mcs.kent.edu.
[2] Department of Computer and Information Science,
Ohio State University
Columbus, OH 43210 USA,
anish@cis.ohio-state.edu

Abstract. Program refinements from an abstract to a concrete model empower designers to reason effectively in the abstract and architects to implement effectively in the concrete. For refinements to be useful, they must not only preserve functionality properties but also dependability properties. In this paper, we focus our attention on refinements that preserve the property of stabilization.

We distinguish between two types of stabilization-preserving refinements — atomicity refinement and semantics refinement — and study the former. Specifically, we present a stabilization-preserving atomicity refinement from a model where a process can atomically access the state of all its neighbors and update its own state, to a model where a process can only atomically access the state of any one of its neighbors or atomically update its own state. (Of course, correctness properties, including termination and fairness, are also preserved.)

Our refinement is based on a low-atomicity, bounded-space, stabilizing solution to the dining philosophers problem. It is readily extended to: (a) solve stabilization-preserving semantics refinement, (b) solve the drinking philosophers problem, and (c) allow further refinement into a message-passing model.

1 Introduction

Concurrent programming involves reasoning about the interleaving of the execution of multiple processes running simultaneously. On one hand, if the grain of atomic (indivisible) actions of a concurrent program is assumed to be coarse, the number of possible interleavings is kept small and the program design is made simple. On the other hand, if the program is to be efficiently implemented, its

---

* This research was supported in part by a grant from the Division of Research and Graduate Studies, Kent State University

** This research was supported in part by an Ameritech Faculty Fellowship and grants from the National Science Foundation, the National Security Agency, and Microsoft Research.

atomic actions must be fine-grain. This motivates the need for refinements from *high-atomicity* programs to *low-atomicity* programs.

Atomicity refinement must preserve the correctness of the high-atomicity program. In other words, the safety (e.g., invariants) and the liveness (e.g., termination and fairness) properties of that program must also hold in the corresponding low-atomicity program. But it is also important to preserve the non-functional properties of the high-atomicity program. In this paper, we concentrate on refinements that, in addition to preserving functionality, preserve the property of stabilization.

Informally speaking, stabilization of a program with respect to a set of legitimate states implies that upon starting from an arbitrary state, every execution of the program eventually reaches a legitimate state and thereafter remains in legitimate states. It follows that a stabilizing program does not necessarily have to be initialized and is able to recover from transient failures.

To be fair, our notion of stabilization-preservation atomicity refinement should be distinguished from what we call stabilization-preservation semantics refinement:

- *Atomicity refinement.* In this case, the atomicity of program actions is refined from high to low, but the semantics of concurrency in program execution is not. For instance, both the high- and low-atomicity programs may be executed in *interleaving* semantics, where only one atomic operation may be executed at a time. Alternatively, both programs may be executed in *power-set* semantics, where any number of processes may each execute an atomic action at a time, or both in *partial-order* semantics, etc.
- *Semantics refinement.* In this case, the semantics of concurrency in program execution is refined, but the program atomicity is not. For instance, a program in interleaving semantics may be refined to execute (with identical actions) in power-set semantics [2]. The program is more easily reasoned about in the former semantics, but more easily implemented in the latter.

An elegant solution for a semantics refinement problem has been proposed by Gouda and Haddix [12]. Their solution does not however achieve atomicity refinement. In this paper, by way of contrast, we focus on an atomicity refinement problem. But, as an aside, we demonstrate that our solution is applicable for semantics refinement as well.

Specifically, we consider atomicity refinement from a model where a process can atomically access the state of all its neighbors and update its own state, to a model where a process can only atomically access the state of any one of its neighbors or atomically update its own state. (We also address further refinement to a message-passing model.) In all models, concurrent execution of actions of processes is in interleaving semantics.

As can be expected, the straightforward division of high-atomicity actions into a sequence of low-atomicity actions does not suffice because each sequence may not execute in isolation. A simple strategy for refinement, therefore, is to execute each sequence in a mutually exclusive manner. Of course, the mechanism for achieving mutual exclusion has to be (i) itself stabilizing, in order for the refinement to be stabilization-preserving, (ii) in low-atomicity, since the refined program is in low atomicity, and (iii) bounded space, to be implemented reasonably.

This simple strategy unfortunately suffers from loss of concurrency, since no two processes can execute sequences concurrently even if these sequences operate on completely disjoint state spaces. We are therefore led to solving the problem of dining philosophers, which requires mutual exclusion only between "neighboring" processes, and thus allows more concurrency.

Although there is a number of stabilizing mutual exclusion programs in the literature [4, 5, 11, 15, 18], none of them is easily generalized to solve dining philosophers. Mizuno and Nesterenko [17] consider dining philosophers in order to solve a problem that has a flavor of atomicity refinement, but their solution uses infinite variables. It is well-known that bounding the state of stabilizing programs is often challenging [3]. This motivates a new solution to the dining philosopher's problem which satisfies the requirements (i)-(iii) above.

Other notable characteristics of our refinement include: It is *sound* and *complete*; i.e. every computation of the low-atomicity program corresponds to a unique computation of the high-atomicity program, and for every computation of the high-atomicity program there is a computation of the low-atomicity program that corresponds to it. It is *fixpoint-preserving*; i.e., terminating computations of the high-atomicity program correspond only to terminating computations of the low atomicity program. It is *fairness-preserving*; i.e., weak-fairness of action execution is preserved, which intuitively implies that the refinement includes a stabilizing, low-atomicity weakly-fair scheduler.

We describe further refinement into a message-passing model. An (unbounded space) transformation from high-atomicity model into message-passing model is presented in [16]. Our solution has bounded space complexity.

The rest of the paper is organized as follows. We define the model, syntax, and semantics of the programs we use in Section 2. We then present a low-atomicity bounded-space dining philosophers program and prove its correctness and stabilization properties, in Section 3. Next, in Section 4, we demonstrate how a high-atomicity program is refined using our dining philosophers program, and show the relationship between the refined program and the original high-atomicity program in terms of soundness, completeness, and fixpoint- and fairness- preservation. We summarize our contribution and discuss extensions of our work in Section 5.

2 Model, Syntax, and Semantics

Model. A *program* consists of a set of processes and a binary reflexive symmetric relation N between them. The processes are assumed to have unique identifiers 1 through n. Processes P_i and P_j are called *neighbor processes* iff $(P_i, P_j) \in N$.

Each process in the system consists of a set of variables, set of parameters, and a set of guarded commands (GC).

Syntax of high-atomicity programs. The syntax of a process P_i has the form:

> **process** P_i
> **par** ⟨declarations⟩
> **var** ⟨declarations⟩
>
> *[
>   ⟨guarded command⟩ [] ... [] ⟨guarded command⟩
>]

Declarations is a comma-separated list of items, each of the form:

$$\langle list\ of\ names \rangle : \langle domain \rangle$$

A variable can be updated (written to) only by the process that contains the variable. A variable can be read by the process that contains the variable or by a neighbor process. We refer to a variable v that belongs to process P_i as v_i.

A parameter is used to define a set of variables and a set of guarded commands as one parameterized variable and guarded command respectively. For example, let a process P_i have parameter j ranging over values 2,5, and 9; then a parameterized variable $x.j$ defines a set of variables $\{x.j \mid j \in \{2,5,9\}\}$ and a parameterized guarded command $GC.j$ defines the set of GCs:

$$GC.(j := 2) \; [] \; GC.(j := 5) \; [] \; GC.(j := 9)$$

A guarded command has the syntax:

$$\langle guard \rangle \longrightarrow \langle command \rangle$$

A guard is a boolean expression containing local and neighbor variables. A command is a finite comma separated sequence of assignment statements updating local variables and branching statements. An assignment statement can be simple or quantified. A quantified assignment statement has the form:

$$(\|\langle range \rangle : \langle assignments \rangle)$$

quantification is a bound variable and the values it contains. Assignments is a comma separated list of assignment statements containing the bound variable. Similar to parameterized GC, a quantified statement represents a set of assignment statements where each assignment statement is obtained by replacing every occurrence of the bound variable in the assignments by its instance from the specified range.

Syntax of low-atomicity programs. The syntax for the low-atomicity program is the same as for the high atomicity program with the following restrictions. The variable declaration section of a process has the following syntax:

> var
>> **private** ⟨declarations⟩
>> **public** ⟨declarations⟩

A variable declared as private can be read only by the process that contains this variable. A public variable can also be read by a neighbor processes. A guarded command can be either *synch* or *update*. A synch GC mentions the public variables of one neighbor process and local private variables only. An update GC mentions local private and public variables.

Let v_i be a private variable of P_i and v_j a public variable of P_j. We say that v_i is an *image* of v_j if there is a synch guard of process P_i that is enabled when $v_i \neq v_j$ and which assigns $v_i := v_j$ and v_i is not updated otherwise. The variable which value is copied to the image variable is called a *source* of the image.

Semantics. The semantics of high- and low-atomicity programs is the same (cf. [1]). An assignment of values to variables of all processes in the concurrent program is a *state* of this program. A GC whose guard is **true** at some state of the program is *enabled* at this state. A *computation* is a maximal fair sequence of steps such that for each state s_i the state s_{i+1} is obtained by executing the command of some GC that is enabled at s_i. The maximality of a computation means that no computation can be a proper prefix of another computation and the set of all computations is suffix-closed. That is a computation either terminates in a state where none of the GCs are enabled or the computation is infinite. The fairness of a computation means that no GC can be enabled in infinitely many consequent states of the computation. A boolean variable is *set* in some state s if the value of this variable is **true** in s, otherwise the variable is *cleared*.

A *state predicate* (or just predicate) is a boolean expression on the state of a program. A state *conforms* to some predicate if this predicate has value **true** at this state. Otherwise, the state *violates* the predicate. By this definition every state conforms to predicate **true** and none conforms to **false**.

Let $\mathcal{P}$ be a program and R and S be state predicates on the states of $\mathcal{P}$. R is *closed* if every state of the computation of $\mathcal{P}$ that starts in a state conforming R also conforms to R. R *converges* to S in $\mathcal{P}$ if R is closed in $\mathcal{P}$, S is closed in $\mathcal{P}$, and any computation starting from a state conforming to R contains a state conforming to S. If **true** converges to R, we say that R just converges. $\mathcal{P}$ *stabilizes* to R iff **true** converges to R in $\mathcal{P}$. In the rest of the paper we omit the name of the program whenever it is clear from the context.

3 Dining Philosophers Program

3.1 Description

process P_i
par $j : (P_i, P_j) \in N$
var
      public
            $ready_i$: boolean,
            $a_i.j, c_i.j : (0..3)$
      private
            request$_i$: boolean,
            $r_i.j, y_i, j$: boolean,
            $b_i.j, d_i.j : (0..3)$

$*[$

(dp1)   **request**$_i \wedge \neg ready_i \wedge (\forall k : a_i.k = d_i.k) \wedge (\forall k > i : \neg y_i.k) \longrightarrow$
        $ready_i := $ **true**,
        $(\| k > i : y_i.k := r_i.k, \; a_i.k := (a_i.k + 1) \bmod 4)$
    $[]$

(dp2) $ready_i \wedge (\forall k : a_i.k = d_i.k) \wedge (\forall k < i : \neg r_i.k) \longrightarrow$
        $/ *$ critical section $* /$
        $ready_i := $ **false**,
        $(\| k < i : a_i.k := (a_i.k + 1) \bmod 4)$
    $[]$

(dp3) $c_i.j \neq b_i.j \longrightarrow$
        $c_i.j := b_i.j$
    $[]$

(dp4) $r_i.j \neq ready_j \vee (b_i.j \neq a_j.i) \vee (d_i.j \neq c_j.i) \vee (j > i \wedge \neg ready_j \wedge y_i.j) \longrightarrow$
        $r_i.j := ready_j,$
        $b_i.j := a_j.i,$
        $d_i.j := c_j.i,$
        if $j > i \wedge \neg ready_j \wedge y_i.j$ **then** $y_i.j := $ **false** **fi**

$]$

Fig. 1. Dining philosophers process

The dining philosophers problem was first stated in [8]. Any process in the system can request the access to a certain portion of code called *critical section*(CS). The objective of the algorithm is to ensure that the following two properties hold:

safety no two neighbor processes have guarded commands that execute CS enabled in one state;
liveness a process requesting to execute CS is eventually allowed to do so.

This section describes a program $\mathcal{DP}$ that solves the dining philosophers problem. Every process P_i of $\mathcal{DP}$ is shown in Figure 1. To refer to a guarded command executed by some process we attach the process identifier to the name of the guarded command shown in Figure 1. For example, guarded command $dp1_i$ sets variable $ready_i$. We sometimes use GCs identifiers in state predicates. For example, $dp1_i$ used in a predicate means that the guard of this GC is enabled.

Every P_i has the following variables:

- $request_i$ - abstracts the reaction of the environment. It is a read-only variable which is used in program composition in later sections. P_i *wants to enter* its CS if $request_i$ is set.
- $ready_i$ - indicates if P_i tries to execute its CS. P_i is *in CS contention* if $ready_i$ is set.
- $r_i.j$ - records whether P_j is in CS contention, it is an image of $ready_j$.
- $y_i.j$ - records if P_j requests CS and needs to be allowed to access it before P_i can request its own CS again. It is maintained for each P_j such that $j > i$; it is called the *yield variable*.
- $a_i.j, b_i.j, c_i.j, d_i.j$ - used for synchronization between neighbor processes; they are called *handshake variables*.

The basic idea of the program is: among the neighbor processes in CS contention the one with the lowest identifier is allowed to proceed. To ensure fairness, when a process joins CS contention it records the neighbors in CS contention with ids greater than its own; after the process exits its CS it is not allowed to request CS again until the recorded neighbors enter their CS.

Let us consider neighbor processes P_i and P_j and the following sequence of handshake variables $H_{ij} = \langle a_i.j, b_j.i, c_j.i, d_i.j \rangle$. We say that $a_i.j$ has a token if $a_i.j$ is equal to $d_i.j$. We say that any of the other variables has a token if it is *not* equal to the variable preceding it in H_{ij}. $\mathcal{DP}$ is constructed so that H_{ij} forms a ring similar to the a ring used in K-state stabilizing protocol described in [9].

Every P_i has the following GCs:

$dp1_i$ - update GC. When P_i wants to enter CS, it is not in CS contention, for every neighbor P_j, $a_i.j$ has a token, and yield variables for processes with identifiers greater than i are not set; then P_i sets $ready_i$ joining CS contention; P_i also sets yield variables for processes who are in CS contention and increments $a_i.j$ for every P_j with identifier greater than i passing the token in the handshake sequence.

Note, that when $a_i.j$ collects the token again P_j is informed of P_i's joining CS contention, that is $r_j.i$ is set. This ensures safety of the program.

$dp2_i$ - update GC. When P_i is in CS contention, every $a_i.j$ has the token and processes with smaller identifiers are not in CS contention then it is safe for P_i to execute its CS. Note, that critical section is put in comments in Figure 1 since no actual CS is executed. P_i clears $ready_i$ and increments $a_i.j$ for every P_j with identifier less than i, again passing the tokens.

Note, that when the tokens are collected every P_j is informed that P_i exited CS and yield variable $y_j.i$ is cleared. This ensures liveness of the program: P_i cannot repeatedly enter CS while P_j is stuck with $y_j.i$ set.

$dp3_i$ - update GC. It sets $c_i.j$ equal to $b_i.j$ thus passing the token from c to d.

$dp4_i$ - synch GC. It passes the tokens from $b_i.j$ to $c_i.j$ and from $d_i.j$ to $a_i.j$. $dp4_i$ also copies the value of $ready_j$ to it's image $r_i.j$ and clears the yield variable $y_i.j$ when P_j is not in CS contention.

3.2 Proof of Correctness of $\mathcal{DP}$

Due to space limitations some of the proofs of the theorems stated are omitted. All proofs are available in the full version of the paper [19].

Stabilization

Let P_u and P_v be any two neighbor processes.

Proposition 1. $\mathcal{DP}$ stabilizes to the following predicate:

$$\text{there can be one and only one token in } H_{uv} \tag{R_1}$$

Lemma 1. $\mathcal{DP}$ stabilizes to the following predicates:

$$((u < v) \land (a_u.v = b_v.u) \land ready_u) \Rightarrow r_v.u \tag{R_2}$$

$$((u > v) \land (a_u.v = b_v.u) \land \neg ready_u) \Rightarrow \neg r_v.u \tag{R_3}$$

Lemma 2. $\mathcal{DP}$ stabilizes to the following predicate:

$$((u > v) \land (a_u.v = b_v.u) \land \neg ready_u) \Rightarrow \neg y_v.u \tag{R_4}$$

We now define a predicate I_{DP} (which stands for invariant of $\mathcal{DP}$) such that every computation of $\mathcal{DP}$ that starts at a state conforming to I_{DP} satisfies safety and liveness. I_{DP} is: for every pair of neighbor processes $R_1 \land R_2 \land R_3 \land R_4$. In other words in every state conforming to I_{DP}, every pair of neighbor processes conforms to every predicate form the above list.

Theorem 1. $\mathcal{DP}$ stabilizes to I_{DP}.

Thus every execution of $\mathcal{DP}$ eventually reaches a state conforming to I_{DP}. In the next two subsections we show that every computation that starts from a state conforming to I_{DP} satisfies safety and liveness properties.

Safety

Theorem 2 (Safety). In a state conforming to I_{DP}, no two neighbor processes have their guarded commands that execute critical section enabled.

Liveness

For a process P_u and its neighbor P_v the value of the variable $a_u.v$ is changed only when all a variables of process P_u have their tokens. The following observation can be made on the basis of Proposition 1.

Proposition 2. All a variables of a process eventually get the tokens. That is a state conforming to: $\exists v : (P_v, P_u) \in N : a_u.v \neq d_u.v$ is eventually followed by a state where: $\forall v : (P_v, P_u) \in N : a_u.v = d_u.v$

Lemma 3. If a process P_u is in CS contention it is eventually allowed to execute its CS.

Lemma 4. If a process P_u wants to enter its CS it eventually joins CS contention.

The following theorem unifies Lemmas 3 and 4.

Theorem 3 (Liveness). If I_{DP} holds, a process that wants to enter its CS is eventually allowed to do so.

4 The Refinement

4.1 High-Atomicity Program

process P_i
var x_i

(h1)
$$*[\quad g_i(x_i, \langle x_k \mid (P_i, P_k) \in N \rangle) \quad \longrightarrow \quad x_i := f_i(x_i, \langle x_k \mid (P_i, P_k) \in N \rangle) \quad]$$

Fig. 2. High-atomicity process

Each process P_i of high-atomicity program ($\mathcal{H}$) is shown in Figure 2. To simplify the presentation we assume that P_i contains only one GC. We provide the generalization to multiple GCs later in the section. Each P_i of $\mathcal{H}$ contains a variable x_i which is updated by $h1_i$. The type of x_i is arbitrary. The guard of this GC is a predicate g_i that depends on the values of x_i and variables of neighbors processes. The command of $h1_i$ assigns a new value to x_i. The value is supplied by a function f_i which again depends on the previous value of x_i as well as on the values of the variables of the neighbors. Recall, that unlike low-atomicity program such as $\mathcal{DP}$, a GC of $\mathcal{H}$ can read any variable of the neighbor process and update its own variable in one GC.

4.2 Composing $\mathcal{DP}$ and $\mathcal{H}$

To produce the refinement C of $\mathcal{H}$ we *superpose* additional commands on the GCs of $\mathcal{DP}$ and demonstrate that C is equivalent to $\mathcal{H}$. Superposition is a type of program composition that preserves safety and liveness properties of the underlying program ($\mathcal{DP}$). C consists of $\mathcal{DP}$, superposition variables, superposition commands and superposition GCs. The superposition variables are disjoint from variables of $\mathcal{DP}$. Each superposition command has the following form:

$$\langle GC \text{ of } \mathcal{DP} \rangle \parallel \langle command \rangle$$

The type of combined GC (synch or update) is the same as the type of the GC of $\mathcal{DP}$. The superposition commands and GCs can read but cannot update the variables of $\mathcal{DP}$. They can update the superposed variables. Operationally speaking a superposed command executes in parallel (synchronously) with the GC of $\mathcal{DP}$ it is based upon, and a superposed GC executes independently (asynchronously) of the other GCs. Refer to [7] for more details on superposition. Superposition preserves liveness and safety properties of the underlying program. In particular, if R is stabilizing for $\mathcal{DP}$ it is also stabilizing for C. Thus, I_{DP} is also an invariant of C.

process P_i
par $j : (P_i, P_j) \in N$
var

      public x_i
      private

          $x_i.j$,
          request_i : boolean
$*[$

(c1) $dp1$
       $[]$

(c2) $dp2 \parallel \left(\begin{array}{l} \text{if } g_i(x_i, \langle x_i.k \mid (P_i, P_k) \in N \rangle) \text{ then } x_i := f_i(x_i, \langle x_i.k \mid (P_i, P_k) \in N \rangle) \text{ fi} \\ \text{request}_i := \text{false} \end{array} \right)$
       $[]$

(c3) $dp3$
       $[]$

(c4) $dp4 \parallel (\text{ if } x_i.j \neq x.j \text{ then } x_i.j := x.j, \text{ request}_i := \text{true fi })$
       $[]$

(c5) $x_i.j \neq x.j \longrightarrow x_i.j := x.j, \text{ request}_i := \text{true}$
       $[]$

(c6) $g_i(x_i, \langle x_i.k \mid (P_i, P_k) \in N \rangle) \wedge \neg\text{request}_i \longrightarrow$
          $\text{request}_i := \text{true}$
     $]$

Fig. 3. Refined process

Each process P_i of the composed program (C) is shown in Figure 3. For brevity, we only list the superposed variables in the variable declaration section. Besides the x_i we add $x_i.j$ which is an image of x_j for every neighbor P_j. Superposed variable request_i is read by $\mathcal{DP}$. Yet it does not violate the liveness and safety properties of $\mathcal{DP}$ since no assumptions about this variable was used when these properties were proven.

The GCs of $\mathcal{DP}$ are shown in abbreviated form. We superpose the execution of $h1$ on $dp2$. Note that $c2$ is an update GC. Therefore, the superposed command cannot read the value of x_j of a neighbor P_j directly as $h1$ does. The image $x_i.j$ is used instead. We superpose copying of the value of x_j into $x_i.j$ on $dp4$. Thus, the images of neighbor variables of $\mathcal{H}$ are equal to the sources when $h1$ is executed by C. We add a superposition GC $c5$ that copies the value of x_j into $x_i.j$. This GC ensures that no deadlock occurs when an image is not equal to its source. request_i is set when one of the images of the superposed variables is found to be different from the sources or when the guard of $h1$ evaluates to **true** ($c6$). request_i is cleared after $h1$ is executed.

So far we assumed that $\mathcal{H}$ has only one GC. The refined program can be extended to multiple GCs. In this case, $c2$ has to select one of the enabled GCs of $\mathcal{H}$ and execute it. $c6$ has to be enabled when at least one of the GCs of $\mathcal{H}$ is enabled. We prove the correctness of C assuming that $\mathcal{H}$ has only one GC. In a straightforward manner, our argument can be extended to encompass multiple GCs.

4.3 Correctness of the Refinement

As with correctness proof of $\mathcal{DP}$ we have to omit proofs of the theorems stated in this section due to space limitations. All proofs are available in the full version of the paper [19].

Throughout this section we assume that P_u and P_v are neighbor processes.

Lemma 5. C stabilizes to the following predicates:

$$((u < v) \wedge (a_u.v = d_u.v) \wedge ready_u) \Rightarrow (x_u.v = x_v) \tag{R_5}$$
$$((u > v) \wedge \neg r_u.v) \Rightarrow (x_u.v = x_v) \tag{R_6}$$

The following corollary can be deduced from the lemma.

Corollary 1. If I_{DP} holds, $c2$ is executed only when the images of the neighbor variables are equal to the sources. That is:

$$\forall (P_u, P_v) \in N : c2_u \Rightarrow (x_u.v = x.v)$$

Lemma 6. C stabilizes to the following predicates:

$$((u < v) \wedge (a_u.v = b_v.u) \wedge \neg ready_u) \Rightarrow (x_u = x_v.u) \tag{R_7}$$
$$((u > v) \wedge (a_u.v = b_v.u) \wedge ready_u) \Rightarrow (x_u = x_v.u) \tag{R_8}$$

We define the invariant for C (denoted I_C) to be the conjunction of I_{DP}, R_5, R_6, R_7, and R_8. On the basis of Theorem 1, Lemma 5, and Lemma 6 we can conclude:

Theorem 4. C stabilizes to I_C.

Recall, that a global state is by definition an assignment of values to all the variables of a concurrent program. If a program is composed of several component programs, then a *component projection* of a global state s is a part of s consisting of the assignment of values to the variables used only in one of the components of the program. *Stuttering* is a sequence of identical states. A component projection of a computation is a sequence of corresponding component projections of all the states of the computation with finite stuttering eliminated. Note, that projection of a computation does not eliminate an infinite sequence of identical states. When we discuss a projection (of a computation or a state) of C onto $\mathcal{H}$ we omit $\mathcal{H}$ and just say a projection of C. A *fixpoint* is a state where none of the GCs of the program are enabled. Thus, a computation either ends in a fixpoint or it is infinite.

Proposition 3. Let s be a fixpoint of C. The following is true in s:

- $a_u.v = b_v.u = c_v.u = d_u.v$
- $r_u.v = ready_v$
- $ready_u$ is cleared;
- if $u < v$ then $y_u.v$ is cleared;
- $x_u.v = x_v$

Theorem 5 (Fixpoint preservation). When I_C holds, a projection of a fixpoint of C is a fixpoint of $\mathcal{H}$; and if a computation of C starts from a state which projection is a fixpoint of $\mathcal{H}$ then this computation ends in a fixpoint.

Let σ_C and σ_H be computations of C and $\mathcal{H}$ respectively.

Lemma 7. If I_C holds and $h1_u$ continually enabled in the projection of σ_C, then $h1_u$ is eventually executed in σ_C.

Theorem 6 (Soundness). If a computation of C, σ_C starts at a state where I_C holds, then the projection of σ_C, σ_H is a computation of $\mathcal{H}$.

We call a state s of C *clean* if for any process P_u, $ready_u$ is cleared and the only guard that is possibly enabled at s is $c6_u$. Let $u < v$. In a clean state only $c6_u$ be enabled in P_u. Thus the following should also be true in every clean state:

- the token is held by $a_u.v$, that is: $a_u.v = b_v.u = c_v.u = d_u.v$;
- since $ready_v$ is cleared, $r_u.v$ and $y_u.v$ are also cleared;
- $x_u.v = x_v$;
- request$_u$ is cleared.

Theorem 7 (Completeness). For every computation σ_H there exists a computation of σ_C the projection of which is σ_H.

The completeness proof is based on the idea that for pair of states s_i and s_{i+1} of σ_H we can find a clean state s_i' of C whose projection is s_i and a sequence of states that leads to a clean state s_{i+1}' whose projection is s_{i+1}. We compose such sequences into σ_C and show that the execution thus created is maximal and fair.

5 Extensions and Concluding Remarks

In this paper we presented a technique for stabilization-preserving atomicity refinement of concurrent programs. The refinement enables design of stabilizing programs in simple but restrictive model and implementation in a more complex but efficient model. Our refinement is based on a stabilizing, bounded-space, dining philosopher program in the more complex model. It is sound and complete, and fixpoint- and fairness-preserving.

In conclusion, we discuss three notable extensions of our refinement.

5.1 Semantics Refinement

Consider the semantics refinement problem where the abstract model employs interleaving semantics and the concrete model employs power-set semantics. We show how our refinement can be used to solve this problem. To demonstrate that our atomicity refinement is applicable to semantics refinement for power-set semantics we show that for a low-atomicity program a power-set computation is equivalent to an interleaving computation.

Two computations are *equivalent* if in both computations every P_u executes the same sequence of GCs and when a GC executes the values of the variables it reads are the same. Recall that in a computation under interleaving semantics (interleaving computation) each consequent state is produced by the execution of one of the GC that is enabled in the preceding state. In a computation under power-set semantics (power-set computation) each consequent state is produced by the execution of any number of GCs that are enabled in the preceding state.

Theorem 8. For every power-set computation of a low-atomicity program there is an equivalent interleaving computation.

Proof: To prove the theorem it is sufficient to demonstrate that for every pair of consequent states (s_1, s_2) of power-set computation there is an equivalent sequence of states of interleaving computation. The GCs executed in s_1 are either synchs or updates. Clearly, if the synchs are executed one after another and followed by the updates the resulting interleaving sequence is equivalent to the pair (s_1, s_2). □

5.2 Generalization to Drinking Philosophers Problem

Our refinement solution can be generalized to drinking philosophers problem [6] to further increase concurrency of the computation of the program. In the argument below we assume that $\mathcal{H}$ has multiple GCs. GCs of $\mathcal{H}$ *conflict* (affect each other) if one of them writes (updates) the variables the other GC reads. $\mathcal{DP}$ enforces MX of execution of GCs of $\mathcal{H}$ among neighbor processes. This is done regardless of whether these GCs actually conflict.

In $\mathcal{DP}$ to ensure MX among neighbor processes every pair of neighbors P_u and P_v maintains a sequence of handshake variables H_{uv}. Sending a token along this handshake sequence is used to inform the neighbor if the process is entering or exiting its CS. In a similar manner, P_u and P_v can have a sequence of handshake variables for every pair of of conflicting guarded commands. Then if a GC of $\mathcal{H}$ gets enabled the tokens are sent along each sequence to prevent the conflicting guarded commands from executing concurrently. [1] In the meantime non-conflicting GCs can execute concurrently.

5.3   Extension to Message-Passing Systems

Our refinement is further extended into message-passing model where the processes communicate via finite capacity lossy channels. To do so the underlying $\mathcal{DP}$ has to be modified so as it works in this model as follows.

The sequence of handshake variables H_{uv} between a pair of neighbors P_u and P_v is used in $\mathcal{DP}$ for process P_u to pass some information to P_v and get an acknowledgment that this information has been received. In message-passing systems an alternating-bit protocol (ABP) can be used for the same purpose. A formal model of dealing with lossy bounded channels in message-passing systems as well as a stabilizing ABP is presented in [14].

In this case P_u sends the value of a handshake variable (together with the rest of its state) to its neighbor in a message. If the message is lost it is retransmitted by a timeout. When P_u receives the message it copies the state of P_v (including the handshake variable) into its image variables and sends a reply back to P_u. When P_u gets the reply it knows that P_v got the original message. It has been proven that the ABP stabilizes when the range of the handshake variables is greater than the sum of the capacity of the channels between P_u and P_v and in the opposite direction [14].

When $\mathcal{H}$ reaches a fixpoint the values of the variables of processes of $\mathcal{C}$ extended to message passing system do not change. Thus $\mathcal{C}$ is in a quiescent state. It is well-known [13] that a stabilizing message-passing program cannot reach a fixpoint. Therefore the extension of $\mathcal{DP}$ to message-passing systems no longer fixpoint-preserving: the timeout has to be executed even if the projection of the program has reached a fixpoint.

References

1. A. Arora and M. G. Gouda. Closure and convergence: a foundation of fault-tolerant computing. *IEEE Transactions on Software Engineering*, 19:1015–1027, 1993.

---

[1] More precisely: the tokens are sent to the processes with higher ids before the GC is executed and to the processes with smaller ids afterwards.

2. A. Arora and M. G. Gouda. Distributed reset. *IEEE Transactions on Computers*, 43:1026–1038, 1994.

3. B. Awerbuch, B. Patt-Shamir, and G. Varghese. Bounding the unbounded (distributed computing protocols). In *Proceedings IEEE INFOCOM 94 The Conference on Computer Communications*, pages 776–783, 1994.

4. G. M. Brown, M. G. Gouda, and C. L. Wu. Token systems that self-stabilize. *IEEE Transactions on Computers*, 38:845–852, 1989.

5. J. E. Burns. Self-stabilizing rings without demons. Technical Report GIT-ICS-87/36, Georgia Tech, 1987.

6. K. M. Chandy and J. Misra. The drinking philosopher's problem. *ACM Transactions on Programming Languages and Systems*, 6(4):632–646, October 1984.

7. K. M. Chandy and J. Misra. *Parallel Program Design : a Foundation*. Addison-Wesley, Reading, Mass., 1988.

8. E. W. Dijkstra. *Hierarchical Ordering of Sequential Processes*, pages 72–93. Academic Press, 1972.

9. E. W. Dijkstra. Self stabilizing systems in spite of distributed control. *Communications of the Association of the Computing Machinery*, 17:643–644, 1974.

10. S. Dolev, M. G. Gouda, and M. Schneider. B Memory requirements for silent stabilization. In *PODC96 Proceedings of the Fifteenth Annual ACM Symposium on Principles of Distributed Computing*, pages 27–34, 1996.

11. S. Dolev, A. Israeli, and S. Moran. Self-stabilization of dynamic systems assuming only read/write atomicity. *Distributed Computing*, 7:3–16, 1993.

12. M. G. Gouda and F. Haddix. The alternator. In *Proceedings of the Fourth Workshop on Self-Stabilizing systems*, 1999. To appear.

13. M. G. Gouda and N. Multari. Stabilizing communication protocols. *IEEE Transactions on Computers*, 40:448–458, 1991.

14. R. R. Howell, M. Nesterenko, and M. Mizuno. Finite-state self-stabilizing protocols in message passing systems. In *Proceedings of the Fourth Workshop on Self-Stabilizing systems*, 1999. To appear.

15. L. Lamport. The mutual exclusion problem: part ii-statement and solutions. *Journal of the Association of the Computing Machinery*, 33:327–348, 1986.

16. M. Mizuno and H. Kakugawa. A timestamp based transformation of self-stabilizing programs for distributed computing environments. In *WDAG96 Distributed Algorithms 10th International Workshop Proceedings, Springer-Verlag LNCS:1151*, pages 304–321, 1996.

17. M. Mizuno and M. Nesterenko. A transformation of self-stabilizing serial model programs for asynchronous parallel computing environments. *Information Processing Letters*, 66(6):285–290, 1998.

18. M. Mizuno, M. Nesterenko, and H. Kakugawa. Lock-based self-stabilizing distributed mutual exclusion algorithms. In *Proceedings of the Sixteenth International Conference on Distributed Computing Systems*, pages 708–716, 1996.

19. M. Nesterenko and A. Arora. Stabilization-preserving atomicity refinement (full version). http://www.mcs.kent.edu/~mikhail/refinement.ps.

Self-Testing/Correcting Protocols

(Extended Abstract)

Matthew Franklin*   Juan A. Garay**   Moti Yung***

Abstract. In this paper we suggest the notion of *self-testing/correcting protocols*. The work initiates the merge of distributed computing and the area of "program checking" introduced by Blum, and specifically employs extended notions from the work of Blum, Luby and Rubinfeld. In this setting, given a protocol P (a collection of programs on a network of n processors) which allegedly implements a distributed function f, a *self-tester* for f is a (simpler) protocol which makes calls to P to estimate the probability that P when executed in a given environment is faulty (i.e., P and f differ in some of the outputs). A *self-correcting* protocol is another protocol which allows for the computation of f correctly on every input (with high probability) as long as P in the same type of environment is not too faulty.

We first consider self-testing/correcting under a basic form of environmental malfunction, that of *crash* failures, and design a self-tester/corrector pair for protocols implementing the agreement "function." Many distributed protocols can be designed "on top" of this primitive, and can be self tested/corrected whenever it can be. We then consider self-testing/correcting under *gossiping* failures, and present a generic self-testing/correcting pair that is *privacy-preserving*. The notion is basic in protocols where secrecy is an issue. A self-corrector for P is privacy-preserving if it is private (with overwhelming probability) whenever P is private (with overwhelming probability).

In the process of our study, we identify the basic components of a protocol self-testing "utility library," which allows for the safe bootstrapping of the self-testing/correcting process.

1   Introduction

Traditional program testing involves running the program on a "random" subset of the possible inputs, for which the correct outputs are already known. There are several drawbacks to this approach. First, it is not clear what "random" means in this context (equally-likely inputs?; a distribution that arises in practice?; is this distribution well defined or known at all?; etc.). Both Kannan [20] and

---

* Xerox PARC, 3333 Coyote Hill Rd., Palo Alto, CA 94304. E-mail: `franklin@ parc.xerox.com`.

** Bell Labs, 600 Mountain Ave, Murray Hill, NJ 07974. E-mail: `garay@research. bell-labs.com`. URL: `www.bell-labs.com/user/garay/`.

*** CerCo Inc., 55 Broad St., New York, NY 10004. E-mail: `moti@cs.columbia.edu`.

Lipton [23] point to the extreme case of a program that is wrong on exactly one input. Such a program is extremely likely to pass the testing stage, and thus when the program is run on the bad instance the program's output is accepted as correct. The second problem concerns the requirement that some of the outputs be known. How is this achieved? In some cases instances are generated that are "small" enough that can be checked by hand and this is insufficient to make an assertion about the general behavior of the program. In other cases a "different" program is used for the same computation. How independent is this program from the one being tested? How was the confidence about the correctness of this program itself obtained?

Attempting to cover some of the above criticism, Blum [4] proposed a new framework called *program result checking* (program checking, for short). Program checking involves writing a result checker program to be run in conjunction with the original program, that checks the work of the program. Program checking is instance specific: each time the program is run on an input, the checker gives us confidence that the program is correct on *that* input. I.e., the program checker does not verify whether the program is correct or buggy as a whole; it verifies whether the program gives the correct answer on the particular inputs on which it is invoked. Since checking is done during each run of the program, it remedies the program verification problem in that the actual running version—i.e., the compiled version and the hardware on which it runs—of the program is evaluated.

Building on program checking, Blum, Luby and Rubinfeld [11] introduced the notion of *self-testing/correcting programs*. A *self-tester* is a (oracle) program that makes calls to the program P to be evaluated to estimate the probability that $f(x) = P(x)$ for random x. Although a program checker can be used to verify whether P is correct on particular inputs, it does not provide a method for computing the correct answer when the program is faulty. A *self-corrector* corrects P as long as P's probability of error, estimated by the self-tester, is sufficiently low. Blum, Luby and Rubinfeld develop general techniques for constructing simple to program self-testing/correcting pairs for a variety of numerical problems [11].

Independently, Lipton [23] also discussed the concept of self-correcting programs and used it to derive a distribution-free theory of random testing; for several problems he constructed testing programs with respect to any distribution assuming that the programs are not too faulty with respect to a particular distribution. Instrumental in both developments above is the *random self-reducibility* property. Informally, a function f is random self-reducible if, for any x, the computation of $f(x)$ can be reduced to the computation of f on other "randomly chosen" inputs.

Protocol self-testing. In this paper we extend the Blum methodology to deal with *distributed protocols*. Such protocols should be understood here as collections of programs running in a network of n processors, one for each processor. Motivated by [11], we introduce the notion of *self-testing/correcting protocols*. Given a protocol P which allegedly implements a distributed function f, a *self-tester* for f is a protocol which makes calls to P to estimate the probability that P is faulty (i.e., P and f differ in some of the outputs). A *self-correcting* protocol is another protocol which allows for the computation of f correctly on every input (with high probability) as long as P is not too faulty.

In such an environment, other things can go wrong besides the faulty behavior due to flaws in the design and coding of the protocol (e.g., processor failures, messages delays, messages being lost, etc.), making the task of evaluating the correctness of a protocol more complicated than in the case of a sequential program. In particular, the benefit of evaluating the running version of a protocol and the "generalized hardware" on which it runs becomes all the more relevant in this context.

As in [11], we require that the self-tester be *different* than any protocol implementing the function under consideration, as well as *simple*, and *efficient* (see Section 2). The first requirement guarantees the independence of the verification step, the second (however difficult to quantify) makes it easier to assess its correctness, while the third assures that the cost for using it is not too high (e.g., big slowdown in the running time) so as to overwhelm the benefits of using it.

We first consider (Section 3) self-testing/correcting under the basic form of environmental malfunction of crash failures, and design a self-tester/corrector pair for the agreement "function" (aka, Byzantine agreement, Distributed Consensus [24]).

In [11, 25], Blum *et al.* discuss the notion of using several programs—a *library*, all of which are possibly faulty, to aid in the testing and correcting. In the process of designing our self-tester/corrector pair for agreement, we identify some of the basic components (co-routines) that a protocol self-testing "utility" library should contain; besides agreement, these include a shared random coin (e.g., [13]) and Crusader agreement [14]. Such a protocol library, together with [11]'s program library, enable the **bootstrapping** of self-testing/correcting for other protocols.

One important class of protocols are those which enable secure multi-party computation [9, 12]. Besides the correctness requirement, such protocols are required to be *t-private*; informally, this means that an adversary viewing the transcripts of any t parties learns nothing about the computation beyond what can be inferred from their inputs together with the result. From a security standpoint, it is important that self-testers and self-correctors do not create new vulnerabilities. We also present in this paper (Section 4) a generic self-testing/correcting pair that is *privacy-preserving*: if a protocol is t-private, then so is its self-testing/correcting pair.

Related work. To the best of our knowledge, this is the first time that the self-testing/correcting of protocols is discussed.

Program checking and self-testing have been extensively investigated, and checkers and self-testers are now known for many problems [10, 2, 19, 26, 27, 17]. Other relevant works include checking the correctness of memory [6], cryptographic program checking [18], and batch checkers [8].

In the related but different area of *self-stabilizing protocols* (e.g., [1, 3, 15, 22]) the notion of "checking" has been considered as an important co-routine.

This setting assumes a "correct protocol control" constantly checking the state of the execution, which stabilizes when faults cease to exist. The self-stabilizing approach as a whole does not propose a "tool" for reliability; rather, it is a "protocol design methodology" for certain faulty environments. Our setting is quite different: we apply our approach as a reliability tool which checks and actively corrects outputs in the presence of faulty control and executional environment.

2 Model and Definitions

The model we consider in this paper is a synchronous, fully connected network of n processors/parties with identities from $\{1, 2, \cdots, n\}$.

The literature on checking calls the problem specification a "function" while the implementation is called a "program." In a distributed environment, a function may admit more than one outcome depending on the environment's "input." This is a behavior which can be specified using relations; however, for consistency with the existing theory of sequential function self-testing/correcting, we continue to model this process using functions, as explained in the following.

Distributed functions and protocols. To model the computation we define an *ideal* distributed function $\phi : V^n \to R^n$, for arbitrary domain V and range R; typically, $V = R$. A prime example of such a function is the addition function where the inputs are values from a given group and the result is the value of the sum of the inputs. Many arithmetic functions like addition have been treated in the sequential case of self-testing/correcting programs.

In a distributed environment, the behavior of individual processors and the communication environment may deviate from an ideal execution. This gives rise to specifying problems under certain assumptions on (partial properties of) the "behavior." Many times we specify that depending on this behavior the computation will take into account only a partial portion of the inputs, or we specify that only the results which are computed by the non-faulty processors be considered. For example, a "distributed addition" in a faulty environment will specify that we sum up only the values of processors that are non-faulty (up to a certain time), and that the summation result will be written by all the non-faulty processors.

We model this process through the notion of an *environment-aware* distributed function $f : W^n \to S^n$. where f corresponds to ϕ, and they agree on ideal environments. W is an extended set of inputs which includes the actual input set V, but also relevant environmental characteristics that tag each processor; these characteristics influence the outcome of the function. S extends R in a similar fashion. A protocol for a distributed function ϕ is a distributed program which implements f.

We use $\mathcal{E}$ to denote the set of *environments* where the protocols run. Examples of sets of environments are adversarial settings where processors may fail; settings where messages may be lost or delayed; etc. We use the expression "running in $\mathcal{E}$" as a shorthand for "running in environments from $\mathcal{E}$." $\mathcal{E}$ implies the relevant environmental characteristics in the specification of the extended input/output pair W/S, though $\mathcal{E}$ may have additional elements and events. For example, we may only be interested in the case of when a processor has failed (e.g., before or after a certain round) in order to characterize the set of relevant inputs; we may be interested only in whether a processor has failed or not in order to specify a condition on its output; we may not be interested in what a failed processor has written in its internal state; etc.

Oracle protocols. We will now discuss a notion of protocol extension where one protocol employs another protocol as an oracle (I/O access only). This is analogous to the formalization of program extension in [11].

Definition 1 (Oracle protocol). *A protocol $\mathcal{P}$ is an oracle protocol if it makes calls to another protocol P that is specified at run time. When a call is made to P, each party learns only its own output, and not any intermediate messages or computations of P (i.e., the call is "black-box"). We let $\mathcal{P}^P$ denote protocol $\mathcal{P}$ making calls to protocol P.*

We let D_V denote the probability distribution according to which the inputs v_i, $1 \le i \le n$, are drawn from V. If P is a protocol, then we denote $P[i]$ the output of P on processor i. Let $\text{error}(f, P, D_V, \mathcal{E})$ denote the probability that $f \ne P$ (i.e., $f[i] \ne P[i]$ for at least some i) on arguments randomly chosen according to probability distribution D_V running in $\mathcal{E}$. Let β be a confidence parameter.

Definition 2 (Self-testing protocol). *Let $0 \le \epsilon_1 < \epsilon_2 \le 1$. An (ϵ_1, ϵ_2)-self-testing protocol for f with respect to D_V in $\mathcal{E}$ is a probabilistic oracle protocol $\mathcal{T}_f$ that for any P running in $\mathcal{E}$ and β:*

1. *If $\text{error}(f, P, D_V, \mathcal{E}) \le \epsilon_1$ then $\mathbf{Pr}(\forall i : \mathcal{T}_f^P[i] = \text{"PASS"}) \ge 1 - \beta$;*
2. *if $\text{error}(f, P, D_V, \mathcal{E}) \ge \epsilon_2$ then $\mathbf{Pr}(\forall i : \mathcal{T}_f^P[i] = \text{"FAIL"}) \ge 1 - \beta$.*

Definition 3 (Self-correcting protocol). *Let $0 \le \epsilon < 1$. An ϵ-self-correcting protocol for f with respect to D_V in $\mathcal{E}$ is a probabilistic oracle protocol $\mathcal{C}_f$ that for any P running in $\mathcal{E}$ and β:*

If $\text{error}(f, P, D_V, \mathcal{E}) \le \epsilon$ then $\mathbf{Pr}(\forall i : \mathcal{C}_f^P[i] = f[i]) \ge 1 - \beta$.

A *self-testing/correcting pair* for f in $\mathcal{E}$ is a pair of probabilistic oracle protocols $(\mathcal{T}_f, \mathcal{C}_f)$ such that there are constants $0 \le \epsilon_1 \le \epsilon_2 \le \epsilon < 1$ such that $\mathcal{T}_f$ is an (ϵ_1, ϵ_2)-self-testing protocol with respect to D_V, and $\mathcal{C}_f$ is an ϵ-self-correcting protocol with respect to D_V.

As in [11], $\epsilon_1 = 0$ is sufficient for assuming that f will be computed correctly. On the other hand, ϵ_2 should be as close to ϵ_1 as possible in order to allow protocols that are as "buggy" as possible, and still have the corrector work properly.

Modes of operation. In order to allow for self-testing/correcting, the oracle protocol is invoked a number of times. We will consider two modes in which the oracle protocols run:

- **The "reset" mode:** The oracle calls are made sequentially and the system is *reset* with every call. Namely, the system starts from an initial state which is presented to the oracle. To allow the processors to make conclusions based on multiple oracle calls, we will assume that each processor has non-volatile memory preserving information across calls.

- **The "parallel" mode:** The oracle calls are made in parallel. Namely, the processors may have a pre-processing stage after which they invoke the oracle, running in parallel a number of executions.

Complexity—the "little oh" constraint. As in [11], we require that the self-tester/corrector be quantifiably *different* from any correct protocol that implements f, in the sense that their complexity, not counting the cost in the calls to P, should be lower than the complexity of any correct protocol for f. In this paper we consider synchronous networks, where the computation proceeds as a series of *rounds*. Thus, we require that the running time (number of rounds) of T_f^P (resp., C_f^P) be $o(R)$, where R is the minimum worst-case running time of protocols that compute f, when calls to P are counted as one round. In fact, the testers and correctors we present in this paper satisfy a stricter requirement, in that their running time is within a small multiplicative constant of the running time of P, when including the running time of P.

A similar notion can be applied to communication (e.g., number of messages).

Property-preserving oracle protocols: When a protocol runs in $\mathcal{E}$ it may satisfy certain properties. For example, it may tolerate a given number of failures of a certain type, or it may be "private" with respect to an adversary who controls the history of the execution and the view of the failing (gossiping) processors.

We would like to claim that a self-testing/correcting protocol, which employs the protocol being tested/corrected as an oracle, satisfies the same property. This notion is captured by the following definition:

Definition 4. *A self-tester T_f (resp., self-corrector C_f) for P is p-preserving if T_f^P (resp., C_f^P) satisfies property p (with overwhelming probability) whenever P satisfies property r (with overwhelming probability).*

3   Self-Testing/Correcting under Environmental Malfunction

In this section we consider environments where some of the processors in the network, up to t, may fail by crashing. The semantics of crash failures is the usual one: when a processor stops sending messages in one round, a subset of the processors receive the message. Initially, we assume that the failing processors are chosen uniformly at random among all subsets of up to t processors. This is the only random choice assumption that we make. We will denote these environments by $\mathcal{C}$. Later on we consider the standard crash failure model.

3.1 The agreement function

We now consider the design of self-tester/corrector pairs for protocols implementing the *agreement* function (BA) [24]. Recall that in this problem a distinguished source s has an initial value $v_s \in V$. It is required that upon termination, all the correct processors output the same value, and if the source is non-faulty these output values coincide with the source's input value, v_s. The problem can be defined as a function as follows: Let V denote the set of input and output values, let $B = \{\text{faulty, nonfaulty}\}$ be the set of possible processor behavior patterns, and let $T = \{\text{true, false}\}$ be the set of possible termination conditions. Then the agreement function $BA : (V \times B)^n \to (V \times T)^n$ such that:

$$\forall i \text{ s.t. } b_i = \text{nonfaulty}, (d_i, t_i) = \begin{cases} (v_s, \text{true}) & \text{if } b_s = \text{nonfaulty}; \\ (v, \text{true}) & \text{where } v \in V, \text{otherwise}. \end{cases}$$

The first condition is usually called the Validity condition, while the second is called the Agreement condition. The behavior components are given as an example; a more refined notion of behavior may specify in which round a processor fails, when it fails which subset of remaining processors receives its message, etc.

We will deal with protocols that implement the agreement function, and their correctness. It is known that every BA protocol in the presence of crash failures requires $\geq t + 1$ rounds of communication in its worst-case run (e.g., [16]). Even in benign adversarial models, like the one considered in this section, this worst-case scenario may happen with a very small probability.

In order to satisfy the "little-oh" constraint, in [11] self-testing/correcting programs are designed with code that is simpler to implement—and verify—than the function being self-tested/corrected. In our case, the simple one-round *Crusader agreement* protocol [14] will play such a role. Recall that in this problem, the sender also has an initial value which it wishes to broadcast to the remaining processors. The goal is a protocol that guarantees the same Validity condition as above, but the Agreement condidion requires that no two nonfaulty processors decide on different values unless at least one of them discovers that the sender is faulty. The definition of the CA function is similar to the one above, and we omit it for brevity.

To implement the above function obviously all the sender has to do is to broadcast its input, and hence every processor can either decide on the sender's value or detect that the sender has crashed, in which case it is allowed to decide on a default value. That is, the problem is solvable in just one round.

3.2 Self-tester for agreement: reset mode

Consider the simple oracle protocol depicted in Figure 1 for assessing *one run* of a BA protocol P. (We assume that P uses a default decision value $\perp \in V$.)

The tester consists of an initial CA call, followed by a call to P on a random input drawn according to D_V, followed by another CA. In the first CA the sender distributes its randomly-chosen input. If the sender does not crash in this round, then all the non-faulty processors learn the sender's value; on the other hand, if the sender crashes, every processor knows either the input or the fact that the sender has crashed, and hence the output of the oracle call must be the default value. In the second CA, every processor i (including the sender) distributes $P[i]$, the outcome obtained by running protocol P, to all other processors. Note that any processor participating in the second CA was not faulty during the call to P. Based on its local view of input and outputs, every processor judges the protocol by deciding on either "fail" or "not fail." It is easy to check that the tests performed cover all the possibilities of protocol malfunction.

Protocol Simple_Agreement_Tester(P, s)

s chooses $v \in_{D_V} V$
$input \leftarrow CA(s, v)$
$P(s, v)$
for $i = 1, \cdots, n$
$\quad output_i \leftarrow CA(i, P[i])$
let $G = \{i : \text{message received in } CA(i, P[i])\}$
if message received in $CA(s, P[s])$
$\quad sender\_alive \leftarrow$ **true**
$fail \leftarrow \quad (\exists\, j, k \in G : output_j \neq output_k) \vee$
$\qquad\qquad (\exists\, j \in G : (output_j \neq input \wedge sender\_alive) \vee$
$\qquad\qquad\qquad (output_j \neq input \wedge output_j \neq \bot))$

Fig. 1. Simple agreement tester for assessing one run; code for proc. i

Assume that the number of failures that may occur in $\mathcal{C}$ is at most $t < n/2$. We can state the following about the tester of Fig. 1:

Claim 1 *If the run of P is corect, then "not fail" holds in all nonfaulty processors.*

Claim 2 *If the run of P is incorrect, then "fail" holds in every nonfaulty processor with probability $\delta > 1/2$.*

In the worst case, the misbehavior of P is witnessed by just one processor, and its probability of failing—and thus not communicating its findings to any other processor—is less than $1/2$.

We will now use the simple tester of Fig. 1 as the basis for a generic self-tester for BA. The self-tester is shown in Figure 2; it is presented in a "generic"

Protocol Agreement_Tester(P, ϵ, β)

$N \leftarrow \frac{32}{\epsilon} \ln(\frac{2n}{\beta})$
$S \leftarrow 0$
for $j = 1, \cdots, N$
{   choose sender s_j
        Simple_Agreement_Tester(P, s_j)
        if *fail*
            $S \leftarrow S + 1$
}
if $\frac{S}{N} > \frac{\epsilon}{4}$
     "FAIL"
else "PASS"

Fig. 2. Generic self-tester for agreement; code for proc. i

form (ϵ as an input parameter). The protocol basically runs the simple tester an adequate number of times in order to guarantee similar conclusions on the nonfaulty processors. In the reset mode, processors that failed are rebooted each time. The way the sender s_j is chosen in each run is left unspecified. In environments from $\mathcal{C}$, the same sender can be used for all calls; however, the ability to choose senders in different ways will allow us to cope with other types of network adversaries (e.g., asymmetric).

Now to the analysis. Let $Y_l[i]$, $1 \le l \le N$, be the 0/1 random variable indicating the event *fail* = **true** in the lth call on processor i. From Claim 2,

$$\mu = E[Y_l[i]] = \delta \cdot \text{error}(BA, P, D_V, \mathcal{C}) .$$

The following lemma quantifies the number of runs after which the assessments of *all* the processors are sufficiently accurate.

Lemma 1. *Let* $\gamma \le 2$ *and* $N \ge \frac{1}{\mu} \cdot \frac{4 \ln(2n/\beta)}{\gamma^2}$. *Then*

$$\Pr(\forall i : (1 - \gamma)\mu \le Y[i] \le (1 + \gamma)\mu) \ge 1 - \beta ,$$

where $Y[i] = \sum_{l=1}^{N} \frac{Y_l[i]}{N}$.

The proof of the lemma follows from a slight variation of the "Zero-One Estimator Theorem" of [21] for identically-distributed 0/1-valued random variables with mean μ, and the linearity of expectation. Similarly to [25], we will make use of the following corollary:

Corollary 1. (1) *Let* $\mu' \le \mu_i$, *for all* i, *and let* $N = \frac{1}{\mu'} \cdot 16 \ln(2n/\beta)$. *Then* $\Pr(\exists i : Y[i] \le \mu'/2) \le \beta$. *(Use* $\gamma = 1/2$.)

(2) *Let $\mu'' \geq \mu_i$, for all i, and let $N = \frac{1}{\mu''} \cdot 4\ln(2n/\beta)$. Then $Pr(\exists i : Y[i] \geq 2\mu'') \leq \beta$. (Use $\gamma = 1$.)*

Theorem 1. *The protocol of Figure 2 is an $(\frac{\epsilon}{8}, \epsilon)$-self-tester for BA.*

Proof (Sketch). The "little-oh" requirement follows from the fact that CA requires $O(1)$ rounds. Regarding correctness, first note that, from Lemma 2, the expected output on processor i is $E[Y[i]] = \mu_i = \delta \cdot \text{error}$, $\frac{1}{2} < \delta \leq 1$. There are two cases to consider:

(error $\geq \epsilon$) Let $\mu' = \frac{\epsilon}{2}$ (taking the lower bound on δ) and $N = \frac{1}{\epsilon} \cdot 32\ln(2n/\beta)$. Corollary 1(1) yields $\mathbf{Pr}(\exists i : Y[i] \leq \frac{\epsilon}{4}) \leq \beta$. On the other hand, in the protocol of Fig. 2 processor i outputs "FAIL" if $Y[i] > \frac{\epsilon}{4}$. Hence, if error $\geq \epsilon$, the protocol outputs "FAIL" on every processor with probability at least $1 - \beta$.

(error $\leq \frac{\epsilon}{8}$) Let $\mu'' = \frac{\epsilon}{8}$ (corresponding to $\delta = 1$) and $N = \frac{1}{\epsilon} \cdot 32\ln(2n/\beta)$. Corollary 1(2) yields $\mathbf{Pr}(\exists i : Y[i] \geq \frac{\epsilon}{4}) \leq \beta$. On the other hand, if $Y[i] < \frac{\epsilon}{4}$ then processor i outputs "PASS." Hence, if error $\leq \frac{\epsilon}{8}$, the protocol outputs "PASS" on every processor with probability at least $1 - \beta$. □

3.3 Self-corrector for agreement: reset mode

In this section we present a self-correcting protocol that given an agrement protocol P whose error probability (as estimated by the self-tester) is sufficiently low, outputs the correct BA function for any input $x \in V$ by making calls to P. For the design we follow the approach of [23]: to self-correct P on input x, the source draws at random a value r from V, processors run $P(r)$ and $P(x-_V r)$, and output $P(r) +_V P(x -_V r)$. (This is a simple case of the random self-reducibility property.) Recall from Section 3.2 that the BA function admits two outputs depending on whether the sender is faulty or not. Thus, it is necessary to guarantee that either good outcome overwhelms the erroneous output.

Assume that we are given a BA protocol P such that $\text{error}(BA, P, D_V, C) \leq \epsilon$ (e.g., $\epsilon = 0.05$). The ϵ-self-corrector for BA is shown in Figure 3. The protocol performs the two calls to P as described above, and then does a case analysis on the possible outcomes; this is repeated an adequate number of times.

We will need the following statement in order to establish the correctness of the self-corrector (we instantiate for reasonable values of α).

Proposition 1. *Let $\alpha \geq \frac{3}{4}$, and let $X_1, X_2, \ldots, X_N$ be independent identically-distributed $0/1$-valued random variables such that $\mathbf{Pr}[X_i = 1] \geq \alpha$, $i = 1, 2, \ldots, N$. Then*

$$\mathbf{Pr}\left[\sum_{i=1}^{N} X_i > \frac{2N}{3}\right] \geq 1 - e^{-\frac{\alpha N}{324}}.$$

The proof follows directly from Chernoff bounds. The "2/3" captures the fact that there are two correct outcomes of the protocol that are to overwhelm the erroneous one.

Protocol Agreement_Corrector$(P, s, x, \epsilon, \beta)$

$N \leftarrow O(\frac{\ln(n/\beta)}{\epsilon})$
for $j = 1, \cdots, N$
$\{\quad$ s chooses $r \in_{D_V} V$
$\quad output_1 \leftarrow P(r)$
$\quad output_2 \leftarrow P(x -_V r)$
$\quad$ **if** $(output_1 = \perp \wedge output_2 = \perp)$
$\quad\quad outcome_j \leftarrow \perp$
$\quad$ **elseif** $(output_1 \neq \perp \wedge output_2 \neq \perp)$
$\quad\quad outcome_j \leftarrow output_1 +_V output_2$
$\quad$ **else** $outcome_j \leftarrow$ '$*$'
$\}$
$P[i] \leftarrow$ most common $outcome_j, 1 \leq j \leq N,$
$\quad\quad$ s.t. $outcome_j \neq$ '$*$'

Fig. 3. Self-corrector for Byzantine agreement; code for processor i

Theorem 2. *The protocol of Figure 3 is an ϵ-self-correcting protocol for BA, for $\epsilon \leq \frac{1}{8}$.*

Proof (Sketch). By assumption, the probability that in a single run the outcome of processor i $P[i] \neq r$ (resp., $P[i] \neq x-r$), for all i, is at most ϵ. Thus, both calls to P return a correct outcome with probability at least $1-2\epsilon$. Letting $\alpha = 1-2\epsilon$, and adjusting the number of runs so that this happens for all processors, the claim follows from Proposition 1. $\qquad\qquad\qquad\qquad\qquad\square$

3.4 Self-tester/corrector for agreement: parallel mode

We now consider the case where the network is not reset between calls, namely, where faults are persistent. The problem in this case is that if a protocol is prone to behave badly at processor i and processor i fails, then the bad behavior of the protocol is "shielded" by the processor failure. We need a mechanism to unshield the protocol behavior, so that the remaining correct processors have enough information to assess its quality.

To this end we suggest the technique we call *ID re-assignment*. The goal of the technique is to enable each and every remaining processor to "impersonate" every other processor in the network. Roughly, the implementation goes as follows. We do n parallel executions of the tester (resp. corrector) presented before, where each execution represents a different cyclic shift of the processors' IDs. This implies that processor 1 runs the protocol as itself, as processor 2, and so on, impersonating all other processors. Each processor collects a decision value for every impersonated ID. A unanimous decision by all impersonated

IDs determines whether the protocol will pass the test (or output the corrected value). Since each run may fail with negligible inverse exponential probability, the combined protocol still succeeds with overwhelming probability.

Remark 1. ID re-assignment can be augmented to a *randomized* ID re-assignment via a shared random coin procedure. In environments with benign failures, such as the ones considered in this section, a shared random coin protocol is relatively easy to design (see, e.g., [5, 13]). Using the shared coin procedure, processors can draw random permutations of their IDs and execute an adequate number of paralle runs under these re-assignments. This allows to self-test/correct under more powerful network adversaries, such as "biased" (asymmetric) or arbitrary (in the latter case, the adversary does not have access to the shared coin).

4 Privacy-Preserving Self-Correctors

The above already teaches us how the design of a self-testing/correcting pair has to take into consideration certain constraints. For example, it can only assume basic utility library routines to be correct. In the domain of distributed protocols other constraints may be posed on the problem and the addition of co-routines should not violate these requirements. This is particularly important in the case of secure protocols, where the design of self-testers and self-correctors should not create new security vulnerabilities.

In this section we consider this aspect versus a *passive* adversary (i.e., the "private" or "gossip failure" setting). We assume the setting of secure distributed computing against an all-powerful adversary. A number of researchers, beginning with Ben-Or *et al.* and Chaum *et al.* [9, 12], have designed distributed protocols for this setting. Informally, a protocol is said to be t-private if an adversary viewing the transcripts of any t parties learns nothing about the computation beyond what can be inferred from their t inputs together with the output.

Following Definition 4, we say that a self-tester (resp., self-corrector) for P is *privacy-preserving* if $\mathcal{T}_f^P$ (resp., $\mathcal{C}_f^P$) is private (with overwhelming probability) whenever P is private (with overwhelming probability).

Assume that the n-ary function f is computed over a finite field F, and can be represented as a polynomial of degree d over F.[1] Let F^n denote the standard n-dimensional vector space over F. In this section we assume that random choices are made according to U_{F^n}, the uniform probability distribution on F^n. We assume, by the library paradigm of [11], that we have reliable programs to compute f *locally*. This is a reasonable assumption, as typically the task of a distributed protocol is conceptually simple, and the whole point is to be able to cope with the unpredictability of its environment.

A generic self-tester for P is given in Figure 4. The protocol simply verifies the local computation of f with the distributed execution of P at a number

---

[1] Most of the protocols performing secure/private computations are—or can be tuned to be—over a finite field. Also, any function over a finite field can be represented as a polynomial.

of randomly chosen inputs. The correctness of the self-tester is clear. Here we concentrate on the privacy issue, so we leave the constants unspecified—but assume that they satisfy the Chernoff bounds.

Our privacy-preserving self-corrector for P is given in Figure 5. It uses the "low-degree polynomial technique" of Beaver and Feigenbaum [7] to transform a function call at the desired (non-random) input into a collection of function calls at uniformly random inputs. The following series of lemmas establish that the self-corrrector is privacy-preserving.

Protocol Private_Self_Tester$(f, P, , \epsilon, \beta)$

$N \leftarrow O(\frac{\ln(n/\beta)}{\epsilon})$
$S \leftarrow 0$
for $m = 1, \cdots, N$ (in parallel)
$\{$ choose $x^{(m)} \in_{U F^n} F^n$;
     compute *locally* $f(x^{(m)})$
     $P(x^{(m)})$
     if $f \neq P$
         $S \leftarrow S + 1$
$\}$
if $S/N > \epsilon/Const$
     "FAIL"
else "PASS"

Fig. 4. Generic self-tester for privacy; code for proc. i

Lemma 2. *If all oracle calls to P are correct, then the self-corrector of Figure 5 outputs $f(x)$.*

Proof (Sketch). By the same construction as in a theorem in [7], it follows that the value returned by $P(v^{(k)})$ corresponds to $g(k)$ for some univariate polynomial g of degree at most d. By the same construction, we know that $g(0) = f(x)$. $\square$

Lemma 3. *If at most one call to the oracle is not t-private, then the self-corrector is t-private.*

The proof follows from the pairwise independence of the $v_i^{(k)}$. Note the importance of performing the interpolation of g from the shares of the $\{w_i\}_i$. Those intermediate values might leak information about the $v_i^{(k)}$ (and hence the x_i) even if the protocol P is perfectly private, depending on the nature of the underlying function f being computed by P.

Protocol Privacy_Preserving_Self_Corrector(P, x, ϵ, β)

$N \leftarrow O(\frac{\ln(n/\beta)}{\epsilon})$
for $m = 1, \cdots, N$
$\{$ choose $\alpha_i \in_U F$
     for $k = 1, \cdots, d+1$
       $v_i^{(k)} \leftarrow \alpha_i k + x_i$
     for $k = 1, \cdots, d+1$ (in parallel)
       $P(v^{(k)})$ (yielding the share of w_k)
     interpret w_k as $g(k)$ for some function g of degree d
     interpolate the function g at the points $1, 2, \ldots, d+1$
       using the shares of $w_1, w_2, \ldots, w_{d+1}$
       answer$_m \leftarrow$ (share of) $g(0)$
$\}$
$P[i] \leftarrow$ most common answer in $answer_m$, $1 \leq m \leq N$

Fig. 5. Privacy-preserving self-corrector; code for proc. i

Theorem 3. *The protocol of Figure 5 is a privacy-preserving $\frac{\epsilon}{(d+1)}$-self-corrector for any function f of degree d (with respect to the distribution U_{F^n}).*

Proof (Sketch). Because $\mathtt{error}(f, P, U_{F^n}, \mathcal{E}) \leq \frac{\epsilon}{(d+1)}$, all $(d+1)$ outputs of P are correct with probability at least $1 - \epsilon$ each time through the loop. If all $(d+1)$ outputs are correct we know by Lemma 2 that answer$_m = f(x)$. Chernoff bounds provide the desired confidence. t-privacy follows from Lemma 3. $\quad\square$

5 Conclusions

This work has initiated the area of *self-testing/correcting protocols*, which gives a methodology to add reliability on-line and *in situ* to protocols by adding simple co-routines. In [11] and its extensions numerous numerical functions have been shown to have sequential self-testers and self-correctors. Applying the library paradigm one can assume that the correct sequential program is available, and use it to design a generic tester for the distributed version of the same numerical function (details deferred to the full version).

Acknowledgements. The authors thank Alain Mayer for his contributions during the initial stages of this research.

References

1. Y. Afek, S. Kutten and M. Yung, "The Local Detection Paradigm and Its Applications to Self-Stabilization." *TCS* 186 (1-2), pp. 199-229 (1997).

2. L. Adleman and K. Kompella. "Fast Checkers for Cryptography." In *CRYPTO '90*, pp. 515-529.
3. B. Awerbuch, B. Patt-Shamir and G. Varghese, "Self Stabilizing by local Checking and Correction." In *FOCS '91*, pp. 268-277.
4. M. Blum, "Designing programs to check their work." *Communications of the ACM*.
5. P. Berman and A. Bharali, "Quick Atomic Broadcast." In *WDAG '93*.
6. M. Blum, W. Evans, P. Gemmell, S. Kannan, and M. Naor. "Checking the Correctness of Memories." In *FOCS '91*, pp. 90-99.
7. D. Beaver and J. Feigenbaum, "Hiding Instances in Multioracle Queries." In *STACS '90*, pp. 37-48.
8. M. Bellare, J. Garay and T. Rabin. "Batch Verification with Applications to Cryptography and Checking" (invited paper). In *LATIN '98*, pp. 170-191.
9. M. Ben-Or, S. Goldwasser, and A. Wigderson, "Completeness Theorems for Non-Cryptographic Fault-Tolerant Distributed Computation." In *STOC '88*, pp. 1-10.
10. M. Blum and S. Kannan, "Designing programs to check their work." In *STOC '89*, pp. 86-97.
11. M. Blum, M. Luby, and R. Rubinfeld, "Self-Testing/Correcting with Applications to Numerical Problems." In *STOC '90*, pp. 73-83.
12. D. Chaum, C. Crepeau and I. Damgard. "Multiparty Unconditionally Secure Protocols." In *STOC '88*, pp. 11-19.
13. B. Chor, M. Merritt, and D. Shmoys, "Simple Constant-Time Consensus Protocols in Realistic Failure Models." In *PODC '85*, pp. 152-162.
14. D. Dolev, "The Byzantine Generals Strike Again," *Journal of Algorithms*, 3(1):14-30, January 1982.
15. S. Dolev, A. Israeli and S. Moran, "Self Stabilization of Dynamic Systems assuming only Read/Write Atomicity." In *PODC '90*, pp. 103-117.
16. C. Dwork and Y. Moses, "Knowledge and common knowledge in a Byzantine environment: crash failures." Information and Computation **88**, pp. 156-186 (1990).
17. F. Ergun, S. Ravi Kumar and R. Rubinfeld. "Approximate Checking of Polynomials and Functional Equations." In *FOCS '96*, pp. 592-601.
18. Y. Frankel, P. Gemmell and M. Yung. "Witness-Based Cryptographic Program Checking and Robust Function Sharing." In *STOC '96*, pp. 499-508.
19. P. Gemmell, R. Lipton, R. Rubinfeld, M. Sudan, and A. Wigderson. "Self-testing/correcting for polynomials and for approximate functions." In *STOC '91*, pp. 32-42.
20. S. Kannan, "Program Checkers for Algebraic Problems." Ph.D. Thesis, ICSI TR-89-064, December 1989.
21. R. Karp, M. Luby, and N. Madras, "Monte-Carlo Approximation Algorithms for Enumeration Problems." *Journal of Algorithms* **10**, pp. 429-448 (1989).
22. S. Katz and K. Perry, "Self-Stabilizing Extensions for Message-Passing Systems." In *PODC '90*, pp. 91-101.
23. R. Lipton, "New Directions in Testing," DIMACS Series in Discrete Mathematics and Theoretical Computer Science, Vol. 2 (1991), pp. 191-202.
24. L. Lamport, R.E. Shostak and M. Pease, "The Byzantine Generals Problem," *ACM ToPLaS*, Vol. 4, No. 3 (1982), pp. 382-401.
25. R. Rubinfeld, "A Mathematical Theory of Self-Checking, Self-Testing and Self-Correcting Programs." Ph.D. Thesis, ICSI TR-90-054, October 1990.
26. R. Rubinfeld. "On the Robustness of Functional Equations." In *FOCS '94*, pp. 2-13.
27. R. Rubinfeld. "Designing Checkers for Programs that Run in Parallel." Algorithmica 15(4), pp. 287-301, 1996.

Randomization Helps to Perform Tasks on Processors Prone to Failures *

Bogdan S. Chlebus and Dariusz R. Kowalski

Instytut Informatyki, Uniwersytet Warszawski, Banacha 2, 02-097 Warszawa, Poland.
Email: {chlebus,darek}@mimuw.edu.pl.

Abstract. The problem of performing t tasks in a distributed system of p processors is studied. The tasks are assumed to be independent, similar (each takes one step to be completed), and idempotent (can be performed many times and concurrently). The processors communicate by passing messages and each of them may fail. This problem is usually called DO-ALL, it was introduced by Dwork, Halpern and Waarts.

The distributed setting considered in this paper is as follows: The system is synchronous, the processors fail by stopping, reliable multicast is available. The occurrence of faults is modeled by an adversary who has to choose at least $c \cdot p$ processors prior to the start of the computation, for a fixed constant $0 < c < 1$, must not fail the selected processors but may fail any of the remaining processors at any time.

The main result is showing that there is a sharp difference between the expected performance of randomized algorithms versus the worst-case deterministic performance of algorithms solving the DO-ALL problem in such a setting.

Performance is measured in terms of work and communication of algorithms. Work is the total number of steps performed by all the processors while they are operational, including idling. Communication is the total number of point-to-point messages exchanged. Let effort be the sum of work and communication. A randomized algorithm is developed which has the expected effort $\mathcal{O}(t + p \cdot (1 + \log^* p - \log^*(p/t)))$, where $\log^*$ is the number of iterations of the log function required to go with the value of function down to 1. For deterministic algorithms and their worst-case behavior, a lower bound $\Omega(t + p \cdot \log t / \log \log t)$ on work holds, and it is matched by the work performed by a simple algorithm.

1 Introduction

The problem of performing t tasks in a distributed system of p processors is considered. The tasks are assumed to be independent, similar, and idempotent. The processors communicate by passing messages and are prone to failures. This problem is usually called DO-ALL.

---

* This research was supported by KBN contract 8 T11C 036 14.

Review of prior work. The problem DO-ALL was introduced by Dwork, Halpern and Waarts [5], and subsequently studied in [3, 4, 6]. In these papers, if processors fail by stopping then the algorithms are required to perform all the tasks even if only one processor survives. Dwork, Halpern and Waarts [5] consider work defined as the total number of tasks performed counting multiplicities, and communication measure defined as the total number of messages sent. They develop three protocols solving the DO-ALL problem, all of them work optimal. They also consider the effort complexity defined as the sum of work and communication. One of their algorithms has effort complexity $\mathcal{O}(t + p\sqrt{p})$. De Prisco, Mayer and Yung [4] consider work defined as the available processor steps, that is, each processor contributes a unit to the measure of work for each step when it is operational. They present algorithm with work $\mathcal{O}(t + (f+1)p)$ and communication $\mathcal{O}((f+1)p)$, where f is the number of faults. In their algorithm, one processor is designated as an active coordinator which allocates tasks and receives reports of their completion. The coordinator may change over time. In [4] a lower bound $\Omega(t + (f+1)p)$ on work is proved for any algorithm that uses the checkpointing strategy. Another algorithm is developed by Galil, Mayer and Yung [6]. Paper [6] presents a solution of the Byzantine Agreement in the presence of crash failures using the optimal linear number of messages. The algorithmic technique used in the solution allows to improve the message complexity of the algorithm in [4] to $\mathcal{O}(fp^\epsilon + \min\{f+1, \log p\}p)$, for any positive ϵ, while achieving the available processor steps $\mathcal{O}(t + (f+1)p)$. Chlebus, De Prisco and Shvartsman [3] present two algorithms based on an aggressive coordination paradigm by which multiple coordinators may be active as the result of failures. One algorithm is tolerant of fail-stop failures, it has available processor steps $\mathcal{O}((t + p\log p/\log\log p)\log f)$ and communication $\mathcal{O}(t + p\log p/\log\log p + fp)$. The other algorithm is the only one known in the literature that tolerates restarts. Its available processor steps complexity is $\mathcal{O}((t + p\log p + f) \cdot \min\{\log p, \log f\})$, and its message complexity is $\mathcal{O}(t + p\log p + fp)$.

Summary of contributions. We present a randomized algorithm solving the DO-ALL problem and show that its expected performance is much better then worst-case behavior of any deterministic algorithm. The system is assumed to be synchronous, and a reliable multicast is available. The processors fail by crashing. The failures are controlled by an adversary who has to choose at least $c \cdot p$ processors prior to the start of the computation, where $0 < c < 1$ is a fixed constant, must not fail the selected processors but may fail any of the remaining processors at arbitrary times. The performance of algorithms is measured by work, which is the available processor steps, and communication, which is the total number of point-to-point messages. Define effort to be work plus communication. Let $\log^*$ be the number of iterations of the log function required to go with the value of function down to 1; formally $\log^{(1)} x = \log x$, $\log^{(k+1)} x = \log(\log^{(k)} x)$, and $\log^* x = \min_k[\log^{(k)} x \le 1]$. Our randomized algorithm has the expected effort $\mathcal{O}(t + p(1 + \log^* p - \log^* \frac{p}{t}))$. The efficiency of this randomized algorithms is compared with the worst-case behavior of deterministic algorithms. A lower bound $\Omega(t + p\log t/\log\log t)$ holds for the amount of work performed in the worst case by any deterministic algorithm. For instance, if $t = \Theta(p)$ then the randomized algorithm has the expected work $\mathcal{O}(p \cdot \log^* p)$, but any deterministic algorithm requires work $\Omega(p \log p / \log \log p)$ in the worst case. Given a deterministic algorithm, the adversary knows the future behavior of processors and may compare all the possible scenarios of failures; in particular if the adversary wants to fail a specific processor at a specific step to prohibit it from performing a certain task at this step, then also all the other processors (if any) assigned for the same task need to be failed simultaneously. Randomization helps because the adversary has no way to guess the pattern of assignments among tasks and processors if it is created on-line in a random fashion. The lower bound on work performed by any deterministic algorithms is matched by the worst-case work performance of a simple algorithm, which has the communication complexity $\mathcal{O}(t + p^2 \log t / \log \log t)$.

Other related work. In shared-memory models there is a natural problem corresponding to DO-ALL. Given an array initialized with zeroes in the shared memory, a task is to change the value stored at a location of the array. The problem of performing all these tasks is called WRITE-ALL, it was introduced by Kanellakis and Shvartsman [9, 10]. Efficient solutions to this problem can be used iteratively to convert arbitrary shared-memory computations into robust ones resilient to processor failures. This was the subject of papers by Kedem, Palem and Spirakis [13], Kedem, Palem, Rabin, and Raghunathan [11], Martel, Park, and Subramonian [15], and Anderson and Woll [1]. A logarithmic lower bound on time to solve WRITE-ALL deterministically was derived by Kedem, Palem, Raghunathan and Spirakis [12], and on expected time of randomized executions by Martel and Subramonian [14]. Kanellakis and Shvartsman [9] proved a lower bound $\Omega(n \log n / \log \log n)$ on available processor steps in the model with memory snapshots, and developed an algorithm with a matching performance, where n denotes both the number of processors and the size of the array. Buss, Kanellakis, Ragde and Shvartsman [2] proved a lower bound $\Omega(n \log n)$ on available processor steps for any deterministic executions controlled by an adversary that can cause both failures and restarts, and developed an algorithm of a matching performance in the model with memory snapshots. For deterministic computations, the most efficient algorithm performs work $\mathcal{O}(n \log^2 n / \log \log n)$, and if restarts are allowed then the best upper bound is $\mathcal{O}(n^{1+\epsilon})$ for arbitrary positive ϵ; the best lower bound is $\Omega(n \log n)$ in both cases. For randomized computations, expected work $\mathcal{O}(n \log n)$ can be achieved even with restarts.

Contents of the paper. Section 2 presents details of the model and algorithmic paradigms. In Section 3 we present a randomized algorithm RA, prove its correctness and analyze its expected performance. Section 4 contains discussion of the deterministic case, in particular a lower bound on work performed in the worst case by any deterministic algorithm, and algorithm DA of a matching work performance. Section 5 contains final remarks.

2 Model and algorithmic preliminaries

Distributed setting. There are p synchronous processors, each having a unique number in the range $[1..p]$. Processors communicate by passing messages. There is no upper bound on the size of messages. A *stage* of computation consists of three clock cycles called *substages*: *receive* (receiving messages), *compute* (performing local computations), and *send* (multicasting a message). A message sent at a clock cycle is received during the next clock cycle. A processor may in one clock cycle multicast a message to any selected subset of processors, or receive all the incoming messages. A local computation may include performing a single task. The broadcast or multicast operations are reliable (cf. [8]), in the sense that if a processor $\mathcal{A}$ is attempting to perform such an operation and fails in this clock cycle then either no processor receives a message sent by $\mathcal{A}$ in this step or the messages sent by $\mathcal{A}$ in this clock cycle are successfully delivered to all the operational recipients (in the next step).

Tasks. There are t tasks to be performed, all the processors know the number t and each processor may at any clock cycle perform any specific task. The tasks are assumed to be independent, what means that any relative order of performing them is allowed. The tasks are similar, this means that each of them takes one step to be completed. Tasks are also idempotent, this means that they can be performed many times and concurrently.

Model of failure. The processors are prone to stop-failures. If a processor crashes then it stops performing any activity, and never restarts. The failures are controlled by an adversary. There is a fixed constant $0 < c < 1$, such that the adversary has to choose at least $c \cdot p$ processors prior to the start of the computation, must not fail the selected processors but may fail any of the remaining ones at any time. The algorithms presented in this paper do not resort to this constant c. Such an adversary has some features of the off-line adversary (choosing a subset of processors prone to failures in advance) and some of the adaptive adversary (failing the processors prone to failures on-line).

Performance measures. Two independent complexity measures are considered: work and communication. *Work* means the available processor steps, as defined by Kanellakis and Shvartsman [9, 10]. It counts all the steps performed by operational processors, including busy waiting; in other words, any operational processor contributes one unit to work for each clock cycle when it is not faulty. *Communication* is measured as the total number of point-to-point messages sent over the network, in particular a processor broadcasting a message to all the other processors contributes $p - 1$ to the communication complexity. *Effort* is the sum of work and communication.

Coordinators and workers. In the course of an algorithm, the processors may be categorized into *coordinators* and the remaining ones, referred to as *workers*. A coordinator maintains this status till the end of computation, unless it fails, but a processor with the current status of a worker may later become a coordinator. The job of a coordinator is to repeatedly collect incoming messages about the progress of work, combine them, and send back to all the processors which are not known to have failed yet. Sending out such a message by a coordinator also serves the purpose of confirming that this coordinator is still alive. A message sent to every coordinator is called a *report*, and a message of a coordinator sent to every processor is a *summary*.

Phases. The computation proceeds in *phases* comprised of four consecutive stages. A phase may be performed in one of two modes: *work* or *election*. In the work mode a phase consists of the following four stages: (1) performing a task and sending reports, (2) receiving reports by the coordinators, combining them into summaries and sending the summaries, (3) receiving summaries, updating the local knowledge, and deciding on the mode of the next phase, (4) a pause. Each processor, including the coordinators, sends a message about the tasks done to every coordinator that either proclaimed itself a coordinator or confirmed its existence in the previous phase. Each processor maintains a list of tasks of which it does not know as being performed yet, and a list of processors of which it does not know as having failed yet. Each time a processor sends a report to the coordinators or a coordinator sends a summary to all the processors then these two whole lists are carried in the message. If a processor is sure that all the tasks have been completed, then it terminates. If no coordinator is heard during a phase then the remaining operational processors start an election process to select new coordinators, this is done by switching to the election mode. During an election phase, a worker may decide to be a coordinator, then it proclaims this by broadcasting a suitable message to all the processors it expects to be operational. More precisely, in the election mode a phase consists of the following four stages: (1) referring to a randomly set local variable to check if having qualified for a new coordinator, and if this is the case then sending out a proclamation, (2) receiving proclamations, updating the list of coordinators, and sending reports to new coordinators, (3) (performed only be the new coordinators) receiving reports, then sending out summaries, (4) receiving summaries, and if having heard from at least one coordinator then switching to the work mode.

Local knowledge. Each processor A maintains three lists: list of outstanding tasks $Tasks_A$, list of operational processors $Processors_A$, list of coordinators $Coordinators_A$. Lists $Tasks_A$ and $Processors_A$ are overestimates of the true situation because if a processor fails then it takes a number of steps for this information to reach every other processor, similarly if a task is performed. At the start of computation, each processor A obtains a list of all the tasks and a list of all the processors, sorts the lists and initializes $Tasks_A$ with the list of all the tasks and $Processors_A$ with the list of all the processors. Then A sets $Coordinators_A$ to be empty. Message M_A that processor A sends includes the following data: the identification of A, the coordinator/worker status of A, and lists $Tasks_A$ and $Processors_A$.

3 Randomized algorithm

3.1 Algorithm RA

Each processor A maintains a number of local variables. One of them is the variable level$_A$, initialized to $1/2$. It is *increased* by replacing the current value x by $2 \cdot x$. Next is the variable coordination_priority$_A$, it is initialized to a random integer value in the range $[1..p]$, and never changed; the values of these variables of distinct processors are independent of each other. All the processors have unique names in the range $[1..p]$, they are used to assign tasks to processors if there are more tasks then processors. The variable coordination_priority$_A$ does not need to be unique, it is used by processor A to decide if it becomes a coordinator. If the inequality level$_A \geq$ coordination_priority$_A$ holds for the first time during a certain phase then processor A is said to *qualify for a coordinator*, after that the processor becomes a coordinator. The summary sent by a coordinator in the first phase when it qualifies for a coordinator is called the *proclamation* of the coordinator. Another variable is the Boolean one mode which takes one of two values *work* and *election*. The computation starts from the election mode.

After initialization of the variables and lists, all the processors repeat four-stage phases in a loop until all of them terminate. Phases are either election or work, according to the mode. The following are detailed descriptions of phases.

Election phase of processor A of algorithm RA

STAGE 1: Receive substage not used. In compute substage increase level$_A$. Then check if the test to qualify for a coordinator is passed. If this is the case then send proclamation M_A in send substage to every processor on list Processors$_A$.

STAGE 2: In receive substage receive all the proclamations. In compute substage, for each proclamation M_B received, add B to list Coordinators$_A$. If this list is nonempty then in send substage send report M_A to every coordinator on it.

STAGE 3: Let A be a new coordinator, otherwise pause in this stage. Receive reports in receive substage. In compute substage update two lists. On list Tasks$_A$: remove any item T such that it is not included in some list Tasks$_B$ contained in message M_B just received. On list Processors$_A$: remove any item B such that no report of processor B was received. In send substage send summary M_A to all the processors on list Processors$_A$.

STAGE 4: In receive substage receive all the summaries. If at least one summary received then in compute substage update three lists. The lists Tasks$_A$ and Processors$_A$ are updated similarly as in stage 3. Updating of list Coordinators$_A$: for any item B on this list, if no summary received from it in the previous stage, then remove B from both lists Coordinators$_A$ and Processors$_A$. If list Coordinators$_A$ nonempty then switch the mode to work. Send substage not used.

Work phase of processor $\mathcal{A}$ of algorithm RA

STAGE 1: Receive substage not used. In compute substage perform a task: if the size of list Tasks$_\mathcal{A}$ is at least as large as the size of list Processors$_\mathcal{A}$ then perform task T such that the rank of T in Tasks$_\mathcal{A}$ is equal to rank of $\mathcal{A}$ in Processors$_\mathcal{A}$, otherwise select a random task from Tasks$_\mathcal{A}$ and perform it. Remove T from Tasks$_\mathcal{A}$. In send substage send report $M_\mathcal{A}$ to every processor on list Coordinators$_\mathcal{A}$.

STAGE 2: Let $\mathcal{A}$ be a coordinator, otherwise pause in this stage. In receive substage receive all the reports. In compute substage: update lists Tasks$_\mathcal{A}$ and Processors$_\mathcal{A}$, similarly as in the election phases. In send substage send the summary $M_\mathcal{A}$ to all the processors on list Processors$_\mathcal{A}$.

STAGE 3: In receive substage receive all the summaries. In compute substage update lists Tasks$_\mathcal{A}$, Processors$_\mathcal{A}$ and Coordinators$_\mathcal{A}$ similarly as in election phases. If list Coordinators$_\mathcal{A}$ is empty then switch the mode to election. If list Tasks$_\mathcal{A}$ is empty then terminate. Send substage not used.

STAGE 4: Pause for the whole stage.

The phases have been designed to facilitate exposition and simplify the correctness proof. Tasks are not performed during election phases, to have task-oriented work separated from coordinator-selection work. Messages sent by processors have always the same form, they include all the information that may sometimes be useful. Hence there is a room for economizing on the size of messages, for instance the coordinator/worker part is not really needed.

Algorithm RA is related to algorithm AN presented in [3]. It uses the same categorizing of processors into workers and coordinators. The main difference is in using randomness to assign tasks to processors and to control the process of promoting workers to coordinators.

3.2 Correctness of RA

A phase is *productive* if it ends in a work mode of some processor. Let *local view* of processor $\mathcal{A}$ consists of the values of variables mode$_\mathcal{A}$ and level$_\mathcal{A}$, and lists Tasks$_\mathcal{A}$, Processors$_\mathcal{A}$ and Coordinators$_\mathcal{A}$.

Lemma 1. *In any execution of RA, the local view of any two operational processors is the same at the end of a productive phase.*

Proof. Induction on the number of phases. A phase is productive if at least one coordinator sent its summaries. They were received by all the processors by the inductive assumption and the reliability of multicast. The summaries were based on the same set of reports, by the same argument, hence updates of local lists of tasks, processors and coordinators produced the same result. The value of variable mode_A depends on list Coordinators_A. It follows that all the processors simultaneously perform either work or election phases. Variable level is increased simultaneously by all the processors during election phases. □

Lemma 2. *Algorithm* RA *terminates after at most* $t + p + 2\log p$ *phases.*

Proof. The number of election phases is at most $\log(1-c)p$ because the instances of variable level are simultaneously increased during each such a phase, by Lemma 1. Each work phase that is not productive precedes an election phase, hence the number of such phases is not larger than the number of election phases. It is enough to count the productive phases. Observe that during such a phase each processor A either removes a task from Tasks_A or adds a processor to Coordinators_A. Namely, if it is a work phase, then each processor performs a task and removes it from its list of tasks, at the end of this phase all the processors have removed the task from their lists of tasks by Lemma 1. If this is an election phase then new coordinators are added to Coordinators_A. It follows that the number of such phases is at most $t + p$. □

Theorem 1. *Algorithm* RA *terminates with all the tasks performed.*

Proof. By Lemma 2, algorithm RA terminates. Processor A terminates if list Tasks_A is empty. Processor A has removed a task from this list either if it performed it itself or received information in a summary that it had been performed. □

3.3 Analysis of RA

When processors select randomly tasks to be performed, the behavior of algorithm RA can be modeled by the following process of *clearing s urns with n balls*: at the start there are s empty urns, a step begins with a random placement of n balls in the given set of urns, then the urns containing at least one ball are removed; such steps are iterated until no urn remains.

Lemma 3. *The process of clearing s urns with n balls, for $n \geq s$, terminates within $\log^* n - \log^* \frac{n}{s} + \mathcal{O}(1)$ steps with the probability at least $1 - e^{-n^{1/5}}$, for sufficiently large n.*

Proof. If k balls are randomly placed in m urns then the expected number of empty urns is

$$m \cdot \left(\frac{m-1}{m}\right)^k = m \cdot \left(1 - \frac{1}{m}\right)^{m \cdot \frac{k}{m}} \leq m \cdot e^{-k/m} .$$

First consider the case $s = n$. Let X_i be the random variable equal to the number of empty urns after step i. We may assume that the balls in a step are placed one by one. Let $X_{i,k}$ be the number of empty urns after the k-th ball has been put in a random urn during step i.

Let $Y_{i,k} = \mathbf{E}[X_{i,k} \mid X_{i,1}, \ldots, X_{i,k-1}]$. Then the sequence $\langle Y_{i,k} \rangle_k$ is a martingale (cf. [7]). Adding one ball changes the number of empty urns by at most 1, hence $|Y_{i,k+1} - Y_{i,k}| \leq 1$. This allows to use the method of bounded differences (cf. [16]), and to estimate probabilities of deviations by the Azuma inequality, which takes the form

$$\mathbf{P}[X_i - \mathbf{E}\,X_i \geq x] \leq \exp(-x^2/2n) , \tag{1}$$

because $X_i = Y_{i,n}$. This inequality holds for any number of urns used in step i.

Let $e^{(k+1)} = e^{e^{(k)}}$, where $e^{(1)} = e$. We have $\mathbf{E}\,X_1 \leq n/e$. Then by (1) the inequality $\mathbf{P}[X_1 > \frac{n}{e} + \epsilon_1 n] \leq e^{-\delta_1 n}$ holds for each sufficiently small $\epsilon_1 > 0$ and some corresponding $\delta_1 > 0$. Let event $\mathcal{A}_1$ hold iff $X_1 < \frac{n}{e} + \epsilon_1 n$. Then

$$\mathbf{E}[X_2 \mid \mathcal{A}_1] \leq n(e^{-1} + \epsilon_1)\exp\left(-\frac{n}{n(e^{-1} + \epsilon_1)}\right) \to \frac{n}{e \cdot e^{(2)}}$$

with $\epsilon_1 \to 0$. Let event $\mathcal{A}_2$ hold iff $X_2 < n/e^{(2)}$. Then $\mathbf{P}[-\mathcal{A}_2 \mid \mathcal{A}_1] < e^{-\delta_2 n}$, for a certain $\delta_2 > 0$. The case of X_3 is similar to X_2, namely

$$\mathbf{E}[X_3 \mid \mathcal{A}_1 \cap \mathcal{A}_2] \leq n/(e^{(2)}e^{(3)}) .$$

Let $\mathcal{A}_3$ hold iff $X_3 < n/e^{(3)}$. We can estimate the probability similarly as before: $\mathbf{P}[-\mathcal{A}_3 \mid \mathcal{A}_1 \cap \mathcal{A}_2] < \exp(-n/2(e^{(3)})^4)$. This leads to a generalization: define $\mathcal{A}_k$ to hold iff $X_k < n/e^{(k)}$, and define

$$a_k = \mathbf{P}[-\mathcal{A}_k \mid \mathcal{A}_1 \cap \cdots \cap \mathcal{A}_{k-1}] .$$

Then the following inequalities hold:

$$\mathbf{E}[X_k \mid \mathcal{A}_1 \cap \cdots \cap \mathcal{A}_{k-1}] \leq \frac{n}{e^{(k-1)}e^{(k)}}$$

and

$$a_k < \exp\left(\frac{-n}{2(e^{(k)})^4}\right) .$$

Partition the n-process into two stages. Let the first stage terminate if the number of empty urns is less than $n/\log n$. If $k < \log^* x$ then $e^{(k)} \leq \log x$. We estimate the probability that the first stage terminates within $\log^* n - 1$ steps. Let $u = \log^* n$. The probability that all events $\mathcal{A}_i$ hold, for $3 \leq i < u = \log^* n$, is at least

$$\prod_{i=3}^{u-1}(1 - a_i) = \exp\left(\ln \prod_{i=3}^{u-1}(1 - a_i)\right) = \exp\left(\sum_{i=3}^{u-1} \ln(1 - a_i)\right) \geq \exp\left(-2\sum_{i=3}^{u-1} a_i\right) ,$$

for $a_i < 1/2$. Also

$$a_i < \exp(-n/2(e^{(i)})^4) \leq \exp(-n/2\log^4 n) \ ,$$

for $3 \leq i < u$. Hence $\sum_{3 \leq i < u} a_i < \log^* n \cdot \exp(-n/2\log^4 n)$. We need to estimate $\mathbf{P}\left[\bigcap_{1 \leq i < \log^* n} A_i\right]$. This number is at least

$$\left(1 - e^{-\delta_1 n}\right)\left(1 - e^{-\delta_2 n}\right)\exp(-2 \cdot \log^* n \cdot e^{-n/2\log^4 n}) = 1 - \mathcal{O}\left(\frac{\log^* n}{e^{n/2\log^4 n}}\right) \ .$$

This is an estimation of the probability that the first stage is completed within $\log^* n - 1$ steps.

In stage two, the first step is of placing n balls into $n/\log n$ urns. Let Z be a random variable equal to the number of empty urns after this step, then

$$\mathbf{E}\,Z = \frac{n}{\log n} \cdot e^{-\log n} = \mathcal{O}(1/\log n) \ .$$

From the Azuma inequality:

$$\mathbf{P}\,[Z - \mathbf{E}\,Z \geq d\sqrt{n}] \leq \exp(-d^2/2) \ .$$

For $d = n^{1/4}$, with probability $\mathcal{O}(e^{-\sqrt{n}})$ there are $\mathcal{O}(n^{3/4})$ empty urns. Consider the next step of the second stage: the probability that a specific urn is empty is $\mathcal{O}((\frac{n^{3/4}-1}{n^{3/4}})^n) = \mathcal{O}(e^{-n^{1/4}})$. With probability $\mathcal{O}(n^{3/4} \cdot e^{-n^{1/4}})$ there is an empty urn after that step.

Thus the overall probability that after at most $1 + \log^* n$ steps there is no empty urn is at least

$$1 - \mathcal{O}\left(\log^* n \cdot \exp\left(-\frac{n}{2\log^4 n}\right)\right) - \mathcal{O}(e^{-\sqrt{n}}) - \mathcal{O}(n^{3/4} \cdot e^{-n^{1/4}}) \geq 1 - e^{-n^{1/5}} \ ,$$

for sufficiently large n.

Finally consider the case $s < n$. We need to count the number of steps needed to have at most $n/\log n$ empty urns. During each of these steps we estimate the conditional expected number of the remaining urns by number of the form $\frac{s}{e^{(k-1)}e^{(k)}}$, which is less than $n/\log n$ for $k = \log^* n - \log^* \frac{n}{s} + \mathcal{O}(1)$. The rest of the proof is the same as in the case $n = s$. $\qquad\square$

Lemma 4. *The expected work of algorithm* RA *is* $\mathcal{O}(t + p \cdot (1 + \log^* p - \log^* \frac{p}{t}))$.

Proof. First consider the productive work phases. If during a phase the number of outstanding tasks is not smaller than the number of operational processors, then each task is performed by at most one processor, which is assigned to the task in a deterministic way. The total amount of work performed in this fashion is $\mathcal{O}(t)$. Now consider the phases when processors select tasks randomly. The number of operational processors is at least cp during each step. The process of diminishing the outstanding tasks is modeled by the process of clearing $\mathcal{O}(p)$ urns with $\Theta(p)$ balls. Hence the work performed is $\mathcal{O}(p(1 + \log^* p - \log^* \frac{p}{t}))$ by Lemma 3.

Next we estimate the number of election phases, which also gives a bound on the number of unproductive work phases. Let X be the minimum value of level_A for all the processors A that never fail. There are at least cp of such processors, and the following estimation holds:

$$\mathbf{E} X = \sum_{i=1}^{p} \mathbf{P}[X \geq i] \leq \sum_{i=1}^{p} \left(1 - \frac{i-1}{p}\right)^{cp} \leq \sum_{i=1}^{p} e^{-c(i-1)} = \mathcal{O}(1) .$$

Hence the expected number of election phases is $\mathcal{O}(1)$ and the expected work during such phases and the unproductive work phases is $\mathcal{O}(p)$. $\qquad\square$

Lemma 5. *The expected number of messages sent while* RA *is executed is* $\mathcal{O}(t + p \cdot (1 + \log^* p - \log^* \frac{p}{t}))$.

Proof. Let X be the minimum value of variable level_A for all the processors A that never fail. Let Y be the number of processors B such that the inequality $\text{level}_B \leq 2^j$ holds, where j is the integer satisfying $2^{j-1} < X \leq 2^j$. Number $\mathbf{E} Y$ is the expected number of coordinators in the course of algorithm. The expected number of phases is $\mathcal{O}(1 + \frac{t}{p} + \log^* p - \log^* \frac{p}{t})$. The expected number of messages sent during a phase is $\mathcal{O}(p \cdot \mathbf{E} Y)$. We estimate $\mathbf{E} Y$ as follows:

$$\mathbf{E}(Y) = \sum_{i=1}^{p} \mathbf{E}(Y|X = i)\mathbf{P}(X = i) \leq \sum_{j=1}^{1+\log p} 2^j \mathbf{P}[2^{j-1} < X \leq 2^j]$$

$$\leq \sum_{j=1}^{1+\log p} 2^j \left(1 - \frac{2^{j-1}}{p}\right)^{cp} \leq \sum_{j=1}^{1+\log p} 2^j \exp\left(-c2^{j-1}\right) \leq \frac{1}{2} \sum_{k=1}^{\infty} k e^{-ck} = \mathcal{O}(1) .$$

Straightforward calculations complete the proof. $\qquad\square$

Lemmas 4 and 5 imply:

Theorem 2. *The expected effort of algorithm* RA *is* $\mathcal{O}(t + p \cdot (1 + \log^* p - \log^* \frac{p}{t}))$.

4 Deterministic computations

In this section we discuss the deterministic case, to compare it with the randomized one. To show that randomization really helps, it is sufficient to restrict our attention to work performance only.

Consider the scenario in which all the processors have complete knowledge of the progress made, in terms of the tasks already completed. This is similar to computations on a PRAM with memory snapshots, solving the WRITE-ALL problem. Kanellakis and Shvartsman [9] proved a lower bound for such computations solving the WRITE-ALL problem (see also [10]). The adversary considered in [9, 10] may fail all but one of the processors. Notice that in our situation the adversary is different, in particular it is prohibited from failing certain $\Omega(p)$ processors. However a lower bound of a similar form can be proved in the model of this paper, by an adaptation of the arguments from [9, 10]. More precisely the following holds:

Theorem 3. *Any deterministic algorithm solving* DO-ALL *problem requires work* $\Omega(t + p \cdot \frac{\log t}{\log \log t})$ *in the worst case.* □

A full proof will be presented in the final version of this paper.

For completeness sake, we present a deterministic algorithm of a matching work performance. Let us call it DA, it is similar to RA. The main differences are as follows: (1) all the processors act as coordinators, and (2) tasks are always performed in a load-balanced way, that is, processor $\mathcal{A}$ of rank i in list Processors$_{\mathcal{A}}$ performs the task of i-th rank mod the length of Tasks$_{\mathcal{A}}$. There are no election phases in DA, only work phases performed in a loop. Work phase consists of the first three stages of the work phase of RA, with Processors$_{\mathcal{A}}$ playing the role of Coordinators$_{\mathcal{A}}$, and the variables needed for elections not used. The correctness of DA is proved similarly as the correctness of RA.

Algorithm DA is related to algorithm AN of [3]. In particular, the load-balancing of processors when assigning them to tasks is similar, as is the role of workers.

Theorem 4. *The algorithm* DA *performs work* $\mathcal{O}(t + \frac{p \log t}{\log \log t})$ *in the worst case.*

Proof. The method of analysis of algorithm AN for the case of failures without restarts, as presented in [3], can be applied here. More precisely, the work of algorithm DA corresponds to the work of algorithm AN during the attended phases. Details will be provided in the final version of this paper. □

By skipping certain communication steps in the initial part of algorithm, the number of messages of algorithm DA can be made equal to $\mathcal{O}(t + p^2 \cdot \frac{\log t}{\log \log t})$.

5 Discussion

We described the performance of algorithm RA in terms of the expected work and communication. If one would like to have bounds on work and communication holding with the probability polynomially close to 1, then such bounds for RA are $\mathcal{O}(t + p \log \log p)$ on work and $\mathcal{O}(t + p \log p)$ on communication.

Optimality of solving DO-ALL by a randomized algorithm in the setting of this paper is an open problem. We claim that the expected work of any such algorithm is $\Omega(p \log^* p)$ for $t = p$.

Acknowledgement. We thank Adam Malinowski for stimulating discussions about randomization in algorithms.

References

1. R.J. Anderson, and H. Woll, Wait-Free Parallel Algorithms for the Union-Find Problem, in *Proc. 23rd Symp. on Theory of Computing*, 1991, pp. 370–380.
2. J. Buss, P.C. Kanellakis, P. Ragde, and A.A. Shvartsman, Parallel Algorithms with Processor Failures and Delays, *J. Algorithms*, 20 (1996) 45–86.
3. B.S. Chlebus, R. De Prisco, and A.A. Shvartsman, Performing Tasks on Restartable Message-Passing Processors, in *Proc. 11th International Workshop on Distributed Algorithms*, 1997, LNCS 1320, pp. 96–110.
4. R. De Prisco, A. Mayer, and M. Yung, Time-Optimal Message-Efficient Work Performance in the Presence of Faults, in *Proc. 13th Symp. on Principles of Distributed Computing*, 1994, pp. 161–172.
5. C. Dwork, J. Halpern, O. Waarts, Performing Work Efficiently in the Presence of Faults, *SIAM J. on Computing*, 27 (1998) 1457–1491.
6. Z. Galil, A. Mayer, and M. Yung, Resolving Message Complexity of Byzantine Agreement and Beyond, in *Proc. 36th Symp. on Foundations of Computer Science*, 1995, pp. 724–733.
7. G. Grimmett, and D. Stirzaker, *"Probability and Random Processes,"* Oxford University Press, 1992.
8. V. Hadzilacos and S. Toueg, Fault-Tolerant Broadcasts and Related Problems, in *"Distributed Systems,"* 2nd Ed., S. Mullender, ed., Addison-Wesley and ACM Press, 1993.
9. P.C. Kanellakis and A.A. Shvartsman, Efficient Parallel Algorithms Can Be Made Robust, *Distributed Computing*, 5 (1992) 201–217.
10. P.C. Kanellakis and A.A. Shvartsman, *"Fault-Tolerant Parallel Computation,"* Kluwer Academic Publishers, 1997.
11. Z.M. Kedem, K.V. Palem, M.O. Rabin, A. Raghunathan, Efficient Program Transformations for Resilient Parallel Computation via Randomization, in *Proc. 24th Symp. on Theory of Comp.*, 1992, pp. 306–318.
12. Z.M. Kedem, K.V. Palem, A. Raghunathan, and P. Spirakis, Combining Tentative and Definite Executions for Dependable Parallel Computing, in *Proc. 23rd Symp. on Theory of Computing*, 1991, pp. 381–390.
13. Z.M. Kedem, K.V. Palem, and P. Spirakis, Efficient Robust Parallel Computations, in *Proc. 22nd Symp. on Theory of Computing*, 1990, pp. 138–148.
14. C. Martel, and R. Subramonian, On the Complexity of Certified Write-All Algorithms, *J. Algorithms*, 16 (1994) 361–387.
15. C. Martel, A. Park, and R. Subramonian, Work-Optimal Asynchronous Algorithms for Shared Memory Parallel Computers, *SIAM J. Comput.*, 21 (1992) 1070–1099.
16. C. McDiarmid, On the Method of Bounded Differences, in J. Siemon, ed., *"Surveys in Combinatorics,"* Cambridge University Press, 1989, pp. 148–188, London Math. Soc. Lecture Note Series 141.

A New Scheduling Algorithm for General Strict Multithreaded Computations*

Panagiota Fatourou and Paul Spirakis

Department of Computer Engineering and Informatics, University of Patras, Patras, Greece & Computer Technology Institute, Patras, Greece
{faturu,spirakis}@cti.gr

Abstract. In this paper, we study the problem of efficiently scheduling a wide class of multithreaded computations, called *strict*; that is, computations in which all dependencies from a thread go to the thread's ancestors in the computation tree. We present the first scheduling algorithm which applies to *any* strict multithreaded computation and is provably efficient in terms of *execution time, space complexity* and *communication cost*. The algorithm is distributed, randomized, works in an asynchronous way and follows the *work-stealing* paradigm. Our analysis applies for both shared-memory and distributed-memory parallel machines and generalizes the one presented in [5], which applies only to *fully strict multithreaded computations*; that is, computations in which all dependencies from a thread go to the thread's parent.

1 Introduction

Dynamically growing multithreaded computations are nowadays quite common for parallel computers. Multithreaded models of parallel computation have typically been proposed as a general approach to model dynamic, unstructured parallelism and have been employed by several parallel programming languages. To specify parallelism, a thread can spawn child threads. Additionally, a thread may synchronize with some or all of its (direct or indirect) descendants by suspending its execution until a descendant reaches a specific point of computation. A multithreaded computation is identified with a directed acyclic graph, henceforth abbreviated as dag. The nodes of this dag represent instructions of threads, while there are three kinds of different edges, *continue edges* for organizing instructions into threads, *spawn edges* for representing spawning of threads from other threads, and *dependency edges* declaring data or synchronization dependencies among different threads (see e.g., Figure 1). Spawn edges organize threads into a rooted tree, called *spawn tree*.

For the execution of a multithreaded computation on a parallel computer, one should specify which processor executes which threads and when each thread should be executed. Apparently, this is not a desirable task to be undertaken by

---

* This work has been supported in part by the European Union's ESPRIT Long Term Research Project ALCOM-IT (contract # 20244).

a programmer. On the other hand transferring the control of these scheduling decisions to the run time system might not be wise, unless the system guarantees that it will make good scheduling decisions in order to execute the program efficiently. A good scheduling technique must ensure that enough threads remain active to keep the processors busy, while at the same time, the concurrently active threads must be within limits in order to control the (dynamic) memory needed. Moreover, in order to reduce the communication among processors, one should try to maintain related threads on the same processor. Apparently, designing a scheduler to achieve all of the above goals is not a trivial task.

Two scheduling paradigms have been considered in the past, *work-sharing* and *work-stealing*. In work-sharing, overutilized processors try to migrate some threads to other (hopefully underutilized) processors. On the contrary, in the work-stealing paradigm, underutilized processors "steal" work from other processors. The work-stealing paradigm dates back at least as far as Burton and Sleep's research [10] on parallel execution of functional programs and Halstead's implementation of Multilisp [15]. Since then a lot of work has been done in this direction (see e.g., [1, 3–7, 12]).

Three important performance parameters of scheduling algorithms for *multithreaded computations* on parallel computers are the required *space*, their *execution time*, and the *communication cost* incurred during the course of an execution; the first is characterized by the amount of storage needed for an execution, the second is the total number of steps needed for executing all threads, while the last is the amount of communication incurred for keeping more than one processors busy and resolving any kind of dependencies that may exist between threads executing on different processors.

An algorithm achieves *linear speedup* if its execution time with P processors is P times faster than the optimal execution time on a one-processor computer. Since a processor can execute only one instruction at each time step, an algorithm that achieves linear speedup is optimal in terms of execution time. An algorithm uses *linear expansion of memory* if its space requirements are not more than P times the space requirements for the execution of the same computation on a one-processor computer. There exist very simple and common multithreaded computations that require linear expansion of memory in order to achieve linear speedup (see e.g., [4, Section 2.3]). Hence, a scheduling algorithm that uses linear expansion of memory is arguably efficient in terms of space complexity.

Say that a multithreaded computation is *fully strict* when all dependencies from a thread go to the thread's parent. Apparently, the class of fully strict multithreaded computations is a rather restricted one. On the opposite extreme, a *general* multithreaded computation allows arbitrary dependencies between threads. There is, in addition, an important middle ground between fully strict and general mulithreaded computations: those in which dependencies from any thread are directed to the thread's ancestors in the spawn tree. Call these computations *strict*. Apparently, the class of strict multithreaded computations is much wider than the class of fully strict ones. Clearly, the first class encompasses all distributed multithreaded applications in which communication between threads and *any* of their ancestors is required.

Blumofe and Leiserson [6] have proved that there exists no scheduling algorithm for general multithreaded computations to achieve both linear speedup and linear expansion of memory. They have presented a multithreaded computation for which every algorithm can not achieve not even a factor of two speedup without avoiding space requirements to grow as a function of the serial execution time. However, they have proved that by restricting to the class of strict multithreaded computations, there exist efficient execution schedules that both achieve linear speedup and use linear expansion of memory. Thus, these results imply that if one wants to find a scheduling algorithm with good execution time and memory complexity, restricting to strict multithreaded computations does the job.

In a pioneering work, Blumofe and Leiserson [5] have considered the class of fully strict multithreaded computations and they have presented the first provably good work-stealing scheduler (in terms of all three performance parameters) for such computations. However, the class of fully strict multithreaded computations is very restricted, compared to the more general class of strict computations. Thus, an interesting question left open by their work is the existence of a provably good scheduling algorithm for (general) strict multithreaded computations. Blumofe and Leiserson [5, Section 7] have pointed out that generalizing their analysis to work for general strict computations is indeed both important and difficult.

In this paper, we show that it is, in fact, possible to enjoy good performance properties for this much wider class of multithreaded computations. Our result significantly enhances the class of multithreaded computations that can be scheduled efficiently in terms of both execution time and memory complexity. More specifically, we present a distributed, asynchronous, work-stealing scheduling algorithm for (general) strict multithreaded computations and we prove good bounds on its performance. Our algorithm enjoys nice locality properties, while simultaneously it achieves to schedule together related threads. Moreover, we prove that our algorithm is efficient in terms of execution time, as well as space complexity. Our analysis applies not only for shared memory computers, but also for distributed memory systems. More significantly, we provide bounds on the communication complexity of our algorithm for such systems.

Our algorithm achieves expected execution time $O(T_1/P + hT_\infty)$, where T_1 is the optimal execution time with one processor, T_∞ is the length of a path of maximum length in the instruction dag, and h is the *dependency height* of the computation; that is, h is the maximum "distance" in the spawn tree between any two threads that need to communicate during the course of the execution. Clearly, no algorithm can achieve execution time better than T_1/P since each processor can execute only one task at a step. Moreover, no algorithm can achieve execution time less than T_∞, since none of the instructions on this path can be executed in parallel with any other instruction on the path. Notice that our algorithm achieves linear speedup, whenever $P \leq T_1/(hT_\infty)$, so that $hT_\infty \leq T_1/P$.

The space complexity of our algorithm is $O(S_1 P)$, where S_1 is the optimal space complexity with one processor. Thus, our algorithm uses *linear expansion of memory*. Recall that an algorithm that uses linear expansion of memory is arguably efficient in terms of space complexity.

The expected communication complexity of our algorithm is $O(PhT_\infty(1 + n_d)S_{max})$, where S_{max} is the maximum size of storage needed by any thread of the computation and n_d is the maximum number of dependency edges entering any thread. Wu and Kung have proved in [19] that there exist fully strict multithreaded computations, such that any algorithm that achieves linear speedup incurs total communication at least $O(PT_\infty S_{max})$. Thus, scheduling algorithms for fully strict multithreaded computations that achieve this amount of communication are optimal in terms of communication cost. Our communication bound diverges by a factor of h from this lower bound. However, we argue that this divergence is not unexpected, since h appears to be a measure of the degree of "strictness" of multithreaded computations. Since for fully strict multithreaded computations $h = 1$, this divergence of our communication bound from the lower bound provided for fully strict multithreaded computations appears to us natural.

We also prove that for any $\epsilon > 0$, with probability at least $1 - \epsilon$ the algorithm has execution time $O(T_1/P + hT_\infty + \log P + \log(1/\epsilon))$ and communication complexity $O(P(hT_\infty + \log(1/\epsilon))(1 + n_d)S_{max})$.

Substantial research (see e.g., [1, 16, 18, 20]) has been reported in the literature concerning the scheduling of multithreaded computations, ignoring though space requirements and communication costs. Burton shows in [9] how to limit space in certain parallel computations without causing deadlock. More recently, Burton [8] has developed and analyzed a scheduling algorithm with provably good time and space bounds. Blelloch *et al.* [2, 3] have also recently developed and analyzed scheduling algorithms with provably good time and space bounds for languages with nested fine-grained parallelism (that is, languages that lead to series-parallel DAGs). All these algorithms are analyzed only for shared-memory machines and do not account for communication cost. On the opposite, our analysis holds even for distributed-memory machines; more significantly, we provide bounds on the communication complexity of our algorithm for such machines.

Fatourou and Spirakis considered in [12] the case of k-strict computations, that is, computations on which any dependency from a thread goes to some of the k ancestors of the thread in the activation tree. They present two scheduling algorithms for k-strict multithreaded computations. Their algorithms work in a different way than the algorithm presented in this paper and require knowledge of k. On the contrary, the algorithm presented in this paper is based on new ideas, which employ timestamps and maintains extra and more complicated data structures in order to keep track of related threads, that is threads that communicate a lot and thus should be placed on the same processor. Proving particular properties on the structure of these data structures appears to be a major challenge of our analysis. These properties does not hold for the algorithms presented in [12], so that those algorithms are not appropriate for the more general case of strict computations.

Recently, Arora *et al.* [1] have proved that the work-stealing algorithm presented in [5] can be analyzed assuming general multithreaded computations. However, their analysis provides only an execution time bound and no bounds for the space complexity. In contrast, our algorithm provides bounds on both execution time and space complexity, albeit for the less general class of strict multithreaded computations. Additionally, the analysis provided in [1] applies only for shared memory computers, while our analysis applies even for distributed memory machines; more significantly, we provide bounds on the communication complexity of our algorithm for such machines.

The algorithm presented in [5] has been implemented in CILK [4] which is a C-based language for programming multithreaded computations. Another tool that employs randomized work-stealing techniques as its load balancing mechanism is VDS [11].

The rest of this paper is organized as follows. Section 2 includes definitions and some preliminary facts, while Section 3 presents our algorithm, exhibits fundamental properties maintained by the algorithm, and provides bounds for its space complexity, its execution time and its communication cost. Many of our proofs have been omitted in this extended abstract. They can be found in [13].

2 The Model

Our definitions closely follows the ones presented in [5, 12]. A *multithreaded computation* is modeled as a graph G, which is called the *instruction graph* of the computation. A multithreaded computation is composed of a set of *threads*, each of which contains unit-time, serially executed *tasks*. The nodes of the instruction graph represent tasks of the multithreaded computation. Tasks are connected to each other via *continue edges* that determine the order in which they are executed. During the course of a thread's execution, the thread may create, or *spawn*, child threads. A thread can spawn as many children as it likes to. If a task γ of a thread Γ_1 spawns another thread Γ_2, a *spawn edge* begins from task γ and ends at the first task of thread Γ_2 in the instruction graph. Spawn edges organize the threads into a rooted tree, which is called the *spawn tree* of the computation. Call the thread that corresponds to the root of this tree the *root thread* of the multithreaded computation. In addition to the continue and spawn edges, the instruction graph may also contain *dependency edges*. Dependency edges model data dependencies, like e.g., producer-consumer dependencies, and allow threads to synchronize. If the execution of a thread arrives at a "consuming" task, before the execution of the corresponding "producing" task, the execution of the consuming thread *stalls*. Once the producing task executes, the dependency is *resolved* and the consuming task is *enabled* to proceed with its execution. For any multithreaded computation G, we denote by $E_d(G)$ the set of the dependency edges of G.

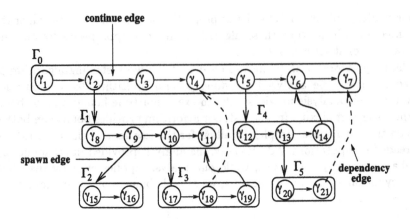

Fig. 1. A multithreaded computation.

Figure 1 presents a multithreaded computation. A thread in this graph is represented by a block of circles, where each circle represents a particular task of the thread. The horizontal edges in Figure 1 are continue edges. Spawn edges are represented by downward-pointing edges. Thus, thread Γ_0 is the parent of threads Γ_1 and Γ_4. Dependency edges are represented by curved arrows between tasks of different threads. For example, task γ_4 of thread Γ_0 is a consuming task. It needs a data item that is produced by task γ_{18} of thread Γ_3. Thus, task γ_4 can not be executed until after task γ_{18}.

Clearly, the execution of a multithreaded computation is possible only if dependency edges do not produce cycles in the instruction graph. Thus, this graph must be a directed acyclic graph or *dag*. We denote by n_d the maximum number of dependency edges entering any specific thread. A thread *dies* when all its tasks have been executed; a *dead* thread is one that has died. A spawned thread that is not *dead* is *alive*.

A multithreaded computation is said to be *strict* if all dependencies from one thread goes to ancestors of the thread in the spawn tree. A *fully-strict multithreaded computation* is one in which all dependencies from a thread go to the thread's parent. Multithreaded computations that contain any other kind of dependencies are called *non-strict* or *general*. Our example computation of Figure 1 is a strict computation. If we remove the dashed dependency edges from the multithreaded computation of Figure 1, it becomes a fully strict multithreaded computation.

For any thread Γ of a multithreaded computation, we define its *height* to be the distance of thread Γ from the root thread in the spawn tree. Clearly, the height of the root thread is 0. We can partition the spawn tree into levels, where level 0 contains only the root thread, level 1 contains all threads of height 1, and generally level i contains all threads of height i. For any thread Γ, we denote by $level(\Gamma)$ the level that Γ is located in the spawn tree of G. Consider any thread Γ located at level j in the spawn tree. For any integer $i \le j$, we define the *i-ancestor* of Γ to be the ancestor of the thread located at level $j - i$ in the spawn tree. For any integer $i \geq 0$, the *i-descendant* of Γ is defined in the natural way.

For any multithreaded computation G and any two threads $\Gamma, \Gamma' \in G$ connected by a dependency edge $e \in E_d(G)$, we define the *dependency height* of edge e, denoted by h_e, to be $h_e = |level(\Gamma) - level(\Gamma')|$. The dependency height of G, denoted $h(G)$, is defined to be $h(G) = \max_{e \in E_d(G)}\{h_e\}$. In the rest of this paper, we use the notation h instead of $h(G)$, that is, we ommit G whenever it is clear from the context.

An execution schedule for a multithreaded computation G, denoted $\mathcal{X}(G, P)$, determines which processors of the parallel computer execute which instructions at each step. A *valid* execution schedule must satisfy all constraints imposed by the continue, spawn and dependency edges of the instruction dag of a multithreaded computation. At any given step t of an execution schedule, a task is *ready* if all of its predecessors in the instruction dag have been executed. Only ready tasks may be executed. We say that an execution schedule maintains the *busy-leaves property* if at each time step, every leaf thread has a processor working on it.

When a task spawns a thread, it allocates an *activation frame*, that is a block of memory, for use by the newly spawned thread. We denote by $S_{max}(G)$ the maximum size of the activation frame of any thread of a multithreaded computation G. We denote by $S_1(G)$ the minimum amount of space required for the execution of G on a one processor machine. The *work* of a computation G is the total number of tasks in the computation. The *dag depth of a task* in G is the length of the longest path of the instruction graph that terminates at the task. The *dag depth of G* is the maximum dag depth of any of its tasks. We denote by $T_1(G)$ the work of the computation, since a one-processor computer can only execute one task at any time step. We denote by $T_\infty(G)$ the dag depth of G, since even with arbitrarily many processors each instruction on a path must execute serially. For any multithreaded computation G, a P-processor ($P > 1$) execution schedule for G may incur an amount of communication when running in a distributed way. Apart from the amount of communication needed for the "distribution" of threads among the different processors, communication may also be required for resolving dependencies among threads residing on different processors. We denote by $C(\mathcal{X}(G, P))$ the total communication required for the execution of the multithreaded computation G by the execution schedule $\mathcal{X}(G, P)$.

A *scheduling algorithm* for a multithreaded computation decides which processors execute which tasks at every time step; that is, for any multithreaded computation G and any integer $P > 0$, a scheduling algorithm Alg takes G and P as input and outputs a schedule $\mathcal{X}_{Alg}(G, P)$. Since more than one threads may be simultaneously ready in a single processor, a mechanism for scheduling threads within a single processor should be provided by any algorithm. Call this mechanism the *internal scheduler*. In order to keep more than one processors working, a scheduling algorithm must dynamically distribute work among processors. Thus, a basic component of any scheduling algorithm is the *external scheduler*, whose job is to schedule threads across different processors. A *work-stealing* external scheduler works as follows. When a processor runs out of work, it becomes a *thief* and steals work from a *victim* processor. The decision of who is going to be the victim processor may be taken either deterministically or in a randomized way, yielding to either deterministic or randomized algorithms, respectively. An algorithm should also provide a mechanism for deciding what actions are made when a dependency is resolved. Call this mechanism the *dependency resolver*.

In this paper, we consider only *distributed* scheduling algorithms, in which a copy of the above three mechanisms runs on each processor independently. If any of the three components of a scheduling algorithm works in a randomized way, the algorithm produces a probability distribution over all execution schedules $\mathcal{X}(G, P)$. In this work, we concentrate on scheduling algorithms with randomized, work-stealing external schedulers. For each such algorithm Alg, we denote by $T_{\mathsf{Alg}}(G, P)$, $S_{\mathsf{Alg}}(G, P)$ and $C_{\mathsf{Alg}}(G, P)$ the random variables denoting the execution time, the total space required, that is the *space complexity*, and the communication incurred, that is the *communication complexity*, during the P-processor execution of a multithreaded computation G by Alg.

The *work of* Alg on a multithreaded computation G is defined to be the number of tasks (instructions) that Alg executes during the execution of G on a P-processor parallel computer. Notice that the work of any scheduling algorithm, whether randomized or not, is always equal to $T_1(G)$. We define the *stealing time of* Alg to be the random variable expressing the number of steal attempts occured during the P-processor execution of Alg on the multithreaded computation G. The *waiting time of* Alg is the random variable expressing the total time that processors wait due to contention caused by stealing at the ready lists of processors.

We continue to describe fundamental analytical tools, which can be proved useful for analysing the complexity of work-stealing, scheduling algorithms.

For any multithreaded computation G, the *augmented instruction dag G'* contains the original graph as a subgraph, but it has some extra edges, which are called *critical edges*. For every set of tasks γ_i, γ_j and γ_m, such that $\langle \gamma_i, \gamma_j \rangle$ is a spawn edge and $\langle \gamma_i, \gamma_m \rangle$ is a continue edge, the critical edge $\langle \gamma_m, \gamma_j \rangle$ is also an edge of G'.

For any time step t during the execution of a multithreaded computation G on a P-processor parallel computer, an unexecuted task γ is said to be *critical* at time step t, if all tasks γ', such that there exists a path from γ' to γ in G', have been executed by time step t. A *critical path* of tasks in G' is a maximal path in G'. We say that a critical path $U(G) = \langle \gamma_1, \ldots, \gamma_L \rangle$ *occurs* during the execution of a multithreaded computation G according to some valid execution schedule $\mathcal{X}(G, P)$, if one and only one of its tasks is critical at each time step of the execution.

A *round of steal attempts* during the execution of some computation G is a set of at least $6hP$ but fewer than $6hP + P$ consecutive steal attempts such that if a steal attempt initiated at time step t occurs in a particular round, then all other steal attempts initiated at time step t are also in the same round. All steal attempts that occur during an execution can be partitioned into rounds as follows. The first round contains all steal attempts initiated at time steps $1, 2, \ldots, t_1$, where t_1 is the earliest time step such that at least $6hP$ steal attempts were initiated at or before t_1. In general, if the ith round ends at time step t_i, then the $(i+1)$st round begins at time step $t_i + 1$ and ends at the earliest time step $t_{i+1} > t_i + 1$ such that at least $6hP$ steal attempts were initiated at time steps between $t_i + 1$ and t_{i+1}, inclusive. We say that a given round of steal attempts *occurs* while some instruction γ is critical if all of the steal attempts that comprise the round are initiated at time steps when γ is critical.

For any multithreaded computation G, a *delay sequence*, denoted by $\mathcal{D}(G)$, is a 3-tuple $\langle U(G), R, \Pi \rangle$ satisfying the following conditions: (1) $U(G) = \langle \gamma_1, \gamma_2, \ldots, \gamma_L \rangle$ is a critical path; (2) R is a positive integer; (3) $\Pi = \langle \pi_1, \pi_1', \pi_2, \pi_2', \ldots, \pi_L, \pi_L' \rangle$ is a partition of the integer R (that is, $R = \sum_{i=1}^{L} (\pi_i + \pi_i')$), such that $\pi_i' \in \{0, 1\}$, for each $i \in [L]$. We define the ith *group* of rounds to be the π_i consecutive rounds starting after the r_ith round, where $r_i = \sum_{j=1}^{i-1} (\pi_j + \pi_j')$.

Assume that Alg is any work-stealing, scheduling algorithm and consider any execution schedule $\mathcal{X}_{\mathsf{Alg}}(G, P)$, produced by Alg for the execution of G on a P-processor parallel computer. A delay sequence $\mathcal{D}(G) = \langle U(G), R, \Pi \rangle$ such that $U(G) = \langle \gamma_1, \ldots, \gamma_L \rangle$ and $\Pi = \langle \pi_1, \pi_1', \ldots, \pi_L, \pi_L' \rangle$, is said to *occur* during the execution of G by some execution schedule $\mathcal{X}_{\mathsf{Alg}}(G, P)$, if the critical path $U(G)$ occurs during the execution and for each $i \in [L]$, all π_i steal attempt rounds in the ith group occur while task γ_i is critical.

3 A Randomized Distributed Scheduling Algorithm

3.1 Description

The algorithm is online, distributed and works in an asynchronous, randomized, work-stealing fashion. Each processor maintains a data structure of ready threads with two endpoints, **top** and **bottom**, which is called *ready list*. The ready list is always sorted, according to the height of the threads it contains. Threads of higher height occupy positions in the ready list closer to the bottom end. We further associate to each thread a timestamp. When a thread is spawned it receives a timestamp equal to the value of the local clock of the processor in whose ready list is placed.

Some of the elements of the ready list of each processor are linked to one another in a way that they comprise a doubly linked list, called the *enabling list*. We will explain which elements of the ready list participate in the construction of the enabling list below. The enabling list has two endpoints, **start** and **end**, and it is always sorted according to the timestamps of threads it contains. Threads of larger timestamps reside in positions closer to the end of the enabling list. Each processor p maintains a pointer, called $\mathbf{uptr}_p$, which points to an appropriate element of p's read list. We will explain how each processor maintains pointer **uptr** below.

Algorithm SRWS is a distributed algorithm; thus, each one of the processors runs its own internal scheduler, external scheduler and dependency resolver. However, these components operate in the same way on every processor. The algorithm starts with all ready lists empty, except from the ready list of the processor where the root thread is initiated. All enabling lists are initially empty, and all uptr pointers are initially null.

The internal scheduler of some processor p pushes and pops threads in its processor's ready list from the bottom, like if it were a stack. More specifically, the internal scheduler of p removes the bottommost thread of its processor's ready list and starts work on it. If this bottommost thread belongs to the enabling list, the internal scheduler updates the appropriate pointers of the enabling list. If pointer $uptr_p$ points to this thread, $uptr_p$ is updated to null. The internal scheduler works on this bottommost thread until it spawns, stalls, dies or enables a stalled thread, in which case it performs according to the following rules: (1) If a thread Γ_i spawns a child thread Γ_j, then Γ_i is placed on the bottom of the ready list, and the internal scheduler continues work on Γ_j. If pointer $uptr_p$ was null before the spawn, it is updated to point to Γ_i. (2) If a thread Γ_i enables a stalled thread Γ_j, the dependency resolver runs. (3) If a thread Γ_i stalls or dies, its internal scheduler checks its ready list. If the list contains any threads, then the internal scheduler removes and begins work on the bottommost thread. If the bottommost thread belongs to the enabling list, the internal scheduler updates the appropriate pointers of the enabling list. If pointer $uptr_p$ points to the bottommost thread, $uptr_p$ is updated to null. If the ready list is empty, the external scheduler runs, and tries to obtain work from other processors. In case a thread enables another thread and dies, the dependency resolver runs first, before the actions for dying.

The dependency resolver of each processor works as follows. If a thread Γ_i enables a stalled thread Γ_j, the now ready thread Γ_j is placed in the proper position, according to its priority, at the ready list of Γ_i's processor. The timestamp of thread Γ_j takes the value of the local clock at the current time step of the processor, in whose ready list Γ_i resides. Moreover, Γ_j participates in the construction of the enabling list (that is, it becomes one of its elements).

The external scheduler of any processor works as a thief and tries to steal work from a victim processor, which has been chosen uniformly at random. The external scheduler queries the ready list of the victim processor[1] and if it is non-empty it steals some thread of the processor's ready list. To choose which thread to steal the thief processor works as follows. The timestamp of the first thread in the enabling list is compared to the timestamp of the thread pointed by pointer uptr and the thread of smallest timestamp between the two is stolen. If pointer start is null, the thread pointed by uptr is stolen. If pointer uptr is null, the thread pointed by start is stolen. If the thread pointed by uptr is stolen, pointer uptr is updated to point to the next element towards the bottommost

---

[1] In message-passing systems, a stealing attempt to the ready list of a victim processor can be implemented by sending a message to this processor. The external scheduler of each processor is then responsible to process this kind of messages.

thread of p's ready list. If there is no such element, it takes the value `null`. If the ready list of the victim processor is empty, the thief processor selects another victim processor uniformly at random and this procedure is repeatedly applied till a victim processor with a non-empty ready list is found. When the external scheduler of a processor achieves to obtain work, the control pass to the internal scheduler of the processor again.

3.2 Properties

For each integer $n \geq 1$, denote $[n] = \{1, \ldots, n\}$. Our first proposition presents important properties of pointer `uptr`. Roughly speaking, Proposition 1 asserts that the threads comprising the enabling list of some processor p occupy the topmost positions in its ready list; moreover, pointer $\texttt{uptr}_p$ points the topmost element in p's ready list that does not belong in the enabling list.

Proposition 1. *Consider any strict multithreaded computation G and let $P > 1$ be any integer. Assume that an arbitrary processor $p \in [P]$ is working on a thread at some given time step during the course of an execution of G according to some execution schedule $\mathcal{X}_{\mathsf{SRWS}}(G, P)$. Let Γ_0 be the thread that p is working on, let n be the number of threads in p's ready list and let $\Gamma_1, \Gamma_2, \ldots, \Gamma_n$ denote the threads in p's ready list ordered from bottom to top, so that Γ_1 is bottommost and Γ_n is topmost. If pointer `uptr` is not `null` and points to thread Γ_m, threads in p's ready list satisfy the following properties:*

(1) *for all $i = 1, \ldots, m$, (a) thread Γ_{i-1} is a child of thread Γ_i in the spawn tree; (b) thread Γ_{i-1} has larger timestamp than thread Γ_i; (c) thread Γ_i has not been worked on since it spawned thread Γ_{i-1}, so that thread Γ_i is not an element of the enabling list;*

(2) *if $n > m$, for all $i = m+1, \ldots, n-1, n$, thread Γ_i is an element of the enabling list.*

Next proposition establishes that a thread can be stolen from some processor's ready list only after all its ancestor threads of smaller timestamp in p's ready list have been stolen.

Proposition 2. *Let G be any multithreaded computation and let $P > 1$ be any integer. Assume that an arbitrary processor $p \in [P]$ is working on a thread at some given time step t during the course of an execution of G by some execution schedule $\mathcal{X}_{\mathsf{SRWS}}(G, P)$. Let Γ, Γ' be threads in p's ready list such that thread Γ is an ancestor of thread Γ' and Γ has a smaller timestamp than Γ'. Then, thread Γ' can not be stolen from p's ready list, unless thread Γ is stolen.*

The following proposition presents fundamental properties of the structure of the ready list of any processor. These properties are very important for proving the performance bounds of our algorithm.

Proposition 3. *Consider any strict multithreaded computation G and let $P > 1$ be any integer. Assume that an arbitrary processor $p \in [P]$ is working on a thread at some given time step during the course of an execution of G according to some execution schedule $\mathcal{X}_{\mathrm{SRWS}}(G, P)$. Let Γ_0 be the thread that p is working on, let n be the number of threads in p's ready list and let $\Gamma_1, \Gamma_2, \ldots, \Gamma_n$ denote the threads in p's ready list ordered from bottom to top, so that Γ_1 is bottommost and Γ_n is topmost. If $n > h+1$, then the threads in p's ready list satisfy the following properties: (1) for all $i = 1, \ldots, n - h$, thread Γ_{i-1} is a child of thread Γ_i in the spawn tree; (2) for all $i = 1, \ldots, n - h - 1$, thread Γ_i has not been worked on since it spawned Γ_{i-1}; (3) if $i \in \{h+1, \ldots, n\}$, for all $l = 0, \ldots, i - h - 1$, thread Γ_l has larger timestamp than thread Γ_i.*

Sketch of Proof. The proof is by induction on execution time. For the basis case, where $t = t_0$, all claims hold vacuously, since the only ready thread is the root thread. For proving the induction step we study several cases on the action taken by the task executed at some processor p one time step before the considered time step. The most difficult case to consider is when the task enables a stalled thread. We use Propositions 1 and 2 to prove a collection of statements, the most important of which are the following: (1) the enabled thread is placed in one of the h topmost positions of p's ready list; (2) for any thread Γ, which has been placed in p's ready list at some time step t for the last time, no l-descendant of Γ, where $l > h$, exists in p's ready list at time step t; moreover, (3) processor p does not commence work-stealing after time step t, while simultaneously (4) it is not possible any such descendant to be placed in p's ready list by enabling. Thus, all these descendants should be spawned in p's read list. We then prove that due to particular properties of both processor's external stealers and dependency resolvers, as well as due to the way timestamps and pointers **uptr** are updated, no such thread can be stolen from p's ready list. We use the above facts to prove the stated claims.

We continue to prove important properties of critical tasks. We start by proving that during the execution of a multithreaded computation by algorithm SRWS, a critical task, residing in the ready list of some processor p, is either an element of p's enabling list or pointer **uptr**$_p$ points to it.

Proposition 4. *Consider a strict multithreaded computation G and let $P > 1$ be any integer. At every time step during the course of an execution of G according to some execution schedule $\mathcal{X}_{\mathrm{SRWS}}(G, P)$, each critical task must be the ready task of a thread that either is an element of the enabling list of some processor p or pointer **uptr**$_p$ points to it.*

The following proposition states that during the execution of any strict multithreaded computation by Algorithm SRWS on a parallel computer with P processors, any critical task executes after at most $(2h + 1)$ steal requests have been serviced on the ready list of the processor that the thread containing this task resides.

Proposition 5. *Consider any strict multithreaded computation G and let $P > 1$ be any integer. Assume that γ is the critical task of a thread Γ residing in the ready list of processor $p \in [P]$, at some time step during the course of an execution of G according to some execution schedule $\mathcal{X}_{\text{SRWS}}(G, P)$. Then, after at most $(2h+1)$ steal requests have been serviced on processor p, task γ executes.*

Sketch of Proof. We prove that there exist at most h ancestors and at most h descendants with larger timestamp than the thread that γ belongs, in one processor's ready list. Moreover, we prove that after $2h$ steal attempts have been serviced by processor p, all these threads have been stolen and either γ has already been executed or it is to be stolen next, as needed.

We next prove that during the execution of any strict multithreaded computation by Algorithm SRWS on a P-processor parallel computer, the probability that $r > 1$ rounds of steal attempts occur while any particular task is critical is exponentially decreasing with hr.

Proposition 6. *Consider any strict multithreaded computation G and let $P > 1$ be any integer. Then, for any task γ and any integer $r > 1$, the probability that r rounds occur during the course of an execution of G according to some execution schedule $\mathcal{X}_{\text{SRWS}}(G, P)$, while γ is critical is at most e^{-2hr}.*

We finally bound the probability that a particular delay sequence occurs during the execution of a strict multithreaded computation by Algorithm SRWS.

Proposition 7. *Consider any multithreaded computation G and let $P > 1$ be any integer. Assume that $\mathcal{D}(G) = \langle U(G), R, \Pi \rangle$ is any arbitrary delay sequence such that $U(G)$ is a critical path of length L. Then, the following holds for the probability that $\mathcal{D}(G)$ occurs during the execution of G according to some execution schedule $\mathcal{X}_{\text{SRWS}}(G, P)$: $\mathbf{P}[\mathcal{D}(G) \text{occurs}] \leq e^{-2h(R-2L)}$.*

3.3 Complexity

In this section, we present upper bounds on the performance of Algorithm SRWS.

Theorem 1. *Consider any strict multithreaded computation G and let $P > 1$ be any integer. Then, (1) $S_{\text{SRWS}}(G, P) \leq S_1 P$; (2) for any $\epsilon > 0$, with probability at least $1 - \epsilon$, the following holds: $T_{\text{SRWS}}(G, P) \in O(T_1/P + hT_\infty + \log P + \log(1/\epsilon))$; moreover, $\mathcal{E}(T_{\text{SRWS}}(G, P)) \in O(T_1/P + hT_\infty)$; (3) for any $\epsilon > 0$, with probability at least $1 - \epsilon$, $C_{\text{SRWS}}(G, P) \in O(P(hT_\infty + \log(1/\epsilon))(1 + n_d)S_{max})$; moreover, $\mathcal{E}(C_{\text{SRWS}}(G, P)) \in O(PhT_\infty(1 + n_d)S_{max})$.*

Sketch of Proof. We prove that all execution schedules produced by SRWS maintain the busy-leaves property. It has been proved [4] that all execution schedules that maintain the busy-leaves property use only linear expansion of memory. In order to bound the execution time of our algorithm, we bound seperately its work, its stealing time and its waiting time. Then, we add up these three factors and divide by P. Clearly, the work of SRWS on G is $T_1(G)$. For bounding the stealing time, we prove that during the execution of any multithreaded computation if a large number of steal attempts are initiated, a delay sequence occurs. However, Proposition 7 implies that the probability of a delay sequence to occur is exponentially decreasing with the number of rounds of steal attempts. Thus, with high probability, a large number of steal attempts does not occur. We use the bound derived for *SRWS*'s steal time to bound its communication complexity. In order to bound the waiting time of *SRWS*, we use a combinatorial balls and bins game introduced and anlyzed in [5].

4 Conclusion

We have presented a provably good randomized, work-stealing algorithm for strict multithreaded computations. We have analyzed the performance of our algorithm in terms not only of execution time, but also of space and communication complexity, and we have proved that our algorithm is arguably efficient in terms of all these parameters. Our analysis generalizes the one presented in [5] and applies for both shared-memory and message-passing systems. Thus, our work answers one of the major open problems raised in [5], namely, whether there exists any provably efficient scheduling algorithm for the general case of strict multithreaded computations.

Acknowledgments: We would like to thank Robert Blumofe and Charles Leiserson whose work [5] has inspired our work. Robert Blumofe gave us valuable feedback on a preliminary version of this paper and we very much thank him.

References

1. N. S. Arora, R. D. Blumofe and C. G. Plaxton, "Thread Scheduling for Multiprogrammed Multiprocessors," *Proceedings of the Tenth Annual ACM Symposium on Parallel Algorithms and Architectures*, Puerto Vallarta, Mexico, June–July 1998.
2. G. E. Blelloch, P.B. Gibbons and Y. Matias, "Provably efficient scheduling for languages with fine-grained parallelism," *Proceedings of the 7th Annual ACM Symposium on Parallel Algorithms and Architectures*, Santa Barbara, California, pp. 1–12, July 1995.
3. G. E. Blelloch, P. B. Gibbons, Y. Matias and G. J. Narlikar, "Space-efficient scheduling of parallelism with synchronization variables," *Proceedings of the 9th Annual ACM Symposium on Parallel Algorithms and Architectures*, Newport, Rhode Island, pp. 12–23, June 1997.
4. R. D. Blumofe, "Executing Multithreaded Programs Efficiently," Ph.D. Thesis, Department of Electrical Engineering and Computer Science, Massachusetts Institute of Technology, September 1995.
5. R. D. Blumofe and C. E. Leiserson, " Scheduling Multithreaded Computations by Work Stealing," *Proceedings of the 35th Annual IEEE Symposium on Foundations of Computer Science*, pp. 356–368, 1994.
6. R. D. Blumofe and C. E. Leiserson, "Space-Efficient Scheduling of Multithreaded Computation," *SIAM Journal on Computing*, Vol. 27, No. 1, pp. 202–229, February 1998.

7. R. D. Blumofe and D. S. Park, "Scheduling large-scale parallel computations on networks of workstations," *Proceedings of the 3rd International Symposium on High Performance Distributed Computing,* pp. 96–105, San Francisco, California, August 1994.

8. F. W. Burton, "Guaranteeing good memory bounds for parallel programs," *IEEE Transactions on Software Engineering,* Vol. 22, No. 10, October 1996.

9. F. W. Burton, "Storage management in virtual tree machines," *IEEE Transactions on Computers,* Vol. 37, No. 3, pp. 321–328, March 1988.

10. F. W. Burton and M. R. Sleep, "Executing functional programs on a virtual tree of processors," *Proceedings of the Conference on Functional Programming Languages and Computer Architecture,* pp. 187–194, Portsmouth, New Hampshire, October 1981.

11. T. Decker, "Virtual Data Space - A Universal Load Balancing Scheme," *Proceedings of the 4th International Symposium on Solving Irregularly Structured Problems in Parallel,* pp. 159-166, 1997.

12. P. Fatourou and P. Spirakis, "Scheduling Algorithms for Strict Multithreaded Computations," *Proceedings of the 10th Internbational Sumposium on Algorithms and Computation,* pp. 407–416, Osaka, Japan, 1996.

13. P. Fatourou and P. Spirakis, "A New Scheduling Algorithms for General Strict Multithreaded Computations," http://students.ceid.upatras.gr/~faturu/public.htm, 1999.

14. W. Feller, *An Introduction to Probability Theory and its Application,* Second Edition, Vol. 1, John Wiley & Sons, Inc., 1957.

15. R. H. Halstead, "Multilisp: A language for concurrent symbolic computation," *ACM Transactions on Programming Languages and Systems,* Vol. 7, No. 4, pp. 501–538, October 1985.

16. R. M. Karp and Y. Zhang, "Randomized parallel algorithms for backtrack search and branch-and-bound computation," *Journal of the ACM,* Vol. 40, No. 3, pp. 765–789, July 1993.

17. P. Liu, W. Aielo and S. Bhatt, "An atomic model for message passing," *Proceedings of the 5th Annual ACM Symposium on Parallel Algorithms and Architectures (SPAA '93),* pp. 154–163, Velen, Germany, June 1993.

18. L. Rudolph, M. Slivkin-Allalouf and E. Upfal, "A simple load balancing scheme for task allocation in parallel machines," *Proceedings of the 3rd Annual ACM Symposium on Parallel Algorithms and Architectures,* pp. 237–245, Hilton Head, California, July 1991.

19. I. C. Wu and H. T. Kung, "Communication complexity for parallel divide-and-conquer," *Proc. of the 32nd Annual IEEE Symposium on Foundations of Computer Science (FOCS '91),* pp. 151–162, San Juan, Puerto Rico, October 1991.

20. Y. Zhang, *Parallel Algorithms for Combinatorial Search Problems,* PhD Thesis, Department of Electrical Engineering and Computer Science, University of California, Berkeley, Technical Report UCB/CSD 89/543, November 1989.

Consensus Numbers of Transactional Objects

Eric Ruppert

University of Toronto
ruppert@cs.utoronto.ca

Abstract. This paper describes the ability of asynchronous shared-memory distributed systems to solve the consensus problem in a wait-free manner if processes are permitted to perform transactions on the shared memory in a single atomic action. It will be shown that transactional memory is often extremely powerful, even if weak types of shared objects are used and the transactions are short. Suppose T is a type of shared object. For any positive integer m, the transactional type trans(T, m) allows processes to perform up to m accesses to a collection of objects of type T in a transaction. The transaction may also include internal process actions that do not affect the shared memory. For any non-trivial type T, trans(T, m) can solve consensus among $\Omega(2^{m/2})$ processes. A stronger lower bound of $\Omega(2^m)$ is given for a large class of objects that includes all non-trivial read-modify-write types T. If the type T is equipped with operations that allow processes to read the state of the object without altering the state, then trans$(T, 2)$ is capable of solving consensus among any number of processes. This paper also gives a consensus algorithm for n^{m-1} processes using trans$(n\text{-consensus}, m)$ and a consensus algorithm for any number of processes that uses trans$(\text{test\&set}, 3)$.

1 Introduction

It is often difficult to design fault-tolerant algorithms for asynchronous distributed systems and prove them correct. This difficulty arises from uncertainty about the behaviour of processes: they run at arbitrarily varying speeds and are subject to failures. One way to make the job of algorithm designers easier is to allow them to specify that certain groups of operations by one process are to be performed without interruptions by other processes [2, 3, 6, 7, 12, 15]. Here, a general model of transactional shared memory will be considered. A transaction is a programmer-specified block of an algorithm that the scheduler is required to treat as a single atomic action. Typically, distributed systems do not provide transactions as primitive operations, so it would be desirable to implement transactions in software from the more basic primitives provided. In this paper, it is shown that giving the programmer the ability to use transactions greatly increases the power of a shared-memory distributed system, where the power is measured by the system's ability to solve the consensus problem in a wait-free way. In particular, this means that one cannot hope, in general, to implement wait-free transactions in software from the corresponding primitive operations.

This paper considers asynchronous shared-memory systems. A scheduler is free to interleave the steps of processes in an arbitrary way, and processes are subject to halting failures. All algorithms are required to be *wait-free* [4]: non-faulty processes must correctly complete their executions even if other processes fail or run at varying speeds. Processes communicate by accessing shared data structures called objects. Read/write `registers`, `queues`, and `compare&swap` objects are examples of different types of shared objects. A type of shared object can be specified formally as an I/O automaton [11]. The object has a state, a set of permissible operations, and a set of possible responses to operations. An operation updates the state of the object and returns a response to the process that invoked the operation, in accordance with a transition function that is part of the object specification. All objects considered in this paper are deterministic.

For any object type T and any positive integer m, one can define the transactional type $trans(T, m)$, where m is an upper bound on the length of a transaction. It consists of a collection of objects of type T, called *base objects*, indexed by the natural numbers. Although a potentially infinite number of base objects are permitted, the number of base objects actually used by the algorithms in this paper is polynomial in the number of processes. The type T is called the *base type* of the transactional type. An operation on the transactional object (called a *transaction*) can be thought of as a block of code where any execution of the code performs at most m operations on the base objects and performs no other shared-memory operations. More formally, a transaction is a collection of m (computable) functions $f_1, \ldots, f_m$, where f_i maps tuples of $i - 1$ responses from objects of type T either to "nil" or to an operation on an object of type T and a natural number. Thus, $f_i(r_1, \ldots, r_{i-1})$ gives the operation to be performed and the index of the base object to be accessed during the ith shared-memory access of the transaction when the responses received from the first $i - 1$ shared-memory accesses in the transaction are $r_1, \ldots, r_{i-1}$. If, during some execution of the transaction, the function f_i evaluates to "nil", this indicates that the transaction should terminate after the first $i - 1$ shared-memory accesses.

The consensus problem has been a very useful tool for comparing the power of different shared-memory systems. In the consensus problem, each process begins with an input value and the processes must all output the same value. This common output value must be the input value of some process. Herlihy [4] showed that objects that solve the n-process consensus problem can be used, with `registers`, to implement any other object type in a system of n processes. Thus, the ability of a shared object type to solve the wait-free consensus problem is an important measure of the type's power to implement other types of shared data structures and to solve problems. This result led to the idea of classifying object types according to their consensus numbers [4, 8]. The *consensus number* of an object type T, denoted $cons(T)$, is the maximum number of processes that can solve consensus using objects of type T and `registers`, or infinity if no such maximum exists. In the latter case, the object type is called *universal*, since it can be used to implement any object in a system with any number of processes. This paper studies how much the consensus number of a type T increases when processes are permitted to perform transactions instead of individual operations.

1.1 Related Results

Afek, Merritt and Taubenfeld [1] defined another type of object, called a multi-object, where processes may perform a number of basic operations as a single atomic action. If T is an object type and m is a positive integer, the multi-object multi(T, m) consists of a collection of base objects of type T, indexed by the natural numbers. [1] An operation on the multi-object is a set of up to m operations on the base objects. As is the case for transactional objects, a multi-object has a potentially infinite number of base objects, but algorithms designed for multi-objects typically use only a polynomial number of base objects. In contrast to the adaptive nature of transactional memory, the m accesses of a multi-object operation must be specified in advance. Thus none of the accesses to base objects may depend on the results from other accesses within the same operation on the multi-object. In addition, the m operations that make up an operation on the multi-object must be applied to distinct base objects. Although the latter restriction is not a part of the definition of transactional object types, all of the algorithms in this paper do perform their operations within a transaction on distinct base objects.

Afek, Merritt and Taubenfeld [1] determined cons(multi(T, m)) for several base types T. Ruppert [14] proved a lower bound on the consensus number of multi(T, m) that applies to any type T with cons(T) > 2, and a stronger bound in the case of readable base types T. These results are summarized in the fourth column of Table 1. Since multi(T, m) is a restricted form of trans(T, m), any lower bound on the consensus number of multi(T, m) is automatically a lower bound on the consensus number of trans(T, m). Jayanti and Khanna [9] considered a related kind of multi-object, where no bound was set on the number of base objects that could be accessed in an atomic action. They showed that the consensus number of such a multi-object is always either 1, 2 or infinity.

A number of researchers have studied transactional objects for particular base types. Most of the research has been focussed on implementing versions of transactional multi-objects from universal object types. One type of universal primitive object that has been considered is the compare&swap object. It is equipped with the operation *compare&swap(old, new)*, which updates the state of the object to *new*, if and only if the current state of the object is *old*. Another type is the LL/SC object, which is equipped with two operations: the *load-linked* (*LL*) operation reads the value stored in the object, and the *store-conditional(v)* (*SC*) operation updates it to a new value v. However, a *SC* operation performed by a process succeeds if and only if the object has not been updated since the last *LL* by that process. Israeli and Rappoport [7] described a variety of implementations of versions of LL/SC and compare&swap objects where the *SC* and *compare&swap* operations are generalized to access several objects in a single atomic action. Shavit and Touitou described how to use LL/SC objects for a non-blocking implementation of atomic transactions on read/write registers. (A non-blocking implementation [5] has a weaker notion of fault-tolerance than

---

[1] The type multi(T, m) has previously been denoted T^m in the literature.

Base Type T	T readable?	cons(T)	cons(multi(T,m)) (for $m > 1$)	cons(trans(T,m)) (for $m > 1$)	
trivial	Yes	1	1	1	
register	Yes	1	$2m - 2$ [4]	∞	Thm 3
toggle	Yes	1	∞ [14]	∞	
test&set	No	2	2 [1]	∞ $(m > 2)$	Prop. 8
queue	No	2	∞ [1]	∞	
any non-trivial T	Maybe	n	$\Omega(n\sqrt{m})$ $(n \geq 3)$ [14]	$\Omega(2^{m/2})$	Thm 9
n-consensus	No	n	$\Theta(n\sqrt{m})$ $(n \geq 3)$ [1]	$\Omega(n^{m-1})$	Prop. 4
any readable T	Yes	n	$\Omega(nm)$ $(n \geq 3)$ [14]	∞ (T non-trivial)	Thm 3
T_n	Yes	$n \geq 3$	$\Theta(nm)$ [14]	∞	Thm 3
toggle $\vee T_n$	Yes	n	∞ [14]	∞	
any RMW T	Maybe	n	$\Omega(n\sqrt{m})$ $(n \geq 3)$ [14]	$\Omega(2^m)$ $(n \geq 2)$	Corol. 7

Table 1. Summary of results

wait-freedom: there can never be an infinite execution in which no operation is completed.) Moir [12] gave a similar wait-free implementation. Attiya and Dagan [3] discussed a non-blocking implementation of operations that can access two base objects in a single action, using LL/SC objects as their primitive. They also showed that *LL* and *SC* operations can be used to solve a problem more efficiently if processes may perform operations on more than one base object in a single atomic action.

1.2 New Results

An object type is called *trivial* if it can be simulated without using shared memory at all. For example, if the only operation permitted is a *read* operation, which simply returns the current state of the object, the object is trivial, since all *read* operations can be simulated by returning the initial state of the object as the response. An object type is called *readable* if it is possible to read the state of the object without altering the state. The read operation need not read the entire state in a single action: instead, it might be possible to read the state piece by piece, as in an array of **registers**, for example. Section 2 contains a proof that, for any non-trivial readable type T, trans(T, 2) is universal. Thus, in the case of readable objects, the transactional model is far more powerful than the multi-object model: a multi(**register**, m) object can only solve consensus among $2m - 2$ processes [4], and there are readable types whose consensus numbers increase only by a factor of $\Theta(m)$ in a multi-object setting [14].

Section 3 studies a specific base type called n-consensus. The n-consensus object is equipped with an operation *propose(v)*, which returns the first value proposed to the object. The object may be accessed at most n times and has consensus number n. Afek, Merritt and Taubenfeld showed that the consensus number of the multi-object multi(n-consensus, m) is $\Theta(n\sqrt{m})$. This result does not extend to transactional objects: Sect. 3 shows that $\text{cons}(\text{trans}(n\text{-consensus}, m))$ is at least n^{m-1}.

Section 4 shows that $\text{cons}(\text{trans}(\text{T}, m)) \geq 2^{m-1}$ for a very large class of base types T, which includes all non-trivial read-modify-write (RMW) types [10]. Many commonly studied objects including compare&swap objects, test&set objects and fetch&add objects are RMW types. Section 4 concludes by considering the base type test&set, which is perhaps the simplest kind of RMW object. A test&set object has two states, 0 and 1. Its single operation, *test&set* sets the state to 1, and returns the old value of the state. This type has consensus number two [4]. In fact, even $\text{multi}(\text{test\&set}, m)$ has consensus number two, for any m [1]. However, $\text{trans}(\text{test\&set}, 3)$ is universal.

Section 5 gives a general lower bound of $2^{\lfloor (m-1)/2 \rfloor}$ on $\text{cons}(\text{trans}(\text{T}, m))$ for any non-trivial base type T.

The results about consensus numbers of transactional objects are summarized in the last column of Table 1. The type T_n is a readable version of the n-consensus type, and the toggle type is a simple three-state readable object [14]. The $\vee$ operator used in the table takes two object types as operands. The type $T_1 \vee T_2$ describes an object that behaves either as an object of type T_1 or as an object of type T_2, depending on its initial state. Using $T_1 \vee T_2$ as the base type in a transactional setting effectively allows transactions that can access objects of both types. Thus, there is no real loss of generality in studying transactional objects that use a single base type instead of a collection of different base types.

2 Readable Base Objects

An object is readable if processes may read the object's state without altering it. It is not necessary that processes be able to read the entire state in a single operation; instead they may be able to read it "piecewise". Formally, a *readable* object O has a state set that is a Cartesian product $Q = \bigtimes_{k \in \Gamma} Q_k$, where Γ is an index set and Q_k is a set for each $k \in \Gamma$. The sets Γ and Q_k need not be finite. For each $k \in \Gamma$, processes may execute the operation $read(O, k)$, which returns component k of the current state of O without changing the state of O. In addition to the *read* operations, the object may be equipped with an arbitrary set of other operations. These other operations are called *update* operations. It is assumed that each update operation can change only a finite number of components of the state.

Any object type with a *read* operation that returns the entire state of the object is readable; in this case, $|\Gamma| = 1$. An array of registers whose elements can be read, copied or swapped atomically is another example of a readable type.

For readable objects, it is possible to give a combinatorial characterization of the object types that are capable of solving consensus among n processes. A readable object is called n-*universal* [13] if a set of n processes can be partitioned into two non-empty teams and a single operation can be assigned to each process so that for any group of processes, if each process performs its own operation on an appropriately initialized object X of type T, then each process in the group could determine which team accessed X first, provided that it could see the final state of X. A more formal definition is given below.

Definition 1. *A readable type* T *is n-universal if there exist*
- *a state $q_0 \in Q$,*
- *a partition of the set of processes $\{P_1, \ldots, P_n\}$ into two non-empty teams A and B, and*
- *an update operation op_i, for $1 \leq i \leq n$,*

such that
$$for\ 1 \leq j \leq n, R_{A,j} \cap R_{B,j} = \emptyset,$$
where $R_{A,j}$ is the set of pairs (r, q) for which there exist distinct process indices $i_1, \ldots, i_\alpha$ including j with $P_{i_1} \in A$ such that if $P_{i_1}, \ldots, P_{i_\alpha}$ each perform their operations (in that order) on an object of type T that is initially in state q_0, P_j gets the result r, and the object ends in state q. The set $R_{B,j}$ is defined similarly.

The property of being n-universal characterizes the readable object types that have consensus number at least n.

Theorem 2. [13] *A readable type can be used with* registers *to solve consensus among n processes if and only if it is n-universal.*

The universality of non-trivial readable types may now be proved. Recall that an object is trivial if it can be simulated without using shared memory.

Theorem 3. *For any non-trivial readable type* T, $\mathrm{cons}(\mathrm{trans}(\mathrm{T}, 2)) = \infty$.

Proof. Since T is non-trivial, there must be some update operation op that changes the state of the object from some state q to some other state r.

First it is shown that $\mathrm{trans}(\mathrm{T}, m)$ is, itself, a readable type. It is possible to read each of the base objects (possibly in a piecewise manner), so it is possible to read any component of the transactional object's state without altering the state. In addition, a transaction will satisfy the technical requirement of updating only a finite number of components of the state of the transactional object, since it accesses at most m base objects, and updates a finite number of components of the state of each of them.

By Theorem 2, it suffices to show that $\mathrm{trans}(\mathrm{T}, m)$ is n-universal (as specified in Definition 1) for every natural number n. The initial state q_0 of the transactional object has every base object in state q. Partition a collection of n processes into two teams $A = \{P_1\}$ and $B = \{P_2, \ldots, P_n\}$. Let the base objects of the transactional object be denoted by $O_1, O_2, \ldots$. The operation op_1 assigned to process P_1 is simply an application of the update operation op to O_1. For $i > 1$, assign to process P_i a transaction as its op_i: it first performs a *read* of O_1 and, if the state returned is q, it then applies op to O_i.

Consider any execution where some group of processes each perform their assigned operations. If the process P_1 on team A takes the first step, all of the objects $O_2, \ldots, O_n$ will always remain in state q. However, if a process P_i

on team B takes the first step, it will change the state of O_i to r, and O_i will remain in state r for the rest of the execution. Thus, one can determine whether a process on team A took the first step from the state of the transactional object by checking whether all of the objects $O_2, \ldots, O_n$ are in state q. The object trans$(T, 2)$ is therefore n-universal for any n. □

It follows from this theorem that a readable type T can be used to implement trans$(T, 2)$ if and only if T is either trivial or universal. Furthermore, transactional objects can be much more powerful than ordinary multi-objects. For example, for any integer m greater than one, the multi-object multi$(\text{register}, m)$, which has consensus number $2m - 2$ [4], is incapable of implementing even trans$(\text{register}, 2)$.

3 Consensus Base Objects

This section considers transactional memory that uses base objects of the type n-consensus (defined in Sect. 1.2). The algorithm presented here shows that the ability to use transactions causes an exponential increase in the consensus number of this type. This contrasts with the multi-object setting, where Afek, Merritt and Taubenfeld showed that if the base objects of type T may be accessed by at most n processes, cons$(\text{multi}(T, m))$ is $O(n\sqrt{m})$.

The algorithm uses a collection of tree data structures. Processes access these trees by starting at a leaf and working towards the root. Each node contains an n-consensus object. The nodes at one level of the tree act as a filter to control access to the nodes at the next higher level. The first value proposed to the first tree's root becomes the output of all processes. However, since each base object in the transactional object can be accessed at most n times, information about the output value must be carefully distributed to all processes using a series of other trees that use similar filtering mechanisms to control access to the nodes. The algorithm given here will be adapted in Sections 4 and 5 to prove more general results.

Proposition 4. *The transactional object* trans$(n$-consensus$, m)$ *can be used to solve consensus among* n^{m-1} *processes.*

Proof. When $n = 1$, the result is trivial, so assume that $n \geq 2$. A consensus protocol for $N = n^{m-1}$ processes, $P_1, \ldots, P_N$, will be constructed using a transactional object of type trans$(n$-consensus$, m)$. Arrange the base objects into trees as follows. The first tree, T, is a complete n-ary tree of height $m - 2$. Each of the remaining trees, T_k^j for $1 \leq k \leq n$ and $1 \leq j < n^{m-2}$, consists of a root with one child which is, itself, the root of a complete n-ary tree of height $m - 3$. The tree T will be used to determine the output of the consensus protocol. The remaining trees will be used to distribute this information to all of the processes. A part of the data structure is shown in Fig. 1. The triangles represent complete n-ary trees of height $m - 3$.

Divide the processes into n^{m-2} groups of size n. Associate each group with a different leaf of the tree T. Let G_k be the set of n^{m-2} processes that are

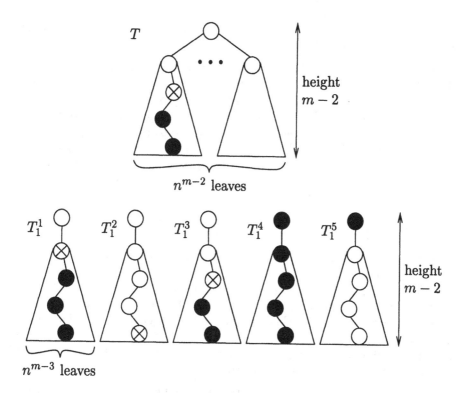

Fig. 1. Accesses to the transactional object by one process

associated with leaf descendants of the kth child of T's root. The trees T_k^j, for $1 \leq j < n^{m-2}$, will be used to distribute information to the processes in G_k. Associate each of the n-process groups in G_k with one of the n^{m-3} leaves of T_k^1. The group is also associated with the corresponding leaf in each of the trees T_k^j, for $2 \leq j < n^{m-2}$.

Process P_i in group G_k begins a transaction in which it will access base objects of the tree T. The process will access several nodes in the tree, each time proposing its own process identifier, i, and receiving a response. The process is said to "win" at a node if the response it receives is the value it proposed, and it is said to "lose" at the node if it receives some other response. First, it accesses the leaf of T with which its group of processes has been associated. If it wins at the leaf, process P_i goes on to access the parent of the leaf, again proposing the value i. It continues in this way, traversing the path from the leaf to the root until it loses. If the process loses at some node below the root, it ends its transaction. If it does reach the root, P_i proposes its own input value (instead of i) to the object located there. Let v be the value that the process P_i receives as a response from the root. The process then proposes the value v to the root of T_k^1, terminates its transaction, outputs v and halts. The access to the root of

T_k^1 has the effect of copying v into that object: any future access to that object will return the value v.

So far, only the processes that accessed the root of T know the outcome. However, this outcome has also been stored in the roots of the trees T_k^1. In an attempt to retrieve this information, each active process in group G_k performs its second transaction on T_k^1. It executes the same algorithm on this tree as it performed on T. (If the process does reach the root of T_k^1, it copies the output value into the root of T_k^2.) The process continues in this way, performing transactions on T_k^2, T_k^3, and so on, until it successfully reaches the root of a tree. Whenever a process accesses the root of a tree T_k^j, it immediately copies the value stored there to the root of the next tree, T_k^{j+1}, as part of the same transaction, outputs the value and then halts. All outputs of this protocol will be the input value of the first process to perform a transaction.

Figure 1 shows the accesses to the transactional object by some process of group G_1 in one execution. The solid circles represent nodes where the process wins. The circles marked with an "X" represent the nodes where it loses. In this example, the process performs five transactions. In the first, it attempts to gain access to the root of T by working its way up from a leaf, but fails. The process then tries unsuccessfully to gain access to the roots of T_1^1, T_1^2 and T_1^3 in its next three transactions. In the final transaction, it successfully reaches the root of T_1^4 and then accesses the root of T_1^5 directly.

It must be shown that the algorithm terminates. Suppose the process P_i attempts to access one of the trees T_k^j, but loses before reaching the root. Then some other process must have performed its transaction on the tree before P_i. The first such process will successfully reach the root and terminate. Thus, each time process P_i fails to access the root of a tree, some other process in G_k terminates. There are $n^{m-2} - 1$ processes in G_k that attempt to access the information from the trees in the set $\{T_k^j : 1 \le j < n^{m-2}\}$, since one process in G_k gets the information directly from the root of T. Thus, process P_i must successfully access the root of one of the $n^{m-2} - 1$ trees T_k^j.

Since any path from a leaf to a root of one of the trees has $m - 1$ nodes, no transaction contains more than m operations on the shared memory. It must also be checked that no more than n processes access any base object, since the behaviour of the base objects is well-defined only under this restriction. For $1 \le j < n^{m-2}$, at most one process will access the root of T_k^j during its $(j+1)$th transaction, since only one process will win at the child of the root. At most one process will access the root of T_k^1 during its first transaction, since only one of G_k's processes can reach the root of T. For $1 < j < n^{m-2}$, at most one process will access the root of T_k^j during its jth transaction, since only one process can reach the root of T_k^{j-1} in its jth transaction. Thus, at most two processes access the root of any tree T_k^j. The leaf of any tree is accessed only by the n processes in the group associated with that leaf. Any other internal node is accessed only by those processes that win at the children of the node, and there are at most n such processes. $\square$

4 Read-Modify-Write Base Types

Consider an object type whose set of possible states is Q. Any function $f : Q \rightarrow Q$ defines a *RMW* operation [10] that updates the state of the object by applying the function f and then returns the previous state of the object. If all operations on the object have this form, the object type is called a RMW type. This class of types includes many important types of objects, such as compare&swap, test&set and fetch&add objects.

To study the consensus power of transactional objects built from RMW types, it is helpful to use a special case of the consensus problem. The team(n_1, n_2) problem is defined to be a restricted version of the general consensus problem among $n_1 + n_2$ processes where the processes are divided (in advance) into two non-empty teams of sizes n_1 and n_2 and all processes on a team receive the same input value. A tournament algorithm was used to prove the following lemma, which says that this restricted version of the consensus problem is just as hard as the general consensus problem.

Lemma 5. [13] *Suppose objects of type* T *and* registers *can be used to solve the team(n_1, n_2) problem for some positive integers n_1 and n_2. Then objects of type* T *can be used, with* registers, *to solve consensus among $n_1 + n_2$ processes.*

Herlihy showed that any non-trivial RMW object type has consensus number at least two [4]. An algorithm similar to the one given in Proposition 4 for the case where $n = 2$ can be used to establish an exponential lower bound on the consensus number of transactional memory built from any non-trivial RMW object type. In fact, the lower bound applies to an even more general class of objects. It is applicable whenever two processes can each apply a single operation and immediately know which operation occurred first. (It will be shown below that any non-trivial RMW type has this property.)

Theorem 6. *Let* T *be any type. Suppose there exist two (not necessarily different) operations op_0 and op_1, and a state q of type* T *so that op_0 and op_1 each return different responses depending on the order that the two operations are performed on an object initially in state q. Then,* $\mathrm{cons}(\mathrm{trans}(\mathrm{T}, m)) \geq 2^{m-1}$.

Proof. For $i = 0, 1$, let R_i be the response returned by op_i when an object of type T is in state q, and R_i' be the response returned by op_i when it is preceded by the other operation, op_{1-i}. The hypothesis requires that $R_0 \neq R_0'$ and $R_1 \neq R_1'$.

Consider a system with 2^{m-1} processes. Partition the set of processes into two non-empty teams, A and B, each with 2^{m-2} processes. By Lemma 5, it suffices to show that $\mathrm{trans}(\mathrm{T}, m)$ can solve the team$(2^{m-2}, 2^{m-2})$ problem.

Arrange the base objects into trees and assign groups of processes to each leaf as in the proof of Proposition 4 for the case where $n = 2$. Processes on team A should be assigned to the left subtree of T, and processes on team B should be assigned to the right subtree of T. Initialize all base objects to the state q.

The team consensus protocol will mimic the operation of the algorithm given in Proposition 4 with $n = 2$. However, instead of agreeing on an input value, the algorithm will be used to agree on the team of the first process to access the transactional object. Once this can be accomplished, it is easy to solve the team$(2^{m-2}, 2^{m-2})$ problem: each process first writes its input value into a register belonging to its team, and when the identity of the winning team is known, the value stored in that team's register is returned as the output.

To simulate the filtering action of a node below the root of a tree, one process that accesses the node performs op_0 and the other process performs op_1. If the process that performed op_i receives the response R_i, then it has won at that node. If it receives the response R_i', then it has lost at that node. The two processes that access the root of T determine which team accessed the root first in exactly the same way.

To simulate the operation that stores a value into the root of T_k^j (during the jth transaction performed by a process), the process applies the operation op_0 to the object if and only if it wants to record the fact that a process from team B took the first step. If it wants to indicate that a process from team A took the first step, it does nothing. To simulate the operation that reads the contents of the root of T_k^j (during the $(j+1)$th transaction performed by a process), the process applies the operation op_1 to the base object located at the root. It interprets the response R_1 as indicating that a process from team A went first, and the response R_1' as indicating that a process from team B went first.

Clearly, each transaction contains at most m operations on base objects. The correctness of the algorithm can be shown in exactly the same way as in the proof of Proposition 4. $\square$

Corollary 7. *For any non-trivial RMW type* T, *cons(trans(T, m))* $\geq 2^{m-1}$.

Proof. Since T is non-trivial, there exists some operation, op, that applies a function f with $f(q) \neq q$ for some state q. Otherwise, one could trivially simulate T without using shared memory by returning the initial state of the object as the response to every operation. The operation op can be used as both operations op_0 and op_1 of Theorem 6. If op is performed when the object is in state q, it returns the response q. However, if op is performed when another op has already been performed on an object in state q, the second op returns a different response, $f(q)$. The lower bound follows from Theorem 6. $\square$

The test&set object defined in Sect. 1.2 is perhaps the most basic non-trivial RMW type. The following proposition demonstrates that this very simple type becomes even more powerful in the transactional setting than Corollary 7 suggests. The algorithm used in the proof has a different flavour from the algorithm in the previous proof. Once a base object has been accessed, further accesses never change its state, so it is not necessary to carefully control access to the base objects to avoid erasing information stored in them.

Proposition 8. *The transactional object* trans(test&set, 3) *is universal.*

Proof. Let n be any integer greater than one. An algorithm will be given that uses trans(test&set, 3) to solve the team$(1, n-1)$ problem. It follows from Lemma 5 that the consensus number of trans(test&set, 3) is infinity. Here, it is described how every process can determine which team first accesses the transactional object. Once this can be done, it is easy to solve team consensus using two additional registers, as in the preceding proof.

Divide the n processes into two teams $A = \{P_1\}$ and $B = \{P_2, \ldots, P_n\}$. The algorithm uses $2n + 1$ base objects, labelled $A_1, \ldots, A_n, B_1, \ldots, B_n$ and C, all of which are initially in state 0.

The object C is used to determine which team wins: every process will eventually discover which team accessed C first. The other objects are used to distribute the information about the winning team to all of the processes. First, the method of distributing this information will be described informally. Processes access the objects $A_1, \ldots, A_n$ in order so that A_{i+1} is never set to 1 while A_i still has value 0. The same comment applies to the objects $B_1, \ldots, B_n$. Consider some moment in the computation. Let a be the largest index such that A_a has been set to 1. Let b be the largest index such that B_b has been set to 1. The information about the first team to access object C is stored in the other base objects by maintaining the following invariant after each complete transaction.

Invariant: If a process from team A accessed the transactional object first, then $a = b + 1$. If a process from team B accessed the transactional object first, then $b = a + 1$.

Each process retrieves information about which team first accessed the base object C by accessing pairs (A_i, B_i) for increasing values of i until it finds a pair where only one of the two base objects is set to 1.

The algorithm will now be described in detail. Process P_1 performs a single transaction. It first performs a *test&set* operation on object C. If it receives the response 1, P_1 knows that some other process has already accessed C, so it can conclude that a process on team B accessed the transactional object first, and it need not perform any further actions. On the other hand, if it receives the response 0, then it knows it is the first process to access the transactional object. It then performs a *test&set* operation on object A_1 to ensure that the invariant holds and performs no further actions.

The algorithm for a process on team B is more complicated. In the first transaction, the process performs a *test&set* operation on the base object C. If the result is 0, it knows that it is the first process to access the transactional object. It then performs the operation *test&set* on B_1 as part of the same transaction in order to satisfy the invariant. If the process receives the result 1 from C, it knows that some other process has already accessed the transactional object. The process must then use the other base objects to determine which team made the first access. The process performs a number of transactions, accessing A_1 and B_1 in the first transaction, then A_2 and B_2 in the second transaction, and so on, until it gets different responses from two objects A_i and B_i. Suppose that A_i returns 1 and B_i returns 0, indicating that a process from team A accessed the transactional object first. To ensure that the invariant remains true, the process performs a *test&set* operation on A_{i+1} as part of the same transaction. It can then halt, knowing that team A performed the first transaction. The case where A_i returns 0 and B_i returns 1 is symmetric.

It must be checked that this algorithm does terminate. The first process to perform a transaction that accesses the pair of objects A_i and B_i will halt at the completion of that transaction. Thus, at most $n - i$ processes on team B will perform the transaction that accesses A_i and B_i. Thus, every process will perform at most n transactions. It is easy to see that the invariant is true after each complete transaction, and the correctness of the algorithm follows. $\qquad \square$

The algorithm given in this proof can easily be adapted to work for any base type that is equipped with an operation whose first invocation returns a response different from any subsequent invocation's response.

5   A General Bound

Theorem 6 gives a lower bound on the consensus numbers of transactional objects that applies to a very large class of base types. In this section it will be shown that a property which is weaker than the hypothesis of Theorem 6 and is satisfied by *any* non-trivial base type can be used to prove a weaker, but still exponential, lower bound on consensus numbers of transactional objects. The hypothesis of Theorem 6 assumed that two processes can each perform a single operation so that both processes can immediately tell which of the two performed its operation first. The following theorem shows that a similar algorithm will solve consensus even if only one of the two processes can determine which process accessed the base object first. Because of the weaker assumption, processes will have to access two base objects at each node, and this has the effect of halving the tree heights and producing a corresponding reduction in the number of processes that can be assigned to the leaves.

Theorem 9. *For any non-trivial base type* T, $\mathrm{cons}(\mathrm{trans}(\mathrm{T}, m)) \geq 2^{\lfloor (m-1)/2 \rfloor}$.

Proof. First, the non-triviality of T will be used to prove that T has a useful property, similar to the hypothesis of Theorem 6. Since T is non-trivial, the response to some operation, op_0 cannot depend entirely on the state in which the object is initialized. Thus, there is some (shortest) sequence of operations that takes the object from a state where it would return the response R to op_0 into a state where it would return a different response R' to op_0. Let op_1 be the last operation in this sequence, and let q be the state of the object just before op_1 is applied. If an object begins in state q and two processes apply the operations op_0 and op_1, the process applying op_0 can tell whether the other process has already taken its step, by checking whether it gets the response R or R'.

Now, consider a system with $2^{\lfloor (m-1)/2 \rfloor}$ processes, partitioned into two teams A and B of equal size. As in the proof of Theorem 6, it suffices to give an algorithm that allows every process to determine whether a process from team A or from team B accesses the transactional object first.

The base objects are organized into trees as in the proof of Proposition 4 for the case when $n = 2$, except the height of the trees are reduced to $\lfloor (m-3)/2 \rfloor$, and nodes of the trees have two base objects instead of one. (However, the roots of the trees T_k^j need only one base object.) The two objects at a node will be referred to as the left and right objects of that node. All base objects are initialized to the state q. Associate groups of two processes with the leaves of the trees as in Proposition 4.

The algorithm to determine the team containing the process that performed the first transaction will mimic the algorithm of Theorem 6. To simulate the filtering action of the nodes below the roots of trees, one process performs op_0 on the left object and op_1 on the right object, and the other process performs op_1 on the left object and op_0 on the right object. If a process receives the response R from op_0, then the process wins at the node, and if the response is R', then the process loses at the node. The winning team at the root of T is determined in the same way.

To simulate an operation that writes the winning team to the root of T_k^j, a process performs op_1 on the object at that node if and only if it wants to indicate that a process from team B took the first step. Otherwise it does nothing. To simulate the operation that reads the contents of the root of T_k^j, the process performs op_0 on the object in the node. The response R indicates that team A took the first step and the response R' indicates that team B took the first step.

In the worst case, a transaction accesses all base objects on some path from a leaf to a root of a tree plus one base object in another tree. Each transaction therefore contains at most $2(\lfloor (m-3)/2 \rfloor + 1) + 1 \le m$ memory accesses, as required. The proof of correctness is the same as in Proposition 4. $\qquad \square$

Corollary 10. *If* T *is neither trivial nor universal, there is some m such that* T *cannot provide a wait-free implementation of* trans(T, m).

Proof. If $m = 2\log_2(\mathrm{cons}(\mathrm{T})) + 3$, then $\mathrm{cons}(\mathrm{trans}(\mathrm{T}, m)) > \mathrm{cons}(\mathrm{T})$, so $\mathrm{trans}(\mathrm{T}, m)$ is strictly more powerful than T. $\qquad \square$

6 Open Questions

It has been shown that the ability to perform even short transactions can greatly increase the consensus numbers of object types. Can corresponding upper bounds on consensus numbers of transactional objects be proved?

In the multi-object model, memory accesses within an atomic operation must be performed on different base objects. In the transactional model, processes are free to access base objects repeatedly during an atomic action, but this ability was not used in the algorithms given here. Is there any case where the ability to access the same base object repeatedly in a transaction really does help?

Another possible setting for transactional objects would be one where each transaction must perform all of the shared-memory accesses on a single base object. How does such a restriction affect the consensus power of objects? In the case of **test&set** base objects, transactions on a single base object give no additional power, since any such transaction has the same effect as doing a single *test&set* operation. Therefore, this single-object version of transactional memory is strictly weaker than general transactional objects.

Acknowledgements I thank my advisor, Faith Fich, for suggesting many improvements. I also thank the anonymous reviewers for their helpful comments.

References

1. YEHUDA AFEK, MICHAEL MERRITT, AND GADI TAUBENFELD. The power of multi-objects. In *Proc. 15th ACM Symposium on Principles of Distributed Computing*, pages 213–222, 1996.

2. JAMES H. ANDERSON AND MARK MOIR. Universal constructions for multi-object operations. In *Proc. 14th ACM Symposium on Principles of Distributed Computing*, pages 184–193, 1995.

3. HAGIT ATTIYA AND EYAL DAGAN. Universal operations: Unary versus binary. In *Proc. 15th ACM Symposium on Principles of Distributed Computing*, pages 223–232, 1996.

4. MAURICE HERLIHY. Wait-free synchronization. *ACM Transactions on Programming Languages and Systems*, 11(1), pages 124–149, January 1991.

5. MAURICE HERLIHY. A methodology for implementing highly concurrent data objects. *ACM Transactions on Programming Languages and Systems*, 15(5), pages 745–770, November 1993.

6. MAURICE HERLIHY AND J. ELIOT B. MOSS. Transactional memory: Architectural support for lock-free data structures. In *Proc. 20th International Symposium on Computer Architecture*, pages 289–300, 1993.

7. AMOS ISRAELI AND LIHU RAPPOPORT. Disjoint-access-parallel implementations of strong shared memory primitives. In *Proc. 13th ACM Symposium on Principles of Distributed Computing*, pages 151–160, 1994.

8. PRASAD JAYANTI. Robust wait-free hierarchies. *Journal of the ACM*, 44(4), pages 592–614, July 1997.

9. PRASAD JAYANTI AND SANJAY KHANNA. On the power of multi-objects. In *Distributed Algorithms, 11th International Workshop*, volume 1320 of *LNCS*, pages 320–332, 1997.

10. CLYDE P. KRUSKAL, LARRY RUDOLPH, AND MARC SNIR. Efficient synchronization on multiprocessors with shared memory. *ACM Transactions on Programming Languages and Systems*, 10(4), pages 579–601, October 1988.

11. NANCY A. LYNCH. *Distributed Algorithms*, chapter 8. Morgan Kaufmann, 1996.

12. MARK MOIR. Transparent support for wait-free transactions. In *Distributed Algorithms, 11th International Workshop*, volume 1320 of *LNCS*, pages 305–319, 1997.

13. ERIC RUPPERT. Determining consensus numbers. In *Proc. 16th ACM Symposium on Principles of Distributed Computing*, pages 93–99, 1997.

14. ERIC RUPPERT. Consensus numbers of multi-objects. In *Proc. 17th ACM Symposium on Principles of Distributed Computing*, pages 211–217, 1998.

15. NIR SHAVIT AND DAN TOUITOU. Software transactional memory. *Distributed Computing*, 10(2), pages 99–116, February 1997.

Linearizability in the Presence of Drifting Clocks and Under Different Delay Assumptions

Maria Eleftheriou[1] and *Marios Mavronicolas*[2]

[1] AMER World Research Ltd., Nicosia, CYPRUS,
`Eleftheriou.Maria@Cyprus.ACNielsen.com`
[2] Department of Computer Science and Engineering, University of Connecticut,
Storrs, CT 06269–3155, USA
`mavronic@engr.uconn.edu`

Abstract. The cost of using message-passing to implement *linearizable read/write objects* for shared memory multiprocessors with *drifting clocks* is studied. We take as cost measures the *response times* for performing read and write operations in distributed implementations of virtual shared memory consisting of such objects. A collection of necessary conditions on these response times are presented for a large family of assumptions on the network delays. The assumptions include the common one of lower and upper bounds on delays, and bounds on the difference between delays in opposite directions. In addition, we consider *broadcast* networks, where each message sent from one node arrives at all other nodes at approximately the same time.

The necessary conditions are stated in the form of "gaps" on the values that the response times may attain in any arbitrary execution of the system; the ends of the gap intervals depend solely on the delays in a particular execution, and on certain fixed parameters of the system that express each specific delay assumptions. The proofs of these necessary conditions are comprehensive and modular; they consist of two major components. The first component is independent of any particular type of delay assumptions; it constructs a "counter-example" execution, which respects the delay assumptions only if it is *not* linearizable. The second component must be tailored for each specific delay assumption; it derives necessary conditions for any linearizable implementation by requiring that the "counter-example" execution does *not* respect the specific delay assumptions.

Our results highlight inherent limitations on the *best* possible cost for each specific execution of a linearizable implementation. Moreover, our results imply lower bounds on the *worst* possible such costs as well; interestingly, for the last two assumptions on mesage delays, these worst-case lower bounds are products of the *drifting factor* of the clocks and the *delay uncertainty* inherent for the specific assumption.

1 Introduction

Shared memory has become a convenient paradigm of interprocessor communication in contemporary computer systems. Perhaps this is so due to its combined features that, first, it facilitates a natural extension of sequential programming, and, second, it is more high-level than message-passing in terms of semantics. This convenience has favored the evolution of concurrent programming on top of shared memory for the solution of many diverse problems. Thus, supporting shared memory in *distributed memory machines* has become a currently major objective.

Unfortunately, implementing shared memory in a distributed memory machine encounters a lot of complications; these complications are due to the high degree of parallelism and the lack of synchronization between dispersed processors, that are both inherent in a distributed architecture. This necessitates the explicit and precise definition of the guarantees provided by shared memory implemented this way; such definition is called a *consistency condition*. *Linearizability* is a basic consistency condition for concurrent objects of shared memory due to Herlihy and Wing [7]. Informally, linearizability requires that each operation, spanning over an interval of time from its invocation to its response, appears to take effect at some instant in this interval. The use of linearizable data abstractions simplifies both the specification and the proofs of multiple instruction/multiple data shared memory algorithms, and enhances compositionality.

In this work, we continue the study of the impact of timing assumptions on the cost of supporting linearizability in distributed systems; this study has been initiated by Attiya and Welch [2], and continued further by Mavronicolas and Roth [12], Chaudhuri *et al.* [3], Friedman [5], and Kosa [9]. We consider a distributed system that introduces non-negligible timing uncertainty in two significant ways: first, in the synchronization with respect to real time of each individual process, and, second, in the communication among different processes.

Following previous work [2, 3, 5, 9, 12], we consider a model consisting of a collection of application programs running concurrently and communicating through virtual shared memory, which consists of a collection of *read/write objects*. These programs are running in a distributed system consisting of a collection of processes located at the nodes of a communication network. The shared memory abstraction is implemented by a *memory consistency system* (MCS), which uses local memory at each process node. Each MCS process executes a protocol, which defines the actions it takes on operation requests by the application programs. Specifically, each application program may submit requests to access shared data to a corresponding MCS process; the MCS process responds to such a request, based, possibly, on information from messages it receives from other MCS processes. In doing so, the MCS must, throughout the network, provide linearizability with respect to the values returned to application programs.

We take as cost measures the *response times* for performing read and write operations on read/write objects in such a distributed system. However, a first major diversion from previous works [2, 3, 5, 9, 12] addressing these particular cost measures is that we show bounds on them that hold for each specific execution of the system, while bounds established in previous work on the same cost measures hold only for the worst execution. Recent research work in distributed computing theory has addressed bounds that hold for each specific execution in the context of the *clock synchronization* [1, 13] and *connection management* [8, 11] problems. A common argument in support of showing such "per-execution" bounds is that for certain kinds of assumptions on network delays, the costs for the worst-case execution may, in fact, have to be unbounded [1], while one may still want to award algorithms that achieve costs that are the *best possible* for each specific instance [1].

A second major diversion from previous related work [2, 3, 5, 9, 12] is with respect to assumptions on message delays; all that work has considered the relatively simple case where there are lower and upper bounds on message delays. Under this assumption, linearizable implementations of shared memory objects have been designed [3, 5, 12], whose efficiency depends critically on the existence of tight lower and upper bounds on message delays. This assumption, however, may not always apply, since it is often the case that there do not exist tight lower and upper bounds on message delays, while there is some other relevant information about the delays. We draw excellent motivation from the work of Attiya *et al.* [1] on clock synchronization under different delay assumptions to study the problem of implementing linearizable read/write objects in message-passing under the following assumptions on message delays (considered in [1]): (1) There is a lower and an upper bound on delays, $d - u$ and u, respectively. (2) There is a bound ε on the difference between delays in opposite directions; this assumption is supported by experimental results revealing that message delays in opposite directions of a bidirectional link usually come very close (cf. [1]). The clock synchronization problem has been already studied under this assumption [1]. (3) There is a bound β on the difference between the times when different processes receive a broadcast message; this assumption is useful for *broadcast networks* that are used in many local area networks. The clock synchronization problem has been studied under this assumption in [1, 6, 14].

A third major diversion from previous related work is with respect to the amount of synchronization of processes to real time. While that work [2, 3, 5, 9, 12] has assumed "perfect" (non-drifting, but possibly translated) clocks to be available to processes, we allow a small "drift" on the processes' clocks; the impact of this assumption on the time complexity of distributed algorithms has already been studied for the clock synchronization problem (see, e.g., [13]), and the connection management problem [8, 11].

The main contribution of our work is a systematic methodology for proving necessary conditions on the response times of read and write operations, that hold for each specific execution of any linearizable implementation, under a variety of message delay assumptions, and allowing a small "drift" on the processes' clocks. This methodology yields a collection of corresponding necssary conditions. Our proof methodology is modular, and consists of two major components. The first component is independent of the specific type of delay assumptions, while the second one addresses each such type in a special way.

In more detail, the first component starts with a linearizable execution that is chosen in a different way for the write operation, the read operation, and their combination, respectively. In each of the three cases, we use the technique of "retiming," originally introduced by Lundelius and Lynch for showing lower bounds for the clock synchronization problem [10], to transform this execution into another *possible* execution of the system that is *not* linearizable. The transformation maintains the view held by each process in the original execution to the result of the transformation; moreover, the clocks in the latter are still drifting. Roughly speaking, retiming is used to change the timing and the ordering of events in an execution of the system, while precluding any particular process from "realizing" the change.

The second component is tailored for each specific assumption on message delays. More specifically, the starting point of the second component is the result of transforming the original execution, and the corresponding message delays in this result. For each specific assumption on message delays, we insist that the resulting delays confirm to the assumption. This yields corresponding upper and lower bounds on the response time of the read and write operations, as a function of the message delays in the original linearizable execution.

Our lower and upper bounds highlight inherent limitations on the *best* possible cost for each specific execution of a linearizable implementation, as a function of the message delays in the execution, and the parameters associated with each specific assumption on message delays. Moreover, our results imply also $\Omega(\rho^2\varepsilon)$ and $\Omega(\rho^2\beta)$ *worst-case* lower bounds on response times for both write and read operations for the bias model and the model of broadcast networks, respectively. These lower bounds indicate that the timing uncertainty ρ^2 in the drifting clocks model must multiply the delay uncertainty (ε and β, respectively) for each of these models. We have not been able to deduce a corresponding fact for the model with lower and upper bounds on delays. (However, for the special case where $\rho = 1$, our general results imply worst-case results that are identical to those in [2, 12].) This model appears to be stronger than the previous two since it does not allow unbounded delays; we conjecture that linearizable implementations allowing for response times $o(\rho^2 u)$ for both write and read operations are possible for this model.

2 Framework

For the system model, we follow [2, 12]. We consider a collection of *application programs* running concurrently and communicating through virtual shared memory, consisting of a collection $\mathcal{X}$ of *read/write objects*, or *objects* for short. Each object $X \in \mathcal{X}$ attains values from a *domain*, a set $\mathcal{V}$ of *values*. We assume a system consisting of a collection of *nodes*, connected via a *communication network*. The shared memory abstraction is implemented by a *memory consistency system* (MCS), consisting of a collection of MCS processes, one at each node, that use local memory, execute some local protocol, and communicate through sending *messages* along the network. Each MCS process p_i, located at node i, is associated with an application program P_i; p_i and P_i interact by using *call* and *response* events.

Call events at p_i represent initiation of operations by the application program P_i; they are $\mathsf{Read}_i(X)$ and $\mathsf{Write}_i(X, v)$, for all objects $X \in \mathcal{X}$ and values $v \in \mathcal{V}$. *Response events* represent responses by p_i to operations initiated by the application program P_i; they are $\mathsf{Return}_i(X, v)$ and $\mathsf{Ack}_i(X)$, for all objects $X \in \mathcal{X}$ and values $v \in \mathcal{V}$. *Message-delivery events* represent delivery of a message from any other MCS process to p_i. *Message-send events* represent sending of a message by p_i to any other MCS process.

For each i, there is a physical, real-time clock at node i, readable by MCS process p_i but not under its control, that may drift away from the rate of real time. Formally, a *clock* is a strictly increasing (hence, unbounded), piece-wise continuous function of real time $\gamma_i : \Re \to \Re$. Denote $\widetilde{\gamma}_i$ the *inverse* of γ. Fix any constant $\rho > 1$, called *drift*. A ρ-*drifting clock*, or *drifting clock* for short, is a clock $\gamma_i : \Re \to \Re$ such that for all real times $t_1, t_2 \in \Re$ with $t_1 < t_2$, $1/\rho \leq (\gamma_i(t_2) - \gamma_i(t_1))/(t_2 - t_1) \leq \rho$. Define ρ^2 to be the *drifting factor* of a ρ-drifting clock. The clocks cannot be modified by the processes. Processes do not have access to real time; instead, each process obtains information about time from its clock. The call, message-delivery and timer-expire events are called *interrupt* events. The response, message-send and timer-set events are called *react* events.

Each MCS process p_i is modeled as an automaton with a (possibly infinite) set of states, including an initial state, and a transition function. Each interrupt event at MCS process p_i causes an application of its transition function, resulting in a *computation step*. The transition function is a function from tuples of a state, a clock time and an interrupt event to tuples of a state and sets of react events. Thus, the transition function takes as input the current state, the local clock time, and an interrupt event, and returns a new state, a set of response events for the corresponding application program, a set of messages to be sent to other MCS processes, and a set of timer-set events. A *history for an MCS process p_i with clock γ_i* is a mapping h_i from $\Re$ (real time) to finite sequences of computation steps by p_i such that: (1) For each real time t, there is only a finite number of times $t' < t$ such that the corresponding sequence of steps $h_i(t')$ is non-empty; thus, the concatenation of all such sequences in real-time order is also a sequence, called the *history sequence*. (2) The old state in the first computation step in the history sequence is p_i's initial state. (3) The old state of each subsequent computation step is the new state of the previous computation step in the history sequence. (4) For each real time t, the clock time component of every computation step in the sequence $h_i(t)$ is equal to $\gamma_i(t)$. (5) For each real time t, there is at most one computation step whose interrupt event is a timer-set event; this step is ordered last in the sequence $h_i(t)$. (6) At most one call event is "pending" at a time; this outlaws pipelining or prefetching at the interface between p_i and P_i. (8) For each call event, there exists a matching response event in some subsequent computation step of the history sequence.

Each pair of matching call and response events forms an *operation*. The call event marks the start of the operation, while the response event marks its end. An operation *op* is *invoked* when the application program issues the appropriate call event for *op*; *op terminates* when the MCS process issues the appropriate response for *op*. For a given MCS, an *execution* σ is a set of histories, one for each MCS process, such that for any pair of MCS processes p_i and p_j, $i \neq j$, there is a one-to-one correspondence between the messages sent by p_i to p_j and those delivered at p_j that were sent by p_i. Use this message correspondence to define the *delay* of any message in an execution to be the real time of delivery minus the real time of sending. By definition of execution, a zero lower bound and an infinite upper bound hold on delay. Define $\Delta_{ij}^{(e)}$ to be the set of delays of messages from MCS process p_i to MCS process p_j in execution e. Two executions are *equivalent* [10] if each process has the same history sequence and associated local clock times in both. Intuitively, equivalent executions are indistinguishable to the processes, and only an "outside observer" with access to real time can tell them apart.

We continue with specific assumptions on the delays, borrowing from [1,13]. Each assumption gives rise to a particular delay model with an associated set of admissible executions. The assumption of lower and upper bounds on the delays [2,5,12] places a lower and an upper bound on the delay for any message exchanged between any pair of processes. Fix some known parameters u and d, $0 \leq u \leq d \leq \infty$; u is the *delay uncertainty*, while d is the *maximum delay*. Execution σ is *admissible* if for each pair of MCS processes p_i and p_j, for every message m in σ from p_i to p_j, $d_\sigma(\mathrm{m}) \in [d - u, d]$.

The assumption of bounds on the round trip delay bias [1, Section 5.2] requires that the difference between the delays of any pair of messages in opposite direction be bounded. Fix any constant $\varepsilon > 0$, called the *delay uncertainty*. Formally, an execution σ is *admissible* if for any pair processes p_i and p_j, and for any pair of messages m and m' received by p_i from p_j and received by p_j from p_i, respectively, $|d_\sigma(\mathrm{m}) - d_\sigma(\mathrm{m}')| \leq \varepsilon$.

The assumption of multicast networks has been studied in [1,4,6,14] in the context of the clock synchronization problem; our presentation follows [1, Section 5.3]. To define this assumption, we replace message-send events by events of the form $\mathsf{Broadcast}_i(\mathrm{m})$ at the MCS process p_i, for all messages m; such events represent a broadcast of m to all MCS processes. The definition of an execution is modified so that for any pair of processes p_i and p_j, $i \neq j$, there is a one-to-one correspondence between the messages broadcast by p_i, and those delivered at p_j and broadcast by p_i. Use this message correspondence to define the *delay of message m to process p_j in execution σ*, denoted $d_\sigma(\mathrm{m}, p_j)$, to be the real time of delivery at p_j in σ minus the real time of broadcast by p_i in σ. Fix any constant $\beta > 0$, called the *broadcast accuracy*. Execution σ is *admissible* if for any process p_i, for any message m broadcast by p_i, $|d_\sigma(\mathrm{m}, p_j) - d_\sigma(\mathrm{m}, p_k)| \leq \beta$; that is, m reaches p_j at most β time units later it reaches p_k, and vice versa.

Each object X has a *serial specification* [7], which describes its behavior in the absence of concurrency and failures. Formally, it defines: (1) A set $Op(X)$ of *operations on X*, which are ordered pairs of *call* and *response* events. Each operation $op \in Op(X)$ has a value $val(op)$ associated with it. (2) A set of *legal operation sequences for X*, which are the allowable sequences of operations on X.

For each process p_i, $Op(X)$ contains a *read* operation $[\mathsf{Read}_i(X), \mathsf{Return}_i(X, v)]$ on X and a *write* operation $[\mathit{Write}_i(X, v), \mathit{Ack}_i(X)]$ on X, for all values $v \in \mathcal{V}$; v is the value associated with each of these operations. The set of legal operation sequences for X contains all sequences of operations on X for which, for any read operation rop in the sequence, either $val(rop) = \bot$ and there is no preceding write operation in the sequence, or $val(wop) = val(rop)$ for the latest preceding write operation wop. A sequence of operations τ for a collection of processes and objects is *legal* if, for every object $X \in \mathcal{X}$, the restriction of τ to operations on X, denoted $\tau \mid X$, is in the set of legal operation sequences for X.

Given an execution σ, let $ops(\sigma)$ be the sequence of call and response events appearing in σ in real-time order, breaking ties for each real time t as follows: First, order all response events whose matching call events occur before time t, using process identification numbers (*ids*) to break any remaining ties. Then, order all operations whose call and response events both occur at time t. Preserve the relative ordering of operations for each process, and break any remaining ties using again process ids. Finally, order all call events whose matching response events occur after time t, using process ids to break any remaining ties. An execution σ specifies a partial order $\xrightarrow{\sigma}$ on the operations appearing in σ: for any operations op_1 and op_2 appearing in σ, $op_1 \xrightarrow{\sigma} op_2$ if the response for op_1 precedes the call for op_2 in $ops(\sigma)$; that is, $op_1 \xrightarrow{\sigma} op_2$ if op_1 completely precedes op_2 in $ops(\sigma)$. Given an execution σ, an operation sequence τ is a *serialization* of σ if it is a permutation of $ops(\sigma)$. A serialization τ of σ is a *linearization* of σ if it extends $\xrightarrow{\sigma}$; that is, if $op_1 \xrightarrow{\sigma} op_2$, then $op_1 \xrightarrow{\tau} op_2$. Let τ be a sequence of operations. Denote by $\tau \mid i$ the restriction of τ to operations at process p_i; similarly, denote by $\tau \mid X$ the restriction of τ to operations on the object X. For an execution σ, these definitions can be extended in the natural way to yield $ops(\sigma) \mid i$ and $ops(\sigma) \mid X$. An execution σ is *linearizable* [7] if there exists a legal linearization τ of σ such that for each MCS process p_i, $ops(\sigma) \mid i = \tau \mid i$. An MCS is a *linearizable implementation* of $\mathcal{X}$ if every admissible execution of the MCS is linearizable.

The efficiency of an implementation $\mathcal{A}$ of $\mathcal{X}$ is measured by the *response time* for any operation on an object $X \in \mathcal{X}$. Given a particular MCS $\mathcal{A}$ and a read/write object X implemented by it, the time $|op_{\mathcal{A}}(X, \sigma)|$ taken by an operation op on X in an admissible execution σ of $\mathcal{A}$ is the maximum difference between the times at which the response and call events of op occur in σ, where the maximum is taken over all occurrences of op in σ. In particular, we denote by $|\mathbf{R}_{\mathcal{A}}(X, \sigma)|$ and $|\mathbf{W}_{\mathcal{A}}(X, \sigma)|$ the maximum time taken by a read and a write operation, respectively, on X in σ, where the maximum is taken over all occurrences of the corresponding operations in σ. Define $|\mathbf{R}_{\mathcal{A}}(X)|$ (resp., $|\mathbf{W}_{\mathcal{A}}(X)|$) to be the maximum of $|\mathbf{R}_{\mathcal{A}}(X, \sigma)|$ (resp., $|\mathbf{W}_{\mathcal{A}}(X, \sigma)|$) over all executions σ of $\mathcal{A}$.

Fix e to be any execution, and let $op = [\mathsf{Call}(op), \mathsf{Response}(op)]$ be any operation in e. We denote by $t_c^{(e)}(op)$ and $t_r^{(e)}(op)$ the (real) times at which $\mathsf{Call}(op)$ and $\mathsf{Response}(op)$, respectively, occur in e. We use $val^{(e)}(op)$ to denote the value associated with the "execution" of operation op in e.

3 Writes

A construction of a non-linearizable, if admissible, execution is presented in Section 3.1; this execution is used in Section 3.2 for deriving necessary conditions for the write operation under specific assumptions on the delays. We refer to any linearizable implementation $\mathcal{A}$ of read/write objects, including an object X with at least two writers p_i and p_j, and a distinct reader p_k.

3.1 A Non-Linearizable, if Admissible, Execution

This construction is based on one in [2, Section 4] and [12, Section 5]. We start with an admissible execution e, in which p_i writes x_i to X, then p_j writes x_j to X, $x_j \neq x_i$, and finally p_k reads x_j from X; moreover, we assume that all clocks in e run at a rate of σ for some constant σ such that $1/\rho \leq \sigma \leq \rho$. If p_i's history is shifted later, while p_j's history is shifted earlier, each by an appropriate amount, while both are either "stretched" or "shrinked" by a factor of σ, depending on whether $1 \leq \sigma \leq \rho$ or $1/\rho \leq \sigma \leq 1$, the result is an execution e', not necessarily admissible, in which the write operation by p_j precedes the write operation by p_i, which, in turn, precedes the read operation by p_k. If, in addition, all clocks are correspondingly "stretched" or "shrinked" by the same factor of σ, all three processes still "see" the same events occurring at the same local time and cannot, therefore, distinguish between e and e'; thus, in particular, p_k still reads x_j from X, which implies that e', if admissible, is not linearizable. We now present some details of the construction.

By the serial specification of X, there exists an admissible execution e of $\mathcal{A}$ consisting of the following operations at processes p_i, p_j, and p_k: p_i performs a write operation wop_i on X with $t_c^{(e)}(wop_i) = 0$ and $val^{(e)}(wop_i) = x_i$; p_j performs a write operation wop_j on X with $t_c^{(e)}(wop_j) = |wop_i|$ and $val^{(e)}(wop_j) = x_j$; p_k performs a read operation rop_k on X with $t_c^{(e)}(rop_k) = |wop_i| + \max\{|wop_i|, |wop_j|\}$; apparently, $\max\{|wop_i|, |wop_j|\} = |\mathbf{W}_{\mathcal{A}}(X, e)|$, so that $t_c^{(e)}(rop_k) = |wop_i| + |\mathbf{W}_{\mathcal{A}}(X, e)|$. Moreover, assume that $\gamma_i^{(e)}(t) = \gamma_j^{(e)}(t) = \gamma_k^{(e)}(t) = \sigma t$ for some positive constant σ such that $1/\rho \leq \sigma \leq \rho$, so that all clocks are ρ-drifting. (We omit reference to clocks of other processes in this extended abstract.)

Since $\mathcal{A}$ is a linearizable implementation and e is an admissible execution, e is a linearizable execution. Thus, there exists a legal linearization τ of e such that for each MCS process p, $ops(e) \mid p = \tau \mid p$. We use the construction of e to show simple properties of the sequence τ, namely that $wop_i \xrightarrow{\tau} wop_j$, and that $wop_j \xrightarrow{\tau} rop_k$. Since τ is a legal operation sequence, these properties imply that $val^{(e)}(rop_k) = val^{(e)}(wop_j) = x_j$.

We now "perturb" the (admissible) execution e in order to obtain another execution e', which is not necessarily admissible; however, we shall show that if e' is admissible, then it is not linearizable. We construct e' as follows. (1) Set $\gamma_i^{(e')}(t) = t/\sigma - \sigma |\mathbf{W}_{\mathcal{A}}(X, e)|$, $\gamma_j^{(e')}(t) = t/\sigma + \sigma |\mathbf{W}_{\mathcal{A}}(X, e)|$, and $\gamma_k^{(e')}(t) =$

t/σ. (2) For any process p_l with clock γ'_l, define a mapping h'_l from $\Re$ to finite sequences of computation steps by p_l as follows. Each step at p_l associated with real time t in h_l is associated with real time $\widetilde{\gamma}_l^{(e')}(\gamma_l^{(e)}(t))$ in e'; in addition, h'_l preserves the ordering of steps in h_l. (3) e' preserves the correspondence between message-delivery and message-send events in e.

Since e is an execution of $\mathcal{A}$, for each MCS process p_l, h_l is a history for p_l with clock $\gamma_l^{(e)}$. By rule (2), this implies that h'_l is a history for p_l with clock $\gamma_l^{(e')}$; moreover, for any real times $t_1, t_2 \in \Re$ with $t_1 < t_2$, $\gamma_l^{(e')}(t_2) - \gamma_l^{(e')}(t_1) = (t_2 - t_1)/\sigma$. Since $1/\rho \le \sigma \le \rho, 1/\rho \le 1/\sigma \le \rho, \gamma_l^{(e')}$ is ρ-drifting; thus, by rule (3), it follows that e' is an execution of $\mathcal{A}$. In addition, rule (2) immediately implies that executions e and e' are equivalent. We continue to establish a fundamental property of the execution e'.

Lemma 1. *Assume that e' is an admissible execution. Then, e' is not linearizable.*

Proof. We give a sketch of the proof. Since $\mathcal{A}$ is a linearizable implementation and e' is an admissible execution of $\mathcal{A}$, e' is a linearizable execution. Thus, there exists a legal linearization τ' of e' such that for each MCS process p, $ops(e') \mid p = \tau' \mid p$. We show simple properties of the sequence τ', namely that $wop_j \xrightarrow{\tau'} wop_i$ and $wop_i \xrightarrow{\tau'} rop_k$. Since τ is a legal operation sequence, these properties imply that $val^{(e')}(rop_k) = val^{(e')}(wop_i) = x_i$. Since $x_i \ne x_j$, it follows that $val^{(e)}(rop_k) \ne val^{(e')}(rop_k)$. However, the equivalence of e and e' implies that $val^{(e)}(rop_k) = val^{(e')}(rop_k)$. A contradiction.

3.2 Results for Specific Models of Delays

Our methodology is as follows. We first calculate message delays in execution e' (independent of specific delay assumptions). Next, we consider separately each specific assumption on delays; requiring that message delays in the execution e' constructed in Section 3.1 satisfy the assumption yields the admissibility of e', which, by Lemma 1, implies the non-linearizability of e'. For the model with lower and upper bounds on delays, we show:

Theorem 1. *Consider the model with lower and upper bounds on the delays. Let $\mathcal{A}$ be any linearizable implementation of read/write objects, including an object X with at least two writers p_i and p_j, and a distinct reader p_k. Fix any parameters $\delta_{ij}, \delta_{ji}, \delta_{ik}, \delta_{ki}, \delta_{jk}, \delta_{kj} > 0$. Then, for any parameter $\sigma \in [1/\rho, \rho]$, there exists an admissible execution e of $\mathcal{A}$ with $\delta_{ij} \in \Delta_{ij}^{(e)}, \delta_{ji} \in \Delta_{ji}^{(e)}, \delta_{ik} \in \Delta_{ik}^{(e)}, \delta_{ki} \in \Delta_{ki}^{(e)}, \delta_{jk} \in \Delta_{jk}^{(e)}, \delta_{kj} \in \Delta_{kj}^{(e)}$, such that either*

$$|\mathbf{W}_{\mathcal{A}}(X, e)|$$
$$< \max\{\frac{\delta_{ij}}{2} - \frac{d}{2\sigma^2}, \frac{d-u}{2\sigma^2} - \frac{\delta_{ji}}{2}, \delta_{ik} - \frac{d}{\sigma^2}, \frac{d-u}{\sigma^2} - \delta_{ki}, \frac{d-u}{\sigma^2} - \delta_{jk}, \delta_{kj} - \frac{d}{\sigma^2}\},$$

or

$$|\mathbf{W}_\mathcal{A}(X,e)|$$
$$> \min\{\frac{\delta_{ij}}{2} - \frac{d-u}{2\sigma^2}, \frac{d}{2\sigma^2} - \frac{\delta_{ji}}{2}, \delta_{ik} - \frac{d-u}{\sigma^2}, \frac{d}{\sigma^2} - \delta_{ki}, \frac{d}{\sigma^2} - \delta_{jk}, \delta_{kj} - \frac{d-u}{\sigma^2}\}.$$

Proof. We give a sketch of the proof. Assume, by way of contradiction, that there exists a linearizable implementation $\mathcal{A}$ of read/write objects, including the object X, such that for any parameter $\sigma \in [1/\rho, \rho]$, for every admissible execution e of $\mathcal{A}$ with $\delta_{ij} \in \Delta_{ij}^{(e)}, \delta_{ji} \in \Delta_{ji}^{(e)}, \delta_{ik} \in \Delta_{ik}^{(e)}, \delta_{ki} \in \Delta_{ki}^{(e)}, \delta_{jk} \in \Delta_{jk}^{(e)}, \delta_{kj} \in \Delta_{kj}^{(e)}$, neither inequality holds. We establish that the execution e' constructed in Section 3.1 is an admissible execution of $\mathcal{A}$; appealing to Lemma 1, this implies that e' is non-linearizable, which contradicts the fact that $\mathcal{A}$ is a linearizable implementation. (To prove that e' is an admissible execution, we show by case analysis that for any pair of processes p_l and p_m, and for any message $\mathbf{m}$ received by p_m from p_l, $d^{(e')}(\mathbf{m}) \in [d-u, d]$.)

Theorem 1 establishes the existence of executions with "gaps" for the response times of write operations. For the model with a bound on the round-trip delay bias, we show:

Theorem 2. *Consider the model with a bound on the round-trip delay bias. Let $\mathcal{A}$ be any linearizable implementation of read/write objects, including an object X with at least two writers p_i and p_j, and a distinct reader p_k. Fix any parameters $\delta_{ij}, \delta_{ji}, \delta_{ik}, \delta_{ki}, \delta_{jk}, \delta_{kj} > 0$. Then, for any parameter $\sigma \in [1/\rho, \rho]$, there exists an admissible execution e of $\mathcal{A}$ with $\delta_{ij} \in \Delta_{ij}^{(e)}, \delta_{ji} \in \Delta_{ji}^{(e)}, \delta_{ik} \in \Delta_{ik}^{(e)}, \delta_{ki} \in \Delta_{ki}^{(e)}, \delta_{jk} \in \Delta_{jk}^{(e)}, \delta_{kj} \in \Delta_{kj}^{(e)}$, such that either*

$$|\mathbf{W}_\mathcal{A}(X,e)| < -\frac{\varepsilon}{4\sigma^2} + \max\{\frac{\delta_{ik} - \delta_{ki}}{2} - \frac{\varepsilon}{4\sigma^2}, \frac{\delta_{kj} - \delta_{jk}}{2} - \frac{\varepsilon}{4\sigma^2}, \frac{\delta_{ij} - \delta_{ji}}{4}\},$$

or

$$|\mathbf{W}_\mathcal{A}(X,e)| > \frac{\varepsilon}{4\sigma^2} + \min\{\frac{\delta_{ik} - \delta_{ki}}{2} + \frac{\varepsilon}{4\sigma^2}, \frac{\delta_{kj} - \delta_{jk}}{2} + \frac{\varepsilon}{4\sigma^2}, \frac{\delta_{ij} - \delta_{ji}}{4}\}.$$

The proof of Theorem 2 is similar to the proof of Theorem 1, and it is omitted. Theorem 2 demonstrates the existence of executions with "gaps" on the response times of write operations. In order to derive a *worst-case* lower bound on the response time for write operations from Theorem 2, we set $\sigma = 1/\rho$, $\delta_{ij} - \delta_{ji} = \varepsilon$, $\delta_{ik} - \delta_{ki} = \varepsilon$, and $\delta_{kj} - \delta_{jk} = \varepsilon$. With these choices, the upper limit on $|\mathbf{W}_\mathcal{A}(X,e)|$ becomes negative, and, therefore, it cannot be met, which implies that the lower limit on $|\mathbf{W}_\mathcal{A}(X,e)|$ must be met, which is positive for these choices. We obtain:

Corollary 1. *Consider the model with a bound on the round-trip delay bias. Let $\mathcal{A}$ be any linearizable implementation of read/write objects, including an object X with at least two writers p_i and p_j, and a distinct reader p_k. Then, $|\mathbf{W}_\mathcal{A}(X)| > \rho^2\varepsilon/4 + \varepsilon/4$.*

For the model of broadcast networks, we show:

Theorem 3. *Consider the model of broadcast networks. Let $\mathcal{A}$ be any lineariz-able implementation of read/write objects, including an object X with at least two writers p_i and p_j, and a distinct reader p_k. Fix any parameters δ_{ij}, δ_{ji}, δ_{ik}, δ_{ki}, δ_{jk}, $\delta_{kj} > 0$. Then, there exists an admissible execution e of $\mathcal{A}$ with $\delta_{ij} \in \Delta_{ij}^{(e)}, \delta_{ji} \in \Delta_{ji}^{(e)}, \delta_{ik} \in \Delta_{ik}^{(e)}, \delta_{ki} \in \Delta_{ki}^{(e)}, \delta_{jk} \in \Delta_{jk}^{(e)}, \delta_{kj} \in \Delta_{kj}^{(e)}$, such that either*

$$|\mathbf{W}_{\mathcal{A}}(X, e)| < -\frac{\beta}{2\sigma^2} + \max\{\delta_{ij} - \delta_{ik} - \frac{\beta}{2\sigma^2}, \delta_{jk} - \delta_{ji} - \frac{\beta}{2\sigma^2}, \frac{\delta_{kj} - \delta_{ki}}{2}\},$$

or

$$|\mathbf{W}_{\mathcal{A}}(X, e)| > \frac{\beta}{2\sigma^2} + \min\{\delta_{ij} - \delta_{ik} + \frac{\beta}{2\sigma^2}, \delta_{jk} - \delta_{ji} + \frac{\beta}{2\sigma^2}, \frac{\delta_{kj} - \delta_{ki}}{2}\}.$$

The proof of Theorem 3 is similar to the proof of Theorem 1, and it is omitted. Theorem 3 demonstrates the existence of executions with "gaps" on the response times of writes operations. In order to derive a *worst-case* lower bound on the response time for write operations from Theorem 3, we set $\sigma = 1/rho$, $\delta_{ij} - \delta_{ik} = \beta$, $\delta_{jk} - \delta_{ji} = \beta$, and $\delta_{kj} - \delta_{ki} = \beta$. With these choices, the upper limit on $|\mathbf{W}_{\mathcal{A}}(X, e)|$ becomes negative, and, therefore, it cannot be met, which implies that the lower limit on $|\mathbf{W}_{\mathcal{A}}(X, e)|$ must be met, which is positive for these choices. We obtain:

Corollary 2. *Consider the model of broadcast networks. Let $\mathcal{A}$ be any lineariz-able implementation of read/write objects, including an object X with at least two writers p_i and p_j, and a distinct reader p_k. Then, $|\mathbf{W}_{\mathcal{A}}(X)| > \rho^2\beta/2 + \beta/2$.*

4 Reads

A construction of a non-linearizable, if admissible, execution is presented in Section 4.1; this execution is used in Section 4.2 for deriving necessary conditions for the read operation under specific assumptions on the delays. We refer to any linearizable implementation $\mathcal{A}$ of read/write objects including an object X with at least two readers p_i and p_j, and a distinct writer p_k.

4.1 A Non-Linearizable, if Admissible, Execution

This construction is based on one in [2, Section 4] and [12, Section 5]. We start with an admissible execution e, in which p_i reads $\perp$ from X, then p_j and p_i alternate reading from X while p_k is writing x to X, and finally p_j reads x from X; moreover, we assume that all clocks in e run at a rate of σ, for some constant σ such that $1/\rho \leq \sigma \leq \rho$. Thus, there exists a read operation rop_0, say by p_i, that returns $\perp$ and is immediately followed by a read operation rop_1 by p_j that returns x. If p_i's history is shifted later by $|\mathbf{R}_{\mathcal{A}}(X, e)|$, while p_j's history is shifted earlier by $|\mathbf{R}_{\mathcal{A}}(X, e)|$, while both are either "swelled" or "shrinked" by a factor of σ, the result is an execution e' in which rop_1 precedes rop_0. If, in addition, all clocks are correspondingly "swelled" or "shrinked" by the same factor σ, all three processes still "see" the same events occurring at the same local time and cannot, therefore, distinguish between e and e'; thus, in particular, p_j and p_i still read x and $\perp$ in their read operations rop_1 and rop_0, respectively, in this order. This implies that e', if admissible, is non-linearizable. We now present some details of the construction.

Let $b = \lceil |\mathbf{W}_A(X)|/2|\mathbf{R}_A(X)| \rceil$. By the serial specification of X, there exists an admissible execution e of A consisting of the following operations at processes p_i, p_j, and p_k. For each integer l, $0 \le l \le b$, p_i performs a read operation $rop_i^{(2l)}$ on X; for each integer l, $0 \le l \le b$, p_j performs a read operation $rop_j^{(2l+1)}$ on X; p_k performs a write operation wop_k on X with $val^{(e)}(wop_k) = x$. For each l, $0 \le l \le 2b+1$, let $rop^{(l)} = rop_i^{(l)}$ if l is even, or $rop_j^{(l)}$ if l is odd. The definition of the call times of read operations in e is inductive. For the basis case, $t_c^{(e)}(rop^{(0)}) = 0$. Assume inductively that we have defined $t_c^{(e)}(rop^{(l)})$ where $0 \le l < 2b+1$. Then, $t_c^{(e)}(rop^{(l+1)}) = t_c^{(e)}(rop^{(l)}) + |rop^{(l)}|$. Set also $t_c(wop_k) = |rop^{(0)}|$. Moreover, assume that $\gamma_i^{(e)}(t) = \gamma_j^{(e)}(t) = \gamma_k^{(e)}(t) = \sigma t$ for some constant σ such that $1/\rho \le \sigma \le \rho$, so that all clocks $\gamma_i^{(e)}, \gamma_j^{(e)}$, and $\gamma_k^{(e)}$ are ρ-drifting. (We omit reference to clocks of other processes in this extended abstract.)

Since A is a linearizable implementation and e is an admissible execution of A, e is a linearizable execution. Thus, there exists a legal linearization τ of e such that for each MCS process p_l, $ops(e) \mid l = \tau \mid l$. We use the construction of e to show simple properties of the operation sequence τ, namely that $rop_i^{(0)} \xrightarrow{\tau} wop_k$ and that $wop_k \xrightarrow{\tau} rop_j^{(2b+1)}$. We show that for each l, $0 \le l \le 2b$, $rop^{(l)} \xrightarrow{\tau} rop^{(l+1)}$. These properties imply that there exists an index l_0, $0 \le l_0 \le 2b$, such that $rop^{(l_0)} \xrightarrow{\tau} wop_k \xrightarrow{\tau} rop^{(l_0+1)}$. Since τ is a legal operation sequence, this implies that $val^{(e)}(rop^{(l_0)}) = \perp$ and $val^{(e)}(rop^{(l_0+1)}) = x$. Assume, without loss of generality, that l_0 is even, so that $rop^{(l_0)}$ is a read operation by process p_i.

We now "perturb" the (admissible) execution e in order to obtain another execution e' which is not necessarily admissible; however, we shall show that if e' is admissible, then it is not linearizable. We construct e' as follows. (1) Set $\gamma_i^{(e')}(t) = t/\sigma - \sigma |\mathbf{R}_A(X, e)|$, $\gamma_j^{(e')}(t) = t/\sigma + \sigma |\mathbf{R}_A(X, e)|$, and $\gamma_k^{(e')}(t) = t/\sigma$. (2) e' preserves the correspondence between message-delivery and message-send events in e. (3) For any process p_l, each step at p_l occurring at real time t in e is scheduled to occur at real time $\widetilde{\gamma}_l^{(e')}(\gamma_l^{(e)}(t))$ in e'; in addition, e' preserves the ordering of steps in e. Since e is an execution of A, for each MCS process p_l, h_l is a history for p_l with clock $\gamma_l^{(e)}$. By rule (2), this implies that h_l' is a history for p_l with clock $\gamma_l^{(e')}$; moreover, for any real times $t_1, t_2 \in \Re$ with $t_1 < t_2$, $\gamma_l^{(e')}(t_2) - \gamma_l^{(e')}(t_1) = (t_2 - t_1)/\sigma$. Since $1/\rho \le \sigma \le \rho$, $1/\rho \le 1/\sigma \le \rho$, so that $\gamma_l^{(e')}$ is ρ-drifting; thus, by rule (3), it follows that e' is an execution of A. In addition, rule (3) immediately implies that executions e and e' are equivalent. We continue to show a fundamental property of the execution e'.

Lemma 2. *Assume that e' is an admissible execution. Then, e' is not linearizable.*

4.2 Results for Specific Models of Delays

We consider separately each specific assumption on message delays; requiring that message delays in the execution e' constructed in Section 4.1 satisfy the assumption yields the admissibility of e', which, by Lemma 2, implies that e' is not linearizable. For the model with lower and upper bounds on the delays, we show:

Theorem 4. *Consider the model with lower and upper bounds on the delays. Let $\mathcal{A}$ be any linearizable implementation of read/write objects, including an object X with at least two readers p_i and p_j, and a distinct writer p_k. Fix any parameters $\delta_{ij}, \delta_{ji}, \delta_{ik}, \delta_{ki}, \delta_{jk}, \delta_{kj} > 0$. Then, there exists an admissible execution e of $\mathcal{A}$ with $\delta_{ij} \in \Delta_{ij}^{(e)}, \delta_{ji} \in \Delta_{ji}^{(e)}, \delta_{ik} \in \Delta_{ik}^{(e)}, \delta_{ki} \in \Delta_{ki}^{(e)}, \delta_{jk} \in \Delta_{jk}^{(e)}, \delta_{kj} \in \Delta_{kj}^{(e)}$, such that either*

$$|\mathbf{R}_{\mathcal{A}}(X, e)|$$
$$< \max\{\frac{\delta_{ij}}{2} - \frac{d}{2\rho^2}, \frac{d-u}{2\rho^2} - \frac{\delta_{ji}}{2}, \delta_{ik} - \frac{d}{\rho^2}, \frac{d-u}{\rho^2} - \delta_{ki}, \frac{d-u}{\rho^2} - \delta_{jk}, \delta_{kj} - \frac{d}{\rho^2}\},$$

or

$$|\mathbf{R}_{\mathcal{A}}(X, e)|$$
$$> \min\{\frac{\delta_{ij}}{2} - \frac{d-u}{2\rho^2}, \frac{d}{2\rho^2} - \frac{\delta_{ji}}{2}, \delta_{ik} - \frac{d-u}{\rho^2}, \frac{d}{\rho^2} - \delta_{ki}, \frac{d}{\rho^2} - \delta_{jk}, \delta_{kj} - \frac{d-u}{\rho^2}\}.$$

For the model with a bound on the round-trip delay bias, we show:

Theorem 5. *Consider the model with a bound on the round-trip delay bias. Let $\mathcal{A}$ be any linearizable implementation of read/write objects, including an object X with at least two readers p_i and p_j, and a distinct writer p_k. Fix any parameters $\delta_{ij}, \delta_{ji}, \delta_{ik}, \delta_{ki}, \delta_{jk}, \delta_{kj} > 0$. Then, there exists an admissible execution e of $\mathcal{A}$ with $\delta_{ij} \in \Delta_{ij}^{(e)}, \delta_{ji} \in \Delta_{ji}^{(e)}, \delta_{ik} \in \Delta_{ik}^{(e)}, \delta_{ki} \in \Delta_{ki}^{(e)}, \delta_{jk} \in \Delta_{jk}^{(e)}, \delta_{kj} \in \Delta_{kj}^{(e)}$, such that either*

$$|\mathbf{R}_{\mathcal{A}}(X, e)| < -\frac{\varepsilon}{4\rho^2} + \max\{\frac{\delta_{ik} - \delta_{ki}}{2} - \frac{\varepsilon}{4\rho^2}, \frac{\delta_{kj} - \delta_{jk}}{2} - \frac{\varepsilon}{4\rho^2}, \frac{\delta_{ij} - \delta_{ji}}{4}\},$$

or

$$|\mathbf{R}_{\mathcal{A}}(X, e)| < \frac{\varepsilon}{4\rho^2} + \min\{\frac{\delta_{ik} - \delta_{ki}}{2} + \frac{\varepsilon}{4\rho^2}, \frac{\delta_{kj} - \delta_{jk}}{2} + \frac{\varepsilon}{4\rho^2}, \frac{\delta_{ij} - \delta_{ji}}{4}\}.$$

Theorem 5 demonstrates the existence of executions with "gaps" on the response times of read operations. In order to derive a *worst-case* lower bound on the response time for read operations from Theorem 5, we set $\sigma = 1/\rho$, $\delta_{ij} - \delta_{ji} = \varepsilon$, $\delta_{ik} - \delta_{ki} = \varepsilon$, and $\delta_{kj} - \delta_{jk} = \varepsilon$. With these choices, the upper limit on $|\mathbf{R}_{\mathcal{A}}(X, e)|$ becomes negative, and, therefore, it cannot be met, which implies that the lower limit on $|\mathbf{R}_{\mathcal{A}}(X, e)|$, which is positive for these choices, must be met. We obtain:

Corollary 3. *Consider the model with a bound on the round-trip delay bias. Let $\mathcal{A}$ be any linearizable implementation of read/write objects, including an object X with at least two readers p_i and p_j, and a distinct writer p_k. Then, $|\mathbf{R}_{\mathcal{A}}(X)| > \rho^2 \varepsilon/4 + \varepsilon/4$.*

For the model of broadcast networks, we show:

Theorem 6. *Consider the model of broadcast networks. Let $\mathcal{A}$ be any linearizable implementation of read/write objects, including an object X with at least two readers p_i and p_j, and a distinct writer p_k. Fix any parameters δ_{ij}, δ_{ji}, δ_{ik}, δ_{ki}, δ_{jk}, $\delta_{kj} > 0$. Then, there exists an admissible execution e of $\mathcal{A}$ with $\delta_{ij} \in \Delta_{ij}^{(e)}, \delta_{ji} \in \Delta_{ji}^{(e)}, \delta_{ik} \in \Delta_{ik}^{(e)}, \delta_{ki} \in \Delta_{ki}^{(e)}, \delta_{jk} \in \Delta_{jk}^{(e)}, \delta_{kj} \in \Delta_{kj}^{(e)}$, such that either*

$$|\mathbf{R}_{\mathcal{A}}(X, e)| < -\frac{\beta}{2\rho^2} + \max\{\delta_{ij} - \delta_{ik} + \frac{\beta}{2\rho^2}, \delta_{jk} - \delta_{ji} + \frac{\beta}{2\rho^2}, \frac{\delta_{kj} - \delta_{ki}}{2}\},$$

or

$$|\mathbf{R}_{\mathcal{A}}(X, e)| > \frac{\beta}{2\rho^2} + \max\{\delta_{ij} - \delta_{ik} + \frac{\beta}{2\rho^2}, \delta_{jk} - \delta_{ji} + \frac{\beta}{2\rho^2}, \frac{\delta_{kj} - \delta_{ki}}{2}\}.$$

Theorem 6 demonstrates the existence of executions with "gaps" on the response times of read operations. In order to derive a *worst-case* lower bound on the response time for read operations from Theorem 6, we set $\sigma = 1/rho$, $\delta_{ij} - \delta_{ik} = \beta$, $\delta_{jk} - \delta_{ji} = \beta$, and $\delta_{kj} - \delta_{ki} = \beta$. With these choices, the upper limit on $|\mathbf{R}_{\mathcal{A}}(X, e)|$ becomes negative, and, therefore, it cannot be met, which implies that the lower limit on $|\mathbf{R}_{\mathcal{A}}(X, e)|$ which is positive for these choices, must be met. We obtain:

Corollary 4. *Consider the model of broadcast networks. Let $\mathcal{A}$ be any linearizable implementation of read/write objects, including an object X with at least two readers p_i and p_j, and a distinct writer p_k. Then, $|\mathbf{R}_{\mathcal{A}}(X)| > \rho^2 \beta/2 + \beta/2$.*

References

1. H. Attiya, A. Herzberg, and S. Rajsbaum, "Optimal Clock Synchronization under Different Delay Assumptions," *SIAM Journal on Computing*, Vol. 25, No. 2, pp. 369–389, April 1996.
2. H. Attiya and J. L. Welch, "Sequential Consistency versus Linearizability," *ACM Transactions on Computer Systems*, Vol. 12, No. 2, pp. 91–122, May 1994.

3. S. Chaudhuri, R. Gawlick, and N. Lynch, "Designing Algorithms for Distributed Systems Using Partially Synchronized Clocks," *Proceedings of the 12th Annual ACM Symposium on Principles of Distributed Computing*, pp. 121–132, August 1993.

4. D. Dolev, R. Reischuk, and H. R. Strong, "Observable Clock Synchronization," *Proceedings of the 13th Annual ACM Symposium on Principles of Distributed Computing*, pp. 284–293, August 1994.

5. R. Friedman, "Implementing High-Level Synchronization Operations in Hybrid Consistency," *Distributed Computing*, Vol. 9, No. 3, pp. 119–129, December 1995.

6. J. Halpern and I. Suzuki, "Clock Synchronization and the Power of Broadcasting," *Proceedings of the 28th Annual Allerton Conference on Communication, Control and Computing*, pp. 588–597, October 1990.

7. M. Herlihy and J. Wing, "Linearizability: A Correctness Condition for Concurrent Objects," *ACM Transactions on Programming Languages and Systems*, Vol. 12, No. 3, pp. 463–492, July 1990.

8. J. Kleinberg, H. Attiya, and N. Lynch, "Trade-offs Between Message Delivery and Quiesce Times in Connection Management Protocols," *Proceedings of the 3rd Israel Symposium on the Theory of Computing and Systems*, pp. 258–267, January 1995.

9. M. J. Kosa, "Making Operations of Concurrent Data Types Fast," *Proceedings of the 13th Annual ACM Symposium on Principles of Distributed Computing*, pp. 32–41, August 1994.

10. J. Lundelius and N. Lynch, "An Upper and Lower Bound for Clock Synchronization," *Information and Control*, Vol. 62, pp. 190–204, August/September 1984.

11. M. Mavronicolas and N. Papadakis, "Trade-off Results for Connection Management," *Proceedings of the 11th International Symposium on Fundamentals of Computation Theory*, pp. 340–351, Lecture Notes in Computer Science, Vol. 1279, Springer-Verlag, Krakow, Poland, September 1997.

12. M. Mavronicolas and D. Roth, "Efficient, Strongly Consistent Implementations of Shared Memory," *Proceedings of the 6th International Workshop on Distributed Algorithms (WDAG'92)*, pp. 346–361, Lecture Notes in Computer Science, Vol. # 647, Springer-Verlag, November 1992.

13. B. Patt-Shamir and S. Rajsbaum, "A Theory of Clock Synchronization," *Proceedings of the 26th Annual ACM Symposium on Theory of Computing*, pp. 810–819, May 1994.

14. K. Sugihara and I. Suzuki, "Nearly Optimal Clock Synchronization under Unbounded Message Transmission Time," *Proceedings of the 3rd International Conference on Parallel Processing*, pp. 14–17, 1988.

Maintenance of a Spanning Tree in Dynamic Networks

Shay Kutten[1] and Avner Porat[2]

[1] IBM T.J Watson Research Center, P.O. BOX 704
Yorktown Heights, NY 10598
and The Davidson Department of Industrial Engineering & Management
Technion, Haifa 3200 Israel
kutten@ie.technion.ac.il
This research was supported by the fund for the promotion of research at the
Technion.
[2] The Davidson Department of Industrial Engineering & Management,
avner@ie.technion.ac.il.

Abstract. Many crucial network tasks such as database maintenance
can be efficiently carried out given a tree that spans the network. By
maintaining such a spanning tree, rather than constructing it "from-
scratch" due to every topology change, one can improve the efficiency
of the tree construction, as well as the efficiency of the protocols that
use the tree. We present a protocol for this task which has communication complexity that is linear in the "actual" size of the biggest connected
component. The time complexity of our protocol has only a polylogarithmic overhead in the "actual" size of the biggest connected component.
The communication complexity of the previous solution, which was considered communication optimal, was linear in the network size, that is,
unbounded as a function of the "actual" size of the biggest connected
component. The overhead in the time measure of the previous solution
was polynomial in the network size.
In an asynchronous network it may not be clear what is the meaning
of the "actual" size of the connected component at a given time. To
capture this notion we define the *virtual component* and show that in
asynchronous networks, in a sense, the notion of the virtual component
is the closest one can get to the notion of the "actual" component.

1 Introduction

1.1 Motivation and Existing Solutions

Maintaining a common database in the local memory of each node is a common
technique in computing a distributed function. An important example is the
case that the replicated information is the set of non-faulty links adjacent to each
node. Maintaining replicas of this information is the classical "Topology Update"
problem, where each node is required to "know" the description of its connected
component of the network [Vis83, BGJ+85, MRR80, SG89, CGKK95, ACK90].

This is one of the most common tasks performed in existing networks since, when the topology gets to be known to all nodes, many distributed tasks can be reduced to sequential tasks. This reduction is conducted by having each node simulate the distributed task on the topology known to it. An Example for a protocol which uses this approach is the Internet OSPF interior routing protocol [OSPF].

In [ACK90] it was shown that the incremental cost of adapting to a single topology change can be smaller than the communication complexity of the previous approach [AAG87] of solving the problem "from scratch". (A variant of the algorithm of [ACK90] was implemented later as a part of the PARIS networking project at IBM [CGKK95].)

In this paper we improve the first subtask of [ACK90]: maintaining a spanning tree in the dynamic network, thus, also improving the database maintaining algorithm. Our algorithm also improves any other algorithm which uses the maintenance spanning tree algorithm as a building block. The amortized communication complexity of the tree maintenance subtask in [ACK90] was $O(V)$, where V was the number of nodes in the network. In a dynamic network the value of this parameter might be much larger than the "actual" size of the biggest connected component.

An example for such a scenario is when all the nodes in the network are separated from each other and only one edge recovers to create a two-node connected component. Therefore, The size of the network is $V/2$ times bigger than the "actual" size of the connected component. Moreover, under this scenario, according to the algorithm in [ACK90], the two nodes of the connected component exchange $O(V)$ messages. Therefore, this scenario demonstrates that the amortized communication complexity in [ACK90] is not bounded as a function of the size of the biggest connected component in the network.

The quiescence time of the algorithm of [ACK90] was high: $O(V^2)$, mainly because the algorithm merged only two trees at a time in each of its phases. Merging more trees in the same iteration of the algorithm of [ACK90] could have violated an important invariant (called the *loop freedom invariant*), the correction of the algorithm relied upon. This was, probably, the reason only two trees were merge at a time in [ACK90].

1.2 Our solution

In this paper we provide a tree maintenance protocol with amortized communication complexity that is linear in the "actual" size A of the connected component in which the algorithm is performed (The message complexity of the previous solution was not bounded as a function of A.) The time complexity overhead of our protocol is only polylogarithmic in the "actual" size of the biggest connected component. (The time overhead of the previous solution was polynomial in the network size).

In an asynchronous network it may not be clear what is the meaning of the "actual" size of the connected component at a given time. To capture this notion we define the *virtual component* and show that in asynchronous networks, in a sense, the notion of the virtual component is the closest one can get to the notion of the "actual" component.

Topological changes may break a tree into several rooted trees. The execution of our algorithm is composed of iterations that are invoked continuously by every root of a tree, until the connected component is spanned. Each iteration of the algorithm is constructed from two phases: in the first phase, referred to as the *Trees Approval* phase, a set of trees is "chosen" and "prepared" for merging. In the second phase, referred to as the *Trees Merge* phase, the actual merge is executed by parallel invocations of the *TREE MERGE* procedure for every tree that was "chosen" in the Trees Approval phase. Some topological changes which occur during the algorithm execution may cause the algorithm to initiate the first phase while other topological change may not influence the algorithm execution. We show that this two-phase structure enables the algorithm to maintain the *loop freedom invariant* of [ACK90] even though our algorithm does merge more than two trees at a time. (This uses especially the fact that a non-"chosen tree" does not participate in the second phase even if an edge from it to a node in a chosen tree has recovered). In that way the algorithm improves the time bottleneck of the algorithm of [ACK90].

The communication improvement is achieved by using a new message exchange policy: exchanging fewer messages between every two merging trees. Our algorithm exchanges only messages that describe the "approved" trees and not the whole local memory of every node as in the algorithm of [ACK90]. We show that sending fewer messages during tree's merging can, in fact, cause additional messages to be sent at later times during the run of the algorithm. (This, probably, is the reason the algorithm of [ACK90] did not try to economize on messages between trees at the time of merging). However, we manage to show that the number of these additional messages is small, leading to the improvement in the total number of messages.

Another difference from the work of [ACK90] is an adaptation we had to make to one of the building blocks used in the algorithm of [ACK90]. This is needed to cope with our algorithm's new message exchange policy.

An additional change that had to be made in our algorithm is the addition of a new message, *range deletion* message, that instructs its receiver to update more than one item in its local database. We show that the use of that new message enables the algorithm to keep its time complexity as a function of the size of the "actual" connected component rather than a function of the number of topological changes that occurred.

The rest of the paper is organized as follows: Section 2 describes the model and the problem. Section 3 presents a high level overview of the algorithm of [ACK90] and the algorithm of [AS91] (which is used as a building block in our algorithm). Section 4 presents Phase 1 of our algorithm (Trees Approval) and Phase 2 (Trees Update). Section 5 contains the correctness and complexity analysis.

2 The Problem

2.1 The Model

The network is represented by a graph G=(V,E) where V is the set of nodes, each having a distinct identity, and $E \subset V \times V$ is the set of edges, or links. We assume that each edge has a distinct finite weight. (If the edge weights are not distinct one simply appends to the edge weight the identities of the two nodes joined by the edge, listing, say, the lower ordered node first [GHS83]).

The network is dynamic: edges may fail or recover. Whenever an edge fails an underlying lower-layer link protocol notifies both endpoints of this edge about the failure, before the edge can recover [MRR80, BGJ+85, ACG+90]. Similarly, a recovery of an edge is also notified to each of its endpoints. A message can be received only over a non-faulty edge.

Messages transmitted over a non-faulty edge eventually arrive, or the edge will fail (in both endpoints). Messages arrive over any given edge according to the FIFO (First In First Out) discipline. The communication is asynchronous.

The complexity measures that are used to evaluate the algorithm performance are: (1) Amortized Communication - the total number of messages (each containing $O(\log V)$ bits) sent by the protocol, divided by the number of topology changes that occurred during the execution. (2) Quiescence Time - the maximum normalized time from the last input change until termination of the protocol. Normalized time is evaluated under the assumption [Awe88] that link delays varies between 0 and 1. This assumption is used only for the purpose of evaluating the performance of the algorithm, but is not used to prove its correctness.

2.2 Problem Definition

In response to *topological changes*, namely, recoveries or failures of edges, the algorithm is required to mark, at each node, a subset of the node's edges. The collection of edges marked by all of the network nodes is called, as in the algorithm of [ACK90], the *real forest*. The requirement imposed on the algorithm is that the real forest is, in fact, a forest at all times. Trees in this forest are called *real trees*. If the input stops changing then the output (the real forest) is required to become eventually a spanning tree of the connected component.

3 Background

3.1 The Tree Maintenance Algorithm of [ACK90]

A failure of a real forest edge causes the edge to become unmarked and disconnects a real tree into two or more real trees. Our model allows multiply edges to fail simultaneously.

In order to span the entire connected component, the algorithm of [ACK90] uses the following scheme to reconnect the tree, until it spans the connected component. Every real tree locates its *minimum outgoing edge*- the edge with the minimum weight among all the edges leading from (nodes of) this real tree to (nodes of) other real trees. If the other endpoint is also the minimum outgoing edge of the other real tree, then it is guaranteed that the endpoints will agree. (Unless, of course, additional topological changes occur, e.g. failure of the minimum edge). Therefore, at each algorithm iteration two distinct real trees are merged into a larger real tree, by marking the minimum edge that connects them. The high level description of the algorithm of [ACK90] appears in figure 1.

Two main distributed subroutines are used in the algorithm (for the full list of the properties of two subroutines refer to section 5):(1) FIND- a subroutine which is used to find the minimum outgoing edge of the real tree using a dynamic data structure maintained by each node. (2) UPDATE- a subroutine that is used to update the mentioned dynamic data structure. The dynamic data structure at each node, v, is v's approximation of the real forest and is called v's *forest replica*. The approximation (a subset of v's forest replica) of Node v's real tree is called v's *tree replica*.

The UPDATE subroutine attempts to keep the tree replicas of all the nodes as "accurate" (i.e. close to the real forest) as possible. To this end a node that performs a change in the marking of its adjacent edges (unmarking as a result of a failure, or marking an edge that the algorithm decided to use to merge two trees) updates its forest replica, and communicates the change over the marked edges to its whole real tree. Observe that in the case that the forest replicas of the endpoints of an edge disagree, it is neither obvious how such an "agreement" is to be reached, nor which one of the endpoints is "more correct" [3] (better reflects the real forest). In order to resolve this conflict, the UPDATE subroutine is based on an idea, which was called the *Tree Belief principle* in [ACK90]. This principle is used between every two neighbors, in order to decide which of their forest replicas is "more correct" regarding every Edge e. In other words, which replica reflects a later (in history) status of Edge e. The two neighboring nodes apply the Tree Belief principle for every topological item that appears in their replicas, namely, for every edge (x, y). Consider a graph, U, which is the union of the tree replicas of nodes u and v. According to this principle, Node v is "more correct" about an edge (x, y) than its neighbor u, if in u the undirected path from u to edge (x, y) starts at Node v. (The intuition is that if Node v is not correct, an indicator for the error should have arrived, sooner or later, over the mentioned path). It is obvious that if for an edge (x, y) there appear two distinct undirected paths from v, one starting with edge (u, v), while the other does not, this principle could not have been applied. Therefore, the following invariant is enforced by the algorithm in order to realized this principle.

Definition 1. The *Loop Freedom invariant* ([ACK90]): For every real tree T, the union of the tree replicas of the nodes of T does not contain a cycle.

---

[3] This is due to the asynchronous nature of network (we do not assume a real time clock) and the bounded size of the message (we cannot aloud to number all the messages using a counter that counts to infinity).

The UPDATE subroutine conducts the correction of the replicas using the Incremental Update technique.

Definition 2. Incremental Update technique- The node with the correct data structure sends each neighbor node a message per error that appears in its neighbor's data structure. The message describes the place of the error in the data structure (thus, the neighbor can correct the error).

This technique is based on the *Neighbor-Knowledge assumption*, namely that each node "knows" the content of the local memory of its network neighbors. This assumption holds for the algorithm of [ACK90] because the algorithm maintains in each node's local memory also an estimate of the forest replicas of its neighbors. Let Node u's *mirror* of node v (denoted by $Mirror_u(v)$) be the data structure, at Node u, that represents the estimate that Node u has for the replica of u's neighbor v.

Whenever a marked edge fails
    Unmark the edge (* at the endpoints *)

Whenever two trees merge or a topological change occurs
    Call UPDATE (* correct tree replicas *)
    call FIND (* choose min outgoing edge *)

Whenever two trees choose same min outgoing edge
    For each of the trees separately call UPDATE
    (* After UPDATE terminates: *)
    Mark the chosen edge at both of its endpoints (*merge*)

Fig. 1. The main Algorithm of [ACK90].

3.2 The Maintenance-of-Common Data Algorithm of [AS91]

In the *TREE MERGE* procedure, which is invoked in our algorithm's second phase (described in section 4.2), a new version of the algorithm of [AS91] is used as a distributed procedure. The purpose of *TREE MERGE* is to update the different replicas at all the nodes of all the *approved Trees* with the topological changes. In the algorithm of [ACK90] this task was conducted, as mentioned earlier, using the UPDATE subroutine. Using a somewhat modified version of the algorithm of [AS91] techniques, Procedure *TREE MERGE* improves the time complexity of our algorithm.

In this section we describe the intuition behind the original version of the algorithm of [AS91] (for full details see [AS91]). The model in [AS91] is a communication network of $n + 1$ nodes arranged in a chain, each holding an m-bit local input array. The first node in the chain (W.l.o.g the left node in the chain) is termed the *broadcaster*. The task of the algorithm is to write in the local memories of all the network nodes the value of the input of the broadcaster. The broadcaster's array is considered to be the "correct" array and the broadcaster is in charge of "correcting" the other "wrong" arrays. We use the term *thread* to denote a single invocation of the algorithm that runs on a single network node at a time (but can migrate). The distributed algorithm is built from such *threads* which can migrate from one node to the node's neighbor in a direction away from the broadcaster, namely, from a node to its right-hand neighbor.

The algorithm places one thread, the first invocation of the algorithm, in charge of the entire protocol - that is, in charge of correcting all the local arrays using an Incremental Update technique (see 2). Namely, this thread starts correcting every error it "knows" about in its neighbor. Only one message per error is sent. Once its neighbor's array is correct the thread moves on to that neighbor and continues its operating. However, this technique can be poor in terms of time complexity due to the fact that the Incremental Update technique puts sever restrictions on the use of pipelining. (Intuitively, only when a node "knows" its neighbor had the opportunity to correct on item but declined, does v "know" that the item is correct; only then can v correct the next neighbor on the chain. To improve the time complexity of the Incremental Update, the algorithm of [AS91] adopts a (very weak) version of message pipelining: each invocation of the algorithm works recursively and creates two "child" threads. Each of the child threads is in charge of correcting half of its parent's array in all the network nodes. The first child thread is in charge of correcting the lower half of its parent array and the second child is in charge of correcting the upper half of its parent array. The second child's correction messages are sent only after the first child has finished sending its correction messages, therefore, keeping the increasing bit order of the correction according to the *incremental update* technique. After a thread finishes to correct the array it is in charge off it delegates to its neighbor. Therefore, the two threads move along the network nodes relative to one another in their work. The parent thread itself tags along just behind its children. In order to correct its smaller replica, a thread runs the same protocol as its parent thread. In particular a child thread can create children that are in charge of arrays that are still smaller than its own, and so forth. Splitting the correction of an array in that manner enables the two threads to work in parallel on different nodes and therefore, improves the algorithm time complexity.

The way in which a thread creates a child threads is by sending a *thread-carrier* message to the right-hand node in the network. This message carries the indexes of the smaller array that the new child thread will be in charge of. Had each thread created child threads immediately, the message complexity of creating these threads could have been a dominant factor in the protocol's message complexity. In such a case there could be arbitrary more *thread-carrier* messages than error-correction messages. The algorithm of [AS91] avoids this problem by allowing a thread to create child threads only if it has corrected "enough" errors in its neighbor's replica. In this manner the algorithm amortized the communication costs associated with the creation of children on the communication cost of the correction messages.

4 Our Algorithm

4.1 Phase 1: Trees Approval

As mentioned earlier, one of the bottlenecks in the time measure in the algorithm of [ACK90] is due to the fact that the algorithm merges only two trees at each iteration. A worst case scenario for this algorithm is a network that is arranged in a chain and in each iteration of the algorithm a tree consisting of a single node merges with the tree in the left side of the chain until in V iterations the whole network is spanned. In this scenario the algorithm's quiescence time is the sum of an algebraic sequence- $O(V^2)$. The first phase of our algorithm, the Trees Approval, removes this bottleneck by enabling more than two trees to merge at a time, and still we manage to avoid violating the *loop freedom invariant*. In this section we describe this phase in detail. The high-level description of the first phase of the algorithm appears in figure 2. For the sake of simplicity we describe our algorithm as a sequential algorithm (the distributed implementation is described in the full paper).

Whenever a tree chooses a minimum outgoing edge it sends over that edge a *request* message, namely, a request to merge, directed at the tree over the other endpoint of the edge. This is the same technique used in the algorithm of [ACK90] (described in section 3.1). The different step taken in our algorithm is conducted whenever two trees have chosen to merge through the same outgoing edge, the *core edge*. Node r, the node with the higher identity between the core edge's endpoints, starts a broadcast wave of a *registration* message[4]. This message propagates over tree edges to all the nodes in r's real tree. Let Nodes u and v be two neighbors that belong to different trees. When the *registration* message reaches u which already got a *request* message from v, Node u marks the request as granted and propagates the *registration* message also to v through (u, v). A merging *request* that arrives at u after the *registration* message is received at u, has to wait for the next *registration* message (namely, for the next algorithm iteration). The registration message is propagated transitively to all the real trees that their *request* messages arrived before the *registration* message (originated from r). We refer to these real trees as the *approved trees*.

---

[4] This *registration* message is substantially different from the *initiate* message of the algorithm of [GHS83]. In the algorithm of [GHS83] Node n that sends a *connect* message to Node n' may merge with n''s tree even though n' has already received the *initiate* message- in certain cases. In our algorithm a tree always has to wait if its merging request has arrived after the *registration* message. This major difference arises from the fact that our model is dynamic. Our algorithm operates in the spirit of "two-phase commit" protocols. It first attempts to "lock" ("approve") some of the trees and only after it stops "approving" it starts allowing them to merge.

When Node r is notified (by the standard Broadcast and Echo technique- the PIF algorithm [Seg83]) that the broadcast of the registration message has terminated, it broadcasts a *start-update* message to the roots of all the approved real trees to invoke the UPDATE' a version of the UPDATE procedure of [ACK90]. This procedure is invoked separately by the root of each approved real tree T on receiving the *start-update* message. This invocation is responsible for updating T's replica as it appears at T's root at all of T's nodes.

The number of failures of edges may be arbitrarily larger than the size of a node's real tree. Therefore, in order to ensure that the number of messages that the algorithm sends is a function of the size of the connected component, a change has to be made in procedure UPDATE. We add a new update message *range deletion* that carries one topological item (u, v). This message instructs its receiver Node w to delete all the topological items that appear in w's tree replica lexicographically after the topological item that appeared in the previous *correction* message. If the *range deletion* message is the first message that the node receives, the node deletes all the topological items that appear in its tree replica lexicographically before (u, v).

When Node r detects, using the termination detection algorithm of [DS80] (the same technique is used in the algorithm of [ACK90]) that all the activation of UPDATE have terminated, it invokes the second phase of the algorithm- Trees Merge (describes in section 4.2).

Whenever a marked edge fails
    Unmark the edge (* at the endpoints *)

Whenever trees merge or a topological change occurs
    Call UPDATE (*correct tree replicas*)
    Call FIND (*choose min outgoing edge*)

Whenever two trees choose the same min outgoing edge
    Broadcast & Echo registration message (*approving trees*)
    Invoke procedure UPDATE' separately for each of the *approved trees*
    Invoke Trees Merge (*second phase*)

Fig. 2. The First Phase - Trees Approval Algorithm.

4.2 Phase 2: Trees Merge

Node r invokes the merge of all the approved trees (the last line of Figure 2) by broadcasting a *start-TREE MERGE* message that propagates to all the nodes of the approved trees. Every local root u of an approved tree T that receives *start-TREE MERGE* message initiates an invocation of the *TREE MERGE* procedure. We refer to Node u as the *broadcaster* of the procedure. Every TREE MERGE procedure is an invocation of a new version of the algorithm of [AS91] where the "correct" replica is the tree replica as it appears in the broadcaster's local memory. The broadcaster is responsible for updating all the local replicas in all the nodes of all the approved trees. Note that there are parallel broadcasts-each broadcast is initiated by a root of an approved tree. Every message of the procedure contains its broadcaster identity, therefore, every node that receives such a message can relate it to its appropriate invocation. Each procedure invocation starts when its broadcaster, say Node u, updates in parallel all of its neighbors in u's real tree. As a part of this update process u also sends its real tree replica over Edge (u, v), over which it got the *registration* message. This is, in fact, an Incremental Update: sending the whole u's tree replica to a neighbor v when $Mirror_u(v)$ is empty.

Recall that the algorithm in [ACK90] required that u sends the whole *forest replica*, namely, sending also replicas of trees that u does not belong to them. Transmitting the real tree replicas, rather than the forest replica, violates the Neighbor Knowledge assumption- a node u no longer holds in its local memory, in $Mirror_u(v)$, an accurate copy of its neighbor v's local replica. Therefore, it is possible that later u will transmit correction messages that describe topological items that already appear in v's forest replica. Note that these sort of duplicate messages cannot be sent in the algorithm of [ACK90]. In section 5.2 we prove that these duplicates do not increase the order of the message complexity of our algorithm.

As was mentioned earlier, the TREE MERGE procedure is a version of the algorithm of [AS91]. However, weakening the neighbor knowledge assumption, that the algorithm in [AS91] relies upon, requires an algorithmic step to be taken in our procedure whenever a node receives a *correction* message. Assume that node w receives a *correction* message from its neighbor, Node z, that tells w to add an edge (x, y) to w's forest replica. Assume further that adding that edge would connect two separate trees that appear in w's forest replica. The new algorithmic step that is taken by w is to remove every edge (y, z) that appears in w's forest replica but does not appear in the mirror of Node z, $Mirror_w(z)$. When a broadcaster u, a root of an approved tree, is notified that the TREE MERGE procedure has terminated, u marks the Edge (u, v) as a real tree edge. Node u also marks Node v as its parent. (This is done only if u is not the node with the higher identity of the two endpoints of the core edge- node r). Every node in every approved tree knows the number, $DOWN\text{-}FLOW$ *counter*, of approved trees to which it and its ancestors in its real tree propagate the *registration* message. If $DOWN\text{-}FLOW$ *counter* equals to zero, then u sends a *termination* message to its parent notifying the parent that the TREE MERGE procedure has terminated. A node w that the number of termination messages it gets is equal to $DOWN\text{-}FLOW$ sends a termination message to its parent. When Node r is notified that all the TREE MERGE procedure invocations have terminated, r starts a new iteration by an invocation of a new search for a minimum outgoing edge for the new tree.

5 Analysis

In this extended abstract we state the lemmas and theorems. The proofs are deferred to the full paper. In our proofs we use the following reworded Lemmas and properties from the algorithm of [ACK90]:

Lemma Lemma C.1 of [ACK90] *FIND subroutine terminates.*

Lemma Lemma C.2 of [ACK90] *UPDATE subroutine terminates.*

Lemma Lemma C.3 of [ACK90] *Upon the termination of UPDATE the tree replica at each node is a subset of the real tree to which the node belonged upon invocation of UPDATE, and a superset of the real tree upon termination of UPDATE.*

In our proofs we use the transition system with asynchronous message passing model of [Tel94]. In order to induce a notion of time in executions we use the following *casual order*:

Definition 3. [Lam78] Let H be an execution. The relation $<$, called the *casual order*, on the events of the execution is the smallest relation that satisfies:
(1) if h and f are different events in the same node and h occurs before f, then $h < f$.
(2) if s is a send event and r the corresponding receive event, then $s < r$.
(3) $<$ is transitive.

5.1 Correctness

As long as the loop-freedom invariant is kept the following three lemmas are follows:

Lemma 4. *The real forest is indeed a forest at all the algorithm execution.*

Lemma 5. *The direction (parent pointer) of every real tree's edges induces only one root at every real tree.*

Lemma 6. *The real trees are disjoint.*

Lemma 7. *The algorithm's first phase, the Trees Approval phase, preserves the loop-freedom invariant.*

Proof Sketch: : During the first phase edges can only be deleted from a node's replica. ∎

Theorem 8. *The algorithm's second phase, the Trees Merge, preserves the loop-freedom invariant.*

Let u and v be two neighboring nodes in a real tree, F_u and F_v be the forest replicas of nodes u and v respectively, and T_u and T_v be u's and v's trees replicas. Let $Mirror_u(v)$ be Node u's mirror of v, and define $Mirror_v(u)$ similarly.

Theorem 9. *When the algorithm's second phase (the Trees Merge phase) terminates, T_u and T_v are identical.*

5.2 Amortized Communication Complexity

The following definition attempts to capture the "maximum information" a node may have on the actual connected component it belongs to. That is, if a node z receives a message that was originated by some far away node x, and every node on the message's way (from x to z) forwarded the message before any fault was detected, then x may still be in Node z's connected component. There is no distributed algorithm that can detect that this is not the case. Thus the message complexity of any algorithm must be based on the assumption that x and z may still be in the same connected component.

Definition 10. Edge (x, y) is a *z-virtual directed edge* if (1) there is a causality chain of *send* and *receive* events ([Lam78]) from Node x, through Node y, $(x, y) = (w_1, w_2)$, (w_2, w_3), (w_3, w_4), ... $(w_{l-1}, w_l) = (w_{l-1}, z)$ to Node z, and (2) between every receive event (on this chain) (w_{i-1}, w_i) and the following (on this chain) send event (w_i, w_{i+1}) there is no event at Node w_i of a failure of edge (w_{i-1}, w_i).

Definition 11. Node z's *Virtual Component*: the set of z-virtual directed edges.

Definition 12. *Physical Component*: The set of nodes that from a global point of view of the network are in the same connected component.

Lemma 13. *Every node that appears in Node u's tree replica is also in u's Virtual Component.*

Lemma 14. *The size of u's tree replica is bounded from above by the size of u's Virtual Component.*

Proof Sketch: : The lemma follows from lemma 13.   ∎

Let A_k be Node k's *Virtual Component* and let Node z Belong to A_k

Lemma 15. *For every execution there exists an equivalent execution ([Lam78]) where Node k's physical component is A_k.*

Theorem 16. *Every algorithm that maintains, in a node, a replica of the node's connected component (if the input stops changing then the output, the node replica, is required to become eventually the node's connected component) cannot maintain a smaller replica than our algorithm's tree replica.*

From Theorem 16 it follows that defining an algorithm measures as a function of the virtual component size is the most accurate according to which measure a distributed algorithm can be measured.

Define A as the union of the trees replicas of all the nodes in the same physical component when the last topological change occurs.

Theorem 17. *Assume that k topological changes occur. Then the number of edges identities exchanged during the algorithm execution is $O(kA)$.*

5.3 Quiescence Time

Lemma 18. *Every invocation of procedure TREE MERGE terminates.*

Lemma 19. *Every edge failure is unmarked in at most one of a given tree node's replica.*

Proof Sketch: : An edge failure disconnects the real tree and the two edge's endpoints become nodes in distinct real trees. ∎

Lemma 20. *The quiescence time of the algorithm's first phase, Trees Approval Algorithm, is $O(A)$.*

Lemma 21. *The quiescence time of the second phase of the algorithm- Trees Merge, is $O(A \log^2 A)$.*

Theorem 22. *The algorithm quiescence time is $O(A \log^3 A)$.*

6 Acknowledgments

We would like to thanks Israel Cidon for helpful discussions.

References

[AAG87]   Yehuda Afek, Baruch Awerbuch and Eli Gafni. Applying static network protocols to dynamic networks. In Proc. 28th IEEE Symp. on Foundations of Computer Science, October 1987.

[ACG+90] Baruch Awerbuch, Israel Cidon, Inder Gopal, Marc Kaplan, and Shay Kutten. DIStributed control for PARIS. In Proc. 9th ACM Symp. on Principles of Distributed Computing, 1990.

[ACK90]   Baruch Awerbuch, Israel Cidon, and Shay Kutten. Optimal maintenance of replicated Information. Proceedings of the 31st Annual IEEE Symposium on Foundations of Computer Science (FOCS 90), St. Louis, MO, USA, pp.492–502, October 1990.

[AS91]   Baruch Awerbuch and Leonard J.Schulman. The maintenance of common data in distributed system. In Proc. 32nd IEEE Symp. On Foundations of Computer Science, October 1991.

[Awe88]   Baruch Awerbuch. On the effects of feedback in dynamic network protocols. In Proc. 29th IEEE Symp. on Foundations of Computer Science, pages 231-245, October 1988.

[BGJ+85] A.E.Baratz, J.P.Gray, P.E.Green Jr., J.M.Jaffe, and D.P.Pozefski. Sna networks of small systems. IEEE journal on Selected Areas in Communications, SAC-3(3):416-426, May 1985.

[CGKK95] Israel Cidon, Inder Gopal, Mark Kaplan, and Shay Kutten. Distributed Control for Fast Networks. IEEE Transactions on Communications,Vol. 43, No. 5, pp. 1950–1960, May 1995.

[DS80]   Edsger W.Dijkstra and C.S.Scholten. Termination detection for diffusing computations. Info. Process. Letters, 11(1):1-4, August 1980.

[GHS83]   R.Gallager, P.Humblet, and P.Spira. A distributed algorithm for minimum weight spanning trees. ACM Transaction on programming language and Systems, 4(1):66-77, January 1983.

[Lam78]   Lamport, L. Time, clocks, and the ordering of events in a distributed system. Commun. ACM 21 (1978), 558-564.

[MRR80]   John McQuillan, Ira Richer, and Eric Rosen. The new routing algorithm for the ARPANET. IEEE Trans. on Commun., 28(5):711-719, May 1980.

[OSPF]   J.Moy. OSPF Version2 RFC1247, October 1991.

[Seg83]   A. Segall. Distributed network protocols. IEEE Transaction on Information Theory, IT-29(1):23-35, January 1983.

[SG89]   John M. Spinelli and Robert G. Gallager. Broadcasting topology information in computer networks. IEEE Trans. on Commun., May 1989.

[Tel94]   Gerard Tel. Introduction to Distributed Algorithms. Cambridge University Press, 1994.

[Vis83]   U.Vishkin. A distributed orientation algorithm. IEEE Trans. on Info. Theory, June 1983.

Author Index

Lecture Notes in Computer Science

For information about Vols. 1–1610
please contact your bookseller or Springer-Verlag

Vol. 1650: K.-D. Althoff, R. Bergmann, L.K. Branting (Eds.), Case-Based Reasoning Research and Development. Proceedings, 1999. XII, 598 pages. 1999. (Subseries LNAI).

Vol. 1651: R.H. Güting, D. Papadias, F. Lochovsky (Eds.), Advances in Spatial Databases. Proceedings, 1999. XI, 371 pages. 1999.

Vol. 1652: M. Klusch, O.M. Shehory, G. Weiss (Eds.), Cooperative Information Agents III. Proceedings, 1999. XI, 404 pages. 1999. (Subseries LNAI).

Vol. 1653: S. Covaci (Ed.), Active Networks. Proceedings, 1999. XIII, 346 pages. 1999.

Vol. 1654: E.R. Hancock, M. Pelillo (Eds.), Energy Minimization Methods in Computer Vision and Pattern Recognition. Proceedings, 1999. IX, 331 pages. 1999.

Vol. 1655: S.-W. Lee, Y. Nakano (Eds.), Document Analysis Systems: Theory and Practice. Proceedings, 1998. XI, 377 pages. 1999.

Vol. 1656: S. Chatterjee, J.F. Prins, L. Carter, J. Ferrante, Z. Li, D. Sehr, P.-C. Yew (Eds.), Languages and Compilers for Parallel Computing. Proceedings, 1998. XI, 384 pages. 1999.

Vol. 1661: C. Freksa, D.M. Mark (Eds.), Spatial Information Theory. Proceedings, 1999. XIII, 477 pages. 1999.

Vol. 1662: V. Malyshkin (Ed.), Parallel Computing Technologies. Proceedings, 1999. XIX, 510 pages. 1999.

Vol. 1663: F. Dehne, A. Gupta. J.-R. Sack, R. Tamassia (Eds.), Algorithms and Data Structures. Proceedings, 1999. IX, 366 pages. 1999.

Vol. 1664: J.C.M. Baeten, S. Mauw (Eds.), CONCUR'99. Concurrency Theory. Proceedings, 1999. XI, 573 pages. 1999.

Vol. 1666: M. Wiener (Ed.), Advances in Cryptology – CRYPTO '99. Proceedings, 1999. XII, 639 pages. 1999.

Vol. 1667: J. Hlavička, E. Maehle, A. Pataricza (Eds.), Dependable Computing – EDCC-3. Proceedings, 1999. XVIII, 455 pages. 1999.

Vol. 1668: J.S. Vitter, C.D. Zaroliagis (Eds.), Algorithm Engineering. Proceedings, 1999. VIII, 361 pages. 1999.

Vol. 1671: D. Hochbaum, K. Jansen, J.D.P. Rolim, A. Sinclair (Eds.), Randomization, Approximation, and Combinatorial Optimization. Proceedings, 1999. IX, 289 pages. 1999.

Vol. 1672: M. Kutylowski, L. Pacholski, T. Wierzbicki (Eds.), Mathematical Foundations of Computer Science 1999. Proceedings, 1999. XII, 455 pages. 1999.

Vol. 1673: P. Lysaght, J. Irvine, R. Hartenstein (Eds.), Field Programmable Logic and Applications. Proceedings, 1999. XI, 541 pages. 1999.

Vol. 1674: D. Floreano, J.-D. Nicoud, F. Mondada (Eds.), Advances in Artificial Life. Proceedings, 1999. XVI, 737 pages. 1999. (Subseries LNAI).

Vol. 1675: J. Estublier (Ed.), System Configuration Management. Proceedings, 1999. VIII, 255 pages. 1999.

Vol. 1976: M. Mohania, A M. Tjoa (Eds.), Data Warehousing and Knowledge Discovery. Proceedings, 1999. XII, 400 pages. 1999.

Vol. 1677: T. Bench-Capon, G. Soda, A M. Tjoa (Eds.), Database and Expert Systems Applications. Proceedings, 1999. XVIII, 1105 pages. 1999.

Vol. 1678: M.H. Böhlen, C.S. Jensen, M.O. Scholl (Eds.), Spatio-Temporal Database Management. Proceedings, 1999. X, 243 pages. 1999.

Vol. 1679: C. Taylor, A. Colchester (Eds.), Medical Image Computing and Computer-Assisted Intervention – MICCAI'99. Proceedings, 1999. XXI, 1240 pages. 1999.

Vol. 1680: D. Dams, R. Gerth, S. Leue, M. Massink (Eds.), Theoretical and Practical Aspects of SPIN Model Checking. Proceedings, 1999. X, 277 pages. 1999.

Vol. 1682: M. Nielsen, P. Johansen, O.F. Olsen, J. Weickert (Eds.), Scale-Space Theories in Computer Vision. Proceedings, 1999. XII, 532 pages. 1999.

Vol. 1684: G. Ciobanu, G. Păun (Eds.), Fundamentals of Computation Theory. Proceedings, 1999. XI, 570 pages. 1999.

Vol. 1685: P. Amestoy, P. Berger, M. Daydé, I. Duff, V. Frayssé, L. Giraud, D. Ruiz (Eds.), Euro-Par'99. Parallel Processing. Proceedings, 1999. XXXII, 1503 pages. 1999.

Vol. 1687: O. Nierstrasz, M. Lemoine (Eds.), Software Engineering – ESEC/FSE '99. Proceedings, 1999. XII, 529 pages. 1999.

Vol. 1688: P. Bouquet, L. Serafini, P. Brézillon, M. Benerecetti, F. Castellani (Eds.), Modeling and Using Context. Proceedings, 1999. XII, 528 pages. 1999. (Subseries LNAI).

Vol. 1689: F. Solina, A. Leonardis (Eds.), Computer Analysis of Images and Patterns. Proceedings, 1999. XIV, 650 pages. 1999.

Vol. 1690: Y. Bertot, G. Dowek, A. Hirschowitz, C. Paulin, L. Théry (Eds.), Theorem Proving in Higher Order Logics. Proceedings, 1999. VIII, 359 pages. 1999.

Vol. 1691: J. Eder, I. Rozman, T. Welzer (Eds.), Advances in Databases and Information Systems. Proceedings, 1999. XIII, 383 pages. 1999.

Vol. 1692: V. Matoušek, P. Mautner, J. Ocelíková, P. Sojka (Eds.), Text, Speech and Dialogue. Proceedings, 1999. XI, 396 pages. 1999. (Subseries LNAI).

Vol. 1693: P. Jayanti (Ed.), Distributed Computing. Proceedings, 1999. X, 357 pages. 1999.

Vol. 1694: A. Cortesi, G. Filé (Eds.), Static Analysis. Proceedings, 1999. VIII, 357 pages. 1999.

Vol. 1698: M. Felici, K. Kanoun, A. Pasquini (Eds.), Computer Safety, Reliability and Security. Proceedings, 1999. XVIII, 482 pages. 1999.

Vol. 1699: S. Albayrak (Ed.), Intelligent Agents for Telecommunication Applications. Proceedings, 1999. IX, 191 pages. 1999. (Subseries LNAI).

Vol. 1701: W. Burgard, T. Christaller, A.B. Cremers (Eds.), KI-99: Advances in Artificial Intelligence. Proceedings, 1999. XI, 311 pages. 1999. (Subseries LNAI).

Vol. 1702: G. Nadathur (Ed.), Principles and Practice of Declarative Programming. Proceedings, 1999. X, 434 pages. 1999.

Vol. 1704: Jan M. Żytkow, J. Rauch (Eds.), Principles of Data Mining and Knowledge Discovery. Proceedings, 1999. XIV, 593 pages. 1999. (Subseries LNAI).

Vol. 1705: H. Ganzinger, D. McAllester, A. Voronkov (Eds.), Logic for Programming and Automated Reasoning. Proceedings, 1999. XII, 397 pages. 1999. (Subseries LNAI).